Exam 70-431: *Microsoft SQL Server 2005—Implementation and Maintenance*

1. Installing and Configuring SQL Server 2005

Objective	Chapter	Lesson
1.1 Install SQL Server 2005		
1.1.1 Verify prerequisites.	1	1, 2
1.1.2 Upgrade from an earlier version of SQL Server.	1	5
1.1.3 Create an instance.	1	3, 4
1.2 Configure SQL Server 2005 instances and databases.		
1.2.1 Configure log files and data files.	2	1
1.2.2 Configure the SQL Server DatabaseMail subsystem for an instance.	2	2
1.2.3 Choose a recovery model for the database.	2	3
1.3 Configure SQL Server security.		
1.3.1 Configure server security principals.	2	4
1.3.2 Configure database securables.	2	5
1.3.3 Configure encryption.	2	6
1.4 Configure linked servers by using SQL Server Management Studio (SSMS).		
1.4.1 Identify the external data source.	2	7
1.4.2 Identify the characteristics of the data source.	2	7
1.4.3 Identify the security model of the data source.	2	7

2. Implementing High Availability and Disaster Recovery

Objective	Chapter	Lesson
2.1 Implement database mirroring.		
2.1.1 Prepare databases for database mirroring.	17	2
2.1.2 Create endpoints.	17	3
2.1.3 Specify database partners.	17	1, 5, 6
2.1.4 Specify a witness server.	17	1
2.1.5 Configure an operating mode.	17	4
2.2 Implement log shipping.		
2.2.1 Initialize a secondary database.	18	2
2.2.2 Configure log shipping options.	18	1, 2, 4
2.2.3 Configure a log shipping mode.	18	3
2.2.4 Configure monitoring.	18	1
2.3 Manage database snapshots.		
2.3.1 Create a snapshot.	16	1
2.3.2 Revert a database from a snapshot.	16	2

3. Supporting Data Consumers

Objective	Chapter	Lesson
3.1 Retrieve data to support ad hoc and recurring queries.		
3.1.1 Construct SQL queries to return data.	5 21	1 4
3.1.2 Format the results of SQL queries.	5	2
3.1.3 Identify collation details.	1	4
3.2 Manipulate relational data.		
3.2.1 Insert, update, and delete data.	5	3
3.2.2 Handle exceptions and errors.	5	4
3.2.3 Manage transactions.	5	4
3.3 Manage XML data.		
3.3.1 Identify the specific structure needed by a consumer.	8	1
3.3.2 Retrieve XML data.	8	2, 3
3.3.3 Modify XML data.	8	4
3.3.4 Convert between XML data and relational data.	8	5
3.3.5 Create an XML index.	8	6
3.3.6 Load an XML schema.	8	1

Objective	Chapter	Lesson
3.4 Implement an HTTP endpoint.		
3.4.1 Create an HTTP endpoint.	13	2
3.4.2 Secure an HTTP endpoint.	13	1
3.5 Implement Service Broker components.		
3.5.1 Create services.	20	1, 3
3.5.2 Create queues.	20	1, 3
3.5.3 Create contracts.	20	1, 2
3.5.4 Create conversations.	20	1, 4
3.5.5 Create message types.	20	1, 2
3.5.6 Send messages to a service.	20	5
3.5.7 Route a message to a service.	20	4
3.5.8 Receive messages from a service.	20	5
3.6 Import and export data from a file.		
3.6.1 Set a database to the bulk-logged recovery model to avoid inflating the transaction log.	10	1
3.6.2 Run the bcp utility.	10	2
3.6.3 Perform a Bulk Insert task.	10	3
3.6.4 Import bulk XML data by using the OPENROWSET function.	10	4
3.6.5 Copy data from one table to another by using the SQL Server 2005 Integration Services (SSIS) Import and Export Wizard.	10	5
3.7 Manage replication.		
3.7.1 Distinguish between replication types.	19	1
3.7.2 Configure a publisher, a distributor, and a subscriber.	19	2
3.7.3 Configure replication security.	19	3
3.7.4 Configure conflict resolution settings for merge replication.	19	4
3.7.5 Monitor replication.	19	5
3.7.6 Improve replication performance.	19	5
3.7.7 Plan for, stop, and restart recovery procedures.	19	2

4. Maintaining Databases

Objective	Chapter	Lesson
4.1 Implement and maintain SQL Server Agent jobs.		
4.1.1 Set a job owner.	14	1
4.1.2 Create a job schedule.	14	1
4.1.3 Create job steps.	14	1
4.1.4 Configure job steps.	14	1
4.1.5 Disable a job.	14	1
4.1.6 Create a maintenance job.	14	2
4.1.7 Set up alerts.	14	4
4.1.8 Configure operators.	14	3
4.1.9 Modify a job.	14	1
4.1.10 Delete a job.	14	1
4.1.11 Manage a job.	14	1
4.2 Manage databases by using Transact-SQL.		
4.2.1 Manage index fragmentation.	12	1
4.2.2 Manage statistics.	12	2
4.2.3 Shrink files.	12	3
4.2.4 Perform database integrity checks by using DBCC CHECKDB.	12	4
4.3 Back up a database.		
4.3.1 Perform a full backup.	11	1
4.3.2 Perform a differential backup.	11	1
4.3.3 Perform a transaction log backup.	11	1
4.3.4 Initialize a media set by using the FORMAT option.	11	1

Microsoft

Exam objectives: The exam objectives listed here are current as of this book's publication date. Exam objectives are subject to change at any time without prior notice and at Microsoft's sole discretion. Please visit the Microsoft Learning Web site for the most current listing of exam objectives: *http://www.microsoft.com/learning/mcp/*.

Microsoft®

MCTS Self-Paced Training Kit (Exam 70-431): Microsoft® SQL Server™ 2005—Implementation and Maintenance

Solid Quality Learning

PUBLISHED BY
Microsoft Press
A Division of Microsoft Corporation
One Microsoft Way
Redmond, Washington 98052-6399

0-7356-2271-X
978-0-7356-2271-5
Library of Congress Control Number 2006924471

Printed and bound in the United States of America.

5 6 7 8 9   QWT   1 0 9 8 7

Distributed in Canada by H.B. Fenn and Company Ltd.

A CIP catalogue record for this book is available from the British Library.

Microsoft Press books are available through booksellers and distributors worldwide. For further information about international editions, contact your local Microsoft Corporation office or contact Microsoft Press International directly at fax (425) 936-7329. Visit our Web site at www.microsoft.com/mspress. Send comments to *tkinput@microsoft.com*.

Acquisitions Editor: Ken Jones
Project Editor: Laura Sackerman
Technical Editors: Rozanne Murphy Whalen and Dan Whalen
Copy Editor: Nancy Sixsmith
Indexer: Ginny Munroe

Body Part No. X12-35101

Acknowledgments

There are always more people to thank than you ever have the space for. But the authors would like to extend their sincere gratitude to the following for making this book possible: A huge thanks to Ken Jones, Laura Sackerman, Jenny Moss Benson, and everyone else at Microsoft Press, as well as Nancy Sixsmith, Dan Whalen, and Rozanne Murphy Whalen—your Herculean efforts have not been missed. Also thanks to Kathy Blomstrom, content development manager for Solid Quality Learning, for her tireless work on the project and to Federico Bazo Alfaro for helping to keep the wheels moving.

In addition, the authors would like to acknowledge the following special people:

Daren Bieniek I would like to thank my mom (MaryAnn), wife (Shara), and daughter (Amelia) for tolerating all of those times that I said, "I can't right now. I'm working."

Mike Hotek I'd like to thank the SQL Server Development Team for creating a product that my life has revolved around for more than 15 years. Thanks to my sister Carrie, brother-in-law Dan, and nieces Tasha and Ashley for the support to keep going. I would have never made it here without my grandparents, whom I've always thought of as my other set of parents, for being a huge part of who I am today. Jen and Gabby, you have provided more smiles than you can ever imagine. Thank you to the many people at Sacred Heart in Eau Claire and Abbott Northwestern in Minneapolis for sending my best friend back—three times. There aren't words in any language to adequately describe what you do every day. And thanks to my best friend—Dad.

Antonio Soto I need to thank my wife, Isabel, for her patience and understanding. She is my raison d'être. Thanks to Fernando Guerrero for placing his trust in me. Thanks to Marcelo Castelo for giving me the opportunity to work with him. Thanks to Solid Quality Learning for its warm welcome. And thanks to Mosqui for making me laugh in the bad moments.

Adolfo Wiernik I definitely must thank Fernando Guerrero, CEO of Solid Quality Learning, for believing in me from the start when I joined this amazing company. Thanks to Michael Rys, SQL Server Program Manager in charge of the XML features in the product, for his mentoring and always answering my mails. Finally, I thank the team at Magen, Microsoft Technology Center in Tel Aviv, Israel, which is where I started working with the XML features in SQL Server 2000 and laid the foundation for who I am.

About the Authors

MCTS Self-Paced Training Kit (Exam 70-431): Microsoft SQL Server 2005–Implementation and Maintenance was written by the following mentors with Solid Quality Learning, a trusted global provider of advanced education and solutions for the Microsoft SQL Server platform:

Daren Bieniek is a mentor with Solid Quality Learning, has 20 years of professional technical experience, and has served in nearly every IT role possible–from systems administrator to developer to database administrator to architect to CEO. During the past 10 years, Daren has focused on data-related roles and technologies, with an emphasis on very large database (VLDB) architecture, design, and implementation.

Randy Dyess is the author of *Transact-SQL Language Reference Guide* and many magazine and newsletter articles about SQL Server security and optimization issues, and has spoken at various international and national conferences. Randy is a member of the Board of Directors for the Professional Association for SQL Server (PASS) and is the Director of Programs for the North Texas SQL Server Users Group. He is also the founder and principle author of *www.TransactSQL.com*.

Mike Hotek has been working with SQL Server since before it was a Microsoft product. He is known throughout the industry for his expertise in replication, high availability, disaster recovery, and performance tuning. Mike has delivered more than 200 sessions at a variety of conferences and has coauthored two other books about SQL Server.

Javier Loria, a mentor with Solid Quality Learning, works primarily with Latin American companies to help them develop business intelligence projects. He is also a trainer and a frequent speaker at Microsoft regional events and loves to write about technology. When not working, Javier enjoys spending time with his wife, Maria, and his five children: Lidia, Javier Jose, Maria Jose, Andrea, and Lucia.

Adam Machanic is an independent database software consultant, writer, and speaker based in Boston, Massachusetts. He has implemented SQL Server solutions for a variety of high-availability online transaction processing (OLTP) and large-scale data warehouse applications, and also specializes in Microsoft .NET data access layer performance optimization. Adam is a Microsoft Most Valuable Professional (MVP) for SQL Server and a Microsoft Certified IT Professional.

Antonio Soto, a database fanatic, has been working with databases since 1994. He has worked with the IT training company Professional Training, in Spain, as a trainer and consultant regarding SQL Server and other Microsoft technologies. Since 2002, Antonio has also been a partner and director of Alcatraz Solutions, which provides security solutions to the IT industry. He writes for various magazines and speaks at many IT conferences in Spain. Antonio is a computer engineer, an MCDBA, an MCSE, an MCAD, and an MCT.

Adolfo Wiernik is director of operations for Solid Quality Learning in Latin America. He previously worked as lead architect at the Microsoft .NET Center in Central America and the Microsoft Technology Center in Tel Aviv, Israel. When not speaking at a local or international event, Adolfo enjoys hiking in the mountains in his home country of Costa Rica.

Contents at a Glance

Table of Contents

Introduction

This training kit is designed for information technology (IT) professionals who plan to take Microsoft Certified Technical Specialist (MCTS) exam 70-431, as well as for IT professionals who need to know how to implement and maintain Microsoft SQL Server 2005 databases. We assume that before you begin using this kit you have a working knowledge of Microsoft Windows, network technologies, relational databases and their design, Transact-SQL, and the SQL Server 2005 client tools.

By using this training kit, you'll learn how to

- Install and configure SQL Server 2005.
- Create and implement database objects.
- Implement high availability and disaster recovery.
- Maintain databases.
- Support data consumers.
- Monitor and troubleshoot SQL Server performance.

Hardware Requirements

We recommend that you use a computer that is not your primary workstation to do the practice exercises in this book because you will make changes to the operating system and application configuration. The following hardware is required to complete the practice exercises:

- Personal computer with a 600 MHz Pentium III–compatible or faster processor; 1 GHz or faster processor recommended
- 512 MB of RAM or more; 1GB or more recommended
- 8 GB of available hard disk space

NOTE Four volumes necessary for some practice exercises

To complete some of the practice exercises in this book, you will need four volumes on your computer. We recommend that you make the C volume the largest, and then use volume sizes of 650 MB for the D, E, and F volumes.

- DVD-ROM drive
- Super VGA (1,024 x 768) or higher resolution video adapter and monitor
- Keyboard and Microsoft mouse, or compatible pointing device

Software Requirements

The following software is required to complete the practice exercises:

- One of the following operating systems:
  - Microsoft Windows 2000 Server with Service Pack (SP) 4 or later
  - Windows 2000 Professional with SP 4 or later
  - Windows XP with SP 2 or later
  - Windows Server 2003 Standard Edition, Enterprise Edition, or Datacenter Edition with SP 1 or later
  - Microsoft Windows Small Business Server 2003 with SP 1 or later
  - Microsoft Windows Server 2003 Standard x64 Edition, Enterprise x64 Edition, or Datacenter x64 Edition with SP 1 or later
  - Windows XP Professional x64 Edition or later running in Windows on Windows
- SQL Server 2005 (A 180-day evaluation edition of Microsoft SQL Server 2005 Enterprise Edition is included on DVD with this book)

CAUTION   Networked computers

If your computer is part of a larger network, verify with your network administrator that the SQL Server instances installed will not interfere with network operations. All instances configured for exercises within this book should be set to allow local connections only to ensure that they will not interact with other resources on your network.

- Microsoft Internet Explorer 6.0 SP 1 or later

Using the CD and DVD

A companion CD and an evaluation software DVD are included with this training kit. The companion CD contains the following:

■ **Practice tests**   You can reinforce your understanding of how to implement and maintain SQL Server 2005 databases by using electronic practice tests you customize to meet your needs from the pool of Lesson Review questions in this book. Or you can practice for the 70-431 certification exam by using tests created from a pool of 295 realistic exam questions, which give you many different practice exams to ensure that you're prepared.

■ **Practice files**   The practice exercises in Chapter 8, "Managing XML Data," are code-intensive. Code for this chapter is included on the companion CD so that you don't have to type it all yourself. Files for you to practice importing in Chapter 10, "Using Flat Files," are also included.

■ **An eBook**   An electronic version (eBook) of this book is included for times when you don't want to carry the printed book with you. The eBook is in Portable Document Format (PDF), and you can view it by using Adobe Acrobat or Adobe Reader.

The evaluation software DVD contains a 180-day evaluation edition of SQL Server 2005 Enterprise Edition, in case you want to use it with this book.

How to Install the Practice Tests

To install the practice test software from the companion CD to your hard disk, do the following:

1.   Insert the companion CD into your CD drive and accept the license agreement. A CD menu appears.

NOTE   If the CD menu doesn't appear

If the CD menu or the license agreement doesn't appear, AutoRun might be disabled on your computer. Refer to the Readme.txt file on the CD-ROM for alternate installation instructions.

---

2.   Click the Practice Tests item and follow the instructions on the screen.

How to Use the Practice Tests

To start the practice test software, follow these steps:

1. Click Start/All Programs/Microsoft Press Training Kit Exam Prep. A window appears that shows all the Microsoft Press training kit exam prep suites installed on your computer.

2. Double-click the lesson review or practice test you want to use.

NOTE   Lesson reviews vs. practice tests

Select the (70-431) Microsoft SQL Server 2005—Implementation and Maintenance *lesson review* to use the questions from the "Lesson Review" sections of this book. Select the (70-431) Microsoft SQL Server 2005—Implementation and Maintenance *practice test* to use a pool of 295 questions similar to those in the 70-431 certification exam.

Lesson Review Options

When you start a lesson review, the Custom Mode dialog box appears so that you can configure your test. You can click OK to accept the defaults or you can customize the number of questions you want, how the practice test software works, which exam objectives you want the questions to relate to, and whether you want your lesson review to be timed. If you're retaking a test, you can select whether you want to see all the questions again or only those questions you missed or didn't answer.

After you click OK, your lesson review starts.

■ To take the test, answer the questions and use the Next, Previous, and Go To buttons to move from question to question.

■ After you answer an individual question, if you want to see which answers are correct—along with an explanation of each correct answer—click Explanation.

■ If you'd rather wait until the end of the test to see how you did, answer all the questions and then click Score Test. You'll see a summary of the exam objectives you chose and the percentage of questions you got right overall and per objective. You can print a copy of your test, review your answers, or retake the test.

Practice Test Options

When you start a practice test, you choose whether to take the test in Certification Mode, Study Mode, or Custom Mode:

- **Certification Mode**   Closely resembles the experience of taking a certification exam. The test has a set number of questions, it's timed, and you can't pause and restart the timer.

- **Study Mode**   Creates an untimed test in which you can review the correct answers and the explanations after you answer each question.

- **Custom Mode**   Gives you full control over the test options so that you can customize them as you like.

In all modes, the user interface when you're taking the test is the basically the same, but different options enabled or disabled depending on the mode. The main options are discussed in the previous section, "Lesson Review Options."

When you review your answer to an individual practice test question, a "References" section is provided that lists where in the training kit you can find the information that relates to that question and provides links to other sources of information. After you click Test Results to score your entire practice test, you can click the Learning Plan tab to see a list of references for every objective.

How to Uninstall the Practice Tests

To uninstall the practice test software for a training kit, use the Add Or Remove Programs option in Windows Control Panel.

Microsoft Certified Professional Program

The Microsoft certifications provide the best method to prove your command of current Microsoft products and technologies. The exams and corresponding certifications are developed to validate your mastery of critical competencies as you design and develop, or implement and support, solutions with Microsoft products and technologies. Computer professionals who become Microsoft-certified are recognized as experts and are sought after industry-wide. Certification brings a variety of benefits to the individual and to employers and organizations.

MORE INFO   All the Microsoft certifications

For a full list of Microsoft certifications, go to *www.microsoft.com/learning/mcp/default.asp*.

Technical Support

Every effort has been made to ensure the accuracy of this book and the contents of the companion CD. If you have comments, questions, or ideas regarding this book or the companion CD, please send them to Microsoft Press by using either of the following methods:

E-mail: tkinput@microsoft.com

Postal Mail:

Microsoft Press
Attn: *MCTS Self-Paced Training Kit (Exam 70-431): Microsoft SQL Server 2005–Implementation and Maintenance* Editor
One Microsoft Way
Redmond, WA 98052–6399

For additional support information regarding this book and the CD-ROM (including answers to commonly asked questions about installation and use), visit the Microsoft Press Technical Support website at *www.microsoft.com/learning/support/ books/*. To connect directly to the Microsoft Knowledge Base and enter a query, visit *http://support.microsoft.com/search/*. For support information regarding Microsoft software, please connect to *http://support.microsoft.com.*

Evaluation Edition Software Support

The 180-day evaluation edition provided with this training kit is not the full retail product and is provided only for the purposes of training and evaluation. Microsoft and Microsoft Technical Support do not support this evaluation edition.

Information about any issues relating to the use of this evaluation edition with this training kit is posted to the Support section of the Microsoft Press Web site (*www.microsoft.com/learning/*support/books/). For information about ordering the full version of any Microsoft software, please call Microsoft Sales at (800) 426-9400 or visit *www.microsoft.com.*

Chapter 1

Installing SQL Server 2005

This chapter prepares you to accomplish one of the common tasks that all database administrators (DBAs) face: installing a new Microsoft SQL Server instance. Not only do you have to select the correct SQL Server edition for your organization's needs but you also have to determine the best hardware and software for the SQL Server installation. After verifying the prerequisites for the different SQL Server 2005 editions, you need to determine whether you will install a default, named, or multiple instances of SQL Server. This chapter shows you how to install a SQL Server 2005 instance from scratch and shares best practices for upgrading to SQL Server 2005 from a previous version of SQL Server. By the end of the chapter, you will understand the decisions you must make before, during, and after a SQL Server 2005 installation—whether the instance you are installing is the first or the tenth instance on the server.

Exam objectives in this chapter:
- Install SQL Server 2005.
  - ❏ Verify prerequisites.
  - ❏ Create an instance.
  - ❏ Upgrade from an earlier version of SQL Server.

Lessons in this chapter:

Before You Begin

To complete the lessons in this chapter, you must have

- A computer that meets or exceeds the minimum hardware requirements for SQL Server 2005 as listed in Lesson 2 of this chapter.
- Microsoft Windows Server 2003 running on your computer on an NTFS file system (NTFS) partition.
- SQL Server 2000 installed to complete the upgrade sections of this chapter.

Real World

Randy Dyess

Having been a DBA for many years in a variety of environments, I have planned and installed hundreds of SQL Server installations. Installing SQL Server is a vital part of a DBA's job role. And you are expected both to determine which SQL Server edition should be installed and to install that SQL Server instance on the correct hardware and software configuration. Keep in mind that the decisions you make as you install SQL Server provide the foundation for an effective database implementation. And as with most decisions you'll make regarding SQL Server, you need to understand the needs of your business users—their current needs and projected future needs—to make sure you install a system that is appropriate for today and that isn't obsolete at your organization's first growth spurt.

Lesson 1: Selecting the Correct SQL Server 2005 Edition

A key part of installing a new SQL Server 2005 instance is selecting the appropriate SQL Server 2005 edition for the installation. Understanding the different SQL Server editions and the features and functionality of each of the editions is key to selecting the right edition for your users' requirements. The edition you select not only determines what you can do with your SQL Server installation but also determines what hardware you must set aside for your installation.

After this lesson, you will be able to:

■ Identify the appropriate SQL Server edition to install for a given environment.

Estimated lesson time: 15 minutes

Understanding SQL Server 2005 Editions

A major part of the installation planning process is determining the SQL Server 2005 edition you need to use. SQL Server 2005 offers five editions—two of which come in either 32-bit or 64-bit versions—each designed for a specific environment. Determining the proper edition to install is critical for meeting the functionality needs of your current environment as well as any future needs you might expect. Here is a description of each edition:

■ **SQL Server 2005 Enterprise Edition (32-bit and 64-bit)** Enterprise Edition is designed to support the largest enterprise online transaction processing (OLTP) environments, highly complex data-analysis requirements, data-warehousing systems, and active Web sites. DBAs designing large database installations should consider only Enterprise Edition.

■ **SQL Server 2005 Standard Edition (32-bit and 64-bit)** Standard Edition includes the essential functionality needed for e-commerce, data warehousing, and line-of-business solutions that most small- and medium-sized organizations use. Organizations with databases that will contain large amounts of data but do not need installations with all the features of Enterprise Edition might want to consider Standard Edition.

- **SQL Server 2005 Workgroup Edition (32-bit only)**   Workgroup Edition is the data-management solution for small organizations that need a database that has no limits on size or number of users and has the capability to serve as a back end to small Web servers and departmental or branch-office operations. DBAs working with small amounts of data on smaller servers might want to consider using Workgroup Edition.

- **SQL Server 2005 Developer Edition (32-bit and 64-bit)**   Developer Edition includes all the functionality of SQL Server 2005 Enterprise Edition, but it is licensed for use as a development and test system, not as a production server. Developer Edition is suited for developers in larger companies who need to develop applications that will use Enterprise Edition but who do not want to install Enterprise Edition on development or test servers.

- **SQL Server 2005 Express Edition (32-bit only)**   SQL Server Express is a free, easy-to-use, and simple-to-manage database that can be redistributed to function as the client database as well as a basic server database. Express Edition is usually suited only for very small data sets. Developers who are developing applications that require a small data store should consider using Express Edition. Express Edition also makes a suitable replacement for Microsoft Access databases.

SQL Server 2005 Features by Edition

To choose the right SQL Server 2005 edition for your installation, you should review the functionality of each edition to determine which one will meet your users' needs. Table 1-1 provides a quick comparison of the features in each SQL Server 2005 edition.

Table 1-1   Feature Set by SQL Server 2005 Edition (Developer Edition has the same feature set as Enterprise Edition)

Feature/Functionality	Express	Workgroup	Standard	Enterprise
Number of CPUs Supported	1; includes support for multicore processor	2; includes support for multicore processor	4; includes support for multicore processor	Unlimited; includes support for multicore processor
Memory	1 GB	3 GB	Limit based on operating system	Limit based on operating system

Table 1-1   Feature Set by SQL Server 2005 Edition (Developer Edition has the same feature set as Enterprise Edition)

Feature/Functionality	Express	Workgroup	Standard	Enterprise
64-bit Support	With Windows on Windows (WOW)	With WOW	Native	Native
Maximum Database Size	4 GB	No Limit	No Limit	No Limit
Partitioning	No	No	No	Yes
Database Mirroring	No	No	Yes	Yes
Failover Clustering	No	No	Yes (two nodes only)	Yes
Log Shipping	No	Yes	Yes	Yes
Management Studio	No	Yes	Yes	Yes
Database Tuning Advisor	No	No	Yes	Yes
Full-Text Search	No	Yes	Yes	Yes
SQL Server Agent Job Scheduling Service	No	Yes	Yes	Yes
Best Practices Analyzer	Yes	Yes	Yes	Yes
Notification Services	No	No	Yes	Yes

Table 1-1   Feature Set by SQL Server 2005 Edition (Developer Edition has the same feature set as Enterprise Edition)

Feature/Functionality	Express	Workgroup	Standard	Enterprise
Service Broker	Yes (Subscriber only)	Yes	Yes	Yes
Merge Replication	Yes (Subscriber only)	Yes (Publish up to 25 Subscribers)	Yes	Yes
Transactional Replication	Yes (Subscriber only)	Yes (Publish up to five Subscribers)	Yes	Yes
Oracle Replication	No	No	No	Yes; transactional replication with an Oracle database as a Publisher
Web Services (HTTP Endpoints)	No	No	Yes	Yes
Report Server	Yes	Yes	Yes	Yes
Report Builder	No	Yes	Yes	Yes
BI Development Studio	Yes (Report Designer only)	Yes (Report Designer only)	Yes	Yes
Enterprise Management Tools	No	Yes	Yes	Yes

Table 1-1   Feature Set by SQL Server 2005 Edition (Developer Edition has the same feature set as Enterprise Edition)

Feature/Functionality	Express	Workgroup	Standard	Enterprise
Native Support for Web Services (Service Oriented Architectures)	Yes (Reporting Services only)	Yes (Reporting Services only)	Yes	Yes
Analysis Services	No	No	Yes	Yes

Quick Check

1. Which SQL Server 2005 edition is free?
2. Which SQL Server 2005 edition has the most features and functionality?

Quick Check Answers

1. Express Edition is free to use and distribute.
2. Enterprise Edition, targeted at organizations with large databases and complex applications, has the most features, including support for partitioning and Oracle replication. It is also licensed for production use. Although Developer Edition includes these same features, it is not licensed for use in a production environment.

Lesson Summary

- SQL Server 2005 includes five editions: Enterprise Edition, Developer Edition, Standard Edition, Workgroup Edition, and Express Edition.

- Enterprise Edition has no limitations and contains all features and functionality.

- Developer Edition has no limitations and contains all features and functionality, but it is not licensed for production.

- Standard Edition has features and functionality suited for larger data sets, but it is limited in the number of nodes it supports for clustering as well as in its capability to use system resources, online indexing, indexed views, fast recovery, online restores, and data partitioning.

- Workgroup Edition does not include the features and functionality needed to operate large databases and is restricted in its capability to support mid-size and large companies.

- Express Edition is useful for small application-installed databases that need to be distributed free of charge. It is not suited for organization-wide databases.

Lesson Review

The following questions are intended to reinforce key information presented in this lesson. The questions are also available on the companion CD if you prefer to review them in electronic form.

NOTE   Answers

Answers to these questions and explanations of why each answer choice is right or wrong are located in the "Answers" section at the end of the book.

---

1. You need to install a new production installation of SQL Server 2005. The server purchased for your installation has four CPUs. Which edition of SQL Server 2005 should you choose to make use of all the CPUs?

   A. SQL Server Express Edition

   B. SQL Server Workgroup Edition

   C. SQL Server Developer Edition

   D. SQL Server Standard Edition

2. During the design process for a new production installation of SQL Server 2005, you determine that you need to partition the database. Which edition supports data partitioning?

   A. SQL Server Express Edition

   B. SQL Server Workgroup Edition

   C. SQL Server Enterprise Edition

   D. SQL Server Standard Edition

3. As a database developer, you need to create an application that will be downloaded from the Internet. The application requires a database to store application data. Which SQL Server edition can you use for your application that does not require application users to purchase a license for SQL Server 2005?

   A. SQL Server Express Edition

   B. SQL Server Workgroup Edition

   C. SQL Server Developer Edition

   D. SQL Server Standard Edition

Lesson 2: Determining Infrastructure Requirements for SQL Server 2005

To select the appropriate infrastructure for your installation, you need to understand the minimum hardware requirements for each SQL Server 2005 edition on each of the supporting Windows operating system (OS) editions. When you review the minimum hardware requirements that this lesson covers, remember that these requirements are a recommended minimum—most production environments go beyond the minimum requirements to ensure an environment that has the speed and capacity the users need. Remember to also keep the future needs of your database environment in mind when determining the appropriate hardware for your situation. Planning for the future helps you avoid common performance problems and eliminate the need for computer hardware upgrades later.

After this lesson, you will be able to:

- Verify hardware prerequisites for a given installation.
- Verify OS prerequisites for a given installation.
- Verify network prerequisites for a given installation.

Estimated lesson time: 25 minutes

Identifying Minimum Hardware, OS, and Network Requirements

In deciding which edition of SQL Server 2005 to install, you need to take into account the processor, Windows OS, memory, hard-disk, and network requirements for both the 32-bit and 64-bit editions of SQL Server 2005. As noted previously, in most SQL Server 2005 production environments, the actual hardware requirements exceed the minimum hardware requirements for each SQL Server 2005 edition. However, it is still important to understand the minimum hardware requirements for the various SQL Server 2005 editions as a baseline to help you decide on the appropriate edition. Let's look at the infrastructure requirements for the 32-bit editions of SQL Server 2005 and then cover the requirements for the 64-bit editions.

32-Bit Editions of SQL Server 2005

- **Minimum processor requirements**   All editions of 32-bit SQL Server 2005 require a Pentium III-compatible, 600-MHz processor with a 1-GHz or faster processor recommended for optimal performance. Remember that this is a minimum requirement, and as with all SQL Server 2005 requirements, DBAs should insist on multiple fast processors for their production installations.

■ **Minimum OS allowed**   Unlike processor speeds, different editions of SQL Server 2005 require different editions and service packs for the Windows OSs. Following is a list of OSs required by each edition of 32-bit SQL Server 2005.

SQL Server 2005 Enterprise Edition

❏ Windows Server 2003 Standard Edition with Service Pack 1 (SP1) or later

❏ Windows Server 2003 Enterprise Edition with SP1 or later

❏ Windows Server 2003 Datacenter Edition with SP1 or later

❏ Windows Small Business Server 2003 Standard Edition with SP1 or later

❏ Windows Small Business Server 2003 Premium Edition with SP1 or later

❏ Windows 2000 Server with SP4

❏ Windows 2000 Advanced Server with SP4

❏ Windows 2000 Datacenter Server with SP4

SQL Server 2005 Standard Edition

❏ Windows Server 2003 Standard Edition with SP1 or later

❏ Windows Server 2003 Enterprise Edition with SP1 or later

❏ Windows Server 2003 Datacenter Edition with SP1 or later

❏ Windows Small Business Server 2003 Standard Edition with SP1 or later

❏ Windows Small Business Server 2003 Premium Edition with SP1 or later

❏ Windows 2000 Server with SP4

❏ Windows 2000 Advanced Server with SP4

❏ Windows 2000 Datacenter Server with SP4

❏ Windows 2000 Professional with SP4

❏ Windows XP Professional with SP2 or later

SQL Server 2005 Workgroup Edition

❏ All OSs listed for Enterprise and Standard editions

❏ Windows XP Media Edition with SP2 or later

❏ Windows XP Tablet Edition with SP2 or later

❏ Windows 2000 Professional with SP4

SQL Server 2005 Express Edition

❑ All OSs listed for Enterprise and Standard editions

❑ All OSs listed for Workgroup Edition

❑ Windows XP Home Edition with SP2 or later

❑ Windows Server 2003 Web Edition with SP1 or later

Developer Edition

❑ All OSs listed for Enterprise and Standard editions

❑ All OSs listed for Workgroup Edition

❑ Windows XP Home Edition with SP2 or later

■ **Memory requirements**   As with OS requirements, different editions of SQL Server 2005 require that you install different amounts of memory to perform effectively. The following list describes the amounts of memory required by each edition of 32-bit SQL Server 2005:

❑ SQL Server 2005 Enterprise Edition: 512 MB; 1 GB or more recommended

❑ SQL Server 2005 Standard Edition: 512 MB; 1 GB or more recommended

❑ SQL Server 2005 Workgroup Edition: 512 MB; 1 GB or more recommended (maximum of 3 GB)

❑ SQL Server 2005 Express Edition: 192 MB; 512 MB or more recommended (maximum of 1 GB)

❑ SQL Server 2005 Developer Edition: 512 MB; 1 GB or more recommended

■ **Hard disk space requirements**   All editions need 350 MB for full installation and an additional 390 MB for installing the sample databases.

■ **Internet and networking requirements**   Table 1-2 lists the Internet and network requirements for the 32-bit version of SQL Server 2005.

Table 1-2   **Internet and Networking Requirements for 32-Bit SQL Server 2005**

Component	Requirement
Internet Software	Microsoft Internet Explorer 6.0 SP1 or later is required for all installations of SQL Server 2005 because Internet Explorer is required for Microsoft Management Console (MMC) and HTML Help. A minimal installation of Internet Explorer is sufficient, and you do not need to configure Internet Explorer as the default browser. However, if you are using the Connectivity Only option and are not connecting to a server that requires encryption, Internet Explorer 4.01 with SP2 is sufficient.
Internet Information Server (IIS)	If you are writing XML applications, you must configure IIS. IIS 5.0 or higher is required for Reporting Services installations.
Network	The OS has built-in network software required for the SQL Server 2005 installation. TCP/IP must be enabled before you install SQL Server 2005.

64-Bit Editions of SQL Server 2005

- **Processor requirements**   Whereas all editions of 32-bit SQL Server 2005 require the same speeds as a minimum for all types of processors, 64-bit systems have different requirements based on the type of processor in the server. The following lists the minimum required speed for each 64-bit processor type:
  - All editions need IA64 minimum: 1 GHz or faster Itanium processor
  - X64 minimum: 1 GHz or faster AMD Opteron, AMD Athlon 64, Intel Xeon with Intel EM64T support, or Intel Pentium IV with EM64T support
- **Minimum OS requirements**   As with 32-bit SQL Server 2005, different editions of SQL Server 2005 64-bit require different editions and service packs of the Windows OSs. The following lists describe the different OSs required by each edition of 64-bit SQL Server 2005.

SQL Server 2005 Enterprise Edition (IA64)

  - Windows Server 2003 64-Bit Itanium Datacenter Edition with SP1 or later
  - Windows Server 2003 64-Bit Itanium Enterprise Edition with SP1 or later

SQL Server 2005 Standard Edition (IA64)

❑ Windows Server 2003 64-Bit Itanium Datacenter Edition with SP1 or later

❑ Windows Server 2003 64-Bit Itanium Enterprise Edition with SP1 or later

SQL Server 2005 Developer Edition (IA64)

❑ Windows Server 2003 64-Bit Itanium Datacenter Edition with SP1 or later

❑ Windows Server 2003 64-Bit Itanium Enterprise Edition with SP1 or later

SQL Server Enterprise Edition (X64)

❑ Windows Server 2003 64-Bit X64 Datacenter Edition with SP1 or later

❑ Windows Server 2003 64-Bit X64 Enterprise Edition with SP1 or later

❑ Windows Server 2003 64-Bit X64 Standard Edition with SP1 or later

SQL Server 2005 Standard Edition (X64)

❑ Windows Server 2003 64-Bit X64 Datacenter Edition with SP1 or later

❑ Windows Server 2003 64-Bit X64 Enterprise Edition with SP1 or later

❑ Windows Server 2003 64-Bit X64 Standard Edition with SP1 or later

SQL Server 2005 Developer Edition (X64)

❑ Windows Server 2003 64-Bit X64 Datacenter Edition with SP1 or later

❑ Windows Server 2003 64-Bit X64 Enterprise Edition with SP1 or later

❑ Windows Server 2003 64-Bit X64 Standard Edition with SP1 or later

SQL Server 2005 Express Edition

❑ All editions listed previously

❑ Windows XP X64 Professional (64-Bit)

- **Memory requirements**   Unlike the 32-bit SQL Server 2005 editions, all editions of SQL Server 2005 64-bit have the same memory requirements. All editions of SQL Server 2005 64-bit require at least 512 MB of memory, with 1 GB of memory recommended.

- **Hard disk space requirements**   All editions need 350 MB for full installation and 390 MB for sample databases.

- **Internet and networking requirements**   Table 1-3 lists the Internet and network requirements for the 64-bit version of SQL Server 2005.

Table 1-3   **Internet and Networking Requirements for 64-Bit SQL Server 2005**

Component	Requirement
Internet Software	Internet Explorer 6.0 SP1 or later is required for all SQL Server 2005 installations because Internet Explorer 6.0 is required for MMC and HTML Help. A minimal installation of Internet Explorer is sufficient, and Internet Explorer is not required to be the default browser. However, if you are using the Connectivity Only option and are not connecting to a server that requires encryption, Internet Explorer 4.01 SP2 is sufficient.
IIS	IIS 5.0 or higher is required for Reporting Services installations. If you are writing XML applications, you must configure IIS.
Network	The OS has built-in network software required for the SQL Server 2005 installation. TCP/IP must be enabled before installing SQL Server 2005.

Quick Check

■ You need to install SQL Server 2005 on a test server to evaluate the new functionality. Which edition do you use if your server has eight CPUs, and you want to use all the CPUs?

Quick Check Answer

■ Both the Enterprise and the Developer editions support eight CPUs; to test the functionality, you should probably select the Developer Edition.

Lesson Summary

■ SQL Server 2005 has editions that support 32-bit and 64-bit environments.

■ Different editions of SQL Server 2005 have different hardware, Windows OS, and networking requirements that you must study before choosing a particular SQL Server 2005 edition.

■ The SQL Server 2005 editions have different memory requirements that you must be familiar with before choosing a particular SQL Server 2005 edition.

■ Most production environments exceed the minimum hardware requirements to ensure satisfactory performance and capacity.

Lesson Review

The following questions are intended to reinforce key information presented in this lesson. The questions are also available on the companion CD if you prefer to review them in electronic form.

NOTE Answers

Answers to these questions and explanations of why each answer choice is right or wrong are located in the "Answers" section at the end of the book.

---

1. Which service pack level is required if you are using Windows 2000 Server for your SQL Server 2005 installation?

   A. SP1

   B. SP2

   C. SP3

   D. SP4

2. Which minimum service pack level is required if you are using Windows 2003 Server for your SQL Server 2005 installation?

   A. SP1

   B. SP2

   C. SP3

   D. SP4

3. Which SQL Server 2005 edition does NOT require at least 512 MB of memory?

   A. SQL Server Express Edition

   B. SQL Server Workgroup Edition

   C. SQL Server Developer Edition

   D. SQL Server Standard Edition

Lesson 3: Using Default, Named, and Multiple Instances of SQL Server 2005

SQL Server 2005 supports the capability to install multiple instances (or copies) of SQL Server 2005 or to install SQL Server 2005 alongside earlier versions of SQL Server on the same server. During the installation process, the DBA can choose to install an instance without a name—in which case, the instance name will take the name of the server—as a default instance. To install multiple instances of SQL Server besides the default instance on the same computer, the DBA must give the additional instances different names . Being able to install multiple instances of SQL Server lets you have system and user databases that are independent of each other. This capability not only lets you work with earlier versions of SQL Server already installed on your computer but also lets you test development software and operate instances of SQL Server 2005 independently of each other. This lesson shows you how to define a default instance and named instances of SQL Server 2005 and covers the advantages and disadvantages of each.

After this lesson, you will be able to:

- Define an instance as either a default or named instance.
- Determine when it is appropriate to create a default or named instance.

Estimated lesson time: 15 minutes

Installing a Default, Named, or Multiple Instances of SQL Server 2005

When you install SQL Server 2005, the Microsoft SQL Server Installation Wizard gives you the option of defining the installation as the default instance or as a named instance. A *named instance* simply means that you define a name for the instance during the installation. You will then have to access that instance by name. Default instances acquire the name of the server you install them on. Thus, you can have only one default instance at a time, but you can have many named instances.

When you start the Microsoft SQL Server Installation Wizard by running the Setup.exe application, it detects whether a default instance already exists on the computer. If the wizard does not detect a default instance, it gives you the choice of installing a default instance or a named instance. To install a named instance, clear the Default check box and type in the name of the named instance, as Figure 1-1 shows.

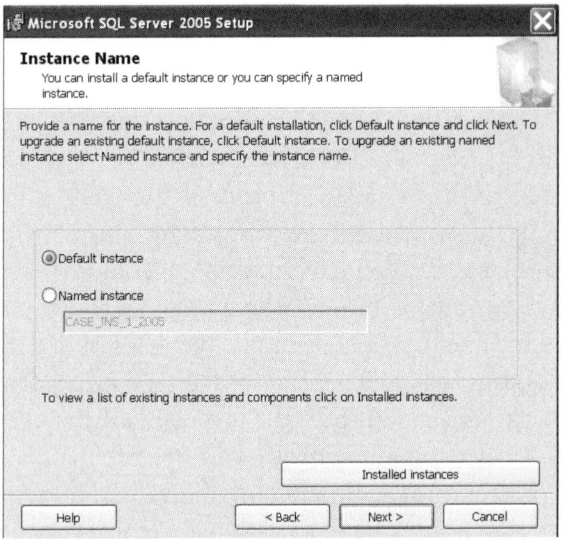

Figure 1-1 Installing a named instance.

NOTE Number of default instances

You can install only one default instance of SQL Server on a server, and you can install only one default instance on a cluster.

Determining When to Use Multiple Instances of SQL Server 2005

Using multiple instances of SQL Server 2005 increases administration overhead and causes duplication of components. Additional instances of the SQL Server and SQL Server Agent services require additional computer resources: memory and processing capacity.

However, in the following scenarios, using multiple instances has advantages over using only a single instance of SQL Server:

- When testing multiple versions of SQL Server on the same computer
- When testing service packs and development databases and applications
- When different customers require their own system and user databases along with full administrative control of their SQL Server instance
- When the desktop engine is embedded in applications because each application can install its own instance independent of instances installed by other applications

> ### Quick Check
> 1. How many default instances of SQL Server can you install on one server?
> 2. When testing multiple versions of SQL Server on the same computer, which type of instance should you install?
>
> #### Quick Check Answers
> 1. Only one default instance can be installed on a server or a cluster.
> 2. In this situation, you should install multiple named instances of SQL Server.

Lesson Summary

- You can install SQL Server 2005 multiple times on one server.

- Only one installation on each server or clustered grouping can be a default instance with no name; additional installations on a server or clustered grouping must be named instances.

- Multiple instances are useful for applying different service packs to different instances for testing purposes.

- Multiple instances are useful for hosting different databases for different customers, with each customer getting a separate instance of SQL Server.

Lesson Review

The following questions are intended to reinforce key information presented in this lesson. The questions are also available on the companion CD if you prefer to review them in electronic form.

NOTE Answers

Answers to these questions and explanations of why each answer choice is right or wrong are located in the "Answers" section at the end of the book.

---

1. You are a DBA at a SQL Server hosting organization. You need to ensure that each of your organization's client installations can operate with different service packs of SQL Server. What can you do to achieve your goals without requiring a different server for each client? (Choose the answer that reflects best practices.)

    A. Create one SQL Server installation and create a different database for each client.

    B. You cannot support different service packs on one server.

    C. Install a different instance of SQL Server for each client on your servers.

    D. Place clients together on servers that have SQL Server installations that have the required service packs.

2. How many default instances can you install on a single SQL Server server?

    A. 1

    B. 2

    C. 3

    D. 4

Lesson 4: Installing a New Instance of SQL Server 2005

During the installation of SQL Server 2005, you face many decisions, ranging from simple questions, such as which drives to install on, to more complex decisions about the installation's security and *collation*. In this lesson, you walk through the decisions you need to make regarding service accounts, authentication mode, and collation settings and see the best practices for determining the configuration most appropriate for your SQL Server 2005 environment.

> **After this lesson, you will be able to:**
> - Determine the service account to use for your installation.
> - Determine the authentication mode to use for your installation.
> - Determine the collation setting to use for your installation.
>
> **Estimated lesson time: 30 minutes**

Determining Service Accounts

One of the important decisions you make when installing SQL Server 2005 is which service accounts to use for the SQL Server and the SQL Server Agent services. These two SQL Server 2005 services run in the security context of a user account, and determining which account to use is an important decision. When installing SQL Server 2005, you need to answer two major questions about the service accounts:

- Should you use separate accounts for the SQL Server service and the SQL Server Agent service, or should you use the same account for both?
- Should you use a built-in system account or a *domain* user account?

Same or Different Accounts for SQL Server and SQL Server Agent Services?

When deciding whether to use the same account or different accounts for the SQL Server service and the SQL Server Agent service, you should take into account the functionality of the SQL Server Agent service. The SQL Server service rarely needs to interact with servers other than the one on which it is installed, but SQL Server jobs, replication processes, log shipping configurations, and other functionality often require that the SQL Server Agent service interact with different servers.

When the SQL Server Agent service must interact with different servers, DBAs typically create separate accounts for these two services to avoid giving the SQL Server service more permissions than it needs.

IMPORTANT   Restricted permissions

The need to restrict permissions of the SQL Server service account is often the determining factor when deciding whether to use one account for the SQL Server service and the SQL Server Agent service or separate accounts for these two services.

Built-In System Account or Domain User Account for the SQL Server and SQL Server Agent Services?

You can choose from among three types of accounts for the SQL Server and SQL Server Agent services: the Network Service account, a local system account, or a dedicated domain user account.

The *Network Service account* is a special built-in system account that is similar to authenticated user accounts. This account has the same level of access to system resources and objects as members of the Users group. Services that run under this account will use the credentials of the computer account to access network resources. It is not recommended that you use this account for either the SQL Server service or the SQL Server Agent service account.

The *local system account* is a Windows OS account that has full administrative rights on the local computer. You can use this account for development or testing of servers that you do not need to integrate with other server applications or to interact with any network resources. But because of the privileges granted to this account, it is not recommended that you use this account for the SQL Server or SQL Server Agent services.

In most SQL Server 2005 production environments, you create and use one or two dedicated domain user accounts for the SQL Server and SQL Server Agent services. Using domain user accounts lets these services communicate with other SQL Server installations, access network resources, and interact with other Windows applications. You can manually grant domain user accounts the permissions needed for the SQL Server service and the SQL Server Agent service, but all rights needed for these accounts will be granted automatically to the domain user accounts you specify when you assign the accounts during SQL Server 2005 setup.

CAUTION System Accounts have too many privileges

The Network Service account and local system account grant too many privileges to the SQL Server and SQL Server Agent services and aren't recommended for use with these services.

Choosing an Authentication Mode

SQL Server 2005 supports two *authentication* modes: Windows authentication and Mixed Mode. The default authentication mode for SQL Server 2005 is Windows authentication, which mandates that the only users who can connect to the SQL Server 2005 instance are users who have previously authenticated to the Windows OS.

The alternative authentication, Mixed Mode, means that SQL Server 2005 supports users who authenticate using either of two authentication methods. The first method is to rely on the Windows OS to authenticate users. The second method is for SQL Server 2005 to authenticate users directly based on the submission of a user name and password to SQL Server 2005 by the client application that is attempting to gain access.

For most SQL Server 2005 environments, you should use Windows authentication mode because it provides the highest level of security. However, legacy applications often do not use Windows user accounts, so they must forward a user name and password to connect to SQL Server. In this case, Mixed Mode authentication lets the legacy application use SQL Server logins to access the instance or if the database environment includes clients on OSs that cannot authenticate with the Windows OS such as Macintosh or UNIX clients. DBAs using Mixed Mode should be aware that using this authentication mode requires the creation of a strong password for the sa account. This account is highly privileged inside of SQL Server and its password is a critical factor when deciding to use Mixed Mode.

NOTE Windows vs. Mixed Mode authentication

Windows authentication mode provides the highest level of security for authenticating user access to a SQL Server instance. But if you have legacy applications that do not use Windows user accounts, you need to use Mixed Mode authentication.

Determining Collation Setting

You define the default collation for a SQL Server 2005 instance at installation time during setup. SQL Server uses the collation setting to determine how non-Unicode character data is stored and how to sort and compare Unicode and non-Unicode data.

To understand SQL Server 2005 collations, you need to start with the Windows OS. When you install a Windows OS, you install a version for the language you want to use, such as English, Greek, or Russian. These various language versions require different characters and different *code pages* to support the character sets and associated keyboard layouts. A Windows locale is also set, based on the version of the Windows OS that you have installed. This Windows locale determines the settings for numbers, currencies, times, and dates on the server.

Although this process might initially seem complicated, determining the *Windows collation* to use for SQL Server 2005 is generally straightforward. You should let the Microsoft SQL Server Installation Wizard determine the default Windows collation based on the Windows locale of the Windows OS unless one of the following conditions exists:

- The primary language supported by the SQL Server 2005 instance you are installing is different from the Windows locale of the computer on which you are installing SQL Server 2005.

- The SQL Server 2005 instance you are installing will participate in a replication scheme with SQL Server 2005 instances supporting a different language.

Quick Check

1. Which authentication mode is often required for legacy applications?

2. Which two accounts are not recommended for use with the SQL Server service and the SQL Server Agent service?

Quick Check Answers

1. Many legacy applications require the use of SQL Server logins, which mandates Mixed Mode authentication.

2. The Network Service account and local system account grant too many privileges and are not recommended for use with the SQL Server and SQL Server Agent services.

PRACTICE Installing a SQL Server 2005 Named Instance

In this practice, you will install a SQL Server 2005 named instance.

1. Start the Microsoft SQL Server Installation Wizard by running the Setup application using the menu that appears when you insert the CD. On the End User License Agreement page, select the I Accept The Licensing Terms And Conditions check box and click Next.

2. On the Installing Prerequisites page, click Next when the installation of the required components completes.

3. On the Welcome To The Microsoft SQL Server Installation Wizard page, click Next.

4. Verify the completion of the System Configuration Checker, as Figure 1-2 shows.

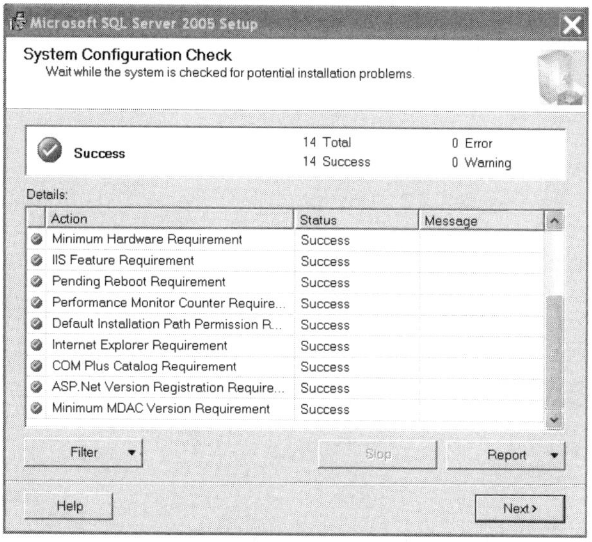

Figure 1-2   Verify the System Configuration Checker.

5. Click Next.

6. Fill in the appropriate user and organization name in the text boxes shown in Figure 1-3.

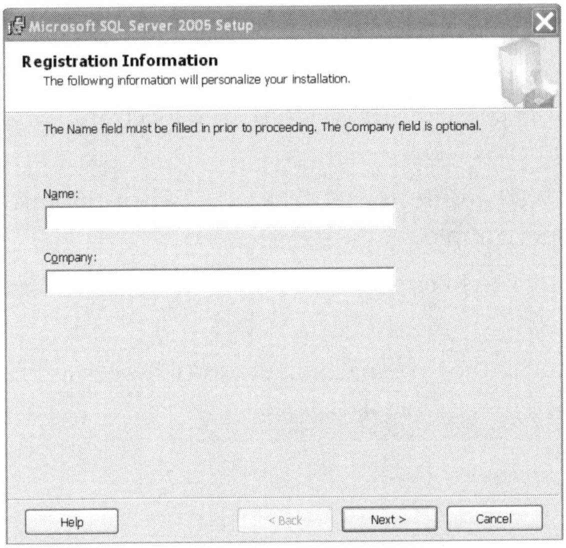

Figure 1-3 Add user and organization name for registration.

7. Click Next.

8. Select the appropriate components to install by checking the box next to the component. For this practice, you should install all the available components (see Figure 1-4).

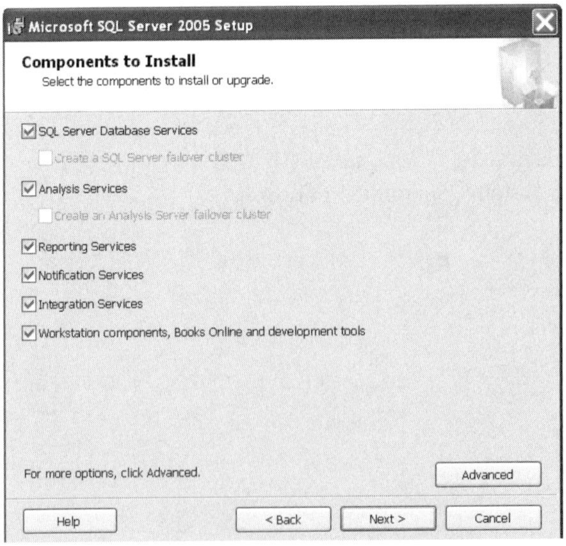

Figure 1-4 Determine appropriate components.

9. Click Advanced. Expand the Documentation, Samples, And Sample Databases tree.

10. From the drop-down list associated with Sample Databases (see Figure 1-5), select Entire Feature Will Be Installed On Local Hard Drive.

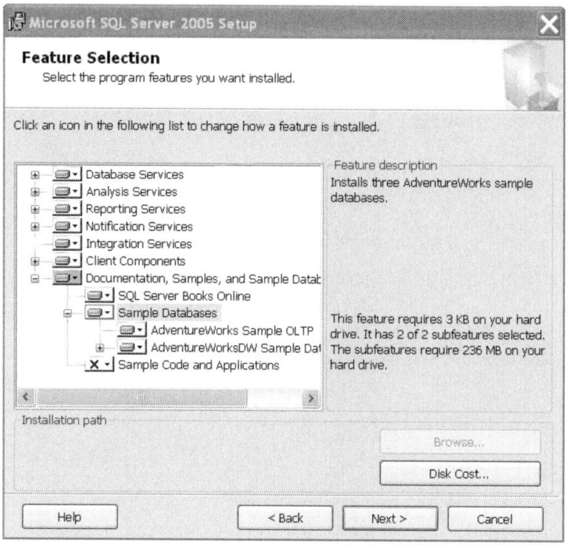

Figure 1-5   Install sample databases.

11. Click Next.

12. Determine which instance names are already in use on the server by clicking Installed Instances, which displays the window shown in Figure 1-6.

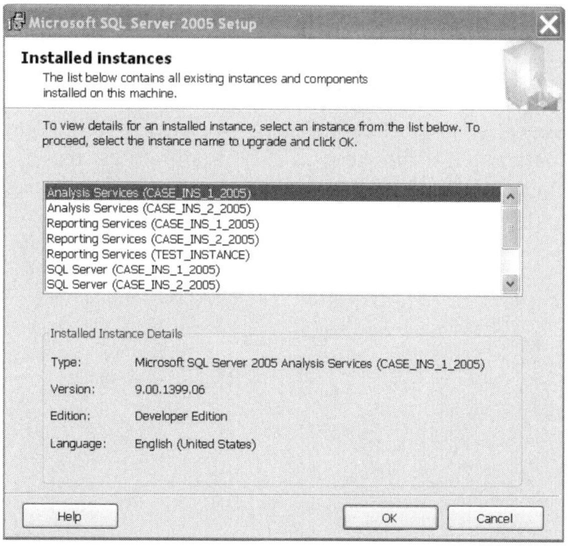

Figure 1-6   Determine names in use.

13. Click OK.

14. Install a default instance, as Figure 1-7 shows.

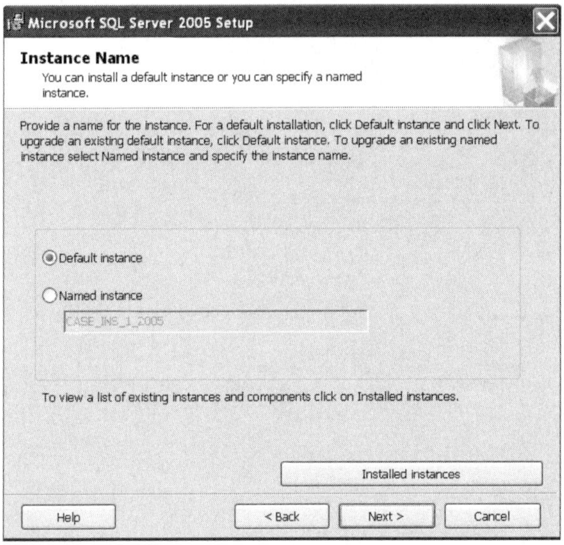

Figure 1-7   Name an instance.

15. Click Next.

16. Review the components that will be installed and click Next.

17. Configure the service account information and the component startup information by selecting Use The Built-In System Account and choosing Local System from the drop-down list, as shown in Figure 1-8.

CAUTION   Local System account vs. domain user account

This practice uses the local system account because we assume that you are working on a computer that is not part of a domain. Keep in mind that the best practices for configuring the service account in a domain environment are to configure these services using a domain user account instead of using the local system account.

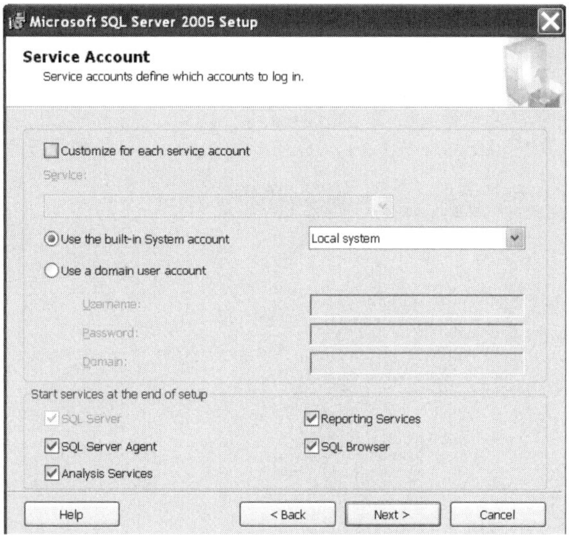

Figure 1-8 Configure service accounts.

18. Select the SQL Server Agent check box.

19. Click Next.

20. Configure the authentication mode by selecting Mixed Mode (Windows Authentication And SQL Server Authentication), as shown in Figure 1-9.

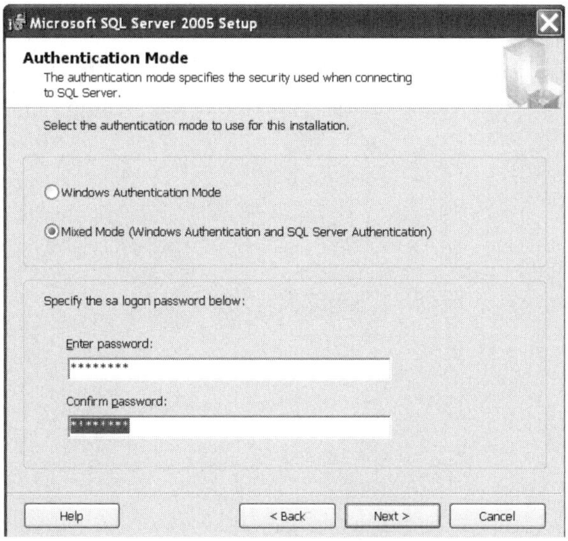

Figure 1-9 Configure authentication mode.

21. Enter a strong password in the password text boxes. This password is used by the sa login ID.

22. Click Next.

23. Review the default collation settings, which Figure 1-10 shows.

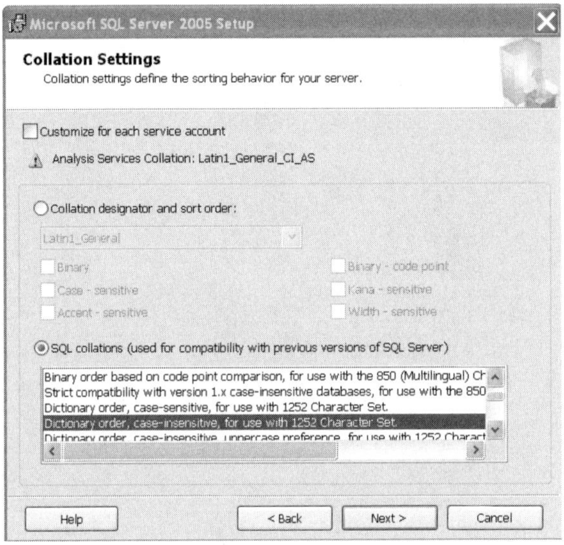

Figure 1-10   Configure the collation.

24. Click Next.

25. Configure error and usage reporting by selecting both the Automatically Send Error Reports and Automatically Send Feature Usage Data check boxes, shown in Figure 1-11.

Figure 1-11   Configure error and usage reporting.

26. Click Next.

27. Verify which components will be installed (see Figure 1-12).

Figure 1-12   Verify which components will be installed.

28. Click Install.

29. Verify that setup is complete (see Figure 1-13).

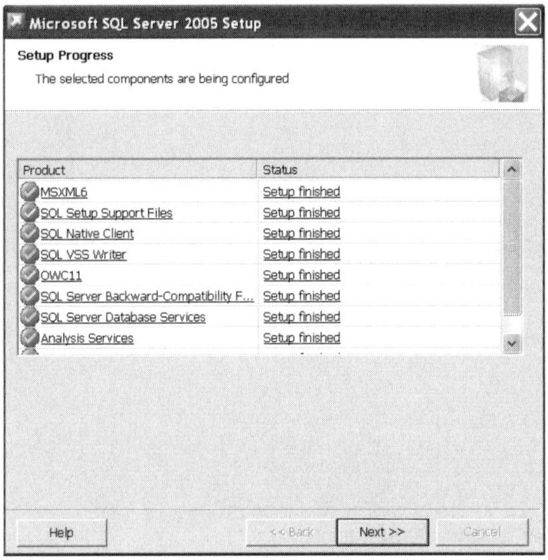

Figure 1-13   Verify that setup is complete.

30. Click Next and then review the completion report.

31. Click Finish.

Lesson Summary

- SQL Server 2005 requires you to select at least one account to use for the SQL Server service and the SQL Server Agent service.

- You must use current business requirements, organization security requirements, and organization database standards to decide whether to install SQL Server 2005 with different service accounts for the SQL Server service and the SQL Server Agent service.

- You must use current business requirements, organization security requirements, and organization database standards to decide whether to install SQL Server 2005 with local system accounts or a domain user account (which is recommended) for the SQL Server service and the SQL Server Agent service.

- When installing SQL Server 2005, Windows authentication mode provides the highest level of security, but legacy applications might require Mixed Mode authentication.

- In most cases, you should let the Microsoft SQL Server Installation Wizard determine which collation to use when installing SQL Server 2005.

Lesson Review

The following questions are intended to reinforce key information presented in this lesson. The questions are also available on the companion CD if you prefer to review them in electronic form.

NOTE Answers

Answers to these questions and explanations of why each answer choice is right or wrong are located in the "Answers" section at the end of the book.

---

1. Which SQL Server 2005 services require that you install them with their own account? (Choose all that apply.)

    A. SQL Server Agent

    B. Log Reader Agent

    C. SQL Server

    D. Replication Agent

2. Which authentication mode lets you use both SQL Server logins and Windows logins?

    A. Kerebos authentication

    B. Windows

    C. Mixed Mode

    D. Network Service account

Lesson 5: Upgrading to a SQL Server 2005 Installation

With the release of SQL Server 2005, many DBAs will want to upgrade their existing databases to the new release to make use of all its new features. As part of this task, DBAs must understand the methods available to perform an upgrade to SQL Server 2005 and must develop a strategy that includes a recovery plan in case the upgrade needs to be rolled back because of problems. In this lesson, you explore the two types of upgrades available, different methods you can use to move files from the old database to the new one, ways to develop testing criteria to make sure the upgrade was successful, and best practices for upgrading.

NOTE   No direct upgrade from SQL Server 6.5

You cannot upgrade a SQL Server 6.5 database environment directly to SQL Server 2005. Instead, you will need to perform a two-step upgrade. First, upgrade from the 6.5 environment to either SQL Server 7.0 or SQL Server 2000, and then upgrade to SQL Server 2005.

> **After this lesson, you will be able to:**
> - Select the appropriate upgrade strategy for your environment.
> - Select an appropriate upgrade method for a side-by-side migration.
> - Develop criteria to test the success of your upgrade.
> - Upgrade from a previous version of SQL Server.
>
> **Estimated lesson time: 20 minutes**

Determining an Appropriate Upgrade Strategy

An essential task of upgrading to SQL Server 2005 is choosing an upgrade strategy, which is the process you use to upgrade the current environment. The strategy not only determines the type of upgrade that you will perform—in-place upgrade or side-by-side migration—but it also determines the upgrade method you use, how you test the upgrade, and what the upgrade success criteria are. The upgrade strategy combines these items with a recovery plan for rolling back the upgrade if you encounter problems that cannot be corrected during the upgrade process.

In-Place Upgrade

Organizations that do not have resources available to host multiple database environments commonly use an in-place upgrade. An in-place upgrade overwrites a previous installation of SQL Server 7.0 or SQL Server 2000 with an installation of SQL Server 2005. During the in-place upgrade, the installation process overwrites previous versions of the SQL Server program files. The upgrade process preserves all user data stored in the previous SQL Server instance, which lets DBAs perform the upgrade without having to move or recover the existing user databases.

Database backups required   Before you perform an in-place upgrade, you should back up all SQL Server databases and other objects associated with your previous SQL Server instances. In addition, be aware that the previous version of SQL Server Books Online will remain intact on the machine after the upgrade.

Side-by-Side Migration

Database environments that have additional server resources can perform a side-by-side migration of their SQL Server 7.0 or SQL Server 2000 installations to SQL Server 2005. Side-by-side migrations involve installing SQL Server 2005 either on the same server or on a different server as your previous SQL Server installations. Having the old environment still active during the upgrade process allows for the continuous operation of the original database environment while you install and test the upgraded environment. Side-by-side migrations can often minimize the amount of downtime for the SQL Server environment. Table 1-4 shows the support for side-by-side migration when upgrading from different versions of SQL Server to SQL Server 2000 (32-bit and 64-bit) and SQL Server 2005 (32-bit and 64-bit).

Table 1-4   Side-by-Side Migration Support

SQL Server Version You Are Upgrading From	SQL Server 2000 (32-bit)*	SQL Server 2000 (64-bit)	SQL Server 2005 (32-bit)*	SQL Server 2005 (64-bit) IA64	SQL Server 2005 (64-bit) X64
SQL Server 7.0	Yes	No	Yes	No	No
SQL Server 2000 (32-bit)	Yes	No	Yes	No	Yes
SQL Server 2000 (64-bit)	No	Yes	No	Yes	No
SQL Server 2005 (32-bit)	Yes	No	Yes	No	Yes
SQL Server 2005 (64-bit) IA64	No	Yes	No	Yes	No
SQL Server 2005 (64-bit) X64	Yes	No	Yes	No	Yes

* The 32-bit editions of SQL Server are supported in WOW64 only on the X64 versions of 64-bit OSs. The 32-bit editions of SQL Server are not supported in WOW64 on the IA64 versions of 64-bit OSs.

A side-by-side migration does not overwrite the SQL Server files on your current installation, nor does it move the databases to your new SQL Server 2005 installation. DBAs need to manually move their databases to the new SQL Server 2005 installation after a side-by-side installation by using one of the upgrade methods that the next section of this lesson discusses.

Choosing an Upgrade Method

DBAs can choose from four methods for moving databases from one SQL Server instance to another during a side-by-side migration: detach/attach, backup/restore, the Copy Database Wizard, and a manual schema rebuild combined with data export/import. The DBA is responsible for performing tests to determine which method is appropriate for the specific database environment. During testing, keep in mind several important factors that can influence your decision to use one method over the other. These factors can include database size, available disk space on source and destination servers, network bandwidth, and speed of the overall operation.

Detach/Attach

When disk storage and source database availability are not a consideration, one common method of moving a database from one server to another is to detach and then attach the database. This process requires that users not be accessing the database, but it has the safety advantage that if an unforeseen problem arises, the DBA can always reattach a copy of the database file to the original SQL Server instance.

Make a copy of the files   It is a best practice to create a copy of the database file for recovery purposes before attaching it to a new instance. After you attach a database file to SQL Server 2005, you can no longer use that file in an earlier version of SQL Server.

You can move a large database from one instance to another on the same server, which requires less disk space than some other methods because it reduces the number of database files that you must create for the upgrade process. However, this method can be unsafe because it doesn't follow the recommendation of creating a copy of the database files.

On systems that use storage area network (SAN) disk configurations, you can detach the SAN volume from the older SQL Server instance and attach it to the new SQL Server 2005 server. This procedure saves you from having to move the database files over the network. It is also possible to clone the disk volume while the original SQL Server is online and then re-create that clone on another disk array. DBAs working with a SAN disk configuration should meet with their disk engineers to discuss possible methods to move the database files without having to perform a copy over the network. DBAs must also take into account the possible inability to revert to the earlier version of SQL Server if something goes wrong after they have upgraded their files, which are then no longer usable by earlier versions of SQL Server.

Backup/Restore

To avoid possible loss of the database files, making a database *backup* to use in the upgrade is a secure alternative method for moving a database from one SQL Server instance to another. You use the following process:

- Create a simple *backup file* through normal database backup methods.
- Move the backup file to the location of the new SQL Server instance.
- Restore the backup file through the SQL Server *database restore* process, changing the file location if necessary.

This process does not interfere with the continuation of activity on the original database environment, nor does it jeopardize the usefulness of the source database files to the original SQL Server version.

Another advantage of using backup and restore is that the backup files are usually smaller than the original database files because the backup process captures only database data, not reserved, unused database space. The decrease in file size usually makes any file transfer faster than transferring the original database file. However, you must take into account the disk space needed for the original database files, the backup files, and the new database files during the upgrade.

Copy Database Wizard

DBAs who want to automate the task of moving a database from one server to another during the upgrade process can use SQL Server's Copy Database Wizard. The Copy Database Wizard gives DBAs a way to move one or more SQL Server 2000 or SQL Server 2005 databases, with their associated objects, while the source database is either online and available for use or offline. This direct copy makes efficient use of disk space while preserving database uptime.

With the Copy Database Wizard, DBAs can

- Select source and destination servers.
- Select one or more databases to be moved and upgraded.
- Specify the file locations for the selected databases.
- Create logins on the destination server.
- Copy supporting environment objects such as jobs, error messages, user-defined stored procedures, and objects.
- Define a schedule for performing the database move or copy.

Manual Schema Rebuild and Data Export/Import

A method not commonly used for database upgrades is the manual method of scripting out the database, scripting the logins associated with that database, scripting all objects associated with that database, and scripting out any other supporting SQL Server objects associated with that database. After executing the script or scripts in the new instance, the DBA must manually move the data from the original database to the new database using Transact-SQL scripts, Data Transformation Services (DTS) or SQL Server Integration Services (SSIS), BCP, or other methods available for moving data from one database to another.

Most DBAs do not choose this mostly manual method to upgrade their databases because of the time and effort it involves. However, manually moving a database has the advantage of letting DBAs modify the database schema, clean up data, and filter the data they move to the upgraded databases.

Quick Check

- What are some of the ways you can move a database from one server to another during an upgrade?

Quick Check Answers

- You can use detach/attach, backup/restore, Copy Database Wizard, or manual methods to move your database from one server to another during an upgrade.

Determining Testing and Success Criteria

As noted earlier in this lesson, you need to define the criteria that determine the success of your database upgrade. The success test might be as simple as manually verifying the existence of an object through the graphical user interface (GUI); or it might be a very complex procedure that executes a set of predetermined queries and scripts to verify that all objects exist, that data has successfully imported, that surrounding database objects such as backup jobs operate normally, and that users have full access to the database. However simple or complex the success criteria, you must define the criteria before upgrading to help ensure a successful upgrade.

To prepare the success criteria, you should review each phase and step of the overall database upgrade plan and ask yourself several questions. The following questions will help you understand what you need to do to declare that the phase or step is successful:

- How can I measure whether this step is successful?
- How can I test that measurement?
- How can I compare my test results against what they would have been in the old database?

Establishing a Recovery Plan

Although creating an upgrade plan reduces the likelihood of problems occurring during the upgrade process, problems do arise that can prevent the upgrade process from completing. Most organizations rely heavily on the data contained in their databases, and having that data unavailable due to an upgrade might cause problems in business operations and even have financial implications. You should create a plan to recover from each phase and step of the upgrade process to help minimize data loss and reduce the time that data might be unavailable. This recovery plan might involve backing up a set of files, creating scripts to move database connections from the upgraded instance back to the original instance, or anything else you feel is necessary to get the old database instance back up and meet business uptime needs while you fix the upgrade problems.

Tips for a Successful Upgrade

The following tips can help you perform a secure and successful upgrade:

- **Create a series of checklists** DBAs and developers should prepare a series of checklists that need to be performed before, during, and after a database upgrade.
- **Back up all important files** Back up all SQL Server database files from the instance to be upgraded, as well as any application files, script files, extract files, and so on so that you can completely restore them if necessary.
- **Ensure database consistency** Run *DBCC CHECKDB* on databases to be upgraded to ensure that they are in a consistent state before performing your upgrade.
- **Reserve enough disk space** Estimate the disk space required to upgrade SQL Server components, user databases, and any database files that might need to be created during the upgrade process. You might need two to four times the amount of disk space during the upgrade process as you will need after the upgrade is finished.

- **Ensure space for system databases** Configure system databases (*master*, *model*, *msdb*, and *tempdb*) to autogrow during the upgrade process, and make sure that they have enough disk space for this growth.

- **Transfer login information** Ensure that all database servers have login information in the *master* database before upgrading the database. This step is important for restoring a database because system login information resides in the *master* database and must be re-created in the new instance.

- **Disable all startup stored procedures** The upgrade process will usually stop and start services multiple times on the SQL Server instance being upgraded. Stored procedures set to execute on startup might block the upgrade process.

- **Stop replication** Stop replication and make sure that the replication log is empty for starting the upgrade process.

- **Quit all applications** Certain applications, including all services with SQL Server dependencies, might cause the upgrade process to fail if local applications are connected to the instance being upgraded.

- **Register your servers after the upgrade** The upgrade process removes registry settings for the previous SQL Server instance. After upgrading, you must reregister your servers.

- **Repopulate full-text catalogs** The upgrade process marks your databases as full-text disabled. Catalogs must be repopulated, but Setup doesn't run this operation automatically because it can be time-consuming. Because this operation enhances the performance of your SQL Server 2005 installation, you should plan to repopulate full-text catalogs at a convenient time after the upgrade.

- **Update statistics** To help optimize query performance, update statistics on all databases following the upgrade.

- **Update usage counters** In earlier versions of SQL Server, the values for the table and index row counts and page counts can become incorrect. To correct any invalid row or page counts, run *DBCC UPDATEUSAGE* on all databases following the upgrade.

- **Configure your new SQL Server installation** To reduce the system's attackable surface area, SQL Server 2005 selectively installs and activates key services and features. You will need to customize this configuration so that you get the optimum security, performance, and functionality for your particular installation. Chapter 2, "Configuring SQL Server 2005," covers the details for configuring your SQL Server implementation.

PRACTICE Using Detach/Attach and Backup/Restore to Move Databases

It is important that DBAs learn to move databases to different servers during the upgrade process. The following two practices take you through the process of moving a database using both the detach/attach method and the backup/restore method.

 Practice 1: Detach and Attach a SQL Server 2000 Database to SQL Server 2005

In this practice, you will detach a SQL Server 2000 database, copy the data file and transaction log file to a new location, and attach the files to SQL Server 2005.

NOTE   SQL Server 2000 required

To complete this practice, you must have SQL Server 2000 installed on your server.

---

1.   Start SQL Server 2000 Enterprise Manager.

2.   Expand the group containing the server that holds your database and then expand the Databases folder.

3.   Right-click the *pubs* database, choose Properties, and click the Data Files tab.

4.   Make a note of the location of the data file for the *pubs* database.

5.   Click the Transaction Log tab.

6.   Make a note of the location of the transaction log file for the *pubs* database. Click Cancel to close the Pubs Properties dialog box.

7.   Right-click the *pubs* database, choose All Tasks, Detach Database, and then click OK twice.

8.   Open Windows Explorer and navigate to the directory containing the data file and log file.

9.   Copy the data file and log file to a new location for SQL Server 2005 databases.

10.   Start SQL Server Management Studio (SSMS), connect to the instance to which you want to attach the database, right-click the Databases folder, and then choose Attach.

11.   Click Add.

12.   Navigate to the location in which you copied the data and transaction log files, click OK, and then click OK again to attach the files to the new database.

13.   Now you can reattach the database to your SQL Server 2000 instance if you want by right-clicking the Databases folder in SQL Server 2000 Enterprise Manager; then choose All Tasks, Attach Database.

14. Click the browser (...) button and navigate to the location of the original data and transaction log files. Select the Pubs.mdf file and click OK twice. Click OK again when the attach completes.

▶ **Practice 2: Back Up and Restore a SQL Server 2000 Database to SQL Server 2005**

In this practice, you will back up a SQL Server 2000 database and restore the file to SQL Server 2005.

NOTE   SQL Server 2000 required

To complete this practice, you must have SQL Server 2000 installed on your server.

---

1. Start SQL Server 2000 Enterprise Manager.

2. Expand the group containing the server that holds your database and expand the Databases folder.

3. Right-click the *pubs* database and choose All Tasks, Backup Database.

4. Create your backup file and click OK to back up the database.

5. Click OK when the database backup completes.

6. Start SSMS.

7. Connect to the instance to which you want to attach the database.

8. Right-click the Databases folder and then choose Restore Database.

9. Type pubs in the To Database text box.

10. Select From Device and then click the browser (...) button.

11. Choose File as the backup media and click Add.

12. Navigate to and select the backup file you just created.

13. Click OK and then click OK again.

14. Select the check box under the Restore column for the backup you want to restore. (If the backup media contains multiple backup sets, you should choose the last backup created.)

15. Select the Options page.

16. Below the Restore As column, type in the location and data file name to which you want to restore the backed up data file. Alternatively, you can use the browser (...) button to navigate to the new location and enter the name you want for the physical file. You should specify .mdf as the extension for all primary files and .ndf as the extension for secondary data files.

17. Repeat the previous step for the transaction log file, specifying .ldf as the extension for all log files.

18. Click OK to restore the backup. When the process is complete, click OK to close the displayed message box.

Lesson Summary

■ When upgrading a SQL Server installation to SQL Server 2005, you have the option of performing an in-place upgrade or a side-by-side upgrade.

■ An in-place upgrade requires the installation of SQL Server 2005 on top of a current installation, replacing the old SQL Server files.

■ A side-by-side upgrade involves installing SQL Server 2005 as a new instance either on the same server as the old instance or on a different server. The databases are then moved to the new SQL Server 2005 instance.

■ Always make a backup copy of your databases before attempting an upgrade.

■ In a side-by-side upgrade, DBAs have multiple ways to move databases from an old SQL Server instance to a SQL Server 2005 instance: detach/attach, backup/ restore, the Copy Database Wizard, and manual.

■ Before upgrading your SQL Server installations, create a testing plan to validate the successful upgrade of your installation.

■ Before upgrading your SQL Server installations, you should create an upgrade rollback plan in case you need to recover from an unsuccessful upgrade.

Lesson Review

The following questions are intended to reinforce key information presented in this lesson. The questions are also available on the companion CD if you prefer to review them in electronic form.

NOTE Answers

Answers to these questions and explanations of why each answer choice is right or wrong are located in the "Answers" section at the end of the book.

1. The term "in-place upgrade" refers to which type of upgrade?

    A. Installing SQL Server 2005 in the same directory as the current installation and replacing the SQL Server files

    B. Installing a new instance of SQL Server 2005 and sharing the older databases between the new instance and the old instance

    C. Installing a new instance of SQL Server 2005 on the same server as the old instance and moving the databases from the old instance to the new instance

    D. Installing a new instance of SQL Server 2005 on a different server from the old instance and moving the databases from the old server to the new server

2. Which upgrade data-movement method requires that users not be accessing the database you want to upgrade?

    A. Copy Database Wizard

    B. Detach/attach

    C. Backup/restore

    D. Manual scripting

3. Which of the following is not recommended when performing a SQL Server upgrade?

    A. Create a series of checklists to ensure that all processes needed before, during, and after an upgrade have been completed.

    B. Reserve enough disk space for the extra copies of database files needed for the upgrade.

    C. Disable all startup stored procedures to prevent the stored procedures from firing multiple times during the upgrade.

    D. Configure system databases not to autogrow to prevent system databases from filling your disks during the upgrade process.

Chapter Review

To further practice and reinforce the skills you learned in this chapter, you can

- Review the chapter summary.
- Review the list of key terms introduced in this chapter.
- Complete the case scenarios. These scenarios set up a real-world situation involving the topics of this chapter and ask you to create solutions.
- Complete the suggested practices.
- Take a practice test.

Chapter Summary

- SQL Server 2005 includes five editions, with each edition having different functionality and feature sets and different infrastructure requirements. Understanding the editions and their hardware, OS, and network requirements is key to selecting the correct edition for your needs.
- You can install a default, unnamed instance of SQL Server 2005 and multiple additional named instances on the same server. Multiple instances can be beneficial for testing purposes and for separating different customers' databases.
- SQL Server 2005 requires at least one account for use by the SQL Server service and the SQL Server Agent service. To make sure that the SQL Server service doesn't have more privileges than necessary, you often need to use a separate account for each service.
- When upgrading a SQL Server installation to SQL Server 2005, you can perform either an in-place upgrade or a side-by-side migration. A side-by-side migration, which allows for the continuous operation of the original database environment while the upgraded environment is being installed and tested, can often minimize downtime for the SQL Server environment.
- You can use detach/attach, backup/restore, the Copy Database Wizard, or manual scripting to move database files in a side-by-side migration. Whichever method you choose, you should make a copy of your original files in case you need to recover your original environment because of an upgrade problem.

Key Terms

Do you know what these key terms mean? You can check your answers by looking up the terms in the glossary at the end of the book.

- authentication
- backup
- backup file
- code page
- collation
- database restore
- domain
- local system account
- named instance
- Network Service account
- Mixed Mode authentication
- Windows collation

Case Scenarios

In the following case scenarios, you will apply what you've learned about how to install SQL Server 2005 as well as how to upgrade current installations of SQL Server to SQL Server 2005. You can find answers to these questions in the "Answers" section at the end of this book.

Case Scenario 1: Installing SQL Server 2005

You are a DBA for a local book publisher. For the past year, you and your team have been designing a new database system to handle ordering information. You have designed your database schema and now need to create an installation plan. To complete the last items of the plan, you need to interview a team of database designers and answer the following questions. Here are the statements from the organization personnel you interviewed:

- **Database Security Lead**   "Most of our database applications have been built to be used with different database platforms. The current application requires the use of a SQL Server login for each component."

- **Database Architecture Lead**   "For this current database installation, we require the ability to partition the database and make use of our eight CPU servers. We also require the ability to place the databases for different retail stores on the same server but with each store being separate from the others."

With the information gained from your interviews, answer the following questions for your manager:

1. Which authentication mode should you use?

2. Should you use a single default instance or multiple named instances?

3. Which edition of SQL Server is the most appropriate?

Case Scenario 2: Upgrading an Instance of SQL Server

You are a DBA for large phone company. The company has decided to upgrade to SQL Server 2005, and you are charged with creating and implementing the upgrade plan. During a planning meeting, your manager asks you questions about your upgrade plan. Answer the following questions for your manager.

1. Given that we are buying new servers, how will we get the databases from the old installation to the new SQL Server 2005 instance without affecting the current online availability?

2. How can we make sure that service will not be interrupted if the upgrade process fails?

3. How can we make sure that the current applications will not have problems once we connect them to the new installation?

Suggested Practices

To successfully master the exam objectives presented in this chapter, complete the following tasks.

Selecting an Edition of SQL Server 2005 to Install

For this task, you should complete both practices to gain experience in deciding which edition of SQL Server 2005 to install.

- **Practice 1**   Review the functionality and feature set of each SQL Server 2005 edition against a current installation or application to determine which features are required in the current installation or by your application.

- **Practice 2**   Review the infrastructure requirements of each edition of SQL Server 2005 against a current installation or application to determine which features are required in the current installation or by your application.

Determining When to Install Default, Named, or Multiple Instances of SQL Server 2005

For this task, you should complete all three practices to gain experience in deciding when to install default, named, or multiple instances of SQL Server 2005.

- **Practice 1**   Review current business requirements and application needs to determine the authentication method needed for an installation of SQL Server 2005.

- **Practice 2**   Review current business requirements and application needs to determine the collation needed for an installation of SQL Server 2005.

- **Practice 3**   Install a default and multiple named instances of SQL Server 2005 on the same server.

Upgrading a SQL Server 2005 Installation

For this task, you should complete all four practices to gain experience upgrading a SQL Server 2005 instance by using the various data-movement methods.

- **Practice 1**   Upgrade an installation of SQL Server by using the detach/attach method of data movement.

- **Practice 2**   Upgrade an installation of SQL Server by using the backup/restore method of data movement.

- **Practice 3**   Upgrade an installation of SQL Server by using the Copy Database Wizard method of data movement.

- **Practice 4**   Upgrade an installation of SQL Server by using the manual scripting method of data movement.

Take a Practice Test

The practice tests on this book's companion CD offer many options. For example, you can test yourself on just the content covered in this chapter, or you can test yourself on all the 70-431 certification exam content. You can set up the test so that it closely simulates the experience of taking a certification exam, or you can set it up in study mode so that you can look at the correct answers and explanations after you answer each question.

MORE INFO   **Practice tests**

For details about all the practice test options available, see "How to Use the Practice Tests" in this book's Introduction.

Chapter 2

Configuring SQL Server 2005

The decisions you make as you configure your Microsoft SQL Server 2005 environment are crucial in setting up a high-performing, secure, and functional system. In this chapter, you will see how to configure data and log files and filegroups and how to select the appropriate redundant array of inexpensive disks (RAID) level for your databases. You'll explore the new Database Mail system that lets the database engine send e-mail messages. And you'll learn the differences between the three recovery models of SQL Server and how to specify the correct model for your situation. This chapter explains the important security concepts of authentication modes, logins, database users, database roles, and schemas; and shows you how to configure a secure system. You'll also learn about the new native encryption facilities of SQL Server 2005 and how to configure linked servers to access external data sources.

Exam objectives in this chapter:

- Configure SQL Server 2005 instances and databases.
    - ❑ Configure log files and data files.
    - ❑ Configure the SQL Server DatabaseMail subsystem for an instance.
    - ❑ Choose a recovery model for the database.
- Configure SQL Server security.
    - ❑ Configure server security principals.
    - ❑ Configure database securables.
    - ❑ Configure encryption.
- Configure linked servers by using SQL Server Management Studio (SSMS).
    - ❑ Identify the external data source.
    - ❑ Identify the characteristics of the data source.
    - ❑ Identify the security model of the data source.

Lessons in this chapter:

Before You Begin

To complete the lessons in this chapter, you must have

- SQL Server 2005 installed.

- A connection to a SQL Server 2005 instance.

- A copy of the *AdventureWorks* sample database installed.

Real World

Antonio Soto

In my work as a database consultant, clients often call me to fix problems that arise from a poor SQL Server configuration. Configuring database files is a fundamental and crucial database administrator (DBA) task. Although SQL Server 2005 provides a default configuration that is valid for a wide range of environments, you should customize database and instance options for your particular environment. Designing and planning a configuration strategy for your storage, security, and linked-server needs gives you a strong base for a high-performing and protected SQL Server environment. And if you pay special attention to the configuration options that this chapter covers, you can deploy an optimum SQL Server environment from the start and avoid a lot of headaches.

Lesson 1: Configuring Log and Data Files

A SQL Server 2005 database has two operating system file types: data files and log files. *Data files* contain data and objects such as tables and indexes; *log files* contain the transaction log for recovering the database's transactions. You can further group data files into filegroups for easier administration and better performance. This lesson explains the different file types, walks you through the configuration options you have, and shares best practices for setting up your files for top performance and recoverability.

After this lesson, you will be able to:

- Configure the data and log files for a SQL Server 2005 database.
- Configure filegroups.
- Determine the best RAID level and configuration for your data and log files.

Estimated lesson time: 20 minutes

Data Files

In a SQL Server 2005 database, you can create two types of data files: primary and secondary.

- The *primary data file* is mandatory and contains startup information for the database catalog and points to the other database files. The primary data file can also contain objects and user data. The recommended extension for the primary data file is .mdf.

- The *secondary data file*, which is optional and user-defined, contains objects and user data. You can put each secondary data file on a different disk drive to boost performance. A database can contain a maximum of 32,766 secondary data files. The recommended extension for a secondary data file is .ndf.

For example, you might have a simple or rarely accessed database that contains just a primary data file that stores catalog information as well as your tables, views, stored procedures, and data. For a larger or more heavily used database, you might configure a primary data file as well as several secondary data files spread across multiple disks for better performance and improved availability and reliability.

BEST PRACTICES   Database files

You should store all data and objects in secondary files and leave the database catalog in the primary file. This configuration helps reduce disk access contention.

Log Files

Every SQL Server 2005 database has a transaction log that records all database modifications that each transaction makes. SQL Server stores this information in log files. You must have at least one log file for each database, and you can create multiple log files per database to facilitate faster recovery. The recommended extension for log files is .ldf.

Filegroups

A *filegroup* is a logical structure that lets DBAs group data files and manage them as a logical unit. To improve performance, you can allocate database objects, such as tables, to specific filegroups. By splitting database objects across several filegroups, you can take advantage of the different disk subsystems and allow SQL Server to perform parallel disk operations. In addition, if you configure multiple filegroups, you can back up and restore files individually.

SQL Server supports two types of filegroups: primary and user-defined.

- A *primary filegroup* contains the primary data file and any secondary data files not stored in another filegroup. All system tables are allocated to the primary filegroup.

- You create a *user-defined filegroup* to group secondary files and assign database objects to filegroups. A database can contain up to 32,766 user-defined filegroups.

> **Quick Check**
> - How many log files can you have in each filegroup?
>
> **Quick Check Answer**
> - None. Filegroups contain only data files.

When managing filegroups, you should pay special attention to the following filegroup properties, which you can set and change from SSMS or by using the *ALTER DATABASE* statement:

- Each database has a *default filegroup*. When you create a database object and do not specify a filegroup, SQL Server allocates the object to the default filegroup.

- You can configure a filegroup as read-only. You can use *read-only filegroups* for database objects that should not be modified, such as historical tables. All filegroups can be configured as read-only except the primary filegroup.

If your database has an access-intensive table—for example, *Order Detail*—you could create multiple secondary data files for the database, store the files on different disk drives, and group these files in a filegroup. Then, you could store the *Order Detail* table in this filegroup so that queries against the table would be spread across the disks.

BEST PRACTICES **Filegroup design**

Create at least one user-defined filegroup to hold secondary data files and database objects. Configure this filegroup as the default filegroup so that SQL Server will store all objects you create in this filegroup.

How to Configure Data Files and Log Files

You can configure data files and log files when you're creating them by using the *CREATE DATABASE* Transact-SQL statement, and you can modify a configuration by using the *ALTER DATABASE* statement. Alternatively, you can configure the files from the Database Properties page in SSMS. Table 2-1 describes the options that you can configure for each file.

Table 2-1 File Configuration Options

Option	Description
Name	The logical name for the file.
Filename	The operating system full path and file name.
Size	The size for the file. When you do not specify a size for the primary file, the database engine uses the size of the primary file on the model database. If you specify a secondary or log file without the size option, the database engine creates files that are 1 MB in size.
Maxsize	The maximum size for the file. If you do not specify maxsize or you specify the UNLIMITED value, the file grows until the drive is full. In SQL Server 2005, a log file has a maximum size of 2 terabytes, and data files have a maximum size of 16 terabytes.
Filegrowth	Specifies the automatic growth allowed for the file. You can specify the value in kilobytes, megabytes, gigabytes, or terabytes; or as a percentage of the actual file size. If you specify a value of 0, the file will not grow.

As a rule, you should create database files as large as possible, based on the maximum amount of data you estimate the database will contain, to accommodate future growth. By creating large files, you can avoid file fragmentation and get better database performance. In many cases, you can let data files grow automatically; just be sure to limit autogrowth by specifying a maximum growth size that leaves some hard disk space available. By putting different filegroups on different disks, you can also help eliminate physical fragmentation of your files as they grow.

The following example creates a database with several files and filegroups, specifying explicit values for each file property:

NOTE   Volumes necessary to run this sample

To run this sample, you need three additional volumes—D, E, and F—with a folder called \Projects_Data on each volume.

```
CREATE DATABASE Projects
ON
PRIMARY
 (NAME = ProjectPrimary,
 FILENAME = 'D:\Projects_Data\ProjectPrimary.mdf',
 SIZE = 100MB,
 MAXSIZE = 200,
 FILEGROWTH = 20),
FILEGROUP ProjectsFG
 ( NAME = ProjectData1,
 FILENAME = 'E:\Projects_Data\ProjectData1.ndf',
 SIZE = 200MB,
 MAXSIZE = 1200,
 FILEGROWTH = 100),
 ( NAME = ProjectData2,
 FILENAME = 'E:\Projects_Data\ProjectData2.ndf',
 SIZE = 200MB,
 MAXSIZE = 1200,
 FILEGROWTH = 100),
FILEGROUP ProjectsHistoryFG
( NAME = ProjectHistory1,
 FILENAME = 'E:\Projects_Data\ProjectHistory1.ndf',
 SIZE = 100MB,
 MAXSIZE = 500,
 FILEGROWTH = 50)
LOG ON
 (NAME = Archlog1,
 FILENAME = 'F:\Projects_Data\ProjectLog.ldf',
 SIZE = 300MB,
 MAXSIZE = 800,
FILEGROWTH = 100)
```

You can add, remove, and modify file properties by using the *ALTER DATABASE* statement. The following example adds a new file to the Projects database:

```
ALTER DATABASE Projects
ADD FILE
 (NAME=ProjectsData4,
 FILENAME='E:\Projects_Data\ProjectData4.ndf',
 SIZE=100MB,
 MAXSIZE=500MB,
 FILEGROWTH=75MB) TO FILEGROUP ProjectsFG
```

You can also configure these file options from SSMS.

MORE INFO   CREATE DATABASE

For more information about the *CREATE DATABASE* and *ALTER DATABASE* syntax, see the topics "CREATE DATABASE (Transact-SQL)" and "ALTER DATABASE (Transact-SQL)" in SQL Server Books Online. SQL Server 2005 Books Online is installed as part of SQL Server 2005. Updates for SQL Server 2005 Books Online are available for download at *www.microsoft.com/technet/prodtechnol/sql/2005/downloads/books.mspx*.

Configuring Database Files with RAID Systems

RAID systems are arrays of disk drives that provide fault tolerance, more storage capacity, and better performance for the disk subsystem, depending on the configuration. Although RAID hardware systems are not part of the SQL Server configuration, they directly affect SQL Server's performance. There are a variety of RAID levels, each of which uses a different algorithm for fault tolerance. The most common RAID levels used with SQL Server are 0, 1, 5, and 10.

- *RAID 0* is also known as disk striping because it creates a disk file system called a stripe set. RAID 0 gives the best performance for read and write operations because it spreads these operations across all the disks in the set. However, RAID 0 does not provide fault tolerance; if one disk fails, you lose access to all the data on the stripe set.

- *RAID 1*, also known as disk mirroring, provides a redundant copy of the selected disk. RAID 1 improves read performance but can degrade the performance of write operations.

- *RAID 5*, the most popular RAID level, stripes the data across the disks of the RAID set as does RAID 0, but it also adds parity information to provide fault tolerance. Parity information is distributed among all the disks. RAID 5 provides better performance than RAID 1. However, when a disk fails, read performance decreases.

- RAID 10, or RAID 1+0, includes both striping without parity and mirroring. RAID 10 offers better availability and performance than RAID 5, especially for write-intensive applications.

The RAID configuration that is best for your database files depends on several factors, including performance and recoverability needs. RAID 10 is the recommended RAID system for transaction log, data, and index files. If you have budget restrictions, keep transaction log files in a RAID 10 system, and store data and index files in a RAID 5 system.

MORE INFO   RAID levels and SQL Server

Selecting the appropriate RAID levels for database files generates a lot of angst in the DBA community, and full coverage of this topic is beyond this lesson. For more information about RAID, see "RAID Levels and SQL Server" at *http://msdn2.microsoft.com/ms190764.aspx* and *Microsoft Windows 2000 Server Administrator's Companion* (Microsoft Press), Chapter 7, "Planning Fault Tolerance and Avoidance," by Charlie Russel and Sharon Crawford, at *http://www.microsoft.com/technet/prodtechnol/windows2000serv/plan/planning.mspx*.

Best Practices

To configure data and log files for best performance, follow these best practices:

- To avoid disk contention, do not put data files on the same drive that contains the operating system files.
- Put transaction log files on a separate drive from data files. This split gives you the best performance by reducing disk contention between data and transaction log files.
- Put the *tempdb* database on a separate drive if possible, preferably on a RAID 10 or RAID 5 system. In environments in which there is intensive use of *tempdb* databases, you can get better performance by putting *tempdb* on a separate drive, which lets SQL Server perform *tempdb* operations in parallel with database operations.

PRACTICE Configuring Database Files and Filegroups

In this practice, you will create a database that contains several files and filegroups and then configure one filegroup as the default filegroup.

NOTE Volumes necessary to run this example

To run this sample properly, you need three volumes—D, E, and F—with a Sales_Data folder on each of them. Also, you need the free space specified to create each file.

---

1. Open SSMS.

2. Connect to the SQL Server instance using Microsoft Windows authentication by clicking OK in the Connect To Server dialog box.

3. Click New Query.

4. Build the first part of a *CREATE DATABASE* statement that creates a database called *Sales*; this database will have three filegroups:

```
CREATE DATABASE Sales
ON
```

5. Build the first part of the code, which creates the primary filegroup to contain the SalesPrimary file, as follows:

```
PRIMARY
    (NAME = SalesPrimary,
    FILENAME = 'D:\Sales_Data\SalesPrimary.mdf',
    SIZE = 50MB,
    MAXSIZE = 200,
    FILEGROWTH = 20),
```

6. Create the part of the code that defines the second filegroup, SalesFG, which will store current data contained in files SalesData1 and SalesData2:

```
FILEGROUP SalesFG
    ( NAME = SalesData1,
    FILENAME = 'E:\Sales_Data\SalesData1.ndf',
    SIZE = 200MB,
    MAXSIZE = 800,
    FILEGROWTH = 100),
    ( NAME = SalesData2,
    FILENAME = 'E:\Sales_Data\SalesData2.ndf',
    SIZE = 400MB,
    MAXSIZE = 1200,
    FILEGROWTH = 300),
```

7. Add the following statement to create the third filegroup, SalesHistoryFG, which will store historical information in the SalesHistory1 file:

```
FILEGROUP SalesHistoryFG
( NAME = SalesHistory1,
    FILENAME = 'E:\Sales_Data\SalesHistory1.ndf',
    SIZE = 100MB,
    MAXSIZE = 500,
    FILEGROWTH = 50)
```

8. Add the code to create a log file called SalesLog:

```
LOG ON
   (NAME = Archlog1,
    FILENAME = 'F:\Sales_Data\SalesLog.ldf',
    SIZE = 300MB,
    MAXSIZE = 800,
    FILEGROWTH = 100)
```

9. Execute the complete *CREATE DATABASE* statement, as shown here:

```
CREATE DATABASE Sales
ON
PRIMARY
   (NAME = SalesPrimary,
    FILENAME = 'D:\Sales_Data\SalesPrimary.mdf',
    SIZE = 50MB,
    MAXSIZE = 200,
    FILEGROWTH = 20),
FILEGROUP SalesFG
   ( NAME = SalesData1,
    FILENAME = 'E:\Sales_Data\SalesData1.ndf',
    SIZE = 200MB,
    MAXSIZE = 800,
    FILEGROWTH = 100),
   ( NAME = SalesData2,
    FILENAME = 'E:\Sales_Data\SalesData2.ndf',
    SIZE = 400MB,
    MAXSIZE = 1200,
    FILEGROWTH = 300),
FILEGROUP SalesHistoryFG
( NAME = SalesHistory1,
    FILENAME = 'E:\Sales_Data\SalesHistory1.ndf',
    SIZE = 100MB,
    MAXSIZE = 500,
    FILEGROWTH = 50)
LOG ON
   (NAME = Archlog1,
    FILENAME = 'F:\Sales_Data\SalesLog.ldf',
    SIZE = 300MB,
    MAXSIZE = 800,
    FILEGROWTH = 100)
```

10. Use the following *ALTER DATABASE* statement to configure the SalesFG file-group as the default filegroup for the Sales database. All database objects created after this change will be stored in SalesFG by default:

```
ALTER DATABASE Sales
MODIFY FILEGROUP SalesFG DEFAULT
```

Lesson Summary

- A SQL Server 2005 database contains three file types: primary data files, secondary data files, and transaction log files.

- You can group data files into filegroups to facilitate administration, such as backup and restore operations, and to provide top performance.

- You can improve your system's performance by using the best RAID level and file configuration for your environment.

Lesson Review

The following questions are intended to reinforce key information presented in this lesson. The questions are also available on the companion CD if you prefer to review them in electronic form.

NOTE Answers

Answers to these questions and explanations of why each answer choice is right or wrong are located in the "Answers" section at the end of the book.

---

1. Which of the following statements can you use to create a filegroup?

    A. *ALTER DATABASE ... ADD FILE*

    B. *.ALTER DATABASE ... MODIFY FILEGROUP*

    C. *ALTER DATABASE ... ADD FILEGROUP*

    D. *ALTER DATABASE ... REMOVE FILEGROUP*

2. You are in charge of designing the physical structure for your company's new server running SQL Server 2005. The server has the following characteristics: two disks in RAID 1, five disks in RAID 5, and another ten disks in RAID 5. Where should you store database files for the best performance?

   A. Use RAID 1 to install the operating system. Use the first RAID 5 disk set to install SQL Server executable files and the second RAID 5 disk set to store database files.

   B. Use RAID 1 to install the operating system. Use the first RAID 5 system to install SQL Server executable files and data and transaction log files. Use the second RAID 5 system to store database backups.

   C. Use RAID 1 to install the operating system and SQL Server executable files. Use the first RAID 5 system to store transaction log files. Use the second RAID 5 system to store data files.

   D. Use the first RAID 5 system to install the operating system and SQL Server executable files. Store data files in the second RAID 5 system and log files in the RAID 1 system.

3. Which of the following are valid filegroup types? (Choose all that apply.)

   A. Read-only

   B. Write-only

   C. Default

   D. Primary

Lesson 2: Configuring Database Mail

Database Mail is a new solution for sending messages from the SQL Server 2005 database engine. Applications that are configured to use Database Mail can send e-mail messages, including HTML messages, query results, and file attachments, to users. Database Mail uses the Simple Mail Transfer Protocol (SMTP) and does not require you to install any Extended MAPI client, such as Microsoft Office Outlook, on SQL Server.

After this lesson, you will be able to:

- Identify Database Mail prerequisites.
- Understand the Database Mail architecture.
- Configure the SQL Server Database Mail subsystem.

Estimated lesson time: 15 minutes

Identifying Database Mail Prerequisites

Before you configure Database Mail, you need to review the following prerequisites:

- **Database Mail must be enabled.**   Database Mail is not enabled by default; you need to enable it by using the SQL Server Surface Area Configuration tool, the Database Mail Configuration Wizard, or the *sp_configure* stored procedure.

- **Service Broker needs to be enabled in the Database Mail host database.** The default Database Mail host database is *msdb*, and Service Broker is enabled on msdb by default.

MORE INFO   Service Broker

You can get a full explanation about Service Broker from *http://msdn.microsoft.com/library/ default.asp?url=/library/en-us/dnsql90/html/sqlsvcbroker.asp.*

- **The Database Mail external executable needs access to the SMTP server.**   If the SMTP server requires authentication, the executable accesses the SMTP server by using the SQL Server service account credentials by default. You should ensure that the SQL Server service account can access the SMTP server.

Understanding the Database Mail Architecture

Database Mail has four main components: configuration components, messaging components, the executable, and logging and auditing components.

- **Configuration components**   There are two configuration components:
  - ❑ A *Database Mail account* contains the information that SQL Server uses to send e-mail messages to the SMTP server, such as the SMTP server name, the authentication type, and the e-mail address.
  - ❑ A *Database Mail profile* is a collection of Database Mail accounts. Applications use Database Mail profiles to send e-mail messages so that the information about the accounts is transparent for applications, which lets DBAs change account information without modifying applications' stored procedures. Database Mail profiles can be private or public. For a private profile, Database Mail maintains a list of users that can use the profile. For a public profile, members of the *msdb* database role *DatabaseMailUserRole* can use the profile.
- **Messaging components**   The main messaging component is the Database Mail host database, which contains all the Database Mail objects. The Database Mail host database is *msdb*.
- **Database Mail executable**   To minimize the impact on SQL Server, Database Mail uses an external executable to process e-mail messages. The executable, called DatabaseMail90.exe, is located in the MSSQL\Binn directory in the SQL Server installation path. Database Mail uses Service Broker activation to start the external program when there are e-mail messages waiting to be processed. The external program connects to the database engine by using Microsoft Windows authentication with the SQL Server service account credentials.
- **Logging and auditing components**   Database Mail stores log information in tables in the Database Mail host database. You can see this log information from the Database Mail Log or by querying the *sysmail_event_log* system view.

How to Configure Database Mail

SSMS provides the Database Mail Configuration Wizard for configuring your Database Mail environment. You can set up Database Mail; manage accounts, profiles, and security; and change system parameters from the wizard, which is shown in Figure 2-1.

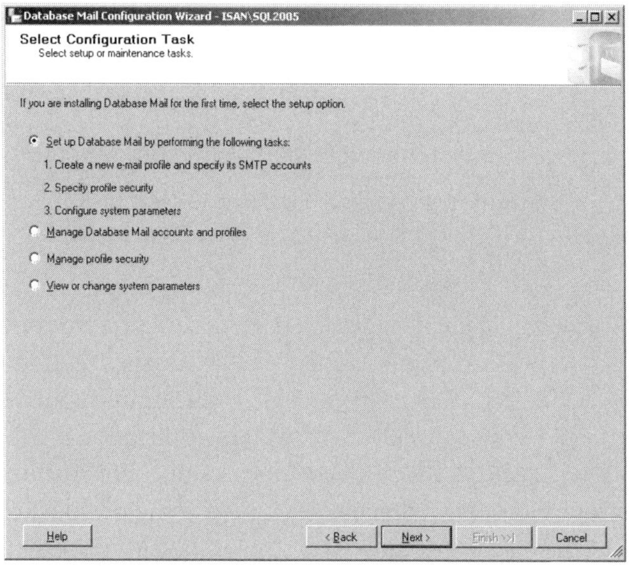

Figure 2-1 Database Mail Configuration Wizard

In the following example, you have an SMTP mail server called *mail.adventure-works.com* and an account on that server with an e-mail address of *sql@adventure-works.com*. To configure a Database Mail profile account for this e-mail account, follow these steps:

1. Expand the *Management* node within Object Explorer in SSMS.

2. Right-click Database Mail and select Configure Database Mail. The Welcome page of the Database Mail Configuration Wizard appears. Click Next.

3. On the Select Configuration Task page, verify that Set Up Database Mail By Performing The Following Tasks is selected and click Next.

4. A warning message appears: The Database Mail feature Is Not Available. Would You Like To Enable This Feature? Click Yes.

5. In the Profile Name text box, type **TestProfile** and click Add to add a new SMTP account.

6. The New Database Mail Account dialog box appears. Fill in the text boxes as Figure 2-2 shows. Click OK and then click Next.

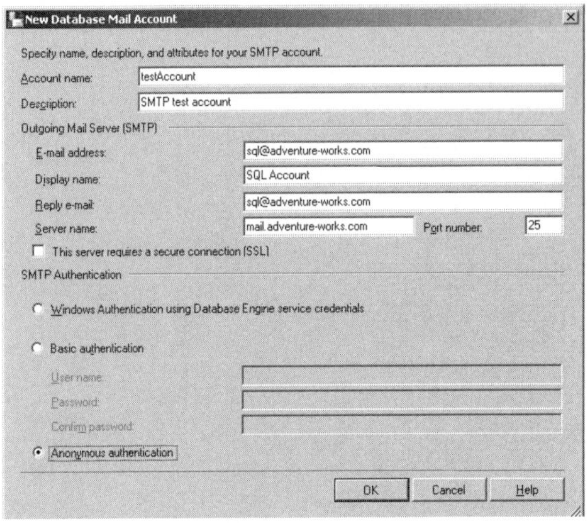

Figure 2-2 New Database Mail Account dialog box

7. In the resulting Manage Profile Security page, you configure public and private profiles. Select the TestProfile check box and click Next.

8. The Configure System Parameters page appears, which enables you to change system-level configurations. Leave the default options and click Next. The Complete The Wizard page appears. Click Finish.

You can also accomplish these tasks by using the Database Mail stored procedures. For example, you can change configuration information by using the *sysmail_configure_sp* stored procedure.

MORE INFO Database Mail stored procedures

For a list of Database Mail stored procedures and what they do, see the "Database Mail and SQL Mail Stored Procedures (Transact-SQL)" topic in SQL Server 2005 Books Online.

NOTE Viewing configuration options

You can view information about Database Mail configuration options by running the Database Mail Wizard or by executing the *sysmail_help_configure_sp msdb* stored procedure.

PRACTICE **Configuring Database Mail**

In this practice, you will use the Database Mail stored procedures to configure Database Mail so that you can send e-mail messages from SQL Server. You will create a Database Mail public profile for an SMTP mail account. The SMTP server is *mail.Adventure-Works.com*, and the e-mail address is *sql@Adventure-Works.com*.

NOTE **Example server name and e-mail address in this code**

SMTP server names and account e-mail addresses used in this code are examples. You should change them to a valid SMTP server name and e-mail address to run the code.

---

1. Execute the *sysmail_add_account* procedure as follows to create a Database Mail account, using *mail.Adventure-works.com* as the mail server and *sql@adventure-works.com* as the e-mail account:

```
EXECUTE msdb.dbo.sysmail_add_account_sp
    @account_name = 'AdventureWorks Mail',
    @description = 'Mail account for Database Mail.',
    @email_address = 'sql@Adventure-Works.com',
    @display_name = 'AdventureWorks Automated Mailer',
    @mailserver_name = 'mail.Adventure-Works.com'
```

2. Use the *sysmail_add_profile* procedure to create a Database Mail profile called AdventureWorks Mail Profile:

```
EXECUTE msdb.dbo.sysmail_add_profile_sp
    @profile_name = 'AdventureWorks Mail Profile',
    @description = 'Profile used for database mail.'
```

3. Execute the *sysmail_add_profileaccount* procedure to add the Database Mail account you created in step 1 to the Database Mail profile you created in step 2:

```
EXECUTE msdb.dbo.sysmail_add_profileaccount_sp
    @profile_name = 'AdventureWorks Mail Profile',
    @account_name = 'AdventureWorks Mail',
    @sequence_number = 1
```

4. Use the *sysmail_add_principalprofile* procedure to grant the Database Mail profile access to the *msdb public* database role and to make the profile the default Database Mail profile:

```
EXECUTE msdb.dbo.sysmail_add_principalprofile_sp
    @profile_name = 'AdventureWorks Mail Profile',
    @principal_name = 'public',
    @is_default = 1 ;
```

Lesson Summary

- Database Mail is the SQL Server 2005 subsystem that lets you send e-mail messages from database applications.

- Database Mail does not need any Extended MAPI client installed on SQL Server because the mail subsystem sends messages directly to an SMTP server.

- You need to have Service Broker enabled to use Database Mail, which uses an external executable to send messages.

- You can configure multiple Database Mail accounts and group them into Database Mail profiles.

- All Database Mail information is stored in the *msdb* database, the default Database Mail host database.

Lesson Review

The following questions are intended to reinforce key information presented in this lesson. The questions are also available on the companion CD if you prefer to review them in electronic form.

NOTE   Answers

Answers to these questions and explanations of why each answer choice is right or wrong are located in the "Answers" section at the end of the book.

---

1. Which of the following is a prerequisite for Database Mail?

   A. Service Broker

   B. Database Mirroring

   C. Extended MAPI Profile

   D. Microsoft Exchange Server

2. Which of the following sentences is true for authentication mechanisms when the SMTP server is being accessed?

   A. Database Mail accesses the SMTP server using the database engine service credentials by default.

   B. Database Mail accesses the SMTP server using the SQL Server Agent service credentials by default.

   C. Database Mail accesses the SMTP server using the SQL Browser service credentials by default.

   D. Database Mail accesses the SMTP server using the SQL Server Active Directory Helper service credentials by default.

3. Which of the following sentences is true for Database Mail?

   A. A Database Mail account is a collection of Database Mail profiles.

   B. Each Mail Database Host user account must have a Database Mail profile associated.

   C. A Database Mail profile is a collection of Mail Database Host user accounts.

   D. A Database Mail profile is a collection of Database Mail accounts.

Lesson 3: Specifying a Recovery Model

A *recovery model* is a database configuration option that controls how transactions are logged, whether the transaction log is backed up, and what restore options are available for the database. The recovery model you choose for your database has both data-recovery implications and performance implications, based on the logging the recovery model performs or doesn't perform.

After this lesson, you will be able to:

- Explain the differences between the recovery models.
- Choose the best recovery model for each SQL Server 2005 database.

Estimated lesson time: 10 minutes

Recovery Models Overview

SQL Server 2005 provides three recovery models for databases: Full, Simple, and Bulk-Logged. These models determine how SQL Server works with the transaction log and selects the operations that it logs and whether it truncates the log. Truncating the transaction log is the process of removing committed transactions and leaving log space to new transactions. The following is a definition of each recovery model:

- In the *Full recovery model*, the database engine logs all operations onto the transaction log, and the database engine never truncates the log. The Full recovery model lets you restore a database to the point of failure (or to an earlier point in time in SQL Server 2005 Enterprise Edition).

- In the *Simple recovery model*, the database engine minimally logs most operations and truncates the transaction log after each checkpoint. In the Simple recovery model, you cannot back up or restore the transaction log. Furthermore, you cannot restore individual data pages.

IMPORTANT   Simple recovery model scenarios

The Simple recovery model is not appropriate for databases in which the loss of recent changes is unacceptable.

- In the *Bulk-Logged recovery model*, the database engine minimally logs bulk operations such as SELECT INTO and BULK INSERT. In this recovery model, if a log backup contains any bulk operation, you can restore the database to the end of the log backup, not to a point in time. The Bulk-Logged recovery model is intended to be used only during large bulk operations.

How to Configure Recovery Models

You can see the recovery model specified for a given database on the Database Properties page in SSMS or by querying the *sys.databases* catalog view, as this basic syntax shows:

```
SELECT name, recovery_model_desc FROM sys.databases
```

To configure the recovery model for a database, you can go to the Database Properties page in SSMS or use the *ALTER DATABASE* statement.

In SSMS, you can change the recovery model by performing the following steps:

1. Expand the *Databases* node within Object Explorer in SSMS.

2. Right-click the database for which you want to set the recovery model and then choose Properties. Select the Options page.

3. You can change the recovery mode from the Recovery model drop-down list, as Figure 2-3 shows.

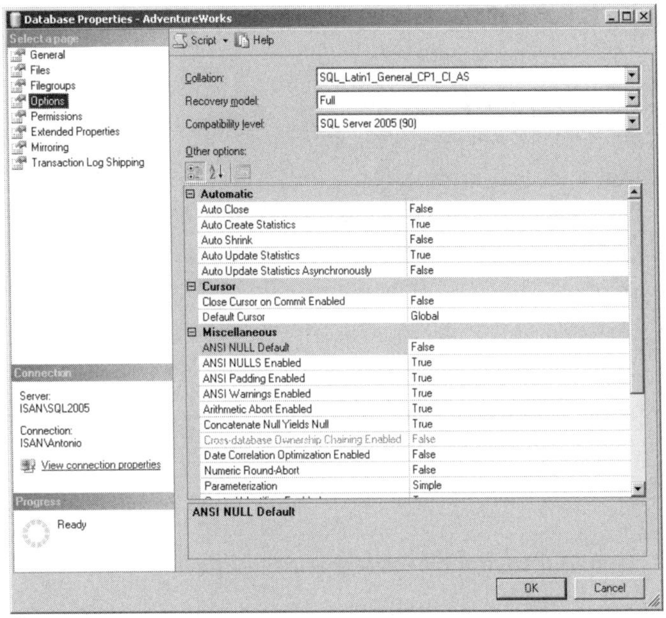

Figure 2-3   Changing the recovery model from SSMS

The basic syntax for configuring the recovery model using *ALTER DATABASE* is as follows:

```
ALTER DATABASE <database_name>
SET RECOVERY FULL | SIMPLE | BULK_LOGGED
```

As noted earlier, Full recovery is the recommended model for a production database because it provides the most recoverable configuration. If you import data periodically by using a bulk mechanism, you can temporarily change the recovery model for your database to Bulk-Logged to get better bulk-load performance. Then, when the import process ends, return your database to the Full recovery model.

PRACTICE **Changing a Database's Recovery Model**

In this practice, you will change the database recovery model to Bulk-Logged to get good performance for a bulk-logged operation and then revert to the Full recovery model.

1. Set the database recovery model for the *AdventureWorks* database to Bulk-Logged by executing the following *ALTER DATABASE* statement. (Before changing the recovery model, do a full backup of the database.)

```
-- Note that you should create the C:\Backup folder at Operating System level before
     running this backup.
BACKUP DATABASE AdventureWorks TO DISK='C:\Backup\AdventureWorks.Bak'
GO
--Change the Recovery Model to Bulk Logged
ALTER DATABASE AdventureWorks
SET RECOVERY BULK_LOGGED
```

2. Type and then run the following *ALTER DATABASE* statement to change the recovery model back to Full after performing the bulk-logged operations; perform another full database backup so that you have a backup of the data that was just loaded:

```
ALTER DATABASE AdventureWorks
SET RECOVERY FULL
--Perform a Full database backup
BACKUP DATABASE AdventureWorks TO DISK='C:\Backup\AdventureWorks.Bak'
GO
```

Lesson Summary

- Recovery models let you control how the database engine logs operations and which restore options are available for a particular database.
- SQL Server provides three recovery models: Full, Simple, and Bulk-Logged.
- The Full recovery model is the default and the recommended recovery model, logging all operations and letting you recover to the point of failure.

- The Simple recovery model minimally logs most operations and doesn't let you back up or restore the transaction log.

- The Bulk-Logged recovery model minimally logs bulk operations and is intended for temporary use during large bulk operations.

- You configure a database's recovery model through the Database Properties window in SSMS or by using the *ALTER DATABASE* Transact-SQL statement.

Lesson Review

The following questions are intended to reinforce key information presented in this lesson. The questions are also available on the companion CD if you prefer to review them in electronic form.

NOTE Answers

Answers to these questions and explanations of why each answer choice is right or wrong are located in the "Answers" section at the end of the book.

---

1. Which of the following sentences is true for recovery models?

    A. In the Simple recovery model, most transactions are minimally logged.

    B. In the Full recovery model, most transactions are minimally logged.

    C. In the Bulk-Logged recovery model, all transactions are logged.

    D. In the Simple recovery model, all transactions are logged.

2. Which of the following methods let you change the database recovery model? (Choose all that apply.)

    A. The *sp_configure* stored procedure

    B. Database properties in SSMS

    C. *ALTER DATABASE*

    D. *CREATE DATABASE*

3. Which of the following restore operations are NOT allowed in the Simple recovery model? (Choose all that apply.)

    A. Point-in-Time Restore

    B. Differential

    C. Full

    D. Page Restore

Lesson 4: Configuring Server Security Principals

SQL Server 2005 provides a strong security model that helps you prevent unauthorized access to your important data resources. This model is based on permissions that you give *principals*—the individuals, groups, and processes that can request SQL Server resources.

SQL Server 2005 authenticates the permissions of all user connections, so all user connections must specify authentication mode and credentials. You can choose between two authentication modes—*Windows authentication* and *Mixed Mode authentication*—that control how application users connect to SQL Server. And you can create two types of SQL Server logins—Windows logins and SQL Server logins—that let you manage access to the SQL Server instance. To help manage the logins of principals that have administrative privileges to SQL Server, you can arrange these logins in *fixed server roles*. Authentication mode and logins are the first security level for SQL Server, so you should take care to configure the most secure option for your environment.

After this lesson, you will be able to:

- Choose between authentication modes.
- Manage SQL Server logins.
- Manage fixed server roles.

Estimated lesson time: 10 minutes

Choosing Between Authentication Modes

SQL Server 2005 provides two modes for authenticating access to database resources: Windows authentication and Mixed Mode authentication.

- **Windows authentication**   When you configure SQL Server 2005 to use Windows authentication, only authenticated Windows users can gain access to the SQL Server instance. You need to add a Windows login for each Windows user or group that needs access to a SQL Server instance. This is the default and recommended authentication mode because you can take advantage of all the centralized security policies of your Active Directory domain.

- **Mixed Mode authentication**   With Mixed Mode authentication, both Windows logins and SQL Server logins (neither of which are mapped to an operating system user) can access the SQL Server instance. You use Mixed Mode authentication when you need to provide access to non-Windows users—for example, when users of another client operating system need access to SQL Server.

You can change the authentication mode by using Server Properties in SSMS by taking the following steps:

1. In SSMS, right-click on your server and choose Properties.

2. Select the Security page.

3. Below Server Authentication, select the authentication mode you want to use on your server. You can select either the Windows authentication mode or the SQL Server And Windows authentication mode.

4. Click OK to save your changes.

5. Click OK to close the message box stating that your changes will not take effect until you restart SQL Server.

6. To restart your server, right-click on your server in Object Explorer and choose Restart.

Quick Check

■ Which authentication mode is the default and recommended mode for security principals?

Quick Check Answer

■ Windows authentication

How to Configure SQL Server Logins

Logins are the server principals that give users access to SQL Server. You can create SQL Server logins graphically in SSMS or by using the *CREATE LOGIN* statement.

The basic *CREATE LOGIN* syntax to create a Windows login is

```
CREATE LOGIN [Domain\User] FROM WINDOWS
```

The syntax to create a SQL Server login is

```
CREATE LOGIN login_name WITH PASSWORD='password'
```

For SQL Server logins, you can specify the following options when creating the login:

■ *MUST_CHANGE*   The login should change the password at the next login.

■ *CHECK_EXPIRATION*   SQL Server will check the Windows expiration policy for the SQL Server login.

■ *CHECK_POLICY*   SQL Server will apply the local Windows password policy on SQL Server logins.

BEST PRACTICES Password policies

To get a secure SQL Server environment, you should use the options to check the Windows expiration policy for SQL Server logins and apply the local Windows password policy on them.

In the following example, you create a SQL Server login and force checking of password expiration and password policy:

```
CREATE LOGIN secureSQL WITH PASSWORD='Ty%6tsfs$g23', CHECK_EXPIRATION=ON,  CHECK_POLICY =ON
```

If you need to change any login property, you can use the *ALTER LOGIN* statement. The following example shows you how to change the password for a SQL Server login:

```
ALTER LOGIN login_name WITH PASSWORD='password'
```

You can disable a login by executing the following:

```
ALTER LOGIN login_name DISABLE
```

When you need to remove a login, you can use the *DROP LOGIN* statement:

```
DROP LOGIN login_name
```

Or use the following to drop a Windows login:

```
DROP LOGIN [Domain\User]
```

To get SQL Server login information such as state or login options, you can query the *sys.sql_logins* catalog view.

CAUTION Removing logins

You cannot drop a login that owns any securable, server-level object, or SQL Server Agent job. You should disable logins before dropping them, and drop logins only when you are sure the action will not affect your environment.

In addition, if the login is mapped to a database user and you drop the login, SQL Server does not automatically remove the user, resulting in an orphaned user.

DBAs commonly need to manage exceptions when providing access to a Windows group. For example, you might need to provide SQL Server access to all the members of a certain Windows group except for one member. To accomplish this task, you should create a Windows login for the Windows group and then deny access to the user who shouldn't receive access. The following example shows the basic syntax for accomplishing these steps:

```
CREATE LOGIN [domain_name\group_name] FROM WINDOWS
DENY CONNECT SQL TO [domain_name\user_name]
```

NOTE Backward compatibility

You can use SQL Server 2000 stored procedures, such as *sp_addlogin*, *sp_droplogin*, and so on, to manage logins. But remember that these stored procedures are in SQL Server 2005 only for backward-compatibility purposes.

Managing Fixed Server Roles

SQL Server provides a set of fixed server roles, such as *sysadmin* and *securityadmin*, which you can use to assign and manage administrative privileges to logins by adding logins as members of these roles. Table 2-2 describes the fixed server roles for SQL Server 2005.

Table 2-2 SQL Server's Fixed Server Roles

Fixed Server Role	Members Can
sysadmin	Perform any activity in SQL Server. The permissions of this role comprise the permissions of all other fixed server roles.
serveradmin	Configure server-wide settings.
setupadmin	Add and remove linked servers and execute some system stored procedures, such as *sp_serveroption*.
securityadmin	Manage server logins.
processadmin	Manage processes running in an instance of SQL Server.
dbcreator	Create and alter databases.
diskadmin	Manage disk files.
bulkadmin	Execute the *BULK INSERT* statement.

To obtain information about logins for a fixed server role, you can query the *sys.server_role_members* catalog view, which returns a row for each member of the server role.

The basic syntax for adding a login to a fixed server role is

```
EXECUTE sp_addsrvrolemember login_name, fixed_server_role
```

You can use the *sp_dropsrvrolemember* stored procedure to remove the login from the fixed server role.

Alternatively, you can use SSMS to add and remove logins from fixed server roles. You can accomplish these tasks by displaying the properties for either a login or a server role.

MORE INFO   Fixed server roles properties

For more information about fixed server roles and their properties, see the "Server-Level Roles" topic in SQL Server 2005 Books Online.

PRACTICE ## Selecting an Authentication Mode and Creating a Login

In these practices, you will change your server's authentication mode to Mixed Mode and create a SQL Server login. You will enforce the password policy and expiration policy for that login and add the login to the sysadmin fixed server role.

▶ **Practice 1: Change Authentication Mode**

In this practice, you will change authentication mode to Mixed Mode.

1. In SSMS, right-click your server and choose Properties.

2. Select the Security page. Below Server Authentication, select SQL Server And Windows Authentication mode. Click OK. A warning message appears informing you that this change will take effect only after you restart SQL Server.

3. Right-click your server and choose Restart so the change will take effect.

▶ **Practice 2: Add a SQL Server Login**

In this practice, you will add a new SQL Server login and enforce the expiration and check policy restrictions. Then you will add the login to the sysadmin fixed server role.

1. Expand the *Security* node, right-click Logins, and then choose New Login. The New Login dialog box appears.

2. In the Login Name text box, type sqlLogin.

3. Select the SQL Server Authentication option; in the Password and Confirm Password text boxes, type the password Pa$$w0rd.

4. Clear the User Must Change Password At Next Login check box.

5. To add the login to the sysadmin fixed server role, select the Server Roles page. Select the Sysadmin check box and click OK.

Lesson Summary

- Server principals provide a mechanism for controlling how SQL Server authenticates user access to database resources.

- SQL Server provides two authentication modes: Windows authentication—the default and recommended mode—and Mixed Mode authentication, which you use only if you need to give access to non-Windows users.

- Each user connection should specify a valid login so that the database engine can authenticate the connection and check the permissions.

- To help manage administrative privileges to SQL Server, you can assign logins to fixed server roles, which define ready-made permissions for members of each role.

Lesson Review

The following questions are intended to reinforce key information presented in this lesson. The questions are also available on the companion CD if you prefer to review them in electronic form.

NOTE Answers

Answers to these questions and explanations of why each answer choice is right or wrong are located in the "Answers" section at the end of the book.

---

1. Which of the following are valid SQL Server principals? (Choose all that apply.)

   A. Database users

   B. Fixed server roles

   C. Windows logins

   D. SQL Server logins

2. Which of the following sentences are true regarding authentication modes? (Choose all that apply.)

   A. Windows authentication is the preferred authentication mode.

   B. Mixed Mode authentication does not let you apply password policies.

   C. Windows authentication is the default authentication mode.

   D. Mixed Mode authentication is the default authentication mode.

3. Which of the following statements let you create a SQL Server login called Peter? (Choose all that apply.)

   A. *CREATE LOGIN Peter FROM SQL*

   B. *CREATE LOGIN Peter WITH PASSWORD='Pa$$w0rd'*

   C. *EXEC sp_addlogin 'Peter', 'Pa$$w0rd'*

   D. *EXEC sp_grantlogin 'Peter', 'Pa$$w0rd'*

Lesson 5: Configuring Database Securables

Although server security principals are the entities requesting access to database resources, server securables are the entities that you allow or disallow principals to access. At the highest securable level are servers and databases, but you can also set permissions at a more granular level. This lesson covers securables at the database level.

After you configure the authentication mode and create logins for the principals, you need to give them appropriate database access. You do this by mapping each database login needing access to the database to a database user. For faster and easier administration, you can add database users as members of database roles.

After this lesson, you will be able to:

- Manage database users.
- Manage database roles.
- Manage schemas.

Estimated lesson time: 20 minutes

Managing Database Users

To give logins access to a database, you need to create a database user for each login that needs access to the database. You should create the user in the database in which the user needs access. The basic syntax to create a database user is

```
CREATE USER user_name FOR LOGIN login_name
```

If you do not specify a login name, SQL Server will try to create a user mapped to a login with the same name.

You can use the *ALTER USER* statement to modify user properties and the *DROP USER* statement to remove database users.

You can also use SSMS to create and manage database users. You can either manage database users from Logins below the *Security* node or Users below each *Database* node.

When a login that doesn't have a database user mapped to it tries to access a database, SQL Server looks for the Guest database user. SQL Server creates a Guest user in each database. By default, the Guest user is not permitted to connect to the database. You can allow guest connections by activating the Guest user, as follows:

```
GRANT CONNECT TO Guest
```

You can revoke guest access by executing the following:

```
REVOKE CONNECT TO Guest
```

Managing Orphaned Users

Orphaned users are database users that are not mapped to a login in the current SQL Server instance. In SQL Server 2005, a user can become orphaned when you drop its mapped login. To obtain information about orphaned users, you can execute the following command:

```
USE AdventureWorks;
GO
EXECUTE sp_change_users_login @Action='Report';
```

CAUTION   Removing database users

The database engine doesn't let you remove database users if they own a schema that contains objects. You need to transfer the schema to another user or role before removing the database user.

Managing Database Roles

If you have many database users, the process of creating them, modifying them, removing them, and ensuring that they have correct permissions can become tedious and time-consuming. To help you manage these tasks, each user database provides a set of fixed database roles that you can use to group like database users. Table 2-3 lists these fixed database roles.

Table 2-3   SQL Server Fixed Database Roles

Fixed Database Role	Database-Level Permission
db_accessadmin	Granted: *ALTER ANY USER, CREATE SCHEMA*
db_accessadmin	Granted with *GRANT* option: *CONNECT*
db_backupoperator	Granted: *BACKUP DATABASE, BACKUP LOG, CHECK-POINT*
db_datareader	Granted: *SELECT*
db_datawriter	Granted: *DELETE, INSERT, UPDATE*

Table 2-3 SQL Server Fixed Database Roles

Fixed Database Role	Database-Level Permission
db_ddladmin	Granted: *ALTER ANY ASSEMBLY, ALTER ANY ASYMMETRIC KEY, ALTER ANY CERTIFICATE, ALTER ANY CONTRACT, ALTER ANY DATABASE DDL TRIGGER, ALTER ANY DATABASE EVENT, NOTIFICATION, ALTER ANY DATASPACE, ALTER ANY FULLTEXT CATALOG, ALTER ANY MESSAGE TYPE, ALTER ANY REMOTE SERVICE BINDING, ALTER ANY ROUTE, ALTER ANY SCHEMA, ALTER ANY SERVICE, ALTER ANY SYMMETRIC KEY, CHECKPOINT, CREATE AGGREGATE, CREATE DEFAULT, CREATE FUNCTION, CREATE PROCEDURE, CREATE QUEUE, CREATE RULE, CREATE SYNONYM, CREATE TABLE, CREATE TYPE, CREATE VIEW, CREATE XML SCHEMA COLLECTION, REFERENCES*
db_denydatareader	Denied: *SELECT*
db_denydatawriter	Denied: *DELETE, INSERT, UPDATE*
db_owner	Granted with *GRANT* option: *CONTROL*
db_securityadmin	Granted: *ALTER ANY APPLICATION ROLE, ALTER ANY ROLE, CREATE SCHEMA, VIEW DEFINITION*

NOTE **Managing database role members**

Members of the *db_owner* and *db_securityadmin* roles can manage members of fixed database roles, but only members of the *db_owner* role can add members to the *db_owner* role.

You can also create your own database roles to group database users who have the same access needs and assign permissions on a per-group basis instead of assigning permissions user by user. For example, you can group users who are members of the Accounting department into a database role called *Accounting* so that you can assign permissions to only that database role and have the permissions applied to all members of that role.

The basic syntax for creating a database role is

```
CREATE ROLE role_name
```

You can modify role properties by using the *ALTER ROLE* statement and remove database roles by using the *DROP ROLE* statement. You can also manage database roles by using SSMS from the *Security* node below each database.

To add a database user to a role, you use the *sp_addrolemember* stored procedure, which has the following basic syntax:

```
EXECUTE sp_addrolemember role_name, user_name
```

Alternatively, you can add a database user to a role via SSMS by modifying the database user's properties or the role's properties.

You can nest database roles, so you can add database roles into other roles. For example, suppose that you want to group managers in the Accounting department into a database role called *AccountingMgr*. You could grant that role the permissions of the entire *Accounting* role by nesting *AccountingMgr* within *Accounting* and then just granting the extra manager permissions to the *AccountingMgr* role. To obtain information about database role members, you can query the *sys.database_role_members* catalog view, which returns one row for each member of the database role.

Quick Check

■ True or False: Database roles are all fixed, giving you a predefined set of permissions that you can grant to a group of like database users.

Quick Check Answer

■ False. Although SQL Server provides a set of fixed database roles, you can also create your own roles.

Managing Schemas

SQL Server 2005 implements the ANSI concept of *schemas*, which are collections of database objects—such as tables, views, stored procedures, and triggers—that form a single namespace. The main benefit of schemas in SQL Server 2005 is that schemas and users are now separate entities. User name is no longer part of object name, as it was in previous versions of SQL Server, so you can remove users or change user names without having to make application changes. Each schema is owned by a user or role, but if you need to drop a user or role, you just transfer the schema ownership from the user or role you're dropping to another new user or role.

The basic syntax to create a schema is

```
CREATE SCHEMA schema_name AUTHORIZATION owner
```

To modify a schema, you can use the *ALTER SCHEMA* statement; to remove a schema, you can use the *DROP SCHEMA* statement. You can also accomplish these tasks from SSMS. To retrieve information about schemas, you can query the *sys.schemas* catalog view.

In addition, you can assign a default schema for each database user. This default schema is used when the user does not specify the schema name when accessing an object. For instance, if user Peter has a default schema of *HumanResources* and wants to access the *Employee* table without specifying a schema, he can just specify Employee instead of having to specify *HumanResources.Employee*.

You assign a default schema by using the *CREATE USER* or *ALTER USER* statement. You also can assign a default schema through SSMS in the user's properties.

PRACTICE Configuring Server Securables

In this practice, you will configure server securables for the *AdventureWorks* database. You will create a login and database user for Peter. Peter needs access to the *Human-Resources* schema objects in *AdventureWorks*.

1. Use the following *CREATE LOGIN* statement to create a SQL Server login and database user named Peter that has access to the *AdventureWorks* database:

```
CREATE LOGIN Peter WITH PASSWORD='Pa$$w0rd'
GO
USE AdventureWorks
GO
CREATE USER Peter FROM LOGIN Peter
```

2. Grant Peter *SELECT* permission to *HumanResources* database objects by coding the following statement (note the :: syntax to specify a schema name):

```
GRANT SELECT ON SCHEMA::[HumanResources] TO [Peter]
```

3. Click New Query. Right-click the query area and choose Connection | Change Connection. Connect using the SQL login Peter with a password of **Pa$$w0rd**.

4. Execute the following query to test SQL Server login Peter's access:

```
USE AdventureWorks
GO
SELECT * FROM Employee
```

5. Notice that you get an Invalid Object error message, meaning that login Peter doesn't have the correct permissions to the *Employee* table. You need to solve this problem by running the following *ALTER USER* statement to assign *Human-Resources* as the default schema for Peter so that he can select the *Employee* table directly without having to use the *HumanResources* schema name to qualify the table name:

    ```
    ALTER USER Peter WITH DEFAULT_SCHEMA=HumanResources
    ```

6. Run the query from step 4 again. You should get a valid result set now.

Lesson Summary

■ Database users, roles, and schemas give you the tools you need to secure database objects.

■ Each login is mapped to a database user for each database that the login needs access to.

■ Database roles let you group users with the same permissions and same database access needs for easy management.

■ Schemas, a new concept in SQL Server 2005, separate schemas (a collection of database objects that form one namespace) from users so that you can now manage these entities individually.

Lesson Review

The following questions are intended to reinforce key information presented in this lesson. The questions are also available on the companion CD if you prefer to review them in electronic form.

NOTE   Answers

Answers to these questions and explanations of why each answer choice is right or wrong are located in the "Answers" section at the end of the book.

---

1. Which of the following sentences is true for database schemas?

    A. Database schemas define the database catalog.

    B. Database schemas group database objects.

    C. Database schemas group databases.

    D. Database schemas define the table catalog.

2. Which of the following statements let you appropriately create a database user called Peter mapped to the login Peter? (Choose all that apply.)

   A. *CREATE USER Peter FROM Peter*

   B. *CREATE USER Peter FOR LOGIN Peter*

   C. *CREATE USER Peter FOR SQL_LOGIN Peter*

   D. *CREATE USER Peter*

3. Which of the following sentences are true when talking about database roles? (Choose all that apply.)

   A. You can nest database roles.

   B. Database roles are fixed.

   C. You can add new database roles.

   D. You can add fixed server roles to database roles.

Lesson 6: Configuring Encryption

SQL Server 2005 provides a hierarchical key infrastructure that lets you encrypt data—offering a new level of security that didn't exist in previous versions of SQL Server. To implement data encryption in earlier versions of the database system, you have to use a third-party solution.

You can encrypt data by using symmetric and asymmetric keys and certificates. Although data encryption is an important feature, especially for certain types of data such as customer credit card information, be careful where you implement encryption. The overhead of encrypting and decrypting data can have a big impact on performance.

After this lesson, you will be able to:

■ Configure the encryption hierarchy.

■ Configure symmetric and asymmetric keys.

■ Configure certificates.

Estimated lesson time: 10 minutes

Configuring the Encryption Hierarchy

SQL Server 2005 provides an encryption hierarchy based on the *service master key*, which is a symmetric key generated automatically when you install a SQL Server 2005 instance. The database engine uses the service master key to encrypt the following:

■ Linked server passwords

■ Connection strings

■ Account credentials

■ All database master keys

You should back up the service master key and store it in a secure offsite location. You can manage the backup and restore of the service master key by using the *BACKUP SERVICE MASTER KEY* and *RESTORE SERVICE MASTER KEY* Transact-SQL statements, as the following sample statements show:

```
BACKUP SERVICE MASTER KEY TO FILE='file_name_path' ENCRYPTION BY PASSWORD = 'password' --
 SQL will use the password to encrypt the backup
RESTORE SERVICE MASTER KEY FROM FILE='file_name_path'
DECRYPTION BY PASSWORD = 'password'
```

You can manage service account changes and key regeneration by using the *ALTER SERVICE MASTER KEY* statement. The following sample statement regenerates the service master key:

```
ALTER SERVICE MASTER KEY REGENERATE
```

The next level in the encryption hierarchy is the *database master key*, which is an optional symmetric key that you can create at the database level to encrypt certificates and keys in the database. You can create the database master key by using the *CREATE MASTER KEY* statement and specifying a password:

```
CREATE MASTER KEY ENCRYPTION BY PASSWORD = 'password'
```

SQL Server stores one copy of the database master key in the master database and the key is encrypted with the service master key. Another copy is stored in the database, encrypted with the password. You require *CONTROL* permission in the database to create the master key.

Quick Check

■ The database engine automatically generates the service master key to encrypt what components?

Quick Check Answer

■ The service master key is used to encrypt linked server passwords, connection strings, account credentials, and all database master keys.

Configuring Symmetric and Asymmetric Keys

The next level in the encryption hierarchy is the data level, which gives you two encryption key options: symmetric and asymmetric. A *symmetric key* is the fastest encryption mechanism for encrypting and decrypting data and is suitable for encrypting frequently accessed data. You can use the *CREATE SYMMETRIC KEY* statement to create a symmetric key:

```
CREATE SYMMETRIC KEY key_name WITH ALGORITHM = AES_256 ENCRYPTION BY PASSWORD='password'
```

To encrypt and decrypt data, you can use the *EncryptByKey* function and the *DecryptByKey* function, respectively. These functions take the key and the data as parameters and return the data encrypted or decrypted.

An *asymmetric key* is a combination of a private key and its corresponding public key. An asymmetric key is stronger than a symmetric key, but it is also more resource-intensive. You can create an asymmetric key by using the *CREATE ASYMMETRIC KEY* statement:

```
CREATE ASYMMETRIC KEY key_name
    WITH ALGORITHM = RSA_2048
    ENCRYPTION BY PASSWORD = 'password'
```

To encrypt and decrypt data, you can use the *EncryptByAsmKey* function and the *DecryptByAsmKey* function, respectively.

Quick Check

What is the fastest data-encryption method?

Quick Check Answer
- A symmetric key is the fastest data-encryption mechanism.

Configuring Certificates

Certificates are the strongest encryption mechanism available. A public key certificate is a digitally signed statement that maps the value of a public key to the identity of the person, device, or service that holds the corresponding private key. SQL Server 2005 can create self-signed certificates that follow the X.509 standard. Although certificates are very secure, they also have a great impact on query performance because of the overhead that they use when they encrypt and decrypt data.

You can use the *CREATE CERTIFICATE* statement to create the certificate by using the following basic syntax:

```
CREATE CERTIFICATE certificate_name
WITH SUBJECT='certificate_subject'
```

You can use the Transact-SQL *EncryptByCert* function to encrypt data and the *DecryptByCert* function to decrypt data. In the following example, you see how to create a certificate and use it to encrypt a string:

```
USE AdventureWorks
GO
CREATE CERTIFICATE testCert WITH SUBJECT='Certificate for testing'
GO
SELECT Title, EncryptbyCert(Cert_id('testCert'),Title)Title_Ecnrypted from
 HumanResources.Employee
```

NOTE Balancing security and performance

To choose the best data-encryption mechanism for your environment, you need to balance security and performance requirements. Although certificates give you the most security, their performance hit might cause them to be inappropriate for your needs. In contrast, symmetric keys are fast but provide less security for your data.

PRACTICE ## Encrypting and Decrypting a Column

In these exercises, you will practice encrypting a column of data by using symmetric encryption. You will add a column called Comments to the *HumanResources.JobCandidate* table. This column will store confidential information about job candidates. You will encrypt the column by using a symmetric key protected with a certificate. This option provides a good balance between security and performance.

▶ **Practice 1: Create the Key Infrastructure**

In this practice, you will create the key infrastructure by creating the database master key, the certificate, and the symmetric key.

1. Open SSMS and connect to your server using Windows authentication.

2. Click New Query.

3. Type and execute the following code to create the database master key:

```
USE AdventureWorks
GO
IF NOT EXISTS (SELECT * FROM sys.symmetric_keys WHERE symmetric_key_id=101)
CREATE MASTER KEY ENCRYPTION BY PASSWORD = 'dkjuw4r$$#1946kcj$ngJKL95Q'
GO
```

4. Create the certificate that you will use to encrypt the symmetric key, and create the symmetric key itself by typing and executing the following code:

```
CREATE CERTIFICATE HRCert
WITH SUBJECT = 'Job Candidate Comments'
GO
CREATE SYMMETRIC KEY CommentKey
WITH ALGORITHM = DES
ENCRYPTION BY CERTIFICATE HRCert
GO
```

▶ **Practice 2: Encrypt the Data**

1. Execute the following code to add the Comments column to the *HumanResources.JobCandidate* table; Comments will store the encrypted data:

```
ALTER TABLE HumanResources.JobCandidate
ADD Comments varbinary(8000)
GO
```

2. Before using the *EncryptByKey* function to encrypt the data, you need to open the symmetric key by using the certificate you created earlier. Execute the following code to both use the certificate to decrypt the symmetric key and then to use *EncryptByKey* to encrypt the Comments column:

```
OPEN SYMMETRIC KEY CommentKey
DECRYPTION BY CERTIFICATE HRCert

UPDATE HumanResources.JobCandidate
SET Comments = EncryptByKey(Key_GUID('CommentKey'), 'No Comments')
GO
```

3. Query the *HumanResources.jobCandidate* table. You can see that the data is encrypted:

```
SELECT JobCandidateID,ModifiedDate, Comments FROM HumanResources.JobCandidate
```

4. To access the data in the encrypted column, you need to decrypt the column by executing the following code:

```
OPEN SYMMETRIC KEY CommentKey
DECRYPTION BY CERTIFICATE HRCert;

SELECT JobCandidateID, ModifiedDate,
CONVERT(varchar, DecryptByKey(Comments))
AS "Decrypted Comments"
FROM HumanResources.JobCandidate
```

Lesson Summary

- The ability to encrypt data is a new feature that is built into SQL Server 2005.

- The database engine gives you a hierarchical encryption infrastructure—ranging from the service master key to symmetric and asymmetric keys to database certificates—that lets you manage encryption in a secure, flexible way.

- To select the appropriate encryption mechanism for your environment, you need to balance your security and performance requirements.

Lesson Review

The following questions are intended to reinforce key information presented in this lesson. The questions are also available on the companion CD if you prefer to review them in electronic form.

NOTE   Answers

Answers to these questions and explanations of why each answer choice is right or wrong are located in the "Answers" section at the end of the book.

1. Which of the following sentences is true for the service master key?

   A. You should create the service master key by using the Surface Area Configuration Tool.

   B. The database engine creates the service master key automatically. The service master key can be opened only by the user account that installs SQL Server.

   C. The database engine creates the service master key automatically. The service master key can be opened only by the user account that starts the SQL Server service.

   D. You should create the service master key automatically from SQL Server Configuration.

2. Which of the following statements enables you to create a database certificate?

   A. *CREATE CERTIFICATE MyCert WITH SUBJECT='Certificate Subject'*

   B. *CREATE CERTIFICATE 'MyCert', 'Certificate Subject'*

   C. *CREATE CERT 'MyCert', 'Certificate Subject'*

   D. *CREATE CERT MyCert WITH TARGET= 'Certificate Subject'*

3. Which of the following sentences are true for the database master key? (Choose all that apply.)

   A. The database master key is optional.

   B. The database master key is mandatory if you want to encrypt data.

   C. The database master key is created automatically when you create the first certificate.

   D. The database master key is created manually.

Lesson 7: Configuring Linked Servers

SQL Server lets you access external data sources from your local Transact-SQL code. You can get ad hoc access to external data sources by using the *OPENROWSET* function. When you need to access data outside your local instance—such as a remote SQL Server; another instance in your server; or a Microsoft Access, Oracle, or other database—on a regular basis, you create a *linked server* to access the external data source. Linked servers also let you configure distributed environments such as replication.

To create a linked server, you need an OLE DB provider that lets you connect to the external data source. The key to good performance for non-SQL Server linked servers, such as AS/400 or Oracle, is to select a good OLE DB provider.

After this lesson, you will be able to:

- Specify the external data source.
- Specify the characteristics of the data source.
- Specify the security model of the data source.

Estimated lesson time: 10 minutes

How to Create a Linked Server

You need to define a linked server for each external data source you want to access and then configure the security context under which your distributed queries will run. After you create a linked server, you can use the Transact-SQL *OPENQUERY* function to execute your distributed queries.

NOTE   Executing a distributed query

When executing a distributed query against a linked server, use a fully qualified, four-part table name—in the form *linked_server_name.catalog.schema.object_name*—for each data source you are querying.

Here are the general steps for creating a linked server:

1. Expand the *Server Objects* node within Object Explorer in SSMS, as Figure 2-4 shows.

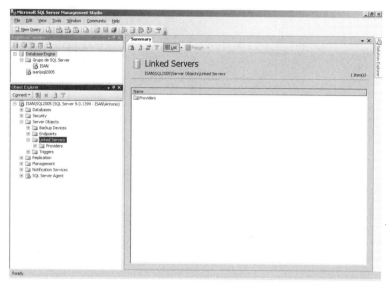

Figure 2-4   Manage Linked Servers from SSMS.

2. Right-click the *Linked Servers* node and choose New Linked Server.

3. Figure 2-5 shows the General Page of the New Linked Server dialog box, in which you choose the linked server type you want to create. If you select SQL Server, the system will use the Microsoft SQL Native Client OLE DB Provider to connect to the linked server. For other data sources, you can select the correct OLE DB provider to use. For example, you select the Microsoft Jet 4.0 OLE DB Provider to connect to an Access database.

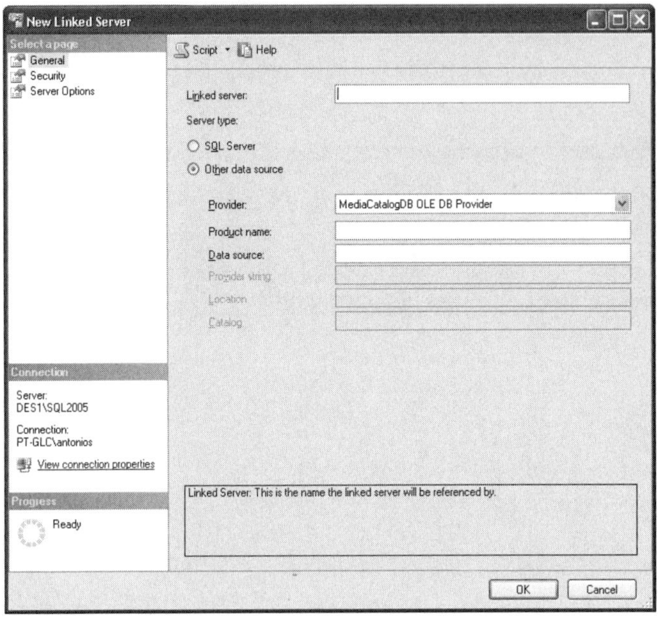

Figure 2-5 Create a new linked server.

4. Select the Security page, which Figure 2-6 shows, to configure the security context that you will use for the linked server.

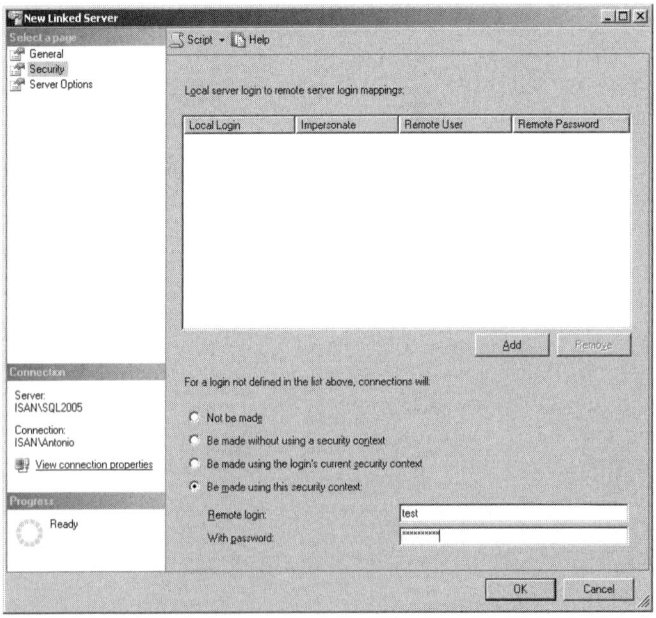

Figure 2-6 Configure the security model for a linked server.

Configuring the Security Model

When you use linked servers to access external data sources, you should pay special attention to the security context for the external connection. You can configure the linked server to use one of the following three security modes:

- **Self-mapping**   When a linked server is created, this mode is added for all local logins, so SQL Server tries to connect to the external data source using the current user's login credentials. The same login and password must exist on the remote server. This is the default behavior.

- **Delegation**   This mode impersonates the Windows local credentials; the connection forwards the credentials of an authenticated Windows user to the linked server. The Windows user account and password must exist on the linked server.

- **Remote Credentials**   This mode lets you map local logins to remote logins on the external data source.

Delegation of operating system logins is the securest mechanism, but you can use it only when the external data source supports Windows authentication. In other cases, you should map local logins to remote credentials to have a secure context for the connection to the external data source.

PRACTICE Creating a Microsoft Access Linked Server

In this practice, you create a linked server, link it to a Microsoft Access database called C:\Practice Files\Northwind.mdb, and then query the *Customer* table on the Access database. You use the *sp_addlinkedserver* stored procedure to accomplish this task. The basic syntax for this stored procedure is

```
sp_addlinkedserver <server_name>,<product_name>,<oledb provider name>, <data source>
```

1. Download the Northwind.mdb database from http://download.microsoft.com/ download/1/1/e/11e8b0ec-db42-4155-92d2-d11049628867/Northwind.exe and copy to C:\Practice Files\Northwind.mdb.

2. Open SQL Server Management Studio. In the Login dialog box, click OK, and then click New Query. Create a linked server called North and link it to the Access database C:\Practice Files\Northwind.mdb by executing the *sp_addlinkedserver* stored procedure, as follows:

```
EXECUTE sp_addlinkedserver 'North', 'OLE DB Provider for Jet',
 'Microsoft.Jet.OLEDB.4.0','C:\Practice Files\Northwind.mdb'
```

3. Test your access to the remote database by issuing the following query against the *Customers* table:

```
SELECT * FROM North...Customers
```

Lesson Summary

- Linked servers are server objects that let you connect and execute commands on remote data sources, including non-SQL Server data sources.

- To define a linked server, you specify the external data source, an OLE DB provider, to connect to that source, and the security context of the connection.

- After creating a linked server, you can access its objects by using the fully qualified, four-part table name.

Lesson Review

The following questions are intended to reinforce key information presented in this lesson. The questions are also available on the companion CD if you prefer to review them in electronic form.

NOTE   Answers

Answers to these questions and explanations of why each answer choice is right or wrong are located in the "Answers" section at the end of the book.

---

1. When do you need to specify an external data source by using a linked server?

    A. When you need to access a different database.

    B. When you need to access a different instance.

    C. When you need to access a different database schema

    D. When you need to access objects of a different user owner.

2. What do you need to specify to create a linked server? (Choose all that apply.)

    A. OLE DB Data Source

    B. ODBC Data Source

    C. ODBC Provider

    D. OLE DB Provider

3. Which of the following sentences are true for linked server security? (Choose all that apply.)

    A. The security mode is defined at the instance level.

    B. The default configuration is self-mapping.

    C. The default configuration is delegation.

    D. The security mode is defined per linked server.

Chapter Review

To further practice and reinforce the skills you learned in this chapter, you can

- Review the chapter summary.
- Review the list of key terms introduced in this chapter.
- Complete the case scenarios. These scenarios set up real-world situations involving the topics of this chapter and ask you to create a solution.
- Complete the suggested practices.
- Take a practice test.

Chapter Summary

- Configuring data and log files is one of the most important tasks in the database design phase. You should evaluate server hardware along with the database structure to define the best approach for your environment.
- Database Mail gives you an easy mechanism for configuring a mail subsystem in SQL Server 2005. Database Mail is an SMTP client that lets your database applications send and receive e-mails without requiring you to install an Extended MAPI client on the server, as was required with previous versions of SQL Server.
- How you configure a database's recovery model has great impact on the database's availability. The Full recovery model is recommended for all production databases, but you can use the Bulk-Logged recovery model temporarily during a bulk load operation.
- In setting up security for your database system, selecting the appropriate authentication mode is your first crucial task. Windows authentication mode provides the most secure mechanism, but for you to use it, all your clients must support Windows authentication.
- To give access to your database, you need to configure database users mapped to logins. You can use SQL Server's fixed database roles or create your own to group users with the same security needs and simplify management.

■ Data encryption, new in SQL Server 2005, provides a highly secure environment, but with a possible high performance cost. You should evaluate the need for encryption carefully and test the impact on your applications.

■ When you need to create a linked server to access an external data source, you should pay special attention to two configuration options: the OLE DB provider you will use to connect to the external data source and the security mechanism that will validate the connections to the external data source.

Key Terms

Do you know what these key terms mean? You can check your answers by looking up the terms in the glossary at the end of the book.

■ asymmetric key

■ Bulk-Logged recovery model

■ certificate

■ Database Mail

■ Database Mail account

■ Database Mail profile

■ database master key

■ database role

■ data file

■ default filegroup

■ filegroup

■ fixed server role

■ Full recovery model

■ linked server

■ log file

■ Mixed Mode authentication

■ primary data file

■ primary filegroup

■ RAID 0

■ RAID 1

- RAID 5
- read-only filegroup
- recovery model
- schema
- secondary data file
- service master key
- Simple recovery model
- symmetric key
- user-defined filegroup
- Windows authentication

Case Scenarios

In the following case scenarios, you will apply what you've learned in this chapter. You can find answers to these questions in the "Answers" section at the end of this book.

Case Scenario 1: Configuring Security

You are working as a senior DBA for a large retail company. Your company plans to implement a new Customer Relationship Management (CRM) application that uses SQL Server 2005 as the database engine. You have Windows XP and Macintosh clients on your Active Directory network, and you need to provide access from both environments to SQL Server. You'll have basically two user types: Sales and Marketing. The CRM solution will store confidential data about clients, so you need to configure an encryption mechanism that has a small impact on performance.

1. What authentication mode and login types should you use?
2. What database users and roles would be appropriate?
3. What encryption architecture should you implement to encrypt the confidential data?

Case Scenario 2: Configuring a Heterogeneous Environment

You work as a senior DBA at an insurance company that has its headquarters in California and branch offices in Seattle, Bogota, Madrid, and Marsella. Your company has an Enterprise Resource Planning (ERP) solution installed on an Oracle server, and you are deploying a call-center application based on SQL Server 2005. The call-center application on SQL Server 2005 needs access to the Oracle server to extract information. Also, you need to send aggregate information to branch offices by e-mail, but you have a UNIX mail server.

1. How should you provide access to the Oracle server from SQL Server 2005?

2. What security solution should you implement to ensure that your connection is as safe as possible?

3. What infrastructure changes are needed to support Database Mail?

Suggested Practices

To help you successfully master the exam objectives presented in this chapter, complete the following practice tasks.

■ **Practice 1: Managing Database Schemas**   Practice creating a schema; then transfer a schema to a new owner and drop the original user who owned the schema.

■ **Practice 2: Managing Recovery Models**   Using the *AdventureWorks* database, compare the performance of the backup performed when the database is configured to use the Simple recovery model versus the Full recovery model.

Take a Practice Test

The practice tests on this book's companion CD offer many options. For example, you can test yourself on just the content covered in this chapter, or you can test yourself on all the 70-431 certification exam content. You can set up the test so that it closely simulates the experience of taking a certification exam, or you can set it up in study mode so that you can look at the correct answers and explanations after you answer each question.

MORE INFO   Practice tests

For details about all the practice test options available, see the section titled "How to Use the Practice Tests" in this book's Introduction.

Chapter 3
Creating Tables, Constraints, and User-Defined Types

The entire purpose of a database is to store and return data. These tasks would not be possible without the structure that database tables provide. Tables are the basic building blocks of a database. And the choices you make when designing a table affect the amount of space consumed on disk, the amount of memory consumed when processing data, and the queries required to manipulate the data for application use. This chapter lays the foundation for building high-performing databases. We begin by looking at how to define the columns within a table to enforce a structure for your data that supports business rules while using minimum storage resources. After you understand how to appropriately define columns, you can create your table and assign permissions to allow access to the table.

This chapter then discusses the Microsoft SQL Server constraints you can use to further enforce business rules, and it ends with coverage of user-defined types (UDTs) that you can create to enforce consistent column definitions within your database or to create entirely new data types that SQL Server doesn't provide.

Exam objectives in this chapter:
- Implement a table.
  - Specify column details.
  - Specify the filegroup.
  - Assign permissions to a role for tables.
- Implement constraints.
  - Specify the scope of a constraint.
  - Create a new constraint.
- Create user-defined types.
  - Create a Transact-SQL user-defined type.
  - Specify details of the data type.
  - Create a CLR user-defined type.

Lessons in this chapter:

Before You Begin

To complete the lessons in this chapter, you must have

- SQL Server 2005 installed.

- A copy of the *AdventureWorks* sample database installed in the instance or an empty database created.

IMPORTANT   Implementing tables

The placement of this chapter creates a "chicken-and-egg" dilemma. You can't have a chicken with-out an egg, and you can't have an egg without a chicken. The same is true for SQL Server tables. You can't define a table without using Transact-SQL. And tables aren't much use if they don't con-tain any data, which you place into the table by using Transact-SQL. However, we can't teach Trans-act-SQL without first explaining tables. In this book, we cover table creation first. And as much as possible, this chapter avoids discussing the details of using Transact-SQL, which is covered in later chapters.

> ### Real World
>
> *Michael Hotek*
>
> Much of my career with SQL Server has focused on either achieving maximum uptime or fixing performance issues. Performance problems manifest them-selves in a variety of ways, but every issue always comes back to a single root cause: resources.
>
> Companies often first try "throwing more hardware at the problem" by changing servers, adding memory, adding disks, and so on. This rarely solves the perfor-mance problem. Most professionals dealing with performance issues start by inves-tigating the code that has been written to access the data, usually identifying a number of changes they can make to improve performance or even solve the issue. Rarely does anyone look into the database table structure, simply because you gen-erally cannot change table structures after a database is in production. Unfortu-nately, structural issues are at the core of almost every performance problem.

I spent two weeks at one customer site, analyzing its environment and documenting all the performance issues the organization was having as its application was having to process larger and larger volumes of data. I found lots of ways to improve queries so that they were more efficient and read less data. And I suggested additional improvements the IT team could make to reduce the amount of code that had to be executed to reach a final result. Over the course of my assignment, I identified hundreds of queries that could be tuned, and I changed several dozen of them myself. However, all the changes combined could not overcome the most fundamental problem with the company's application: poor table design.

The company's application revolved around dates and scheduling items into time blocks. However, the application never dealt with actual dates; instead it dealt with either minutes or seconds. Unfortunately, when the database tables were designed, everything was stored in a *datetime* data type. So every query running in the system had to call a function that converted the data into minutes and seconds that could be used by the application. And every time a change had to be made, the application had to convert the minutes and seconds that it used back into a *datetime* value to be stored in the database. (Because of a nonstandard business week definition, the company couldn't use any of the date or time functions in SQL Server.) After further analysis, we determined that more than 80 percent of the total resources being consumed—processor, memory, and input/output (I/O)—was involved in this conversion process.

We created a simple test database that converted all the *datetime* columns into integers, stripped out all the conversion code, and then ran several tests. Queries that were taking seconds to execute dropped to 50 milliseconds or less. Queries taking minutes dropped to a few seconds. In the most extreme case, a batch process that ran several times per day and previously took as long as four hours in a given run took less than five minutes to finish, regardless of the amount of data that needed to be processed.

Unfortunately, the application data is still stored in *datetime* columns, and the application still spends 80 percent or more of the total resources that it consumes converting the *datetime* values into usable values for the application. To change this fundamental structure would have required a complete rewrite of more than 80 percent of the stored procedure code and would have affected almost all the database tables.

So when someone tells me that the choice of data types for a table really doesn't matter because storage space is cheap, I wonder just how long it will be before their performance becomes a problem—and a problem whose root cause can't be fixed because of business constraints. Disk space might be reasonably inexpensive and essentially limitless, but all the data still has to be moved through memory and processors, and there is a maximum amount of memory and processors that current hardware can support. Every byte wasted when data is stored needlessly consumes a byte of memory along with processor cycles when it is processed. Although a single byte here or there won't do much harm, losing a single byte per row in a table that contains millions of rows of data adds up very quickly to memory pressure and high processor utilization.

Lesson 1: Creating Tables

The basic analogy for a database *table* is that it is like a single worksheet within a spreadsheet. As you work with a worksheet, you enter information in rows and columns. Well-designed spreadsheets generally have column headers that give you an idea of the kind of data you find in a column. The problem with working with data in a worksheet, however, is that it doesn't enforce any structure. You can place any type of data in any column without limitation.

Database tables also store rows of data in columns. And each of these columns has a name associated with it to provide an easy way to reference a particular piece of data. But what sets a table and database apart from a Microsoft Office Excel worksheet or spreadsheet, for example, is the strict enforcement of the data that you can enter in a column. SQL Server enforces this data structure by using data types as well as properties that you can add to further define a column. In this lesson, you will learn how to make the best choices when defining data types and properties for columns, how to create a table, and then how to assign appropriate permissions to allow access to a table.

> **After this lesson, you will be able to:**
> - Specify column details including data type.
> - Specify the filegroup.
> - Implement a table.
> - Assign permissions to a role for tables.
>
> **Estimated lesson time: 30 minutes**

Understanding Data Types

Data types limit the type of data that you can store in a column and, in some cases, even limit the range of possible values in the column. The data type that you choose for a column is the most critical decision that you make within your database. If you choose a data type that is too restrictive, applications cannot store the data they are supposed to process, leading to a large design effort. If you choose too broad a data type, however, you wind up consuming more space than necessary on disk and in memory, which can create a resource and performance issue.

When selecting a data type for a column, you should choose the data type that allows all the data values that you expect to be stored while doing so in the least amount of space possible. SQL Server data types fall into seven general categories, which Table 3-1 describes.

Table 3-1   Seven Categories of SQL Server Data Types

Data Type Category	General Purpose
Exact numeric	Stores precise numbers either with or without decimals
Approximate numeric	Stores numeric values with or without decimals
Monetary	Stores numeric values with decimal places; used specifically for currency values with up to four decimal places
Date and time	Stores date and time information and enables special chronological enforcement, such as rejecting a value of February 30
Character	Stores character-based values of varying lengths
Binary	Stores data in a strict binary (0 and 1) representation
Special purpose	Complex data types that require specialized handling, such as XML documents or globally unique identifiers (GUIDs)

Let's look at each of these data type categories to see how you can use the different data types to provide the basic definition of each column in a table. You use these data types when defining permanent tables, temporary tables, table variables, and variables. There are few restrictions to the data types that you can use in stored procedures, triggers, and functions.

MORE INFO   Data type definitions

For more detailed information about each data type, including explicit storage details and restrictions, see the SQL Server 2005 Books Online topics "Data Types (Transact-SQL)" and "Data Type Conversion (Database Engine)." SQL Server 2005 Books Online is installed as part of SQL Server 2005. Updates for SQL Server 2005 Books Online are available for download at *www.microsoft.com/technet/prodtechnol/sql/2005/downloads/books.mspx*.

Exact Numeric Data Types

You use exact numeric data types to store numbers that have zero or more decimal places. You can manipulate the numbers that you store in these data types by using any mathematical operation without requiring any special handling. The storage is also precisely defined, so any data stored in these data types returns and calculates to the same value on either an Intel or an AMD processor architecture. Table 3-2 lists the exact numeric data types that SQL Server supports.

Table 3-2   Exact Numeric Data Types

Data Type	Storage	Value Range	Purpose
bigint	8 bytes	$-2E63$ to $2E63 -1$	Stores very large whole numbers that can be positive or negative
int	4 bytes	$-2E31$ to $2E31 -1$	Stores whole numbers that can be positive or negative
smallint	2 bytes	$-32,768$ to $32,767$	Stores whole numbers that can be positive or negative
tinyint	1 byte	0 to 255	Stores a small range of positive whole numbers
decimal(p,s)	5–17 bytes depending on the precision	$-10E38 + 1$ to $10E38 -1$	Stores decimals up to a maximum of 38 places
numeric(p,s)	5–17 bytes depending on the precision	$-10E38 + 1$ to $10E38 -1$	Functionally equivalent to decimal, and can be used interchangeably with decimal

The *decimal* and *numeric* data types accept parameters to complete the data type definition. These parameters define the precision and scale for the data type. For example, *decimal*(12,4) defines a decimal value that can have up to 12 total digits, with four of those digits after the decimal.

The most common data types from this group are *int* and *decimal*. You can use a *decimal* data type to store integer values, but doing so requires extra bytes of storage per row and should not be used for this purpose.

Although *int* data types can store both positive and negative numbers, the negative portion is very rarely used. The *int* data types are commonly used—and commonly misused. If the range of values you plan to store in a column do not exceed 32,767, you can save two bytes for every row by using *smallint* instead of *int*. If the values are going to range only from 0 to 255, you can save three bytes for every row by using *tinyint*.

IMPORTANT   Space utilization

Saving two or three bytes of storage per row doesn't seem like a lot compared to the 250+ GB hard drives that you can now purchase for a few hundred dollars, pounds, euros, yen, or whatever currency you are working with. However, hard disk storage is a minor concern. If you store 1 million rows of data in a table, which is very common, the bytes per row saved would add up to 2 or 3 MB. Although that does not sound like much, consider that you also save that much space in memory if a user executes a query that returns all the rows in the table. You also save thousands of processor cycles at the same time.

The space issue becomes even larger when you join two tables together. Joining two *int* columns together consumes eight bytes of memory as well as the corresponding calculation on the processor. If both tables hold 1 million rows and need to be read completely, the operation consumes about 8 MB of memory space. If you could have stored the data in a *smallint* or *tinyint* column instead, the memory savings for this query would be 4–6 MB. And that is the savings for only a single query. Consider what would happen if thousands of queries are being processed against the database, and you can see how one or two bytes of savings per row based on the data type you use can quickly make the difference between an environment with good performance and one with very poor performance.

Approximate Numeric Data Types

Approximate numeric data types can store decimal values. However, data stored in a *float* or *real* data type is exact only to the precision specified in the data type definition. Any digits to the right are not guaranteed to be stored exactly. For example, if you stored 1.00015454 in a data type defined as *float*(8), the column is guaranteed to return only 1.000154 accurately. SQL Server rounds off any digits further to the right when it stores the data. Therefore, calculations involving these data types compound rounding errors. Transferring databases containing tables with these data types between Intel and AMD processors also introduces errors. Table 3-3 lists SQL Server's approximate numeric data types.

Table 3-3   Approximate Numeric Data Types

Data Type	Storage	Value Range	Purpose
float(p)	4 or 8 bytes	−2.23E308 to 2.23E308	Stores large, floating point numbers that exceed the capacity of a decimal data type
real	4 bytes	−3.4E38 to 3.4E38	Still valid, but replaced by float to meet the SQL-92 standard

The *float* data types accept a parameter in the definition that determines the number of digits to store precisely. For example, a *float*(8) column precisely stores seven digits, and anything exceeding that is subject to rounding errors.

Because of the imprecision associated with these data types, they are rarely used. You should consider using *float* only in cases in which an exact numeric data type is not large enough to store the values.

Monetary Data Types

Monetary data types are designed to store currency values with four decimal places of precision. Table 3-4 lists SQL Server's monetary data types.

Table 3-4   Monetary Data Types

Data Type	Storage	Value Range	Purpose
money	8 bytes	−922,337,203,685,477.5808 to 922,337,203,685,477.5807	Stores large currency values
smallmoney	4 bytes	−214,748.3648 to 214,748.3647	Stores small currency values

The *smallmoney* data types are rarely defined in databases, even though this data type is the most accurate choice for many applications that deal with products and orders. It is much more common for these databases to incorrectly use the *money* data type and waste four bytes of storage for each row stored.

Although *money* and *smallmoney* data types are designed to store currency values, they are rarely used in financial applications. Instead, these applications use a *decimal* data type because they need to perform accurate calculations to 6, 8, and even 12 decimal places.

Date and Time Data Types

In storing data, nothing generates more controversy than figuring out how to store dates and times. Some applications need to store only a date. Other applications need to store only a time. And still other applications need to store both dates and times together. Unfortunately, SQL Server stores this type of data only together as both a date and a time—for example, 2006-03-14 20:53:36.153, which is the precise millisecond on the system clock when I started writing this sentence. Table 3-5 lists SQL Server's date and time data types.

Table 3-5   Date and Time Data Types

Data Type	Storage	Value Range	Purpose
datetime	8 bytes	January 1, 1753, through December 31, 9999, with an accuracy of 3.33 milliseconds	Stores large date and time values.
smalldatetime	4 bytes	January 1, 1900, through June 6, 2079, with an accuracy of 1 minute	Stores a smaller range of date and time values

The *datetime* and *smalldatetime* data types are stored internally as integers. The *datetime* data type is stored as a pair of four-byte integers, which together represent the number of milliseconds since midnight on January 1, 1753. The first four bytes store the date, and the second four bytes store the time. The *smalldatetime* data type is stored as a pair of two-byte integers, which together represent the number of minutes since midnight on January 1, 1900. The first two bytes store the date, and the second two bytes store the time.

Character Data Types

To store character data, you select one of the data types designed for this purpose. Each one consumes either one or two bytes of storage for each character, depending on whether the data type uses American National Standards Institute (ANSI) encoding or Unicode encoding.

Before looking at the character data types, let's look briefly at the background behind the ANSI and Unicode encodings. To handle the wide variety of languages in the world, computer technologists needed a way to store the many different characters of a language in a standard format. So, the ANSI standards body developed an encoding standard that required eight bits to represent the range of letters. The only problem was that every character could not be specified within a single eight-bit encoding. Thus, dozens of character sets were created that specified the acceptable characters for a given encoding. This approach worked well until you started transferring data between systems that used different character sets. If a character in one encoding did not exist in a different encoding, it was lost in the translation process. In addition to the encoding-translation issues, the eight-bit encoding couldn't capture several languages.

These problems led to the creation of the Unicode standard. The Unicode standard uses 2 bytes to represent each character. This extra space meant that all the character sets in use in the ANSI standard could be eliminated. Now, each unique character could be expressed within a single encoding schema. And because with Unicode there's just one encoding scheme, no encoding translation is necessary when transferring data between systems set for different languages. This makes character data completely transportable. The only downside is that Unicode data types require two bytes to store each character, so Unicode data types require twice as much space as their ANSI counterparts.

Unicode data types are preceded with an *n*. For example, *nchar* is the Unicode counterpart to the *char* data type, which uses the ANSI encoding. When defining a character data type, you specify the maximum number of bytes the column is allowed to store. Table 3-6 lists SQL Server character data types.

Table 3-6   Character Data Types

Data Type	Storage	Number of Characters	Purpose
char(n)	1–8,000 bytes	Maximum of 8,000 characters	ANSI data type that is fixed width
nchar(n)	2–8,000 bytes	Maximum of 4,000 characters	Unicode data type that is fixed width

Table 3-6   **Character Data Types**

Data Type	Storage	Number of Characters	Purpose
varchar(n)	1–8,000 bytes	Maximum of 8,000 characters	ANSI data type that is variable width
varchar(max)	Up to 2 GB	Up to 2,147,483,647 characters	ANSI data type that is variable width
nvarchar(n)	2–8,000 bytes	Maximum of 4,000 characters	Unicode data type that is variable width
nvarchar(max)	Up to 2 GB	Up to 1,073,741,823 characters	Unicode data type that is variable width
text	Up to 2 GB	Up to 2,147,483,647 characters	ANSI data type that is variable width
ntext	Up to 2 GB	Up to 1,073,741,823 characters	Unicode data type that is variable width

Why are there so many character data types that appear to be equivalent to each other? The differences in the data types might be subtle, but they can be important. A *char* data type, either ANSI or Unicode, is a fixed-width data type. Therefore, it consumes the same amount of storage space regardless of the number of characters that are stored in the column. For example, a *char*(30) column consumes 30 bytes of storage space regardless of whether you store one character or 30 characters in the column. Any unused space is padded with spaces up to the maximum storage specified for the column. However, a *varchar*(30) column consumes only one byte for each character that is stored in the column.

The *text* and *ntext* data types are designed to store large amounts of character-based data. However, *text* and *ntext* columns aren't allowed with many operations. For example, you cannot use them with an equality operator or join them together. Many system functions also cannot use *text* and *ntext* data types.

Because of these limitations, SQL Server 2005 introduced the *varchar*(max) and *nvarchar*(max) data types. These data types combine the capabilities of both *text/ntext* and *varchar/nvarchar* data types. They can store up to 2 GB of data and do not have any restrictions on the operations that you can perform with them or on the functions you can use them with.

Binary Data Types

There are many times when you need to store binary data. So SQL Server provides three data types that let you store various amounts of binary data in a table. Table 3-7 lists SQL Server's binary data types.

Table 3-7   Binary Data Types

Data Type	Storage	Purpose
binary(n)	1–8,000 bytes	Stores fixed-size binary data
varbinary(n)	1–8,000 bytes	Stores variable-size binary data
varbinary(max)	Up to 2 GB	Stores variable-size binary data
image	Up to 2 GB	Stores variable-size binary data

You use the *binary* data types essentially to store files within SQL Server. You use the *binary/varbinary* data types for storing small files, such as a group of 4 KB or 6 KB files containing a variety of data in native format.

The most popular data type within this group is the *image* data type. This data type has an unfortunate name; it is not used exclusively to store images, such as a library of pictures from a recent vacation. Although you can store pictures in an *image* data type, you can also use this data type to store Word, Excel, PDF, and Visio documents. You can store any file that is 2 GB or less in size in an *image* data type. One of the most famous implementations of this data type is the TerraServer project, which is a multi-terabyte database of terrestrial images that you can access at *www.terraserver.com*.

The *varbinary*(max) data type is new to SQL Server 2005. It can store the same amount of data as an *image* data type, and you can use it with all the operations and functions that you can use with *binary/varbinary* data types.

Specialized Data Types

In addition to the preceding standard data types, SQL Server provides seven additional data types for very specific purposes. Table 3-8 describes these specialized data types.

Table 3-8   Specialized Date Types

Data Type	Purpose
bit	Stores a 0, 1, or *null*. Used for basic "flag" values. TRUE is converted to 1, and FALSE is converted to 0.
timestamp	An automatically generated value. Each database contains an internal counter that designates a relative time counter not associated with an actual clock. A table can have only one *timestamp* column, which is set to the database timestamp when the row is inserted or modified.
uniqueidentifier	A 16-bit GUID used to globally identify a row across databases, instances, and servers.
sql_variant	Can change the data type based on the data that is stored within it. Stores a maximum of 8,000 bytes.
cursor	Used by applications that declare cursors. Contains a reference to the cursor that can be used for operations. This data type cannot be used in a table.
table	Used to hold a result set for subsequent processing. This data type cannot be used for a column. The only time you use this data type is when declaring table variables in triggers, stored procedures, and functions.
Xml	Stores an XML document of up to 2 GB in size. You can specify options to force only well-formed documents to be stored in the column.

CAUTION   sql_variant: just say no

The *sql_variant* data type, new in SQL Server 2005, is a dangerous data type that, in my opinion, should never have been added to SQL Server. This data type enables you to declare a column or variable without having to decide what type of data will be stored in it. The *sql_variant* data type then automatically "converts" itself into the type of data that is written into it.

Databases are useful because all data is explicitly declared and explicitly typed. By allowing a data type that has no defined type, all kinds of data-mismatch issues can arise. We *very strongly* recommend that you never use *sql_variant*.

MORE INFO sql_variant

For more information about the *sql_variant* data type, see the SQL Server 2005 Books Online article "sql_variant (Transact-SQL)."

> ## Quick Check
> - What are the six categories of standard data types that you can use to define columns in tables, and what is the general purpose of each category?
>
> ### Quick Check Answer
> - *Exact numeric data types* store precise integer or decimal values.
> - *Approximate numeric data types* store floating-point numbers.
> - *Monetary data types* store currency accurate to four decimal places.
> - *Datetime* data types store dates and times.
> - *Character data types* store text values.
> - *Binary data types* store binary streams, normally files.

Nullability

The second characteristic of any column definition is whether it requires a value to be stored. Databases have a special construct called a *null* that you can use to denote the absence of a value—something similar to "unknown" or "not applicable." A *null* is not a value, nor does it consume storage. The best way to understand this construct is to look at an example.

Let's say that you are designing a table to store addresses of your company's customers. You have decided that each address can have up to three lines for the street address. Each address can also have a city, a state or province, a postal code, and a country. So you create a table that contains seven columns. Not every customer needs all three address lines to capture the street address, so one or two of these columns are not necessary for some addresses. Some customers live in countries that do not have states or provinces, so this column is also not necessary for every customer. In addition, when users input addresses, they might not know the postal code of certain customers, but they still need to be able to save all of the data that is known. These issues create a basic dilemma. You could stick a dummy value in the columns that either don't have values or the values aren't known when the data was entered. However, inserting dummy data can cause even more problems because you are adding invalid data to your table—data that might be seen and used by an employee or customer. Generally, you would have users just omit the data. Because the data was not explicitly specified, it is either unknown or not applicable. In the database, the column would be *null* to designate this unknown state.

When you define columns, you can specify whether or not *nulls* are allowed. If you disallow *nulls*, a user is required to specify a value for the column.

Note that because it is impossible for the absence of something to equal the absence of something—in other words, one *null* cannot equal another *null*—you cannot use a null in comparisons.

MORE INFO   Nulls

For more details about *nulls*, see the SQL Server 2005 Books Online article "Null Values."

Identity

When defining columns, you also have the ability to specify a special identity property for a single column in a table. Defining a column with the identity property causes SQL Server to generate an automatically incrementing number. The identity property takes two parameters: seed and increment. The seed value designates the starting value that SQL Server uses. The increment value specifies what number SQL Server adds to this starting value when generating each successive value. This property is equivalent to autonumber or autoincrement values in other languages.

You can use the identity property with the exact numeric data types: *bigint*, *int*, *smallint*, *tinyint*, *decimal*, and *numeric*. If you use *decimal* or *numeric* data types with the identity property, you must define them with 0 decimal places.

Computed Columns

You can also create a special type of column called a *computed* column, which contains a computation involving one or more other columns in the table.

By default, the computed column contains a definition for the computation but does not physically store data by default. When the data is returned, the computation is applied to return a result.

However, you can force a computed column to physically store data by using the *PERSISTED* keyword. This keyword causes the computation to occur when the row is inserted or modified, and the result of the computation is then physically stored in the table.

Creating a Table

Now that you have seen all the column details you can specify to define the structure of a table, you are ready to actually create a table. You can create three different types of tables in SQL Server: permanent, temporary, and table variables.

MORE INFO Normalization, naming conventions, and table design

Normalization, naming conventions, and various table-design methods are beyond the scope of this book. For information about these topics, see *MCITP Self-Paced Training Kit (Exam 70-443): Designing a Database Server Infrastructure by Using Microsoft SQL Server 2005,* Microsoft Press, 2007.

Permanent Tables

To create a table, you use the *CREATE TABLE* Transact-SQL command. The general syntax of this command is as follows:

```
CREATE TABLE
    [ database_name . [ schema_name ] . | schema_name . ] table_name
        ( { <column_definition> | <computed_column_definition> }
        [ <table_constraint> ] [ ,...n ] )
    [ ON { partition_scheme_name ( partition_column_name ) | filegroup
        | "default" } ]
    [ { TEXTIMAGE_ON { filegroup | "default" } ]
[ ; ]
```

To execute this command, you must be a member of the sysadmin fixed server role, a member of the database owner fixed database role, or have been granted the *CREATE TABLE* permission. When you use this command, you create a table in the database that can be accessed by any user with the appropriate permissions.

The *ON* clause specifies where the table will reside on physical storage. If you do not specify a filegroup, SQL Server creates the table on the default filegroup.

Using our earlier example, you could use the *CREATE TABLE* command to create the *CustomerAddress* table as follows:

```
CREATE TABLE dbo.CustomerAddress
(AddressLine1          varchar(30)    NOT NULL,
AddressLine2           varchar(30)    NULL,
AddressLine3           varchar(30)    NULL,
City                   varchar(50)    NOT NULL,
StateProvinceID        int            NULL,
PostalCode             char(10)       NULL,
CountryID              int            NULL)
```

This table definition specifies the following:

- The table will be created in the *dbo* schema.

- A minimum of one address line that has a maximum of 30 characters must be specified for every customer. The storage space consumed will be equal to the number of characters in the column.

- One or two optional address lines can be specified, each holding up to 30 characters and consuming storage space equal to the number of characters in the column.

- A customer record must have a city specified; the City column can hold a value up to 50 characters in length and consumes storage equal to the number of characters in the column.

- A customer can have an optional state/province specified. The column consumes four bytes of storage and contains an integer value.

- A customer can have an optional postal code specified. Each column consumes 10 bytes of storage.

- A customer can have an optional country specified. The column consumes four bytes of storage and contains an integer value.

Although the preceding table definition accurately captures the necessary data, you might have noticed a few problems. A customer might have one or more home addresses, one or more business addresses, and one or more shipping addresses. A customer might also want to designate a particular address as the primary address. So you might be tempted to add a lot of additional columns to handle these situations. But that would be thinking in terms of a spreadsheet, not a database. Instead, you can simply add a column to the table that designates the type of address and a column to designate the primary address, as the following example shows:

```
CREATE TABLE dbo.CustomerAddress
(AddressType           char(4)        NOT NULL,
PrimaryAddressFlag     bit            NOT NULL,
AddressLine1           varchar(30)    NOT NULL,
AddressLine2           varchar(30)    NULL,
AddressLine3           varchar(30)    NULL,
City                   varchar(50)    NOT NULL,
StateProvinceID        int            NULL,
PostalCode             char(10)       NULL,
CountryID              int            NULL)
```

For now, we will ignore the questions concerning the StateProvinceID and CountryID columns because we will cover them in the next lesson on constraints.

But there is still one other problem with this table definition. We are capturing addresses, but we have no way of knowing which address corresponds with which customer. To complete the table structure and allow an address to be associated with a customer, we need to add one more column to the table: the CustomerAddressID *int* column, defined with the identity property. The complete table definition is as follows:

```
CREATE TABLE dbo.CustomerAddress
(CustomerAddressID       int          IDENTITY(1,1),
AddressType              char(4)      NOT NULL,
PrimaryAddressFlag       bit          NOT NULL,
AddressLine1             varchar(30)  NOT NULL,
AddressLine2             varchar(30)  NULL,
AddressLine3             varchar(30)  NULL,
City                     varchar(50)  NOT NULL,
StateProvinceID          int          NULL,
PostalCode               char(10)     NULL,
CountryID                int          NULL)
```

NOTE   Deleting tables

You use the *DELETE* command to remove rows from a table. And to remove an entire table, you use the *DROP TABLE* command. To execute this command, you must be a member of the sysadmin fixed server role, a member of the database owner fixed database role, or the owner of the table.

Temporary Tables

Temporary tables, as their name suggests, are temporary table structures. Temporary tables can be either global or local and can be created by any user. All temporary tables are created in the *tempdb* database.

A local temporary table is visible only to the user who created the table and only within the connection that was used to create the table. Local temporary tables are automatically dropped when the connection they are associated with is closed. You create a local temporary table by using the *CREATE TABLE* command and prepending a pound sign (#) to the table name.

The following example shows the command to create the earlier *CustomerAddress* table as a local temporary table:

```
CREATE TABLE #CustomerAddress
(CustomerAddressID       int          IDENTITY(1,1),
AddressType              char(4)      NOT NULL,
PrimaryAddressFlag       bit          NOT NULL,
AddressLine1             varchar(30)  NOT NULL,
```

```
AddressLine2          varchar(30)      NULL,
AddressLine3          varchar(30)      NULL,
City                  varchar(50)      NOT NULL,
StateProvinceID       int              NULL,
PostalCode            char(10)         NULL,
CountryID             int              NULL)
```

A global temporary table, in contrast, is visible to any user within the SQL Server instance. Global temporary tables are dropped when the last connection accessing the table is closed. You create a global temporary table by using the *CREATE TABLE* command and prepending two pound signs (##) to the table name, as the following example shows:

```
CREATE TABLE ##CustomerAddress
(CustomerAddressID    int              IDENTITY(1,1),
AddressType           char(4)          NOT NULL,
PrimaryAddressFlag    bit              NOT NULL,
AddressLine1          varchar(30)      NOT NULL,
AddressLine2          varchar(30)      NULL,
AddressLine3          varchar(30)      NULL,
City                  varchar(50)      NOT NULL,
StateProvinceID       int              NULL,
PostalCode            char(10)         NULL,
CountryID             int              NULL)
```

BEST PRACTICES   **Cleaning up**

Everything you read related to programming should have one recurring theme: "If you create it, you should delete it." This mantra applies to all temporary objects that you ever create. If you create a temporary table, you should drop it when you no longer need it. This allows resources to be reclaimed and ensures that structures are not left hanging around. You should never rely on a connection being closed to clean up any temporary tables, particularly because many applications use connection pools in which the connections are never closed. Explicitly dropping a temporary table after you finish using it ensures that you never receive any errors because of attempting to create the temporary table a second time.

Table Variables

Table variables provide an alternative to temporary tables and can be used in functions, triggers, and stored procedures. Instead of storing the table and all data within the table in the *tempdb* database on disk, a table variable and all associated data is stored in memory. However, if the amount of data placed into the table variable causes it to require more storage space than is available in memory, the overflow will be spooled to disk within *tempdb*.

Table variables are local to the function, trigger, or stored procedure they were created in and are automatically deallocated when the object is exited.

You create the customer address table as a table variable by declaring the table as a variable, which you denote by prepending the table name with the @ character, as follows:

```
DECLARE @CustomerAddress TABLE
(CustomerAddressID      int          IDENTITY(1,1),
AddressType             char(4)      NOT NULL,
PrimaryAddressFlag      bit          NOT NULL,
AddressLine1            varchar(30)  NOT NULL,
AddressLine2            varchar(30)  NULL,
AddressLine3            varchar(30)  NULL,
City                    varchar(50)  NOT NULL,
StateProvinceID         int          NULL,
PostalCode              char(10)     NULL,
CountryID               int          NULL)
```

Assigning Permissions

Now that you've created your table, you need to provide permissions for users to access it. As you learned in Chapter 2, "Configuring SQL Server 2005," all objects in SQL Server are secured. Furthermore, SQL Server does not provide any access unless permission has been explicitly granted.

A member of the sysadmin fixed server role has already been granted unlimited rights to any object within the SQL Server instance, so a member of this role can perform any operation on a table. A member of the database owner fixed database role has already been granted permission to perform any operation on any object within the database that is owned, so a member of this role can perform any operation on a table. Additionally, the owner of a table has already been granted explicit authority to perform any operation against a table that he or she owns. All other users must be assigned permissions to work with a table.

BEST PRACTICES   Security assignments

Security best practices dictate that you never grant permissions directly to a user. Therefore, you should add a Microsoft Windows login to a Windows group and the Windows group as a login to SQL Server. You then add this group as a user in a database. Next, create roles in a database corresponding to various job functions, and assign database users to the appropriate role. Finally, assign security permissions on objects in the database to the database role. It is assumed that for all examples regarding security, you are implementing security best practices.

There are seven permissions that you can assign for a table, as listed in Table 3-9.

Table 3-9   Table Permissions

Permission	Purpose
CREATE TABLE	Gives the authority to create any table in the database.
ALTER TABLE	Gives the authority to change the structure of any table in the database.
SELECT	Allows rows to be retrieved from the specified table.
INSERT	Allows rows to be inserted in a specified table. Requires the *SELECT* permission to be granted as well.
UPDATE	Allows rows to be modified in a specified table. Requires the *SELECT* permission to be granted as well.
DELETE	Allows rows to be deleted from a specified table. Requires the *SELECT* permission to be granted as well.
REFERENCES	Used with foreign key constraints; to be discussed in the next lesson.

You can use the special keyword *ALL* to grant every permission shown in the table to a specified role. However, you should always explicitly list each permission that you will allow. The general statement to assign permissions is the following:

```
GRANT { ALL [ PRIVILEGES ] }
     | permission [ ( column [ ,...n ] ) ] [ ,...n ]
     [ ON [ class :: ] securable ] TO principal [ ,...n ]
     [ WITH GRANT OPTION ] [ AS principal ]
```

The *ON* clause specifies the object that you are granting permission to, whereas the *TO* clause specifies the database role the permissions are assigned to.

For tables, it is possible to grant permissions on a subset of the columns in the table. There is no facility to grant permissions to a subset of rows in a table.

The *WITH GRANT* option enables you to grant permissions to a role whose members can then grant permissions to other users or roles. You should never use this option because it takes control of security out of the hands of the owner of the table.

For the *CustomerAddress* table, the command to grant *SELECT*, *INSERT*, *UPDATE*, and *DELETE* permissions to a role is as follows:

```
GRANT SELECT, INSERT, UPDATE, DELETE ON CustomerAddress TO <database role>
```

PRACTICE **Create a Table**

In this practice, you will create three additional tables—*Customer*, *StateProvince*, and *Country*—for use with the *CustomerAddress* table we created in this lesson.

NOTE **If you didn't create the *CustomerAddress* table**

The instructions for creating the CustomerAddress table are earlier in this lesson, under the heading "Permanent Tables."

The *Customer* table will contain the customer name, a value for the customer's credit line, a value for the customer's outstanding balance, a computation for available credit, and the date the customer record was created. The *StateProvince* table will contain a text-based column that will store a list of the valid states or provinces recognized by this company. The *Country* table will contain a text-based column that will store a list of the valid countries. Remember to create a column to reference each of the rows the same way we did with the *CustomerAddress* table.

NOTE **Database context**

This practice can be done in either the *AdventureWorks* database or another database of your choice.

---

1. Launch SQL Server Management Studio (SSMS), connect to your instance, and then open a new query window.

2. Construct a *CREATE TABLE* statement for the *Customer* table as follows:

```
CREATE TABLE dbo.Customer
(CustomerID              int           IDENTITY(1,1),
CustomerName             varchar(50)   NOT NULL,
CreditLine               smallmoney    NULL,
OutstandingBalance       smallmoney    NULL,
AvailableCredit AS (CreditLine - OutstandingBalance),
CreationDate             datetime      NOT NULL)
```

3. Construct a *CREATE TABLE* statement for the *StateProvince* table as follows:

```
CREATE TABLE dbo.StateProvince
(StateProvinceID         int           IDENTITY(1,1),
StateProvince            varchar(50)   NOT NULL)
```

4. Construct a *CREATE TABLE* statement for the *Country* table, as follows:

```
CREATE TABLE dbo.Country
(CountryID          int          IDENTITY(1,1),
Country             varchar(50)  NOT NULL)
```

Lesson Summary

- Tables, the building blocks for every database, store all the data in SQL Server.

- To provide the necessary structure to a table, you must choose between the available *numeric*, *text*, *datetime*, and *binary* data types so that data can be properly stored.

- You can also define special properties for columns to allow *nulls*, define a column as a unique identifier column, and allow a column to store a computation or computed data.

- After a table is defined, you must grant permissions on the table to allow users to retrieve and manipulate data.

Lesson Review

The following questions are intended to reinforce key information presented in this lesson. The questions are also available on the companion CD if you prefer to review them in electronic form.

NOTE   Answers

Answers to these questions and explanations of why each answer choice is right or wrong are located in the "Answers" section at the end of the book.

---

1. Which data type would you use to store up to 2 GB of text data and still be able to query and manipulate it by using standard functions and operators?

    A. *text*

    B. *varbinary*

    C. *varchar*(max)

    D. *varchar*

Lesson 2: Implementing Constraints

Designing a database is really an exercise in implementing business rules. You might not have realized it, but the entire first lesson implemented a variety of business rules. For example, in Lesson 1, we implemented a business rule stating that a customer can have more than one address, but an address is not valid unless there is at least one address line and a city.

Constraints provide a second level of business-rule implementation by preventing users from entering data into tables that is outside the allowed boundaries. Examples of this type of business rule include one that prohibits a customer's credit line from exceeding $50,000 and one that prevents users from entering countries that do not exist in a standardized list.

This lesson explains the six types of constraints that you can create to enforce business rules and shares best practices for when to implement each type of constraint.

After this lesson, you will be able to:

- Implement constraints.
- Specify the scope of a constraint.
- Create a new constraint.

Estimated lesson time: 20 minutes

Check Constraints

You use check constraints to limit the range of possible values in a column or to enforce specific patterns for data. All check constraints must evaluate to a Boolean True/False and cannot reference columns in another table.

You can create check constraints at two different levels:

- *Column-level* check constraints are applied only to the column and cannot reference data in another other column.

- *Table-level* check constraints can reference any column within a table but cannot reference columns in other tables.

The most basic constraint compares the data in a column to a specified value—for example, *CHECK CreditLine <= 50000*. You can create any number of check constraints separated by *AND*, *OR*, or *NOT* to create more complex conditions.

You can also use check constraints to enforce patterns within data. Using a check constraint this way, you might enforce the pattern that an EmployeeID is required to start with an uppercase letter, followed by three digits and then six additional letters. Another example is to require an e-mail address to contain, in order, any number of characters or digits, an @ symbol, a number of characters or digits, a period (.), and then either three characters or two characters with a period (.) plus two more characters.

The wildcard characters for pattern matching are the underscore (_), which designates one value that can be a character, number, or special character; and a percent symbol (%), which designates any number of characters, numbers, or special characters. For example, a table-level check constraint to validate an e-mail address might look like this:

```
CONSTRAINT chkEmail CHECK (Email like '%@%.[a-z][a-z][a-z]' or Email like '%@%.[a-z]
[a-z].[a-z][a-z]')
```

A column-level check constraint for the EmployeeID looks like this:

```
CHECK (EmployeeID like '[A-Z][0-9][0-9][0-9][A-Z][A-Z][A-Z][A-Z][A-Z][A-Z]')
```

MORE INFO   Constraints and pattern matching

Creating pattern matches can become complex. For more information about the allowed operators and wildcards, see the SQL Server 2005 Books Online topics "CHECK Constraints" and "CREATE RULE (Transact-SQL)."

Rules

You define check constraints within the table definition and cannot reuse them. Rules provide the same functionality as check constraints, except that you create them as a separate object.

Because rules are not associated with a specific table or column when you create them, they cannot reference columns or tables in their definition. Instead, you use variables as placeholders. Rules provide the same features and complex comparisons via *AND*, *OR*, and *NOT* as check constraints and allow pattern matching.

The following examples show the previous two check constraints implemented as rules:

```
CREATE RULE EmailValidator
AS
@value like '%@%.[a-z][a-z][a-z]' or @value like '%@%.[a-z][a-z].[a-z][a-z]';
```

```
CREATE RULE EmployeeIDValidator
AS
@column like '[A-Z][0-9][0-9][0-9][A-Z][A-Z][A-Z][A-Z][A-Z][A-Z]';
```

After defining a rule, you then bind it to columns or user-defined data types by using the *sp_bindrule* system stored procedure.

MORE INFO   **Binding rules**

For complete information about binding rules to columns or user-defined data types, see the SQL Server 2005 Books Online article "CREATE RULE (Transact-SQL)."

Default Constraints

Another mechanism for enforcing a business rule in a table is a default constraint, which enables SQL Server to write a value to a column when the user doesn't specify a value. Common uses for a default constraint are when a "typical" value or very "common" value exists for a column, but that value is not necessarily the only possible choice. For example, let's say the company we have been creating tables for is a retail store located in Grand Prairie, TX. Most customers have an address with a city of Grand Prairie. However, customers might still come into the store from nearby Arlington or Irving.

You can add a default constraint to the City column in the *CustomerAddress* table using the following example:

```
CREATE TABLE dbo.CustomerAddress
(CustomerAddressID      int              IDENTITY(1,1),
AddressType             char(4)          NOT NULL,
PrimaryAddressFlag      bit              NOT NULL,
AddressLine1            varchar(30)      NOT NULL,
AddressLine2            varchar(30)      NULL,
AddressLine3            varchar(30)      NULL,
City                    varchar(50)      NOT NULL DEFAULT 'Grand Prairie',
StateProvinceID         int              NULL,
PostalCode              char(10)         NULL,
CountryID               int              NULL)
```

Unique Constraints

A unique constraint prohibits a column or combination of columns from allowing duplicate values. You might use a unique constraint to enforce a business rule stating that each customer name must be unique.

You can add a unique constraint to the CustomerName column in the *Customer* table by using the following:

```
CREATE TABLE dbo.Customer
(CustomerID              int          IDENTITY(1,1),
CustomerName             varchar(50)  NOT NULL UNIQUE NONCLUSTERED,
CreditLine               smallmoney   NULL,
OutstandingBalance       smallmoney   NULL,
AvailableCredit AS (CreditLine - OutstandingBalance),
CreationDate             datetime     NOT NULL)
```

NOTE   Clustered and nonclustered indexes

A unique constraint is physically implemented in the database as a unique index. Indexes can be either clustered or nonclustered. Within this chapter, we are explicitly avoiding the discussion of indexes, including clustered and nonclustered indexes. Chapter 4, "Creating Indexes," covers these topics in detail.

Primary Key Constraints

Your choice of primary key constraint is critical in creating a sound structure for a table. A *primary key* defines the column or combination of columns that allow a row to be uniquely identified.

MORE INFO   Primary key choice

Choosing the columns for a primary key is beyond the scope of this book, as is the discussion of whether a primary key should have business meaning or be implemented as an internal database structure. For details on these topics, see *MCITP Self-Paced Training Kit (Exam 70-443): Designing a Database Server Infrastructure by Using Microsoft SQL Server 2005,* Microsoft Press, 2007.

You implement a primary key on the StateProvinceID column of the *StateProvince* table as follows:

```
CREATE TABLE dbo.StateProvince
(StateProvinceID         int          IDENTITY(1,1)  PRIMARY KEY,
StateProvince            varchar(50)  NOT NULL)
```

Foreign Key Constraints

You use foreign key constraints to implement a concept called referential integrity. *Foreign keys* ensure that the values that can be entered in a particular column exist in a specified table. Users cannot enter values in this column that do not exist in the specified table.

For example, the *CustomerAddress* table should be allowed to specify only valid values for the StateProvince column. Providing a valid list of states and provinces for a user to select from and enforcing the range of available values ensures that data is not only consistent but also valid.

To enforce referential integrity on the StateProvince column in the *CustomerAddress* table, you could use the following code, which uses the *REFERENCES* keyword:

```
CREATE TABLE dbo.CustomerAddress
(CustomerAddressID       int           IDENTITY(1,1),
AddressType              char(4)       NOT NULL,
PrimaryAddressFlag       bit           NOT NULL,
AddressLine1             varchar(30)   NOT NULL,
AddressLine2             varchar(30)   NULL,
AddressLine3             varchar(30)   NULL,
City                     varchar(50)   NOT NULL DEFAULT 'Grand Prairie',
StateProvinceID          int           NULL REFERENCES dbo.StateProvince(StateProvinceID),
PostalCode               char(10)      NULL,
CountryID                int           NULL)
```

Or you could use the following code, which uses the *FOREIGN KEY* keyword:

```
CREATE TABLE dbo.CustomerAddress
(CustomerAddressID       int           IDENTITY(1,1),
AddressType              char(4)       NOT NULL,
PrimaryAddressFlag       bit           NOT NULL,
AddressLine1             varchar(30)   NOT NULL,
AddressLine2             varchar(30)   NULL,
AddressLine3             varchar(30)   NULL,
City                     varchar(50)   NOT NULL DEFAULT 'Grand Prairie',
StateProvinceID          int           NULL FOREIGN KEY (StateProvinceID)
 REFERENCES dbo.StateProvince(StateProvinceID),
PostalCode               char(10)      NULL,
CountryID                int           NULL)
```

When you add a foreign key to a table, it not only enforces the values that can be used in a column but it also enforces a dependency chain. You cannot drop a foreign key table unless you do one of the following first:

- Drop the table that references it.
- Remove the foreign key constraint with an *ALTER TABLE* statement.

For example, you could not drop the *StateProvince* table without either dropping the *CustomerAddress* table first or removing the foreign key constraint from the *Customer-Address* table.

IMPORTANT   Referencing tables

For a foreign key to work, it must be able to uniquely identify each row in the referenced table. Therefore, you must create a primary key on the column that is used to enforce referential integrity.

Foreign Keys vs. Check Constraints

A foreign key constraint is really nothing more than a check constraint with a list of allowed values. So the question becomes, when should you use a check constraint and when should you use a foreign key?

You should use check constraints when you need to validate patterns, perform calculations to compare against, or use comparison operators such as >, <, >=, and so on.

You should always use foreign keys when you need to validate the column against a list of acceptable values. Even if the list contains only one or two values, you should still implement it as a foreign key.

If you implement a list validation as a check constraint, whenever you want to add a new value to the list, you have to modify the table structure by using an *ALTER TABLE* command. By implementing the list as a foreign key, you simply insert the new value into the table.

Using a foreign key for list validation also leads to a maintainable design. When a database is initially designed, you might not know the list of acceptable values. Or the list might be completely valid at the time it was created, but five years later, the list of valid values might have changed. Application developers can easily add a maintenance screen into an application to allow one or more designated users to modify the list of allowed values, and the foreign key constraint prevents a value from being removed from the table if it has been used. Adding a new value to the table then becomes a simple action performed by a user instead of becoming a request to the database administrator (DBA) team, as would happen if the list were in a check constraint.

Quick Check

- What are the six types of constraints, and what purpose does each serve?

Quick Check Answer

- *Check constraints* restrict the allowable values in a column.

- *Rules* implement the same functionality as check constraints but are implemented as objects separate from a specific table, so a rule can be created once and used in many places.

- A *default constraint* causes a value to be entered into a column when one is not specified by a user.

- A *unique constaint* ensures that duplicate values do not exist in a column or combination of columns.

- A *primary key* ensures that each row in a table can be uniquely identified by the column or a combination of specified columns. Only one primary key can exist on a table, whereas multiple unique constraints can be created.

- A *foreign key* forces a column to allow only values that exist in a referenced table.

PRACTICE **Implement Constraints**

In this practice, you will apply a variety of constraints to the *Customer, CustomerAddress, StateProvince,* and *Country* tables so that they more closely match what you would see in an actual production environment.

1. If necessary, launch SSMS, connect to your instance, and open a new query window.

2. Before you begin this exercise, drop all the tables that you created previously by using the following batch:

```
DROP TABLE dbo.CustomerAddress;
DROP TABLE dbo.Customer;
DROP TABLE dbo.Country;
DROP TABLE dbo.StateProvince;
```

NOTE Errors

If you receive any errors when executing the preceding batch, you can ignore them. Any error you might receive will say something like "could not drop table because it does not exist." Chapter 9, "Creating Functions, Stored Procedures, and Triggers," explains how to write batches that contain error checking and handling.

---

3. Re-create the *Country* and *StateProvince* tables with primary keys, as follows:

```
CREATE TABLE dbo.StateProvince
(StateProvinceID         int         IDENTITY(1,1)  PRIMARY KEY CLUSTERED,
StateProvince            varchar(50) NOT NULL);

CREATE TABLE dbo.Country
(CountryID               int         IDENTITY(1,1) PRIMARY KEY CLUSTERED,
Country                  varchar(50) NOT NULL);
```

4. Create a new table for the list of allowed address types, as follows:

```
CREATE TABLE dbo.AddressType
(AddressTypeID           tinyint     IDENTITY(1,1) PRIMARY KEY CLUSTERED,
AddressType              varchar(20) NOT NULL);
```

5. Create the *CustomerAddress* table with a primary key and enforce referential integrity for the StateProvinceID, CountryID, and AddressType columns, as follows:

```
CREATE TABLE dbo.CustomerAddress
(CustomerAddressID       int         IDENTITY(1,1) PRIMARY KEY CLUSTERED,
AddressType              char(4)     NOT NULL FOREIGN KEY (AddressType) REFERENCE
S dbo.AddressType(AddressTypeID),
PrimaryAddressFlag       bit         NOT NULL,
AddressLine1             varchar(30) NOT NULL,
AddressLine2             varchar(30) NULL,
AddressLine3             varchar(30) NULL,
City                     varchar(50) NOT NULL,
StateProvinceID          int         NULL FOREIGN KEY (StateProvinceID) REFERENCE
S dbo.StateProvince(StateProvinceID),
PostalCode               char(10)    NULL,
CountryID                int         NULL FOREIGN KEY (CountryID) REFERENCES dbo.
Country(CountryID));
```

NOTE Data type mismatches

You should have received an error message when trying to create this table. Before reading on, can you explain why?

The AddressType column is defined as a *char*(4), but the foreign key references an integer column in the *AddressType* table. A character value cannot be implicitly converted to a *tinyint* for comparison. Although the column name in the *CustomerAddress* table does not have to match the column name in the *AddressType* table, the data types must be compatible. However, for consistency and readability, the columns names should match.

---

6. Fix the error by redefining the *CustomerAddress* table, as follows:

```
CREATE TABLE dbo.CustomerAddress
(CustomerAddressID       int         IDENTITY(1,1) PRIMARY KEY CLUSTERED,
AddressTypeID            tinyint     NOT NULL FOREIGN KEY (AddressTypeID) REFEREN
CES dbo.AddressType(AddressTypeID),
PrimaryAddressFlag       bit         NOT NULL,
AddressLine1             varchar(30) NOT NULL,
```

```
AddressLine2                varchar(30)    NULL,
AddressLine3                varchar(30)    NULL,
City                        varchar(50)    NOT NULL,
StateProvinceID             int            NULL FOREIGN KEY (StateProvinceID)
  REFERENCES dbo.StateProvince(StateProvinceID),
PostalCode                  char(10)       NULL,
CountryID                   int            NULL FOREIGN KEY (CountryID) REFERENCES
  dbo.Country(CountryID));
```

7. Create the *Customer* table with a primary key, enforcing no duplicate customer names and a credit line between 0 and 50,000. Default the available balance to 0, and default the creation date to the current date and time, as follows:

```
CREATE TABLE dbo.Customer
(CustomerID                 int            IDENTITY(1,1) PRIMARY KEY CLUSTERED,
CustomerName                varchar(50)    NOT NULL UNIQUE NONCLUSTERED,
CreditLine                  smallmoney     NULL CHECK (CreditLine >= 0 AND CreditLine <
= 50000),
OutstandingBalance          smallmoney     NULL DEFAULT 0,
AvailableCredit AS (CreditLine - OutstandingBalance),
CreationDate                datetime       NOT NULL DEFAULT getdate());
```

8. Our customer minidatabase is looking pretty good at this point, but there is one problem. Customers can be entered, and addresses can be entered, but there is no way to associate a customer to an address. Create a table that provides an association between the *Customer* and *CustomerAddress* tables, as follows:

```
CREATE TABLE dbo.CustomerToCustomerAddress
(CustomerID                 int    NOT NULL FOREIGN KEY (CustomerID) REFERENCES
  dbo.Customer(CustomerID),
CustomerAddressID           int    NOT NULL FOREIGN KEY (CustomerAddressID)
  REFERENCES dbo.CustomerAddress(CustomerAddressID),
CONSTRAINT PK_CustomerToCustomerAddress PRIMARY KEY CLUSTERED(CustomerID,
  CustomerAddressID));
```

NOTE Cross-reference tables

The *CustomerToCustomerAddress* table is generally referred to as a *cross-reference* table. You could have linked the *Customer* and *CustomerAddress* tables together by adding a CustomerID column to the *CustomerAddress* table. However, the cross-reference table allows flexibility in the design and minimizes the amount of data that needs to be stored. For example, you could have multiple customers at the same address, such as with multiple people in the same household. If the CustomerID column were added to the *CustomerAddress* table, each customer at the same address would require you to duplicate the address in the *CustomerAddress* table. However, the cross-reference table allows you to associate a single row in the *CustomerAddress* table with one or more customers. The opposite is also true: you can associate a single customer with multiple addresses.

Lesson Summary

- You use constraints to enforce additional business rules within a table.

- You can use constraints to ensure that duplicate values cannot be entered into a column or that a column can allow only values that meet a specified condition.

- You can use constraints to enforce complex pattern matching such as the Vehicle Identification Number (VIN) that is used to uniquely identify every vehicle.

- You can also create constraints to ensure that a value cannot be entered in one table unless it already exists in another table, for example, not allowing an address to be entered unless a customer already exists for the address.

Lesson Review

The following questions are intended to reinforce key information presented in this lesson. The questions are also available on the companion CD if you prefer to review them in electronic form.

NOTE   Answers

Answers to these questions and explanations of why each answer choice is right or wrong are located in the "Answers" section at the end of the book.

---

1. Which of the following objects can you use in a check constraint? (Choose all that apply.)

    A. System function

    B. Stored procedure

    C. User-defined function (UDF)

    D. View

Lesson 3: Creating User-Defined Types

User-defined types (UDTs) have two purposes in SQL Server 2005. You can use Transact-SQL-based UDTs to enforce consistency in table definitions, and you can use Common Language Runtime (CLR) UDTs to create new data types that do not exist in SQL Server. In this lesson, you see how and when to create each type of UDT.

> **After this lesson, you will be able to:**
> - Explain the differences between Transact-SQL and CLR UDTs.
> - Create a Transact-SQL UDT.
> - Create a CLR UDT.
>
> **Estimated lesson time: 20 minutes**

Transact-SQL UDTs

You use Transact-SQL UDTs essentially as an aliasing mechanism to provide consistency in table definitions within a database. For example, you might have customers, vendors, manufacturers, and employees stored in the same database. Because of differences in the data that you store for each entity, you might have separate address tables for each one. Even though you have four different address tables, a City column exists in each one. The City column holds variable-length character data with a maximum size of 30 characters.

You could implement the City column as a *varchar*(30) in each table, or you could use a Transact-SQL UDT to ensure that all City columns are defined the same. To create a UDT, you use the *CREATE TYPE* command as follows:

```
CREATE TYPE [ schema_name. ] type_name
{
    FROM base_type
    [ ( precision [ , scale ] ) ]
    [ NULL | NOT NULL ]
  | EXTERNAL NAME assembly_name [ .class_name ]
} [ ; ]
```

The following command would create a UDT for the City column discussed previously:

```
CREATE TYPE udt_city
FROM varchar(30) NOT NULL ;
```

You could then use this UDT when you are defining a table, as follows:

```
CREATE TABLE dbo.CustomerAddress
(CustomerAddressID        int         IDENTITY(1,1) PRIMARY KEY CLUSTERED,
AddressTypeID             tinyint     NOT NULL FOREIGN KEY (AddressTypeID) REFERENCES
 dbo.AddressType(AddressTypeID),
PrimaryAddressFlag        bit         NOT NULL,
AddressLine1              varchar(30) NOT NULL,
AddressLine2              varchar(30) NULL,
AddressLine3              varchar(30) NULL,
City                      udt_city    NOT NULL,
StateProvinceID           int         NULL FOREIGN KEY (StateProvinceID) REFERENCES
 dbo.StateProvince(StateProvinceID),
PostalCode                char(10)    NULL,
CountryID                 int         NULL FOREIGN KEY (CountryID) REFERENCES
 dbo.Country(CountryID));
```

Transact-SQL UDTs are always created using base data types.

CLR UDTs

You can use the CLR integration in SQL Server 2005 to create your own data types beyond those that already exist within SQL Server.

Defining New Data Types

There is at least one person reading this whose brain shifted into overdrive when they read that you can create new data types in SQL Server 2005. So before we get started on this topic, we need to do a serious reality check.

First, you cannot create CLR UDTs unless you turn on CLR capability by using the Surface Area Configuration utility.

Second, SQL Server is NOT an object database. Thousands of developers have invested tens of thousands of man-years of development in SQL Server. The same goes for Oracle, DB2, and Sybase. Together, these four database management systems (DBMSs) represent nearly all the database market. And none of these DBMSs has support for object data types. That doesn't mean that someone can't come up with a way to do create such data types; it simply means that if an actual market existed for such things, at least one of the vendors would have written it by now or at least licensed an implementation from someone and added into their product.

Before you go out and spend several hundred hours creating the *Person* data type or the *Customer* data type, carefully consider exactly what you are imposing on your system. CLR data types must be written to a specification that places 15 very stringent requirements on the interfaces and code specification. You must also create your own methods to serialize and deserialize all data being stored in your new data type. That means every time SQL Server reads or writes data into a column or variable that uses your new data type, it must make a call to your code to process the request. As the complexity of your logic increases, the performance dramatically decreases. With very large result sets, performance can grind to a screeching halt.

So, what are good choices for CLR data types? Date and time should be at the top of everyone's list because they have been on feature request lists since before Microsoft licensed the first version of SQL Server from Sybase. Other good choices are compressed encodings or custom encryption algorithms. In other words, you should consider using CLR data types only for small, discrete types of data that have clearly defined value domains requiring a minimal amount of code in the data type definition.

To use a CLR UDT, you must first enable the CLR within the Surface Area Configuration utility. If the CLR is ever disabled, all columns defined with CLR UDTs will no longer be accessible.

To create a CLR UDT, you must create a class by using one of the Microsoft .NET programming languages, such as C#, that conforms to the UDT specification. You need to compile the class to a dynamic-link library (DLL), and a member of the sysadmin fixed server role must register the assembly in the SQL Server instance. Only then can a CLR UDT be implemented within a database.

NOTE   Creating CLR UDTs

Full coverage of CLR UDTs is beyond the scope of this book and the 70-431 exam. For comprehensive information about CLR UDTs, including specifications, restrictions, and code samples, see the SQL Server 2005 Books Online article "CLR User-Defined Types."

Quick Check
- What are the two classes of UDTs, and what is the purpose of each?

Quick Check Answer
- *Transact-SQL UDTs* give you a way to standardize data type definition based on a native SQL Server data type that can then be used within tables to ensure consistency within a database.
- *CLR UDTs* let you introduce new data types that do not exist within SQL Server, such as geospatial coordinates.

Implement a Transact-SQL UDT

In this exercise, you will create a Transact-SQL UDT for the City column in our *CustomerAddress* table so that any other tables in our database that store a city will have a consistent definition.

1. If necessary, launch SSMS, connect to your instance, and open a new query window.

2. Drop the previously created *CustomerAddress* and *CustomerToCustomer* tables:

   ```
   DROP TABLE dbo.CustomerToCustomerAddress
   DROP TABLE dbo.CustomerAddress;
   ```

3. Create the *city* data type by using the following code:

   ```
   CREATE TYPE udt_city
   FROM varchar(50) NOT NULL ;
   ```

4. Use the following code to re-create the *CustomerAddress* table with the new UDT and to create the *CustomerToCustomerAddress* table:

```
CREATE TABLE dbo.CustomerAddress
(CustomerAddressID      int           IDENTITY(1,1) PRIMARY KEY CLUSTERED,
AddressTypeID           tinyint       NOT NULL FOREIGN KEY (AddressTypeID) REFERENCES
 dbo.AddressType(AddressTypeID),
PrimaryAddressFlag      bit           NOT NULL,
AddressLine1            varchar(30)   NOT NULL,
AddressLine2            varchar(30)   NULL,
AddressLine3            varchar(30)   NULL,
City                    udt_city      NOT NULL,
StateProvinceID         int           NULL FOREIGN KEY (StateProvinceID) REFERENCES
 dbo.StateProvince(StateProvinceID),
PostalCode              char(10)      NULL,
CountryID               int           NULL FOREIGN KEY (CountryID) REFERENCES
 dbo.Country(CountryID));

CREATE TABLE dbo.CustomerToCustomerAddress
(CustomerID             int       NOT NULL FOREIGN KEY (CustomerID) REFERENCES
 dbo.Customer(CustomerID),
CustomerAddressID       int       NOT NULL FOREIGN KEY (CustomerAddressID) REFERENCES
 dbo.CustomerAddress(CustomerAddressID),
CONSTRAINT PK_CustomerToCustomerAddress PRIMARY KEY CLUSTERED(CustomerID,
 CustomerAddressID));
```

Lesson Summary

- Transact-SQL UDTs provide a means for enforcing consistency in data type definitions across multiple tables.

- One of the most exciting new capabilities in SQL Server 2005 is the capability to use the CLR to define UDTs that are not native to SQL Server, such as latitudes and longitudes or geometric coordinates. However, beware of performance issues if you decide to create something like a customer or order data type.

Lesson Review

The following questions are intended to reinforce key information presented in this lesson. The questions are also available on the companion CD if you prefer to review them in electronic form.

NOTE Answers

Answers to these questions and explanations of why each answer choice is right or wrong are located in the "Answers" section at the end of the book.

---

1. What are the requirements to create a CLR based user-defined type? (Choose all that apply.)

   A. The CLR must be enabled for the database.

   B. The CLR must be enabled for the instance.

   C. A class created with a Microsoft .NET language.

   D. A class created with a CLR-compatible language.

Chapter Review

To further practice and reinforce the skills you learned in this chapter, you can

- Review the chapter summary.
- Review the list of key terms introduced in this chapter.
- Complete the case scenario. This scenario sets up a real-world situation involving the topics of this chapter and asks you to create a solution.
- Complete the suggested practices.
- Take a practice test.

Chapter Summary

- Without tables in a database, you cannot store data. Therefore, tables become the base of everything you do with SQL Server. However, you need to do more than simply create a bunch of tables and start throwing data into them. Without a structure to the data, your applications will be difficult to write, and performing comparisons among the data will become difficult, if not impossible.

- The initial structure for data is provided by a set of data types that define the type as well as basic limitations on the data. The broad categories of data types are as follows:

  - **Exact numeric** Stores precise numbers either with or without decimals.
  - **Approximate numeric** Stores numeric values with or without decimals.
  - **Monetary** Stores numeric values with decimal places. Used specifically for currency values with up to four decimal places.
  - **Date and time** Stores date and time information and enables special chronological enforcement, such as rejecting a value of February 30.
  - **Character** Stores character-based values of varying lengths.
  - **Binary** Stores data in a strict binary (0 and 1) representation.
  - **Special purpose** Complex data types for data that requires specialized handling, such as XML documents or GUIDs.

- You can further enforce business rules by using constraints. The set of SQL Server constraints that you can use are the following:

  - **Check** Enforces boundary values on a column and can also force specific formatting requirements for data.

❑ **Rule** Functionally equivalent to check constraints, but can be reused for more than one column.

❑ **Default** Provides a value to a column when one is not specified by the user.

❑ **Unique** Ensures that duplicate values cannot be stored in a column or group of columns.

❑ **Primary key** Provides a way to uniquely identify each row in a table.

❑ **Foreign key** Forces all values entered into a column to exist in another table.

■ You can use Transact-SQL UDTs to create a consistent definition for columns based on a native SQL Server data type. When the native SQL Server data types are not sufficient, you can define your own data types with custom processing by using the CLR integration.

Key Terms

Do you know what these key terms mean? You can check your answers by looking up the terms in the glossary at the end of the book.

■ constraint

■ foreign key

■ primary key

■ table

Case Scenario: Designing a Database

In the following case scenario, you will apply what you've learned in this chapter. You can find answers to these questions in the "Answers" section at the end of this book.

Contoso Limited, a health care company located in Bothell, WA, manages patient claims data. To support the business, you need to create a database to store the wide variety of data related to patient claims.

You need to create structures for basic patient data, such as name, address, date of birth, and Social Security number. The database also needs to store the companies that Contoso works with, including the company name, address, and people to contact. Each patient claim must be associated with a company in the database. And the database needs to associate a list of doctors with a claim and also store various supporting documents.

All pieces of data need to be uniquely identified within the tables. Referential integrity is crucial to the successful operation of the database application.

How would you define the table structures to meet the needs of the patient claims database?

Suggested Practices

Before doing the following suggested practices, skip forward in this book to read Chapter 5, "Working with Transact-SQL." This chapter familiarizes you with the basics of adding data to a table as well as retrieving it. Understanding these functions is important for performing the practice tasks, which will help you see how the various table structures interact with data.

Creating Tables

- **Practice 1**   Insert some data into the *StateProvince*, *Country*, and *AddressType* tables. Retrieve the data from the table and inspect the identity column. Change the seed, increment, or both for the identity column and insert more rows. Retrieve the data from the table. Are the values in the identity column what you expected?

- **Practice 2**   Concatenate the City, StateProvince, and PostalCode columns together. Change the data type of the resulting new column from a *varchar* to a *char*. Execute the same query you used in Practice 1. Why do the results differ?

Creating Constraints

- **Practice 1**   Insert some data into the *CustomerAddress* table. What happens when you do not specify an AddressType? What happens when you do not specify either a Country or StateProvince?

- **Practice 2**   Change the value in one of the foreign key columns to another value that exists in the referenced table. What happens? Change the value to something that does not exist in the referenced table. What happens? Is this what you expected?

- **Practice 3**   Try to insert a row into the *Customer* table that has a negative value for the credit line. Are the results what you expected?

- **Practice 4**   Insert a row into the *Customer* table without specifying a value for the outstanding balance. Retrieve the row. What are the values for the outstanding balance and available credit? Are they what you expected?

Take a Practice Test

The practice tests on this book's companion CD offer many options. For example, you can test yourself on just the content covered in this chapter, or you can test yourself on all the 70-431 certification exam content. You can set up the test so that it closely simulates the experience of taking a certification exam, or you can set it up in study mode so that you can look at the correct answers and explanations after you answer each question.

MORE INFO   **Practice tests**

For details about all the practice test options available, see the "How to Use the Practice Tests" section in this book's Introduction.

Chapter 4
Creating Indexes

As you saw in Chapter 3, "Creating Tables, Constraints, and User-Defined Types," creating tables is the first step of building a useful database. You then need to add data to the tables. However, if you never retrieve the data in the table, you are simply wasting storage space. SQL Server does not need to have indexes on a table to retrieve data. It can simply scan a table to find the piece of data that is requested. However, most organizations store massive amounts of data in a table and need to be able to retrieve data instantly. To allow rapid data retrieval while ensuring that performance does not decline as users add rows to a table, you need to add indexes to your tables.

Indexes are not a new concept or strictly a database concept. We use indexes every day. At the back of this book, you will find an index in printed form. If you wanted to read about full-text indexes to prepare for your exam, you could find the information in two different ways. You could open this book, start at page 1, and scan each page until you found the information you needed. Or you could turn to the index at the back of the book, locate full-text indexing, and then go directly to the corresponding page or pages that discuss this topic. You find the information either way, but using the index is much more efficient. In this chapter, you will explore how SQL Server builds and uses indexes to ensure fast data retrieval and performance stability. You will then learn how to build clustered, nonclustered, and covering indexes on your tables to achieve the optimal balance between speed and required index maintenance overhead.

Exam objectives in this chapter:
- Implement indexes.
  - ❏ Specify the filegroup.
  - ❏ Specify the index type.
  - ❏ Specify relational index options.
  - ❏ Specify columns.
  - ❏ Disable an index.
  - ❏ Create an online index by using an ONLINE argument.

Lessons in this chapter:

Before You Begin

To complete the lessons in this chapter, you must have

- SQL Server 2005 installed.
- A copy of the *AdventureWorks* sample database installed in the instance.

Real World

Michael Hotek

Several years ago, after SQL Server 6.5 had been on the market for awhile, I started a project with a new company in the Chicago area. This company had the great idea to help people find apartments in the area that met the customers' criteria. One of the employees had read about a programming language called Visual Basic that would enable them to create the type of application they needed to manage the hundreds of apartment complexes in the area. The application was created, tested, and put in production. Four months later, the business was growing rapidly, and the company opened offices in several dozen other cities.

This is when the company started having problems. Finding apartments by using the SQL Server database application was taking longer and longer. Many associates were getting so frustrated that they started keeping their own paper-based files. The developer had reviewed all the code and couldn't reproduce the problem. So the company called me to take a look at the SQL Server side of the equation.

The first thing I did was ask the developer whether he had reviewed the indexes on the tables in SQL Server. I had my answer to the performance problem when the developer asked what an index was. It took me an hour to get to the customer's office downtown, and the performance problem was solved 15 minutes later with the addition of some key indexes. I spent the rest of the day indexing the other tables so they wouldn't become problems in the future and explaining to the developer what an index was, why it would help, and how to determine what should be indexed.

Lesson 1: Understanding Index Structure

An index is useful only if it can help find data quickly regardless of the volume of data stored. Take a look at the index at the back of this book. The index contains only a small sampling of the words in the book, so it provides a compact way to search for information. If the index were organized based on the pages that a word appears on, you would have to read many entries and pages to find your information. Instead, the index is organized alphabetically, which means you can go to a specific place in the index to find what you need. It also enables you to scan down to the word you are looking for. After you find the word you are looking for, you know that you don't have to search any further. The way an index is organized in SQL Server is very similar. In this lesson, you will see how SQL Server uses the B-tree structure to build indexes that provide fast data retrieval even with extremely large tables.

After this lesson, you will be able to:

■ Explain SQL Server's index structure.

Estimated lesson time: 20 minutes

Exploring B-Trees

The structure that SQL Server uses to build and maintain indexes is called a Balanced tree, or *B-tree*. The illustration in Figure 4-1 shows an example of a B-tree.

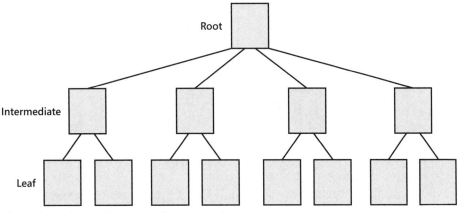

Figure 4-1   General index architecture

A B-tree consists of a *root node* that contains a single page of data, zero or more *intermediate levels* containing additional pages, and a *leaf level*.

The leaf-level pages contain entries in sorted order that correspond to the data being indexed. The number of index rows on a page is determined by the storage space required by the columns defined in the index. For example, an index defined on a 4-byte integer column will have fifteen times as many values per page as an index defined on a char(60) column that requires 60 bytes of storage per page.

SQL Server creates the intermediate levels by taking the first entry on each leaf-level page and storing the entries in a page with a pointer to the leaf-level page. The root page is constructed in the same manner.

MORE INFO   **Index internals**

For a detailed explanation of the entries on an index page as well as how an index is constructed, see *Inside Microsoft SQL Server 2005: The Storage Engine* by Kalen Delaney (Microsoft Press, 2006) and *Inside Microsoft SQL Server 2005: T-SQL Querying* by Itzik Ben-Gan (Microsoft Press, 2006).

By constructing an index in this manner, SQL Server can search tables that have billions of rows of data just as quickly it can tables that have a few hundred rows of data. Let's look at the B-tree in Figure 4-2 to see how a query uses an index to quickly find data.

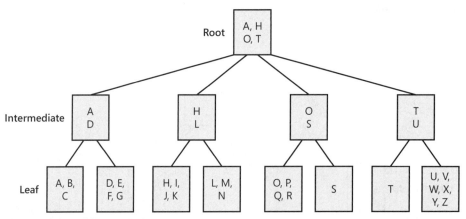

Figure 4-2   Building an index

If you were looking for the term "SQL Server," the query would scan the root page. It would find the value O as well as the value T. Because S comes before T, the query knows that it needs to look on page O to find the data it needs. The query would then move to the intermediate-level page that entry O points to. Note that this single operation has immediately eliminated three-fourths of the possible pages by scanning a very small subset of values. The query would scan the intermediate-level page and find the value S. It would then jump to the page that this entry points to. At this point, the query has scanned exactly two pages in the index to find the data that was requested. Notice that no matter which letter you choose, locating the page that contains the words that start with that letter requires scanning exactly two pages.

This behavior is why the index structure is called a B-tree. Every search performed always transits the same number of levels in the index—and the same number of pages in the index—to locate the piece of data you are interested in.

Inside Index Levels

The number of levels in an index, as well as the number of pages within each level of an index, is determined by simple mathematics. As previous chapters explained, a data page in SQL Server is 8,192 bytes in size and can store up to 8,060 bytes of actual user data.

If you built an index on a char(60) column, each row in the table would require 60 bytes of storage. That also means 60 bytes of storage for each row within the index.

If there are only 100 rows of data in the table, you would need 6,000 bytes of storage. Because all the entries would fit on a single page of data, the index would have a single page that would be the root page as well as the leaf page. In fact, you could store 134 rows in the table and still allocate only a single page to the index.

As soon as you add the 135th row, all the entries can no longer fit on a single page, so SQL Server creates two additional pages. This operation creates an index with a root page and two leaf-level pages. The first leaf-level page contains the first half of the entries, the second leaf-level page contains the second half of the entries, and the root page contains two rows of data. This index does not need an intermediate level because the root page can contain all the values at the beginning of the leaf-level pages. At this point, a query needs to scan exactly two pages in the index to locate any row in the table.

You can continue to add rows to the table without affecting the number of levels in the index until you reach 17,957 rows. At 17,956 rows, you have 134 leaf-level pages containing 134 entries each. The root page has 134 entries corresponding to the first row on each of the leaf-level pages. When you add the 17,957th row of data to the table, SQL Server needs to allocate another page to the index at the leaf level, but the root page cannot hold 135 entries because this would exceed the 8,060 bytes allowed per page. So SQL Server adds an intermediate level that contains two pages. The first page contains the initial entry for the first half of the leaf-level pages, and the second page contains the initial entry for the second half of the leaf pages. The root page now contains two rows, corresponding to the initial value for each of the two intermediate-level pages.

The next time SQL Server would have to introduce another intermediate level would occur when the 2,406,105[th] row of data is added to the table.

As you can see, this type of structure allows SQL Server to very quickly locate the rows that satisfy queries, even in extremely large tables. In this example, finding a row in a table that has nearly 2.5 million rows requires SQL Server to scan only three pages of data. And the table could grow to more than 300 million rows before SQL Server would have to read four pages to find any row.

Keep in mind that this example uses a char(60) column. If you created the index on an int column requiring 4 bytes of storage, SQL Server would have to read just one page to locate a row until the 2,016[th] row was entered. You could add a little more than 4 million rows to the table and still need to read only two pages to find a row. It would take more than 8 billion rows in the table before SQL Server would need to read three pages to find the data you were looking for.

Quick Check

- What structure guarantees that every search performed will always transit the same number of levels in the index—and the same number of pages in the index—to locate the piece of data you are interested in?

Quick Check Answer

- The B-tree structure that SQL Server uses to build its indexes.

Lesson Summary

- A SQL Server index is constructed as a B-tree, which enables SQL Server to search very large volumes of data without affecting the performance from one query to the next.

- The B-tree structure delivers this performance stability by ensuring that each search will have to transit exactly the same number of pages in the index, regardless of the value being searched on.

- At the same time, the B-tree structure results in very rapid data retrieval by enabling large segments of a table to be excluded based on the page traversal in the index.

Lesson Review

The following questions are intended to reinforce key information presented in this lesson. The questions are also available on the companion CD if you prefer to review them in electronic form.

NOTE **Answers**

Answers to these questions and explanations of why each answer choice is right or wrong are located in the "Answers" section at the end of the book.

---

1. Which levels of the index can have multiple pages? (Choose all that apply.)

    A. Root

    B. Intermediate

    C. Leaf

    D. B-tree

Lesson 2: Creating Clustered Indexes

The first type of index you should create on a table is a *clustered index*. As a general rule of thumb, every table should have a clustered index. And each table can have only one clustered index. In this lesson, you will see how to create a clustered index by using the *CREATE INDEX* Transact-SQL command, including which options you can specify for the command. You will also learn how to disable and then reenable a clustered index.

After this lesson, you will be able to:

■ Implement clustered indexes.

■ Disable and reenable an index.

Estimated lesson time: 20 minutes

Implementing Clustered Indexes

The columns you define for a clustered index are called the *clustering key*. A clustered index causes SQL Server to order the data in the table according to the clustering key. Because a table can be sorted only one way, you can create only one clustered index on a table.

In addition, the leaf level of a clustered index is the actual data within the table. So when the leaf level of a clustered index is reached, SQL Server does not have to use a pointer to access the actual data in the table because it has already reached the actual data pages in the table.

IMPORTANT   Physical ordering

It is a common misconception that a clustered index causes the data to be physically ordered in a table. That is not entirely correct: A clustered index causes the rows in a table as well as the data pages in the doubly linked list that stores all the table data to be ordered according to the clustering key. However, this ordering is still logical. The table rows can be stored on the physical disk platters all over the place. If a clustered index caused a physical ordering of data on disk, it would create a prohibitive amount of disk activity.

As a general rule of thumb, every table should have a clustered index, and this clustered index should also be the primary key.

IMPORTANT Clustered index selection

Several readers probably turned purple when they read that the clustered index should also be the primary key. General rule of thumb does not mean "always." The primary key is not always the best choice for a clustered index. However, we don't have the hundreds of pages in this book to explain all the permutations and considerations for selecting the perfect clustering key. Even if we did have the space to devote to the topic, we would still end up with the same general rule of thumb. Clustering the primary key is always a better choice than not having a clustered index at all. You can read all the considerations required to make the appropriate choice for clustered index in the "Inside SQL Server" book series from Microsoft Press.

You use the *CREATE...INDEX* Transact-SQL command to create a clustered index. The general syntax for this command is as follows:

```
CREATE [ UNIQUE ] [ CLUSTERED | NONCLUSTERED ] INDEX index_name
    ON <object> ( column [ ASC | DESC ] [ ,...n ] )
    [ INCLUDE ( column_name [ ,...n ] ) ]
    [ WITH ( <relational_index_option> [ ,...n ] ) ]
    [ ON { partition_scheme_name ( column_name )
        | filegroup_name
        | default
        }
    ][ ; ]
```

We already covered the *UNIQUE* keyword in Chapter 3. All primary keys and unique constraints are implemented as unique indexes.

The *CLUSTERED* and *NONCLUSTERED* options designate the type of index you are creating. We will cover the *NONCLUSTERED* option in Lesson 3, "Creating Nonclustered Indexes," of this chapter.

After you specify that you want to create a clustered index, you need to specify a name for your index. Every index must have a name that conforms to the rules for object identifiers.

Next, you use the *ON* clause to specify the object to create the index against. You can create an index on either a table or a view (we cover indexed views in Chapter 7, "Implementing Views"). After you specify the table or view to create the index against, you specify in parentheses the columns on which you will create the index. The *ASC* and *DESC* keywords specify whether the sort order should be ascending or descending.

You also use the *ON* clause to specify the physical storage on which you want to place the index. You can specify either a filegroup or a partition scheme for the index (we cover partition schemes in Chapter 6, "Creating Partitions"). If you do not specify a location, and the table or view is not partitioned, SQL Server creates the index on the same filegroup as the underlying table or view.

The next part of the *CREATE INDEX* command enables you to specify relational index options. Covering each option in detail is beyond the scope of this book, but Table 4-1 briefly describes the relational options you can set for an index.

Table 4-1   Relational Index Options

Option	Description
PAD_INDEX	Specifies index padding. When set to *ON*, this option applies the percentage of free space specified by the *FILLFACTOR* option to the intermediate-level pages of the index. When set to *OFF* (the default) or when *FILLFACTOR* isn't specified, the intermediate-level pages are filled to near capacity, leaving enough space for at least one row of the maximum size the index can have.
FILLFACTOR	Specifies a percentage (0–100) that indicates how full the database engine should make the leaf level of each index page during index creation or rebuild.
SORT_IN_TEMPDB	Specifies whether to store temporary sort results in the *tempdb* database. The default is *OFF*, meaning intermediate sort results are stored in the same database as the index.
IGNORE_DUP_KEY	Specifies the error response to duplicate key values in a multiple-row insert operation on a unique clustered or unique nonclustered index. The default is *OFF*, which means an error message is issued and the entire *INSERT* transaction is rolled back. When this option is set to *ON*, a warning message is issued, and only the rows violating the unique index fail.

Table 4-1   **Relational Index Options**

Option	Description
STATISTICS_NORECOMPUTE	Specifies whether distribution statistics are recomputed. When set to *OFF*, the default, automatic statistics updating is enabled. When set to *ON*, out-of-date statistics are not automatically recomputed.
DROP_EXISTING	When set to *ON*, specifies that the named, preexisting clustered or nonclustered index is dropped and rebuilt. The default is *OFF*.
ONLINE	When set to *ON*, specifies that underlying tables and associated indexes are available for queries and data modification during the index operation. The default is *OFF*.
ALLOW_ROW_LOCKS	When set to *ON*, the default, specifies that row locks are allowed.
ALLOW_PAGE_LOCKS	When set to *ON*, the default, specifies that page locks are allowed.
MAXDOP	Overrides the *max degree of parallelism* configuration option for the duration of the index operation. *MAXDOP* limits the number of processors used in a parallel plan execution. The maximum is 64 processors. (Parallel index operations are available only in SQL Server 2005 Enterprise Edition.)

Of these options, let's look a little more closely at the *ONLINE* option, which is new in SQL Server 2005. As the table description notes, this option enables you to specify whether SQL Server creates indexes online or offline. The default is *ONLINE OFF*. When a clustered index is built offline, SQL Server locks the table, and users cannot select or modify data. If a nonclustered index is built offline, SQL Server acquires a shared table lock, which allows *SELECT* statements but no data modification.

When you specify *ONLINE ON*, during index creation, *SELECT* queries and data-modification statements can access the underlying table or view. When SQL Server creates an index online, it uses row-versioning functionality to ensure that it can build the index without conflicting with other operations on the table. *Online index creation* is available only in SQL Server 2005 Enterprise Edition.

MORE INFO   Index options

For more information about the options available to create an index, see the SQL Server 2005 Books Online topic "CREATE INDEX (Transact-SQL)." SQL Server 2005 Books Online is installed as part of SQL Server 2005. Updates for SQL Server 2005 Books Online are available for download at *www.microsoft.com/technet/prodtechnol/sql/2005/downloads/books.mspx.*

Disabling an Index

You can disable an index by using the *ALTER INDEX* Transact-SQL statement, as follows:

```
ALTER INDEX { index_name | ALL }
    ON <object>
    DISABLE [ ; ]
```

When you disable an index, the index definition remains in the system catalog, but SQL Server no longer uses it. SQL Server does not maintain the index as data in the table changes, and the index cannot be used to satisfy queries. And if you disable a clustered index, the entire table becomes inaccessible.

To enable an index, you must drop it and then re-create it to regenerate and populate the B-tree structure. You can do this by using the following *ALTER INDEX* command, which uses the *REBUILD* clause:

```
ALTER INDEX { index_name | ALL }
    ON <object>
    REBUILD [ ; ]
```

Quick Check
■ What requirement does a clustered index impose on logical storage of a table?

Quick Check Answer
■ A clustered index forces rows on data pages, as well as data pages within the doubly linked list, to be sorted by the clustering key.

PRACTICE **Create a Clustered Index**

In this practice, you will create a clustered index. You will then disable the index and reenable it.

1. Launch SQL Server Management Studio (SSMS), connect to your instance, and open a new query window.

2. Change the context to the *AdventureWorks* database.

3. Create a clustered index on the PostTime column of the *DatabaseLog* table by executing the following command:

```
CREATE CLUSTERED INDEX ci_postdate
ON dbo.DatabaseLog(PostTime);
```

4. Run the following query to verify that data can be retrieved from the table:

```
SELECT * from dbo.DatabaseLog;
```

5. Disable the index by executing the following command:

```
ALTER INDEX ci_postdate ON dbo.DatabaseLog DISABLE;
```

6. Verify that the table is now inaccessible by executing the following query:

```
SELECT * from dbo.DatabaseLog;
```

7. Reenable the clustered index and verify that the table can be accessed by executing the following query:

```
ALTER INDEX ci_postdate ON dbo.DatabaseLog REBUILD;
GO
SELECT * from dbo.DatabaseLog;
```

Lesson Summary

- You can create only one clustered index on a table.

- The clustered index, generally the primary key, causes the data in the table to be sorted according to the clustering key.

- When a clustered index is used to locate data, the leaf level of the index is also the data pages of the table.

- New in SQL Server 2005, you can specify online index creation, which enables users to continue to select and update data during the operation.

Lesson Review

The following questions are intended to reinforce key information presented in this lesson. The questions are also available on the companion CD if you prefer to review them in electronic form.

NOTE Answers

Answers to these questions and explanations of why each answer choice is right or wrong are located in the "Answers" section at the end of the book.

---

1. Which type of index physically orders the rows in a table?

     A. Unique index

     B. Clustered index

     C. Nonclustered index

     D. Foreign key

2. Which index option causes SQL Server to create an index with empty space on the leaf level of the index?

     A. *PAD_INDEX*

     B. *FILLFACTOR*

     C. *MAXDOP*

     D. *IGNORE_DUP_KEY*

Lesson 3: Creating Nonclustered Indexes

After you build your clustered index, you can create nonclustered indexes on the table. In contrast with a clustered index, a *nonclustered index* does not force a sort order on the data in a table. In addition, you can create multiple nonclustered indexes to most efficiently return results based on the most common queries you execute against the table. In this lesson, you will see how to create nonclustered indexes, including how to build a covering index that can satisfy a query by itself. And you will learn the importance of balancing the number of indexes you create with the overhead needed to maintain them.

After this lesson, you will be able to:

- Implement nonclustered indexes.
- Build a covering index.
- Balance index creation with maintenance requirements.

Estimated lesson time: 20 minutes

Implementing a Nonclustered Index

Because a nonclustered index does not impose a sort order on a table, you can create as many as 249 nonclustered indexes on a single table. Nonclustered indexes, just like clustered indexes, create a B-tree structure. However, unlike a clustered index, in a nonclustered index, the leaf level of the index contains a pointer to the data instead of the actual data.

This pointer can reference one of two items. If the table has a clustered index, the pointer points to the clustering key. If the table does not have a clustered index, the pointer points at a relative identifier (RID), which is a reference to the physical location of the data within a data page.

When the pointer references a nonclustered index, the query transits the B-tree structure of the index. When the query reaches the leaf level, it uses the pointer to find the clustering key. The query then transits the clustered index to reach the actual row of data. If a clustered index does not exist on the table, the pointer returns a RID, which causes SQL Server to scan an internal allocation map to locate the page referenced by the RID so that it can return the requested data.

You use the same *CREATE...INDEX* command to create a nonclustered index as you do to create a clustered index, except that you specify the *NONCLUSTERED* keyword.

Creating a Covering Index

An index contains all the values contained in the column or columns that define the index. SQL Server stores this data in a sorted format on pages in a doubly linked list. So an index is essentially a miniature representation of a table.

This structure can have an interesting effect on certain queries. If the query needs to return data from only columns within an index, it does not need to access the data pages of the actual table. By transiting the index, it has already located all the data it requires.

For example, let's say you are using the *Customer* table that we created in Chapter 3 to find the names of all customers who have a credit line greater than $10,000. SQL Server would scan the table to locate all the rows with a value greater than 10,000 in the Credit Line column, which would be very inefficient. If you then created an index on the Credit Line column, SQL Server would use the index to quickly locate all the rows that matched this criterion. Then it would transit the primary key, because it is clustered, to return the customer names. However, if you created a nonclustered index that had two columns in it—Credit Line and Customer Name—SQL Server would not have to access the clustered index to locate the rows of data. When SQL Server used the nonclustered index to find all the rows where the credit line was greater than 10,000, it also located all the customer names.

An index that SQL Server can use to satisfy a query without having to access the table is called a *covering index*.

Even more interesting, SQL Server can use more than one index for a given query. In the preceding example, you could create nonclustered indexes on the credit line and on the customer name, which SQL Server could then use together to satisfy a query.

NOTE Index selection

SQL Server determines whether to use an index by examining only the first column defined in the index. For example, if you defined an index on FirstName, LastName and a query were looking for LastName, this index would not be used to satisfy the query.

Balancing Index Maintenance

Why wouldn't you just create dozens or hundreds of indexes on a table? At first glance, knowing how useful indexes are, this approach might seem like a good idea. However, remember how an index is constructed. The values from the column that the index is created on are used to build the index. And the values within the index are also sorted. Now, let's say a new row is added to the table. Before the operation can complete, the value from this new row must be added to the correct location within the index.

If you have only one index on the table, one write to the table also causes one write to the index. If there are 30 indexes on the table, one write to the table causes 30 additional writes to the indexes.

It gets a little more complicated. If the leaf-level index page does not have room for the new value, SQL Server has to perform an operation called a *page split*. During this operation, SQL Server allocates an empty page to the index, moving half the values on the page that was filled to the new page. If this page split also causes an intermediate-level index page to overflow, a page split occurs at that level as well. And if the new row causes the root page to overflow, SQL Server splits the root page into a new intermediate level, causing a new root page to be created.

As you can see, indexes can improve query performance, but each index you create degrades performance on all data-manipulation operations. Therefore, you need to carefully balance the number of indexes for optimal operations. As a general rule of thumb, if you have five or more indexes on a table designed for online transactional processing (OLTP) operations, you probably need to reevaluate why those indexes exist. Tables designed for read operations or data warehouse types of queries generally have 10 or more indexes because you don't have to worry about the impact of write operations.

Using Included Columns

In addition to considering the performance degradation caused by write operation, keep in mind that indexes are limited to a maximum of 900 bytes. This limit can create a challenge in constructing more complex covering indexes.

An interesting new indexing feature in SQL Server 2005 called included columns helps you deal with this challenge. Included columns become part of the index at the leaf level only. Values from included columns do not appear in the root or intermediate levels of an index and do not count against the 900-byte limit for an index.

> ## Quick Check
> - What are the two most important things to consider for nonclustered indexes?
>
> **Quick Check Answer**
> - The number of indexes must be balanced against the overhead required to maintain them when rows are added, removed, or modified in the table.
> - You need to make sure that the order of the columns defined in the index match what the queries need, ensuring that the first column in the index is used in the query so that the query optimizer will use the index.

PRACTICE **Create Nonclustered Indexes**

In this practice, you will add a nonclustered index to the tables that you created in Chapter 3.

1. If necessary, launch SSMS, connect to your instance, and open a new query window.

2. Because users commonly search for a customer by city, add a nonclustered index to the *CustomerAddress* table on the City column, as follows:

```
CREATE NONCLUSTERED INDEX idx_CustomerAddress_City ON dbo.CustomerAddress(City);
```

Lesson Summary

- You can create up to 249 nonclustered indexes on a table.

- The number of indexes you create must be balanced against the overhead incurred when data is modified.

- An important factor to consider when creating indexes is whether an index can be used to satisfy a query in its entirety, thereby saving additional reads from either the clustered index or data pages in the table. Such an index is called a covering index.

- SQL Server 2005's new included columns indexing feature enables you to add values to the leaf level of an index only so that you can create more complex index implementations within the index size limit.

Lesson Review

The following questions are intended to reinforce key information presented in this lesson. The questions are also available on the companion CD if you prefer to review them in electronic form.

NOTE Answers

Answers to these questions and explanations of why each answer choice is right or wrong are located in the "Answers" section at the end of the book.

---

1. Which index option causes an index to be created with empty space on the intermediate levels of the index?

    A. *PAD_INDEX*

    B. *FILLFACTOR*

    C. *MAXDOP*

    D. *IGNORE_DUP_KEY*

Chapter Review

To further practice and reinforce the skills you learned in this chapter, you can

- Review the chapter summary.
- Review the list of key terms introduced in this chapter.
- Complete the case scenario. This scenario sets up a real-world situation involving the topics of this chapter and asks you to create a solution.
- Complete the suggested practices.
- Take a practice test.

Chapter Summary

- Indexes on SQL Server tables, just like indexes on books, provide a way to quickly access the data you are looking for—even in very large tables.
- Clustered indexes cause rows to be sorted according to the clustering key. In general, every table should have a clustered index. And you can have only one clustered index per table, usually built on the primary key.
- Nonclustered indexes do not sort rows in a table, and you can create up to 249 per table to help quickly satisfy the most common queries.
- By constructing covering indexes, you can satisfy queries without needing to access the underlying table.

Key Terms

Do you know what these key terms mean? You can check your answers by looking up the terms in the glossary at the end of the book.

- B-tree
- clustered index
- clustering key
- covering index
- intermediate level
- leaf level
- nonclustered index
- online index creation

- page split
- root node

Case Scenario: Indexing a Database

In the following case scenario, you will apply what you've learned in this chapter. You can find answers to these questions in the "Answers" section at the end of this book.

Contoso Limited, a health care company located in Bothell, WA, has just implemented a new patient claims database. Over the course of one month, more than 100 employees entered all the records that used to be contained in massive filing cabinets in the basements of several new clients.

Contoso formed a temporary department to validate all the data entry. As soon as the data-validation process started, the IT staff began to receive user complaints about the new database's performance.

As the new database administrator (DBA) for the company, everything that occurs with the data is in your domain, and you need to resolve the performance problem. You sit down with several employees to determine what they are searching for. Armed with this knowledge, what should you do?

Suggested Practices

To help you successfully master the exam objectives presented in this chapter, complete the following practice tasks.

Creating Indexes

- **Practice 1** Locate all the tables in your databases that do not have primary keys. Add a primary key to each of these tables.
- **Practice 2** Locate all the tables in your databases that do not have clustered indexes. Add a clustered index or change the primary key to clustered for each of these tables.
- **Practice 3** Identify poorly performing queries in your environment. Create non-clustered indexes that the query optimizer can use to satisfy these queries.
- **Practice 4** Identify the queries that can take advantage of covering indexes. If indexes do not already exist that cover the queries, use the included columns clause to add additional columns to the appropriate index to turn it into a covering index.

Take a Practice Test

The practice tests on this book's companion CD offer many options. For example, you can test yourself on just the content covered in this chapter, or you can test yourself on all the 70-431 certification exam content. You can set up the test so that it closely simulates the experience of taking a certification exam, or you can set it up in study mode so that you can look at the correct answers and explanations after you answer each question.

MORE INFO   Practice tests

For details about all the practice test options available, see the "How to Use the Practice Tests" section in this book's Introduction.

Chapter 5

Working with Transact-SQL

The query language that Microsoft SQL Server uses is a variant of the ANSI-standard Structured Query Language, SQL. The SQL Server variant is called Transact-SQL. Database administrators and database developers must have a thorough knowledge of Transact-SQL to read data from and write data to SQL Server databases. Using Transact-SQL is the only way to work with the data.

Exam objectives in this chapter:

- Retrieve data to support ad hoc and recurring queries.
  - ❑ Construct SQL queries to return data.
  - ❑ Format the results of SQL queries.
  - ❑ Identify collation details.
- Manipulate relational data.
  - ❑ Insert, update, and delete data.
  - ❑ Handle exceptions and errors.
  - ❑ Manage transactions.

Lessons in this chapter:

Before You Begin

To complete the lessons in this chapter, you must have

- SQL Server 2005 installed.
- A connection to a SQL Server 2005 instance in SQL Server Management Studio (SSMS).
- The *AdventureWorks* database installed.

Real World

Adam Machanic

In my work as a database consultant, I am frequently asked by clients to review queries that aren't performing well. More often than not, the problem is simple: Whoever wrote the query clearly did not understand how Transact-SQL works or how best to use it to solve problems.

Transact-SQL is a fairly simple language; writing a basic query requires knowledge of only four keywords! Yet many developers don't spend the time to understand it, and they end up writing less-than-desirable code.

If you feel like your query is getting more complex than it should be, it probably is. Take a step back and rethink the problem. The key to creating well-performing Transact-SQL queries is to think in terms of sets instead of row-by-row operations, as you would in a procedural system.

Lesson 1: Querying Data

Data in a database would not be very useful if you could not get it back out in a desired format. One of the main purposes of Transact-SQL is to enable database developers to write queries to return data in many different ways.

In this lesson, you will learn various methods of querying data by using Transact-SQL, including some of the more advanced options that you can use to more easily get data back from your databases.

After this lesson, you will be able to:

- Determine which tables to use in the query.
- Determine which join types to use.
- Determine the columns to return.
- Create subqueries.
- Create queries that use complex criteria.
- Create queries that use aggregate functions.
- Create queries that format data by using the PIVOT and UNPIVOT operators.
- Create queries that use Full-Text Search (FTS).
- Limit returned results by using the TABLESAMPLE clause.

Estimated lesson time: 35 minutes

Determining Which Tables to Use in the Query

The foundations of any query are the tables that contain the data needed to satisfy the request. Therefore, your first job when writing a query is to carefully decide which tables to use in the query. A database developer must ensure that queries use as few tables as possible to satisfy the data requirements. Joining extra tables can cause performance problems, making the server do more work than is necessary to return the data to the data consumer.

Avoid the temptation of creating monolithic, do-everything queries that can be used to satisfy the requirements of many different parts of the application or that return data from additional tables just in case it might be necessary in the future. For instance, some developers are tempted to create views that join virtually every table in the database to simplify data access code in the application layer. Instead, you should carefully partition your queries based on specific application data requirements, returning data only from the tables that are necessary. Should data requirements change in the future, you can modify the query to include additional tables.

By choosing only the tables that are needed, database developers can create more maintainable and better-performing queries.

Determining Which Join Types to Use

When working with multiple tables in a query, you join the tables to one another to produce tabular output result sets. You have two primary choices for join types when working in Transact-SQL: inner joins and outer joins. *Inner joins* return only the data that satisfies the join condition; nonmatching rows are not returned. *Outer joins*, on the other hand, let you return nonmatching rows in addition to matching rows.

Inner joins are the most straightforward to understand. The following query uses an inner join to return all columns from both the *Employee* and *EmployeeAddress* tables. Only rows that exist in both tables with the same value for the EmployeeId column are returned:

```
SELECT *
FROM HumanResources.Employee AS E
INNER JOIN HumanResources.EmployeeAddress AS EA ON
    E.EmployeeId = EA.EmployeeId
```

NOTE Table alias names

This query uses the AS clause to create a table alias name for each table involved in the query. Creating an alias name can simplify your queries and mean less typing—instead of having to type "HumanResources.Employee" every time the table is referenced, the alias name, "E", can be used.

Outer joins return rows with matching data as well as rows with nonmatching data. There are three types of outer joins available to Transact-SQL developers: left outer joins, right outer joins, and full outer joins. A left outer join returns all the rows from the left table in the join, whether or not there are any matching rows in the right table. For any matching rows in the right table, the data for those rows will be returned. For nonmatching rows, the columns in the right table will return NULL. Consider the following query:

```
SELECT *
FROM HumanResources.Employee AS E
LEFT OUTER JOIN HumanResources.EmployeeAddress AS EA ON
    E.EmployeeId = EA.EmployeeId
```

This query will return one row for every employee in the *Employee* table. For each row of the *Employee* table, if a corresponding row exists in the *EmployeeAddress* table, the data from that table will also be returned. However, if for a row of the *Employee* table no corresponding row exists in *EmployeeAddress*, the row from the *Employee* table will still be returned, with NULL values for each column that would have been returned from the *EmployeeAddress* table.

A right outer join is similar to a left outer join except that all rows from the right table will be returned, instead of rows from the left table. The following query is, therefore, identical to the query listed previously:

```
SELECT *
FROM HumanResources.EmployeeAddress AS EA
RIGHT OUTER JOIN HumanResources.Employee AS E ON
    E.EmployeeId = EA.EmployeeId
```

The final outer join type is the full outer join, which returns all rows from both tables, whether or not matching rows exist. Where matching rows do exist, the rows will be joined. Where matching rows do not exist, NULL values will be returned for whichever table does not contain corresponding values.

Generally speaking, inner joins are the most common join type you'll use when working with SQL Server. You should use inner joins whenever you are querying two tables and know that both tables have matching data or would not want to return missing data. For instance, assume that you have an *Employee* table and an *EmployeePhoneNumber* table. The *EmployeePhoneNumber* table might or might not contain a phone number for each employee. If you want to return a list of employees and their phone numbers and not return employees without phone numbers, use an inner join.

You use outer joins whenever you need to return nonmatching data. In the example of the *Employee* and *EmployeePhoneNumber* tables, you probably want a full list of employees—including those without phone numbers. In that case, you use an outer join instead of an inner join.

Determining the Columns to Return

Just as it's important to limit the tables your queries use, it's also important when writing a query to return only the columns absolutely necessary to satisfy the request. Returning extra unnecessary columns in a query can have a surprisingly negative effect on query performance.

The performance impact of choosing extra columns is related to two factors: network utilization and indexing. From a network standpoint, bringing back extra data with each query means that your network might have to do a lot more work than necessary to get the data to the client. The smaller the amount of data you send across the network, the faster the transmission will go. By returning only necessary columns and not returning additional columns just in case, you will preserve bandwidth.

The other cause of performance problems is index utilization. In many cases, SQL Server can use nonclustered indexes to satisfy queries that use only a subset of the columns from a table. This is called index covering. If you add additional columns to a query, the query might no longer be covered by the index, and therefore performance will decrease. For more information about indexing, see Chapter 4, "Creating Indexes."

BEST PRACTICES   Queries

Whenever possible, avoid using SELECT * queries, which return all columns from the specified tables. Instead, always specify a column list, which will ensure that you don't bring back any more columns than you're intending to, even as additional columns are added to underlying tables.

MORE INFO   Learning query basics

For more information about writing queries, see the "Query Fundamentals" topic in SQL Server 2005 Books Online, which is installed as part of SQL Server 2005. Updates for SQL Server 2005 Books Online are available for download at www.microsoft.com/technet/prodtechnol/sql/2005/downloads/books.mspx.

How to Create Subqueries

Subqueries are queries that are nested in other queries and relate in some way to the data in the query in which they are nested. The query in which a subquery participates is called the outer query. As you work with Transact-SQL, you will find that you often have many ways to write a query to get the same output, and each method will have different performance characteristics. For example, in many cases, you can use subqueries instead of joins to tune difficult queries.

You can use subqueries in a variety of different ways and in any of the clauses of a *SELECT* statement. There are several types of subqueries available to database developers.

The most straightforward subquery form is a noncorrelated subquery. Noncorrelated means that the subquery does not use any columns from the tables in the outer query. For instance, the following query selects all the employees from the *Employee* table if the employee's ID is in the *EmployeeAddress* table:

```
SELECT *
FROM HumanResources.Employee AS E
WHERE E.EmployeeId IN
(
    SELECT EmployeeId
    FROM HumanResources.EmployeeAddress
)
```

The outer query in this case selects from the *Employee* table, whereas the subquery selects from the *EmployeeAddress* table.

You can also write this query using the correlated form of a subquery. Correlated means that the subquery uses one or more columns from the outer query. The following query is logically equivalent to the preceding noncorrelated version:

```
SELECT *
FROM HumanResources.Employee AS E
WHERE EXISTS
(
    SELECT *
    FROM HumanResources.EmployeeAddress EA
    WHERE E.EmployeeId = EA.EmployeeId
)
```

In this case, the subquery correlates the outer query's *EmployeeId* value to the subquery's *EmployeeId* value. The *EXISTS* predicate returns true if at least one row is returned by the subquery. Although they are logically equivalent, the two queries might perform differently depending on your data or indexes. If you're not sure whether to use a correlated or noncorrelated subquery when tuning a query, test both options and compare their performances.

You can also use subqueries in the *SELECT* list. The following query returns every employee's ID from the *Employee* table and uses a correlated subquery to return the employee's address ID:

```
SELECT
    EmployeeId,
    (
        SELECT EA.AddressId
        FROM HumanResources.EmployeeAddress EA
        WHERE EA.EmployeeId = E.EmployeeId
    ) AS AddressId
FROM HumanResources.Employee AS E
```

Note that in this case, if the employee did not have an address in the *EmployeeAddress* table, the AddressId column would return NULL for that employee. In many cases such as this, you can use correlated subqueries and outer joins interchangeably to return the same data.

Quick Check

- What is the difference between a correlated and noncorrelated subquery?

Quick Check Answer

- A correlated subquery references columns from the outer query; a noncorrelated subquery does not.

Creating Queries That Use Complex Criteria

You often must write queries to express intricate business logic. The key to effectively doing this is to use a Transact-SQL feature called a *case expression*, which lets you build conditional logic into a query. Like subqueries, you can use case expressions in virtually all parts of a query, including the *SELECT* list and the *WHERE* clause.

As an example of when to use a case expression, consider a business requirement that salaried employees receive a certain number of vacation hours and sick-leave hours per year, and nonsalaried employees receive only sick-leave hours. The following query uses this business rule to return the total number of hours of paid time off for each employee in the *Employee* table:

```
SELECT
    EmployeeId,
    CASE SalariedFlag
        WHEN 1 THEN VacationHours + SickLeaveHours
        ELSE SickLeaveHours
    END AS PaidTimeOff
FROM HumanResources.Employee
```

MORE INFO   Case expression syntax

If you're not familiar with the SQL case expression, see the "CASE (Transact-SQL)" topic in SQL Server 2005 Books Online.

This query conditionally checks the value of the SalariedFlag column, returning the total of the VacationHours and SickLeaveHours columns if the employee is salaried. Otherwise, only the SickLeaveHours column value is returned.

IMPORTANT **Case expression output paths**

All possible output paths of a case expression must be of the same data type. If all the columns you need to output are not the same type, make sure to use the CAST or CONVERT functions to make them uniform. See the section titled "Using System Functions" later in this chapter for more information.

Creating Queries That Use Aggregate Functions

You can often aggregate data stored in tables within a database to produce important types of business information. For instance, you might not be interested in a list of employees in the database but instead want to know the average salary for all the employees. You perform this type of calculation by using *aggregate functions*. Aggregate functions operate on groups of rows rather than individual rows; the aggregate function processes a group of rows to produce a single output value.

Transact-SQL has several built-in aggregate functions, and you can also define aggregate functions by using Microsoft .NET languages. Table 5-1 lists commonly used built-in aggregate functions and what they do.

Table 5-1 Commonly Used Built-in Aggregate Functions

Function	Description
AVG	Returns the average value of the rows in the group.
COUNT/COUNT_BIG	Returns the count of the rows in the group. *COUNT* returns its output typed as an integer, whereas *COUNT_BIG* returns its output typed as a bigint.
MAX/MIN	*MAX* returns the maximum value in the group. *MIN* returns the minimum value in the group.
SUM	Returns the sum of the rows in the group.
STDEV	Returns the standard deviation of the rows in the group.
VAR	Returns the statistical variance of the rows in the group.

As an example, the following query uses the *AVG* aggregate function to return the average number of vacation hours for all employees in the *Employee* table:

```
SELECT AVG(VacationHours)
FROM HumanResources.Employee
```

If you need to return aggregated data alongside nonaggregated data, you must use aggregate functions in conjunction with a *GROUP BY* clause. You use the nonaggregated columns to define the groups for aggregation. Each distinct combination of nonaggregated data will comprise one group. For instance, the following query returns the average number of vacation hours for the employees in the *Employee* table, grouped by the employees' salary status:

```
SELECT SalariedFlag, AVG(VacationHours)
FROM HumanResources.Employee
GROUP BY SalariedFlag
```

Because there are two distinct salary statuses in the Employee table—salaried and non-salaried—the results of this query are two rows. One row contains the average number of vacation hours for salaried employees, and the other contains the average number of vacation hours for nonsalaried employees.

Creating Queries That Format Data by Using PIVOT and UNPIVOT Operators

Business users often want to see data formatted in what's known as a *cross-tabulation*. This is a special type of aggregate query in which the grouped rows for one of the columns become columns themselves. For instance, the final query in the last section returned two rows: one containing the average number of vacation hours for salaried employees and one containing the average number of vacation hours for nonsalaried employees. A business user might instead want the output formatted as a single row with two columns: one column for the average vacation hours for salaried employees and one for the average vacation hours for nonsalaried employees.

You can use the *PIVOT* operator to produce this output. To use the *PIVOT* operator, perform the following steps:

1. Select the data you need by using a special type of subquery called a *derived table*.
2. After you define the derived table, apply the *PIVOT* operator and specify an aggregate function to use.
3. Define which columns you want to include in the output.

The following query shows how to produce the average number of vacation hours for all salaried and nonsalaried employees in the *Employee* table in a single output row:

```
SELECT [0], [1]
FROM
(
    SELECT SalariedFlag, VacationHours
    FROM HumanResources.Employee
) AS H
PIVOT
(
    AVG(VacationHours)
    FOR SalariedFlag IN ([0], [1])
) AS Pvt
```

In this example, the data from the *Employee* table is first selected in the derived table called *H*. The data from the table is pivoted using the *AVG* aggregate to produce two columns—0 and 1—each corresponding to one of the two salary types in the *Employee* table. Note that the same identifiers used to define the pivot columns must also be used in the SELECT list if you want to return the columns' values to the user.

The *UNPIVOT* operator does the exact opposite of the *PIVOT* operator. It turns columns back into rows. This operator is useful when you are normalizing tables that have more than one column of the same type defined.

Creating Queries That Use Full-Text Search

If your database contains many columns that use string data types such as *VARCHAR* or *NVARCHAR*, you might find that searching these columns for data by using the Transact-SQL = and *LIKE* operators does not perform well. A more efficient way to search text data is to use the SQL Server FTS capabilities.

To do full-text searching, you first must enable full-text indexes for the tables you want to query. To query a full-text index, you use a special set of functions that differ from the operators that you use to search other types of data. The main functions for full-text search are *CONTAINS* and *FREETEXT*.

The *CONTAINS* function searches for exact word matches and word prefix matches. For instance, the following query can be used to search for any address containing the word "Stone":

```
SELECT *
FROM Person.Address
WHERE CONTAINS(AddressLine1, 'Stone')
```

This query would find an address at "1 Stone Way", but to match "23 Stoneview Drive" you need to add the prefix identifier, *, as in the following example:

```
SELECT *
FROM Person.Address
WHERE CONTAINS(AddressLine1, '"Stone*"')
```

Note that you must also use double quotes if you use the prefix identifier. If the double quotes are not included, the string will be searched as an exact match, including the prefix identifier.

If you need a less-exact match, use the *FREETEXT* function instead. This function uses a fuzzy match to get more results when the search term is inexact. For instance, the following query would find an address at "1 Stones Way", even though the search string "Stone" is not exact:

```
SELECT *
FROM Person.Address
WHERE FREETEXT(AddressLine1, 'Stone')
```

FREETEXT works by generating various forms of the search term, breaking single words into parts as they might appear in documents and generating possible synonyms using thesaurus functionality. This predicate is useful when you want to let users search based on the term's meaning, rather than only exact strings.

Both *CONTAINS* and *FREETEXT* also have table-valued versions: *CONTAINSTABLE* and *FREETEXTTABLE*, respectively. The table-valued versions have the added benefit of returning additional data along with the results, including the rank of each result in a column called RANK. The rank is higher for closer matches, so you can order results for users based on relevance. You can join to the result table by using the generic KEY column, which joins to whatever column in your base table was used as the unique index when creating the full-text index.

MORE INFO Creating full-text indexes

For information on creating full-text indexes, see the "CREATE FULLTEXT INDEX (Transact-SQL)" topic in SQL Server 2005 Books Online.

> **Quick Check**
> - Which function should you use to query exact or prefix string matches?
>
> **Quick Check Answer**
> - The *CONTAINS* function lets you query either exact matches or matches based on a prefix.

Limiting Returned Results by Using the TABLESAMPLE Clause

In some cases, you might want to evaluate only a small random subset of the returned values for a certain query. This can be especially relevant, for instance, when testing large queries. Instead of seeing the entire result set, you might want to analyze only a fraction of its rows.

The *TABLESAMPLE* clause lets you specify a target number of rows or percentage of rows to be returned. The SQL Server query engine randomly determines the segment from which the rows will be taken.

The following query returns approximately 10 percent of the addresses in the *Address* table:

```
SELECT *
FROM Person.Address
TABLESAMPLE(10 PERCENT)
```

CAUTION   TABLESAMPLE returns random rows

The TABLESAMPLE clause works by returning rows from a random subset of data pages determined by the percentage specified. Because some data pages contain more rows than others, this means that the number of returned rows will almost never be exact. When using the TABLESAMPLE clause, do not write queries that expect an exact number of rows to be returned.

PRACTICE **Query and Pivot Employees' Pay Rates**

In the following practice exercises, you will write queries that retrieve employees' pay rate information using aggregate functions and then pivot the data using the *PIVOT* operator.

▶ **Practice 1: Retrieve Employees' Current Pay Rate Information**

In this exercise, you will practice writing a query that uses aggregate functions to get employees' current pay rate information from the *AdventureWorks* database.

1. Open SSMS and connect to your SQL Server.

2. Open a new query window and select *AdventureWorks* as the active database.

3. Type the following query and execute it:

```
SELECT
    EPH.EmployeeId,
    EPH.Rate,
    EPH.RateChangeDate
FROM HumanResources.EmployeePayHistory EPH
```

4. This shows that the table *EmployeePayHistory* has one row for each employee's pay rate and the date it changed.

5. To find the current pay rate, you need to determine which change date is the maximum for each employee.

6. Type the following query and execute it:

```
SELECT
    EPH.EmployeeId,
    EPH.Rate,
    EPH.RateChangeDate
FROM HumanResources.EmployeePayHistory EPH
WHERE EPH.RateChangeDate =
(
    SELECT MAX(EPH1.RateChangeDate)
    FROM HumanResources.EmployeePayHistory EPH1
)
```

7. This query, however, returns rows for only a few of the employees; it uses a non-correlated subquery, which gets the most recent *RateChangeDate* for the whole table. So only employees who had their rate changed on that day are returned. Instead, you need to use a correlated subquery. For each employee, the query needs to compare the most recent *RateChangeDate*.

8. Type the following query and execute it:

```
SELECT
    EPH.EmployeeId,
    EPH.Rate,
    EPH.RateChangeDate
FROM HumanResources.EmployeePayHistory EPH
WHERE EPH.RateChangeDate =
(
    SELECT MAX(EPH1.RateChangeDate)
    FROM HumanResources.EmployeePayHistory EPH1
    WHERE EPH1.EmployeeId = EPH.EmployeeId
)
```

9. This query, which uses the correlated subquery, returns the most recent pay rate for every employee.

▶ **Practice 2: Pivot Employees' Pay Rate History**

In this exercise, you will practice writing a query that uses the *PIVOT* operator to create a report that shows each employee's pay rate changes in each year.

1. If necessary, open SSMS and connect to your SQL Server.

2. Open a new query window and select *AdventureWorks* as the active database.

3. Type the following query and execute it:

```
SELECT
    EmployeeId,
    YEAR(RateChangeDate) AS ChangeYear,
    Rate
FROM HumanResources.EmployeePayHistory
```

4. This query returns the rate of each change made for each employee, along with the year in which the change was made.

5. Next, you need to store this information in a derived table, as the following query shows:

```
SELECT *
FROM
(
    SELECT
        EmployeeId,
        YEAR(RateChangeDate) AS ChangeYear,
        Rate
    FROM HumanResources.EmployeePayHistory
) AS EmpRates
```

6. Execute the query and then analyze the years returned. Notice that the data ranges between 1996 and 2003.

7. You can now pivot this derived table. One requirement of *PIVOT* is to use an aggregate function on the data being pivoted. Because that data is employee salary, the most obvious function is *MAX*, which would report the maximum change for each year.

8. Based on the date range in the data and the chosen aggregate function, the following *PIVOT* query can be written:

```
SELECT *
FROM
(
    SELECT
        EmployeeId,
        YEAR(RateChangeDate) AS ChangeYear,
        Rate
    FROM HumanResources.EmployeePayHistory
) AS EmpRates
PIVOT
(
    MAX(Rate)
    FOR ChangeYear IN
    (
        [1996],
        [1997],
        [1998],
        [1999],
        [2000],
        [2001],
        [2002],
        [2003]
    )
) AS Pvt
```

9. Executing this query returns a report with a column for each year, showing whether or not the employee received a pay rate change during that year. Years without changes show NULL for that employee.

Lesson Summary

- Avoid including unnecessary tables and columns in queries.
- Subqueries and outer joins can often be used interchangeably to query for matching and nonmatching data.
- Aggregate functions and the *PIVOT* operator can assist in creating more useful output for business users.
- The FTS functions can be used to more efficiently query text data.

Lesson Review

The following questions are intended to reinforce key information presented in this lesson. The questions are also available on the companion CD if you prefer to review them in electronic form.

NOTE Answers

Answers to these questions and explanations of why each answer choice is right or wrong are located in the "Answers" section at the end of this book.

---

1. Which types of joins let you retrieve nonmatching data? (Choose all that apply.)

   A. Full outer join

   B. Inner join

   C. Right outer join

   D. Left outer join

2. Which of the following aggregate functions returns a row count as an integer?

   A. *AVG*

   B. *COUNT_BIG*

   C. *STDEV*

   D. *COUNT*

3. You need to find all matches from your *Product* table in which the Description column includes either the words "book" or "booklet". Which of the following FTS syntaxes should you use?

   A. *FREETEXT(Description, "'Book'")*

   B. *FREETEXT(Description, "'Book*'")*

   C. *CONTAINS(Description, "'Book'")*

   D. *CONTAINS(Description, "'Book*'")*

Lesson 2: Formatting Result Sets

Lesson 1 covered many of the finer points for basic data querying. However, this knowledge is not enough for most projects. In many cases, you will need to do more than just query the data; you'll have to return it in a useful format so that your users can understand it.

In this lesson, you will learn how to format data using functions, query Common Language Runtime (CLR) user-defined data types, and use alias columns to make data easier for your users to consume.

After this lesson, you will be able to:

■ Use system functions.

■ Use user-defined functions (UDFs).

■ Query CLR user-defined types (UDTs).

■ Create column aliases.

Estimated lesson time: 20 minutes

Using System Functions

SQL Server includes a variety of built-in functions that can help with data formatting. Table 5-2 describes the most commonly used functions.

Table 5-2 Commonly Used Data-Formatting Functions

Function	Description
CAST/CONVERT	The *CAST* and *CONVERT* functions let you convert between data types. *CONVERT* is especially useful because it lets you change formatting when converting certain types (for example, datetime) to strings.
DAY/MONTH/ YEAR/DATENAME	The *DAY*, *MONTH*, and *YEAR* functions return the numeric value corresponding to the day, month, or year represented by a datetime data type. The *DATENAME* function returns the localized name for whatever part of the date is specified.
REPLACE	The *REPLACE* function replaces occurrences of a substring in a string with another string.

Table 5-2 Commonly Used Data-Formatting Functions

Function	Description
STUFF	The *STUFF* function lets you insert strings inside of other strings at the specified position.
SUBSTRING/LEFT/ RIGHT	The *SUBSTRING* function returns a slice of a string starting at a specified position. *LEFT* and *RIGHT* return slices of the string from the left or right, respectively.
STR	The *STR* function converts numeric types into strings.

These functions are most commonly used in a query's *SELECT* list to modify the output of the query to satisfy user requirements. For instance, the following query uses the *CONVERT* function to convert all the birth dates in the *Employee* table to the ANSI two-digit year format:

```
SELECT CONVERT(CHAR(10), BirthDate, 2)
FROM HumanResources.Employee
```

CAUTION   Do not use functions in WHERE clauses

Avoid using formatting functions in your queries' WHERE clauses. Using such functions can cause performance problems by making it difficult for the query engine to use indexes.

Using User-Defined Functions in Queries

In addition to the system functions available for formatting, database developers can create custom functions called user-defined functions (UDFs). Once defined, you can use these functions anywhere that you can use a built-in function. The only difference between using a built-in function and a UDF is that UDFs must be scoped by the name of the database schema in which they participate. The following query uses the *ufnGet-ProductListPrice* UDF that is defined in the *dbo* schema of the *AdventureWorks* database:

```
SELECT
    ProductId,
    dbo.ufnGetProductListPrice(ProductId, ModifiedDate)
FROM Sales.SalesOrderDetail
```

The function has two parameters—product ID and order date—and returns the price for the given product as of the order date. Because the function is in the *dbo* schema, to call the function, you must prefix it with *dbo*. This prefix tells SQL Server that you're using a UDF rather than a system function.

Quick Check

■ What is the main difference between querying a UDF and a built-in function?

Quick Check Answer

■ When querying a UDF, you must specify the function's schema. Built-in functions do not participate in schemas.

Querying CLR User-Defined Types

You can use .NET CLR user-defined types (UDTs) to programmatically extend SQL Server's type system. Querying CLR UDTs is not quite the same as querying built-in types. If you need the results returned as a string, you must use the *ToString* method that all CLR UDTs define. Assume that the PhoneNumber column of the *ContactInformation* table uses a UDT. The following query would return the phone numbers as strings if your database used a UDT for the PhoneNumber column:

```
SELECT PhoneNumber.ToString()
FROM ContactInformation
```

In addition to exposing the *ToString* method for returning strings, CLR UDTs can have additional methods and properties defined that can help to retrieve data in various ways. For instance, the *PhoneNumber* type might have a property called *AreaCode* that returns only the area code for the phone number. In that case, you could use the following query to get all the area codes from the *ContactInformation* table, again only if your database used a UDT for the PhoneNumber column:

```
SELECT PhoneNumber.AreaCode
FROM ContactInformation
```

Quick Check

■ How do you return the value of a CLR UDT as a string?

Quick Check Answer

■ All CLR UDTs expose a method called *ToString*, which you can call to retrieve a string representation of the type.

Creating Column Aliases

When writing queries, you often need to change the name of output columns to make them more user-friendly. You do this by using the *AS* modifier. For instance, in the following query, the SalariedFlag column will appear to the user as a column called "IsSalaried":

```
SELECT
    EmployeeId,
    SalariedFlag AS IsSalaried
FROM HumanResources.Employee
```

You can also use the *AS* modifier to define a column name whenever one doesn't exist. For example, if you use an expression or a scalar function to define the column, the column name by default will be NULL.

BEST PRACTICES   **Use distinct column names**

It's a good idea to make sure that every output column of a query has a distinct column name. Applications should always be able to rely on column names for programmatically retrieving data from a query and should not be forced to use column ordinal position.

PRACTICE Formatting Column Output

In this exercise, you will practice using some of the system functions available for formatting column output.

Assume that you have the following business requirement: Write a query that returns for every employee in the *Employee* table that employee's hire date formatted using the ANSI date format, number of vacation hours, and the employee's login ID, without the standard prefix. All data must be concatenated for each employee into a single comma-delimited string, and the column should be called "EmpData".

1. If necessary, open SSMS and connect to your SQL Server.

2. Open a new query window and select *AdventureWorks* as the active database.

3. Type the following query and execute it:

```
SELECT
    HireDate,
    VacationHours,
    LoginId
FROM HumanResources.Employee
```

4. Note the formatting problems: HireDate is not formatted according to the ANSI date format, and LoginId needs to have the "adventure-works\" prefix removed.

5. First, format HireDate according to the ANSI date format by using the *CONVERT* function. Type the following query and execute it:

```
SELECT
    CONVERT(CHAR(10), HireDate, 2),
    VacationHours,
    LoginId
FROM HumanResources.Employee
```

6. Next, remove the prefix from the login ID. You can do this easily by using the *REPLACE*, *SUBSTRING*, or *STUFF* function. The following code example shows how to remove the prefix by using *REPLACE* to replace the prefix with an empty string:

```
SELECT
    CONVERT(CHAR(10), HireDate, 2),
    VacationHours,
    REPLACE(LoginId, 'adventure-works\', '')
FROM HumanResources.Employee
```

7. Before concatenating the information, you need to convert VacationHours into a string:

```
SELECT
    CONVERT(CHAR(10), HireDate, 2),
    STR(VacationHours),
    REPLACE(LoginId, 'adventure-works\', '')
FROM HumanResources.Employee
```

8. Now you can concatenate the data by using the concatenation operator (+):

```
SELECT
    CONVERT(CHAR(10), HireDate, 2) + ', ' +
    STR(VacationHours) + ', ' +
    REPLACE(LoginId, 'adventure-works\', '')
FROM HumanResources.Employee
```

9. Finally, you apply the column alias:

```
SELECT
    CONVERT(CHAR(10), HireDate, 2) + ', ' +
    STR(VacationHours) + ', ' +
    REPLACE(LoginId, 'adventure-works\', '') AS EmpData
FROM HumanResources.Employee
```

Lesson Summary

- Use system functions and UDFs to format your data for more useful query output.

- UDTs can expose methods and properties to make data formatting much easier.

- Use column aliases to provide better column names for your data consumers.

Lesson Review

The following questions are intended to reinforce key information presented in this lesson. The questions are also available on the companion CD if you prefer to review them in electronic form.

NOTE **Answers**

Answers to these questions and explanations of why each answer choice is right or wrong are located in the "Answers" section at the end of this book.

1. Which of the following functions can you use to convert integers into strings? (Choose all that apply.)

    A. *STR*

    B. *STUFF*

    C. *CAST*

    D. *CONVERT*

2. Which of the following methods is exposed by all CLR UDTs for returning the UDT data as a string?

    A. *GetString*

    B. *ConvertString*

    C. *ToString*

    D. *MakeString*

3. Which keyword is used to create a column alias?

    A. *STR*

    B. *AS*

    C. *FROM*

    D. *COLUMN*

Lesson 3: Modifying Data

In addition to knowing how to select and format data, database developers need to understand how to modify the data in the database. In this lesson, you will learn some of the best practices to consider when writing data-modification code so that you can create efficient, maintainable queries.

After this lesson, you will be able to:

- Understand cursors.
- Create local and global temporary tables.
- Use the SELECT INTO command.

Estimated lesson time: 20 minutes

Understanding Cursors

One of the most important foundations of quality Transact-SQL programming is an understanding of how to think in terms of sets instead of procedurally. In almost every case, data access inside of SQL Server can be performed using set-based techniques—that is, using standard *SELECT* statements. Even when working with very complex formatting requirements, this holds true.

However, you can develop nonset-based SQL Server code by using cursors. Cursors operate by iterating through a data set one row at a time, letting the developer operate on individual rows rather than on sets of data.

SQL Server supports three types of cursors: static, keyset, and dynamic. Each uses more resources than the last to detect changes to the data being queried. Static cursors use few resources because they do not detect any changes during processing. Keyset cursors detect some changes and, therefore, use more resources. Dynamic cursors detect all changes to the underlying data and are the most resource-intensive.

SQL Server's query optimizer cannot generate query plans for cursors, so they are often much slower than set-based queries. Add to this the fact that keyset and dynamic cursors often must hold locks on underlying rows for the entire scope of the cursor, and it is not hard to see why cursors are considered the SQL of last resort. The combination of slow processing and holding locks during the entire course of that processing can result in extreme blocking issues, decreasing overall database performance and scalability.

MORE INFO Locks

If you're not familiar with the SQL Server locking mechanisms, see the "Locking in the Database Engine" topic in SQL Server 2005 Books Online.

BEST PRACTICES Try to steer clear of cursors

Avoid cursors whenever possible. Ideally, cursors should be used only for administrative purposes when a set-based solution is impossible to implement.

> ## Quick Check
> ■ Which cursor types can detect changes to the underlying data?
>
> ## Quick Check Answer
> ■ Keyset and dynamic cursors can detect changes to the underlying data.

Creating Local and Global Temporary Tables

When working with complex queries, it is often helpful to break up the logic into smaller, more manageable chunks. Breaking the logic can help simplify queries and stored procedures, especially when iterative logic is necessary. It can also help performance in many cases. If you need to apply the results of a complex query to other queries, it is often cheaper to cache the results of the query in a temporary table and reuse them than to reexecute the complex query each time.

You can cache intermediate results in special tables called *temporary tables*. These tables act just like other SQL Server tables, but they are actually created in the *tempdb* system database. When you are finished using temporary tables, you do not have to drop them; they are automatically dropped when the connection using them is closed.

SQL Server has two types of temporary tables: local and global. Local temporary tables are visible only to the connection that created them. Global temporary tables, on the other hand, are visible to all connections.

Create a local temporary table by using the *CREATE TABLE* command and prefixing the table name with #:

```
CREATE TABLE #LocalTempTable
(
    Column1 INT,
    Column2 VARCHAR(20)
)
```

Create global temporary tables by prefixing the table name with ##:

```
CREATE TABLE ##GlobalTempTable
(
    Column1 INT,
    Column2 VARCHAR(20)
)
```

Using the SELECT INTO Command

In many situations, developers need to create tables that have the same column definition as a table that already exists. Or developers might need to create a table based on the results of a query. In either case, you can use the *SELECT INTO* command to create a new table.

By adding the *INTO* clause to a *SELECT* statement after the *SELECT* list, SQL Server creates the table name in the *INTO* clause, using the results of the *SELECT*, if the table does not already exist. If the table already exists, SQL Server returns an exception.

To create a table that has the same columns and data as another table already in the system, use *SELECT INTO* with *SELECT **. The following query creates a table called *Address2* from the data in the *Address* table:

```
SELECT *
INTO Address2
FROM Person.Address
```

SELECT INTO is commonly used in stored procedures to create local temporary tables. Instead of using the *CREATE TABLE* syntax and inserting the data into the temporary table, developers can use the *SELECT INTO* command to do both operations. The following query creates a local temporary table called *#FemaleEmployees* that contains all employee IDs for female employees in the *Employee* table:

```
SELECT EmployeeId
INTO #FemaleEmployees
FROM HumanResources.Employee
WHERE Gender = 'F'
```

Quick Check

■ Should you use *SELECT INTO* to insert data into tables that already exist?

Quick Check Answer

■ No. If you use *SELECT INTO*, and the target table already exists, an error will be returned.

PRACTICE **Create and Use a Temporary Table**

In this practice, you will create a temporary table and use it to join to another table.

Assume that you need to find all addresses for salaried employees.

1. If necessary, open SSMS and connect to your SQL Server.

2. Open a new query window and select *AdventureWorks* as the active database.

3. Type the following query and execute it:

```
SELECT EmployeeId
FROM HumanResources.Employee
WHERE SalariedFlag = 1
```

4. This query returns all employee IDs for salaried employees. To create a temporary table with this data, you can use *SELECT INTO*. Type and execute the following query:

```
SELECT EmployeeId
INTO #SalariedEmployees
FROM HumanResources.Employee
WHERE SalariedFlag = 1
```

5. A local temporary table called *#SalariedEmployees* now exists. You can see the employee IDs in the table by using the following query:

```
SELECT EmployeeId
FROM #SalariedEmployees
```

6. The following query returns all addresses from the *EmployeeAddress* table:

```
SELECT *
FROM HumanResources.EmployeeAddress
```

7. Add a *WHERE* clause to the query that includes a noncorrelated subquery using the *IN* predicate:

```
SELECT *
FROM HumanResources.EmployeeAddress
WHERE EmployeeId IN
(
    SELECT EmployeeId
    FROM #SalariedEmployees
)
```

8. Execute the query.

Lesson Summary

- Use cursors as sparingly as possible, preferably only for administrative tasks.

- Temporary tables can make it easier to express complex logic in a maintainable way and improve performance, letting you cache intermediate results.

- *SELECT INTO* lets you create tables that have the same column definition as a table that already exists or to create a table based on the results of a query.

Lesson Review

The following questions are intended to reinforce key information presented in this lesson. The questions are also available on the companion CD if you prefer to review them in electronic form.

NOTE Answers

Answers to these questions and explanations of why each answer choice is right or wrong are located in the "Answers" section at the end of this book.

---

1. What are the three types of cursors available in SQL Server? (Choose all that apply.)

    A. Static

    B. Firehose

    C. Dynamic

    D. Keyset

2. Which of the following syntaxes will create a global temporary table?

    A. *CREATE TABLE #TableName (Column INT)*

    B. *CREATE TABLE ##TableName (Column INT)*

    C. *DECLARE @TableName TABLE (Column INT)*

    D. *SELECT CONVERT (INT, NULL) INTO #TableName*

3. Which situations can you use *SELECT INTO* for? (Choose all that apply.)

    A. Create a new local temporary table.

    B. Create a new permanent table.

    C. Insert data into an existing global temporary table.

    D. Create a new global temporary table.

Lesson 4: Working with Transactions

When modifying data, it's important to ensure that only correct data gets written to the database. By controlling transactions and handling errors, developers can make sure that if problems do occur when modifying data, incorrect data can be selectively kept out of the database.

After this lesson, you will be able to:

■ Begin and commit or roll back transactions.

■ Programmatically handle errors.

Estimated lesson time: 20 minutes

Beginning and Committing or Rolling Back Transactions

When modifying data in the database, one of the most important things developers need to consider is how best to keep the data in a consistent state. Consistent state means that all data in the database should be correct at all times—incorrect data must be removed or, better yet, not inserted at all.

Transactions are the primary mechanism by which you can programmatically enforce data consistency. When you begin a transaction, any data changes you make are, by default, visible only to your connection. Other connections reading the data cannot see the changes you make and have to wait until you either commit the transaction—thereby saving the changes to the database—or roll it back, thereby removing the changes and restoring the data to the state it was in before the transaction started.

The basic process to use when working with transactions is as follows:

1. Start transactions by using the *BEGIN TRANSACTION* command.

2. After you start a transaction by using *BEGIN TRANSACTION*, the transaction will encompass all data modifications made by your connection, including inserts, updates, and deletes.

3. The transaction ends only when you either commit it or roll it back.

You can commit a transaction, saving the changes, by using the *COMMIT TRANSAC-TION* command. You roll back a transaction by using the *ROLLBACK TRANSACTION* command. If at any time after the start of the transaction you detect that a problem has occurred, you can use *ROLLBACK TRANSACTION* to return the data to its original state.

BEST PRACTICES Use transactions for testing

Transactions can be very useful if you're testing code that modifies data in the database. Begin a transaction before running your code, and then roll back the transaction when you're done testing. Your data will be in the same state it was in when you started.

Programmatically Handle Errors

The ability to begin transactions and selectively commit them or roll them back is not quite enough to be able to effectively deal with problems when they occur. The other necessary component is the ability to programmatically detect and handle errors.

You perform error checking in Transact-SQL by using the *TRY* and *CATCH* control-of-flow statements. *TRY* defines a block within which you place code that might cause an error. If any of the code in the block causes an error, processing immediately halts, and the code in the *CATCH* block is run. The following code shows the basic *TRY/ CATCH* format:

```
BEGIN TRY
  --Put error-prone code here
END TRY
BEGIN CATCH
  --Put error handling code here
END CATCH
```

Within the *CATCH* block, you can determine what caused the error and get information about the error by using the Transact-SQL error handling system functions. The most commonly used of these functions are *ERROR_NUMBER* and *ERROR_MESSAGE*, which return the error number for the error and the text description for the error, respectively. Other available functions include *ERROR_LINE*, *ERROR_SEVERITY*, and *ERROR_STATE*. By using these functions in the *CATCH* block, you can determine whether you need to use *ROLLBACK* to roll back your transaction.

Quick Check
- Into which block should you place code that might cause an error?

Quick Check Answer
- Code that might cause an error should be put into the *TRY* block.

PRACTICE **Seeing the Effect of Transactions**

In this practice, you will see how transactions affect other connections.

1. If necessary, open SSMS and connect to your SQL Server.

2. Open a new query window and select *AdventureWorks* as the active database.

3. Type the following query and execute it:

   ```
   BEGIN TRANSACTION
   ```

4. A transaction starts. Any data modification you do will not be visible to other connections.

5. Type the following query and execute it:

   ```
   UPDATE HumanResources.Employee
   SET Title = 'TestTitle'
   WHERE EmployeeId = 150
   ```

6. To verify the modification, type the following query and execute it:

   ```
   SELECT Title
   FROM HumanResources.Employee
   WHERE EmployeeId = 150
   ```

7. "TestTitle" should be returned. You updated the data, but it is visible only to your connection.

8. Open a new query window and select *AdventureWorks* as the active database.

9. In the new window, type the following query and execute it:

   ```
   SELECT Title
   FROM HumanResources.Employee
   WHERE EmployeeId = 150
   ```

10. The query does not return because it is waiting for the transaction started in the other window. Go back to the first window, type the following query, and execute it:

    ```
    ROLLBACK
    ```

11. The data modification has now been rolled back. Return to the second window, and notice that the query will have completed, returning the data "Network Manager".

Lesson Summary

- Use transactions to help ensure that inconsistent data does not get written to the database.
- Use *TRY* and *CATCH* blocks for error handling and to gain better control over transactions.

Lesson Review

The following questions are intended to reinforce key information presented in this lesson. The questions are also available on the companion CD if you prefer to review them in electronic form.

NOTE Answers

Answers to these questions and explanations of why each answer choice is right or wrong are located in the "Answers" section at the end of the book.

---

1. Which command is used to save the data modified in a transaction so that other connections can see it?

   A. *DELETE FROM TRANSACTION*

   B. *COMMIT TRANSACTION*

   C. *UPDATE TRANSACTION*

   D. *SELECT TRANSACTION*

2. Which function can be used inside the *CATCH* block to find out the number for the error that occurred?

   A. *ERROR_STATE*

   B. *ERROR_MESSAGE*

   C. *ERROR_SEVERITY*

   D. *ERROR_NUMBER*

Chapter Review

To further practice and reinforce the skills you learned in this chapter, you can

- Review the chapter summary.
- Review the list of key terms introduced in this chapter.
- Complete the case scenarios. These scenarios set up real-world situations involving the topics of this chapter and ask you to create solutions.
- Complete the suggested practices.
- Take a practice test.

Chapter Summary

- To improve query performance, don't include extraneous tables or columns in queries.
- Use correlated subqueries or inner joins to return information from other tables with matching data. Use noncorrelated subqueries or outer joins when other tables have nonmatching data.
- Use the FTS functions to efficiently search text data.
- Use system functions, UDFs, and aggregate functions to help format output data for business requirements.
- Avoid cursors; instead, use temporary tables if you need to break up query logic.
- Use transactions and error handling code to keep inconsistent data out of the database.

Key Terms

Do you know what these key terms mean? You can check your answers by looking up the terms in the glossary at the end of the book.

- aggregate function
- case expression
- cross-tabulation
- derived table
- inner join
- outer join
- subquery
- temporary table

Case Scenarios

In the following case scenarios, you will apply what you've learned in this chapter. You can find answers to these questions in the "Answers" section at the end of this book.

Case Scenario 1: Database-Backed Authoring Application

Proseware, a textbook organization in San Francisco, CA, is writing a new database-backed application for authors to use to submit text and various types of changes.

The application must take special care to ensure that only well-formed data gets into the database. The database developers have written a series of data-validation stored procedures that throw exceptions if there are issues.

Management requires a variety of reports, including the number of submissions by each author and a quarterly report that shows the number of submissions by each author every week for the quarter.

1. How should Proseware write data-insertion code to make sure that no invalid data is stored in the database?

2. What aggregate function can be used to determine how many submissions each author had?

3. How should the quarterly report be created?

Case Scenario 2: Banking Corporation

Northwind Partners is a new banking organization in the southeastern United States. The firm has decided to write its own custom back-end software for running most of its business.

Because the software deals with financial data, it is imperative that errors do not affect data modifications. Should an error occur, any modification already made should be backed out, and the error should be logged.

An important part of the application will be used by the bank's customer service department when creating new accounts. The customer service agents need to be able to search by name or parts of addresses and find whether the customer has a preexisting account. Because the agents sometimes make typos, and the bank wants to reduce the probability of mistakes, the system must do its best to match existing data, even if it's slightly different than what was typed in.

1. Northwind Partners needs to write code to transfer funds between accounts. How can this code be written to ensure that data modifications can be backed out in the event of a problem?

2. How can Northwind Partners make sure that all errors that occur are logged?

3. How should the search functionality be written so that slight differences in input text still match the correct preexisting customer data?

Suggested Practices

To help you successfully master the exam objectives presented in this chapter, complete the following practice tasks.

Writing Queries Against the Sales Schema of the AdventureWorks Database

For this task, write the following queries in order to practice using various query techniques.

Practice 1

- Write a query that uses an aggregate function to return the total sales per customer from the *SalesOrderHeader* table.

Practice 2

- Rewrite the query from Practice 1 to return customers' names along with the aggregated data. Make sure that customers who have not made purchases are also included in the output results.

Practice 3

- Rewrite the query from Practice 2 as many different ways as you can, making sure that it always returns the same results. Try using different combinations of subqueries and join types.

- You can store the results of different queries you come up with in temporary tables so that you can verify that the results are the same.

Take a Practice Test

The practice tests on this book's companion CD offer many options. For example, you can test yourself on just the content covered in this chapter, or you can test yourself on all the 70-431 certification exam content. You can set up the test so that it closely simulates the experience of taking a certification exam, or you can set it up in study mode so that you can look at the correct answers and explanations after you answer each question.

MORE INFO   Practice tests

For details about all the practice test options available, see the section titled "How to Use the Practice Tests" in this book's Introduction.

Chapter 6
Creating Partitions

Microsoft SQL Server 2005 introduces a new functionality called partitioning. Partitioning lets you split a table across multiple storage units called filegroups, based on a user specification. Database administrators (DBAs) have been able to separate tables and even indexes onto specific filegroups since SQL Server 7.0, so what is so important about partitions?

By using partitions, you can place a subset of a table or index on a designated filegroup. This capability lets you separate specific pieces of a table or index onto individual filegroups and effectively manage file input/output (I/O) for volatile tables. Additionally, as organizations collect more and more data and keep it longer for analysis purposes, tables continue to grow larger and larger. Managing such massive tables can be difficult. With partitioning, however, you can segregate data within a table based on age, which lets you target backups at only a subset of a table. The final and most important reason for partitions is that they enable you to easily manage archival routines and data-loading operations.

To partition a table or index, you perform the following tasks:

1. Create a partition function.
2. Create a partition scheme mapped to a partition function.
3. Create the table or index on the partition scheme.

This chapter walks you through these tasks and shows you how to query and manage partitions.

Exam objectives in this chapter:
-   Implement partitions.

Lessons in this chapter:

Before You Begin

To complete the lessons in this chapter, you must have

- SQL Server 2005 installed

Real World

Michael Hotek

As I was writing this chapter, I received an instant message from one of the mentors within our company: Solid Quality Learning. He was working with a customer on a very large data warehouse and running into problems with the daily data-load operations.

The table contained millions of rows of data. Each day, operations would load the most recent set of rows to the table and remove data older than 90 days. Because each operation involved hundreds of thousands or millions of rows, each was a reasonably challenging operation but nothing that using regular insert and delete processes couldn't handle.

The real challenge was that the table had a large number of indexes. The customer couldn't drop the indexes for the insert operation because re-creating them would cause several hours of downtime on the table. (The company wasn't aware of the *ONLINE* option for creating indexes.) Loading the data into the table with the indexes in place required hours, with much of that time spent in index maintenance that also caused severe blocking. Archiving data older than 90 days caused similar problems.

If only there were a way to load this data into the table without incurring any of the index maintenance overhead and then incrementally build the portion of the index for the new data. With SQL Server 2005, there is.

SQL Server 2005 introduces a feature called table partitioning. By using this feature, regardless of the number of rows inserted, this company could add data to the operational table in less than one second without requiring indexes to be rebuilt or causing any contention. The same process could be applied to archiving the data, which would allow the company to remove as many rows as it wants in less than a second, also without requiring indexes to be rebuilt or incurring any contention. How does this feature work? Read Lesson 5, "Managing Partitions," in this chapter to find out.

NOTE   Partitioning and SQL Server Management Studio (SSMS)

Partitioning is one SQL Server 2005 feature that does not have a graphical user interface (GUI) in SSMS. You must use code to perform all operations related to partitions.

Lesson 1: Creating a Partition Function

A *partition function* is a stand-alone object in the database that defines the boundary points for partitioning data. Creating a partition function is the first step of partitioning a table, index, or indexed view. These are the only objects that you can partition because they are the only objects that store data in a database. In this lesson, you will see how to create a partition function to define the boundary points for partitioning data.

After this lesson, you will be able to:

■ Create a partition function.

Estimated lesson time: 20 minutes

How to Create a Partition Function

You use the *CREATE PARTITION FUNCTION* Transact-SQL command to create a partition function. The general syntax for this command is as follows:

```
CREATE PARTITION FUNCTION partition_function_name ( input_parameter_type )
AS RANGE [ LEFT | RIGHT ]
FOR VALUES ( [ boundary_value [ ,...n ] ] ) [ ; ]
```

You first give the partition function a name that conforms to the rules for object identifiers. Then you must specify a data type for the input parameter. You can use any data type except *text, ntext, varchar(max), image, xml, timestamp, nvarchar(max), varbinary(max)*, Transact-SQL user-defined data types (UDTs), and common language runtime (CLR) data types.

Range partitioning is the only type of partitioning that SQL Server 2005 supports. In the command's *RANGE* clause, you specify a value of either *RIGHT* or *LEFT* to specify which partition a boundary point value belongs in. And in the *VALUES* clause, you specify the list of boundary points for the partition function.

To explain how to use this command, let's look at the following example:

```
CREATE PARTITION FUNCTION partfunc (int) AS
RANGE LEFT FOR VALUES (1000, 2000, 3000, 4000, 5000);
```

This command creates a partition function named *partfunc* that is applied to values of data type *integer*. This means that you cannot apply the function to columns that either are not defined as an *integer* data type or are not implicitly converted to an *integer* data type.

The *RANGE LEFT* clause in the example specifies that each boundary point defined for the function resides in the left-hand partition. The *VALUES* clause defines the boundary points for the partitions. A partition function always maps the entire range of allowed values without any holes, so every possible value is always defined to a specific partition. The partition function *partfunc* defines six partitions, as Table 6-1 shows.

Table 6-1   Partition Function *partfunc*'s Six Partitions

Partition ID	Range of Values
1	−infinity to 1,000
2	1,001 to 2,000
3	2,001 to 3,000
4	3,001 to 4,000
5	4,001 to 5,000
6	5,001 to +infinity

If you defined the partition function as *RANGE RIGHT* instead of *RANGE LEFT*, the values would map as shown in Table 6-2.

Table 6-2   Partition Values If Partition Function Were Defined as *RANGE RIGHT*

Partition ID	Range of Values
1	−infinity to 999
2	1,000 to 1,999
3	2,000 to 2,999
4	3,000 to 3,999
5	4,000 to 4,999
6	5,000 to +infinity

Note that a partition function does not do the following:

- Specify a table, index, or indexed view
- Specify a filegroup
- Reference physical data of any kind

The partition scheme and table or index creation statement uses a stand-alone database object to implement partitioning.

Quick Check

1. What does the *RANGE* clause of the *CREATE PARTITION FUNCTION* command define?

2. What does the *VALUES* clause of the *CREATE PARTITION FUNCTION* command define?

Quick Check Answers

1. The *RANGE* clause specifies the partition that boundary values belong to.

2. The *VALUES* clause defines the boundary points for the partition function.

PRACTICE Create a Partition Function

In this practice, you will create a partition function to use in subsequent practices. To simplify this, we use a test database.

1. Launch SSMS, connect to your instance, and open a new query window.

2. If you have not already created a directory called C:\test, create it now.

3. Create a new database called *partitiontest* by using the following script:

```
USE master
GO
CREATE DATABASE partitiontest
ON PRIMARY
( NAME = db_dat,
    FILENAME = 'c:\test\db.mdf',
    SIZE = 2MB),
FILEGROUP FG1
( NAME = FG1_dat,
    FILENAME = 'c:\test\FG1.ndf',
    SIZE = 2MB),
FILEGROUP FG2
( NAME = FG2_dat,
    FILENAME = 'c:\test\FG2.ndf',
    SIZE = 2MB),
```

```
FILEGROUP FG3
( NAME = FG3_dat,
    FILENAME = 'c:\test\FG3.ndf',
    SIZE = 2MB),
FILEGROUP FG4
( NAME = FG4_dat,
    FILENAME = 'c:\test\FG4.ndf',
    SIZE = 2MB)
LOG ON
( NAME = db_log,
    FILENAME = 'c:\test\log.ndf',
    SIZE = 2MB,
    FILEGROWTH = 10% );
GO
USE partitiontest
GO
```

4. Create a partition function by using the following command:

```
CREATE PARTITION FUNCTION partfunc (int) AS
RANGE LEFT FOR VALUES (1000, 2000)
GO
```

5. View the results of executing this command by executing the following query:

```
SELECT * FROM sys.partition_range_values;
```

Lesson Summary

- Defining a partition function is the first step of partitioning a table, index, or indexed view.

- Partition functions are stand-alone objects that define the boundary points that are used to partition data.

- The *CREATE PARTITION FUNCTION* statement's *RANGE* clause specifies the partition that boundary values belong to, and the *VALUES* clause defines the boundary points for the partition function.

Lesson Review

The following questions are intended to reinforce key information presented in this lesson. The questions are also available on the companion CD if you prefer to review them in electronic form.

NOTE Answers

Answers to these questions and explanations of why each answer choice is right or wrong are located in the "Answers" section at the end of the book.

1. What does a partition function define?

   A. Boundary points for a partition

   B. Physical storage for a partition

   C. A rowset that returns the values in a partition

   D. The number of the partition containing a specified value

Lesson 2: Creating a Partition Scheme

The second step of partitioning a table, index, or indexed view is creating a partition scheme. The *partition scheme* defines the physical storage structures, or filegroups, that will be used with a specific partition function. In this lesson, you will see how to create a partition scheme that maps partitions to filegroups.

After this lesson, you will be able to:

■ Create a partition function.

Estimated lesson time: 20 minutes

How to Create a Partition Scheme

You use the *CREATE PARTITION SCHEME* Transact-SQL command to create a partition scheme. The general syntax for this command is as follows:

```
CREATE PARTITION SCHEME partition_scheme_name
AS PARTITION partition_function_name
TO ( { file_group_name | [ PRIMARY ] } [ ,...n ] )[ ; ]
```

You begin by naming your partition scheme according to the rules for object identifiers. You then use the *PARTITION* clause to specify the name of the partition function that will be mapped to this partition scheme.

In the command's *TO* clause, you specify the list of filegroups that define the on-disk storage for any data using the partition scheme. Any filegroups you specify in this clause must already be added to the database, must have at least one file assigned to them, and must not be marked read-only.

The following example shows how to use the command to define a partition scheme called *partscheme*:

```
CREATE PARTITION SCHEME partscheme AS
PARTITION partfunc TO
([FG1], [FG2], [FG3], [FG4], [FG5], [FG6])
GO
```

Notice that we still have not specified a table, index, or indexed view or referenced any other object in the database with the exception of the partition function. A partition scheme simply specifies a name for a physical storage structure.

How does this partition scheme work with the partition function from Lesson 1? The partition function *partfunc* had six partitions. Based on the partition scheme definition, SQL Server stores any values that reside in Partition 1 in FG1, values in Partition 2 in FG2, values in Partition 3 in FG3, and so on. So by carefully designing your partition functions and partition schemes, you can determine the exact set of data within a table, index, or indexed view that resides within a particular filegroup.

Quick Check

1. What does a partition scheme define?

2. What are the requirements for creating a partition scheme?

Quick Check Answers

1. A partition scheme defines a physical storage structure composed of one or more filegroups.

2. The filegroups defined in the partition scheme must already be part of the database, must have a file assigned to them, and must not be marked read-only.

PRACTICE **Create a Partition Scheme**

In this practice, you create the partition scheme for the partition function you created in the practice of Lesson 1.

1. If necessary, launch SSMS, connect to your instance, open a new query window, and change the context to the *partitiontest* database.

2. Create a partition scheme by executing the following command:

```
CREATE PARTITION SCHEME partscheme AS
PARTITION partfunc TO
([FG1], [FG2], [FG3]);
```

3. View the results of executing the command by running the following query:

```
SELECT * FROM sys.partition_schemes;
```

Lesson Summary

- A partition scheme maps a partition function to a physical storage structure.

- Any object that uses the partition function will store its data within the associated partition scheme.

Lesson Review

The following questions are intended to reinforce key information presented in this lesson. The questions are also available on the companion CD if you prefer to review them in electronic form.

NOTE Answers

Answers to these questions and explanations of why each answer choice is right or wrong are located in the "Answers" section at the end of the book.

---

1. What does a partition scheme define?

    A. Boundary points for a partition

    B. Physical storage for a partition

    C. A rowset that returns the values in a partition

    D. The number of the partition containing a specified value

Lesson 3: Partitioning Tables and Indexes

After you create a partition function and a partition scheme, you are ready to partition a table, index, or indexed view. In this lesson, you learn how to partition a table as you create the table, how to partition an index as you create the index, and how to partition an existing table or index.

> **After this lesson, you will be able to:**
> - Specify a partition scheme when creating a table.
> - Specify a partition scheme when creating an index.
>
> **Estimated lesson time: 20 minutes**

Creating a Partitioned Table, Index, or Indexed View

To create a partitioned table or index, you use the same syntax as when you create a regular table or index. Partitioning an indexed view is simply a matter of partitioning the index for the view. The general syntax of the *CREATE TABLE* Transact-SQL command is as follows:

```
CREATE TABLE
    [ database_name . [ schema_name ] . | schema_name . ] table_name
        ( { <column_definition> | <computed_column_definition> }
        [ <table_constraint> ] [ ,...n ] )
    [ ON { partition_scheme_name ( partition_column_name ) | filegroup
        | "default" } ]
    [ { TEXTIMAGE_ON { filegroup | "default" } ] [ ; ]
```

The general syntax of the *CREATE INDEX* Transact-SQL command is as follows:

```
CREATE [ UNIQUE ] [ CLUSTERED | NONCLUSTERED ] INDEX index_name
    ON <object> ( column [ ASC | DESC ] [ ,...n ] )
    [ INCLUDE ( column_name [ ,...n ] ) ]
    [ WITH ( <relational_index_option> [ ,...n ] ) ]
    [ ON { partition_scheme_name ( column_name )
        | filegroup_name | default } ][ ; ]
```

The important partition-related clause in each command is the *ON* clause. To partition a table or index, instead of specifying a filegroup for the *ON* clause, you specify a partition scheme.

The following code example shows the *CREATE PARTITION FUNCTION*, *CREATE PARTITION SCHEME*, and *CREATE TABLE* statements you would use to partition the *CustomerAddress* table:

```
CREATE PARTITION FUNCTION partfunc (int) AS
RANGE LEFT FOR VALUES (1000, 2000, 3000, 4000, 5000);
```

```
GO

CREATE PARTITION SCHEME partscheme AS
PARTITION partfunc TO
([FG1], [FG2], [FG3], [FG4], [FG5], [FG6])
GO

CREATE TABLE dbo.CustomerAddress
(CustomerAddressID        int          IDENTITY(1,1) PRIMARY KEY CLUSTERED,
AddressTypeID             tinyint      NOT NULL,
PrimaryAddressFlag        bit          NOT NULL,
AddressLine1              varchar(30)  NOT NULL,
AddressLine2              varchar(30)  NULL,
AddressLine3              varchar(30)  NULL,
City                      varchar(50)  NOT NULL,
StateProvinceID           int          NULL,
PostalCode                char(10)     NULL,
CountryID                 int          NULL)
ON partscheme(CustomerAddressID);
```

This example does the following:

- Creates a partition function called *partfunc*
- Creates a partition scheme called *partscheme*
- Creates the *dbo.CustomerAddress* table with the specified definition
- Stores the table on the partition scheme *partscheme*
- Uses the CustomerAddressID column in the table to determine which rows in the table belong within a given partition

As data is added to the table, any rows with a CustomerAddressID of 1,000 or less will fall into Partition 1 and be stored on FG1, addresses with an ID of 1,001 to 2,000 will fall into Partition 2 and be stored on FG2, and so on.

Partitioned Indexes and Included Columns

The following example shows how to create a partitioned index on the same table:

```
CREATE NONCLUSTERED INDEX idx_CustomerAddress_City ON dbo.CustomerAddress(City)
ON partscheme(CustomerAddressID);
```

The interesting piece of syntax here is that the index is defined on the City column. However, the index is partitioned by the CustomerAddressID column, which does not exist in the index definition. Partitioning takes advantage of the included columns feature that Chapter 4, "Creating Indexes," discusses. With the included columns feature, any columns that make up the clustered index are automatically migrated into any index created against the table. This lets you partition the indexes the same way you partition the table. In Lesson 5 of this chapter, we will discuss why this is important.

When you create this index, SQL Server stores the portion of the index that corresponds to a CustomerAddressID less than or equal to 1,000 in FG1, stores the portion from 1,001 to 2,000 in FG2, and so on.

Partitioning an Existing Table or Index

You can partition an existing table or index without dropping and re-creating the table or index. Instead, if you drop a clustered index and re-create it on another filegroup, SQL Server moves the entire contents of the table into the same filegroup as the clustered index.

You can use this process to partition a table or index that already exists by performing the following steps:

1. Create a partition function.
2. Create a partition scheme.
3. Drop the existing clustered index.
4. Re-create the clustered index on the partition scheme.

By following this process, the table is automatically partitioned according to the partition scheme that the clustered index is placed on, using the partition function that is mapped to the partition scheme. The clustering key is automatically migrated into each nonclustered index as an included column, and each nonclustered index is partitioned the same way as the table.

You can partition each nonclustered index by using a different partition function and scheme than the table. However, you cannot partition the clustered index differently from the table.

Quick Check
- Which clause do you use to partition a table or index?

Quick Check Answer
- You use the *ON* clause of the *CREATE TABLE* or *CREATE INDEX* command to partition tables and indexes, respectively. Instead of specifying a filegroup for this clause, you specify a partition scheme.

PRACTICE **Create a Partitioned Table**

In this practice, you create a partitioned table on the partition scheme you created in Lesson 2.

1. If necessary, launch SSMS, connect to your instance, open a new query window, and change the context to the *partitiontest* database.

2. Create a partitioned test table by executing the following code, which specifies the partition scheme *partscheme* in the *ON* clause:

```
CREATE TABLE dbo.t1 (
   id INT
   , v CHAR(1000) DEFAULT 'aaaa',
   CONSTRAINT ci_t1_id PRIMARY KEY CLUSTERED (id))
    ON partscheme(id);
```

3. View the results of executing this command by running the following query:

```
SELECT * FROM sys.partitions
WHERE object_id = OBJECT_ID('dbo.t1');
```

4. Next, add some rows of data to the table by executing the following batch:

```
SET NOCOUNT ON
DECLARE @i INT
SET @i=10
WHILE @i<=3000
BEGIN
INSERT dbo.t1 (id) SELECT @i
SET @i=@i+10
END
GO
```

5. View the data in the table by executing the following query:

```
SELECT * from dbo.t1
```

6. View the state of the partitions by executing the following query:

```
SELECT * FROM sys.partitions
WHERE object_id = OBJECT_ID('dbo.t1');
```

Lesson Summary

■ You create partitioned tables and indexes by using the same commands that you use to create unpartitioned tables and indexes: *CREATE TABLE* and *CREATE INDEX*. An unpartitioned table or index specifies a filegroup in the commands' *ON* clause. A partitioned table or index specifies a partition scheme in the *ON* clause.

■ Nonclustered indexes can be partitioned using a different partition function and/or partition scheme than the table, but you must partition a clustered index the same way that you partition the table.

Lesson Review

The following questions are intended to reinforce key information presented in this lesson. The questions are also available on the companion CD if you prefer to review them in electronic form.

NOTE   Answers

Answers to these questions and explanations of why each answer choice is right or wrong are located in the "Answers" section at the end of the book.

---

1. Which objects can you partition?

    A. Tables

    B. Indexes

    C. Views

    D. Databases

Lesson 4: Querying Partitions

A nice feature of partitioning is that the process is completely hidden from developers. Data in a table is retrieved and modified in exactly the same way for both partitioned tables and nonpartitioned tables. However, you can query the internals of a partition to determine its structural elements or to restrict a result set to a particular partition. This lesson shows you how to use the *$PARTITION* function to determine the partition number that a particular value would correspond to or to restrict a query to a specific partition.

After this lesson, you will be able to:

■ Query partitions.

Estimated lesson time: 10 minutes

How to Query Partitions

You can query partitions by using a special function called *$PARTITION*. The general syntax for this function is as follows:

```
[ database_name. ] $PARTITION.partition_function_name(expression)
```

The *$PARTITION* function returns a partition number based on the column values for a particular partition function. The most common ways to use this function are the following:

■ Determine the partition number to which a particular value would correspond.

■ Restrict a query to a specific partition.

The following *SELECT* query shows how you could use the *$PARTITION* function to determine the partition number for a given value:

```
SELECT $partition.partfunc (2784) as [PartitionNum];
```

The following code example shows how to use *$PARTITION* to restrict a query to a specific partition, in this case, partition number 3:

```
SELECT * FROM dbo.CustomerAddress
WHERE $partition.partfunc (CustomerAddressID) = 3
```

> **Quick Check**
> - What does the *$PARTITION* function return?
>
> **Quick Check Answer**
> - The *$PARTITION* function returns the number of the partition correspond-
>   ing to the column values for a given partition function.

PRACTICE Query Partitions

In this practice, you use the *$PARTITION* function to return the partition number for
a given value, the number of rows in each partition that contain data, and all the rows
within a specified partition.

1. If necessary, launch SSMS, connect to your instance, open a new query window,
   and change the context to the *partitiontest* database.

2. Return the number of rows for each partition by executing the following query:

   ```
   SELECT $partition.partfunc(id) AS [PartitionNum], count(*) [NumRows]
   FROM dbo.t1 GROUP BY $partition.partfunc(id)
   ORDER BY $partition.partfunc(id);
   ```

3. Return the partition that the value 4,000 would belong to by executing the
   following query:

   ```
   SELECT $partition.partfunc(4000) as [PartitionNum];
   ```

4. Return all the rows in partition number 2 by executing the following query:

   ```
   SELECT * FROM dbo.t1
   WHERE $partition.partfunc(id)=2
   ```

5. Now, add data to the table and view the results by executing the following batch:

   ```
   SET NOCOUNT ON
   DECLARE @i INT, @max INT
   SELECT @max=MAX(id) + 10 FROM dbo.t1
   SET @i= @max
   WHILE @i<= @max + 3000 - 10
   BEGIN
   INSERT dbo.t1 (id) SELECT @i
   SET @i=@i+10
   END
   GO

   --What is the data distribution in the table now?
   SELECT $partition.partfunc(id) AS [PartitionNum], count(*) [NumRows]
   FROM dbo.t1 GROUP BY $partition.partfunc(id)
   ORDER BY $partition.partfunc(id)
   GO
   ```

NOTE   Even data distribution

SQL Server does not evenly distribute data between the partitions. The even distribution of data in the initial examples was an accident of how the data was inserted. Data is partitioned on the boundary points only. If a particular partition contains more data than another, it is because more rows match the range defined for the partition. If you want to rebalance the way data is distributed between partitions, you must manually rebalance the distribution by using the operations we will discuss in Lesson 5.

Lesson Summary

- You can use the *$PARTITION* function in a *SELECT* query to
  - ❏ Determine the partition number to which a particular value belongs.
  - ❏ Restrict queries to a specific partition number.

Lesson Review

The following questions are intended to reinforce key information presented in this lesson. The questions are also available on the companion CD if you prefer to review them in electronic form.

NOTE   Answers

Answers to these questions and explanations of why each answer choice is right or wrong are located in the "Answers" section at the end of the book.

1. What does the *$PARTITION* function define?
   A. Boundary points to a partition
   B. Physical storage for a partition
   C. A rowset that returns the values in a partition
   D. The number of the partition containing a specified value

Lesson 5: Managing Partitions

After you partition a table, index, or indexed view, data modifications cause SQL Server to place rows into the appropriate partition and hence into a specific filegroup on disk. However, partitioning is not a static process. In this lesson, you see how to manage partitions by using three operators: *SPLIT*, *MERGE*, and *SWITCH*.

> **After this lesson, you will be able to:**
> - Use the *SPLIT* or *MERGE* operator to add or remove partitions.
> - Use the *SWITCH* operator to add and remove rows from a table.
>
> **Estimated lesson time: 20 minutes**

Split and Merge

You use the *SPLIT* and *MERGE* operators with the *ALTER PARTITION FUNCTION* Transact-SQL command to introduce new boundary points or remove boundary points from a partition function, respectively. The general syntax is as follows:

```
ALTER PARTITION FUNCTION partition_function_name()
{
    SPLIT RANGE ( boundary_value )
  | MERGE RANGE ( boundary_value )
} [ ; ]
```

The following example command introduces a new boundary point to the partition function named *partfunc*:

```
ALTER PARTITION FUNCTION partfunc ()
SPLIT RANGE (6000);
```

This statement causes the number of partitions for the table to be increased by one. Any data with a value greater than 6,000 that existed in the table would be moved to the new partition. Note that this operation could cause a large number of writes as SQL Server moves the rows to a different filegroup.

The following example removes a boundary point from the partition function named *partfunc*.

```
ALTER PARTITION FUNCTION partfunc ()
MERGE RANGE (1000);
```

This statement causes the number of partitions for the table to decrease by one. Any data that existed in the partition that was removed would be combined into a single partition. This also could cause a large number of writes as SQL Server moves the rows to a different filegroup.

SWITCH

You can use the *SWITCH* operator of the *ALTER TABLE* Transact-SQL command to perform two actions:

- Add rows to a table.
- Remove rows from a table.

You can add rows to a table by using an *INSERT* statement and remove them by using a *DELETE* statement. So what is so special about the *SWITCH* operator? An *INSERT* or *DELETE* operation causes SQL Server to acquire locks on a table, which blocks other processes. If you are adding or removing a large number of rows from a table, the operation can result in severe contention and take a long time to complete.

The *SWITCH* operator, in contrast, is infinitely scalable and does not cause blocking on a table. It also lets you add or remove any number of rows in less than one second.

To understand how *SWITCH* works, you first need to understand how data is stored within SQL Server. All data is stored on a series of 8-KB pages within a database. Each table and each index has its own series of 8-KB pages, which are constructed in a doubly linked list. A doubly linked list simply means that each page points to the previous page as well as the next page within the chain (for example, page 3 points to pages 2 and 4, whereas page 4 points to pages 3 and 5).

When a table is partitioned, SQL Server splits the data structure across filegroups so that each partition contains a sequential series of pages. If you were to go into the last page within a partition and remove the entry that points to the first page in the next partition, the entire series of pages within that partition would immediately disappear from the table. At the same time, if you were to go into the last page in a table (whose next page pointer would be null, indicating that it is the last page in the table) and change the next page entry to a page in another partition, the entire series of pages in that partition would immediately become part of the table.

Remember that a *SWITCH* operation occurs between tables. Let's look at a simple example to see what happens when you perform a *SWITCH* operation. Suppose that you have a reporting application that allows queries against the orders. The table contains only the last 12 months of orders, and orders are added to this table once per month. You create two tables: *Orders* and *Orderstage*. Orders for the current month are added into the *Orderstage* table. As long as the *Orders* and *Orderstage* tables have the same definition and the same indexes, the only difference is that the data resides in two different tables. Let's say that you go to the last page of the *Orders* table and change the next page pointer to the first page in the *Orderstage* table, while also changing the first page in the *Orderstage* table to the last page in the *Orders* table. All the pages of the *Orderstage* table would immediately be associated with the *Orders* table, and the *Orderstage* table would have no pages associated with it. This is a very simple example. In practice, the process is slightly more complicated because a table must have at least one page attached to it, but this example explains what occurs.

To ensure that a *SWITCH* operation is infinitely scalable, only a metadata operation occurs when the command is executed. In other words, the operation modifies only page pointers. If SQL Server must move data during this operation, the *SWITCH* fails. This architecture places several restrictions on a *SWITCH* operation. Some of these restrictions are as follows:

- A full partition must be switched with an empty partition.
- Both tables must be aligned (that is, must use the same partition function and partition scheme).
- Both tables must have exactly the same structure for tables as well as indexes.
- The range of values in the partition being switched must not exist in the target table.

MORE INFO   *SWITCH* Requirements

For the full list of requirements for the *SWITCH* operation, see the SQL Server 2005 Books Online topic "Transferring Data Efficiently by Using Partition Switching." SQL Server 2005 Books Online is installed as part of SQL Server 2005. Updates for SQL Server 2005 Books Online are available for download at *www.microsoft.com/technet/prodtechnol/sql/2005/downloads/books.mspx*.

The general syntax for a *SWITCH* operation is as follows:

```
ALTER TABLE [ database_name . [ schema_name ] . | schema_name . ] table_name
SWITCH [ PARTITION source_partition_number_expression ]
       TO [ schema_name. ] target_table
       [ PARTITION target_partition_number_expression ] [ ; ]
```

You can find a specific example of using *SWITCH* in this lesson's practice.

> ## Quick Check
> - What are the three operations you can use to manage partitions, and what is the purpose of each?
>
> ### Quick Check Answer
> - *SPLIT* introduces a new boundary point for a partition function.
> - *MERGE* removes a boundary point for a partition function.
> - *SWITCH* exchanges partitions between two tables.

PRACTICE **Manage Partitions**

In this practice, you merge two partitions, split partitions, load data into a staging table, and use the *SWITCH* operator to merge this data into a master table.

1. If necessary, launch SSMS, connect to your instance, open a new query window, and change the context to the *partitiontest* database.

2. Combine Partitions 1 and 2 by executing the following command:

```
ALTER PARTITION FUNCTION partfunc()
MERGE RANGE (1000);
```

3. View the results of this operation by executing the following queries:

```
SELECT * FROM sys.partitions
WHERE object_id = OBJECT_ID('dbo.t1')

SELECT $partition.partfunc(id) AS [PartitionNum], count(*) [NumRows]
FROM dbo.t1 GROUP BY $partition.partfunc(id)
ORDER BY $partition.partfunc(id)
GO
```

4. Add another filegroup to the partition scheme by executing the following command, which also designates that the next partition created be assigned to this filegroup:

```
ALTER PARTITION SCHEME partscheme
NEXT USED [FG4];
```

5. Introduce a new boundary point into the partition function:

```
ALTER PARTITION FUNCTION partfunc()
SPLIT RANGE (4000);
```

6. View the results of this operation by executing the following queries:

```
SELECT * FROM sys.partitions
WHERE object_id = OBJECT_ID('dbo.t1')
```

```
SELECT $partition.partfunc(id) AS [PartitionNum], count(*) [NumRows]
FROM dbo.t1 GROUP BY $partition.partfunc(id)
ORDER BY $partition.partfunc(id)
```

7. Create a staging table and add some data to it:

```
CREATE TABLE dbo.t2 (
    id INT
    , v CHAR(1000) DEFAULT 'bbbb',
    CONSTRAINT ci_t2_id PRIMARY KEY CLUSTERED (id)
    , CONSTRAINT check_t2 CHECK (ID>6000)
    ) ON [FG3]
GO

--Insert rows into staging table t2.
SET NOCOUNT ON
DECLARE @i INT, @max INT
SELECT @max=MAX(id) + 10 FROM dbo.t1
SET @i= @max
WHILE @i<= @max + 6000 - 10
BEGIN
    INSERT dbo.t2 (id) SELECT @i
    SET @i=@i+10
END
GO
```

8. Add a new filegroup and file to the database and alter the partition scheme for this new filegroup by executing the following batch:

```
--Add a new filegroup to the database and add a file to that new filegroup.
ALTER DATABASE [partitiontest]
ADD FILEGROUP [FG5]
GO

ALTER DATABASE [partitiontest]
ADD FILE
( NAME = db5_dat,
    FILENAME = 'c:\test\FG5.ndf',
    SIZE = 2MB)
TO FILEGROUP [FG5]
GO

--Alter the partition scheme to include the newly created and empty
--filegroup just added to the database.
ALTER PARTITION SCHEME partscheme
NEXT USED [FG5];
GO
```

9. Split the range to introduce a new empty partition, as follows:

```
ALTER PARTITION FUNCTION partfunc()
SPLIT RANGE (6000);
```

10. View the partitions on the *t1* table by executing the following commands:

```
SELECT * FROM sys.partitions
WHERE object_id = OBJECT_ID('dbo.t1')

SELECT $partition.partfunc(id) AS [PartitionNum], count(*) [NumRows]
FROM dbo.t1 GROUP BY $partition.partfunc(id)
ORDER BY $partition.partfunc(id)
GO
```

11. Verify the number of rows in the two tables at this point as well as the *MIN* and *MAX* values by executing the following queries:

```
SELECT COUNT(*), MIN(id), MAX(id) FROM dbo.t2
GO
SELECT COUNT(*), MIN(id), MAX(id) FROM dbo.t1
GO
```

12. Now add the rows in *t2* to *t1* by executing the following command:

```
/*Now, instead of performing a heavy insert operation to move data from the staging
table to the warehouse table, use a partition feature to move the data in table t2
into the empty partition in table t1. This is a full data swap. At the end of this
operation, which is infinitely scalable, nearly instantaneous, and incurs ZERO locking
overhead, table t2 will be empty and table t1 will contain its original data plus the
data that was loaded into t2.*/
ALTER TABLE dbo.t2
SWITCH TO dbo.t1 PARTITION 4
GO
```

13. Verify the number of rows in the two tables at this point as well as the *MIN* and *MAX* values by executing the following queries:

```
SELECT COUNT(*), MIN(id), MAX(id) FROM dbo.t2
GO
SELECT COUNT(*), MIN(id), MAX(id) FROM dbo.t1
GO
```

Lesson Summary

- You use *SPLIT* to introduce a new boundary point into a partition function.

- You use *MERGE* to remove a boundary point from a partition function.

- The most powerful partitioning operator is *SWITCH*. As long as a table and its associated indexes are aligned, you can use *SWITCH* to either add an entire partition already populated with data to a table or to remove all the data from a table that corresponds to a particular partition. The *SWITCH* operation is infinitely scalable and does not incur any locking overhead on the table.

Lesson Review

The following questions are intended to reinforce key information presented in this lesson. The questions are also available on the companion CD if you prefer to review them in electronic form.

NOTE Answers

Answers to these questions and explanations of why each answer choice is right or wrong are located in the "Answers" section at the end of the book.

---

1. Which operator do you use to move partitions between tables?

    A. *SWITCH*

    B. *MERGE*

    C. *SPLIT*

    D. *INTERSECT*

Chapter Review

To further practice and reinforce the skills you learned in this chapter, you can

- Review the chapter summary.
- Review the list of key terms introduced in this chapter.
- Complete the case scenario. This scenario sets up a real-world situation involving the topics of this chapter and asks you to create a solution.
- Complete the suggested practices.
- Take a practice test.

Chapter Summary

- The partitioning capability of SQL Server 2005 enables you to divide the data in a table, index, or indexed view into multiple filegroups based on user-defined criteria.
- To partition a table, index, or indexed view, you perform the following tasks:
  1. Create a partition function.
  2. Create a partition scheme mapped to a partition function.
  3. Create a table or index mapped to the partition scheme.
- You can use the *$PARTITION* function to determine the number of a partition that contains a specific value or to restrict a query to a particular partition.
- To manage partitioning, SQL Server provides the following operators: *SPLIT*, to introduce a new boundary point into a partition function; *MERGE*, to remove a boundary point from a partition function, and *SWITCH*, to scalably add a set of rows to a table or remove a set of rows from a table.

Key Terms

Do you know what these key terms mean? You can check your answers by looking up the terms in the glossary at the end of the book.

- $PARTITION
- alignment
- boundary points

- MERGE
- partition function
- partition scheme
- SPLIT
- SWITCH

Case Scenario: Archiving Data

In the following case scenario, you will apply what you've learned in this chapter. You can find answers to these questions in the "Answers" section at the end of this book.

Contoso Limited, a health care company located in Bothell, WA, manages patient claims data. The company keeps claims in the online transaction processing (OLTP) database for 12 months before archiving them to a separate server used for research.

How can you design the process of archiving data from the *Claims* table in the OLTP database to the *Research* database on a separate server without causing locking contention in the table?

Suggested Practice

To help you successfully master the exam objectives presented in this chapter, complete the following task.

Partitioning Tables

- **Practice 1**   Create three tables in a database that all use the same partition function and partition scheme and that have the same structure. Name the tables *Stage*, *Main*, and *Archive*. Add data into *Main*. Using the *SPLIT*, *MERGE*, and *SWITCH* operations, remove data from *Main* and add it to *Archive*. Move data from *Archive* into *Stage*.

Take a Practice Test

The practice tests on this book's companion CD offer many options. For example, you can test yourself on just the content covered in this chapter, or you can test yourself on all the 70-431 certification exam content. You can set up the test so that it closely simulates the experience of taking a certification exam, or you can set it up in study mode so that you can look at the correct answers and explanations after you answer each question.

MORE INFO   **Practice tests**

For details about all the practice test options available, see the "How to Use the Practice Tests" section in this book's Introduction.

Chapter 7
Implementing Views

A *view* is simply a *SELECT* statement that has a name and is stored in Microsoft SQL Server. Views act as virtual tables to provide several benefits. A view gives developers a standardized way to execute queries, enabling them to write certain common queries once as views and then include the views in application code so that all applications use the same version of a query. A view can also provide a level of security by giving users access to just a subset of data contained in the base tables that the view is built over and can give users a more friendly, logical view of data in a database. In addition, a view with indexes created on it can provide dramatic performance improvements, especially for certain types of complex queries. Most views allow only read operations on underlying data, but you can also create updateable views that let users modify data via the view. This chapter shows you how to leverage the power and flexibility of views by creating regular views, updateable views, and indexed views.

Exam objectives in this chapter:
- Implement a view.
    - Create an indexed view.
    - Create an updateable view.
    - Assign permissions to a role or schema for a view.

Lessons in this chapter:

Before You Begin

To complete the lessons in this chapter, you must have

- SQL Server 2005 installed.
- A copy of the *AdventureWorks* sample database installed in the instance.

Real World

Michael Hotek

A couple of years ago, I had a two-week project with a customer who was experiencing performance issues. When I started looking into the database, I knew I was in for a big challenge. There were tens of thousands of lines of code spread among almost 2,000 stored procedures, functions, and triggers—along with about 350 tables. What really stood out at first glance were the more than 800 views in the database.

Having a large number of views in a database isn't necessarily a problem. But having more than twice as many views as tables told me that either the tables were poorly designed or the views were not being properly used. Unfortunately, in this case, it was both—but that is a story for a different day.

As I investigated, I found views that did nothing more than select a handful of columns from a single table by using a simple *WHERE* clause. After looking at about the 50th view, I discovered that something wasn't right. Cross-referencing back to the views I already looked at, I found a duplicate. Then I found another and another and another. In one instance, I found 23 views that all did the same thing.

It turns out that the developers were in a hurry to create applications and deploy new features. At some point, one of the database administrators (DBAs) dictated that all data access had to be through views because the DBA mistakenly thought that a view gave a performance improvement. So several years later, the company had hundreds of views embedded in the applications. And finding anything was so difficult that developers simply created new views whenever they needed anything, making a bad situation even worse.

Fortunately, the applications were not directly accessing tables or views; data access was through stored procedures. So the first step in the process was to wade through the stored procedure, function, and trigger code for references to duplicate views. By removing all the duplicates, we could drop more than 400 views.

We then took the second step of eliminating anything that really shouldn't have been a view in the first place. We defined unnecessary views as views that accessed only one table through a simple *WHERE* clause; views that implemented things that did not belong in a view, such as a hard-coded list of states; and views that contained simple logic that any developer should understand.

The end result of this process was a database that contained only 34 views. The only views that survived contained complex calculations or complex joins that needed to be encapsulated either to ensure consistency or to avoid a significant amount of effort in correctly constructing the query in the future.

The lesson learned by the developers was that SQL Server gives you a lot of tools to accomplish a task. But just because you can do something doesn't necessarily mean that you should. Before creating an object in a database, you have to understand how it will improve the application and be able to justify why creating the object is the best approach.

Lesson 1: Creating a View

Certain SQL Server objects are necessary or generally recommended. For example, you must have database tables to store data, and you should create certain indexes on your tables to improve performance. However, you should create views only when there is a clear advantage to having them. Views that don't have demonstrated benefits just take up space. Suppose that you need to return the name of a customer who has a credit line in excess of $10,000. A view would provide no advantage in this case because the *SELECT* statement to generate this result is simple and straightforward. However, if you need to return the name of a customer with the primary address and most recent payment, while keeping in the output all of the customers who have not made a payment, creating a view is probably useful because generating this result requires a combination of inner and outer joins to at least five different tables. In this lesson, you see how to define a view over one or more tables. You also learn why it is important to ensure that you have appropriate permissions assigned for the view and any underlying tables the view is based on.

After this lesson, you will be able to:

- Create a view.
- Assign permissions to a role or schema for a view.

Estimated lesson time: 20 minutes

How to Create a View

You use the Transact-SQL *CREATE VIEW* command to create a view over one or more tables. The syntax for the command follows:

```
CREATE VIEW [ schema_name . ] view_name [ (column [ ,...n ] ) ]
[ WITH <view_attribute> [ ,...n ] ]
AS select_statement [ ; ]
[ WITH CHECK OPTION ]

<view_attribute> ::=
{
    [ ENCRYPTION ]
    [ SCHEMABINDING ]
    [ VIEW_METADATA ]     }
```

You begin by naming your view. As with all objects, a view must have a name that meets the rules for identifiers.

The command's first *WITH* clause lets you apply three different options to the view: *ENCRYPTION, SCHEMABINDING,* and *VIEW_METADATA. ENCRYPTION* specifies that SQL Server should encrypt the definition of the view when it is stored in the database. The definition of an encrypted view is not visible to anyone, including a member of the sysadmin fixed server role. So when you encrypt a view, you must ensure that you keep the original source code somewhere because you cannot decrypt the definition.

When you specify the *SCHEMABINDING* option, you cannot drop any tables, views, or functions referenced by the view without first dropping the view.

BEST PRACTICES   **Schema binding trick**

An old trick that many DBAs use in a production environment is to create a view for each table that selects all columns in the table and specifies the *SCHEMABINDING* option. These views are never used with any application or by any user. The only purpose of the views is to prevent a DBA from accidentally dropping a table or a column within a table. This trick does not prevent a DBA from purposefully dropping a table because the DBA can also drop the view and then drop the table. But dropping an object on purpose that should not be dropped is a security issue.

The *VIEW_METADATA* option returns metadata about a view to client-side data access libraries.

You use the command's *AS* clause to specify the *SELECT* statement that defines the view. The *SELECT* statement can be of any complexity as long as the query is valid and can reference tables, views, user-defined functions (UDFs), and system functions. The only restrictions are that the view's *SELECT* statement CANNOT do the following:

■ Use the *COMPUTE* or *COMPUTE BY* clause

■ Use the *INTO* keyword

■ Use the *OPTION* clause

■ Reference a temporary table or table variable

■ Use the *ORDER BY* clause unless it also specifies the *TOP* operator

The command's last option, *WITH CHECK OPTION*, is something you use to create an updateable view. Lesson 2, "Modifying Data Through Views," covers this option.

After you have created a view, you can use it just like any table in a database. However, a view does NOT contain any data. A view is simply a *SELECT* statement that has a name associated with it. So when a view is referenced in a *SELECT* statement, the query optimizer substitutes the reference with the definition of the view in the *SELECT* statement before generating an execution plan.

For example, consider the following code:

```
CREATE VIEW v_CustomerAddress
AS
SELECT a.CustomerID, a.CustomerName, c.AddressLine1, c.AddressLine2, c.AddressLine3,
 c.City, d.StateProvince, c.PostalCode, e.Country
FROM dbo.Customer a INNER JOIN dbo.CustomerToCustomerAddress b ON a.CustomerID =
 b.CustomerID
    INNER JOIN dbo.CustomerAddress c ON b.CustomerAddressID = c.CustomerAddressID
    INNER JOIN dbo.StateProvince d ON c.StateProvinceID = d.StateProvinceID
    INNER JOIN dbo.Country e ON c.CountryID = e.CountryID;

SELECT a.CustomerName, b.CreditLine FROM v_CustomerAddress a INNER JOIN dbo.Customer b
 ON a.CustomerID = b.CustomerID;
```

The optimizer would locate the reference to the *v_CustomerAddress* view and substitute the view definition, rewriting the submitted query into a query similar to the following:

```
SELECT a.CustomerName, f.CreditLine
FROM dbo.Customer a INNER JOIN dbo.CustomerToCustomerAddress b ON a.CustomerID =
 b.CustomerID
    INNER JOIN dbo.CustomerAddress c ON b.CustomerAddressID = c.CustomerAddressID
    INNER JOIN dbo.StateProvince d ON c.StateProvinceID = d.StateProvinceID
    INNER JOIN dbo.Country e ON c.CountryID = e.CountryID
    INNER JOIN dbo.Customer f ON a.CustomerID = f.CustomerID;
```

Understanding Ownership Chains

Because a view references other objects, there is the potential for permission issues. Consider the objects and object owners that the diagram in Figure 7-1 shows.

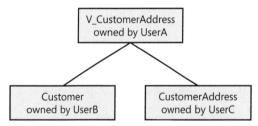

Figure 7-1   Defining an ownership chain

Let's say that *UserA* grants *SELECT* permission to *UserD* on the *v_CustomerAddress* view. Even though *UserD* has permission to execute a *SELECT* statement against the view, this user would receive an error when he attempts to use the view because the view is defined against the *Customer* and *CustomerAddress* tables, which are owned by a different user than either *UserA* or *UserD*. When the ownership across a chain of dependent objects causes an error due to insufficient permissions, you have a *broken ownership chain*.

For *UserD* to be able to execute a *SELECT* statement against the *v_CustomerAddress* view, the following has to occur:

- *UserA* grants *UserD SELECT* permission to the view.
- *UserB* grants *UserD SELECT* permission to *dbo.Customer*.
- *UserC* grants *UserD SELECT* permission to *dbo.CustomerAddress*.

MORE INFO   **Ownership chains**

For more information about *ownership chains*, see the SQL Server 2005 Books Online topic "Ownership Chains." SQL Server 2005 Books Online is installed as part of SQL Server 2005. Updates for SQL Server 2005 Books Online are available for download at *www.microsoft.com/technet/prodtechnol/sql/2005/downloads/books.mspx*.

> ## Quick Check
> - What are the restrictions on the *SELECT* statement within a view?
>
> ### Quick Check Answer
> - *COMPUTE* or *COMPUTE BY* clauses are not allowed. You cannot use the *INTO* keyword or *OPTION* clause. Temporary tables and table variables cannot be referenced. An *ORDER BY* clause cannot be specified unless the *TOP* operator is also used.

PRACTICE Create a View

In this practice, you use the database that contains the tables you created in Chapter 3, "Creating Tables, Constraints, and User-Defined Types," to create a view to return customer information for customers who live in Canada.

1. Launch SQL Server Management Studio (SSMS), connect to your instance, open a new query window, and change context to the database containing the tables you created in Chapter 3.

2. Create a view to return information for customers who live in Canada by executing the following statement:

```
CREATE VIEW v_CanadaCustomerAddress
AS
SELECT a.CustomerID, a.CustomerName, c.AddressLine1, c.AddressLine2, c.AddressLine3,
 c.City, d.StateProvince, c.PostalCode, e.Country
```

```
FROM dbo.Customer a INNER JOIN dbo.CustomerToCustomerAddress b ON a.CustomerID =
b.CustomerID
    INNER JOIN dbo.CustomerAddress c ON b.CustomerAddressID = c.CustomerAddressID
    INNER JOIN dbo.StateProvince d ON c.StateProvinceID = d.StateProvinceID
    INNER JOIN dbo.Country e ON c.CountryID = e.CountryID
WHERE e.Country = 'Canada'
    AND PrimaryAddressFlag = 1;
```

3. Construct a *SELECT* statement to verify that the view returns only customers from Canada.

Lesson Summary

- A view is simply a *SELECT* statement that you name and store in SQL Server as a sort of "virtual table" that lets you give users access to just a subset of data and that lets you improve performance, especially for complex queries.

- After it's defined, the view can be referenced in a *SELECT* statement just like a table, although it does not contain any data.

- When granting permissions to a view, you must pay careful attention to the ownership chain to ensure that the user has access to the view as well as all underlying objects that the view is built on.

Lesson Review

The following questions are intended to reinforce key information presented in this lesson. The questions are also available on the companion CD if you prefer to review them in electronic form.

NOTE Answers

Answers to these questions and explanations of why each answer choice is right or wrong are located in the "Answers" section at the end of the book.

---

1. Which of the following options can prevent a table from being dropped?

    A. *CHECK OPTION*

    B. *SCHEMABINDING*

    C. *UNION*

    D. *QUOTED_IDENTIFIER*

Lesson 2: Modifying Data Through Views

As noted previously, a view is just a named *SELECT* statement. In effect, a view is a pass-through reference to one or more base tables. Although most views provide read access to underlying data, because a view is a pass-through you can also make data modifications through it. A view that enables you to modify data is called an *updateable view*. This lesson explains how you can perform *INSERT, UPDATE, DELETE, BCP,* and *BULK INSERT* operations against a view.

After this lesson, you will be able to:

■   Create an updateable view.

Estimated lesson time: 20 minutes

Creating Updateable Views

Although you can define a view based on more than one table, SQL Server restricts any data modifications you execute through the view to a single table. In addition, all changes must directly reference columns and not derivations of a column.

Thus, you cannot modify columns that are derived through an aggregate function, such as *AVG, COUNT, SUM, MIN,* or *MAX,* or through a computation that involves other columns or operations on a column, such as *SUBSTRING.* Changes cannot reference columns generated by using operators such as *UNION, CROSSJOIN,* and *INTERSECT.* In addition, the view definition cannot contain a *GROUP BY, HAVING,* or *DISTINCT* clause. And you cannot use *TOP* when you specify *WITH CHECK OPTION.*

BEST PRACTICES   Using views to modify data

Although you can use views to insert, update, and delete data, views are almost never used for that purpose. Stored procedures are always a better option because you can more easily validate changes via stored procedures. Stored procedures are also more flexible.

In your view definition, you can include a *WHERE* clause that limits the range of rows that the view returns. However, the *WHERE* clause does not restrict the changes that users can make through the view. To restrict the changes that users can make, you use the *CREATE VIEW* command's *WITH CHECK OPTION* clause when defining the view.

Let's look at a brief example to see how the *CHECK OPTION* clause works. Suppose that you define a view that shows customers who have a credit line greater than $1,000. A user could insert a new customer who has a credit line of $500 and not cause an error. However, doing so could cause confusion because although the insert was successful, the view cannot display the inserted data, and a user might think that the data had been lost. So to restrict the changes that users can make so that the data is always visible through the view, you should define the view by using the *WITH CHECK OPTION* clause. If you define the preceding view with the *CHECK OPTION* clause, a user's attempt to insert a customer with a credit line of $1,000 or less causes an error to be returned.

You can also create triggers on a view, which are useful for performing data-modification operations. You create a special kind of trigger on views called an *INSTEAD OF* trigger. *INSTEAD OF* triggers operate exactly as you would expect: Instead of SQL Server performing the operation against the view, SQL Server executes the trigger to perform an alternative operation.

MORE INFO   *INSTEAD OF* triggers

For more information about triggers, see Chapter 9, "Creating Functions, Stored Procedures, and Triggers."

> ## Quick Check
> - Which clause should you use to make data modifications visible through the view?
>
> ### Quick Check Answer
> - The *WITH CHECK OPTION* clause places a constraint on *INSERT*, *UPDATE*, *DELETE*, *BCP*, and *BULK INSERT* statements, so the operations can occur only on the set of rows that match the criteria in the view's *WHERE* clause.

PRACTICE Create an Updateable View

In this practice, you create a view that you can use to make changes to the *Customer* table for any customer who has a credit line greater than $1,000.

1. If necessary, launch SSMS, connect to your instance, open a new query window, and change the context to the database that contains the customer tables you created in Chapter 3.

2. Create a Customer view on the *Customer* table by executing the following statement:

```
CREATE VIEW dbo.v_Customer
AS
SELECT CustomerID, CustomerName, CreditLine, AvailableCredit
FROM dbo.Customer
WHERE CreditLine > 1000
WITH CHECK OPTION;
```

3. Execute the following *INSERT* statement and observe the results:

```
INSERT INTO dbo.Customer
(CustomerName, CreditLine)
VALUES('Customer1',5000);
```

4. Execute the following *INSERT* statement and observe the results:

```
INSERT INTO dbo.v_Customer
(CustomerName, CreditLine)
VALUES('Customer2',300);
```

Lesson Summary

■ Although stored procedures are a better alternative for performing data modifications, you can use views to *INSERT, UPDATE, DELETE, BCP,* or *BULK INSERT*
   data.

■ The view is used as a pass-through to apply the changes directly to a single base
   table.

■ To constrain the changes to only the set of rows that match the view's *WHERE*
   clause, you use the *WITH CHECK OPTION* clause when creating the view.

Lesson Review

The following questions are intended to reinforce key information presented in this
lesson. The questions are also available on the companion CD if you prefer to review
them in electronic form.

NOTE Answers

Answers to these questions and explanations of why each answer choice is right or wrong are
located in the "Answers" section at the end of the book.

---

1. Which of the following options restricts changes to data to conform to the select
    criteria of a view?

    A. *SCHEMABINDING*

    B. *CHECK OPTION*

    C. *ANSI_NULLS*

    D. *QUOTED_IDENTIFIER*

Lesson 3: Creating an Indexed View

As you saw earlier in this chapter, when a query references a regular view, the query optimizer replaces the reference with the stored definition of the view before executing the *SELECT* statement. However, SQL Server still computes any joins or aggregations for the query at execution time. *Indexed views* provide a way to precalculate the result set a view returns. Using indexed views becomes valuable when the cost for SQL Server to constantly execute the query far outweighs the cost required to maintain the results of the *SELECT* statement in a view as data is modified. This lesson explains how to create an indexed view and some appropriate situations for indexed views.

After this lesson, you will be able to:

■ Create an indexed view.

Estimated lesson time: 20 minutes

Prerequisites for an Indexed View

In theory, creating an indexed view is simply a process of creating a view and then creating a clustered index on the view. In practice, the process is not so straightforward.

To create an indexed view, the base tables for the view must meet many criteria. The view then has additional restrictions. Finally, the index has even more restrictions.

MORE INFO   **Restrictions on creating an indexed view**

For details about all the requirements and restrictions for creating an indexed view, see the SQL Server 2005 Books Online topic "Creating Indexed Views."

The purpose of all these restrictions is to ensure that SQL Server can perform a consistent calculation. An indexed view, also called a materialized view, causes SQL Server to execute the *SELECT* statement in the view definition. SQL Server then builds a clustered index on the view's results, and stores the data and index within the database. As you change data in the base tables, SQL Server propagates these changes to the indexed view. If the result of the view could change from one execution to another or could change if different query options were set, the entire set of data SQL Server calculated and stored would be invalidated. Therefore, all the operators or functions that can cause varying results are disallowed.

Some examples of these restrictions are as follows:

- The *SELECT* statement cannot reference other views.
- All functions must be deterministic. For example, you cannot use *getdate()* because every time it is executed, it returns a different date result.
- *AVG*, *MIN*, *MAX*, and *STDEV* are not allowed.

You use the *CREATE INDEX* Transact-SQL command to create a clustered index on a view. For details about this command, see Chapter 4, "Creating Indexes." You can also create nonclustered indexes on a view to give the query optimizer more options for satisfying a query. You also use the *CREATE INDEX* command to create nonclustered indexes on a view.

Query Substitution

Lesson 1, "Creating a View," discussed the query substitution that happens when a *SELECT* statement references a regular view. Indexed views work differently because an indexed view is, in fact, a table. So queries that reference the indexed view return the data directly from the view. The query optimizer *does not* substitute the view definition into the query.

Although you can create an indexed view in any version of SQL Server 2005, Enterprise Edition contains an interesting optimizer feature. If the optimizer determines that it can use an indexed view more efficiently to satisfy a query than a base table, it will rewrite the query to use the indexed view instead. You do not even have to specify the indexed view in the query; the query needs to specify only a table on which you have defined an indexed view. The practice in this lesson demonstrates this substitution behavior, which is available only if you are using the Enterprise or Developer editions of SQL Server 2005. To use an indexed view in any other edition of SQL Server, you must explicitly reference it in the query.

Quick Check

- What is the difference between a regular view and an indexed view?

Quick Check Answer

- A regular view is a *SELECT* statement that is referenced by a name and stored in SQL Server. It does not contain any data. An indexed view is a view that has a clustered index created against it, which causes SQL Server to materialize and store the results of the query defined in the view on disk. An indexed view must meet very stringent requirements for the view, the base tables that the view references, and the index on the view.

Create an Indexed View

In this practice, you create an indexed view in the *AdventureWorks* database.

1. If necessary, launch SSMS, connect to your instance, open a new query window, and change the context to the *AdventureWorks* database.

2. Create an indexed view called Orders by executing the following code:

```
--Set the options to support indexed views.
SET NUMERIC_ROUNDABORT OFF;
SET ANSI_PADDING, ANSI_WARNINGS, CONCAT_NULL_YIELDS_NULL, ARITHABORT,
    QUOTED_IDENTIFIER, ANSI_NULLS ON;
GO
--Create view with schemabinding.
IF OBJECT_ID ('Sales.vOrders', 'view') IS NOT NULL
DROP VIEW Sales.vOrders ;
GO
CREATE VIEW Sales.vOrders
WITH SCHEMABINDING
AS
    SELECT SUM(UnitPrice*OrderQty*(1.00-UnitPriceDiscount)) AS Revenue,
        OrderDate, ProductID, COUNT_BIG(*) AS COUNT
    FROM Sales.SalesOrderDetail AS od, Sales.SalesOrderHeader AS o
    WHERE od.SalesOrderID = o.SalesOrderID
    GROUP BY OrderDate, ProductID;
GO
--Create an index on the view.
CREATE UNIQUE CLUSTERED INDEX IDX_V1
    ON Sales.vOrders (OrderDate, ProductID);
GO
```

3. Execute the following queries, which use the indexed view even though the view is not explicitly referenced in the queries:

```
SELECT SUM(UnitPrice*OrderQty*(1.00-UnitPriceDiscount)) AS Rev,
    OrderDate, ProductID
FROM Sales.SalesOrderDetail AS od
    JOIN Sales.SalesOrderHeader AS o ON od.SalesOrderID=o.SalesOrderID
        AND ProductID BETWEEN 700 and 800
        AND OrderDate >= CONVERT(datetime,'05/01/2002',101)
GROUP BY OrderDate, ProductID
ORDER BY Rev DESC;

SELECT  OrderDate, SUM(UnitPrice*OrderQty*(1.00-UnitPriceDiscount)) AS Rev
FROM Sales.SalesOrderDetail AS od
    JOIN Sales.SalesOrderHeader AS o ON od.SalesOrderID=o.SalesOrderID
        AND DATEPART(mm,OrderDate)= 3
        AND DATEPART(yy,OrderDate) = 2002
GROUP BY OrderDate
ORDER BY OrderDate ASC;
```

Lesson Summary

- You create an indexed view by creating a clustered index on the view.

- By creating a clustered index on a view, SQL Server stores the result set of querying the view on disk, which can dramatically improve performance, especially for queries that perform aggregations or computations.

- If you are using SQL Server 2005 Enterprise Edition, the query optimizer will automatically rewrite a query to use an indexed view if it determines that the indexed view would be more efficient than the base table in satisfying the query.

Lesson Review

The following questions are intended to reinforce key information presented in this lesson. The questions are also available on the companion CD if you prefer to review them in electronic form.

NOTE Answers

Answers to these questions and explanations of why each answer choice is right or wrong are located in the "Answers" section at the end of the book.

---

1. Which of the following settings are required to create an indexed view? (Choose all that apply.)

   A. *QUOTED_IDENTIFIER ON*

   B. Three-part names

   C. *SCHEMABINDING*

   D. *ANSI_NULLS OFF*

Chapter Review

To further practice and reinforce the skills you learned in this chapter, you can

- Review the chapter summary.
- Review the list of key terms introduced in this chapter.
- Complete the case scenario. This scenario sets up a real-world situation involving the topics of this chapter and asks you to create a solution.
- Complete the suggested practices.
- Take a practice test.

Chapter Summary

- Views are simply a named *SELECT* statement stored in SQL Server.
- You can use a view just like a table without having to be concerned about the complexity of the underlying *SELECT* statement.
- Because views depend on underlying base tables to access the data, you must pay attention to the chain of permissions that are required to return data.
- To safely use views to insert, update, and delete data in a single base table, use the *WITH CHECK OPTION* clause on the *CREATE VIEW* command to constrain the changes to only the set of rows that match the view's *WHERE* clause.
- You can improve performance by creating a clustered index on a view. Indexed views cause the returned data, including aggregations and calculations, to be materialized on disk instead of computed at execution time. SQL Server 2005 Enterprise Edition can use an indexed view, even if it is not directly referenced in a *SELECT* statement.

Key Terms

Do you know what these key terms mean? You can check your answers by looking up the terms in the glossary at the end of the book.

- broken ownership chain
- indexed view
- ownership chain
- updateable view
- view

Case Scenario: Creating Views

In the following case scenario, you will apply what you've learned in this chapter. You can find answers to these questions in the "Answers" section at the end of this book.

Contoso Limited, an insurance company located in Bothell, WA, handles insurance policies and claims for individuals. The development group has been evaluating select pieces of code within applications that perform the same function but return different results. The group has also identified several complex queries that perform poorly because of the large number of tables that they join together.

To fix the issues, the development team needs to standardize queries and improve the performance of key queries. How should the group solve these problems?

Suggested Practices

To help you successfully master the exam objectives presented in this chapter, complete the following practice tasks.

Creating a View

- **Practice 1**   Take several of your more complex queries and turn them into views. Substitute these new views back into your code.

Creating an Indexed View

- **Practice 1**   Take one of the views that you created in Practice 1 and turn it into an indexed view. Compare the performance of the indexed view against the performance of the underlying *SELECT* statement.

Take a Practice Test

The practice tests on this book's companion CD offer many options. For example, you can test yourself on just the content covered in this chapter, or you can test yourself on all the 70-431 certification exam content. You can set up the test so that it closely simulates the experience of taking a certification exam, or you can set it up in study mode so that you can look at the correct answers and explanations after you answer each question.

MORE INFO   **Practice tests**

For details about all the practice test options available, see the "How to Use the Practice Tests" section in this book's Introduction.

Chapter 8
Managing XML Data

The addition of native XML support in Microsoft SQL Server 2005 represents a learning curve for database specialists who are used to relational data representation. But the effort is worth it. XML is a multipurpose, extensible data representation technology that expands the possibilities for how applications can consume and manipulate data. Unlike relational data, XML data can represent structured, semistructured, and unstructured data. XML support in SQL Server 2005 is fully integrated with the relational engine and query optimizer, allowing the retrieval and modification of XML data and even the conversion between XML and relational data representations.

This chapter covers the key aspects of working with XML structures, shows you how to retrieve and modify XML data, and describes how to convert between XML and relational data. You also see how you can optimize the new XML data type in SQL Server 2005 for data retrieval by using different types of indexes.

Exam objectives in this chapter:
- Manage XML data.
    - Identify the specific structure needed by a consumer.
    - Retrieve XML data.
    - Modify XML data.
    - Convert between XML data and relational data.
    - Create an XML index.
    - Load an XML schema.

Lessons in this chapter:

Before You Begin

To complete the lessons in this chapter, you must have

- A general understanding of XML and its related technologies, specifically XML schemas and XPATH.

- A general understanding of the supported XML data features in previous versions of SQL Server.

- The SQL Server 2005 *AdventureWorks* sample database installed.

- Microsoft Visual Studio 2005 or Microsoft Visual C# 2005 Express Edition installed. You can download Visual C# 2005 Express Edition from *http://msdn.microsoft.com/vstudio/express/*.

Real World

Adolfo Wiernik

As a software architect, I've had to create the necessary database schema in an entity-relationship diagram to model structured data for relational databases. To represent some kinds of complex data in a relational format, I've had to use models that relax the rules of normalization. But I've also worked with data—such as order-dependent data, hierarchical data, complex object graphs, and recursive data—that is difficult to fit into the homogeneous structure of a relational model.

In the past, I usually ended up representing in the database only the structured data and choosing for the unstructured data another data source, such as an XML file on the file system. However, the implementation of a native XML data type in SQL Server 2005 gives me the ability to represent all my data in the same relational data source and use all the power built into the relational query engine to favor other types of data. Although you might need to spend some time to become comfortable with the XML features in SQL Server, the flexibility and extensibility they can provide will make it well worth your while.

Lesson 1: Working with XML Structures

XML is a platform-independent, data-representation format that offers certain bene-fits over a relational format for specific data-representation requirements. XML has been widely used in user-interface rendering and data-transformation scenarios but has not been used much as a data-storage format. Until recently, relational databases didn't support XML data manipulation (other than composing XML documents from a relational representation). In 2003, the International Organization for Standardiza-tion (ISO) and the American National Standards Institute (ANSI) released Part 14 of the SQL Standard XML-Related Specifications (SQLXML), which specifies how a rela-tional database can natively manage XML data. And SQL Server 2005 embraces this specification to give database administrators (DBAs) and developers more flexibility in working with different types of data. This lesson focuses on the strategies you can use to store XML data in a SQL Server 2005 relational database and the structures required to efficiently support this storage.

After this lesson, you will be able to:

- Choose the proper XML storage option.
- Define table columns, parameters, and Transact-SQL variables by using the XML data type.
- Add type information to an XML data type column, parameter, or variable by using an XML schema.

Estimated lesson time: 30 minutes

Storage Options for XML data

Storing data as XML offers several benefits. First, XML is self-describing, so applica-tions can consume XML data without knowing its schema or structure. XML data is always arranged hierarchically as a tree structure. XML tree structures must always have a root, or parent, node that is known as an XML document. If a set of XML nodes doesn't have a root node, it is said to be an XML fragment.

Second, XML maintains document ordering. Because XML structure is hierarchical, maintaining node order is important because it dictates the distance between nodes inside the tree structure.

Third, schema declaration provides type information and structure validation. XML Schema language is a standard language that you use to define a valid structure for a specific XML document or fragment. XML schemas also provide type information to the data in the XML structure. XML Schema enables you to declare optional sections inside the schema or generic types that accept any XML fragment. This capability means you can represent not only structured data but also semistructured and unstructured data.

Fourth, XML data is searchable. Because of XML's hierarchical structure, you can apply multiple algorithms to search inside tree structures. XQUERY and XPATH are query languages designed to search XML data.

And fifth, XML data is extensible. You can manipulate XML data by inserting, modifying, or deleting nodes. This capability means that you can create new XML instances out of existing XML structures.

NOTE Data representation types

Here are definitions of the three data representation types:

- **Structured data**   Homogeneous static data structure in which all instances of the data follow the same structure.
- **Semistructured data**   Heterogeneous data structure that can contain dynamic or optional structures. Instances can look completely different from each other but still conform to the same schema.
- **Unstructured data**   Heterogeneous data that does not conform to a schema. In XML, data can exist without having a schema to define its structure.

Applications that manipulate XML execute a variety of actions on data, such as creating new XML documents, filtering an XML document and extracting relevant nodes based on a filter expression, transforming an XML fragment into another XML structure, and updating or modifying the current data inside the XML structure.

The way applications store XML data affects which of these possible actions are at your disposal. SQL Server 2005 enables you to store XML data in two ways:

- As XML in the database in a text column
- As XML in the database in an XML data type column

MORE INFO Storing XML data as relational data

Lesson 5 in this chapter covers storing data as a relational representation and applying composition and shredding techniques to transform relational data into XML and back.

Storing XML in Text Columns

You can store XML data in a text column by using the *(n)char*, *(n)varchar*, or *varbinary* data types. For these data types, SQL Server 2005 introduces the MAX argument, which allocates a maximum storage size of 2 GB. The following code example stores XML data in the *nvarchar* data type:

```
DECLARE @myXML AS nvarchar(max)
SET @myXML = '<log><application>Sales</application><description>The connection timed
 out</description></log>'
```

CAUTION **Deprecated data types**

Microsoft intends to drop support for the *text*, *ntext*, and *image* data types in upcoming SQL Server versions. For this reason, Microsoft recommends that you stop using these data types.

The key benefits of storing XML data in SQL Server 2005 text columns are the following:

- XML provides textual fidelity. All details such as comments and white space are preserved.

- It does not depend on database capabilities.

- It reduces the processing workload on the database server because all processing of XML data happens in a middle tier.

- It provides the best performance for document-level insertion and retrieval. Document-level means that if you want to execute operations at the node level, you are forced to work with the complete XML document because SQL Server is not aware of what is stored in this column.

Some limitations of storing XML in SQL Server 2005 text columns are as follows:

- Coding complexity (and related higher maintenance cost) is added in the middle tier.

- You can't manipulate, extract, or modify XML data at the node level.

- Searching XML data always involves reading the entire document because XML is interpreted as text by the database server.

- XML validation, well-formedness, and type checking must be executed in the middle tier.

MORE INFO   Well-formed XML

Well-formed XML is an XML document that meets a set of constraints specified by the World Wide Web Consortium (W3C) Recommendation for XML 1.0. For example, well-formed XML must contain a root-level element, and any other nested elements must open and close properly without intermixing.

SQL Server 2005 validates some of the well-formedness constraints. Some rules, such as the requirement for a root-level element, are not enforced.

For a complete list of well-formedness requirements, read the W3C Recommendation for XML 1.0 at *http://www.w3.org/TR/REC-xml*.

Quick Check

1. What are two benefits of storing XML in a text column in SQL Server 2005?

2. What are two disadvantages of storing XML in a text column in SQL Server 2005?

Quick Check Answers

1. Possible answers include the following: XML provides textual fidelity, does not depend on database capabilities, reduces the processing workload on the database server, and provides the best performance for document-level insertion and retrieval.

2. Possible answers include the following: it's impossible to manipulate, extract, or modify the data at the node level; searching XML data always involves reading the entire document; XML validation must be executed in the middle tier; and there is extra coding complexity in the middle tier.

Storing XML in XML Data Type Columns

You can use the new XML data type in SQL Server 2005 as you use any other native SQL Server data type: to define columns on tables, to define parameters for functions and stored procedures, and to create variables. As the following code example demonstrates, the XML data type column accepts both XML documents and XML fragments; this behavior is specified in the SQL/XML ISO-ANSI Standard Part 14.

```
CREATE TABLE UniversalLog(recordID int, description XML)

INSERT UniversalLog(recordID, description)
VALUES(1, '<log><application>Sales</application><description>The connection timed
 out.</description></log>')

INSERT UniversalLog(recordID, description)
VALUES(1, 'database unavailable')
```

You can also use the XML data type to define parameters and variables, as the following code example demonstrates:

```
CREATE PROCEDURE AddRecordToLog (@record AS XML)
AS
  -- procedure body
GO

DECLARE @logRecord AS XML
SET @logRecord = '<log><application>Sales</
application><description>The connection timed out.</description></log>'

EXEC AddRecordToLog @logRecord
```

SQL Server automatically converts the data types *(n)char*, *(n)varchar*, *(n)text*, *varbinary*, and *image* to the XML data type when assigning values to an XML parameter, column, or variable.

The benefits of storing XML data by using the XML data type in SQL Server 2005 are as follows:

- The XML data type is fully integrated with the SQL Server query engine and all other SQL Server services. The same query processor and query optimizer are used for both relational and XML queries.

- The data is stored and manipulated natively as XML.

- SQL Server 2005 provides fine-grained support for selecting, inserting, modifying, or deleting at the node level.

- Performance improves for data-retrieval operations because multiple indexing is possible with the XML data type, so SQL Server reads only relevant nodes.

- Document order and structure are preserved.

Limitations of storing XML using the XML data type in SQL Server 2005 include the following:

- Textual fidelity is not preserved. White space, the XML declaration at the top of the document, comments in the XML, attribute ordering, and other nondata elements are removed from the structure.

- The maximum allowed node depth is 128 levels.

- The maximum allowed storage size is 2 GB.

Quick Check

1. Which of the following *INSERT* statements will fail? (Choose all that apply.)

    A. INSERT UniversalLog(recordID, description) VALUES (1, '<ROOT/>')

    B. INSERT UniversalLog(recordID, description) VALUES (1, 'ROOT')

    C. INSERT UniversalLog(recordID, description) VALUES (1, '<ROOT>')

    D. INSERT UniversalLog(recordID, description) VALUES (1, '<ROOT>
    <A><b></a></B></ROOT>')

Quick Check Answers

1. **Will succeed:** Represents a single-node XML document.

2. **Will succeed:** Represents an XML fragment.

3. **Will fail:** SQL Server validates the well-formedness of the XML document. The *<ROOT>* node is opened but never closed.

4. **Will fail:** SQL Server validates the well-formedness of the XML document. The hierarchy constructed by the *A* and *B* nodes is not closed properly. Also, XML is case sensitive, so the *A* node is not the same as the *a* node.

Typing and Validating XML Data with XML Schemas

An XML schema describes the structure and constrains the contents of XML documents. Additionally, XML schemas provide type information that describes the nature of the data in elements and attributes. SQL Server 2005 supports *untyped XML data* and *typed XML data.* By binding an XML data type variable, column, or parameter to an XML schema, SQL Server gets input that lets it validate the correctness of the XML instance and to strongly type the nodes and contents of the XML instance.

If an XML document conforms to what is declared inside an XML schema, the XML document is said to be valid. An invalid XML document does not conform to what is declared inside an XML schema.

XML schemas are declared at the database level and deployed to SQL Server. XML schemas are valuable to SQL Server because they provide metadata that defines and constrains XML data types. After creating the XML schema as the following code shows, you can type and validate any XML data type column, variable, or parameter according to the XML schema collection.

Creating an XML Schema in SQL Server 2005

```
CREATE XML SCHEMA COLLECTION LogRecordSchema AS
'<schema xmlns="http://www.w3.org/2001/XMLSchema">
    <element name="log">
        <complexType>
            <sequence>
                <element name="application" type="string"/>
                <element name="description" type="string"/>
            </sequence>
        </complexType>
    </element>
</schema>'
```

In the following code example, SQL Server validates the contents of the *@myXML* variable by the rules specified in all the XML schemas that compose the LogRecord-Schema schema collection:

```
DECLARE @myXML AS XML(LogRecordSchema)
SET @myXML = '<log><date>2005-11-07</date></log>'
```

The assignment in the example fails because the XML instance does not conform to the XML structure declared by the XML schema collection.

NOTE Loading an XML schema from a file

In most cases, instead of retyping the complete XML schema, it is easier to load it from an XML schema file (extension .xsd). Use the *OPENROWSET* command in SQL Server 2005 to load the file into a variable of type XML:

```
DECLARE @schema XML
SELECT @schema = c FROM OPENROWSET (
    BULK 'MyXMLSchema.xsd', SINGLE_BLOB) AS TEMP(c)
CREATE XML SCHEMA COLLECTION MySchema AS @schema
```

PRACTICE **Creating a New Database**

In this practice, you will create a new database. In the database, you will create a new XML schema collection, loading it from an .xsd file. Then, you will create a table with columns of XML data type and constrain the XML columns to the XML schema collection. Finally, you will load data into the table. This database is the basic database you will use in the other lessons in this chapter.

NOTE Code available on the companion CD

The practices for this chapter are code intensive. So that you don't have to type in the code examples in the practices, the Practice Files\Chapter8 folder provides the code needed for all the practices in this chapter. For solutions to the exercises in the Lesson 1 practice, see the Practice Files\Chapter8\Lesson 1\CompleteLesson1.sql file on the CD.

▶ **Practice 1: Create the TK431Chapter8 Database, UniversalLog Table, and XML Schema**

In this exercise, you will create the necessary database schema elements to support typed XML data inside a database.

1. Open SQL Server Management Studio (SSMS) and open a connection to SQL Server 2005.

2. Issue a *CREATE DATABASE* statement to create a new database called *TK431Chapter8*.

   ```
   CREATE DATABASE TK431Chapter8
   GO
   ```

3. Copy the Chapter8 folder from the companion CD to the root of the C drive. Then create an XML schema collection called LogRecordSchema. Your code might look like the following:

   ```
   USE TK431Chapter8
   GO

   declare @schema XML
   SELECT @schema = c FROM OPENROWSET (
       BULK 'C:\Chapter8\Lesson 1\logRecordSchema.xsd', SINGLE_BLOB) AS TEMP(c)
   CREATE XML SCHEMA COLLECTION LogRecordSchema AS @schema
   ```

4. Load the XML schema from the .xsd file in the C:\Chapter8 folder. The following code shows the LogRecordSchema XML schema:

   ```
   <?xml version="1.0" encoding="utf-8"?>
   <xsd:schema xmlns:xsd="http://www.w3.org/2001/XMLSchema">
       <xsd:element name="logRecord" type="logRecordType" />

       <xsd:simpleType name="flagEnum">
           <xsd:restriction base="xsd:string">
               <xsd:enumeration value="warning" />
               <xsd:enumeration value="information" />
               <xsd:enumeration value="failure" />
               <xsd:enumeration value="custom" />
           </xsd:restriction>
       </xsd:simpleType>

       <xsd:simpleType name="eventEnum">
           <xsd:restriction base="xsd:string">
               <xsd:enumeration value="appStart"/>
               <xsd:enumeration value="appClose"/>
               <xsd:enumeration value="logIn"/>
               <xsd:enumeration value="logOut"/>
           </xsd:restriction>
       </xsd:simpleType>
   ```

```
<xsd:complexType name="logRecordType">
    <xsd:choice maxOccurs="unbounded">
        <xsd:element name="information" type="informationType"/>
        <xsd:element name="error" type="errorType"/>
        <xsd:element name="post" type="postType"/>
    </xsd:choice>
    <xsd:attribute name="machine" type="xsd:string" />
    <xsd:attribute name="timestamp" type="xsd:dateTime" />
</xsd:complexType>

<xsd:complexType name="postType">
    <xsd:sequence>
        <xsd:element name="moreInformation" type="xsd:string" maxOccurs="1"
         minOccurs="0"/>
    </xsd:sequence>
    <xsd:attribute name="eventType" type="eventEnum"/>
</xsd:complexType>

<xsd:complexType name="informationType">
    <xsd:sequence>
        <xsd:element name="message" type="xsd:string" />
    </xsd:sequence>
    <xsd:attribute name="flag" type="flagEnum" />
</xsd:complexType>

<xsd:complexType name="errorType">
    <xsd:sequence>
        <xsd:element name="message" type="xsd:string" />
        <xsd:element name="module" type="xsd:string" />
    </xsd:sequence>
    <xsd:attribute name="number" type="xsd:int" />
</xsd:complexType>
</xsd:schema>
```

5. Issue a *CREATE TABLE* statement to create a new table called *UniversalLog* that contains the following columns:

   ❑ ID: *INT* data type. Set it as an identity column. Do not accept null values.

   ❑ LogDateTime: *DATETIME* data type. Default to current date and time. Do not accept null values.

   ❑ ApplicationName: *NVARCHAR (50)* data type. Do not accept null values.

   ❑ LogRecord: XML data type. Accept null values and bind the column to the LogRecordSchema schema collection.

   Your code should look like this:

```
CREATE TABLE UniversalLog
( ID INT IDENTITY(1,1) NOT NULL,
  LogDateTime DATETIME NOT NULL CONSTRAINT [DF_UniversalLog_LogDateTime]
     DEFAULT (GetDate()),
  ApplicationName NVARCHAR(50) NOT NULL,
  LogRecord XML(LogRecordSchema) NULL )
```

NOTE   Altering the LogRecord column

If you created the table first and then the XML schema collection, you can alter the column in the table to map it to the XML schema by using the following code:

```
ALTER TABLE UniversalLog ALTER COLUMN LogRecord XML (LogRecordSchema)
```

▶ **Practice 2: Insert Log Records into the UniversalLog Table**

In this exercise, you will insert XML data representing log records into the *Universal-Log* table you created in Practice 1.

1. If necessary, open SSMS and open a connection to SQL Server 2005.

2. Connect to the *TK431Chapter8* database you created in Practice 1.

3. Open the LogRecordsXML.sql file in the C:\Chapter8 folder. The file contains the following *INSERT* statements:

```
INSERT UniversalLog(ApplicationName, LogRecord)
VALUES ('SalesApp',
  '<logRecord machine="server1" timestamp="2000-01-12T12:13:14Z"/>')

INSERT UniversalLog(ApplicationName, LogRecord)
VALUES ('SalesApp',
  '<logRecord machine="server1"><information/></logRecord>')

INSERT UniversalLog(ID, ApplicationName, LogRecord)
VALUES (1, 'SalesApp',
  '<logRecord machine="server1" timestamp="2000-01-12T12:13:14Z">
  <post eventType="appStart">
      <moreInformation>All Services starting</moreInformation>
  </post>
</logRecord>')

INSERT UniversalLog(ID,ApplicationName, LogRecord)
VALUES (2, 'Inventory',
  '<logRecord machine="server2" timestamp="2000-01-13T12:13:14Z">
  <post eventType="appStart"/>
  <information flag="warning">
      <message>Duplicate IP address</message>
  </information>
</logRecord>')

INSERT UniversalLog(ID,ApplicationName, LogRecord)
VALUES (3, 'HR',
  '<logRecord machine="server1" timestamp="2000-01-14T12:13:14Z">
  <error number="1001">
      <message>The user does not have enough permissions to execute query</message>
      <module>DataAccessLayer</module>
  </error>
</logRecord>')
```

```
INSERT UniversalLog(ID,ApplicationName, LogRecord)
VALUES (4, 'CustomerService',
   '<logRecord machine="server2" timestamp="2000-01-15T12:13:14Z">
   <post eventType="logOut"/>
   <information flag="custom">
         <message>User must change password on next login</message>
   </information>
</logRecord>')

INSERT UniversalLog(ID,ApplicationName, LogRecord)
VALUES (5, 'HoursReport',
   '<logRecord machine="server2" timestamp="2000-01-11T12:13:14Z">
   <information flag="failure">
         <message>Hard Disk with ID #87230283 is not responding</message>
   </information>
   <error number="18763">
         <message>Application can not start</message>
         <module>AppLoader</module>
   </error>
   <post eventType="appStart"/>
</logRecord>')
```

4. Execute each of the *INSERT* code segments in the file in turn by selecting the code and pressing F5 to execute. The first two *INSERT* statements are meant to return validation errors because the XML data does not conform to the XML schema collection. Pay attention to the messages SQL Server returns.

Lesson Summary

- The XML data-representation format is used to represent semistructured and unstructured data that you cannot represent relationally.

- SQL Server 2005 provides a new XML data type for native storage of XML documents and fragments in the relational database.

- XML data can be typed and untyped. Typed XML is constrained by the declarations in an XML schema registered in an XML schema collection.

Lesson Review

The following questions are intended to reinforce key information presented in this lesson. The questions are also available on the companion CD if you prefer to review them in electronic form.

NOTE Answers

Answers to these questions and explanations of why each answer choice is right or wrong are located in the "Answers" section at the end of this book.

---

1. You are developing a book-management application for your city's public library. You are required to store each book's index structure as XML data so that you can display the indexes to users in a Web page. You decide to store this information in a text column. Which of the following statements best justify this decision? (Choose all that apply.)

   A. Preserves document order and structure

   B. Allows complex queries involving mixing relational and XML data

   C. Doesn't require node-level modifications or filtering

   D. Allows indexing for fast retrieval

2. XML schemas provide which functions? (Choose all that apply.)

   A. Indexes to improve performance

   B. Validation constraints for the XML instance

   C. Data type information about the XML instance

   D. Methods to insert, delete, and update XML data

Lesson 2: Retrieving XML Data by Using SQL Server Server-Side Technologies

SQL Server 2005 offers multiple options for retrieving XML data. This lesson covers the various techniques for retrieving XML data from SQL Server 2005, regardless of whether the data is stored in a relational representation, as a textual column, or in an XML data type column. In this lesson, you will see how to use the *FOR XML* construct in Transact-SQL to retrieve relational data by using an XML representation. This lesson also covers the various methods implemented by the XML data type. Some of these methods are used to extract XML data stored as XML in an XML data type by executing an XQUERY or XPATH query instruction.

After this lesson, you will be able to:

- Choose the proper *FOR XML* mode (*RAW, AUTO, PATH, EXPLICIT*), depending on the required result.
- Define nested queries to create complex multilevel XML documents.
- Extract XML fragments from the data contained inside an XML data type column, variable, or parameter.
- Transform existing XML fragments into new XML structures by using the XQUERY query language.
- Combine relational and XML structures into new result sets, and choose the proper representation—either tabular format or XML format.

Estimated lesson time: 60 minutes

Converting Relational Data to XML

Both SQL Server 2000 and SQL Server 2005 enable you to compose relational data into an XML representation by using the *FOR XML* clause in the *SELECT* statement. SQL Server 2005 extends the *FOR XML* capabilities, making it easier to represent complex hierarchical structures, and adds new keywords to modify the resulting XML structure.

The *FOR XML* clause converts the result sets from a query into an XML structure, and it provides different modes of formatting:

- *FOR XML RAW*
- *FOR XML AUTO*
- *FOR XML PATH*
- *FOR XML EXPLICIT*

Let's look into the differences between them.

Using FOR XML RAW

The default behavior for the *FOR XML RAW* mode creates a new XML element identified as *<row>* for each row found in the result set. An XML attribute is added to the *<row>* element for each column in the *SELECT* statement, using the column name as the attribute name.

To rename the *<row>* element, you can specify a new tag name right after the *RAW* keyword. To rename each attribute, you can specify an alias for each column. To change the formatting from attribute-centric to element-centric (create a new element for each column, instead of attributes), specify the *ELEMENTS* keyword after the *FOR XML RAW* clause.

The following code example applies all these techniques. The query uses the *Human-Resources.Department* and the *HumanResources.EmployeeDepartmentHistory* tables in the *AdventureWorks* sample database to list all the employees ordered by time in department, from the employee who has worked longest in each department to the department's most recently hired employee.

```
SELECT Department.[DepartmentID]
     ,History.[EmployeeID]
     ,History.[StartDate]
     ,Department.[Name] AS DepartmentName
     ,DATEDIFF(year, History.[StartDate], GetDate()) AS YearsToDate
  FROM HumanResources.Department, HumanResources.EmployeeDepartmentHistory History
  WHERE Department.DepartmentID = History.DepartmentID
  AND History.EndDate IS NULL
ORDER BY Department.[DepartmentID], History.[StartDate]
FOR XML RAW('OldestEmployeeByDepartment'), ELEMENTS
```

A partial result of executing this query is as follows:

NOTE   Viewing XML results in SSMS

If you are using SSMS to execute this sample Transact-SQL code, configure the results pane to show the results in grid view. The XML data will be displayed as a link. When you click this link, the complete XML result will open in an independent window.

```
<OldestEmployeeByDepartment>
  <DepartmentID>1</DepartmentID>
  <EmployeeID>3</EmployeeID>
  <StartDate>1997-12-12T00:00:00</StartDate>
  <DepartmentName>Engineering</DepartmentName>
  <YearsToDate>9</YearsToDate>
</OldestEmployeeByDepartment>
```

```
<OldestEmployeeByDepartment>
  <DepartmentID>1</DepartmentID>
  <EmployeeID>9</EmployeeID>
  <StartDate>1998-02-06T00:00:00</StartDate>
  <DepartmentName>Engineering</DepartmentName>
  <YearsToDate>8</YearsToDate>
</OldestEmployeeByDepartment>
```

NOTE Using *XML RAW*

FOR XML RAW provides limited formatting capabilities, but it is the easiest way to retrieve basic XML structures out of relational representation in SQL Server 2005.

Here are some important observations to note about *XML RAW* formatting:

- No root node is provided, so the XML structure is not a well-formed XML document. It represents an XML fragment.

- All the columns must be formatted in the same way. It is impossible to set some columns as XML attributes and other columns as XML elements.

- *XML RAW* generates a one-level hierarchy. Notice that all elements are at the same level. To construct complex nested XML structures, SQL Server supports nested *FOR XML* queries (explained later in this lesson).

MORE INFO Using *FOR XML RAW*

For more information about the settings available to *FOR XML RAW*, read the topic "Using RAW Mode" in SQL Server 2005 Books Online. SQL Server 2005 Books Online is installed as part of SQL Server 2005. Updates for SQL Server 2005 Books Online are available for download at *www.microsoft.com/technet/prodtechnol/sql/2005/downloads/books.mspx*.

Using *FOR XML AUTO*

FOR XML AUTO creates nested XML structures. For each table you specify in the *SELECT* query, *FOR XML AUTO* creates a new level in the XML structure. The order for nesting the XML data is based on the column order as you declared it in the *SELECT* clause.

As in *XML RAW*, the default formatting is attribute-centric. To change the formatting from attribute-centric to element-centric (and create a new element for each column, instead of attributes), specify the *ELEMENTS* keyword after the *XML AUTO* clause. With *XML AUTO*, the XML tags take their names from the table and column names you declare in the *SELECT* clause.

Exam Tip If you declared a table by using a four-part name in the FROM clause of the SELECT query, the XML elements will be named with a three-part name when queried from the local computer and with a four-part name when queried from a remote server. In the following code, MyServerName represents the name of a SQL Server instance:

```
SELECT TOP 2 [Name]

FROM MyServerName.AdventureWorks.HumanResources.Department

FOR XML AUTO
```

It returns the following when executed from the local server:

```
<AdventureWorks.HumanResources.Department Name="Document Control" />
<AdventureWorks.HumanResources.Department Name="Engineering" />
```

And it returns the following code when executed from a remote server:

```
<MyServerName.AdventureWorks.HumanResources.Department Name="Document Control" />
<MyServerName.AdventureWorks.HumanResources.Department Name="Engineering" />
```

To implement a more predictable outcome, use two-part names, or use table aliases in the query.

The following code example uses the same query as the previous example, but instead of *XML RAW*, it is formatted as *XML AUTO*:

```
SELECT Department.[DepartmentID]
      ,History.[EmployeeID]
      ,History.[StartDate]
      ,Department.[Name] AS DepartmentName
      ,DATEDIFF(year, History.[StartDate], GetDate()) AS YearsToDate
  FROM HumanResources.Department, HumanResources.EmployeeDepartmentHistory History
  WHERE Department.DepartmentID = History.DepartmentID
  AND History.EndDate IS NULL
ORDER BY Department.[DepartmentID], History.[StartDate] FOR XML AUTO, ELEMENTS
```

A partial result of executing this query is as follows:

```
<HumanResources.Department>
  <DepartmentID>1</DepartmentID>
  <DepartmentName>Engineering</DepartmentName>
  <History>
    <EmployeeID>3</EmployeeID>
    <StartDate>1997-12-12T00:00:00</StartDate>
    <YearsToDate>9</YearsToDate>
  </History>
  <History>
    <EmployeeID>9</EmployeeID>
    <StartDate>1998-02-06T00:00:00</StartDate>
    <YearsToDate>8</YearsToDate>
  </History>
</HumanResources.Department>
```

Important observations to note about *XML AUTO* formatting include the following:

- No root node is provided, so the XML structure is not a well-formed XML document. It represents an XML fragment.

- All the columns must be formatted in the same way. It is impossible to set some columns as XML attributes and other columns as XML elements.

- *XML AUTO* generates a new hierarchy level for each table in the SELECT query, constructed in the following order:

  ❑ The first level in the XML structure is mapped to the table that owns the first column declared on the SELECT query. The second level in the XML structure is mapped to the table that owns the next column declared on the SELECT query, and so on to the other levels. Notice in the previous example that Department.[DepartmentID] is the first column declared. It means that Department elements will be the first level in the XML structure and EmployeeDepartmentHistory will be nested inside the Department elements.

  ❑ If columns are mixed in with the SELECT query, *XML AUTO* will reorder the XML nodes so that all nodes belonging to the same level are grouped under the same parent node. Notice in the previous example that the Department.[Name] column is declared fourth in the SELECT query, but it appears before History.[EmployeeID] in the XML structure.

- *FOR XML AUTO* does not provide a renaming mechanism the way *XML RAW* does. *XML AUTO* uses the table and column names and aliases if present. (See the History nodes in the previous example.)

- The formatting is applied by row; to construct complex nested XML structures, SQL Server supports nested FOR XML queries (explained later in this lesson).

Figure 8-1 shows these facts.

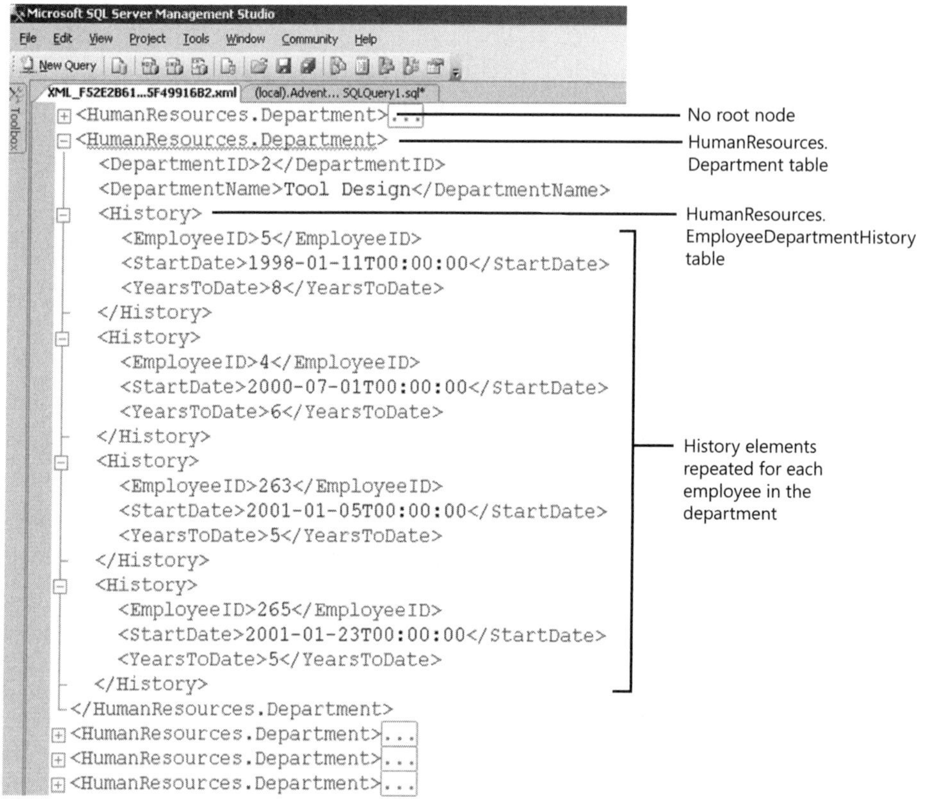

Figure 8-1   Using XML AUTO when joining multiple tables

MORE INFO   Using *FOR XML AUTO*

For more information about the different settings available to *FOR XML AUTO,* read the topic "Using AUTO Mode" in SQL Server 2005 Books Online.

Using *FOR XML PATH*

FOR XML PATH is new to SQL Server 2005. With *XML PATH*, developers have full control over how the XML structure is generated, including having some columns as attributes and others as elements. Each column is configured independently.

Each column is given a column alias that tells SQL Server where to locate this node in the XML hierarchy. If a column doesn't receive a column alias, the default node <*row*> is used (as in *XML RAW*). You declare column aliases by using pseudo-XPATH expressions. Table 8-1 describes some of the different options for configuring columns in *FOR XML PATH*.

Table 8-1 Configuring Columns in *FOR XML PATH*

Option	Description
'elementName'	An XML element, <elementName>, is created with the content of that column on the context node.
'@attributeName'	An XML attribute, attributeName, is created with the content of that column on the context node.
'elementName/nestedElement'	An XML element, <elementName>, is created; beneath it, a <nestedElement> XML element is created with the content of that column.
'elementName/@attributeName'	An XML element, <elementName>, is created, and an XML attribute, attributeName, is created with the content of that column.
text()	Inserts the content of that column as a text node in the XML structure.
comment()	Inserts the content of that column as an XML comment in the XML structure.
node()	The content of that column is inserted as if no column name were specified.
data()	The content of that column is treated as an atomic value. A space character is added to the XML if the next item in the serialization is also an atomic value.

The following code example is based on the same query as the previous examples. The order of the column declarations in the *SELECT* statement has been changed a little to show the most important features of using *XML PATH*.

```
SELECT History.[StartDate] '@StartDate'
      ,Department.[DepartmentID] 'Department/@id'
      ,Department.[Name] 'comment()'
      ,History.[EmployeeID] 'Department/Employee/@id'
      ,'Years in role:' 'Department/Employee/data()'
      ,DATEDIFF(year, History.[StartDate], GetDate()) 'Department/Employee/data()'
  FROM HumanResources.Department, HumanResources.EmployeeDepartmentHistory History
  WHERE Department.DepartmentID = History.DepartmentID
  AND History.EndDate IS NULL
ORDER BY Department.[DepartmentID], History.[StartDate] FOR XML PATH ('ForEachRow')
```

Here is a partial result of executing this query:

```
<ForEachRow StartDate="2001-02-18T00:00:00">
  <Department id="1" />
  <!--Engineering-->
  <Department>
    <Employee id="270">Years in role: 5</Employee>
  </Department>
</ForEachRow>
<ForEachRow StartDate="1998-01-11T00:00:00">
  <Department id="2" />
  <!--Tool Design-->
  <Department>
    <Employee id="5">Years in role: 8</Employee>
  </Department>
</ForEachRow>
<ForEachRow StartDate="2000-07-01T00:00:00">
  <Department id="2" />
  <!--Tool Design-->
  <Department>
    <Employee id="4">Years in role: 6</Employee>
  </Department>
</ForEachRow>
```

In the previous example

- The *XML PATH* instruction renames the default <*row*> element to <*ForEachRow*>.

- The StartDate column is formatted as the *'StartDate'* attribute. Because it does not specify where to locate the attribute in the XML structure, it is created on the context node, the <*ForEachRow*> element.

- The DepartmentID column is formatted as the *'id'* attribute for the <*Department*> element that is created beneath the <*ForEachRow*> element.

- The Name column is formatted as a comment. Because it does not specify where to locate the comment in the XML structure, it is created under the context node, the <*Department*> element.

- The EmployeeID column is formatted as the *'id'* attribute for the <*Employee*> element that is created under the <*Department*> element. The <*Department*> element is created beneath the <*ForEachRow*> element.

- A constant value column is formatted as an atomic value for the <*Employee*> element that is created under the <*Department*> element. The <*Department*> element is created under the <*ForEachRow*> element.

- The computed column is formatted as an atomic value for the <*Employee*> element that is created under the <*Department*> element, which is created under the <*ForEachRow*> element. Because the previous column is also an atomic value in exactly the same location, SQL Server will add an extra space between the two values.

Note the following important observations about *XML PATH* formatting:

- No root node is provided, so the XML structure is not a well-formed XML document. It represents an XML fragment.

- The declared XML structure is repeated for each of the rows. To construct complex nesting XML structures, SQL Server supports nested FOR XML queries (explained later in this lesson).

- Developers have full control over the number of levels that the XML structure will have.

- The XML attribute declarations must be declared before the XML element declarations, so column order does matter. Column order also indicates the context node to locate column values that do not specify their position in the XML structure.

- Table aliases are ignored by the formatting mechanism in *XML PATH*.

MORE INFO   Using *FOR XML PATH*

For more information about the different settings available to FOR XML PATH, read the topic "Using PATH Mode" in SQL Server 2005 Books Online.

Adding a Root Node

All the examples shown so far in this lesson represent XML fragments. The results of these queries do not represent an XML document because the result is not well-formed; it is missing a root node to contain all the nested elements.

When you declare a ROOT instruction after the *FOR XML* clause, SQL Server adds a node containing the resulting XML structure, so the XML will be ready for consumption by calling applications. Developers can give the ROOT instruction a name tag, so instead of using the default *<root>* node, developers can specify a proper node name for the root node.

You can use the ROOT instruction with all formatting modes. The following code example shows how to use it with *FOR XML RAW*:

```
SELECT TOP 1 Department.[DepartmentID]
     ,History.[EmployeeID]
     ,History.[StartDate]
     ,Department.[Name] AS DepartmentName
     ,DATEDIFF(year, History.[StartDate], GetDate()) AS YearsToDate
  FROM HumanResources.Department, HumanResources.EmployeeDepartmentHistory History
  WHERE Department.DepartmentID = History.DepartmentID
  AND History.EndDate IS NULL
ORDER BY Department.[DepartmentID], History.[StartDate]
FOR XML RAW('OldestEmployeeByDepartment'), ELEMENTS, ROOT('QueryResult')
```

The result of executing this query is the following:

```
<QueryResult>
  <OldestEmployeeByDepartment>
    <DepartmentID>1</DepartmentID>
    <EmployeeID>3</EmployeeID>
    <StartDate>1997-12-12T00:00:00</StartDate>
    <DepartmentName>Engineering</DepartmentName>
    <YearsToDate>9</YearsToDate>
  </OldestEmployeeByDepartment>
</QueryResult>
```

Adding Support for NULL Values in XML

By default, the XML formatting mechanism of SQL Server 2005 ignores NULL values. When using element-centric formatting, you can instruct SQL Server to generate empty rows for columns with NULL values.

In the following example, *col3* contains the constant value NULL:

```
SELECT    100 'col1',
          200 'col2',
          NULL 'col3',
          400 'col4'
FOR XML RAW, ELEMENTS
```

The result of executing this query is as follows:

```
<row>
  <col1>100</col1>
  <col2>200</col2>
  <col4>400</col4>
</row>
```

If you add the XSINIL instruction to the *ELEMENTS* clause in the *FOR XML* construction, SQL Server 2005 generates an empty XML element for NULL values.

In the following example, *col3* contains the constant NULL, but ELEMENTS XSINIL is specified:

```
SELECT    100 'col1',
          200 'col2',
          NULL 'col3',
          400 'col4'
FOR XML RAW, ELEMENTS XSINIL
```

The result of executing this query is the following:

```
<row xmlns:xsi="http://www.w3.org/2001/XMLSchema-instance">
  <col1>100</col1>
  <col2>200</col2>
  <col3 xsi:nil="true" />
  <col4>400</col4>
</row>
```

Returning XML as an XML Data Type Instance

In its default execution mode, the *FOR XML* construction returns the resulting XML as text. This result could be assigned to a literal type variable or to an XML data type variable. In the former case, the XML fragment is converted automatically to the XML data type, as the following example shows:

```
DECLARE @myXML NVARCHAR(MAX)
SET @myXML = (SELECT 100 'col1',
                     200 'col2',
                     NULL 'col3',
                     400 'col4'
               FOR XML RAW, ELEMENTS XSINIL)
SELECT @myXML
```

In SQL Server 2005, the FOR XML construction supports the TYPE instruction, which tells SQL Server to return the result of the FOR XML query as an XML data type instead of text. This capability opens greater manipulation possibilities, as we cover later in this lesson. The XML data type provides a set of methods to execute XQUERY and XPATH queries as well as methods to update the XML.

The following example shows how to use the TYPE instruction:

```
DECLARE @myXML XML
SET @myXML = (SELECT 100 'col1',
                     200 'col2',
                     NULL 'col3',
                     400 'col4'
               FOR XML RAW, ELEMENTS XSINIL, TYPE)
SELECT @myXML
```

Using Nested Queries to Create Complex Hierarchical Structures

As you saw in previous examples, *FOR XML RAW*, *AUTO*, and *PATH* all provide different capabilities for creating complex hierarchical XML structures. *XML RAW* enables you to create one-level XML structures only. *XML AUTO* creates a new level per participating table, but the structure is repeated per row. *XML PATH* allows each column to specify its location in the XML structure, but again, the structure is repeated per row.

By using nested queries, you can modify the XML structure so that a set of nodes can really be contained by a parent node; not for each row, but for a set of rows.

The following example retrieves the same information as the *FOR XML RAW* example shown previously in this lesson. The difference is that by using a nested query, we can create sublevels in the resulting XML structure:

```
SELECT Department.[DepartmentID],
     Department.[Name],
     (
          SELECT EmployeeDepartmentHistory.[EmployeeID]
            ,EmployeeDepartmentHistory.[StartDate]
            ,DATEDIFF(year, EmployeeDepartmentHistory.[StartDate], GetDate()) AS
             YearsToDate
          FROM HumanResources.EmployeeDepartmentHistory
          WHERE Department.DepartmentID = EmployeeDepartmentHistory.DepartmentID
               AND EmployeeDepartmentHistory.EndDate IS NULL
          ORDER BY EmployeeDepartmentHistory.[StartDate]
          FOR XML RAW('Employee'), TYPE
        ) AS Employees
  FROM HumanResources.Department
ORDER BY Department.[DepartmentID]
FOR XML RAW('Department'), ELEMENTS, ROOT ('OldestEmployeeByDepartment')
```

A partial result of executing this query follows:

```
<OldestEmployeeByDepartment>
  <Department>
    <DepartmentID>15</DepartmentID>
  <Name>Shipping and Receiving</Name>
<Employees>
    <Employee EmployeeID="34" StartDate="1999-01-08T00:00:00" YearsToDate="7" />
    <Employee EmployeeID="35" StartDate="1999-01-08T00:00:00" YearsToDate="7" />
    <Employee EmployeeID="72" StartDate="1999-01-27T00:00:00" YearsToDate="7" />
    <Employee EmployeeID="85" StartDate="1999-02-03T00:00:00" YearsToDate="7" />
    <Employee EmployeeID="121" StartDate="1999-02-21T00:00:00" YearsToDate="7" />
    <Employee EmployeeID="195" StartDate="1999-03-30T00:00:00" YearsToDate="7" />
  </Employees>
</Department>
<Department>
  <DepartmentID>16</DepartmentID>
  <Name>Executive</Name>
  <Employees>
    <Employee EmployeeID="109" StartDate="1999-02-15T00:00:00" YearsToDate="7" />
    <Employee EmployeeID="140" StartDate="2003-12-16T00:00:00" YearsToDate="3" />
  </Employees>
</Department>
</OldestEmployeeByDepartment>
```

Compare this XML structure with the previous structures shown for *FOR XML RAW*, *FOR XML AUTO*, and *FOR XML PATH*. This is a much more intuitive and rich structure.

- Department information is formatted as element-centric, and Employee information is formatted as attribute-centric.

- The departments are under the root node, each contained in a parent *<Department>* node.

- The employees are nested together by department and contained in a parent *<Employees>* node.

- The ordering of the department information can be different from the ordering of the employee information.

NOTE Using TYPE in nested FOR XML queries

Because you use the TYPE instruction in the *FOR XML* clause in nested queries, SQL Server interprets and manipulates the resulting XML as an *XML* type instead of simply copying it as text in the containing node.

Using *FOR XML EXPLICIT*

The formatting mode *FOR XML EXPLICIT* provides the greater degree of control for developers to be able to generate complex XML structures. For *FOR XML EXPLICIT* to work, the query result set must follow a specific pattern called a *Universal Table*.

The Universal Table requires specific columns that must be provided, and columns aliases must be formatted using a specific pattern. This formatting provides metadata for the XML formatter in SQL Server 2005 to construct the XML, as Table 8-2 describes.

Table 8-2 *FOR XML EXPLICIT* Result Set Requirements

Option	Description
Tag column	Must be the first column in the result set. The Tag column indicates the depth in the XML structure, starting from 1.
Parent column	Must be the second column in the result set. The Parent column indicates the node parent in the XML structure. The node parent is identified by its Tag identifier.

Table 8-2 *FOR XML EXPLICIT* Result Set Requirements

Option	Description
Column name pattern: *ElementName!Tag-Number!AttributeName!Directive*	Data columns must provide an alias following this pattern. *ElementName* is the name you want to assign to the XML element. *TagNumber* indicates the level (according to the tag column) at which this node must be located. *AttributeName* is optional if you indicate a directive; it indicates the name to provide to the XML attribute that holds the value. *Directive* is optional; it provides more information to the XML formatting mechanism. Some of its possible values include these: ■ *hide*: Indicates that this column should not be included in the resulting XML structure. Use this value for columns you might need just for ordering purposes. ■ *element*: Generate the column value as an XML element, not as an XML attribute. NULL values will be ignored. ■ *elementxsinil*: Generate the column value as an XML element, not as an XML attribute. NULL values will not be ignored; an empty element will be provided. ■ *cdata*: Generate the column value as an XML comment inside a CDATA section.

The Universal Table also requires specific ordering for the rows in the result set. The XML structure is constructed following row order; the rows in the result set must be ordered so that each parent node is immediately followed by its child nodes.

```
SELECT 1 as Tag,
   NULL as Parent,
   Department.[DepartmentID] as [Department!1!id],
   Department.[Name] as [Department!1!name],
```

```
      NULL as [Employee!2!id],
      NULL as [Employee!2!StartDate],
      NULL as [Employee!2!YearsInRole]
FROM HumanResources.Department
UNION ALL
SELECT 2 as Tag,
      1 as Parent,
      Department.[DepartmentID],
      NULL,
      History.EmployeeID,
      History.StartDate,
      DATEDIFF(year, History.[StartDate], GetDate())
FROM HumanResources.EmployeeDepartmentHistory History, HumanResources.Department
WHERE Department.DepartmentID = History.DepartmentID
      AND History.EndDate IS NULL
ORDER BY [Department!1!id], [Employee!2!YearsInRole]
FOR XML EXPLICIT, ROOT('OldestEmployeeByDepartment')
```

A partial result of executing this query is as follows:

```
<OldestEmployeeByDepartment>
  <Department id="1" name="Engineering">
    <Employee id="267" StartDate="2001-01-30T00:00:00" YearsInRole="5" />
    <Employee id="270" StartDate="2001-02-18T00:00:00" YearsInRole="5" />
    <Employee id="11" StartDate="1998-02-24T00:00:00" YearsInRole="8" />
    <Employee id="12" StartDate="1998-03-03T00:00:00" YearsInRole="8" />
    <Employee id="9" StartDate="1998-02-06T00:00:00" YearsInRole="8" />
    <Employee id="3" StartDate="1997-12-12T00:00:00" YearsInRole="9" />
  </Department>
  <Department id="2" name="Tool Design">
    <Employee id="265" StartDate="2001-01-23T00:00:00" YearsInRole="5" />
    <Employee id="263" StartDate="2001-01-05T00:00:00" YearsInRole="5" />
    <Employee id="4" StartDate="2000-07-01T00:00:00" YearsInRole="6" />
    <Employee id="5" StartDate="1998-01-11T00:00:00" YearsInRole="8" />
  </Department>
</OldestEmployeeByDepartment>
```

If you execute the same query without the *FOR XML EXPLICIT* clause, you can see the Universal Table format, as Figure 8-2 shows.

	Tag	Parent	Department!1!id	Department!1!name	Employee!2!id	Employee!2!StartDate	Employee!2!YearsInRole
1	1	NULL	1	Engineering	NULL	NULL	NULL
2	2	1	1	NULL	267	2001-01-30 00:00:00.000	5
3	2	1	1	NULL	270	2001-02-18 00:00:00.000	5
4	2	1	1	NULL	11	1998-02-24 00:00:00.000	8
5	2	1	1	NULL	12	1998-03-03 00:00:00.000	8
6	2	1	1	NULL	9	1998-02-06 00:00:00.000	8
7	2	1	1	NULL	3	1997-12-12 00:00:00.000	9
8	1	NULL	2	Tool Design	NULL	NULL	NULL
9	2	1	2	NULL	265	2001-01-23 00:00:00.000	5
10	2	1	2	NULL	263	2001-01-05 00:00:00.000	5
11	2	1	2	NULL	4	2000-07-01 00:00:00.000	6
12	2	1	2	NULL	5	1998-01-11 00:00:00.000	8
13	1	NULL	3	Sales	NULL	NULL	NULL
14	2	1	3	NULL	288	2003-04-15 00:00:00.000	3
15	2	1	3	NULL	289	2003-07-01 00:00:00.000	3
16	2	1	3	NULL	290	2003-07-01 00:00:00.000	3
17	2	1	3	NULL	284	2002-05-18 00:00:00.000	4
18	2	1	3	NULL	285	2002-07-01 00:00:00.000	4
19	2	1	3	NULL	286	2002-07-01 00:00:00.000	4
20	2	1	3	NULL	287	2002-11-01 00:00:00.000	4
21	2	1	3	NULL	273	2001-03-18 00:00:00.000	5
22	2	1	3	NULL	275	2001-07-01 00:00:00.000	5
23	2	1	3	NULL	276	2001-07-01 00:00:00.000	5

Figure 8-2   Universal Table format

Here are some important observations to note about *XML EXPLICIT* formatting:

- You can combine multiple queries by a *UNION* operator to provide a complete Universal Table. There is one query for each level in the hierarchy.

- No root node is provided, so the XML structure is not a well-formed XML document. It represents an XML fragment unless you specify the ROOT instruction.

- Developers have full control over the number of levels that the XML structure will have.

- Column order in the *SELECT* clause is unimportant.

- Table aliases are ignored by the formatting mechanism.

MORE INFO   Using *FOR XML EXPLICIT*

For more information about the different settings available to FOR XML EXPLICIT, read the topic "Using EXPLICIT Mode" in SQL Server 2005 Books Online.

Quick Check

1. What *FOR XML* modes support mixing XML elements and attributes?

2. What instruction is used to return well-formed XML documents instead of XML fragments when using *FOR XML*?

Quick Check Answers

1. Only *FOR XML PATH* and *FOR XML EXPLICIT* allow you to choose independently the column formatting in an XML element or an XML attribute.

2. The ROOT('rootNodeName') instruction allows you declare that the resulting XML must have a root element.

Retrieving XML Data from the XML Data Type

The XML data type provides greater searching and querying capabilities over an XML structure. More importantly, it provides developers with the ability to transform an XML instance into another XML instance; extract a value into the SQL type system; test for the existence of nodes and values inside the XML structure; and modify an existing XML structure by adding, updating, or deleting existing nodes.

The XML data type provides five methods that enable you to manipulate the XML fragment. Table 8-3 lists these methods.

Table 8-3   XML Data Type Methods

Method	Description
query()	Provides the ability to execute an XPATH or XQUERY expression and returns the resulting XML fragment.
value()	Provides the ability to execute an XPATH or XQUERY expression and returns a single scalar value that is converted into a SQL type.
exist()	Provides the ability to execute an XPATH or XQUERY expression to check for the existence of nodes. If the query returns a node collection, the *exist()* method returns true; otherwise, the *exist()* method returns false.
modify()	Provides XML data-manipulation capabilities (covered in later lessons).
nodes()	Provides the ability to execute an XPATH or XQUERY expression and returns the resulting XML fragment shredded into a row set (covered in later lessons).

You will see how to use the *query()*, *value()*, and *exist()* methods later in this lesson. And following lessons cover the use of the *modify()* and *nodes()* methods.

XQUERY and XPATH

The W3C has created two querying languages, *XQUERY* and *XPATH*, which combine to provide powerful capabilities for manipulating XML structures.

XQUERY is a query language designed to query XML data. It has been designed around the following principles:

- **Compositionality**   The result of an expression can be used as the input for another expression, much as in a functional programming language.

- **Closure**   It has been designed as a closed language with no extensibility points.

- **Integration**   It is aligned to existing and broadly used XML technologies such as XML Schema Definition (XSD) files and XPATH to use existing knowledge.

- **Simplicity**   The language declares a small set of keywords to keep its development simple, yet provides very powerful capabilities.

- **Completeness**   The language allows for the declaration of a broad range of queries.

- **Static analysis**   XQUERY is a compiled language, and as such, a static analysis is first executed on the XQUERY expressions before they are executed.

MORE INFO   XQUERY specification and SQL Server 2005

An XQUERY working draft was accepted as a candidate recommendation in November 2005. SQL Server 2005 is aligned to the July 2004 working draft of XQUERY. For more information, read "XQuery 1.0: An XML Query Language" at www.w3.org/TR/xquery/.

The most important XQUERY expression is the *FLWOR expression*. By declaring a FLWOR expression, developers can write complex query logic that iterates through a set of nodes that match a specified filter. For each matching node, the developer can apply different data-manipulation functions, extraction methods, and constructors.

You build a FLWOR expression by using the following clauses:

- *FOR*   One or more FOR expressions can be applied to an XQUERY expression. The *FOR* clause declares variables that contain a sequence of nodes resulting from an XPATH expression. This sequence is the input sequence for the XQUERY expression to process. The *FOR* clause will iterate through all the items in the set of nodes; for each one of them, the FLWOR expression will return a result.

- **LET** Not supported in SQL Server 2005. In the XQUERY recommendation, it is used to declare variables that contain a single value or a sequence of nodes that match a specific XPATH expression. The difference about the *FOR* clause is that the FLWOR expression does not iterate through the items in the *LET* variables.

- **WHERE** An optional clause. It gives the XQUERY expression the capability to filter further the input sequences that use different types of operators (for example, *conditional* and *logical comparison* operators) and functions (for example, *aggregate*, *numeric*, and *boolean* functions).

- **ORDER BY** An optional clause. It gives the XQUERY expression the capability to order the output sequence in a different order than the input sequence. The input sequence is processed in document order as generated by the XPATH expression in the *FOR* clause.

- **RETURN** Only one is permitted. It declares the structure of the output sequence (the resulting XML fragment). The return section of the XQUERY expression allows developers to extract and manipulate data coming from the input sequence and to create new XML structures by means of XQUERY constructors (special functions used to create new XML elements, attributes, and other XML structures).

MORE INFO   XQUERY

XQUERY is a complete programming language and is beyond the scope of this book. A recommended starting point is to read the subtopics under the section "XQuery Against the xml Data Type" in SQL Server 2005 Books Online.

Using the *query()* Method

You use the *query()* method to execute an XQUERY or an XPATH expression over the XML structure contained inside a column, parameters, or variables of type XML. The result of executing a *query()* method is an untyped instance of XML data type. It is said to be untyped because SQL Server does not verify whether it conforms to an XML schema.

The following code blocks show an example of using a *query()* method to execute a FLWOR expression. The first code block declares a variable of type XML and assigns to it the result of a FOR XML PATH query, typing the resulting XML as XML data type by using the TYPE instruction:

```
DECLARE @EMPLOYEES XML
SET @EMPLOYEES = (SELECT Department.[DepartmentID] 'Department/@id',
    Department.[Name] 'Department/@name',
```

```
        (
        SELECT History.[EmployeeID] 'Employee/@id'
                    ,History.[StartDate] 'Employee/@StartDate'
                    ,DATEDIFF(year, History.[StartDate], GetDate()) 'Employee/@YearsInRole'
        FROM HumanResources.EmployeeDepartmentHistory History
        WHERE Department.DepartmentID = History.DepartmentID
          AND History.EndDate IS NULL
        ORDER BY History.[StartDate]
        FOR XML PATH(''), TYPE
        ) 'Department/Employees'
  FROM HumanResources.Department
  ORDER BY Department.[DepartmentID]
FOR XML PATH (''), TYPE)
```

The next code block issues a *SELECT* statement and uses the *query()* method of the XML variable to execute a FLWOR expression:

```
SELECT @EMPLOYEES.query('
   for $dept in /Department,
       $emp in $dept/Employees/Employee[1]
   where count($dept/Employees/Employee) >= 10
   order by number($emp/@YearsInRole) descending
   return
        <BigDepartment employees="{count($dept/Employees/Employee)}"
            averageYears="{avg($dept/Employees/Employee/@YearsInRole)}">
              <SeniorEmployee firstDay="{$emp/@StartDate}"
                    yearsInRole="{$emp/@YearsInRole}">
                  {data($emp/@id)}
              </SeniorEmployee>
        </BigDepartment>')
FOR XML PATH(''), ROOT('Departments')
```

In the previous code example, the *for* clause declares two variables: *$dept* and *$emp*. (You must precede all variables in XQUERY with the dollar sign [$].) The *$dept* variable contains a sequence of *Department* nodes as a result from the /Department XPATH expression, which returns all nodes of type *Department*.

The *$emp* variable contains a sequence of a single *Employee* node resulting from the execution of the *$dept/Employees/Employee[1]* XPATH expression. When the Employee XML elements were generated, they were ordered by History.[StartDate] so that the first employee found always represents the employee who has been with the department the longest.

The FLWOR expression iterates through each of the nodes returned by the XPATH expressions.

The *where* clause filters the input sequence further by ignoring all departments with fewer than 10 employees.

The *order by* clause orders the output sequence of nodes. In this example, the output XML fragment is ordered according to the number of years that the employee has worked for that department, starting from the employee who has worked there the longest to the most recent employee.

The *return* clause declares the structure of the resulting XML sequence as a constant. Dynamic content is created by enclosing the code in curly braces ({*code*}). By using the variables $dept and $emp, the code is referencing the current node being processed, also known as the *context node*.

A *BigDepartment* XML element will be created with two XML attributes: *employees* and *averageYears*. The *employees* attribute will contain the number of employees in that department, and the *averageYears* attribute will contain the average number of years that all the employees combined have worked for the department. Notice the use of the *count* and *avg* XQUERY functions.

The *BigDepartment* element contains a nested XML element called *SeniorEmployee*, which is created with two XML attributes: *firstDay* and *yearsInRole*. The *firstDay* attribute contains the employee's work start date, and the *yearsInRole* contains the number of years that the employee has worked in that department.

The employee ID is created as the *SeniorEmployee* element's data. By using the *data()* function, the value of the *id* attribute is extracted and inserted in the new resulting structure as the node value for the *SeniorEmployee* element.

The result should be similar to this structure:

```
<Departments>
  <BigDepartment employees="179" averageYears="6.89944134078212">
    <SeniorEmployee firstDay="1996-07-31T00:00:00" yearsInRole="10">1</SeniorEmployee>
  </BigDepartment>
  <BigDepartment employees="12" averageYears="5.83333333333333">
    <SeniorEmployee firstDay="1999-03-14T00:00:00" yearsInRole="7">164</SeniorEmployee>
  </BigDepartment>
  <BigDepartment employees="10" averageYears="7">
    <SeniorEmployee firstDay="1999-01-19T00:00:00" yearsInRole="7">59</SeniorEmployee>
  </BigDepartment>
  <BigDepartment employees="10" averageYears="7">
    <SeniorEmployee firstDay="1999-01-05T00:00:00" yearsInRole="7">28</SeniorEmployee>
  </BigDepartment>
  <BigDepartment employees="18" averageYears="4.44444444444444">
    <SeniorEmployee firstDay="2001-02-04T00:00:00" yearsInRole="5">268</SeniorEmployee>
  </BigDepartment>
</Departments>
```

Sql:Variable and Sql:Column

The XQUERY implementation in SQL Server 2005 has been extended to support the scenarios in which the XML data must interact with data coming from outside the XQUERY expression, as Transact-SQL parameters or even with data coming from the relational environment, such as a column value.

By using the *sql:variable* function, you can include outside values coming from Transact-SQL variables inside an XQUERY and XPATH expression.

By using the *sql:column* function, you can include outside values coming from an existing column in a table inside an XQUERY and XPATH expression.

Using the *value()* Method

You use the *value()* method to execute an XQUERY or an XPATH expression over the XML structure contained inside a column, parameters, or variables of type XML. The difference is that the *value()* method must return a scalar value.

The resulting value of the value method is then converted to a Transact-SQL type. Developers must be careful to write the XQUERY/XPATH expression correctly for it to return a single value.

Examples of scalar values in XPATH could be the result of executing a *count()* function or a predicate specified in an expression to return a single result.

The following example is based on the same query shown in the last code example. It returns the value of the *name* attribute in a *Department* element and an *id* attribute with a value of 5 (*"Purchasing"*); the result is converted to a Transact-SQL *nvarchar(max)* data type:

```
SELECT @EMPLOYEES.value('(/Department[@id=5]/@name)[1]','nvarchar(max)')
```

Even if there is a single Department XML element in the XML structure with *id* with a value of 5, you must specify the *[1]* predicate. When SQL Server compiles the XPATH expression, the *[1]* indicates the cardinality of the result of executing such expression, and the value method validates that there is only one result.

Using the *exist()* Method

You use the *exist()* method to execute an XQUERY or an XPATH expression on the XML structure contained inside a column, parameters, or variable of type XML. The result of executing the *exist()* method is a Boolean value of 1 or 0. A 1 is returned when the XQUERY or XPATH expression returned at least one resulting node. A 0 is returned when the XQUERY or XPATH expression did not return any resulting node.

The *exist()* method is usually used in the *WHERE* clause of the *SELECT* statement in Transact-SQL to validate that the expression actually has matching nodes.

The following code sections walk you through an example of how to apply several XML manipulation techniques:

1. Create a new table with an XML column:

```
--CREATE TABLE
CREATE TABLE OLDEMPLOYEES(ID INT IDENTITY, EMPLOYEE_DATA XML)
GO
```

2. Create a new variable of type XML, initialize the variable with the result of a FOR XML query, and insert the XML stored in the variable into the table declared in step 1:

```
DECLARE @EMPLOYEES XML
SET @EMPLOYEES = (SELECT Department.[DepartmentID] 'Department/@id'
     ,Department.[Name] 'Department/@name',
        (
        SELECT History.[EmployeeID] 'Employee/@id'
                   ,History.[StartDate] 'Employee/@StartDate'
                   ,DATEDIFF(year, History.[StartDate], GetDate())
'Employee/@YearsInRole'
        FROM HumanResources.EmployeeDepartmentHistory History
        WHERE Department.DepartmentID = History.DepartmentID
          AND History.EndDate IS NULL
        ORDER BY History.[StartDate]
        FOR XML PATH(''), TYPE
        ) 'Department/Employees'
  FROM HumanResources.Department
  ORDER BY Department.[DepartmentID]
FOR XML PATH (''), TYPE)

INSERT OLDEMPLOYEES(EMPLOYEE_DATA)
VALUES (@EMPLOYEES)
```

3. Execute an XPATH expression on the XML data stored in the table:

```
DECLARE @YEARS INT
SET @YEARS = 7
SELECT EMPLOYEE_DATA.query(
'/Department[@name = sql:column("D.Name")]//
Employee[@YearsInRole>sql:variable("@YEARS")]')
FROM HumanResources.Department D, OLDEMPLOYEES
```

```
WHERE D.DepartmentID in
    (
        SELECT DepartmentID
        FROM HumanResources.Department
        WHERE GroupName = 'Manufacturing'
    ) AND
    EMPLOYEE_DATA.exist(
    '/Department[@name = sql:column("D.Name")]//
    Employee[@YearsInRole>sql:variable("@YEARS")]') = 1
    FOR XML RAW('Candidates'), ROOT('Bonus')
```

Notice the use of the *query()* method, the use of the *sql:variable* function, the use of the *sql:column* function, and the use of the *exist()* method.

The result you see should be similar to this structure:

```
<Bonus>
  <Candidates>
    <Employee id="1" StartDate="1996-07-31T00:00:00" YearsInRole="10" />
    <Employee id="7" StartDate="1998-01-26T00:00:00" YearsInRole="8" />
    <Employee id="8" StartDate="1998-02-06T00:00:00" YearsInRole="8" />
    <Employee id="10" StartDate="1998-02-07T00:00:00" YearsInRole="8" />
    <Employee id="13" StartDate="1998-03-05T00:00:00" YearsInRole="8" />
    <Employee id="14" StartDate="1998-03-11T00:00:00" YearsInRole="8" />
    <Employee id="15" StartDate="1998-03-23T00:00:00" YearsInRole="8" />
    <Employee id="16" StartDate="1998-03-30T00:00:00" YearsInRole="8" />
    <Employee id="17" StartDate="1998-04-11T00:00:00" YearsInRole="8" />
    <Employee id="18" StartDate="1998-04-18T00:00:00" YearsInRole="8" />
    <Employee id="19" StartDate="1998-04-29T00:00:00" YearsInRole="8" />
  </Candidates>
</Bonus>
```

Quick Check

1. What is the main difference between using the *query()* method and using the *value()* method of the XML data type?

2. What function is used to input external values into an XQUERY FLWOR expression?

Quick Check Answers

1. The *query()* method returns an untyped XML fragment as a result. The *value()* method returns a scalar Transact-SQL typed value.

2. There are two functions—*sql:variable* and *sql:column*—that enable you to include external values from the relational context into the XML expression.

PRACTICE **Use XQUERY to Query the UniversalLog Table**

This practice uses the results of the Lesson 1 practice. If you have not completed that practice, please go back and follow the instructions to complete it.

In this exercise, you query the data in the *UniversalLog* table in the *TK431Chapter8* database. You create the appropriate queries to return the results in the requested format. Remember that the LogRecord column in the *UniversalLog* table is of type XML.

NOTE Code available on the companion CD

For solutions to the exercises in the Lesson 2 practice, see the Practice Files\Chapter8\Lesson 2\ CompleteLesson2.sql file on the companion CD.

---

1. Create a query to retrieve all records from the *UniversalLog* table by using the *query()* method and XPATH. The result should resemble this structure:

```
<UniversalLog>
  <logRecord machine="server1" timestamp="2000-01-12T12:13:14Z">
    <post eventType="appStart">
      <moreInformation>All Services starting</moreInformation>
    </post>
  </logRecord>
  <logRecord machine="server2" timestamp="2000-01-13T12:13:14Z">
    <post eventType="appStart" />
    <information flag="warning">
      <message>Duplicate IP address</message>
    </information>
  </logRecord>
..........
<UniversalLog>
```

2. Retrieve records from the *UniversalLog* table by using the *query()* method and XPATH. Filter the results for log records that apply to Server2. The result should resemble this structure:

```
<UniversalLog>
  <logRecord machine="server2" timestamp="2000-01-13T12:13:14Z">
    <post eventType="appStart" />
    <information flag="warning">
      <message>Duplicate IP address</message>
    </information>
  </logRecord>
..........
<UniversalLog>
```

3. Retrieve records from the *UniversalLog* table by using the *query()* method and XPATH. Filter the results for log records that notify about a failure. The result should resemble this structure:

```
<UniversalLog>
  <logRecord machine="server2" timestamp="2000-01-11T12:13:14Z">
    <information flag="failure">
      <message>Hard Disk with ID #87230283 is not responding</message>
    </information>
    <error number="18763">
      <message>Application can not start</message>
      <module>AppLoader</module>
    </error>
    <post eventType="appStart" />
  </logRecord>
</UniversalLog>
```

4. Retrieve records from the *UniversalLog* table by using the *query()* method and XPATH, but include in the XML structure data stored in the relational infrastructure; for example, include the LogDateTime and ApplicationName columns. The result should resemble this structure:

```
<UniversalLog>
  <LogDateTime>2006-01-27T19:29:44.420</LogDateTime>
  <ApplicationName>SalesApp</ApplicationName>
  <logRecord machine="server2" timestamp="2000-01-11T12:13:14Z">
    <information flag="failure">
      <message>Hard Disk with ID #87230283 is not responding</message>
    </information>
    <error number="18763">
      <message>Application can not start</message>
      <module>AppLoader</module>
    </error>
    <post eventType="appStart" />
  </logRecord>
</UniversalLog>
```

5. Retrieve records from the *UniversalLog* table by using the *query()* method and XQUERY. Return an XML structure representing a report with all logged errors. The result should resemble this structure:

```
<UniversalLog>
  <errorReport issuedby="dbo" date="Jan 27 2006 11:59PM" />
  <error number="1001" timestamp="2000-01-14T12:13:14Z" server="server1">
    <message>The user does not have enough permissions to execute query</message>
    <module>DataAccessLayer</module>
  </error>
  <error number="18763" timestamp="2000-01-11T12:13:14Z" server="server2">
    <message>Application can not start</message>
    <module>AppLoader</module>
  </error>
</UniversalLog>
```

6. Retrieve independent values from the *UniversalLog* table by using the *value()* method and XPATH. Return a tabular structure representing a report with all logged errors. The result should resemble the following structure:

Error-Number	TimeStamp	Server-Name	Message	Module
1001	2000-01-14T12:13:14Z	server1	The user does not have enough permissions to execute query	DataAccess-Layer
18763	2000-01-11T12:13:14Z	server2	Application cannot start	AppLoader

Lesson Summary

- SQL Server 2005 provides multiple Transact-SQL constructs you can use to compose relational data into XML structures, to transform XML fragments into new XML formats, and to extract data out of existing XML fragments.

- The *FOR XML* clause enables you to compose relational data into an XML representation. There are four different formatting modes: *RAW*, *AUTO*, *PATH*, and *EXPLICIT*.

- By using nested queries in SQL Server 2005, developers can return complex multilevel XML structures that were impossible to create previously.

- The XML data type provides five methods that you can use to manipulate the contained XML fragment: *query()*, *value()*, *exist()*, *modify()*, and *nodes()*. The input to the XML data type's methods can be XQUERY and XPATH expressions.

- XQUERY and XPATH provide a complete query language for XML structures.

Lesson Review

The following questions are intended to reinforce key information presented in this lesson. The questions are also available on the companion CD if you prefer to review them in electronic form.

NOTE Answers

Answers to these questions and explanations of why each answer choice is right or wrong are located in the "Answers" section at the end of this book.

---

1. You are a database developer for your company. Your database contains one table to store Contact information in the following columns: ID, FirstName, Last-Name, and Company. You are asked to return an XML structure needed to bind this data to a Web page. The XML structure should look like this:

```
<ContactList>
  <Contact>
    <CompanyName> company </CompanyName>
    <NumberOfContacts> 1 </NumberOfContacts>
    <Contacts>
      <Contacts FirstName="fName" LastName="lName" />
    </Contacts>
  </Contact>
........
<ContactList>
```

Which of the following queries will return the desired structure?

A.

```
SELECT Contact.Company AS [CompanyName], COUNT(Contact.ID) AS [NumberOfContacts],
 FirstName, LastName
FROM Contacts AS Contact
GROUP BY Company, FirstName, LastName
FOR XML AUTO, ELEMENTS, ROOT('ContactList')
```

B.

```
SELECT Contact.Company AS [CompanyName], COUNT(Contact.ID) AS [NumberOfContacts],
(
    SELECT FirstName, LastName
    FROM Contacts
    WHERE Contact.Company = Contact.Company
    FOR XML AUTO
) AS [ContactList]
FROM Contacts AS Contact
GROUP BY Contact.Company
FOR XML AUTO
```

C.

```
SELECT Contact.Company AS [CompanyName], COUNT(Contact.ID) AS [NumberOfContacts],
(
    SELECT FirstName, LastName
    FROM Contacts
    WHERE Contacts.Company = Contact.Company
    FOR XML AUTO, TYPE, ROOT('Contacts')
)
FROM Contacts AS Contact
GROUP BY Contact.Company
FOR XML AUTO, ELEMENTS, ROOT('ContactList')
```

D.

```
SELECT Contact.Company AS [CompanyName], COUNT(Contact.ID) AS [NumberOfContacts],
(
    SELECT FirstName, LastName
    FROM Contacts
    WHERE Contacts.Company = Contact.Company
    FOR XML AUTO, ELEMENTS, TYPE, ROOT('Contacts')
)
FROM Contacts AS Contact
GROUP BY Contact.Company
FOR XML AUTO, ROOT('ContactList')
```

2. Which of the methods implemented by the XML data type enables you to execute the following XQUERY expression? (Choose all that apply.)

```
for $c in /companies
where $c/company/@profit > 1000000
return
    <successful>
        <company ticker="{data($c/@StockSymbol)}">
            {data($c/company/@profit)}
        </company>
    </successful>
```

   A. *exist()*

   B. *modify()*

   C. *value()*

   D. *query()*

Lesson 3: Retrieving XML Data by Using SQL Server Middle-Tier Technologies

In Lesson 2, you saw how to use the *FOR XML* construct in Transact-SQL to retrieve relational data by using an XML representation and how to execute XQUERY and XPATH query instructions to extract data stored as XML in the XML data type. SQL Server 2005 also comes with SQLXML 4.0, a COM middle-tier application programming interface (API) that gives client applications the capability to extract XML data out of relational data without requiring you to write any Transact-SQL code.

At the core of SQLXML is the capability to define annotated XSD language schemas. By annotating a regular XSD schema with special keywords, you define a mapping between the XML schema and a database schema that enables developers to manipulate relational data without having to write Transact-SQL code. SQLXML generates all the required Transact-SQL code based on the activities executed against the XML structure.

Using annotated XSD schemas enables you to do the following:

- Extract information from the database and generate an XML instance.
- Execute XPATH queries over the annotated XSD schema.
- Update information in the database based on changes executed on an XML instance. If nodes have been added, updated, or removed, those activities will generate the required *INSERT*, *UPDATE*, and *DELETE* statements.
- Bulk load XML data from a file into a database.

This lesson covers how to use annotated XSD schemas and how to query them by using XML view files.

MORE INFO   Using SQLXML to modify and bulk load data

For information about how to use SQLXML to update data, see Lesson 4 in this chapter. For information about bulk loading XML data into the database using a mapping schema, see Lesson 5.

> **After this lesson, you will be able to:**
> - Create annotated XSD schemas.
> - Create XML views.
> - Use SQLXML 4.0 to query XSD schemas and XML views.
>
> **Estimated lesson time: 30 minutes**

Using SQLXML-Annotated XSD Schemas

Annotated XSD schemas declare a mapping between an XML schema and a relational schema so that SQLXML components can infer the relational operations to execute on the database based on the operations executed against the XML structure.

NOTE **Different uses of the term "schema"**

For the rest of this lesson, we will use the following terms to refer to different types of schemas:

■ The declaration of the physical structure of data is called a "schema."

■ Data in XML format is referred to as an "XML schema."

■ Data in a relational-tabular format is referred to as a "relational schema."

■ The SQLXML mapping mechanism is called an "annotated XSD schema."

You build annotated XSD schemas by enhancing regular XSD schemas with specific keywords. The annotated keywords are defined in the *xmlns:sql="urn:schemas-microsoft-com:mapping-schema"* XML namespace and namespace prefix. Table 8-4 describes the most common keywords you use to annotate XSD schemas.

Table 8-4 Common Annotated Keywords

Keyword	Description
sql:relation	Maps XML element declarations to tables in the database.
sql:fields	Maps XML content elements and attributes to columns in a table in the database.
sql:key-fields	Declares the primary keys from a table in the database so that SQLXML can formulate Transact-SQL queries by using the correct keys to filter data.
sql:relationship	Declares the relationship between two tables and is used when the XML code has nested elements that are related to different tables. It is translated into a Transact-SQL join.
sql:is-constant	Declares that the XML element should be copied as-is to the resulting structure. It does not map to any table or column in the database.

MORE INFO   Mapping keywords

For information about all the mapping keywords available and how to use each of them, see the topic "Using Annotations in XSD Schemas" in SQL Server 2005 Books Online.

Here is an example of an annotated XML schema that returns all employees, grouped by their department, as in previous examples:

```xml
<?xml version="1.0"?>
<xsd:schema id="EmployeeHiredDate"
    xmlns:sql="urn:schemas-microsoft-com:mapping-schema"
    xmlns:xsd="http://www.w3.org/2001/XMLSchema">
<xsd:element name="EmployeesByDepartment" sql:is-constant="true">
<xsd:complexType>
    <xsd:sequence minOccurs="0" maxOccurs="unbounded">
        <xsd:element name="Department" sql:relation="HumanResources.Department"
    sql:key-fields="DepartmentID">
            <xsd:complexType>
                <xsd:sequence minOccurs="0" maxOccurs="unbounded">
                    <xsd:element name="Employee" sql:relation="HumanResources.Employee"
                        sql:key-fields="EmployeeID">
                        <xsd:annotation>
                        <xsd:appinfo>
                        <sql:relationship    parent="HumanResources.Department"
parent-key="DepartmentID"
    child="HumanResources.EmployeeDepartmentHistory"
        child-key="DepartmentID" />
                        <sql:relationship
    parent="HumanResources.EmployeeDepartmentHistory"
        parent-key="EmployeeID"
        child="HumanResources.Employee" child-key="EmployeeID" />
                        </xsd:appinfo>
                        </xsd:annotation>
                        <xsd:complexType>
                            <xsd:sequence>
                                <xsd:element name="Title"/>
                                <xsd:element name="HireDate"/>
                            </xsd:sequence>
                            <xsd:attribute name="ID" sql:field="EmployeeID"/>
                            <xsd:attribute name="LoginID"/>
                        </xsd:complexType>
                    </xsd:element>
                </xsd:sequence>
                <xsd:attribute name="ID" sql:field="DepartmentID"/>
                <xsd:attribute name="Name"/>
            </xsd:complexType>
        </xsd:element>
    </xsd:sequence>
</xsd:complexType>
</xsd:element>
</xsd:schema>
```

The *is-constant* attribute is added to the *EmployeesByDepartment* root node because it does not map to any table in the database.

Notice that the *sql:relationship* elements declare a many-to-many relationship between the *HumanResources.Department* table and the *HumanResources.EmployeeDepartment-History* table and then between the *HumanResources.EmployeeDepartmentHistory* table and the *HumanResources.Employee* table.

An implicit mapping is applied when an element or attribute does not declare its source table or column. An explicit mapping is applied when the *sql:relation* or *sql:field* attributes are used, as you can see by looking at the ID attributes in the *Employee* element in the above example.

A partial result of retrieving XML by using this annotated XML schema looks like this:

```
<EmployeesByDepartment>
...
<Department ID="2" Name="Tool Design">
 <Employee ID="4" LoginID="adventure-works\rob0">
  <Title>Senior Tool Designer</Title>
  <HireDate>1998-01-05T00:00:00</HireDate>
  </Employee>
 <Employee ID="5" LoginID="adventure-works\thierry0">
  <Title>Tool Designer</Title>
  <HireDate>1998-01-11T00:00:00</HireDate>
  </Employee>
 <Employee ID="263" LoginID="adventure-works\ovidiu0">
  <Title>Senior Tool Designer</Title>
  <HireDate>2001-01-05T00:00:00</HireDate>
  </Employee>
 <Employee ID="265" LoginID="adventure-works\janice0">
  <Title>Tool Designer</Title>
  <HireDate>2001-01-23T00:00:00</HireDate>
  </Employee>
  </Department>
...
</EmployeesByDepartment>
```

A clear benefit of using SQLXML-annotated XML schemas is that developers can design the structure of the XML data to fit their own needs.

Using SQLXML XML Views

A SQLXML XML view is an XML file that declares optional input parameters, a query, and a resulting XML structure. The result of executing an XML view is an XML fragment.

The input parameters enable you to accept external values that you can then use as arguments in the queries declared inside the XML view. The queries inside an XML view can be of two types: XPATH queries, which are executed over an annotated XSD schema, or Transact-SQL queries that use the FOR XML expression. You can write any number of queries inside the XML view, and different queries can fill in different sections of the resulting XML structure.

The following sample XML view combines all these features:

```
<BonusCandidates xmlns:sql="urn:schemas-microsoft-com:xml-sql">
<sql:header>
   <sql:param name="DeptID">1</sql:param>
</sql:header>
<NineAndTenYears>
  <sql:query>
   SELECT EmployeeID, StartDate, DATEDIFF(year, StartDate, GETDATE()) AS 'YearsInRole'
   FROM  HumanResources.EmployeeDepartmentHistory AS Employee
   WHERE (EndDate IS NULL) AND (DATEDIFF(year, StartDate, GETDATE()) > 8)
   ORDER BY StartDate
   FOR XML AUTO
  </sql:query>
</NineAndTenYears>
<DepartmentOfTheMonth>
  <sql:xpath-query mapping-schema="EmployeeHiredDate.xsd">
   EmployeesByDepartment/Department[@ID=$DeptID]
  </sql:xpath-query>
</DepartmentOfTheMonth>
</BonusCandidates>
```

The result of executing this XML view is the following:

```
<BonusCandidates xmlns:sql="urn:schemas-microsoft-com:xml-sql">
   <NineAndTenYears>
        <Employee EmployeeID="1" StartDate="1996-07-31T00:00:00" YearsInRole="10"/>
        <Employee EmployeeID="2" StartDate="1997-02-26T00:00:00" YearsInRole="9"/>
        <Employee EmployeeID="3" StartDate="1997-12-12T00:00:00" YearsInRole="9"/>
   </NineAndTenYears>
   <DepartmentOfTheMonth>
        <Department ID="2" Name="Tool Design">
            <Employee ID="4" LoginID="adventure-works\rob0">
                <Title>Senior Tool Designer</Title>
                <HireDate>1998-01-05T00:00:00</HireDate>
            </Employee>
            <Employee ID="5" LoginID="adventure-works\thierry0">
                <Title>Tool Designer</Title>
                <HireDate>1998-01-11T00:00:00</HireDate>
            </Employee>
            <Employee ID="263" LoginID="adventure-works\ovidiu0">
                <Title>Senior Tool Designer</Title>
                <HireDate>2001-01-05T00:00:00</HireDate>
            </Employee>
```

```
            <Employee ID="265" LoginID="adventure-works\janice0">
                  <Title>Tool Designer</Title>
                  <HireDate>2001-01-23T00:00:00</HireDate>
            </Employee>
        </Department>
    </DepartmentOfTheMonth>
</BonusCandidates>
```

XML view files accept the keywords that Table 8-5 describes.

Table 8-5 Keywords for XML View Files

Keyword	Description
sql:header	Declares a header section used to declare input parameters.
sql:param	Declares an input parameter. The *name* attribute indicates the parameter's identification name. The *content* value represents the default value in case the parameter is not sent when the view is executed.
sql:query	Declares a section in which a Transact-SQL query can be written. This query statement is sent as-is to the database server, so you have access to all query features supported by SQL Server 2005, including the different FOR XML modes explained previously.
sql:xpath-query	Declares a section in which an XPATH expression can be written. The *mapping-schema* attribute points to an annotated XSD schema to be used as source. Note in the previous example that the *DeptID* attribute is prefixed with the dollar sign ($) when used inside the query.

Some important restrictions that exist when using XML views include these:

- SQLXML 4.0 does not support all XPATH functions and syntaxes. For example, SQLXML 4.0 does not support the root query (/). Every XPATH query must begin at the top-level element in the schema.

- In SQLXML 4.0, document order is not always maintained, so XPATH numeric predicates and axes that use document order are not implemented. *XPATH axes* represent a step in an XPATH expression that defines the set of nodes that the expression should return. And *XPATH predicates* represent a conditional filter applied to the collection of nodes defined by the axes in an XPATH expression.

Only matching nodes will be returned by the XPATH expression. For example, the XPATH expression *Customer[1]* indicates that only the first *Customer* element found should be retrieved. This expression is illegal in SQLXML 4.0.

- SQLXML 4.0 does not support cross-product XPATH queries. For example, SQLXML does not support the following query, which selects all *Customers* with any *Order* for which the *OrderDate* equals the *ShipDate* of any *Order*: *Customers[Order/@OrderDate=Order/@ShipDate]*.

- Some XPATH expressions that might contain characters with special meanings in XML (for example, <, >, &, ', ") must be written as escape sequences in the XPATH expressions (for example, &lt for less than, &gt for greater than, &amp for ampersand, &apos for apostrophe, and &quot for quotation mark).

Quick Check
- What is the result of executing an XML view?

Quick Check Answer
- The result of executing an XML view is an XML fragment.

Querying Annotated XML Schemas and XML Views from .NET

SQLXML provides a managed API to execute queries against annotated XML schemas and XML views. Following the same object model as the ADO.NET classes, the API provides Command, DataAdapter, and Parameter classes that specialize in querying annotated XSD schemas. The SQLXML API is defined inside the Microsoft.Data.SqlXml dynamic-link library (DLL).

IMPORTANT   Use SqlOleDB provider

When connecting to a database by using the SQLXML classes, you must use the SqlOleDB provider.

To use SQLXML to execute an XPATH query against an annotated XSD schema, use the following code:

```
SqlXmlCommand cmd = new SqlXmlCommand("connection_string");
cmd.CommandText = "XPATH_expression";
cmd.CommandType = SqlXmlCommandType.XPath;
cmd.SchemaPath = "Annotated_XML_Schema_file.xml";
Stream s = cmd.ExecuteStream();
```

To execute an XML view file, use the following code:

```
SqlXmlCommand cmd = new SqlXmlCommand("connection_string");
cmd.CommandText = "XML_View_file.xml";
cmd.CommandType = SqlXmlCommandType.TemplateFile;
System.Xml.XmlReader xr = cmd.ExecuteXmlReader();
```

The *SqlXmlCommand.CommandType* property indicates the type of command that will be processed next. Note that the result of executing an XML view file can be processed by either a *System.IO.Stream* object or a *System.Xml.XmlReader* object.

The following example shows how to consume the result by using a *System.Data.DataSet* and how to pass input parameters to an XML view file:

```
SqlXmlCommand cmd = new SqlXmlCommand("connection_string");
cmd.CommandText = "XML_View_file.xml";
cmd.CommandType = SqlXmlCommandType.TemplateFile;

SqlXmlParameter param = cmd.CreateParameter();
param.Name = "@param_name";
param.Value = "param_value";

SqlXmlAdapter da = new SqlXmlAdapter(cmd);
System.Data.DataSet ds = new System.Data.DataSet();
da.Fill(ds);
```

The main benefit of using XML views and annotated XML schemas to query XML data is that they are easy to maintain because they are stored as files on the file system; any changes you make to the queries do not require recompiling the application. Another benefit is that the XML rendering happens where the XML views and annotated XML schemas are deployed, which can be on a different machine than the database server.

PRACTICE **Use SQLXML to Query the *UniversalLog* Table**

In this practice, you create an annotated XSD schema for the *UniversalLog* table. Then you execute multiple XPATH queries directly from the annotated XSD schema by using an XML view file. For solutions to the steps in this practice, see the Practice Files\Chapter8\Lesson 3\SQLXMLViews\SQLXMLViews.csproj Visual Studio 2005 project file on the companion CD.

1. Annotate the following XSD schema with the proper keywords to make this schema valid as an SQLXML-annotated XSD schema for the *UniversalLog* table:

```
<?xml version="1.0"?>
<xsd:schema id="UniversalLogSchema" xmlns:xsd="http://www.w3.org/2001/XMLSchema">
   <xsd:element name="Log">
      <xsd:complexType>
```

```
            <xsd:sequence>
                    <xsd:element name="Application" />
                    <xsd:element name="Details"/>
            </xsd:sequence>
            <xsd:attribute name="ID"/>
            <xsd:attribute name="Timestamp" />
        </xsd:complexType>
    </xsd:element>
</xsd:schema>
```

❑ The *Application* element maps to the ApplicationName column.

❑ The *Details* element maps to the LogRecord column. Because it is an XML-typed column, it must be marked with the *sql:datatype="xml"* attribute in the annotated XSD schema.

❑ The *ID* attribute maps to the ID column.

❑ The *Timestamp* attribute maps to the LogDateTime column.

2. Create an XML view file with the following XPATH query: *Log[Application= "SalesApp"]*

3. Create a console application in Visual Studio 2005 to execute the XPATH query directly against the annotated XSD schema or through the XML view file.

4. To create a console application, open Visual Studio 2005 or Visual C# 2005 Express Edition.

5. Point to New in the File Menu and choose Project.

6. In the New Project dialog box, select the Console Application template and click OK.

7. In the Project menu, choose Add Reference. When the Add Reference dialog box opens, scroll down and select Microsoft.Data.SqlXml and click OK.

8. Add the following code at the beginning of the file:

```
using Microsoft.Data.SqlXml;
using System.IO;
```

9. Add the following code inside the Main method:

```
string connectionString = "Provider=sqloledb; Data Source=(local);";
connectionString += "Initial Catalog=TK431Chapter8; User Id=sa;";
SqlXmlCommand cmd = new SqlXmlCommand(connectionString);
cmd.CommandText = "Log";
cmd.CommandType = SqlXmlCommandType.XPath;
cmd.SchemaPath = "UniversalLogSchema.xsd";
cmd.RootTag = "UniversalLog";

StreamReader r = new StreamReader(cmd.ExecuteStream());

Console.WriteLine(r.ReadToEnd());
Console.ReadLine();
```

Notice that for this code to work, you must modify the connection string to your specific environment. Set the Data Source to point to the correct SQL Server instance that you will be connecting, and set the User ID and Password to a correct credential with permissions to execute queries on the *TK431Chapter8* database.

10. Make sure that the connection string in the code points to the correct server and is using the correct identity to connect to the SQL Server instance.

11. Make sure to copy the UniversalLogSchema.xsd file and the UniversalLog-View.xml file to the C:\Chapter8\Lesson 3\SQLXMLViews\bin\Debug directory before running it.

12. Press F5 to start running the sample application.

Lesson Summary

- SQLXML is a middle-tier COM component that can compose relational data into XML data by using annotated XSD schemas and XML views.

- Annotated XSD schemas declare a mapping between an XML schema and a relational schema so that SQLXML components can infer the relational operations to execute on the database based on the operations executed against the XML structure.

- SQLXML provides a managed API that provides Command, DataAdapter, and Parameter classes that specialize in querying annotated XSD schemas. The SQLXML API is defined inside the Microsoft.Data.SqlXml DLL.

- SQLXML XML view files provide an easy way to manage the format of the resulting XML of multiple Transact-SQL and XPATH queries within the same file.

Lesson Review

The following questions are intended to reinforce key information presented in this lesson. The questions are also available on the companion CD if you prefer to review them in electronic form.

NOTE Answers

Answers to these questions and explanations of why each answer choice is right or wrong are located in the "Answers" section at the end of this book.

---

1. What is the mechanism you use to define a mapping between the XML schema and a relational schema that enables developers to manipulate relational data without having to write Transact-SQL code?

    A. *exist()* method

    B. XML schema collection

    C. Annotated XML schema

    D. Relational schema

2. What are the main benefits of using XML views and annotated XML schemas to query XML data? (Choose all that apply.)

    A. XML views and annotated XML schemas validate your XML.

    B. They are stored as files on the file system, so you don't have to recompile the application if you change the files.

    C. The XML rendering happens where you deploy the XML views and annotated XML schemas, which can be on a different machine than the database server.

    D. XML views and annotated XML schemas compare the original and current views of the XML data and automatically create the required Transact-SQL commands to synchronize the changes from the XML data into relational data in the database.

Lesson 4: Modifying XML Data

SQL Server 2005 offers two technologies that give you the capability to modify an XML instance by deleting, adding, or updating nodes in the XML structure or by changing the node contents. The XML data type implements XML data manipulation language (XML DML) as an extension to the XQUERY and XPATH expressions already supported. And the SQLXML middle-tier API gives you the option of using updategrams, so instead of declaring the actual queries to execute, applications just need to provide the final view of the XML instance. By comparing the original and the final versions of the XML structure, SQLXML can formulate the set of Transact-SQL operations required to synchronize the XML data with the relational data.

This lesson covers the most important techniques for updating XML data in SQL Server 2005 and, when appropriate, provides references to external documentation so that you can learn more about a specific feature. All the code examples in this lesson use the *AdventureWorks* sample database installed by the SQL Server 2005 Setup.

After this lesson, you will be able to:

- Choose whether to use the XML data type or SQLXML to modify XML data.
- Use the *modify()* method of the XML data type to insert, modify, or delete XML content and XML structure elements.
- Use SQLXML updategrams to generate Transact-SQL *INSERT*, *UPDATE*, and *DELETE* statements without writing any Transact-SQL code.

Estimated lesson time: 30 minutes

Real World

Adolfo Wiernik

Previous versions of SQL Server did not provide a way to update XML data at the node level. The only technology available was SQLXML updategrams, which are covered in this lesson. But updategrams enable you to modify relational data represented as XML data. Updategrams provide modification capabilities for data viewed as XML and not stored as XML. Another possibility was to use OPENXML, convert the XML structure into a tabular format, update it, and then convert it back into XML. Of course, this caused heavy processor and memory usage. The last and easiest solution was to update the XML data by using a middle-tier technology such as *Document Object Model (DOM)* or *Simple API for XML (SAX)*, but this meant that the database was not aware of the changes being made.

> But with SQL Server 2005, I have another, easier, option. I can store data in the new XML data type and use the *modify()* method to insert, delete, or update the XML data. And what's great about the *modify()* method is that it enables me to modify both values inside XML nodes and the XML structure.

Modifying XML Values and XML Structure

Depending on how XML data is stored, SQL Server 2005 offers two different technologies for modifying the data:

- If the data is stored in an XML data type, use the *modify()* method to insert, delete, or update the XML data. The *modify()* method supports modifying both the values inside XML nodes and the structure of the XML fragment.

- If the data is stored in a relational structure but processed as XML, by using either the *FOR XML* statements or an annotated XSD schema, use the SQLXML Updategrams feature, which supports modifying the XML values inside the XML nodes. Because the data is not stored natively as XML, it does not support modifying the XML structure.

Using the modify() Method in the XML Data Type

The XQUERY language does not provide data-manipulation keywords. But Microsoft has extended the XQUERY capabilities in SQL Server 2005 by including a set of instructions that you can use to add, update, or delete XML data (XML DML). The *modify()* method of the XML data type receives a single input parameter that must be a valid XML DML expression and executes it over the XML fragment that it contains.

The XML DML language provided by SQL Server 2005 supports the following keywords:

- *insert* Instructs SQL Server 2005 to insert one or more nodes as children or siblings of a specified node. The *insert* construction is made of two expressions and an operator. The first expression can return a single node or a set of nodes. The second expression must return a single node. Both expressions can be constructed by using constant values or by providing an XQUERY expression. The operator that joins both expressions can be one of the following:
  - ❏ *into* Indicates that the nodes must be inserted as children of the node identified by the second expression. If the node already has child nodes, the XML DML expression could indicate whether the new nodes should be

inserted as the first nodes (by specifying *as first into*) or as the last nodes (by specifying *as last into*, which is the default).

❑ ***after*** Indicates that the nodes must be inserted after the node identified by the second expression so that they become siblings.

❑ ***before*** Indicates that the nodes must be inserted before the node identified by the second expression so that they become siblings.

❑ ***replace value of*** Instructs SQL Server 2005 to update the value of a specified node. The *replace value of* construction comprises two expressions. The first expression must be a single node. The second expression can be constructed by using constant values or by providing an XQUERY expression that returns a set of nodes.

❑ ***delete*** Instructs SQL Server 2005 to delete one or more nodes from the XML structure. The *delete* construction is made of a single XQUERY expression that returns a set of nodes to be removed from the XML instance.

You call the *modify()* method of the XML data type by using the SET expression, either as a stand-alone expression or as part of an *UPDATE* statement.

When modifying a typed XML instance, the final XML format must be a valid instance of that type as declared on an XML schema collection. Otherwise, a validation error is returned.

The examples in this lesson are based on the following initial query from Lesson 2 in this chapter:

```
USE AdventureWorks
GO
DECLARE @X XML

SET @X = ( SELECT Department.[DepartmentID] 'Department/@id'
    ,Department.[Name] 'Department/@name',
        (
        SELECT History.[EmployeeID] 'Employee/@id'
                ,History.[StartDate] 'Employee/@StartDate'
                ,DATEDIFF(year, History.[StartDate], GetDate()) 'Employee/@YearsInRole'
        FROM HumanResources.EmployeeDepartmentHistory History
        WHERE Department.DepartmentID = History.DepartmentID
          AND History.EndDate IS NULL
        ORDER BY History.[StartDate]
        FOR XML PATH(''), TYPE
        ) 'Department/Employees'
  FROM HumanResources.Department
  ORDER BY Department.[DepartmentID]
FOR XML PATH (''),ROOT('Departments'), TYPE)
```

If you display the contents of the @*X* variable, you see the following partial result:

```
<Departments>
...
  <Department id="2" name="Tool Design">
    <Employees>
      <Employee id="5" StartDate="1998-01-11T00:00:00" YearsInRole="8" />
      <Employee id="4" StartDate="2000-07-01T00:00:00" YearsInRole="6" />
      <Employee id="263" StartDate="2001-01-05T00:00:00" YearsInRole="5" />
      <Employee id="265" StartDate="2001-01-23T00:00:00" YearsInRole="5" />
    </Employees>
  </Department>
...
</Departments>
```

To demonstrate the *modify()* method and the XML DML keywords, let's walk through a short series of scenarios. Suppose you were assigned the task of creating a new department for customer service. Because customer service is very important, all employees who have been working for the company more than eight years will be assigned to that department. The following XML DML expression uses the *insert* keyword with the *before* operator to insert a new *Department* node:

```
SET @X.modify('
    insert <Department id="17" name="Customer Service"><Employees/></Department>
    before (/Departments/Department)[1]')
```

The next XML DML expression uses the *insert* keyword with the *into* operator to insert all employees who have been working for the company more than eight years into the newly created department node:

```
SET @X.modify('
    insert /Departments/Department/Employees/Employee[@YearsInRole>8]
    into (/Departments/Department[@id=17]/Employees)[1]')
```

The following XML DML *modify()* expression uses *insert* with the *into* operator to modify the XML structure by adding a new bonus attribute for the employees who have been with the company the longest as an incentive for moving into the new department:

```
SET @X.modify('
    insert attribute bonus {"true"}
    into (/Departments/Department[@id=17]/Employees/Employee[@YearsInRole =
    max(/Departments/Department[@id=17]/Employees/*/@YearsInRole)])[1]')
```

If you display the contents of the @*X* variable, you see the following partial result:

```
<Departments>
  <Department id="17" name="Customer Service">
    <Employees>
      <Employee id="3" StartDate="1997-12-12T00:00:00" YearsInRole="9" />
```

```
      <Employee id="2" StartDate="1997-02-26T00:00:00" YearsInRole="9" />
      <Employee bonus="true" id="1" StartDate="1996-07-31T00:00:00" YearsInRole="10" />
    </Employees>
  </Department>
...
<Departments>
```

Now, let's say that you must remove the *Employee* nodes with IDs 1, 2, and 3 from their previous departments (7, 4, 1) by using the *delete* keyword:

```
SET @X.modify('delete /Departments/Department[@id=7]/Employees/Employee[@id=1]')
SET @X.modify('delete /Departments/Department[@id=4]/Employees/Employee[@id=2]')
SET @X.modify('delete /Departments/Department[@id=1]/Employees/Employee[@id=3]')
```

And management has also decided that the new department should not be called *Customer Service*; you need to use the *replace value of* keyword to change its name to *Customer Assistance*:

```
SET @X.modify('
   replace value of (/Departments/Department[@id=17]/@name)[1]
   with "Customer Assistance"')
```

Quick Check

1. What are the three keywords in XML DML as defined by SQL Server 2005?
2. How would you use the *modify()* method in a Transact-SQL *UPDATE* statement?

Quick Check Answers

1. The three XML DML keywords in SQL Server 2005 are *insert*, *replace value of*, and *delete*.
2. The following code example shows how you would use the *modify()* method in a Transact-SQL *UPDATE* statement:

```
UPDATE UniversalLog
SET LogRecord.modify('
   replace value of (logRecord/error/module)[1]
   with "BusinessLayerComponent" ')
WHERE ID = 5
```

Using SQLXML Updategrams

An updategram is an XML fragment that declares an original and a current view of an XML structure. By comparing the original and current views of the XML data, SQLXML can create the required Transact-SQL commands to synchronize the changes from the XML data into relational data in the database.

An annotated XSD schema can support an updategram, so SQLXML can be aware of the mapping between the XML schema and the relational schema. If an annotated XSD schema is not available, the updategram implementation in SQLXML tries to do an implicit mapping, taking the names of the XML nodes as table and column names.

An updategram comprises three sections:

- **Namespace declaration**   The following namespace declares the reserved update-gram keywords: *xmlns:updg="urn:schemas-microsoft-com:xml-updategram"*

- **Optional *header* section**   As in the XML views, the optional *header* section allows for the declaration of input parameters in the updategram.

- **One or more *sync* sections**   Each *sync* section declares a transaction scope. All the operations inside each *sync* section are executed as an atomic operation: they must either all succeed or all fail. Each *sync* section can be associated with a different annotated XSD schema by using the *mapping-schema* attribute. The *sync* section contains any number of *before* and *after* sections (they should be declared in pairs). The *before* section represents the original version of the XML data; the *after* section represents the current version of the XML data.

When using SQLXML updategrams to generate Transact-SQL statements to insert, delete, and update data, remember the following requirements:

- If you want to generate a Transact-SQL *INSERT* statement, the XML fragment must be in the *after* section. The *before* section can be omitted.

- If you want to generate a Transact-SQL *DELETE* statement, the XML fragment must be in the *before* section. The *after* section can be omitted.

- If you want to generate a Transact-SQL *UPDATE* statement, the *before* section and the *after* section must be declared. Based on the differences between them, SQLXML formulates the *UPDATE* statement.

MORE INFO   **Special updategram keywords for Insert, Update, and Delete**

Special keywords enable you to execute different tasks such as handling null values, handling automatic values such as Identity columns or globally unique identifier (GUID) columns, and matching a specific *before* version of the data with an *after* version of the data when multiple *before* and *after* nodes are provided inside the same *sync* section.

Read the following sections in SQL Server 2005 Books Online for more information about the special keywords that you can specify in the XML structure:

❑   "Inserting Data Using XML Updategrams"

❑   "Updating Data Using XML Updategrams"

❑   "Deleting Data Using XML Updategrams"

Let's take the same example we used for the *modify()* method of the XML data type and adjust it to use updategrams. First, let's create an annotated XSD schema called Department.xsd for the *HumanResources.Departments* table in the *AdventureWorks* database:

```xml
<?xml version="1.0"?>
<xs:schema id="Department" xmlns:sql="urn:schemas-microsoft-com:mapping-schema"
           xmlns:xs="http://www.w3.org/2001/XMLSchema">
  <xs:element name="NewDepartment" sql:relation="HumanResources.Department">
        <xs:complexType>
            <xs:sequence>
                <xs:element name="ID" sql:field="DepartmentID" />
                <xs:element name="Name"   />
                <xs:element name="GroupName" />
            </xs:sequence>
        </xs:complexType>
    </xs:element>
</xs:schema>
```

Now we can create an updategram to insert a new department, saved in a file called DepartmentUpdg.xml:

```xml
<ROOT xmlns:updg="urn:schemas-microsoft-com:xml-updategram">
   <updg:header>
        <updg:param name="DepartmentName"></updg:param>
   </updg:header>
   <updg:sync mapping-schema="Department.xsd">
   <updg:before>
   </updg:before>
   <updg:after>
        <NewDepartment>
             <Name>@DepartmentName</Name>
             <GroupName>Quality Assurance</GroupName>
        </NewDepartment>
   </updg:after>
   </updg:sync>
</ROOT>
```

And last, let's create a .NET application to execute the updategram. Remember to add a reference to Microsoft.Data.dll:

```csharp
SqlXmlCommand cmd = new SqlXmlCommand("connection_string");

cmd.CommandStream = new FileStream("DepartmentUpdg.xml", FileMode.Open, FileAccess.Read);
cmd.CommandType = SqlXmlCommandType.DiffGram;

SqlXmlParameter p = cmd.CreateParameter();
p.Name = "@DepartmentName";
p.Value = "Customer Assistance";

cmd.ExecuteNonQuery();
```

When you execute this code, it generates the following dynamic Transact-SQL code to be executed by SQL Server 2005:

```
exec sp_executesql N' SET XACT_ABORT ON
BEGIN TRAN
DECLARE @eip INT, @r__ int, @e__ int
SET @eip = 0
INSERT HumanResources.Department (Name, GroupName) VALUES (N''@DepartmentName'', N''Quality
 Assurance''); SELECT @e__ = @@ERROR, @r__ = @@ROWCOUNT
 IF (@e__ != 0 OR @r__ != 1) SET @eip = 1

IF (@eip != 0) ROLLBACK ELSE COMMIT
SET XACT_ABORT OFF
 ',N'@DepartmentName nvarchar(19)',N'Customer Assistance'
```

MORE INFO   Be careful when handling database concurrency issues

If one user alters the data in the database right before another user, it could be that both the *before* and *after* sections of data are out of date. Updategrams take an optimistic concurrency approach to handling concurrent updates to data in the database. This topic is beyond the scope of this chapter, but to learn how to handle database concurrency issues in updategrams, see the topic "Handling Database Concurrency Issues in Updategrams" in SQL Server 2005 Books Online.

PRACTICE Modifying XML Data

This practice is constructed over the results of the previous practices in Lessons 2 and 3. If you have not completed these practices, please go back and follow the instructions to complete them. In this practice, you modify the XML data inside the *UniversalLog* table by using XML DML. Then you create an updategram to insert new records into the *UniversalLog* table.

NOTE   Code available on the companion CD

The Practice Files\Chapter8\Lesson 4\CompleteLesson4.sql file provides the solution for the exercises in Practice 1 in this lesson.

▶ **Practice 1: Modify XML Data by Using XML DML**

In this exercise, you create the Transact-SQL statements to modify the contents of the *UniversalLog* table. If you completed the practices from previous lessons, the *UniversalLog* table contains five rows.

1. The first row is from the SalesApp application. The LogRecord column contains the following XML fragment:

```
<logRecord machine="server1" timestamp="2000-01-12T12:13:14Z">
  <post eventType="appStart">
```

```
    <moreInformation>All Services starting</moreInformation>
  </post>
</logRecord>
```

2. Issue an *UPDATE* statement by using the *modify()* method of the XML data type to modify this XML into a fragment that looks like this:

```
<logRecord machine="server1" timestamp="2000-01-12T12:13:14Z">
  <post eventType="appStart">
    <moreInformation>All Services starting</moreInformation>
  </post>
<information flag="custom">
    <message>SQL Server service is starting</message>
  </information>
</logRecord>
```

3. The fifth row is from the HoursReport application. Update the XML data contained in the LogRecord column. Change the information message in the *logRecord/information/message* XML element to be "Not enough memory."

4. The fourth row is from the CustomerService application. Update the XML data contained in the LogRecord column. Delete the *logRecord/post* XML element.

5. Execute a *SELECT* statement to read all data from the *UniversalLog* table and verify that the changes were applied.

NOTE   Code available on the companion CD

The files in the Chapter8\Lesson 4\Updategram\Updategram.csproj Visual Studio project provide the solution for the exercises in Practice 2 in this lesson.

▶ **Practice 2: Insert New Rows by Using a SQLXML Updategram**

In the practice in Lesson 3, you created an annotated XSD schema for the *Universal-Log* table. In this exercise, you create an updategram that matches that schema and use it to insert new records into the *UniversalLog* table.

1. Create an updategram to insert new values into the *UniversalLog* table. Use this updategram as a reference:

```
<ROOT xmlns:updg="urn:schemas-microsoft-com:xml-updategram">
  <updg:header>
        <updg:param name="AppName"></updg:param>
        <updg:param name="Message"></updg:param>
  </updg:header>
  <updg:sync mapping-schema="UniversalLogSchema.xsd">
  <updg:before>
  </updg:before>
```

```
<updg:after>
      <Log Timestamp="2000-01-01T06:00:00.000">
            <Application>$AppName</Application>
            <Details>$Message</Details>
      </Log>
</updg:after>
</updg:sync>
</ROOT>
```

2. Create a console application in Visual Studio 2005 to execute this updategram. Your code should look like this:

```
SqlXmlCommand cmd = new SqlXmlCommand("Provider=sqloledb;Data Source=(local);
    Initial Catalog=TK431Chapter8;User Id=sa;");

cmd.CommandStream = new FileStream("NewLogRecordUpdategram.xml",
    FileMode.Open, FileAccess.Read);
cmd.CommandType = SqlXmlCommandType.DiffGram;

SqlXmlParameter appName = cmd.CreateParameter();
appName.Name = "@AppName";
appName.Value = "CustomerAssistance";

SqlXmlParameter message = cmd.CreateParameter();
message.Name = "@Message";
message.Value = @"<logRecord machine='WebHostingServer' timestamp='2000-01-
01T06:00:00Z'>
    <post eventType='appStart'><moreInformation>The web server is under attack</
moreInformation>
    </post></logRecord>";

cmd.ExecuteNonQuery();
```

Lesson Summary

- SQL Server 2005 supports updating XML documents. It supports modifying both XML values and the XML structure.

- The XML data type in SQL Server 2005 implements the *modify()* method to allow updating of XML data. The *modify()* method accepts as input parameters an XQUERY language extension for data manipulation.

- SQLXML updategrams enable you to update relational data represented as XML data. SQLXML updategrams are XML documents that compare the original and current versions of XML data. They then execute Transact-SQL *INSERT*, *UPDATE*, and *DELETE* statements based on the differences between the versions.

- You can execute updategrams from .NET applications.

Lesson Review

The following questions are intended to reinforce key information presented in this lesson. The questions are also available on the companion CD if you prefer to review them in electronic form.

NOTE   Answers

Answers to these questions and explanations of why each answer choice is right or wrong are located in the "Answers" section at the end of this book.

---

1. Which of the following technologies would you use to update the XML values as well as the XML structure of an XML document?

   A. SQLXML-annotated XSD schemas

   B. SQLXML updategrams

   C. The *modify()* method of the XML data type with XML DML

   D. OPENXML in an *UPDATE* statement

2. What is the result of executing the following XML DML expression?

   ```
   SET @X.modify('
      insert
            for $e in /Departments/Department[@id=1]/Employees/Employee
            return $e
      before (/Departments/Department[@id=1]/Employees/Employee)[1]')
   ```

   A. Inserts the constant expression *"for $e in /Departments/Department [@id=1]/Employees/Employee return $e"* as a child of the */Departments/ Department[@id=1]/Employees/Employee* node.

   B. Duplicates the nodes contained inside */Departments/Department[@id=1]/ Employees/Employee*.

   C. Copies the contents of the */Departments/Department[@id=1]/Employees/ Employee* node into the first *Employee* node found under *Employees*, under *Department*, and under *Departments*.

   D. Returns an error: XQUERY not supported with the insert XML DML keyword.

Lesson 5: Converting Between XML Data and Relational Data

Previous lessons examined the various techniques you can use to retrieve XML data from SQL Server 2005. This lesson focuses on the opposite operation: converting XML data into relational data, often called *shredding*. SQL Server 2005 offers three options for shredding XML data:

- Use OPENXML and the XML stored procedures.
- Use the XML data type's *nodes()* method along with the *APPLY* operators.
- Use the SQLXML middle-tier API to bulk load XML data.

This lesson covers the most important techniques for converting XML data into relational data and, where appropriate, references external documentation so that you can learn more about a specific feature. All code examples in this lesson use the *AdventureWorks* sample database installed by SQL Server 2005 Setup.

After this lesson, you will be able to:

- Choose the proper strategy between using OPENXML, the *nodes()* method in the XML data type, and SQLXML-annotated XSD schemas when shredding XML data.
- Decide when to use implicit or explicit mapping when using OPENXML.
- Use the *APPLY* operators when querying an XML data type column.
- Create annotated XSD schemas and bulk load XML data into the database.

Estimated lesson time: 40 minutes

Shredding XML Using OPENXML and XML Stored Procedures

SQL Server 2000 first provided support for shredding XML data into a relational representation by using the OPENXML Transact-SQL instructions and XML stored procedures. SQL Server provides two important stored procedures for shredding XML documents:

- *sp_xml_preparedocument* takes an XML document, *parses* it using an XML parser, and loads it into memory in a DOM-like structure. The stored procedure returns a memory handle to the in-memory parsed structure as an output parameter.
- *sp_xml_removedocument* receives a memory handle to a parsed XML structure; then deallocates and cleans up the memory space.

Between these two calls, developers must use the *OPENXML* statement to transform the loaded XML structure into tabular format.

The *OPENXML* statement returns a result set, so you can use it wherever a result set is expected inside the Transact-SQL language—for example, in the *FROM* clause of a *SELECT* statement.

SQL Server 2005 implements two important changes to the way OPENXML works:

- It adds support to the new data types available in SQL Server 2005, including the XML data type and the *(n)varchar(max)* data types.

- It uses a new version of the MSXML parser that is used to parse the input XML, optimized especially for SQL Server loading requirements.

CAUTION   Memory requirements for using OPENXML

One of the most important issues in using OPENXML is that you need to fully load the XML document into memory before shredding it into relational data. Depending on the size of the XML document, this process can allocate a lot of memory from the database server. You need to run tests to ensure that loading the XML document into memory will not overly tax your installation.

Using OPENXML

The *OPENXML* statement receives three input parameters: the handle to the in-memory parsed XML structure, an XPATH expression that filters the XML nodes to be processed, and an optional mapping scheme. The mapping scheme is used to define the relationship between the XML elements and attributes and a table schema. OPENXML supports two mapping modes: implicit mapping and explicit mapping.

The *OPENXML* statement also enables you to declare a table schema to define the table format that should be returned by the execution of the *OPENXML* statement.

The examples in this lesson will be based on the initial query from Lesson 2 in this chapter:

```
USE AdventureWorks
GO
DECLARE @X XML

SET @X = ( SELECT Department.[DepartmentID] 'Department/@id'
    ,Department.[Name] 'Department/@name',
        (
        SELECT History.[EmployeeID] 'Employee/@id'
                ,History.[StartDate] 'Employee/@StartDate'
                ,DATEDIFF(year, History.[StartDate], GetDate()) 'Employee/@YearsInRole'
```

```
        FROM HumanResources.EmployeeDepartmentHistory History
        WHERE Department.DepartmentID = History.DepartmentID
          AND History.EndDate IS NULL
        ORDER BY History.[StartDate]
        FOR XML PATH(''), TYPE
        ) 'Department/Employees'
  FROM HumanResources.Department
  ORDER BY Department.[DepartmentID]
FOR XML PATH (''),ROOT('Departments'), TYPE)
```

A partial result of executing this query is as follows:

```
<Departments>
...
  <Department id="2" name="Tool Design">
    <Employees>
      <Employee id="5" StartDate="1998-01-11T00:00:00" YearsInRole="8" />
      <Employee id="4" StartDate="2000-07-01T00:00:00" YearsInRole="6" />
      <Employee id="263" StartDate="2001-01-05T00:00:00" YearsInRole="5" />
      <Employee id="265" StartDate="2001-01-23T00:00:00" YearsInRole="5" />
    </Employees>
  </Department>
...
</Departments>
```

Implicit Mapping in OPENXML

The *OPENXML* statement provides an implicit XML mapping infrastructure in which
SQL Server tries to automatically map XML elements and attributes into columns.
The mapping is based on two items:

- A flag value that tells SQL Server to interpret the XML as an attribute-centric structure, as an element-centric structure, or as a combination of the two. Table 8-6
  describes the key values to specify in the flags parameter.

Table 8-6   Flag Values for Implicit Mapping in OPENXML

Value	Description
0	SQL Server 2005 will try to extract the values by using attribute-centric mapping. Each XML attribute will be converted into a column.
1	SQL Server 2005 will try to extract the values by using attribute-centric mapping. Each XML attribute will be converted into a column. If columns are not mapped yet, element-centric mapping is applied.
2	SQL Server 2005 will try to extract the values by using element-centric mapping. Each XML element will be converted into a column.

- The (case sensitive) names of the elements in the XML structure, which must match the name of the columns as declared on the returning table schema.

The following code example shows how to use OPENXML properly with implicit mapping:

```
DECLARE @h INT

EXEC sp_xml_preparedocument @h OUTPUT, @X
SELECT *
FROM OPENXML( @h , '/Departments/Department/Employees/Employee', 0)
WITH (   id INT,
         YearsInRole int,
         StartDate datetime)
WHERE YearsInRole >= 8

EXEC sp_xml_removedocument @h
GO
```

The *@h* variable will contain the memory handle to the parsed XML structure. The *@X* variable contains the XML structure. It is of type XML. The *OPENXML* statement filters the XML structure by executing the given XPATH query. The resulting XML nodes are converted into the table structure declared inside the *WITH* clause. Figure 8-3 shows the result of this query.

id	YearsInRole	StartDate
3	9	1997-12-12 00:00:00.000
9	8	1998-02-06 00:00:00.000
11	8	1998-02-24 00:00:00.000
12	8	1998-03-03 00:00:00.000
5	8	1998-01-11 00:00:00.000
2	9	1997-02-26 00:00:00.000
1	10	1996-07-31 00:00:00.000
7	8	1998-01-26 00:00:00.000
8	8	1998-02-06 00:00:00.000
10	8	1998-02-07 00:00:00.000
13	8	1998-03-05 00:00:00.000
14	8	1998-03-11 00:00:00.000
15	8	1998-03-23 00:00:00.000
16	8	1998-03-30 00:00:00.000
17	8	1998-04-11 00:00:00.000
18	8	1998-04-18 00:00:00.000
19	8	1998-04-29 00:00:00.000

Figure 8-3 Result of running example OPENXML query with implicit mapping

Explicit Mapping in OPENXML

Using the explicit XML mapping syntax, developers can manually specify the relationship between an XML structure and the return table schema. Instead of using the flags parameter and the element names, you must provide a column mapping pattern to explicitly specify how to map each column to the XML data, as shown in the following code example:

```
DECLARE @h INT

EXEC sp_xml_preparedocument @h OUTPUT, @X

SELECT *
FROM OPENXML( @h , '/Departments/Department/Employees/Employee')
WITH (
        ID INT '../../@id',
        StartDate datetime,
        [Name] nvarchar(max) '../../@name',
        YearsInRole int)
WHERE YearsInRole = 8

EXEC sp_xml_removedocument @h
GO
```

Notice that the column declarations inside the *WITH* clause explicitly indicate how to extract the values from the values contained inside the XML document. The *ID* column is mapped to the *ID* attribute of the *Department* element, and the Name column is mapped to the *name* attribute of the *Department* element. Figure 8-4 shows the result of this query.

ID	StartDate	Name	YearsInRole
1	1998-02-06 00:00:00.000	Engineering	8
1	1998-02-24 00:00:00.000	Engineering	8
1	1998-03-03 00:00:00.000	Engineering	8
2	1998-01-11 00:00:00.000	Tool Design	8
7	1998-01-26 00:00:00.000	Production	8
7	1998-02-06 00:00:00.000	Production	8
7	1998-02-07 00:00:00.000	Production	8
7	1998-03-05 00:00:00.000	Production	8
7	1998-03-11 00:00:00.000	Production	8
7	1998-03-23 00:00:00.000	Production	8
7	1998-03-30 00:00:00.000	Production	8
7	1998-04-11 00:00:00.000	Production	8
7	1998-04-18 00:00:00.000	Production	8
7	1998-04-29 00:00:00.000	Production	8

Figure 8-4   Result of running example OPENXML query with explicit mapping

---

MORE INFO   Edge Table

If the *WITH* clause is not specified in the *OPENXML* statement, SQL Server returns an internal relational representation of the XML data called an *Edge Table*. The Edge Table can be further queried to get information about the structure of the XML data. To learn about the structure of the Edge Table, see the topic "OPENXML (Transact-SQL)" in SQL Server 2005 Books Online.

Shredding XML by Using the XML Data Type's *nodes()* Method

With the inclusion of the XML data type in SQL Server 2005, Microsoft had to solve a new problem: how to shred the contained XML data from the XML data type instance into a tabular-relational format. Instead of having to convert the XML data into a string type and paying the high price of loading the whole XML structure into memory by using OPENXML, the XML data type provides its own shredding mechanism: the *nodes()* method.

The *nodes()* method returns a tabular result set. This result set represents a table containing a single column of type XML. A new row is returned for each XML node that matches a given XQUERY expression.

Because the result set returned from the *nodes()* method contains a single column of type XML, you should apply the other methods available in the XML data type—*value()*, *query()*, *exist()*—to extract data out of each row.

The following code shows how to use the *nodes()* method:

```
SELECT   C.value('@id','int') AS ID,
         C.value('@name','nvarchar(max)') AS [NAME],
         C.value('count(./Employees/*)', 'int') AS EMPLOYEE_COUNT,
         C.query('./Employees') AS EMPLOYEE_LIST
FROM @X.nodes('/Departments/Department') T(C)
GO
```

Figure 8-5 shows the result of this query.

ID	NAME	EMPLOYEE_COUNT	EMPLOYEE_LIST
1	Engineering	6	<Employees><Employee id="3" StartDate="1997-12-1...
2	Tool Design	4	<Employees><Employee id="5" StartDate="1998-01-1...
3	Sales	18	<Employees><Employee id="268" StartDate="2001-02...
4	Marketing	9	<Employees><Employee id="2" StartDate="1997-02-2...
5	Purchasing	12	<Employees><Employee id="164" StartDate="1999-03...
6	Research and Development	4	<Employees><Employee id="79" StartDate="1999-01-...
7	Production	179	<Employees><Employee id="1" StartDate="1996-07-3...
8	Production Control	6	<Employees><Employee id="21" StartDate="1999-01-...
9	Human Resources	6	<Employees><Employee id="30" StartDate="1999-01-...
10	Finance	10	<Employees><Employee id="59" StartDate="1999-01-...
11	Information Services	10	<Employees><Employee id="28" StartDate="1999-01-...
12	Document Control	5	<Employees><Employee id="54" StartDate="1999-01-...
13	Quality Assurance	6	<Employees><Employee id="41" StartDate="1999-01-...
14	Facilities and Maintenance	7	<Employees><Employee id="49" StartDate="1999-01-...
15	Shipping and Receiving	6	<Employees><Employee id="34" StartDate="1999-01-...
16	Executive	2	<Employees><Employee id="109" StartDate="1999-02...

Figure 8-5   Result of query that uses the nodes() method

NOTE   OPENXML and *nodes()* method performance

The *nodes()* method is more efficient than the *OPENXML* statement because it does not have to load into memory and parse the XML structure before querying and shredding it. The XML data type in SQL Server 2005 stores the XML data in an internal structure that looks very similar to an Edge Table.

Using CROSS APPLY and OUTER APPLY Operators

When a table contains a column of type XML, you cannot call the *nodes()* method in the SELECT expression. Because the *nodes()* method returns a result set, the SELECT expression will not permit you to call it; thus, you cannot use a query like the following example:

```
-- Create a new table
CREATE TABLE T(C1 XML);

-- Query the table
SELECT C1.nodes('XQUERY expression')
FROM T
```

Because the *nodes()* method must be called at the XML column, it is also impossible to call the nodes method in the *FROM* section of a SELECT expression, so you can't use the following query, either:

```
-- Create a new table
CREATE TABLE T(C1 XML);

-- Query the table
SELECT *
FROM T.C1.nodes('XQUERY expression')
```

To call the *nodes()* method on an XML type column, you must use the *APPLY* operators, which enable you to invoke a function for each row returned from a query.

The *CROSS APPLY* operator returns from the invoked function only those results that are not NULL. The *OUTER APPLY* operator returns all results, even if they are NULL. By using the *APPLY* operators, you can invoke the *nodes()* method for each row returned from a query.

The following code shows how to use the *nodes()* method from an XML type column by using the *CROSS APPLY* operator:

```
SELECT  T.C.value('@id','int') AS ID,
        T.C.value('@name','nvarchar(max)') AS [NAME],
        T.C.value('count(./Employees/*)', 'int') AS TOTAL_EMPLOYEE_COUNT,
        T2.C.query('.') EMPLOYEES_OLDER_THAN_7
FROM @X.nodes('/Departments/Department') T(C)
CROSS APPLY T.C.nodes('./Employees[Employee/@YearsInRole>7]') T2(C)
```

Figure 8-6 shows the result of this query.

	ID	NAME	TOTAL_EMPLOYEE_COUNT	EMPLOYEES_OLDER_THAN_7
1	1	Engineering	6	\<Employees\>\<Employee id="3" StartDate="1997-12-1...
2	2	Tool Design	4	\<Employees\>\<Employee id="5" StartDate="1998-01-1...
3	4	Marketing	9	\<Employees\>\<Employee id="2" StartDate="1997-02-2...
4	7	Production	179	\<Employees\>\<Employee id="1" StartDate="1996-07-3...

Figure 8-6   Results of query that uses the nodes() method with the CROSS APPLY operator

The following code shows how to use the *nodes()* method from an XML type column by using the *OUTER APPLY* operator:

```
SELECT    T.C.value('@id','int') AS ID,
          T.C.value('@name','nvarchar(max)') AS [NAME],
          T.C.value('count(./Employees/*)', 'int') AS TOTAL_EMPLOYEE_COUNT,
          T2.C.query('.') EMPLOYEES_OLDER_THAN_7
FROM @X.nodes('/Departments/Department') T(C)
OUTER APPLY T.C.nodes('./Employees[Employee/@YearsInRole>7]') T2(C)
```

Figure 8-7 shows the result of this query.

ID	NAME	TOTAL_EMPLOYEE_COUNT	EMPLOYEES_OLDER_THAN_7
1	Engineering	6	\<Employees\>\<Employee id="3" StartDate="1997-12-1...
2	Tool Design	4	\<Employees\>\<Employee id="5" StartDate="1998-01-1...
3	Sales	18	NULL
4	Marketing	9	\<Employees\>\<Employee id="2" StartDate="1997-02-2...
5	Purchasing	12	NULL
6	Research and Development	4	NULL
7	Production	179	\<Employees\>\<Employee id="1" StartDate="1996-07-3...
8	Production Control	6	NULL
9	Human Resources	6	NULL
10	Finance	10	NULL
11	Information Services	10	NULL
12	Document Control	5	NULL
13	Quality Assurance	6	NULL
14	Facilities and Maintenance	7	NULL
15	Shipping and Receiving	6	NULL
16	Executive	2	NULL

Figure 8-7   Results of query using the nodes() method with the Outer Apply operator

---

Quick Check

■ Why are the *APPLY* operators necessary?

Quick Check Answer

■ You need the *APPLY* operators to correlate the results from the *nodes()* method with the results of other XML data type methods being called in the *SELECT* statement. Otherwise, you would not be able to call any of the XML data type methods.

Shredding XML by Using SQLXML

SQLXML-annotated XSD schemas enable you to bulk load XML data coming from a file into a database and to transform that data into tabular-relational format when the data is inserted. To bulk load XML data by using SQLXML, you must execute the following steps:

1. Create the database schema by issuing the required *CREATE DATABASE* and *CREATE TABLE* statements.

2. Update the XML schema file with the necessary annotations to create an annotated XSD schema, as you learned in Lesson 3.

3. Use the SQLXML API to load both the annotated schema and to bulk load the XML data into the database. To do this, follow these steps:

   A. Open a .NET Framework 2.0 SDK command-line window and navigate to C:\Program Files\Common Files\System\Ole DB.

   B. Type **tlbimp xblkld4.dll** to generate a proxy for the COM library; then press Enter to execute it.

   C. The utility should print *"Type library imported to SQLXMLBULKLOADLib.dll"* if it succeeded.

   D. Add a reference to the SQLXMLBULKLOADLib.dll assembly from the Visual Studio 2005 project in which you want to bulk load XML data.

   E. If the project is an executable assembly, add the *[STAThread]* attribute to the *Main* method. If the *SQLXMLBULKLOADLib.SQLXMLBulkLoad4Class* object is being called from a custom secondary thread, use the *Thread.Set-ApartmentState(ApartmentState.MTA)* method before starting the thread. If the project is a Web application, set the *ASPCompat* attribute of the *@Page* directive like this: *<%@ Page AspCompat="true">*

   F. Add the following code to execute the bulk load:

```
string connectionString = "Provider=sqloledb; Data Source=SERVER;
Initial Catalog=DATABASE; User Id=USER; Password=PWD";

SQLXMLBULKLOADLib.SQLXMLBulkLoad4Class objBL =
new SQLXMLBULKLOADLib.SQLXMLBulkLoad4Class();
objBL.ConnectionString = connectionString;
objBL.Execute("annotated_XSD_schema.xsd", "XML_data_file.xml");
```

The *SQLXMLBULKLOADLib.SQLXMLBulkLoad4Class* object provides different flags that you can set to enable different functionality, which Table 8-7 describes.

Table 8-7   Properties from the SQLXMLBULKLOADLib.SQLXMLBulkLoad4Class Class

Property	Description
BulkLoad *SchemaGen* *SGDropTables*	The combination of these three properties enables you to configure the bulk-load mechanism to generate the relational schema based on the annotated XSD schema. ■ Set the *BulkLoad* property to false so that no XML data will be loaded into the database. ■ Set the *SchemaGen* property to true so that SQLXML will issue the required CREATE TABLE Transact-SQL code based on what is declared on the mapping schema. ■ Set the *SGDropTables* property to true so that SQLXML will drop the tables before creating them if they already exist.
XMLFragment	If you set the *XMLFragment* property to true, SQLXML enables you to bulk load XML fragments (XML data without a root node) instead of XML documents.
ErrorLogFile	Set the *ErrorLogFile* property to a file name. SQLXML will log in this file any unhandled errors that occurred during XML bulk loading.
Transaction *ForceTableLock*	SQLXML uses default implicit transactions, so each *BULK INSERT* statement will execute in its own transaction. ■ Set the *Transaction* property to true so that all XML loading will occur in a single transaction. ■ If necessary, set the *ForceTableLock* property to true to force a table-level lock during the bulk insert operation.

MORE INFO   Bulk Loading XML

For more information about the bulk-loading API, see the "SQL Server XML Bulk Load Object Model" topic in SQL Server Books Online.

PRACTICE **Bulk Loading XML Files**

In this practice, you use OPENXML and SQLXML Bulk Load to upload two XML files into the database. Then you query the data in the *UniversalLog* table to build some reports. The queries require you to shred XML into relational data by using the *nodes()* method of the XML data type.

NOTE **Code available on the companion CD**

The Practice Files\Chapter8\Lesson 5\CompleteLesson5.sql file provides the solution for Practice 1 and Practice 3 in this lesson.

▶ **Practice 1: Use OPENXML to Load XML Data**

The *UniversalLog* administrator found an XML file that contains old data that must be uploaded into the database. The XML file must be loaded into memory by using the SQLXML XML stored procedures. You then need to insert the data into the *Universal-Log* table.

1. The C:\Chapter8\Lesson5\UniversalLog.xml file contains 500 log entries that you need to upload into the *UniversalLog* table.

2. Load the UniversalLog.xml file into a XML-typed variable in SQL Server. (Lesson 1 covered how to load XML files by using the OPENROWSET function in Transact-SQL.)

3. Use the *sp_xml_preparedocument* stored procedure to load the XML data into memory.

4. Issue an *INSERT..SELECT* statement to insert into the *UniversalLog* table the data read by using OPENXML. Remember that you must use explicit mapping in the OPENXML declaration because the XML is in a different format.

5. Use the *sp_xml_removedocument* stored procedure to clean up the server memory.

6. Execute the queries and then use a *SELECT COUNT* statement to validate that the data has been inserted into the table.

NOTE **Code available on the companion CD**

The Practice Files\Chapter8\Lesson 5\ BulkLoad\SQLXMLBulkLoad.csproj Visual Studio project file provides the solution for Practice 2 in this lesson.

▶ **Practice 2: Use SQLXML Bulk Load to Load XML Data**

The *UniversalLog* administrator found another XML file that contains old data that must be uploaded into the database. The XML file must be loaded into memory by using the SQLXML Bulk Load COM component, so you need to write a .NET application to do this. The data should be inserted into the *UniversalLog* table.

1. The C:\Chapter8\Lesson 5\ForBulkLoad.xml file contains 500 log entries that you need to upload into the *UniversalLog* table.

2. Use Visual Studio 2005 to write a console application to load the file into memory. The console application must use the SQL Server Bulk Load component. Add the following code to execute the bulk load:

```
SQLXMLBULKLOADLib.SQLXMLBulkLoad4Class objBL =
new SQLXMLBULKLOADLib.SQLXMLBulkLoad4Class();
objBL.ConnectionString = "Provider=sqloledb;Data Source=DEMOS;Initial Catalog=
TK431Chapter8;User Id=sa;";
objBL.Execute("UniversalLogSchema.xsd", "ForBulkLoad.xml");
```

3. Use the provided C:\Chapter8\Lesson 5\ UniversalLogSchema.xsd annotated XSD schema to map the XML data to the relational database.

4. Run the application to upload the XML data into the database.

5. Validate the data load by running a *SELECT COUNT* statement in SSMS.

▶ **Practice 3: Shred XML Data by Using the *nodes()* Method**

The *UniversalLog* administrator needs to build a reporting application to analyze the most common errors raised by applications logging into the *UniversalLog* table. You need to develop the queries that extract the information needed by the reporting application.

1. The first report must show four columns, with the application name in the first column and the logRecord data from all the logged messages divided into three columns: Error Messages, Post Messages, and Informational Messages.

```
SELECT
   ApplicationName,
   LogRecord.value('(/logRecord//error/
message)[1]','nvarchar(max)') As 'Error Messages',
   LogRecord.value('(/logRecord//post/
moreInformation)[1]','nvarchar(max)') As 'Post Messages',
   LogRecord.value('(/logRecord//information/
message)[1]','nvarchar(max)') As 'Informational Messages'
FROM UniversalLog
```

2. Use the *CROSS APPLY* operator to show log records that contain all three types of messages.

```
SELECT
    ApplicationName,
    Errors.C.value('./message','nvarchar(max)') As 'Error Messages',
    Posts.C.value('./moreInformation','nvarchar(max)') As 'Post Messages',
    Info.C.value('./message','nvarchar(max)') As 'Informational Messages'
FROM UniversalLog
CROSS APPLY LogRecord.nodes('/logRecord//error') Errors(C)
CROSS APPLY LogRecord.nodes('/logRecord//post') Posts(C)
CROSS APPLY LogRecord.nodes('/logRecord//information') Info(C)
```

3. Use the *OUTER APPLY* operator to show all log records and to see the messages for each record.

```
SELECT
    ApplicationName,
    Errors.C.value('./message','nvarchar(max)') As 'Error Messages',
    Posts.C.value('./moreInformation','nvarchar(max)') As 'Post Messages',
    Info.C.value('./message','nvarchar(max)') As 'Informational Messages'
FROM UniversalLog
OUTER APPLY LogRecord.nodes('/logRecord//error') Errors(C)
OUTER APPLY LogRecord.nodes('/logRecord//post') Posts(C)
OUTER APPLY LogRecord.nodes('/logRecord//information') Info(C)
```

Lesson Summary

- OPENXML supports implicit and explicit mapping.
- Always remember to call the *sp_xml_removedocument* after using OPENXML.
- OPENXML loads the whole XML structure into memory.
- The *nodes()* method of the XML data type returns a new row for each XML node that matches a given XQUERY expression. Use the *value()*, *query()*, and *exist()* methods available in the XML data type to extract data from each row.
- The *APPLY* operator enables you to invoke a function for each row returned from a query.
- The *CROSS APPLY* operator returns from the invoked function only those results that are not NULL.
- The *OUTER APPLY* operator returns all results, even if they are NULL.

Lesson Review

The following questions are intended to reinforce key information presented in this lesson. The questions are also available on the companion CD if you prefer to review them in electronic form.

NOTE Answers

Answers to these questions and explanations of why each answer choice is right or wrong are located in the "Answers" section at the end of this book.

1. An application you wrote uses OPENXML to parse XML data into a relational table. As soon as the XML data got bigger, you started to see that SQL Server was running out of memory, and your OPENXML query started to return memory errors. What can you do to improve performance? (Choose all that apply.)

    A. When possible, process all XML documents at once instead of splitting the documents into multiple smaller files.

    B. Check that you are calling *sp_xml_removedocument* as soon as possible after executing OPENXML.

    C. Reduce the size of the XML files by making the XML tag names smaller.

    D. When possible, split the XML data into multiple smaller files and process each of them independently.

2. Under which circumstances should you use the *nodes()* method instead of OPENXML? (Choose all that apply.)

    A. The XML data is already stored in an XML data type column.

    B. You need to extract XML data out of multiple columns, not just a single source.

    C. You need to use an XPATH expression not supported by OPENXML but supported by the XML data type implementation.

    D. You are migrating stored procedure code from a previous version of SQL Server.

Lesson 6: Creating XML Indexes

Lessons 2 and 3 examined different alternatives for retrieving XML data out of SQL Server 2005. Depending on the size of this data, extraction can be a costly operation. By implementing different indexing options on the XML data type, you can have SQL Server 2005 resolve queries on XML data types by inspecting only a certain set of nodes and not navigating through the complete XML document or fragment. In this lesson, you see the benefits of indexing XML data as well as the best indexes to use for different scenarios.

> **After this lesson, you will be able to:**
> - Describe the benefits of creating a primary XML index.
> - Define a strategy to create secondary indexes.
> - Choose the appropriate secondary index based on the queries to be executed.
> - Create XML indexes.
>
> **Estimated lesson time: 30 minutes**

Indexing an XML Data Type Instance

The XML data type in SQL Server 2005 can store a maximum of 2-GB of information. When XML data is assigned to an XML data type instance, it is transformed into an internal binary large object (BLOB) representation. When you use XML data type methods to query the XML data, SQL Server performs a lookup on the table data rows to extract the required nodes.

You can gain a performance improvement when you index the XML internal structure. Instead of having to look up the queried data in the 2 GB binary representation of all the XML data, the SQL Server query processor can perform an index lookup and probe fewer memory pages to serve the query. You can create two general types of indexes on the XML data type: a primary index and a secondary index (of which there are three types).

Indexes improve performance when reading data because fewer data pages must be read into memory to return the desired result. On the other hand, performance can be affected under a heavy load of insert, update, and delete operations because of SQL Server having to update the index structures in addition to the table itself.

Creating an XML Data Type Primary Index

XML data type instances can have only one primary index. The primary index analyzes the complete XML structure, so the number of rows in the index is approximately equal to the number of nodes in the XML BLOB.

The primary index in an XML data type instance maintains the information that Table 8-8 describes.

Table 8-8   XML Data Type Primary Index Columns

Column	Description
Ordering Information	The primary index is clustered by this column. Order is maintained by a special structure called ORDPATH, which keeps the node hierarchy.
Primary Key	This column corresponds to the base table primary key. It is duplicated to maintain a reference to the relational data associated with the XML instance.
Tag	This column maintains the XML node tag name. Instead of keeping the string characters, it is tokenized, so it keeps a reference to the real node tag name in the BLOB structure.
Node Type	This column maintains the node's XSD type, indicating whether the node is an XML element, an XML attribute, XML text, and so on.
Node Value	This column holds the node contents.
Path	This column maintains the complete path from the root node to the current node. It is used for path-based lookups.

The primary index maintains document order and document structure. It is built in reverse order, so lookups can be recursive and work when only the path suffix is known—for example, when you use // in XPATH. You can rebuild the XML data by using the information in the primary index.

You can create a primary XML index for each XML column in a table. The primary index is built on the relational B+ tree structure of a clustered index on the table's primary key column, so you must create the table's clustered index first.

MORE INFO   SQL Server 2005 indexing features

Please refer to Chapter 4, "Creating Indexes," for more information on SQL Server 2005 indexing features.

You create XML indexes by using the same Transact-SQL data definition language (DDL) statements you use to create relational indexes. The syntax for creating a primary XML index is as follows:

```
CREATE PRIMARY XML INDEX Index_Identifier
ON table_name (XML_typed_column_name);
```

Creating XML Data Type Secondary Indexes

Having a primary index improves performance because instead of having to navigate the BLOB structure, the SQL Server query processor can execute lookups on the primary index. Those lookups are executed sequentially based on the primary index key.

However, you can achieve further performance gains by declaring secondary indexes that let SQL Server avoid sequential lookups on the primary index. Secondary indexes are built on top of the primary index, so they provide different lookup schemes depending on the secondary index keys. Table 8-9 lists the three types of secondary indexes you can create.

Table 8-9   Three Types of XML Data Type Secondary Indexes

Secondary Index Type	Description
PATH	This type of XML secondary index uses the Path and Node Value columns from the primary index. Those two columns allow for more efficient seeks when SQL Server is searching for paths in the XML data. Instead of having to search sequentially for a path in the primary index, SQL Server can fully serve from the secondary index any query that executes path-based queries.

Table 8-9   Three Types of XML Data Type Secondary Indexes

Secondary Index Type	Description
VALUE	You build this type of XML secondary index by using the Node Value and Path columns from the primary index. Those two columns produce more efficient seeks when searching for specific values in the XML data. Instead of having to search sequentially for a value in the primary index, SQL Server can fully serve from the secondary index a query that executes value-based queries.
PROPERTY	This type of XML secondary index is based on the Primary Key, Node Value, and Path columns from the primary index. Those three columns give more efficient seeks when SQL Server is searching for specific values that must be associated with their parent row in the base table.

Here is the syntax to create a secondary PATH XML index:

```
CREATE XML INDEX Secondary_Index_Identifier
ON table_name (XML_typed_column_name);
USING XML INDEX Primary_Index_Identifier
FOR PATH
```

The syntax to create a secondary VALUE XML index is as follows:

```
CREATE XML INDEX Secondary_Index_Identifier
ON table_name (XML_typed_column_name);
USING XML INDEX Primary_Index_Identifier
FOR VALUE
```

And the syntax to create a secondary PROPERTY XML index is the following:

```
CREATE XML INDEX Secondary_Index_Identifier
ON table_name (XML_typed_column_name);
USING XML INDEX Primary_Index_Identifier
FOR PROPERTY
```

Choosing Secondary XML Indexes

The PATH secondary index is best used for queries that filter based on the XML structure or for queries for which the complete XML path is unknown. It can also be used for queries that combine path-based queries and value filtering. For example, the query */Employees/Employee[@Bonus]* retrieves all *Employee* elements that have a

Bonus attribute. And */Departments/Department[@ID = 10]* retrieves all nodes under the *Departments* element that have an *ID* attribute with the value *10*.

The VALUE secondary index works best for queries that filter based on values and if the path is not fully specified or if it includes a wildcard. For example, *// Employee[@YearsInRole = 8]* retrieves all *Employee* elements (no matter where they appear in the XML structure) that have a *YearsInRole* attribute with a value of *8*. And *//Employees/Employee[@* = "Smith"]* retrieves all *Employee* elements that have any attribute with the value *Smith*.

The PROPERTY secondary index is best used for queries that use the value method of the XML data type and that filter based on the table's primary key, as this example shows:

```
SELECT EmployeeData.value('(/Employee/FirstName)[1]', 'nvarchar(100)')
   FROM EmployeesTable
   WHERE EmployeeID = 101
```

Quick Check

- Which type of secondary index works best for queries that filter based on values and if the path is not fully specified or if it includes a wildcard?

Quick Check Answer

- The VALUE secondary index works best for those types of queries.

PRACTICE   Create Appropriate Indexes for XML Data

In this practice, you will create the appropriate indexes on the LogRecord XML column in the *UniversalLog* table.

1. In the TK431Chapter8 database, modify the *UniversalLog* table and add a clustered primary key constraint on the ID column:

   ```
   ALTER TABLE UniversalLog
   ADD CONSTRAINT ULogPK PRIMARY KEY CLUSTERED (ID)
   ```

2. Execute a *CREATE INDEX* statement to create the XML primary index:

   ```
   CREATE PRIMARY XML INDEX LogRecordPrimaryIdx
   ON UniversalLog (LogRecord);
   ```

3. Execute a *CREATE INDEX* statement to create an XML PATH secondary index:

   ```
   CREATE XML INDEX LogRecordSecondaryIdxPath
   ON UniversalLog (LogRecord)
   USING XML INDEX LogRecordPrimaryIdx
   FOR PATH;
   ```

4. Execute a *CREATE INDEX* statement to create the XML VALUE secondary index:

```
CREATE XML INDEX LogRecordSecondaryIdxValue
ON UniversalLog (LogRecord)
USING XML INDEX LogRecordPrimaryIdx
FOR VALUE;
```

5. Execute a *CREATE INDEX* statement to create the XML PROPERTY secondary index:

```
CREATE XML INDEX LogRecordSecondaryIdxProperty
ON UniversalLog (LogRecord)
USING XML INDEX LogRecordPrimaryIdx
FOR PROPERTY;
```

Lesson Summary

- Indexes help the SQL Server query engine optimize the query execution plan.

- The XML data type primary index requires a clustered index on the base table's primary key column.

- XML data type columns accept one primary index and three types of secondary indexes.

- Create secondary indexes based on the type of queries that will be executed: PATH, VALUE, or PROPERTY.

Lesson Review

The following questions are intended to reinforce key information presented in this lesson. The questions are also available on the companion CD if you prefer to review them in electronic form.

NOTE Answers

Answers to these questions and explanations of why each answer choice is right or wrong are located in the "Answers" section at the end of this book.

---

1. Users of the sales application have been complaining about the time it takes to generate the TotalSalesPerDay report. The report is created from the *SalesByDate* XML data type column in the Sales tables. The TotalSalesPerDay report is fed by the *TotalSalesPerDaySP* stored procedure, which executes the following query:

```
SELECT SalesByDate.query('/Sales[//@reportDate = sql:variable("@today")]')
FROM Sales
```

How can you improve the performance on this query?

A. Create a PATH secondary XML index.

B. Create a PROPERTY secondary XML index.

C. Create a VALUE secondary XML index.

D. Create a clustered index on the XML column.

2. The end of the fiscal year is coming up, and users of the accounting application are inserting 200 new records per minute. Each record is made up of four XML documents representing different tax forms that need to be filled in. The users have been complaining because the rate of inserted records per minute was three times higher last year at this time. Which action would provide the best performance in this application?

A. Create a PROPERTY secondary XML index.

B. Drop the secondary indexes on the XML columns.

C. Create a PATH secondary XML index.

D. Drop all indexes on the XML columns.

Chapter Review

To further practice and reinforce the skills you learned in this chapter, you can

- Review the chapter summary.
- Review the list of key terms introduced in this chapter.
- Complete the case scenarios. These scenarios set up real-world situations involving the topics of this chapter and ask you to create a solution.
- Complete the suggested practices.
- Take a practice test.

Chapter Summary

- SQL Server 2005 takes the XML feature set provided by SQL Server 2000 and adds the capability to manipulate XML in and out of the database server, to compose relational data into XML data, and to shred XML data into relational data.
- The biggest benefit of SQL Server 2005's XML capabilities is that you can represent data in whichever format is best for that specific data—whether it is structured data, semi-structured data, or unstructured data—and still use the same query engine to return query results.
- The new XML data type is central in SQL Server 2005's XML infrastructure, giving you methods for manipulating XML data and structure through XQUERY and XPATH query expressions.
- SQLXML, a middle-tier COM component, enables you to compose relational data into XML data by using annotated XSD schemas and XML views, which give you an easy way to manage the XML result from multiple Transact-SQL and XPATH queries in just one file.
- You can create indexes on the XML data type column to help the SQL Server query engine optimize the query execution plan. The XML data type column accepts one primary index and three types of secondary indexes.

Key Terms

Do you know what these key terms mean? You can check your answers by looking up the terms in the glossary at the end of the book.

- composition
- Document Object Model (DOM)

- Edge Table
- FLWOR expression
- parse
- semistructured data
- shredding
- Simple API for XML (SAX)
- structured data
- typed XML data
- unstructured data
- untyped XML data
- updategram
- XML validation
- XPATH
- XPATH axes
- XPATH predicates
- XQUERY

Case Scenarios

In the following case scenarios, you will apply what you've learned in this chapter. You can find answers to these questions in the "Answers" section at the end of this book.

Case Scenario 1: Troubleshooting XML Performance by Choosing the Correct Indexing Strategy

You are a database developer for one of the biggest news syndication agencies in the country. Your application subscribes to RSS feeds from diverse sources spread around the world. Your customers subscribe to your syndication service by providing specific keywords that they are interested in being notified about when they occur in any feed from any source.

Your application scans nearly 2,000 sources every 5 minutes for new feeds. The results of such scanning are saved in XML format in a SQL Server 2005 database, in which a second process probes for the keywords defined by customers. The second process uses the XQUERY language through the *query()* method in the XML data type.

You wrote the following function to probe for the keywords:

```
CREATE FUNCTION fn_FindKeyword(@keyword AS nvarchar(100))
RETURNS @xml TABLE ( result XML )
AS
BEGIN

INSERT INTO @xml
    SELECT FEED.query('
        for $item in /rss/channel/item,
$title in $item/title,
$desc in $item/desc
        return
            <result>
            {
            if (fn:contains(string($title), sql:variable("@keyword")) or
             fn:contains(string($desc), sql:variable("@keyword")))
then
                <found/>
             else
                <notfound/>
            }
            </result>
    ')
    FROM RSS
RETURN
END
GO
```

The *fn_FindKeyword* function is called by the following code:

```
SELECT * FROM Customer_Keywords CK
CROSS APPLY dbo.fn_FindKeyword (CK.keywords)
```

To enhance query performance, you created an XML VALUE index on the FEED column.

1. Will this index provide the best performance?

2. Which other XML index could you use to improve performance?

3. Are there any other search alternatives that would meet the requirements for this specific case scenario?

Case Scenario 2: Handling Data as XML or as Relational Representation

You are working as a database developer for a global company with offices in more than 150 countries. The Human Resources (HR) department must evaluate every employee at the end of the fiscal year. To do so, the HR department asks you to develop an Employee Evaluation questionnaire application.

The application must handle approximatly 1500 questions. Each question can be cat-alogued, given a different evaluation weight, and use different answer formats. For example, some questions are answered on a 1–10 scale, and other questions require conditional answers (depending on the response in previous questions, different answer choices must appear).

Your manager, who has worked at the company for 25 years, wants to implement the solution by using Microsoft Office Word documents saved in the file system and sent to each employee by e-mail. The employee must fill in the Word document and send it back to a reply e-mail address.

You proposed instead to use the Smart Document features in Office 2003 so that the Word document can communicate to the server via XML Web services. This way, the document content would be generated dynamically, based on the questions and answers stored as XML in a SQL Server 2005 database.

Your manager does not understand very much XML yet but has been working with relational databases for the past 25 years. What justifications would you use to per-suade your manager to use the Smart Document features and XML Web services?

Suggested Practices

To help you successfully master the exam objectives presented in this chapter, com-plete the following practice tasks.

Working with XML Structures

For this task, you should complete at least Practices 1 and 3. If you want hands-on experience with every aspect of the exam objectives, complete all four practices.

Practice 1

- Use SSMS to define a new table that has multiple columns of type XML. Try inserting information into the table by using different types of XML structures.

Practice 2

- Use SSMS to define a new stored procedure and a user-defined function (UDF) with multiple parameters of type XML. Try to call the stored procedure by using different types of XML structures.

Practice 3

- Use SSMS to define a new XML schema collection. Load multiple schemas on the same collection. Try loading an in-line XML schema and a schema loaded from a file.

Practice 4

- Alter some of the columns in the table you defined in Practice 1 and then bind the XML columns to the XML schema collection that you created in Practice 3. Try inserting information into the table by using different types of XML structures.

Retrieving XML Data

For this task, you should complete all the practices to exercise the different skills needed to retrieve XML data.

Practice 1

- Apply the different FOR XML modes by using an existing complex query that contains at least two joins.

- Design an XML schema that uses complex nesting, and try to generate XML that matches that schema by using FOR XML modes and nested queries.

Practice 2

- Take the XML structure that resulted from Practice 1 and assign it to an XML data type variable. Execute different XQUERY expressions against the XML variable by using the XML data type *query()* method so that the resulting information will be in XML format. Use the *exist()* method of the XML data type to further filter the results.

- Take the XML structure that resulted from Practice 1 and assign it to an XML data type variable. Execute different XQUERY expressions against the XML variable by using the XML data type *value()* method so that the resulting information will be in tabular format. Use the *exist()* method of the XML data type to further filter the results.

Practice 3

- Annotate the XML schema that you created in Practice 1 with the necessary keywords to map its structure to a table in a database.

- Create XML views that reuse the annotated XML schema and query it using the SQLXML API.

Modifying XML Data

For this task, you should complete at least Practice 1. If you want a more well-rounded understanding of how to use updategrams, also complete Practice 2.

Practice 1

- Use the XML data type's *modify()* method to insert new nodes in an XML document. Extend the exercise to include inserting a new attribute in an existing XML element. Try inserting new data instead of using a new structure.

- Use the *modify()* method in the XML data type to delete nodes from an XML document. Extend the exercise to include deleting attributes in an existing XML element. Try deleting data instead of the structure.

- Use the *modify()* method in the XML data type to update existing nodes in an XML document. Extend the exercise to include updating an existing attribute in an existing XML element. Try updating data instead of the structure.

Practice 2

- Create an annotated XML schema. Then create an updategram to insert new nodes, update existing nodes, and delete nodes.

- Use the SQLXML API to execute the updategram.

Converting Between XML Data and Relational Data

For this task, you should complete Practice 1 to practice using the *nodes()* method of the XML data type. If you want a more well-rounded understanding of using the *nodes()* method, you should also complete Practice 2. Practice 3 covers using the SQLXML Bulkload API to insert an XML document in the database.

Practice 1

- Use the OPENXML Transact-SQL instruction and the XML stored procedures to load an existing XML document and insert the data into a database. Use different sample XML documents—one with an element-centric structure, another with an attribute-centric structure, and another combining elements and attributes in a complex nesting structure.

Practice 2

■ Create an XML data type variable and then use the *nodes()* method to execute an XQUERY expression. Extract the resulting data by using the *value()* method.

■ Create a new table and create a column of the XML data type. Load the column with data and then use the *nodes()* method to execute an XQUERY expression. Extract the resulting data by using the *value()* method. Remember that you must use the *APPLY* operators.

Practice 3

■ Using the XML document from Practice 1, write a .NET application that uses the SQXML Bulkload API to insert the XML document into a database. Remember that you must write an annotated XSD schema.

Creating XML Indexes

For this task, complete all three practices to get a well-rounded understanding of indexing options.

Practice 1

■ Create a complex XQUERY expression and execute it by using the *query()* method of the XML data type. The XQUERY expression must filter the data by its structure—for example, by querying if an attribute appears in the XML structure. Time the execution as you process a fairly large amount of XML data.

■ Create an XML PATH index, reexecute the query, and time it again.

Practice 2

■ Create a complex XQUERY expression, and execute it by using the *query()* method of the XML data type. The XQUERY expression must filter the data by its content—for example, by querying the value of an existing attribute that appears in the XML structure. Do not fully specify the path to the attribute; instead, use //. Time the execution as you process a fairly large amount of XML data.

■ Create an XML VALUE index, reexecute the query, and then time it again.

Practice 3

■ Create a complex XQUERY expression, and execute it by using the *value()* method of the XML data type and filtering by the table's primary key. The

XQUERY expression must filter the data by its content—for example, by querying the value of an existing attribute that appears in the XML structure. Time the execution as you process a fairly large amount of XML data.

■ Create an XML PROPERTY index, reexecute the query, and then time it again.

Take a Practice Test

The practice tests on this book's companion CD offer many options. For example, you can test yourself on just the content covered in this chapter, or you can test yourself on all the 70-431 certification exam content. You can set up the test so that it closely simulates the experience of taking a certification exam, or you can set it up in study mode so that you can look at the correct answers and explanations after you answer each question.

MORE INFO   Practice tests

For details about all the practice test options available, see the "How to Use the Practice Tests" section in this book's Introduction.

Chapter 9

Creating Functions, Stored Procedures, and Triggers

SQL Server provides three types of programmable objects: functions, stored procedures, and triggers. Instead of executing a single statement or command, these objects support the creation of rich programming logic, including looping, flow control, decision making, and branching. In addition to the built-in set of functions in SQL Server, you can create user-defined functions (UDFs) to encapsulate commonly used code for reuse in multiple programs. You use stored procedures, which are saved batches of code, as the interface for all application access to a database, letting you control data access and ease maintenance by avoiding hard-coding SQL into applications. And you use triggers to automatically execute code in response to certain database events. New in SQL Server 2005, you can write the code for each of these objects by using either Transact-SQL or a Microsoft .NET Framework–supported language such as C# or Visual Basic.

MORE INFO Language coverage

For the sake of brevity, we cover the core programming structures of SQL Server by using Transact-SQL code instead of common language runtime (CLR) code. For more information about implementing triggers, functions, and stored procedures by using the CLR, see the following SQL Server 2005 Books Online articles "CLR Stored Procedures," "CLR Triggers," and "CLR User-Defined Functions." SQL Server 2005 Books Online is installed as part of SQL Server 2005. Updates for SQL Server 2005 Books Online are available for download at *www.microsoft.com/technet/prodtechnol/sql/2005/downloads/books.mspx*.

Exam objectives in this chapter:
- Implement functions.

  Create a function.

  Identify deterministic versus nondeterministic functions.
- Implement stored procedures.

  Create a stored procedure.

  Recompile a stored procedure.

  Assign permissions to a role for a stored procedure.

- Implement triggers.

  Create a trigger.

  Create DDL triggers for responding to database structure changes.

  Identify recursive triggers.

  Identify nested triggers.

Lessons in this chapter:

Before You Begin

To complete the lessons in this chapter, you must have

- SQL Server 2005 installed.

- A copy of the *AdventureWorks* sample database installed in the instance.

Real World

Michael Hotek

A customer of mine was having some major performance issues with its applications. After discussing the issues the company was encountering, we started digging around in the database. There were a lot of tables, very few indexes, and not a single stored procedure. Although stored procedures don't necessarily mean better performance, the lack of procedures meant that any performance tuning would be extremely invasive within the application.

Using SQL Server Profiler (which Chapter 15, "Monitoring and Troubleshooting SQL Server Performance," discusses), we captured all the queries being issued against the database in a 30-minute window to get a snapshot of what was going on. The results were staggering. An application that only 15 users were working in had generated more than 300,000 queries in just 30 minutes. Something was clearly wrong. So we connected to a test system for further investigation and found some interesting behavior. A user would click a button that would return four rows of data—and execute more than 1,500 queries.

It turns out that the developers used a development environment that "does everything for you" and never paid attention to what was going on in the database. But, of course, the performance problem was "SQL Server's fault." Although everyone wanted to blame SQL Server, executing more than 1,500 queries to retrieve 4 rows of data was clearly the application's fault.

After figuring out what the users really needed, we wrote a stored procedure to return the results. We went back to the test system and clicked the button; almost instantly, the results popped up in the application. However, instead of listening and waiting until the solution was complete, the customer shoved the new code directly into production, where it promptly blew up. Why? To point the application at the stored procedure, it was necessary to rewrite a section of the application code and recompile it. The new code was never tested, and no one noticed that the developer had inadvertently disabled a critical piece of functionality.

Over the next four months, we systematically ripped apart every section of the application and replaced the ad hoc SQL code with stored procedures. In the end, the process required rewriting the entire application and going through full functional testing, load testing, and user-acceptance testing. When we finally deployed the application, it had only slightly better performance than before because we hadn't had the time to optimize everything. But over the next week, we were able to systematically tune each of the stored procedures and deploy them directly into production without having to touch a single line of application code.

The moral of the story is that even if stored procedures do not directly improve performance, if you use them, any subsequent tuning does not require developers to rip apart their applications, retest, and run the risk of breaking something that is currently working.

Lesson 1: Implementing Functions

SQL Server provides a set of built-in functions that you can plug into your applications to provide common functionality. For example, you can use the *GETDATE()* function to return the current system date and time in the SQL Server 2005 standard internal format for *datetime* values. Although SQL Server provides a nice variety of built-in functions, you can also build your own functions to encapsulate pieces of commonly used code, letting you develop the code once and reuse it across applications. Typically, you create UDFs to encapsulate complex pieces of code so that the implementation is seamless to applications. In this lesson, you see how to implement two types of UDFs: *scalar functions*, which return a scalar value result, and *table-valued functions*, which return a result in the form of a table. You also learn how to identify deterministic and nondeterministic functions, which affect whether you can define indexes on the results the functions return.

> **After this lesson, you will be able to:**
> - Create a function.
> - Identify deterministic vs. nondeterministic functions.
>
> **Estimated lesson time: 20 minutes**

Scalar Functions

Scalar functions accept 0 or more input parameters and return a single scalar value. You use the *CREATE FUNCTION* Transact-SQL statement to create a function. The general syntax of the statement is as follows:

```
CREATE FUNCTION [ schema_name. ] function_name
( [ { @parameter_name [ AS ][ type_schema_name. ] parameter_data_type
    [ = default ] }
    [ ,...n ]
  ]
)
RETURNS return_data_type
    [ WITH <function_option> [ ,...n ] ]
    [ AS ]
    BEGIN
               function_body
        RETURN scalar_expression
    END [ ; ]
<function_option>::=
{
    [ ENCRYPTION ]
  | [ SCHEMABINDING ]
  | [ EXECUTE_AS_Clause ]
}
```

Each function must have a unique name that conforms to the rules for object identifiers.

Although you do not have to define input parameters for functions, it is rare for UDFs to not have input parameters. So you will usually specify one or more input parameters along with the data type of each parameter.

You use the statement's *RETURNS* clause to specify the data type of the scalar value that the function will return. There are several options that you can specify for this clause. When you specify *ENCRYPTION*, SQL Server encrypts the definition of the function when it is stored. The *SCHEMABINDING* option prevents any objects that the function depends on from being dropped. The *EXECUTE AS* option specifies the security context of the function.

The body of the function is delimited by a *BEGIN...END* construct, which must include a *RETURN* clause that is used to output the value that the function calculates.

The body of the function is obviously where all the interesting work happens. Although you can execute virtually any valid batch of code within a function, functions do have some restrictions. The most significant restriction is that you cannot use a function to change the state of any object in a database or the database itself. Therefore, you cannot insert, update, or delete data in tables, nor can you create, alter, or drop objects in the database. However, you can create one or more table variables and issue *INSERT*, *UPDATE*, and *DELETE* statements against the table variable.

MORE INFO   Table variables

A *table variable* is a special type of variable used to temporarily store a set of rows that will be returned as the result of a table-valued function. For information about table variables, see the SQL Server 2005 Books Online topic "Table (Transact-SQL)."

Because scalar functions return a single value, you normally use them in the column list of a *SELECT* statement and can use them in the *WHERE* clause as well.

The following example shows you how to define a scalar-valued function that returns the stock level for a given product ID:

```
CREATE FUNCTION [dbo].[ufnGetStock](@ProductID [int])
RETURNS [int]
AS
-- Returns the stock level for the product. This function is used
-- internally only.
BEGIN
    DECLARE @ret int;
```

```
        SELECT @ret = SUM(p.[Quantity])
        FROM [Production].[ProductInventory] p
        WHERE p.[ProductID] = @ProductID
            AND p.[LocationID] = '6'; -- Only look at inventory in the
                                      -- misc storage.
        IF (@ret IS NULL)
            SET @ret = 0
        RETURN @ret
END;
```

You can then use the function in a query, as follows:

```
SELECT *, dbo.ufnGetStock(Production.Product.ProductID)
FROM Production.Product;
```

Table-Valued Functions

Table-valued functions adhere to the same rules as scalar functions. The difference is that table-valued functions return a table as output. Therefore, they are generally used in the *FROM* clause of a *SELECT* statement and possibly joined to other tables or views.

The general syntax of a table-valued function is as follows:

```
CREATE FUNCTION [ schema_name. ] function_name
( [ { @parameter_name [ AS ] [ type_schema_name. ] parameter_data_type
    [ = default ] }
    [ ,...n ]
  ]
)
RETURNS @return_variable TABLE < table_type_definition >
    [ WITH <function_option> [ ,...n ] ]
    [ AS ]
    BEGIN
                function_body
        RETURN
    END [ ; ]
```

The following code shows an example of a table-valued function that takes a contact ID and returns contact information (contact ID, first name, last name, job title, and contact type) in the form of a table:

```
CREATE FUNCTION [dbo].[ufnGetContactInformation](@ContactID int)
RETURNS @retContactInformation TABLE
(
    -- Columns returned by the function:
    [ContactID] int PRIMARY KEY NOT NULL,
    [FirstName] [nvarchar](50) NULL,
    [LastName] [nvarchar](50) NULL,
    [JobTitle] [nvarchar](50) NULL,
    [ContactType] [nvarchar](50) NULL
)
```

```
AS
-- Returns the first name, last name, job title, and contact type
-- for the specified contact.
BEGIN
    DECLARE
        @FirstName [nvarchar](50),
        @LastName [nvarchar](50),
        @JobTitle [nvarchar](50),
        @ContactType [nvarchar](50);

    -- Get common contact information.
    SELECT
        @ContactID = ContactID,
        @FirstName = FirstName,
        @LastName = LastName
    FROM [Person].[Contact]
    WHERE [ContactID] = @ContactID;

    SET @JobTitle =
        CASE
            -- Check for employee.
            WHEN EXISTS(SELECT * FROM [HumanResources].[Employee] e
                WHERE e.[ContactID] = @ContactID)
                THEN (SELECT [Title]
                    FROM [HumanResources].[Employee]
                    WHERE [ContactID] = @ContactID)

            -- Check for vendor.
            WHEN EXISTS(SELECT * FROM [Purchasing].[VendorContact] vc
                    INNER JOIN [Person].[ContactType] ct
                    ON vc.[ContactTypeID] = ct.[ContactTypeID]
                WHERE vc.[ContactID] = @ContactID)
                THEN (SELECT ct.[Name]
                    FROM [Purchasing].[VendorContact] vc
                        INNER JOIN [Person].[ContactType] ct
                        ON vc.[ContactTypeID] = ct.[ContactTypeID]
                    WHERE vc.[ContactID] = @ContactID)

            -- Check for store.
            WHEN EXISTS(SELECT * FROM [Sales].[StoreContact] sc
                    INNER JOIN [Person].[ContactType] ct
                    ON sc.[ContactTypeID] = ct.[ContactTypeID]
                WHERE sc.[ContactID] = @ContactID)
                THEN (SELECT ct.[Name]
                    FROM [Sales].[StoreContact] sc
                        INNER JOIN [Person].[ContactType] ct
                        ON sc.[ContactTypeID] = ct.[ContactTypeID]
                    WHERE [ContactID] = @ContactID)

            ELSE NULL
        END;
```

```
        SET @ContactType =
            CASE
                -- Check for employee.
                WHEN EXISTS(SELECT * FROM [HumanResources].[Employee] e
                    WHERE e.[ContactID] = @ContactID)
                    THEN 'Employee'

                -- Check for vendor.
                WHEN EXISTS(SELECT * FROM [Purchasing].[VendorContact] vc
                        INNER JOIN [Person].[ContactType] ct
                        ON vc.[ContactTypeID] = ct.[ContactTypeID]
                    WHERE vc.[ContactID] = @ContactID)
                    THEN 'Vendor Contact'

                -- Check for store.
                WHEN EXISTS(SELECT * FROM [Sales].[StoreContact] sc
                        INNER JOIN [Person].[ContactType] ct
                        ON sc.[ContactTypeID] = ct.[ContactTypeID]
                    WHERE sc.[ContactID] = @ContactID)
                    THEN 'Store Contact'

                -- Check for individual consumer.
                WHEN EXISTS(SELECT * FROM [Sales].[Individual] i
                    WHERE i.[ContactID] = @ContactID)
                    THEN 'Consumer'
            END;

    -- Return the information to the caller.
    IF @ContactID IS NOT NULL
    BEGIN
        INSERT @retContactInformation
        SELECT @ContactID, @FirstName, @LastName, @JobTitle, @ContactType;
    END;

    RETURN;
END;
SELECT * FROM dbo.ufnGetContactInformation(1);
```

Deterministic vs. Nondeterministic Functions

When working with functions, it's important to know whether the function you are using is deterministic or nondeterministic. *Deterministic functions* return, for the same set of input values, the same value every time you call them. The SQL Server built-in function *COS*, which returns the trigonometric cosine of the specified angle, is an example of a deterministic function. In contrast, a *nondeterministic function* can return a different result every time you call it. An example of a nondeterministic function is the SQL Server built-in function *GETDATE()*, which returns the current system time and date. SQL Server also considers a function nondeterministic if the function calls a nondeterministic function or if the function calls an extended stored procedure.

Whether a function is deterministic or not also determines whether you can build an index on the results the function returns and whether you can define a clustered index on a view that references the function. If the function is nondeterministic, you cannot index the results of the function, either through indexes on computed columns that call the function or through indexed views that reference the function.

Quick Check

- What are the two types of UDFs, and how are they used?

Quick Check Answer

- Scalar functions return a single value and are generally used in column lists and *WHERE* clauses.

- Table-valued functions return a table variable and are used in the *FROM* clause.

PRACTICE **Create a Function**

In this practice, you create a scalar function to return the model name for a product given a particular product ID. You then create a table-valued function to return the contents of the *Product* table for a given model ID.

1. Launch SQL Server Management Studio (SSMS), connect to your instance, open a new query window, and change the context to the *AdventureWorks* database.

2. Create and test the *GetModelNameForProduct* scalar function by executing the following code:

```
CREATE FUNCTION dbo.GetModelNameForProduct (@ProductID int)
RETURNS nvarchar(50)
WITH EXECUTE AS CALLER
AS
BEGIN
    DECLARE @ModelName nvarchar(50)

    SELECT @ModelName = Production.ProductModel.Name
    FROM Production.Product INNER JOIN Production.ProductModel
        ON Production.Product.ProductModelID =
Production.ProductModel.ProductModelID
    WHERE Production.Product.ProductID = @ProductID
```

```
        RETURN(@ModelName)
END;
GO

SELECT dbo.GetModelNameForProduct(717);
```

3. Create and test the table-valued function *GetProductsForModelID* by executing the following code:

```
CREATE FUNCTION dbo.GetProductsForModelID (@ProductModelID int)
RETURNS @Products TABLE
(
ProductID               int             NOT NULL,
Name                    dbo.Name        NOT NULL,
ProductNumber           nvarchar(25)    NOT NULL,
MakeFlag                dbo.Flag        NOT NULL,
FinishedGoodsFlag       dbo.Flag        NOT NULL,
Color                   nvarchar(15)    NULL,
SafetyStockLevel        smallint        NOT NULL,
ReorderPoint            smallint        NOT NULL,
StandardCost            money           NOT NULL,
ListPrice               money           NOT NULL,
Size                    nvarchar(5)     NULL,
SizeUnitMeasureCode     nchar(3)        NULL,
WeightUnitMeasureCode   nchar(3)        NULL,
Weight                  decimal(8, 2)   NULL,
DaysToManufacture       int             NOT NULL,
ProductLine             nchar(2)        NULL,
Class                   nchar(2)        NULL,
Style                   nchar(2)        NULL,
ProductSubcategoryID    int             NULL,
ProductModelID          int             NULL,
SellStartDate           datetime        NOT NULL,
SellEndDate             datetime        NULL,
DiscontinuedDate        datetime        NULL,
rowguid                 uniqueidentifier NOT NULL,
ModifiedDate            datetime        NOT NULL
)
WITH EXECUTE AS CALLER
AS
BEGIN
    INSERT INTO @Products
    SELECT ProductID, Name, ProductNumber, MakeFlag, FinishedGoodsFlag,
        Color, SafetyStockLevel, ReorderPoint, StandardCost, ListPrice,
        Size, SizeUnitMeasureCode, WeightUnitMeasureCode, Weight,
        DaysToManufacture, ProductLine, Class, Style,
        ProductSubcategoryID, ProductModelID, SellStartDate, SellEndDate,
        DiscontinuedDate, rowguid, ModifiedDate
    FROM Production.Product
    WHERE Production.Product.ProductModelID = @ProductModelID
```

```
      RETURN
END;
GO

SELECT * FROM dbo.GetProductsForModelID(6);
```

Lesson Summary

- SQL Server lets you create two types of UDFs—scalar and table-valued—to encapsulate complex queries for reuse.

- Scalar functions return a single value.

- Table-valued functions return a table variable.

- Computed columns or views based on deterministic functions, which return the same value every time they are called, can be indexed. Those using nondeterministic functions, which can return different results every time they are called, cannot be indexed.

Lesson Review

The following questions are intended to reinforce key information presented in this lesson. The questions are also available on the companion CD if you prefer to review them in electronic form.

NOTE   Answers

Answers to these questions and explanations of why each answer choice is right or wrong are located in the "Answers" section at the end of the book.

1. Which of the following are valid commands to use within a function?

   A. *UPDATE Table1 SET Column1 = 1*

   B. *SELECT Column1 FROM Table2 WHERE Column2 = 5*

   C. *EXEC sp_myproc*

   D. *INSERT INTO @var VALUES (1)*

Lesson 2: Implementing Stored Procedures

Stored procedures are the most-used programmatic structures within a database. A procedure is simply a name associated with a batch of SQL code that is stored and executed on the server. Stored procedures, which can return scalar values or result sets, are the primary interface that applications should use to access any data within a database. Not only do stored procedures enable you to control access to the database, they also let you isolate database code for easy maintenance instead of requiring you to find hard-coded SQL statements throughout an application if you need to make changes. In this lesson, you see how to create a stored procedure, recompile a stored procedure, and assign permissions to a role for a stored procedure.

After this lesson, you will be able to:

- Create a stored procedure.
- Recompile a stored procedure.
- Assign permissions to a role for a stored procedure.

Estimated lesson time: 20 minutes

Creating a Stored Procedure

Stored procedures can contain virtually any construct or command that is possible to execute within SQL Server. You can use procedures to modify data, return scalar values, or return entire result sets.

Stored procedures also provide a very important security function within a database. You can grant users permission to execute stored procedures that access data without having to grant them the ability to directly access the data. Even more important, stored procedures hide the structure of a database from a user as well as only permit users to perform operations that are coded within the stored procedure.

The general Transact-SQL syntax for creating a stored procedure is the following:

```
CREATE { PROC | PROCEDURE } [schema_name.] procedure_name [ ; number ]
    [ { @parameter [ type_schema_name. ] data_type }
        [ OUT | OUTPUT ]
    ] [ ,...n ]
[ WITH <procedure_option> [ ,...n ] ]
[ FOR REPLICATION ]
AS { <sql_statement> [;][ ...n ] | <method_specifier> }
[;]
```

```
<procedure_option> ::=
    [ ENCRYPTION ]
    [ RECOMPILE ]
    [ EXECUTE_AS_Clause ]

<sql_statement> ::=
{ [ BEGIN ] statements [ END ] }

<method_specifier> ::=
EXTERNAL NAME assembly_name.class_name.method_name
```

Each procedure must have a name that is unique within the database and that conforms to the rules for object identifiers.

Procedures can accept any number of *input parameters*, which are used within the stored procedure as local variables. You can also specify *output parameters*, which let a stored procedure pass one or more scalar values back to the routine that called the procedure.

You can create procedures with three options. When you create a procedure with the *ENCRYPTION* option, SQL Server encrypts the procedure definition. Specifying the *RECOMPILE* option forces SQL Server to recompile the stored procedure each time the procedure is executed. The *EXECUTE AS* option provides a security context for the procedure.

BEST PRACTICES   Recompilation

Stored procedures are compiled into the query cache when executed. Compilation creates a query plan as well as an execution plan. SQL Server can reuse the query plan for subsequent executions, which conserves resources. But the *RECOMPILE* option forces SQL Server to discard the query plan each time the procedure is executed and create a new query plan. There are only a few extremely rare cases when recompiling at each execution is beneficial, such as if you add a new index from which the stored procedure might benefit. Thus, you typically should not add the *RECOMPILE* option to a procedure when you create it.

The body of the stored procedure contains the batch of commands you want to execute within the procedure. The following are the only commands that you cannot execute within a stored procedure:

- *SET SHOWPLAN_TEXT*
- *SET SHOWPLAN_ALL*
- *USE <database>*

The following code shows a sample stored procedure that logs errors in a table called *ErrorLog*:

```
CREATE PROCEDURE [dbo].[uspLogError]
    @ErrorLogID [int] = 0 OUTPUT -- contains the ErrorLogID of the row
                                 -- inserted by uspLogError in the
AS                               -- ErrorLog table.
BEGIN
    SET NOCOUNT ON;

    -- Output parameter value of 0 indicates that error
    -- information was not logged.
    SET @ErrorLogID = 0;

    BEGIN TRY
        -- Return if there is no error information to log.
        IF ERROR_NUMBER() IS NULL
            RETURN;

        -- Return if inside an uncommittable transaction.
        -- Data insertion/modification is not allowed when
        -- a transaction is in an uncommittable state.
        IF XACT_STATE() = -1
        BEGIN
            PRINT 'Cannot log error since the current transaction is in an uncommittable
              state. '
                + 'Rollback the transaction before executing uspLogError in order to
                  successfully log error information.';
            RETURN;
        END

        INSERT [dbo].[ErrorLog]
            (
            [UserName],
            [ErrorNumber],
            [ErrorSeverity],
            [ErrorState],
            [ErrorProcedure],
            [ErrorLine],
            [ErrorMessage]
            )
        VALUES
            (
            CONVERT(sysname, CURRENT_USER),
            ERROR_NUMBER(),
            ERROR_SEVERITY(),
            ERROR_STATE(),
            ERROR_PROCEDURE(),
            ERROR_LINE(),
            ERROR_MESSAGE()
            );
```

```
        -- Pass back the ErrorLogID of the row inserted
        SET @ErrorLogID = @@IDENTITY;
    END TRY
    BEGIN CATCH
        PRINT 'An error occurred in stored procedure uspLogError: ';
        EXECUTE [dbo].[uspPrintError];
        RETURN -1;
    END CATCH
END;
```

Assign Permissions to a Role for a Stored Procedure

As with all objects and operations in SQL Server, you must explicitly grant a user permission to use an object or execute an operation. To allow users to execute a stored procedure, you use the following general syntax:

```
GRANT EXECUTE ON <stored procedure> TO <database principal>
```

Chapter 2, "Configuring SQL Server 2005," covers the *GRANT* statement and database principals.

The use of permissions with stored procedures is an interesting security mechanism. Any user granted execute permissions on a stored procedure is automatically delegated permissions to the objects and commands referenced inside the stored procedure based on the permission set of the user who created the stored procedure.

To understand this delegation behavior, consider the previous example code. The stored procedure *dbo.uspLogError* inserts rows into the *dbo.ErrorLog* table. UserA has insert permissions on *dbo.ErrorLog* and also created this stored procedure. UserB does not have any permissions on *dbo.ErrorLog*. However, when UserA grants *EXECUTE* permissions on the *dbo.uspLogError* procedure, UserB can execute this procedure without receiving any errors because the *SELECT* and *INSERT* permissions necessary to add the row to the *dbo.ErrorLog* table are delegated to UserB. However, UserB receives those permissions only when executing the stored procedure and still cannot directly access the *dbo.ErrorLog* table.

The permission delegation possible with stored procedures provides a very powerful security mechanism within SQL Server. If all data access—insertions, deletions, updates, or selects—were performed through stored procedures, users could not directly access any table in the database. Only by executing the stored procedures would users be able to perform the actions necessary to manage the database. And although users would have the permissions delegated through the stored procedures, they would still be bound to the code within the stored procedure, which can perform actions such as the following:

- Allowing certain operations to be performed only by users who are on a specified list, which is maintained in another table by a user functioning in an administrative role

- Validating input parameters to prevent security attacks such as SQL injection.

Quick Check

1. What is a stored procedure?

2. Which operations can a stored procedure perform?

Quick Check Answers

1. A stored procedure is a name for a batch of Transact-SQL or CLR code that is stored within SQL Server.

2. A procedure can execute any commands within the Transact-SQL language except *USE, SET SHOWPLAN_TEXT ON,* and *SET SHOWPLAN_ALL ON.*

PRACTICE Create a Stored Procedure

In this practice, you create two stored procedures that will update the hire date for all employees to today's date and then compare the procedures.

1. If necessary, launch SSMS, connect to your instance, open a new query window, and change the context to the *AdventureWorks* database.

2. Create a stored procedure to update the hire date by executing the following code:

```
CREATE PROCEDURE dbo.usp_UpdateEmployeeHireDateInefficiently
AS
DECLARE  @EmployeeID  int

DECLARE curemp CURSOR FOR SELECT EmployeeID FROM HumanResources.Employee
OPEN curemp
FETCH curemp INTO @EmployeeID

WHILE @@FETCH_STATUS = 0
BEGIN

    UPDATE HumanResources.Employee
    SET HireDate = GETDATE()
    WHERE EmployeeID = @EmployeeID
```

```
        FETCH curemp INTO @EmployeeID
    END

    CLOSE curemp
    DEALLOCATE curemp
```

3. Create a second stored procedure to update the hire date by executing the following code:

```
CREATE PROCEDURE dbo.usp_UpdateEmployeeHireDateEfficiently
AS
DECLARE  @now  DATETIME

SET @now = GETDATE()

UPDATE HumanResources.Employee
SET HireDate = @now
```

4. Compare the execution between the two procedures by executing each of the queries in the following code separately:

```
EXEC dbo.usp_UpdateEmployeeHireDateInefficiently
EXEC dbo.usp_UpdateEmployeeHireDateEfficiently
```

BEST PRACTICES   Code efficiency

Databases are built and optimized for set-oriented processes instead of row-at-a-time processes. When constructing stored procedures, you always want to use the minimum amount of code that also minimizes the amount of work performed. Although both of the procedures in this practice accomplish the requirement to change all employees' hire dates, the second procedure executes significantly faster. The first procedure not only reads in the entire list of employees, but it also executes an update as well as a call to a function for each employee. The second procedure executes the *GETDATE()* function only once and performs a single update operation.

Lesson Summary

- Stored procedures are stored batches of code that are compiled when executed.

- Procedures can be used to execute almost any valid command while also providing a security layer between a user and the tables within a database.

Lesson Review

The following questions are intended to reinforce key information presented in this lesson. The questions are also available on the companion CD if you prefer to review them in electronic form.

NOTE Answers

Answers to these questions and explanations of why each answer choice is right or wrong are located in the "Answers" section at the end of the book.

1. Which stored procedure option regenerates the query plan every time a procedure is executed?

    A. *ENCRYPTION*

    B. *RECOMPILE*

    C. *VARYING*

    D. *EXECUTE AS*

Lesson 3: Implementing Triggers

A *trigger* is a specialized implementation of a Transact-SQL or CLR batch that automatically runs in response to an event within the database. You can create two types of triggers in SQL Server 2005: *data manipulation language (DML) triggers* and *data definition language (DDL)* triggers. DML triggers run when *INSERT, UPDATE,* or *DELETE* statements modify data in a specified table or view. DDL triggers, which run in response to DDL events that occur on the server such as creating, altering, or dropping an object, are used for database administration tasks such as auditing and controlling object access. In this lesson, you see how to create *AFTER* and *INSTEAD OF* DML triggers, how to identify and manage recursive and nested triggers, and how to create DDL triggers to perform administration tasks.

After this lesson, you will be able to:

- Create DML triggers.
- Create DDL triggers.
- Identify recursive and nested triggers.

Estimated lesson time: 20 minutes

DML Triggers

Unlike stored procedures and functions, DML triggers are not stand-alone objects, and you cannot directly execute them. A DML trigger is attached to a specific table or view and defined for a particular event. When the event occurs, SQL Server automatically executes the code within the trigger, known as "firing the trigger." The events that can cause a trigger to fire are *INSERT, UPDATE,* and *DELETE* operations.

Triggers can fire in two different modes: *AFTER* and *INSTEAD OF.*

An *AFTER* trigger fires after SQL Server completes all actions successfully. For example, if you insert a row into a table, a trigger defined for the *INSERT* operation fires only after the row passes all constraints defined by primary keys, unique indexes, constraints, rules, and foreign keys. If the insert fails any of these validations, SQL Server does not execute the trigger. You can define *AFTER* triggers only on tables. And you can create any number of *AFTER* triggers on a table.

An *INSTEAD OF* trigger causes SQL Server to execute the code in the trigger instead of the operation that caused the trigger to fire. If you were to define an *INSTEAD OF* trigger on the table in the previous example, the insert would not be performed, so none of the validation checks would be performed. SQL Server would execute the code in the trigger instead. You can create *INSTEAD OF* triggers on views and tables. The most common usage is to use *INSTEAD OF* triggers on views to update multiple base tables through a view. You can define only one *INSTEAD OF* trigger for each *INSERT*, *UPDATE*, or *DELETE* event for a view or table.

The code within a trigger can be composed of any statements and constructs valid for a batch, with some exceptions. Following is a brief list of some of the more important commands or constructs that you cannot use within a trigger:

- Databases cannot be created, altered, dropped, backed up, or restored.

- Structural changes cannot be made to the table that caused the trigger to fire, such as *CREATE/ALTER/DROP INDEX*, *ALTER/DROP TABLE*, and so on.

MORE INFO Trigger exceptions

You can find the full list of commands and constructs that are not allowed within a trigger in the SQL Server 2005 Books Online article "CREATE TRIGGER (Transact-SQL)."

SQL Server does not support triggers against system objects such as system tables and dynamic management views. Also, triggers will fire only in response to logged operations. Minimally logged operations such as *TRUNCATE* and *WRITETEXT* do not cause a trigger to fire.

BEST PRACTICES Referential integrity

You can use triggers to enforce referential integrity. However, you should not use triggers in place of declarative referential integrity (DRI) via a *FOREIGN KEY* constraint. DRI is enforced when the modification is made, before the change is part of the table, and is much more efficient than executing trigger code. However, you cannot define *FOREIGN KEY* constraints across databases. To enforce referential integrity across databases, you must use triggers.

Triggers have access to two special tables that are dynamically generated: *INSERTED* and *DELETED*. *INSERTED* and *DELETED* tables can be viewed by using an OUTPUT clause. The structure of the *INSERTED* and *DELETED* tables exactly matches the column definition of the table on which the trigger was created. Therefore, you can reference columns by using the same name as the table for which the trigger was defined.

When you execute an *INSERT* operation, the *INSERTED* table contains each row that was inserted into the table, whereas the *DELETED* table does not contain any rows. When you execute a *DELETE* statement, the *DELETED* table contains each row that was deleted from the table, whereas the *INSERTED* table does not contain any rows. When you execute an *UPDATE* statement, the *INSERTED* table contains the after image of each row you updated, and the *DELETED* table contains the before image of each row that you updated. The before image is simply a copy of the row as it existed before you executed the *UPDATE* statement. The after image reflects the data in the row after the *UPDATE* statement has changed appropriate values.

The general Transact-SQL syntax for creating a DML trigger is as follows:

```
CREATE TRIGGER [ schema_name . ]trigger_name
ON { table | view }
[ WITH <dml_trigger_option> [ ,...n ] ]
{ FOR | AFTER | INSTEAD OF }
{ [ INSERT ] [ , ] [ UPDATE ] [ , ] [ DELETE ] }
[ WITH APPEND ]
[ NOT FOR REPLICATION ]
AS { sql_statement  [ ; ] [ ,...n ] | EXTERNAL NAME <method specifier [ ; ] > }

<dml_trigger_option> ::=
    [ ENCRYPTION ]
    [ EXECUTE AS Clause ]
```

Every trigger must have a name that conforms to the rules for object identifiers.

You use the *ON* clause to specify the table or view that the trigger will be created against. If the table or view is dropped, any triggers that were created against the table are also dropped.

Using the *WITH* clause, you can do the following:

- Specify whether the code in the trigger will be encrypted when it is created.
- Specify an execution context.

The *FOR* clause specifies whether the trigger is an *AFTER* or *INSTEAD OF* trigger as well as the event(s) that cause the trigger to fire. You can specify more than one event for a given trigger if you choose.

Most people can ignore the *WITH APPEND* clause, which applies only to 65 compatibility mode, because most organizations should have upgraded their SQL Server 6.5 databases by now. The *NOT FOR REPLICATION* clause is covered in Chapter 19, "Managing Replication."

Following the *AS* clause, you specify the code that you want to execute when the trigger is fired.

Let's look at an example of how to use triggers. Human Resources has a strict policy that requires any changes to an employee's pay rate to be audited. The audit must include prior pay rate, current pay rate, the date the change was made, and the name of the person who made the change. You could accomplish the audit process within an application, but you cannot guarantee that all pay rate changes take place through applications that you control. So you decide to implement a trigger on the *Employee* table that fires on an *UPDATE* operation and logs pay-rate audit information into the *EmployeeAudit* table:

```
CREATE TRIGGER tu_employeepayaudit
ON dbo.Employee
FOR UPDATE
AS

DECLARE @now  DATETIME

SET @now = getdate()

BEGIN TRY
    INSERT INTO dbo.EmployeeAudit
    (RowImage, PayRate, ChangeDate, ChangeUser)
    SELECT 'BEFORE', INSERTED.PayRate, @now, suser_sname()
    FROM DELETED

    INSERT INTO dbo.EmployeeAudit
    (RowImage, PayRate, ChangeDate, ChangeUser)
    SELECT 'AFTER', INSERTED.PayRate, @now, suser_sname()
    FROM INSERTED
END TRY

BEGIN CATCH
    --Some error handling code
    ROLLBACK TRANSACTION
END CATCH
```

Recursive and Nested Triggers

Because triggers fire in response to a DML operation and can also perform additional DML operations, there is the possibility for a trigger to cause itself to fire or to fire additional triggers in a chain.

A trigger causing itself to fire is called *recursion*. For example, suppose that an *UPDATE TRIGGER* is created on the *Customers* table that modifies a column in the *Customers* table. The modification in the trigger causes the trigger to fire again. The trigger modifies the *Customers* table again, causing the trigger to be fired yet again. Because this recursion can lead to an unending chain of transactions, SQL Server has a mechanism to control *recursive triggers*. The *RECURSIVE_TRIGGERS* option of a database is normally set to *OFF*, preventing recursion by default. If you want triggers to fire recursively, you must explicitly turn on this option.

NOTE   *INSTEAD OF* **triggers**

An *INSTEAD OF* trigger does not fire recursively.

Recursion can also occur indirectly. For example, suppose that an *UPDATE* operation on the *Customers* table causes a trigger to fire to update the *Orders* table. The update to the *Orders* table then fires a trigger that updates the *Customers* table. Indirect recursion is a subset of the cases referred to as *nested triggers*.

The most general case of nested triggers is when a trigger makes a change that causes another trigger to fire. By setting the *NESTED TRIGGERS* option to 0 at the server level, you can disable all forms of nested triggers.

DDL Triggers

New in SQL Server 2005 is the ability to create triggers for DDL operations, such as when a table is created, a login is added to the instance, or a new database is created. The main purposes of DDL triggers are to audit and regulate actions performed on a database. DDL triggers let you restrict DDL operations even if a user might normally have the permission to execute the DDL command.

For example, you might want to prevent anyone, including members of the sysadmin fixed server role, from altering or dropping tables in a production environment. You can create a DDL trigger for the *ALTER TABLE* and *DROP TABLE* events that causes the commands to be rolled back and a message returned telling the users that approval is needed before they can alter or drop the table.

The general syntax for creating a DDL trigger is as follows:

```
CREATE TRIGGER trigger_name
ON { ALL SERVER | DATABASE }
[ WITH <ddl_trigger_option> [ ,...n ] ]
{ FOR | AFTER } { event_type | event_group } [ ,...n ]
AS { sql_statement  [ ; ] [ ,...n ] | EXTERNAL NAME < method specifier >  [ ; ] }

<ddl_trigger_option> ::=
    [ ENCRYPTION ]
    [ EXECUTE AS Clause ]

<method_specifier> ::=
    assembly_name.class_name.method_name
```

MORE INFO Event groups

You can find the events that are valid for DDL triggers in the SQL Server 2005 Books Online article "Event Groups for Use with DDL Triggers."

An example of a DDL trigger to prevent the dropping or altering of a table is as follows:

```
CREATE TRIGGER tddl_tabledropalterprevent
ON DATABASE
FOR DROP_TABLE, ALTER_TABLE
AS
    PRINT 'Tables cannot be dropped or altered!'
    ROLLBACK ;
```

> ## Quick Check
> 1. What are the two types of triggers?
> 2. What are they generally used for?
>
> ### Quick Check Answers
> 1. SQL Server 2005 provides DML and DDL triggers.
> 2. DML triggers fire in response to *INSERT*, *UPDATE*, and *DELETE* statements executed against a specific table. DML triggers are generally used to perform operations against the data that was modified in a table. DDL triggers fire in response to DDL commands being executed on the server. DDL triggers are used mainly for security and auditing purposes.

PRACTICE Creating DML and DDL Triggers

In these practices, you create a DML trigger that audits list-price changes and a DDL trigger that prevents dropping tables in a database.

▶ Practice 1: Create a DML Trigger

In this practice, you create a DML trigger on the *Production.Product* table that audits when the list price changes.

1. If necessary, launch SSMS, connect to your instance, open a new query window, and change the database context to the *AdventureWorks* database.

2. Create an auditing table by executing the following command:

```
CREATE TABLE  Production.ProductAudit
(AuditID            int       identity(1,1) PRIMARY KEY,
ProductID           int       NOT NULL,
ListPriceBefore     money     NOT NULL,
ListPriceAfter      money     NOT NULL,
AuditDate           datetime  NOT NULL,
ChangeUser          sysname   NOT NULL);
```

3. Create a trigger against the *Production.Product* table that logs all changes in the audit table. For simplicity, store everything in an XML column:

```
CREATE TRIGGER tuid_ProductAudit
ON Production.Product
FOR UPDATE
AS
INSERT INTO Production.ProductAudit
(ProductID, ListPriceBefore, ListPriceAfter, AuditDate, ChangeUser)
SELECT INSERTED.ProductID, DELETED.ListPrice, INSERTED.ListPrice, getdate(),
suser_sname()
FROM INSERTED INNER JOIN DELETED ON INSERTED.ProductID = DELETED.ProductID;
```

4. Change a row of data in the *Production.Product* table.

5. Observe the effect of the trigger by selecting the data from the audit table.

6. Can you explain why there are two rows of data in the *Production.ProductAudit* table for each row that is changed?

▶ **Practice 2: Create a DDL Trigger**

In this practice, you create a DDL trigger that prevents any table from being dropped.

1. If necessary, launch SSMS, connect to your instance, open a new query window, and change the database context to the *AdventureWorks* database.

2. Create the DDL trigger by executing the following code:

```
CREATE TRIGGER tddl_tabledropprevent
ON DATABASE
FOR DROP_TABLE
AS
    PRINT 'Tables cannot be dropped!'
    ROLLBACK ;
```

3. Create a table for testing purposes, as follows:

```
CREATE TABLE dbo.DropTest
(ID    int   NOT NULL);
```

4. Try to drop the table you just created by executing the following code:

    ```
    DROP TABLE dbo.DropTest;
    ```

5. Verify that the table still exists by executing the following code:

    ```
    SELECT ID from dbo.DropTest
    ```

Lesson Summary

- SQL Server supports two types of triggers: DML and DDL.

- DML triggers can be either *AFTER* or *INSTEAD OF* triggers. You can create any number of *AFTER* triggers for a table or view, but you can create only one *INSTEAD OF* trigger for each data-modification operation for a table or view. When DML triggers fire, they have access to special tables named *INSERTED* and *DELETED*.

- DDL triggers fire in response to DDL events that occur on the server, such as creating, altering, or dropping an object. The main purposes of DDL triggers are to provide an additional means of security and to audit any DDL commands issued against a database.

Lesson Review

The following questions are intended to reinforce key information presented in this lesson. The questions are also available on the companion CD if you prefer to review them in electronic form.

NOTE   Answers

Answers to these questions and explanations of why each answer choice is right or wrong are located in the "Answers" section at the end of the book.

---

1. Which of the following operators is allowed in a trigger when it is used against the table or view that is the target of the triggering action?

    A. *CREATE INDEX*

    B. *RESTORE DATABASE*

    C. *INSERT*

    D. *ALTER DATABASE*

Chapter Review

To further practice and reinforce the skills you learned in this chapter, you can

- Review the chapter summary.
- Review the list of key terms introduced in this chapter.
- Complete the case scenario. This scenario sets up a real-world situation involving the topics of this chapter and asks you to create a solution.
- Complete the suggested practices.
- Take a practice test.

Chapter Summary

- UDFs, stored procedures, and triggers are the programmatic constructs used within SQL Server.
- You use UDFs to encapsulate complex functionality and return either a single value or a table variable. Functions cannot make changes that cause the state of the database or server to change.
- You use stored procedures to perform any programmatic actions on a server. Stored procedures, which can return scalar values or result sets, are the primary interface that applications should use to access any data within a database.
- Triggers are a special type of stored procedure that you use to execute code in response to specified actions. DML triggers execute in response to *INSERT*, *UPDATE*, and *DELETE* operations. DDL triggers execute in response to DDL commands.

Key Terms

Do you know what these key terms mean? You can check your answers by looking up the terms in the glossary at the end of the book.

- data definition language (DDL) trigger
- data manipulation language (DML) trigger
- deterministic function
- function
- input parameter

- nested trigger
- nondeterministic function
- output parameter
- recursive trigger
- scalar function
- stored procedure
- table-valued function
- trigger

Case Scenario: Creating Triggers, Functions, and Stored Procedures

In the following case scenario you will apply what you've learned in this chapter. You can find answers to these questions in the "Answers" section at the end of this book.

Contoso Limited, a health care company located in Bothell, WA, has completed the initial design of its new patient claims database. All the table structures are defined, along with the necessary indexes, views, and partitioning. The company now has to implement all the rest of the parts of the application, including auditing all changes, calculating patient risk scores (a common calculation), and providing access to the data. What should Contoso be designing in the database?

Suggested Practices

To help you successfully master the exam objectives presented in this chapter, complete the following tasks.

Creating Functions

- **Practice 1** Within your existing databases, locate a calculation or result set that is generated on a frequent basis and that isn't straightforward to re-create each time. Encapsulate this code into a function and adjust your application code to use the function instead of using ad hoc SQL code.

Creating Stored Procedures

- **Practice 1** Move all the ad hoc SQL code from your applications into stored procedures and call the procedures to perform the actions. Once all access (*INSERT/UPDATE/DELETE/SELECT*) is through stored procedures, remove all direct permissions to any base tables from all users.

Creating Triggers

- **Practice 1** Add triggers to your databases that audit changes made to data within your databases.

- **Practice 2** Add triggers to your production SQL Server instances for all *DROP* operations that cause the action to be rolled back. Create DDL triggers for *CREATE* and *ALTER* actions that also roll back those operations. This process creates a structure that prevents any accidental changes to objects within any database on the server. To perform these operations, a sysadmin would have to disable the DDL trigger first. Make sure that you do not prevent yourself from altering a DDL trigger; if you do, you won't be able to make any changes.

Take a Practice Test

The practice tests on this book's companion CD offer many options. For example, you can test yourself on just the content covered in this chapter, or you can test yourself on all the 70-431 certification exam content. You can set up the test so that it closely simulates the experience of taking a certification exam, or you can set it up in study mode so that you can look at the correct answers and explanations after you answer each question.

MORE INFO **Practice tests**

For details about all the practice test options available, see the "How to Use the Practice Tests" section in this book's Introduction.

Chapter 10

Working with Flat Files

A common task when working with a database is importing data from other sources. One of the most frequently used methods of transferring data is by using one or more flat files. A *flat file* is a file that is not hierarchical in nature or a file that contains data meant for a single table in the database. Using flat files for data import and export is beneficial because the format is often common between the source and destination systems. Flat files can also provide a layer of abstraction between the source and destination. This chapter covers the factors you need to consider before performing any data-load operations. It then covers the different methods you can use to efficiently import files into SQL Server, including bulk copy program (*bcp*), the *BULK INSERT* Transact-SQL command, the *OPENROWSET* Transact-SQL function, and the SQL Server Integration Services (SSIS) Import/Export Wizard.

Exam objectives in this chapter:

- Import and export data from a file.

  - ❏ Set a database to the bulk-logged recovery model to avoid inflating the transaction log.

  - ❏ Run the *bcp* utility.

  - ❏ Perform a Bulk Insert task.

  - ❏ Import bulk XML data by using the *OPENROWSET* function.

  - ❏ Copy data from one table to another by using the SQL Server 2005 Integration Services (SSIS) Import/Export Wizard.

Lessons in this chapter:

Before You Begin

To complete the lessons in this chapter, you must have

- A computer that meets the hardware and software requirements for Microsoft SQL Server 2005.

- SQL Server 2005 Developer, Workgroup, Standard, or Enterprise Edition installed.

Real World

Daren Bieniek

My work since the mid-1990s has focused mostly on business intelligence (BI) and data warehousing, so I have loaded a lot of flat files into many databases. In fact, I have loaded hundreds of terabytes of data from flat files (nearly all into SQL Server), and I consider flat files an excellent choice for loading databases large or small.

From my experience, here is a quick story about the importance of using the appropriate file formats for data loads. I was working with a client who was bringing in data from several systems, more than 25 GB a week in flat files, and the client suggested that we leave behind the "old" flat files and move to the "newer" XML files. The client could not give me any good reasons why he wanted to change, other than saying it was a general industry direction. I protested and told the client that this is not one of XML's strengths and that the company would incur unnecessary overhead. However, the client insisted that we run a test, and I did.

First, the client's 25 GB in flat files grew to more than 100 GB as XML files because of XML's tag overhead, so we now needed four times the storage and bringing the file across the network took more than four times as long. Second, while loading from the XML files, processor utilization increased substantially (from the overhead of XML tag parsing because tags now made up more than 75 percent of the files' size), and other resources were also more heavily taxed during this time. Additionally, the load time tripled, causing the load to now extend past the maintenance window. Having learned his lesson, the client immediately decided that it was best to stay with the flat files. The moral of this story is that you should use the format that best fits the data you are loading; not switch to the "latest" format just because it is there.

Lesson 1: Preparing to Work with Flat Files

Before starting the file imports, it is important to review the factors that influence logging behavior and performance of the bulk data loads. You need to consider factors related to the source of the import, the import mechanism you are using, and the destination of the data. You also need to make sure the database you're loading into is set to the Bulk-Logged recovery model.

After this lesson, you will be able to:

- List items that affect the logging and performance of bulk operations.
- Explain the impact of recovery models during bulk loads.
- Change the recovery model for a database in preparation for a bulk load.

Estimated lesson time: 15 minutes

Source File Location

The *source* of the data is important because it is a major determining factor in the speed and complexity of the import. For example, if the source is a flat file on a network share, other factors outside of the import server's control can influence performance. These factors include network performance and file server performance. Regardless of how fast the import mechanisms and data destination, the import will run only as fast as the source data can be read. Therefore, it is important to consider the performance of the data source as a factor in determining overall import performance. As with any operation on a computer, the process is only as fast as the slowest component involved.

Import Mechanism

The import mechanism (*bcp*, *BULK INSERT*, *OPENROWSET*, or SSIS) you choose is important in many ways, most of which we will explore later in this chapter. However, keep in mind that although there is substantial overlap in the functionality of the different import mechanisms, they each have their place for certain types of imports.

Data Destination

The destination of the data is probably the single most important factor in determining not only the performance of your import, but also its overall impact on the server. Included in the definition of data destination are the database server, the database, and the data structure. The database server in general is important because its overall design and usage plays a major role in determining the method and performance of the data load. However, a discussion of server design is outside of the scope of this book. The next factor is the database itself. You need to ask many questions about your database to determine which data-load mechanism works best. What level of uptime is needed? Is there a maintenance window during which you can load the data? What *recovery model* is being used? Many other database factors can affect your decision. The last data destination item that affects the data import is the data structure, or table design, itself. Does the table have clustered and/or nonclustered indexes? Does the table have active constraints or triggers? Does the table already have several million rows, or is it empty? Is the table a source for replication?

A Best-Case Scenario

The best-case scenario is bulk-loading data into an empty heap (a table with no indexes) that is not involved in replication, with no constraints or triggers, with the database placed into the Bulk-Logged recovery model, and during a maintenance window. Here is what makes this a best-case scenario.

First, the database is using the Bulk-Logged recovery model. This model differs from the Full recovery model in many ways, one of which is that bulk-load operations are minimally logged so the transaction log will not be filled by the bulk-load operation. There are several caveats surrounding minimal logging. For example, if the table that is being bulk-loaded already has data and has a clustered index, the bulk load will be fully logged, even if the database is using the Bulk-Logged recovery model. (See the sidebar titled "Ensuring Minimal Logging" for more information.)

Ensuring Minimal Logging

You use the Bulk-Logged recovery model to minimize bloating the transaction log during bulk loads. However, it is important to remember that simply setting the recovery model to Bulk-Logged is not enough. Other conditions must be met for minimal logging to occur. The following conditions are necessary for minimal logging:

- Database recovery model is set to Bulk-Logged.
- Table is not replicated.
- TABLOCK hint is used.
- Destination table meets population and indexing requirements (as shown in Table 10-1).

Table 10-1 shows the level of logging (Minimal, Index, or Full) that will occur under different circumstances.

Table 10-1   Logging Level Under Different Conditions

		Clustered Index		Nonclustered Indexes	
		Yes	No	Yes	No
Table	Empty	Minimal	Minimal	Minimal	Minimal
	Has Data	Full	Minimal	Index	Minimal

Note that the table population and indexing criteria are applied at the batch level, not the load level. Therefore, if you load 100,000 rows in 10 batches with 10,000 rows per batch into an empty table with a clustered index, SQL Server logs the first 10,000 rows minimally and fully logs the remaining rows (90,000).

Quick Check

- Why is it useful to switch the recovery mode to Bulk-Logged before bulk-loading data?

Quick Check Answer

- Switching logging modes from Full to Bulk-Logged lets the database possibly perform minimal logging during the data load. Data that is loaded during a bulk load usually has no need for the *point-in-time recovery* capability of the Full recovery model. Decreasing the volume of log writes improves performance and helps alleviate the log bloat that occurs during bulk loads.

It is important to performance that you complete the bulk load during a maintenance window. The obvious reason is so that the bulk load won't have to contend with users for server resources. But the less obvious reasons are that the bulk load can use a table lock, and the recovery model can be altered. The load operation can acquire a table lock instead of the more granular locks that it would acquire otherwise. A table lock is not only more efficient, it is also required for minimal logging to occur. Additionally, most databases operate using the Full recovery model during normal usage. Therefore, if you perform the bulk load during a maintenance window, you can switch the database to the Bulk-Logged recovery model. Although you can switch the database to the Bulk-Logged recovery model during normal usage, certain recovery capabilities are lost, such as point-in-time recovery. To switch to the Bulk-Logged recovery model, use either the *ALTER DATABASE* Transact-SQL command or SQL Server Management Studio (SSMS). An example of using *ALTER DATABASE* to set the recovery model to Bulk-Logged follows:

```
ALTER DATABASE AdventureWorks SET RECOVERY BULK_LOGGED;
```

After you complete the bulk loads, you should switch the database back to the Full recovery model and immediately perform a transaction log backup. Doing so reenables point-in-time recovery from the time of the log backup forward. This log backup not only stores the minimal logging that occurred during the bulk load but also places a copy of the bulk-loaded data into the log backup. This distinction is important because the log backup needs access to the log files and the data files that were the destination of the bulk load. Starting a log backup while a bulk load is occurring to the same data file might introduce contention, which causes both operations to occur more slowly than they would separately. Therefore, it is usually wise to wait until you have finished the bulk loads and placed the database back into Full recovery mode before starting the log backup.

SQL Server Recovery Models

SQL Server provides three recovery models: Full, Bulk-Logged, and Simple. For the most part, the recovery model affects the way SQL Server uses and manages a database's transaction log.

The Full recovery model records every change caused by every transaction at a granular level, which allows for point-in-time recovery. You must back up the transaction log to allow SQL Server to reuse log space.

The Bulk-Logged recovery model is similar to the Full recovery model, but varies when you bulk load data. If certain conditions are met, the Bulk-Logged recovery model does not record the row inserts at a granular level; instead, it logs only extent allocations, which saves a significant amount of log space. Like the Full recovery model, you must perform a transaction log backup for SQL Server to reuse log space.

The Simple recovery model is the same as Bulk-Logged, except that you do not need to back up the transaction log for space to be cleared and reused. Therefore, when using the Simple recovery model, transaction log backups are unreliable.

For more information about recovery models, see Chapter 2, "Configuring SQL Server 2005."

PRACTICE Change the Recovery Model

In this practice, you will change the recovery model of the *AdventureWorks* database from Full to Bulk-Logged and back again.

1. Open SSMS.

2. In the Connect To Server window, specify a Server type of Database Engine, enter the appropriate Server name, and use the appropriate Authentication information for your environment. Click Connect.

3. Press Ctrl+N to open a new query window.

4. To see the current recovery model that *AdventureWorks* is using, type the following command:

```
SELECT DATABASEPROPERTYEX('AdventureWorks', 'Recovery');
```

   If you are still using the default recovery model, the query should return 'FULL'. If anything else is returned, just use the command from step 7 to change the recovery model back to Full.

5. In the query window, above the *SELECT* command from step 4, type the following command to set the recovery model to Bulk-Logged:

```
ALTER DATABASE AdventureWorks SET RECOVERY BULK_LOGGED;
```

   Now, the query window should look like the following:

```
ALTER DATABASE AdventureWorks SET RECOVERY BULK_LOGGED;
SELECT DATABASEPROPERTYEX('AdventureWorks', 'Recovery');
```

6. Click Execute, and the result set should now show 'BULK_LOGGED', which means that you have successfully changed the recovery model to Bulk-Logged.

7. In the query window, replace the words BULK_LOGGED with FULL so that the query window now reads as follows:

```
ALTER DATABASE AdventureWorks SET RECOVERY FULL;
SELECT DATABASEPROPERTYEX('AdventureWorks', 'Recovery');
```

8. Click Execute, and the result set should now show 'FULL', meaning that you have successfully changed the recovery model back to Full.

Lesson Summary

- Many factors are involved in efficiently bulk-loading data, including the characteristics of the data source, the bulk-load mechanism, and the destination of the import.

- Placing a database into the Bulk-Logged recovery model helps to minimize the bloating of the transaction log during a bulk load, but only if several other requirements are met.

Lesson Review

The following questions are intended to reinforce key information presented in this lesson. The questions are also available on the companion CD if you prefer to review them in electronic form.

NOTE   Answers

Answers to these questions and explanations of why each answer choice is right or wrong are located in the "Answers" section at the end of the book.

---

1. Why is it best to bulk load data during a maintenance cycle? (Choose all that apply.)

    A. It is safer to set the recovery model of a database to Bulk-Logged when it is not in use by end users.

    B. Minimal logging requires that a table have a clustered index, and clustered indexes can be created only when the database is in single-user mode.

    C. A table lock must be acquired to minimize logging, and this is not practical during regular usage.

    D. *bcp* can be run only when the database is in single-user mode.

Lesson 2: Running the *bcp* Utility

One of the oldest and most well-known methods of bulk loading data into a SQL Server database is by using the *bcp* command-line utility. Many people consider *bcp* to be the "quick and easy" method of bulk loading data, and they are mostly right. In this lesson, you learn what *bcp* is good for and what it is not good for. Then you will see how to use *bcp* to import data into SQL Server.

After this lesson, you will be able to:

■ Explain the use of the *bcp* command-line utility.

■ Explain certain situations when *bcp* should not be used.

■ List certain common *bcp* parameters and explain their use.

■ List the permissions necessary for a user to bulk-load data into a table by using *bcp*.

■ Execute the *bcp* command to import data.

Estimated lesson time: 15 minutes

What Is *bcp*?

The abbreviation *bcp* stands for bulk copy program. Because *bcp* is a program, you do not execute it from within a query window or batch but rather from the command line. It is an external program, which means it runs outside of the SQL Server process. As its name indicates, you use *bcp* to bulk copy data either into or out of SQL Server. However, this lesson primarily explores the import or loading of data.

Here are two limitations to keep in mind about *bcp*:

■ ***bcp* has limited data-transformation capabilities.**   If the data that you are loading needs to go through complex transforms or validations, *bcp* is not the correct tool to use.

■ ***bcp* has limited error handling capabilities.**   *bcp* might know that an error occurred while loading a given row, but it has limited reaction options. Based on the settings you use during the *bcp* load, *bcp* can react to an erroneous row by either erroring out of the *bcp* load or by logging the row and error (up to a user-specified maximum count) and then erroring out of the *bcp* load. The program does not have the native capability to recover and retry a given row or set of rows during the same load process, as SSIS might do, or to send a notification to someone about the errors that occurred.

bcp Command-Line Syntax

The syntax for the *bcp* command is as follows:

```
bcp {[[database_name.][owner].]{table_name | view_name} | "query"}
    {in | out | queryout | format} data_file
    [-mmax_errors] [-fformat_file] [-x] [-eerr_file]
    [-Ffirst_row] [-Llast_row] [-bbatch_size]
    [-n] [-c] [-w] [-N] [-V (60 | 65 | 70 | 80)] [-6]
    [-q] [-C { ACP | OEM | RAW | code_page } ] [-tfield_term]
    [-rrow_term] [-iinput_file] [-ooutput_file] [-apacket_size]
    [-Sserver_name[\instance_name]] [-Ulogin_id] [-Ppassword]
    [-T] [-v] [-R] [-k] [-E] [-h"hint [,...n]"]
```

As you can see, there are many parameters and options. The following discussion centers on the most frequently used *bcp* parameters.

MORE INFO   *bcp* parameters

For a full description of all the parameters available for *bcp*, see the SQL Server 2005 Books Online topic "bcp Utility." SQL Server 2005 Books Online is installed as part of SQL Server 2005. Updates for SQL Server 2005 Books Online are available for download at *www.microsoft.com/technet/ prodtechnol/sql/2005/downloads/books.mspx.*

Flat files can come in many formats: with or without header rows, varying field delimiters or row delimiters, and so on. Some of the parameters that help with these variances are *-t*, *-r*, and *-F*.

IMPORTANT   Parameters are case-sensitive

Note that *bcp* parameters are case-sensitive. Therefore, *-t* and *-T* are different and unrelated parameters.

-t defines the column delimiter or field "t"erminator. The default for this parameter is \t (tab character), or tab delimited. If you are familiar with importing and exporting files in Microsoft Office Excel, you are probably familiar with tab-delimited files.

-r defines the "r"ow delimiter or "r"ow terminator. The default for this parameter is \n (newline character).

-F defines the number of the "F"irst row to import from the data file. This parameter can be useful in many ways, including telling *bcp* to skip the first row because it is the file header. You can also use *-F* in a case in which part of a file has been processed and you want to restart processing where it left off.

NOTE Most common *bcp* parameters

The *bcp* parameters *-t*, *-r*, and *-F* are the most commonly used parameters for bulk importing an ASCII character file.

---

bcp Hint Parameter

In addition to the previously mentioned commonly used *bcp* parameters, the *-h* or "h"int parameter can have a substantial impact on both performance and logging overhead of the data-load operation. Unlike some of the other *bcp* parameters, you use the *-h* parameter to specify a set of hints for use during the bulk import. There are several hints you can use, including TABLOCK and ORDER. You use the TABLOCK hint to tell the *bcp* command to use a table lock while loading data into the destination table. As noted before, using a table lock decreases locking overhead and allows the Bulk-Logged recovery model to perform minimal logging. Use the ORDER hint to specify that the records in the data file are ordered by certain columns. If the order of the data file matches the order of the clustered index of the destination table, bulk-import performance is enhanced. If the order of the data file is not specified or does not exactly match the ordering of the clustered index of the destination table, the ORDER hint is ignored.

Exam Tip   The *Hint* parameter applies only to importing data from a file to a table. When used with *out*, *queryout*, or *format*, the *Hint* parameter is ignored.

Exam Tip   Both the *bcp* TABLOCK and ORDER hints are important for import performance. But ORDER is useful only if it exactly matches the sort order of the destination table's clustered index.

---

bcp Permissions

The minimum security permissions a user needs to successfully import data to a table by using *bcp* are the *SELECT/INSERT* permissions. However, unlike SQL Server 2000, SQL Server 2005 requires that the user have *ALTER TABLE* permissions to suspend trigger execution, to suspend constraint checking, or to use the *KEEPIDENTITY* option.

> **Quick Check**
>
> - What permissions are needed to run the following *bcp* command?
>
>   ```
>   bcp Table1 in c:\test.txt -T -c
>   ```
>
> **Quick Check Answer**
>
> - First, the *-T* parameter instructs *bcp* to use a trusted connection, which means that all database work will be done using the permissions granted to the Microsoft Windows user executing the command. Second, to import data with *bcp*, the user must have *SELECT* and *INSERT* permissions on the target table. Finally, the defaults that are implied by the command are that triggers and constraints will be disabled; therefore, the user also needs *ALTER TABLE* permission.

PRACTICE Importing Data by Using bcp

In this practice, you create the necessary objects and run a *bcp* import to a table.

NOTE See the companion CD for practice files

Lessons 2, 3, and 4 in this chapter use the files in the \Practice Files\Chapter 10 folder on the companion CD.

▶ **Practice 1: Prepare the Environment**

In this practice, you create a database, a table, a folder, and a file to be used for testing purposes. The folder stores the import file and text files that contain the script to create the table and some commands that are pretyped to help you move quickly through the exercise.

1. In the root folder of the C drive, create a folder named FileImportPractice.

2. Copy all the files in the \Practice Files\Chapter 10 folder on the companion CD to the folder you just created.

3. Open SSMS and connect to the Database Engine.

4. Create a database named *FileImportDB*. It does not need to be very large (10 MB should be enough), and for our learning purposes, you should configure the database to use the Simple recovery model.

5. Using Windows Explorer, in the FileImportPractice folder, double-click the ExamTableCreateScript.sql file.

6. A Connect To Database Engine dialog box opens. Make sure that you connect to the test server in which you created the *FileImportDB* database.

7. Click Execute to run the script and create a table named Exam within the *FileImportDB* database.

8. Verify that the script ran without error and that the Exam table was created.

9. Become familiar with the ExamImportFile.txt file. (Open the file in Notepad.) It is ANSI character data, with four columns separated (delimited) by tabs, and rows delimited by the newline character. Also note that the fourth column is always empty (NULL in our case). You will use the fourth column in a later practice. The four columns in the file are ExamID, ExamName, ExamDescription, and ExamXML, in that order.

10. Don't open any of the *bcp*, BulkInsert, or OpenRowSet command files yet. They are included in case you have difficulty in later practices.

▶ **Practice 2: Run *bcp***

In this practice, you run the *bcp* command to import 500 rows into the new Exam table that you created in Practice 1.

1. Open Notepad.

2. Try to formulate the proper *bcp* command to copy the ExamImportFile.txt into the *FileImportDB..Exam* table. Remember that the defaults for column and row terminators are /t (tab) and /n (newline), respectively.

3. When you think you have the right command, paste it into a command prompt and run it. It doesn't matter if the data is imported more than once, so you do not need to clear the table between attempts.

4. Hints: If you are having trouble, remember that there are actually several ways to form the *bcp* command properly. However, the quickest is to use the -c parameter, which means that the import file is character data and defaults to using /t (tab) and /n (newline) as column and row terminators.

5. You also need to specify how to connect to the SQL Server. The easiest and best way to do this is to simply use the -T parameter, which instructs *bcp* to connect using a trusted connection (Windows Authentication).

6. Therefore, here is the simplest command:

```
bcp FileImportDB..Exam in "c:\FileImportPractice\ExamImportFile.txt" -T -c
```

7. If you like, the command is also available in the bcpImportCommand.txt file. Simply copy it to the command prompt and run it. You should get a message saying that 500 rows were imported. The message also tells you how long the import took and how many rows per second it extrapolates to.

Lesson Summary

- *bcp* is an out-of-process command-line utility for importing or exporting data quickly to or from a file.

- *bcp* has extremely limited data-transformation and error-handling capabilities.

- *bcp* provides numerous parameters that give you substantial flexibility in using the utility. The *-t*, *-r*, and *-F* parameters are the most commonly used parameters for bulk importing an ASCII character file.

- Certain *bcp* hints, such as TABLOCK, must be used for minimal logging to occur.

Lesson Review

The following questions are intended to reinforce key information presented in this lesson. The questions are also available on the companion CD if you prefer to review them in electronic form.

NOTE Answers

Answers to these questions and explanations of why each answer choice is right or wrong are located in the "Answers" section at the end of the book.

---

1. When loading data from a file that uses a comma for the field delimiter and newline for the row delimiter, and the file has a header row at the beginning, which arguments MUST you specify? (Choose all that apply.)

    A. *-T*

    B. *-t*

    C. *-r*

    D. *-F*

Lesson 3: Performing a BULK INSERT Task

BULK INSERT is the in-process brother to the out-of-process *bcp* utility. The *BULK INSERT* Transact-SQL command uses many of the same switches that *bcp* uses, although in a less cryptic format. For example, instead of using *-t* to designate the column terminator, as it is in *bcp*, you can use *FIELDTERMINATOR* = , which is much easier to read and remember. In this lesson, you learn the differences between *bcp* and *BULK INSERT*, and see how to use *BULK INSERT* to insert data into a SQL Server table.

After this lesson, you will be able to:

- Explain the differences between *bcp* and *BULK INSERT*.
- Explain certain situations when *BULK INSERT* should not be used.
- List certain common *BULK INSERT* parameters and explain their use.
- List the permissions necessary for a user to bulk load data into a table by using *BULK INSERT*.
- Execute a *BULK INSERT* command to import data into SQL Server.

Estimated lesson time: 15 minutes

Differences Between *BULK INSERT* and *bcp*

Two of the biggest differences between *bcp* and *BULK INSERT* are that *BULK INSERT* can only import data and it executes inside SQL Server. Whereas *bcp* can either import or export data, *BULK INSERT* (as its name implies) can only import (insert) data into a SQL Server database. Also, *bcp* is executed from the command line and runs outside of the SQL Server process space, meaning that all communications between *bcp* and SQL Server are done via InterProcess Communications (IPC). In contrast, *BULK INSERT* runs inside the SQL Server process space and is executed from a query window or query batch. Other than these two differences and some minor variations in security, the commands behave almost exactly the same.

NOTE *bcp* vs. *BULK INSERT*

bcp runs out-of-process and is executed from the command line, whereas *BULK INSERT* runs in-process and is executed from a query window or Transact-SQL batch.

All of the caveats that apply to *bcp* for minimal logging—for example, there can be no clustered index on a populated table and you must use the TABLOCK hint—also apply to *BULK INSERT*.

Following is the syntax for the *BULK INSERT* command:

```
BULK INSERT
  [ database_name . [ schema_name ] . | schema_name . ] [ table_name | view_name ]
    FROM 'data_file'
   [ WITH
  (
  [ [ , ] BATCHSIZE = batch_size ]
  [ [ , ] CHECK_CONSTRAINTS ]
  [ [ , ] CODEPAGE = { 'ACP' | 'OEM' | 'RAW' | 'code_page' } ]
  [ [ , ] DATAFILETYPE =
    { 'char' | 'native'| 'widechar' | 'widenative' } ]
  [ [ , ] FIELDTERMINATOR = 'field_terminator' ]
  [ [ , ] FIRSTROW  = first_row ]
  [ [ , ] FIRE_TRIGGERS ]
  [ [ , ] FORMATFILE = 'format_file_path' ]
  [ [ , ] KEEPIDENTITY ]
  [ [ , ] KEEPNULLS ]
  [ [ , ] KILOBYTES_PER_BATCH = kilobytes_per_batch ]
  [ [ , ] LASTROW = last_row ]
  [ [ , ] MAXERRORS = max_errors ]
  [ [ , ] ORDER ( { column [ ASC | DESC ] } [ ,...n ] ) ]
  [ [ , ] ROWS_PER_BATCH = rows_per_batch ]
  [ [ , ] ROWTERMINATOR = 'row_terminator' ]
  [ [ , ] TABLOCK ]
  [ [ , ] ERRORFILE = 'file_name' ]
  )]
```

The *BULK INSERT* command uses nearly all the same parameters as *bcp*, but in a less cryptic fashion. Additionally, you can use any format files you create for *bcp* with *BULK INSERT*. And any files you extract from a SQL Server database by using *bcp*, including those you extract in native formats, you can load into a SQL Server database by using *BULK INSERT*.

MORE INFO *BULK INSERT* parameters

For a detailed description of the *BULK INSERT* command's many options, see the SQL Server 2005 Books Online topic "BULK INSERT (Transact-SQL)."

Let's look at the same parameters we discussed for *bcp* to compare what they look like in *BULK INSERT*.

- *FIELDTERMINATOR*   Specifies the field or column terminator or delimiter. As with the *bcp -t* parameter, the default value is \t (tab character). To explicitly declare a different field terminator, such as | (the pipe character), you would specify the following as part of the *BULK INSERT* command:

```
FIELDTERMINATOR = '|'
```

- *ROWTERMINATOR*   Specifies the row terminator or delimiter. As with the *bcp -r* parameter, the default value is \n (newline character). To explicitly declare a different row terminator, such as |>| (the pipe, greater than, and pipe characters concatenated together), you specify the following as part of the *BULK INSERT* command:

```
ROWTERMINATOR = '|>|'
```

- *FIRSTROW*   Specifies the first row in the file that will be inserted into the table. As with the *bcp -F* parameter, *FIRSTROW* can be used to skip a header row or to restart the loading of a file at a certain row number. To explicitly declare a row to start at, such as row 2, you would specify the following as part of the *BULK INSERT* command:

```
FIRSTROW = 2
```

BULK INSERT Permissions

When it comes to *BULK INSERT* security, there are a few things to note, especially because SQL Server 2005 handles security differently from SQL Server 2000. SQL Server 2005 varies from SQL Server 2000 in how it verifies file access permissions. In SQL Server 2000, it didn't matter what type of login was used (Windows user or SQL login); the *BULK INSERT* command would access the import file by using the security privileges of the SQL Server service account. This was a potential security issue that might allow users to get access to a file that their Windows user accounts could not get to directly. In SQL Server 2005, using an integrated login, the *BULK INSERT* command uses the file access privileges of the user account that is executing the query, not the SQL Server service account. The only exception to this is if SQL Server is operating in Mixed Mode, and the *BULK INSERT* command is executed by a SQL Server login that does not map to a Windows user account. In this case, SQL Server still uses the file access permissions of the SQL Server service account.

In addition, to use the *BULK INSERT* command, the user executing the *BULK INSERT* command must have at least *INSERT* and *ADMINISTER BULK OPERATION* permissions. And if the *BULK INSERT* command will suspend trigger execution, suspend constraint checking, or use the *KEEPIDENTITY* option, the user must also have *ALTER TABLE* permissions.

Quick Check

■ What permissions are needed to run the following *BULK INSERT* command?

```
BULK INSERT Table1 FROM 'c:\test.txt'
```

Quick Check Answer

■ To import data by using the *BULK INSERT* command, the user must have *INSERT* permissions on the target table and *ADMINISTER BULK OPERATION* permission on the server. Additionally, the defaults that are implied by the preceding command are that triggers and constraints will be disabled; therefore, the user also needs *ALTER TABLE* permission.

PRACTICE Import Data by Using *BULK INSERT*
====

In this practice, you run the *BULK INSERT* command to import 500 rows into the *Exam* table in the *FileImportDB* database.

IMPORTANT   Perform Lesson 2, Practice 1 first

The necessary database, table, and files for this practice were created or copied during Practice 1, "Prepare the Environment," in Lesson 2 of this chapter. Perform that practice before attempting the following exercise.

---

1. If necessary, open SSMS and connect to the server that you are using for these exercises.

2. Open a new query window by pressing Ctrl+N.

3. Try to formulate the proper *BULK INSERT* command to copy the ExamImportFile.txt into the *FileImportDB..Exam* table. Remember that the defaults for column and row terminators are \t (tab) and \n (newline), respectively.

4. When you think you have the right command, try executing it in the SQL window. It doesn't matter whether the data is imported more than once, so there is no need to clear the table between attempts.

5. Hints: If you are having trouble, remember that there are several ways to form the *BULK INSERT* command properly. However, unlike the *bcp* command, you do not have to specify that it is character data because that is the default for *BULK INSERT*.

6. Here is the simplest command:

```
BULK INSERT FileImportDB..Exam FROM 'c:\FileImportPractice\ExamImportFile.txt'
```

You can also include the TABLOCK hint by appending WITH (TABLOCK) to the end of the command.

7. If you like, the command is also available in the BulkInsertCommand.sql file. Simply copy the command to the SQL window and execute it, or double-click the file for a new SQL window and connection; then execute the command. You should get a message saying that 500 row(s) were affected.

Lesson Summary

- The *BULK INSERT* Transact-SQL command is the in-process brother to *bcp*.
- *BULK INSERT* has similar arguments to *bcp*, but they are less cryptic.
- The *BULK INSERT* permissions have changed from SQL Server 2000 to SQL Server 2005.
- Similar to *bcp*, certain hints, such as TABLOCK, must be used with *BULK INSERT* for minimal logging to occur.

Lesson Review

The following questions are intended to reinforce key information presented in this lesson. The questions are also available on the companion CD if you prefer to review them in electronic form.

NOTE Answers

Answers to these questions and explanations of why each answer choice is right or wrong are located in the "Answers" section at the end of the book.

---

1. When loading data from a file by using *BULK INSERT* on a SQL Server 2005 instance that uses only Windows Authentication, file access permissions are verified based on which user's credentials?

   A. The user account that the SQL Server service is running as.

   B. The user account of the person executing the *BULK INSERT* command.

   C. The user account of the SQL Server Agent service.

   D. File permissions are ignored because a program, not a person, is trying to access the file.

Lesson 4: Importing Bulk XML Data

SQL Server provides several options for importing XML documents. You can use the *OPENROWSET* Transact-SQL function to read data, including XML data, from a file. SQL Server also offers OPENXML and XML stored procedures; the XML data type's *nodes()* method; or the SQLXML middle-tier API to load XML data as relational data, a process called shredding. Lesson 5 of Chapter 8, "Managing XML Data," covers the shredding methods for loading XML data. This lesson discusses using the *BULK* rowset provider for *OPENROWSET* to read data from a file without having to load the data into a target table. With this method, you can use *OPENROWSET* with a simple *SELECT* statement.

> **After this lesson, you will be able to:**
> - List the main uses of the *OPENROWSET* function.
> - Load an XML file into a table by using the *OPENROWSET* function.
> - Explain some of the options and parameters of the *OPENROWSET* function.
>
> **Estimated lesson time: 10 minutes**

OPENROWSET Function

You can use the *OPENROWSET* function in any standard SQL statement as a table reference, thus enabling you to use data from any valid OLE DB data source in a query without first having to load it into a table. The syntax of the function is the following:

```
OPENROWSET
( { 'provider_name' , { 'datasource' ; 'user_id' ; 'password'
   | 'provider_string' }
      , { [ catalog. ] [ schema. ] object
       | 'query'
      }
   | BULK 'data_file' ,
       { FORMATFILE = 'format_file_path' [ <bulk_options> ]
       | SINGLE_BLOB | SINGLE_CLOB | SINGLE_NCLOB } 
} )

 <bulk_options> ::=
   [ , CODEPAGE = { 'ACP' | 'OEM' | 'RAW' | 'code_page' } ]
   [ , ERRORFILE = 'file_name' ]
   [ , FIRSTROW = first_row ]
   [ , LASTROW = last_row ]
   [ , MAXERRORS = maximum_errors ]
   [ , ROWS_PER_BATCH = rows_per_batch ]
```

There are many uses of the *OPENROWSET* function, including using the function as a target of an *INSERT*, *UPDATE*, or *DELETE* query. For example, you can use this function to make a flat file appear to be a table and then you can treat the file as a table by using joins, *WHERE* clauses, *SELECT* statements, and so on without having to load the data in a table first. Or you can use *OPENROWSET* with a different data provider to allow a SQL query to see data in an Analysis Services Measure Group as a flattened table, and all the same uses apply. However, the focus of this chapter and lesson is importing data from files.

To use *OPENROWSET* to bulk load XML data, you use the *BULK* option, which lets you specify where to start and end reading data, how to deal with errors, and how to interpret data. For example, when importing a single XML document into a column of one row, you specify the *BULK* option along with the *SINGLE_BLOB* format. A sample statement to perform this task is the following:

```
INSERT INTO Documents(XmlCol)
SELECT * FROM OPENROWSET(
   BULK 'c:\XMLDocs\XMLDoc9.txt',
   SINGLE_BLOB) AS x
```

This statement bulk imports the contents of the 'c:\XMLDocs\XMLDoc9.txt' file as a *SINGLE_BLOB* and inserts that *BLOB* into the XmlCol of a single row in the Documents table.

The *SINGLE_BLOB* format tells the *OPENROWSET* function to treat the entire file as a single unit, rather than parsing it in some way.

MORE INFO   *OPENROWSET*

For comprehensive coverage of *OPENROWSET*, see the SQL Server 2005 Books Online topic "OPENROWSET (Transact-SQL)."

Quick Check

- Can *OPENROWSET* be used only to load data from XML files?

Quick Check Answer

- No. You can use *OPENROWSET* to make data from many different data providers available for use inside a query.

PRACTICE **Import Data by Using *OPENROWSET***

In this practice, you use the *OPENROWSET* function in an *UPDATE* statement to import data from a text file that contains an XML fragment and update specific rows in the *Exam* table with the imported XML fragment.

IMPORTANT   Work through the Lessons 2 and 3 practices first

The necessary database, table, and files for this practice were created or copied during Practice 1, "Prepare the Environment," in Lesson 2 of this chapter. Be sure to finish that exercise before attempting the following practice. Also, you need to perform at least one of the *bcp* or *BULK INSERT* import exercises before doing this practice.

---

1. If necessary, open SSMS and connect to the server that you are using for these exercises.

2. Open a new query window by pressing Ctrl+N.

3. Here is the base *UPDATE* statement you use:

```
UPDATE EXAM
SET ExamXML = (SELECT A.Col1
FROM OPENROWSET(
   …) AS A(Col1))
WHERE ExamID=1
```

4. Try to formulate the proper *OPENROWSET* section of the preceding *UPDATE* statement. Remember that the defaults for column and row terminators are /t (tab) and /n (newline), respectively.

5. When you think you have the right command, try executing it in the SQL window. It doesn't matter if you run the command more than once, so there is no need to reset any rows between attempts, and you can always change which ExamID the statement is updating.

6. Here is the complete *UPDATE* statement:

```
UPDATE EXAM
SET ExamXML = (SELECT A.Col1
FROM OPENROWSET(
   BULK 'c:\FileImportPractice\XMLTest.txt',
   SINGLE_BLOB) AS A(Col1))
WHERE ExamID=1
```

7. If you like, the statement is also available in the OpenRowsetCommand.sql file. Simply copy the command to the SQL window and execute it, or double-click the file for a new SQL window and connection and then execute the command. You should get a message saying that a few row(s) were affected. The number of affected rows depends on how many times you ran the *bcp* and *BULK INSERT* commands in previous exercises.

Lesson Summary

- The *OPENROWSET* function, which can be used with an OLE DB data provider, allows you to use data from a file in a query without having to load it into a table first.

- To import an XML file into a single column and row, use *OPENROWSET* with the *BULK* option and *SINGLE_BLOB* format.

Lesson Review

The following questions are intended to reinforce key information presented in this lesson. The questions are also available on the companion CD if you prefer to review them in electronic form.

NOTE Answers

Answers to these questions and explanations of why each answer choice is right or wrong are located in the "Answers" section at the end of the book.

1. Which of the following are valid places to use the *OPENROWSET* function? (Choose all that apply.)
    A. In the *FROM* clause of a query in place of a regular table
    B. In *bcp* as a data source for import into SQL Server 2005
    C. In *BULK INSERT* as a data source for import into SQL Server 2005
    D. As the target of an *INSERT*, *UPDATE*, or *DELETE* query

Lesson 5: Using the SSIS Import/Export Wizard

The most robust way to import or export data is with SSIS. SSIS is the SQL Server 2005 successor to the popular Data Transformation Services (DTS) *extraction, transformation, and loading (ETL)* tool that ships as part of SQL Server 2000 and SQL Server 7.0. Exploring the full power, flexibility, and usage of SSIS are well beyond the scope of this book, but this lesson provides a basic overview of the SSIS Import/Export Wizard as it pertains to importing a flat file.

After this lesson, you will be able to:

- List ways to start the SSIS Import/Export Wizard.
- Explain the wizard's screens.
- Explain how starting the wizard from different applications alters its behavior.

Estimated lesson time: 15 minutes

How to Start the SSIS Import/Export Wizard

There are several ways to instantiate the SSIS Import/Export Wizard. You can start it by going through SSMS, Business Intelligence Development Studio (BIDS), or the command prompt.

SSMS

Starting the SSIS Import/Export Wizard from within SSMS is similar to how you access the Import/Export Wizard in SQL Server 2000 Enterprise Manager. To start the SSIS Import/Export Wizard in SSMS, begin by connecting to a Database Engine server type in the object browser. Under the Databases node, right-click any database container in the tree, choose Tasks, and then choose either Import Data or Export Data, as Figure 10-1 shows.

BIDS

There are two ways to start the SSIS Import/Export Wizard from within BIDS. The first method is to right-click the SSIS Packages folder and then choose SSIS Import And Export Wizard. The second method is to click SSIS Import And Export Wizard on the Project menu.

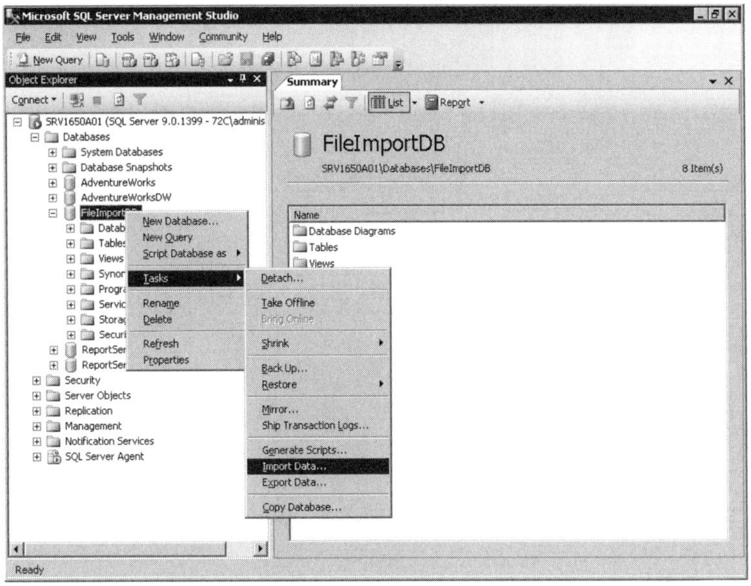

Figure 10-1   Starting the SSIS Import/Export Wizard from within SSMS

Command Prompt

You can also start the SSIS Import/Export Wizard by running DTSWizard.exe, which by default is located in C:\Program Files\Microsoft SQL Server\90\DTS\Binn. After typing the command, the standard graphical user interface (GUI) for the wizard is launched.

Walking Through the Import/Export Wizard

After displaying the Welcome screen, the wizard guides you through selecting the data source, destination, mapping, and package save and execution options.

Choose a Data Source

The wizard first has you specify a data source and its related options. There are many options for a data source, which vary based on the data providers installed. Because this chapter is about importing flat files, Figure 10-2 shows Flat File Source selected as the data source.

When you select Flat File Source as your data source, the SQL Server Import And Export Wizard displays the options that pertain to a flat file, including an option to select the file for import, the types of delimeters used, and whether or not the file contains headers. After you have set up everything properly for your situation, click Next.

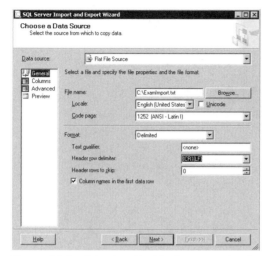

Figure 10-2   Selecting Flat File Source as the data source for the import

Choose a Destination

The next page, Choose A Destination, enables you to select the destination for the data import. Again, this can be any valid data provider. Using the example of importing data from a flat file into a SQL Server table, you use the default destination of SQL Native Client, shown in Figure 10-3.

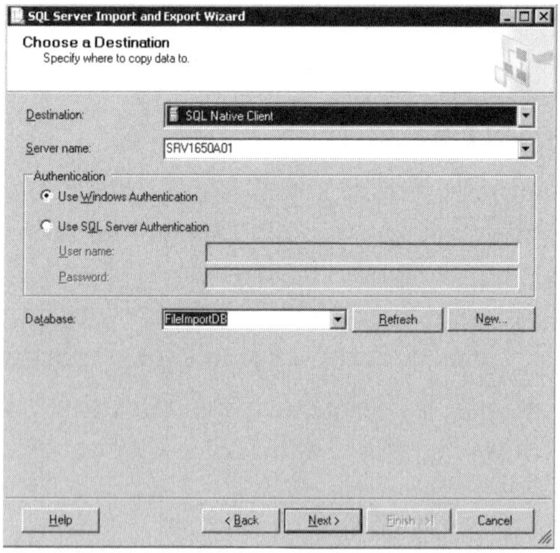

Figure 10-3   Selecting SQL Native Client as the destination for the import

As before, after you select the provider, the wizard shows provider-specific options, which in this case include Server Name, Authentication Method, and Database. After you configure the options, click Next.

Select Source Tables And Views

The Select Source Tables And Views page, as Figure 10-4 shows, enables you to specify which source you want to map to which destination and how you want that mapping to occur. For the flat file import example, you use a single source and single destination. Clicking Edit in the Mapping column lets you specify column-level mapping and other options such as Identity Insert.

Figure 10-4   Mapping source and destination for the import

Save And Execute Package

In the next page, Save And Execute Package, you specify whether you want to execute the import now and/or save the package for later. Selecting the Execute Immediately check box (see Figure 10-5) means that SQL Server executes the import when you complete the wizard. Selecting the Save SSIS Package check box enables you to save the import package for later use.

Saving the package is useful for several reasons, including tracing data lineage, reusing the package, and using the package as a base for other packages. You can use the package for a basic form of data lineage in which someone can open the package and see what transformations and mappings occurred during the import. Also, you can reuse the package for additional imports, possibly with minor variations such as a different file name or source file path. Finally, many people use the wizard to create a base package for performing complex imports. They use the wizard to create the basic package with minimal transforms; then they can edit the saved package within SSIS to make it more robust.

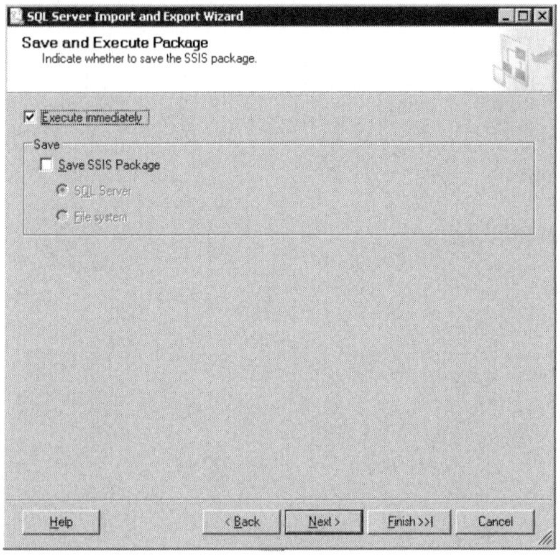

Figure 10-5   Specifying execution options for the import

NOTE   Different option if wizard started from within BIDS

If you start the SQL Server Import And Export Wizard from an Integration Services project in BIDS, you cannot run the package immediately. Instead, the wizard adds the package to the project and then you can run the package in BIDS.

Complete The Wizard

The Complete The Wizard screen gives you a high-level review of the options that you selected before implementing your choices, as Figure 10-6 shows.

From this screen, clicking Finish executes the package and returns a window that reports whether the tasks were successful, shown in Figure 10-7.

Figure 10-6   Reviewing your data-import options

Figure 10-7   Reporting success or failure of the data import tasks

---

Quick Check

- Why is it useful to save the SSIS package created by the Import/Export Wizard?

Quick Check Answer

- Saving the package is useful for several reasons, including being able to trace data lineage, reuse the package, and use the package as a base for other packages.

Lesson Summary

- The SSIS Import/Export Wizard can be started from SSMS, BIDS, or the command prompt.

- When the wizard is started from within BIDS, the package cannot be immediately executed by the wizard.

- The wizard can use many data providers (flat file, SQL Native Client, Microsoft OLE DB for SQL Server, and so on) as the source of the data load, the destination of the data load, or both.

- The packages created by the wizard can either be immediately executed and discarded or saved for later use.

- You can use the wizard to get a "jump start" on more robust data-load projects.

Lesson Review

The following questions are intended to reinforce key information presented in this lesson. The questions are also available on the companion CD if you prefer to review them in electronic form.

NOTE Answers

Answers to these questions and explanations of why each answer choice is right or wrong are located in the "Answers" section at the end of the book.

---

1. When you start the SSIS Import/Export Wizard from a command prompt rather than from within BIDS, which of the following are different in the wizard?

    A. The interface. When you start the wizard from the command line, it has a non-GUI command-line interface. When you start it from within BIDS, it has a graphical interface.

    B. When you start the wizard from within BIDS, several additional options are added to the wizard.

    C. You cannot start the wizard from the command prompt.

    D. When you start the wizard from BIDS, the option to immediately execute the package is removed from the wizard.

Chapter Review

To further practice and reinforce the skills you learned in this chapter, you can

- Review the chapter summary.
- Review the list of key terms introduced in this chapter.
- Complete the case scenario. This scenario sets up a real-world situation involving the topics of this chapter and asks you to create a solution.
- Complete the suggested practices.
- Take a practice test.

Chapter Summary

- Setting the recovery model of a database to Bulk-Logged before bulk loading data can significantly decrease logging overhead, as long as certain other conditions are met.
- Although *bcp* is an efficient but cryptic command-line tool that you can use to load and unload data from a database, it has limited data-transformation and error-handling capabilities.
- *BULK INSERT* is similar to *bcp* except that it runs in-process, has less-cryptic parameters, and can only import data into a database.
- *OPENROWSET* can be used to import or export data (if the provider is capable of it) and can use data from an external source without having to put it in a table first.
- The SSIS Import/Export Wizard can take data from any provider (for example, SQL Server, Oracle, or flat file) as a source and can transform it and put the data into a destination using any provider (SQL Server, Oracle, or flat file). The package created by the wizard can be used immediately (in most cases) or can be saved for later use or as a base to build more-robust SSIS packages from it.

Key Terms

Do you know what these key terms mean? You can check your answers by looking up the terms in the glossary at the end of the book.

- bcp
- BULK INSERT

- extraction, transformation, and loading (ETL)
- flat file
- point-in-time recovery
- recovery model
- source
- target or destination

Case Scenario: Fixing a Bloated Transaction Log

In the following case scenario, you will apply what you've learned in this chapter. You can find answers to these questions in the "Answers" section at the end of this book.

A company has data in several flat files that it loads into its *Logging* table once per week. The IT team does the load during a weekly maintenance window, during which it also performs backups. Members of the team want to do the backups after the data load is complete, but they have found that the database log files are nearly full after about 70 percent of the files are loaded. Therefore, they have to complete a log backup before the loading can finish, which puzzles the database administrators (DBAs) because they are setting the recovery model of the database to Bulk-Logged before the loads start.

The *Logging* table contains five weeks' worth of logs, and before the latest week is loaded, the oldest week is deleted. The company is currently working on a partitioning strategy, but needs help in the meantime. The company is loading the data by using the *BULK INSERT* command. The *Logging* table has a clustered index on the primary key, which is an identity column, and four nonclustered indexes.

You review the loading scripts and find that the *BULK INSERT* commands are not using any hints and that the scripts do not do anything to the table except delete and bulk insert data. You also find that the beginning and ending identity value for each week's load is stored in another table. What should you do to help minimize logging during the data loads?

Suggested Practices

To help you successfully master the exam objectives presented in this chapter, complete the following tasks.

Using *bcp* and *BULK INSERT* to Load Tables

- **Practice 1**   Create a data file, practice loading this file by using *bcp* with different parameters, and note the differences in load behavior.

- **Practice 2**   Using the same data file as in Practice 1, practice loading the file by using *BULK INSERT* with different options and note the difference in load behavior.

Using SSIS to Load Tables

- **Practice 1**   Using the same file as the previous practices, try loading the table by using the SSIS Import/Export Wizard. Be sure to save the package created by the wizard for later review.

- **Practice 2**   Open the SSIS package that was saved in the preceding practice and review the data flow to see how the wizard constructed the import. Try changing several options in the package designer and note what happens when you run the package.

Take a Practice Test

The practice tests on this book's companion CD offer many options. For example, you can test yourself on just the content covered in this chapter, or you can test yourself on all the 70-431 certification exam content. You can set up the test so that it closely simulates the experience of taking a certification exam, or you can set it up in study mode so that you can look at the correct answers and explanations after you answer each question.

MORE INFO   Practice tests

For details about all the practice test options available, see the "How to Use the Practice Tests" section in this book's Introduction.

Chapter 11

Backing Up, Restoring, and Moving a Database

Maintaining at least one copy of an operational database in case of a disaster is the most fundamental task a database administrator (DBA) can perform. And performing a database backup is the most common method for accomplishing this task. Just because performing a database backup is a common operation, however, does not mean it is unimportant. This chapter emphasizes how important database backups are to your *restore strategy*, which defines how you can recover your database while meeting business requirements for allowed amounts of downtime and maximum data loss. Without a restore strategy, backing up a database has virtually no purpose. After describing Microsoft SQL Server's flexible options for backing up a database, this chapter explains how to restore those backups to recover data up to a specific point in time. You will also learn how to move databases by using backup/restore, detach/attach, or the Copy Database Wizard.

MORE INFO   **SSMS backup and restore facilities**

In this chapter, we explore all the SQL Server 2005 backup and restore features by using the command syntax. Although you can access most of the features we cover via the SQL Server Management Studio (SSMS) graphical interface, walking through the screens does little to explain this subject. In addition, you cannot perform some options and restore processes through the graphical user interface (GUI).

For details about using the SSMS backup and restore facilities, see the SQL Server 2005 Books Online reference page "Backing Up and Restoring How-to Topics." SQL Server 2005 Books Online is installed as part of SQL Server 2005. Updates for SQL Server 2005 Books Online are available for download at *www.microsoft.com/technet/prodtechnol/sql/2005/downloads/books.mspx*.

Exam objectives in this chapter:

- Back up a database.
  - ❏ Perform a full backup.
  - ❏ Perform a differential backup.
  - ❏ Perform a transaction log backup.
  - ❏ Initialize a media set by using the *FORMAT* option.
  - ❏ Append or overwrite an existing media set.
  - ❏ Create a backup device.
  - ❏ Back up filegroups.
- Restore a database.
  - ❏ Identify which files are needed from the backup strategy.
  - ❏ Restore a database from a single file and from multiple files.
  - ❏ Choose an appropriate restore method.
- Move a database between servers.
  - ❏ Choose an appropriate method for moving a database.

Lessons in this chapter:

Before You Begin

To complete the lessons in this chapter, you must have

- SQL Server 2005 installed.
- A connection to a SQL Server 2005 instance.
- A copy of the *AdventureWorks* sample database.
- Completed Chapter 2, "Configuring SQL Server 2005," in this book.

Real World

Michael Hotek

I finally was going to be home for more than a couple of days straight and was looking forward to spending the day working on new projects on the lathe. But on my way through the house and to the woodshop, the phone rang. I didn't know the desperate caller, who was from an organization that I had never heard of. But a DBA from an organization that I had worked with a couple of years ago had given him my phone number.

The organization had a big problem: A disk in its drive array had failed, and the person who swapped in a new drive unfortunately chose the wrong drive and caused the entire system to shut down with a completely unrecoverable redundant array of inexpensive disks (RAID) array. I was apparently the organization's last resort to try to fix a problem no one else had been able to solve. I've spent almost two decades doing emergency disaster recovery for hundreds of organizations around the globe, with a pretty high success rate. Most of the projects involved working to recover production systems that I had never seen before. The damages were caused by nearly every disaster you could think of: flood, fire, tornado, hurricane, tsunami, lightning, earthquake, water immersion, explosives, bullets, every "normal" hardware failure imaginable, security breeches, and even end-user error.

After a virtual private network (VPN) into the organization's system and a several-hour-long conference call to work through everything, we managed to reconstruct just about everything by using a combination of backups, data extracts to other systems, and Lumigent Technologies' Log Explorer product. We could not recover a small amount of data that was damaged during an initial failed recovery operation, but the organization could manually reconstruct the data.

About the time I was finishing up with this customer, an e-mail popped into my inbox, asking if I could help yet another organization. It seems its hosting provider had toasted the drive array on which its data was sitting. Even better, there were no backups for the database. For the hundredth time, I had to ask myself, when were people ever going to learn? Having a functional, tested backup and restore strategy, and deploying that strategy correctly, is the most fundamental part of any database implementation. Thankfully, I typically don't get several of these calls daily and have even managed an entire month in the last decade when I didn't have to deal with one. But I would have really liked to have spent a nice, relaxing day at my lathe, creating something that didn't have to do with a computer...

Lesson 1: Backing Up a Database

Maintaining a duplicate copy of data that you can recover in the event of data loss is critical. And SQL Server 2005 provides a variety of features that you can use to accomplish this goal. The most common way to maintain duplicate copies of data is by using the backup capabilities built into SQL Server. Some of these capabilities will be familiar to anyone who has used a previous version of SQL Server. In addition, SQL Server 2005 includes a significant step forward in providing greater flexibility with ways to perform backups. This lesson will explain the basics of each option that is available within the SQL Server backup engine.

IMPORTANT   Understanding database and log structures

To get a better understanding of the backup and restore architecture, you first need to be familiar with the basic structure of SQL Server databases, filegroups, extents, data pages, and transaction logs. Refer to Chapter 2 before starting this lesson.

> **After this lesson, you will be able to:**
> - Perform a full backup.
> - Perform a differential backup.
> - Perform a transaction log backup.
> - Perform a filegroup backup.
> - Initialize a media set by using the *FORMAT* option.
> - Append or overwrite an existing media set.
> - Create a backup device.
>
> **Estimated lesson time: 45 minutes**

NOTE   Backup permissions

Unlike previous SQL Server versions, SQL Server 2005 aims to strengthen security by implementing the principle of least privilege, using only the minimum set of permissions required to perform an operation. So you need to know what permissions are required to execute backups. Backups, no matter how you initiate them, execute within the database engine under the security context of the SQL Server service account. You need to grant this account permissions to read and write to any directories or tape devices that you will be using to back up to; otherwise, your backups will fail due to insufficient permissions. To grant a user permissions to back up the database without allowing additional access, add the user as a member of the *db_backupoperator* role, which is allowed only to back up the database, log, or checkpoint in the database. No other access is allowed.

Performing Full Backups

The purpose of a *full database backup* is to capture all the data that is stored in the database. The backup engine accomplishes this task by extracting every extent in the database that is allocated to an object. You can then use a full backup by itself to re-create the entire database. Note that this backup method is always available, regardless of the *recovery model* you configure for a database.

NOTE Inside backup granularity

You will find many books that say a SQL Server backup backs up a data page instead of an extent. This is inaccurate. SQL Server does not allocate a single data page to an object that needs space; it allocates a full extent. The backup engine works on the same principle. It extracts any pages allocated to an object, and because allocation occurs one extent at a time, the backup engine is in fact backing up all extents that SQL Server has allocated to objects, regardless of whether SQL Server has written data to all the pages within the extent.

The backup engine is configured to perform a backup as quickly as possible while using a minimum of resources. When you initiate a backup, the backup engine writes pages to the *backup device* without regard to the order of pages. Because the backup is not concerned with the precise ordering of pages, SQL Server can open multiple threads to write data as fast as it can be accepted by the media. The only limiting factor in the backup speed is how fast data can be written to a device.

Because a backup is not instantaneous and can occur while users are connected to the database and issuing queries, logical inconsistency in the database is a possibility. If a page of data were written to the backup media and then modified by another request, for example, restoring this backup would place the database in an inconsistent state.

SQL Server, however, does not allow this to happen because it enforces the following specific series of steps during a full backup:

1. Lock the database, blocking all transactions.
2. Place a mark in the transaction log.
3. Release the database lock.
4. Back up all pages in the database.
5. Lock the database, blocking all transactions.
6. Place a mark in the transaction log.
7. Release the database lock.
8. Extract all transactions between the two log marks and append to the backup.

This process ensures that the database is completely consistent as of the time that the backup completes.

The basic command to back up a database is as follows:

```
BACKUP DATABASE <database name> TO DISK = '<directory>\<filename>' WITH INIT
```

You use the *TO* clause in the *BACKUP DATABASE* command to specify the backup device to send the backup to, which can be the name of a logical backup device that is created, or you can specify an explicit path to either *DISK* or *TAPE*. The *WITH* clause has more than a dozen parameters, all of which are optional. The *INIT* parameter, which is the most common, tells SQL Server to overwrite anything in the backup device that might already exist before starting the backup operation.

MORE INFO   Backup syntax

For a complete discussion of the *BACKUP DATABASE* command, including all possible options, see the article "BACKUP (Transact-SQL)" in SQL Server 2005 Books Online.

Performing Differential Backups

A *differential backup* captures all the extents that have changed since the last full backup. And the main purpose of a differential backup is to reduce the number of *transaction log backups* that need to be restored. You use a differential backup along with a full backup. If a full backup does not exist, you cannot create a differential backup. As with a full backup, you can perform a differential backup of a database no matter what recovery model is specified for the database.

Note that a differential backup is NOT an incremental backup. An incremental backup captures any changes since the previous incremental backup. Therefore, restoring an incremental backup requires all other incremental backups. A differential backup always captures every extent that has changed since the last full backup. So each differential backup contains everything that any previous differential backup taken after a full backup contains. For example, suppose that a full backup occurs at midnight, with differential backups taken every four hours during the day. The differential backup at 04:00 contains all extents that have changed since midnight. The differential backup at 08:00 contains all extents that have changed since midnight. And the noon differential backup contains all extents that have changed since midnight.

To determine the extents that need to be backed up by a differential backup, SQL Server maintains an extent map. An extent map is just another data page within the database, with each bit on the page representing an extent. When SQL Server changes an extent, it changes the corresponding bit for that extent from 0 to 1. When you perform a full backup, SQL Server resets all bits to 0. In this way, SQL Server has to interrogate only this page to determine which extents it needs to back up. Because databases can be an unlimited size and data pages are only 8 KB in size, SQL Server creates one of these mapping pages for approximately every 8,192 extents that it allocates to objects in the database. So a single page can cover thousands of data pages.

The simplest command to perform a differential backup is as follows:

```
BACKUP DATABASE <database name> TO DISK = '<directory>\<filename>' WITH DIFFERENTIAL
```

This command is almost exactly the same as the command to perform a full database backup except that it requires use of the *DIFFERENTIAL* parameter. All other options are the same as with a full backup.

Transaction Log Backups

You can perform transaction log backups only for databases you have configured to use the Full or Bulk-Logged recovery model and that have not yet had a minimally logged transaction executed. Transaction log backups are also allowed only after a full backup has been performed. A transaction log backup contains only a subset of data and requires that you also have at least a full backup to recover the database.

A log backup backs up the *active log*. It starts at the Log Sequence Number (LSN) at which the previous log backup completed. SQL Server then backs up all subsequent transactions until the backup encounters an open transaction. After SQL Server encounters an open transaction, the log backup completes. Any LSNs that are backed up are then allowed to be removed from the transaction log, which enables the system to reuse log space.

NOTE Transaction log, replication, and database mirroring

If you are implementing either transactional replication or database mirroring, an additional requirement is imposed on a transaction log. Both these features guarantee delivery of data and therefore must ensure that data is successfully delivered before SQL Server can remove a transaction from the log, regardless of whether it has been backed up. When you are using these features, a transaction can be removed only when

---

1. It has been successfully committed to the distribution database.
2. It has been successfully committed on the mirror database.

The simplest way to execute a transaction log backup is to issue the following statement (see the SQL Server 2005 Books Online article noted previously for syntax details):

```
BACKUP LOG <database name> TO DISK = '<directory>\<filename>' WITH INIT
```

Quick Check
- How do full, differential, and transaction log backups interact with each other?

Quick Check Answer
- A full backup is required before you can perform either a differential or a transaction log backup. Differential and transaction log backups occur independently of each other. The main purpose of a differential backup is to reduce the number of transaction log backups that you must restore in the event of a database failure.

Performing Filegroup Backups

Filegroup backups provide an alternative *backup strategy* to full backups. Instead of backing up the entire database, you can perform a filegroup backup to back up individual filegroups within the database. The starting point for a filegroup backup strategy must include a backup of all filegroups within the database so that you can reassemble all the filegroups within that database.

BEST PRACTICES   Using filegroup backups

You should select a filegroup backup method when the size of a database makes it impractical to either back up or restore an entire database while still meeting your recovery requirements.

Because a filegroup backup enables you to back up portions of a database, it requires you to configure the database in the Full or Bulk-Logged recovery model so that you can perform a filegroup backup that is read/write. To restore, you can then use filegroup, differential, and transaction log backups.

NOTE   Recovering from a filegroup backup

If you are restoring one or more filegroups with backups taken at different times, transaction log backups are a minimum requirement to roll all filegroups forward to a consistent point in time.

The simplest way to perform a filegroup backup is as follows:

```
BACKUP DATABASE <database name> FILEGROUP = '<filegroup name>' TO DISK = '<directory>\<filen
ame>'
```

You can also take a differential backup on either a database or filegroup basis. The simplest form of a filegroup differential backup command is this:

```
BACKUP DATABASE <database name> FILEGROUP = '<filegroup name>' TO DISK = '<directory>\<filen
ame>' WITH DIFFERENTIAL
```

Performing Mirrored Backups

Each backup operation creates a single copy of data on either disk or tape. It is then up to an administrator to create additional copies to protect your organization from media failure. This duplication process can be tedious and time-consuming, and the single backup becomes a potential single point of failure during the process.

SQL Server 2005 introduces a new capability to the *BACKUP* command. You can create additional copies of a backup called mirrors during the backup operation. You accomplish this operation by using the following optional clause in the *BACKUP* command:

```
[[MIRROR TO <backup_device> [ ,...n ]][ ...next-mirror]]
```

You can create up to four mirrors, with three being specified in the *MIRROR TO* clause. A mirrored backup also places some restrictions on the media that you use. The media for each mirror must be of the same type as well as have the same number of devices. Each must also possess similar properties. For example, if you are backing up to disk, all mirrors must also be disks; if you are backing up to tape, all mirrors must be tape.

NOTE Inside backup striping

A *media set* generally contains a single physical device, such as a file or tape drive. However, a media set can be constructed of up to 64 devices. When a media set encompasses multiple physical devices, the backup engine spawns one thread per physical device and writes a portion of the data within the backup to each device. This is not the same as the striping capability present in RAID technology, but it is similar in concept to what occurs with RAID 0. Each mirror must be identical. Therefore, if you specify a media set that contains two disk devices, each mirror must also contain two disk devices. Similarly, if your media set contains 64 tape devices, the mirror must specify 64 tape devices.

When you use *mirrored backups*, SQL Server reads the page from the data files once and then creates multiple copies as it writes the page to disk or tape. This process has the effect of writing the same page of data to each mirror at the same time. The restriction on each mirror being of the same device type with similar properties is to ensure minimal performance impact when using this capability.

NOTE   **Backup locations**

A common misconception is that devices you are using for backups must be physically attached to the SQL Server machine. Backups can be sent to locally attached devices. You can also send backups to a Universal Naming Convention (UNC) path. When sending backups to a UNC path, you must consider the backup's impact on the network bandwidth.

The following example backs up the *PUBS* database to a two-disk media set and creates three mirrors of the backup. The first backup occurs to a locally attached disk, whereas each of the mirrors is a network resource accessed via a UNC path.

```
BACKUP DATABASE PUBS TO DISK='C:\DEMO\BACKUP\PUBS1A.BAK', DISK='C:\DEMO\BACKUP\PUBS1B.BAK'
    MIRROR TO DISK='\\BAKSERVER1\BACKUP\PUBSMIRROR1A.BAK', DISK='\\BAKSERVER1\BACKUP\
    PUBSMIRROR1B.BAK'
    MIRROR TO DISK='\\BAKSERVER2\BACKUP\PUBSMIRROR2A.BAK', DISK='\\BAKSERVER2\BACKUP\
    PUBSMIRROR2B.BAK'
    MIRROR TO DISK='\\BAKSERVER3\BACKUP\PUBSMIRROR3A.BAK', DISK='\\BAKSERVER3\BACKUP\
    PUBSMIRROR3B.BAK'
WITH FORMAT
GO
```

NOTE   *FORMAT* **clause**

The *FORMAT* clause is normally an optional parameter. This parameter writes a new media header to each media set, overwriting the previous header and invalidating any other backups contained on the media. However, the *FORMAT* clause is required for a mirrored backup.

Partial Backups

It is possible to have databases in which some of the filegroups can be written to, whereas others are read-only. In previous versions of SQL Server, a full backup captured all allocated extents in a database, even when a filegroup was marked as read-only, which meant that there were no changes to the data. SQL Server 2005 introduces an additional parameter to the *BACKUP* command to handle this situation. The *READ_WRITE_FILEGROUPS* clause causes the backup engine to skip any filegroups that are marked as read-only, saving time and space in the backup by having the backup engine gather only the set of extents that could change.

An example of a statement to execute a *partial backup* is the following:

```
BACKUP DATABASE PUBS READ_WRITE_FILEGROUPS TO DISK='C:\DEMO\BACKUP\PUBS1.BAK'
```

PRACTICE Backing Up a Database by Using Full/Differential/Transaction Log and Filegroup/Filegroup Differential/Transaction Log Backups

In this practice, you will create backups for the *AdventureWorks* database using two different methods: full/differential/transaction log and filegroup/differential/transaction log.

▶ **Practice 1: Back Up a Database by Using Full, Differential, and Transaction Log Backups**

In this practice, you will back up the *AdventureWorks* database by using a series of full, differential, and transaction log backups.

1. Launch SSMS, connect to your SQL Server instance, and open a new query window.

2. Create a directory named c:\test.

3. Execute the following command to create a full database backup:

   ```
   BACKUP DATABASE AdventureWorks TO DISK = 'C:\TEST\AW.BAK'
   ```

4. Make a change to the *Production.Product* table in the *AdventureWorks* database.

5. Execute the following command to back up the transaction log and capture the change you just made:

   ```
   BACKUP LOG AdventureWorks TO DISK = 'C:\TEST\AW1.TRN'
   ```

6. Make another change to the *Production.Product* table.

7. Execute the following command to perform a differential backup of the database:

   ```
   BACKUP DATABASE AdventureWorks TO DISK = 'C:\TEST\AWDIFF1.BAK' WITH DIFFERENTIAL
   ```

8. Make another change to the *Production.Product* table.

9. Execute the following command to perform a full transaction log backup to the specified disk location:

   ```
   BACKUP LOG AdventureWorks TO DISK = 'C:\TEST\AW2.TRN'
   ```

▶ **Practice 2: Back Up a Database by Using Filegroup, Filegroup Differential, and Transaction Log Backups**

In this practice, you will add a second filegroup to the *AdventureWorks* database and then perform a series of full filegroup, differential filegroup, and transaction log backups.

1. If necessary, launch SSMS, connect to your SQL Server instance, and open a new query window.

2. If necessary, create a directory named c:\test.

3. Execute the following batch to add the filegroup FG1:

```
ALTER DATABASE [AdventureWorks]
ADD FILEGROUP [FG1]
GO

ALTER DATABASE [AdventureWorks]
ADD FILE
( NAME = AW1DATA,
    FILENAME = 'C:\TEST\FG1.NDF',
    SIZE = 5MB)
TO FILEGROUP [FG1]
GO

--Now, create a testing table on the filegroup.
CREATE TABLE dbo.t1 (
   id INT
   , v CHAR(1000) DEFAULT 'bbbb',
   ) ON [FG1]
GO
```

4. To perform a full filegroup backup, execute the following command:

```
BACKUP DATABASE AdventureWorks FILEGROUP = 'PRIMARY' TO DISK = 'C:\TEST\AWPRI.BAK'
go
BACKUP DATABASE AdventureWorks FILEGROUP = 'FG1' to disk = 'C:\TEST\AWFG1.BAK'
go
```

5. Insert a row of data into the *dbo.t1* table.

6. To perform a transaction log backup of the database, execute the following command:

```
BACKUP LOG AdventureWorks TO DISK = 'C:\TEST\AW3.TRN'
```

7. Insert another row into the *dbo.t1* table.

8. Now perform a differential filegroup backup by executing the following command:

```
BACKUP DATABASE AdventureWorks FILEGROUP = 'FG1' TO DISK = 'C:\TEST\FG1DIFF1.BAK' WITH
 DIFFERENTIAL
```

9. Insert another row into the *dbo.t1* table.

10. Execute the following command to perform another transaction log backup to capture the latest data change:

```
BACKUP LOG AdventureWorks TO DISK = 'C:\TEST\AW4.TRN'
```

Lesson Summary

- The backup engine in SQL Server 2005 provides a flexible set of tools to ensure that your data is backed up and available for restore to provide protection in case of a disaster.

- You can use full backups with differential and transaction log backups to capture the entire database as well as any changes occurring since the last full backup.

- You can use filegroup backups in conjunction with differential and transaction log backups to target portions of a database for backup.

- You can also mirror each type of backup to as many as three devices, enabling you to use a single command to create up to four equivalent backups simultaneously.

Lesson Review

The following questions are intended to reinforce key information presented in this lesson. The questions are also available on the companion CD if you prefer to review them in electronic form.

NOTE Answers

Answers to these questions and explanations of why each answer choice is right or wrong are located in the "Answers" section at the end of the book.

---

1. If you want to let a member of your technical support staff back up a database without having to grant any other permission to a database or SQL Server instance, to which role should you add the staff member?

   A. *db_accessadmin*

   B. *db_owner*

   C. *db_backupoperator*

   D. *sysadmin*

2. You perform a differential backup of the *AdventureWorks* database every four hours starting at 04:00, with a full backup being run at midnight. What data does the differential backup taken at noon contain?

   A. The data pages that have changed since midnight.

   B. The extents that have changed since midnight.

   C. The data pages that have changed since 08:00.

   D. The extents that have changed since 08:00.

3. You perform a full backup of the *AdventureWorks* database that completes at midnight. Differential backups are scheduled to run every four hours beginning at 04:00. Transaction log backups are scheduled to run every five minutes. What information does the transaction log backup created at 09:15 contain?

   A. All transactions that have been issued since 09:10.

   B. Transactions that have been committed since 09:10.

   C. Pages that have changed since 09:10.

   D. Extents that have changed since 09:10.

Lesson 2: Restoring a Database

The ability to restore a backup determines how quickly your databases can resume responding to business requests after damage occurs. This lesson explains all the options that are now available in SQL Server 2005 to restore all or part of a database. You can use this lesson to form the basis of any disaster recovery planning that is performed within your organization.

After this lesson, you will be able to:

- Identify which files are needed from the backup strategy.
- Restore a database from a single file and from multiple files.
- Choose an appropriate restore method.

Estimated lesson time: 45 minutes

IMPORTANT Recovery-oriented planning

Don't be confused by the fact that restoring a database is the second lesson in this chapter. Restoring is the most important concept for you to master. The topic is covered second because you first need to know what types of backups you can create to design a *restore strategy*. The restore strategy is what makes any backup useful. As the saying goes, "If you have never restored a backup, you do not have any backups."

Restoring a Full Backup

Most restore operations begin by re-creating the database at a specific point in time and then applying subsequent backups to bring the database up to a particular point in time. This process begins with a restore of a full backup.

As explained previously, a full backup contains the entire contents of a database. To reconstruct a database, the restore operation must place the pages back into the database in sequential order. This process ensures a completely coherent database when finished. It also takes additional time. Restoring a full backup generally requires about 30 percent more time to complete than the backup being restored took to generate.

BEST PRACTICES   Overwriting and moving databases

Restoring a full backup overwrites a database of the same name, if it already exists on the instance. If the database does not exist, the restore operation creates the files and filegroups for the database before restoring pages. Because creating the files from scratch can consume a significant amount of time, you should not drop a database before a restore if you are going to overwrite it. If you are using backup and restore to move a database to a different server with a different directory structure or the directory structure has changed, you can use the *WITH MOVE* option to cause the restore operation to create the underlying files in a path different from the original backup.

An example of the syntax for a full database restore is as follows:

```
RESTORE DATABASE PUBS FROM DISK = 'C:\DEMO\BACKUP\PUBSFULL.BAK' WITH REPLACE, STANDBY = 'C:\
DEMO\BACKUP\PUBSSTANDBY.STN'
```

This command uses the contents of the *PUBSFULL.BAK* file for the restore operation. The *REPLACE* option tells SQL Server to overwrite the existing database named *PUBS*. The *STANDBY* option leaves the database in a restoring state: Writes are not allowed to occur in the database, but users can connect to the database and issue *SELECT* statements.

The other important clauses in any restore command are *WITH RECOVERY* or *WITH NORECOVERY*.

When a restore operation uses the *WITH RECOVERY* option, the database is brought online, the LSN is rolled forward, and then the database is allowed to accept transactions. No further restore operations are allowed after you recover a database by using the *WITH RECOVERY* option.

When a restore operation uses the *WITH NORECOVERY* option, the database or filegroup state remains set to *RESTORING*. In this state, you can restore additional backups, such as differential and transaction log backups, to apply any changes that have occurred since the full backup was taken.

NOTE   Inside restore operations

A restore operation can be a single step in which a full backup is restored and then the database is recovered and allowed to process transactions. However, in most production environments, a restore operation consists of multiple backup files that are restored one after another to place a database in a particular state and ensure recovery of the maximum amount of data. To accomplish this, the *RESTORE* command must enable the user to explicitly specify when the last restore operation has completed, and the database should be recovered and placed into service.

Restoring a Differential Backup

To restore a differential backup, you must first restore a full backup while ensuring that the database is NOT recovered. The most recent differential backup is then applied to the database.

NOTE Filegroup *differential restore*

The process for restoring a filegroup differential backup is very similar to restoring a differential backup. It requires that you execute a full *filegroup restore* first and that you do not recover the file-group.

Consider the following example of this sequence of operations for a full backup followed by a differential backup:

```
RESTORE DATABASE PUBS FROM DISK = 'C:\DEMO\BACKUP\PUBSFULL.BAK' WITH NORECOVERY
RESTORE DATABASE PUBS FROM DISK = 'C:\DEMO\BACKUP\PUBSDIFF.BAK' WITH RECOVERY
```

The first command restores the full backup, leaving the database unrecovered. The second command applies a differential backup and then recovers the database.

NOTE Restoring a differential backup

The syntax to restore a full backup is the same as it is to restore a differential backup. SQL Server simply takes the extents from the differential backup and writes them into the database.

An example of this sequence of operations for a filegroup backup, along with a filegroup differential backup, is as follows:

```
RESTORE DATABASE AdventureWorks FILEGROUP = 'FG1' FROM DISK = 'C:\TEST\AWFG1.BAK' WITH
   NORECOVERY
RESTORE DATABASE AdventureWorks FROM DISK = 'C:\TEST\FG1DIFF1.BAK' WITH RECOVERY
```

When restoring a differential backup to roll a filegroup restore forward, you do not need to specify the filegroup to which the differential is being applied. SQL Server automatically recognizes the filegroups that are in a *RESTORING* state as well as the extents within the differential backup that can be applied to the filegroup. Any extents that do not correspond to a filegroup that is in a *RESTORING* state are ignored.

Restoring a Transaction Log Backup

You use transaction log backups to roll a database forward to a specific point in time. This point in time is generally the last operation that was executed against the database, but you can select a different point. Transaction logs can be applied to a full backup or after a differential backup has been restored.

A transaction log backup contains a sequence of transactions identified by an LSN. Transactions can also be explicitly named by placing a mark in the transaction log. The exact time a transaction was executed is logged along with the change that was made.

CAUTION   Restoring to a specific point

You can use the *STOPAT* option to restore a database to a particular LSN, named transaction, or point in time. This capability enables a database to be restored so that it does not contain all the transactions up to the most recent. You usually choose this option when restoring a database that has become corrupted so that you can restore to just before the corruption occurred. You can also use it to recover a database in which data has been accidentally deleted; you restore the database to a point in time just before the delete was executed. But because this process causes any transactions after this point to be lost, you must use it with caution.

Transaction Log Chains

When a database is created, the LSN starts at 1 and increments to infinity. This LSN is written into the header of each file that comprises a database. As long as a database is never switched to the Simple recovery model or the *BACKUP LOG...WITH TRUNCATE_ONLY* command is not issued, the transaction log backups executed against a database form a continuous chain back to when the database was created.

This log chain crosses every full, differential, and filegroup backup that is ever performed. As long as you keep all full backups and all subsequent transaction log backups, you can always recover a database to a point in time by starting with any full backup and then applying every subsequent transaction log backup.

In extreme cases, databases have even been recovered by restoring a full backup that was created years before and then subsequently restoring the thousands of transaction log backups that had been created over a several-year time span.

An example of two different restore sequences follows:

```
--Restore sequence using a full, differential, and transaction log backup.
--Full
RESTORE DATABASE AdventureWorks FILEGROUP = 'FG1' FROM DISK = 'C:\TEST\AWFG1.BAK' WITH
 NORECOVERY
--Differential
RESTORE DATABASE AdventureWorks FROM DISK = 'C:\TEST\FG1DIFF1.BAK' WITH NORECOVERY
--Transaction log
RESTORE LOG AdventureWorks FROM DISK = 'C:\TEST\AW2.TRN' WITH RECOVERY

--Restore sequence using a full backup and multiple transaction log backups.
--Full
RESTORE DATABASE AdventureWorks FILEGROUP = 'FG1' FROM DISK = 'C:\TEST\AWFG1.BAK' WITH
 NORECOVERY
--Transaction log
RESTORE LOG AdventureWorks FROM DISK = 'C:\TEST\AW1.TRN' WITH NORECOVERY
RESTORE LOG AdventureWorks FROM DISK = 'C:\TEST\AW2.TRN' WITH RECOVERY
```

BEST PRACTICES **Recovering to a point in time following a disaster**

Recovering databases without any data loss would be much easier if problems always occurred just after you completed a backup and before your application issued any additional transactions. Alas, we are never that lucky. So in any disaster scenario, you always have transactions in the log that have not yet been backed up.

For this reason, your first step in any recovery operation is to issue one final *BACKUP LOG* command. This process captures all remaining committed transactions that have not been backed up and is commonly referred to as backing up the *tail of the log*. Because you can issue a *BACKUP LOG* command against a database even if every data file, including the primary data file, is no longer available, the only excuse for not backing up the tail of the log would be when the transaction log no longer exists.

The backup of the tail of the log then becomes the final transaction log that you apply in a restore process, enabling the database to be recovered without any loss of data.

Quick Check

- What is required to restore multiple backups to a database?

Quick Check Answer

- You must start with a full backup or a filegroup backup. These backups are restored while specifying the *WITH NORECOVERY* option. Additional differential and/or transaction log backups are applied, also using the *WITH NORECOVERY* option. The final restore operation specifies the *WITH RECOVERY* option, which rolls the LSN forward, places the database into service, and prevents any additional differential or transaction log backups from being applied.

Performing a Partial Restore

A new capability in SQL Server 2005 enables you to partially restore a database while the remainder of the database is accessible to requests. As long as a query does not request data within the filegroup(s) you are restoring, users do not even know anything is happening.

This *partial restore* is accomplished by taking advantage of the fact that each filegroup, except the primary filegroup, has a state that is independent of the database. You accomplish partial restores always by using filegroup backups.

NOTE   Restore granularity

Depending on how your database is constructed, the restore of a filegroup can affect multiple tables, a single table, or—in the case of partitioning—a portion of a table.

After the filegroups are restored to the database, you can apply differential and/or transaction log backups to bring the database current with all of the other filegroups. It is not possible to restore a portion of a database to a specific point in time because all filegroups within a database must be rolled forward to the current LSN to enable a write to a particular filegroup to occur.

Restoring a Corrupt Page

Although not common, corruption to one or more pages in a table can occur. In previous SQL Server versions, this corruption caused a severe error and could take the entire database offline. Fixing this type of error depended on the specific page that became corrupted. If the corruption happened on an index page, the index could be dropped and re-created. However, if it was corruption in a data page, you had to restore a backup, which would take the entire database offline during the restore process.

SQL Server 2005 provides an alternative to this process: the *PAGE_VERIFY CHECK-SUM* option. After enabling this verification in the database, any page that becomes corrupted is logged and quarantined, which is commonly referred to as a *corrupt page quarantine*. To enable verification, execute the following command:

```
ALTER DATABASE <database name> SET PAGE_VERIFY CHECKSUM
```

This option is off by default because it does incur a small amount of overhead for reads and writes to any page in the database. After it is enabled, each time a data page needs to be read or written to, SQL Server calculates a checksum for the page. If this checksum does not match the checksum previously stored on the page, the page has become corrupted. This mismatch causes an error to be thrown, and the transaction encountering the corrupt page is rolled back. The page is then logged into the *suspect_pages* table in the *msdb* database.

To fix the problem, you can restore the individual page from a backup. An example of the set of commands to perform a restore of a corrupt page is as follows:

```
--Back up tail of log.
BACKUP LOG PUBS TO DISK='C:\HA\DEMO\BACKUP\PUBS1.TRN' WITH INIT
GO


--Restore corrupt page from a recent backup.
--Note: This command requires all users to be out of the database,
--       so it will incur a very brief outage of generally 1 - 2 seconds.
USE MASTER
GO
RESTORE DATABASE PUBS PAGE = '1:88'
FROM DISK='C:\HA\DEMO\BACKUP\PUBSMIRROR1.BAK'
WITH RECOVERY
GO


--Additional transaction logs are applied to roll the page forward.
--Apply tail of the log to bring database to current point in time.
USE MASTER
GO
RESTORE LOG PUBS
FROM DISK = 'C:\HA\DEMO\BACKUP\PUBS1.TRN'
WITH RECOVERY
GO
```

Restoring with Media Errors

The most difficult problem to overcome during a restore is having media that has been damaged. In previous SQL Server versions, media damage always made a bad situation even worse. Damage to the backup media is rarely detected before a backup begins. And after a restore starts, it wipes out everything that had previously existed in the database. If the restore operation were to abort, you would be left with a completely invalid database. Unfortunately, this is what occurs when the backup media is damaged.

SQL Server 2005 now has an option for the *RESTORE* command that enables SQL Server to skip damaged media sectors and finish the restore operation. By using the *WITH CONTINUE_AFTER_ERROR* option, damaged media sectors are skipped, and any readable parts of the media will be restored.

Although the restore operation completes, it does not guarantee that the database will be usable or that it will even contain any data. At the completion of a *RESTORE* operation in which media errors have occurred, the database is placed in emergency mode. In this mode, you can make a connection to the database and execute *SELECT* statements, but you cannot make changes to the data. If you determine that the database is intact and operational, you can change the state to allow normal operations. In a worst-case scenario, any intact data can be extracted from the database.

Although this solution isn't perfect, it is better than nothing. That is why this feature is more popularly known as a *best-effort restore*.

Validating a Backup

You have performed several backups, but how do you know the backups are usable? The only way to guarantee that a backup is usable is to restore it and verify all the data. This process can be very time-consuming and is rarely practical. However, SQL Server provides a way to verify the integrity of a backup. Although not the same as actually restoring a database, it provides a very thorough check of the backup integrity.

You use the following command to verify a backup's integrity:

```
RESTORE VERIFYONLY FROM <backup_device> [ ,...n ]
```

When you execute this command, SQL Server checks the media header to ensure that it is intact. It then verifies the backup checksum, reads the internal page chains, and recalculates the backup checksum for comparison. A variety of checks are performed to ensure that the backup is intact. However, SQL Server does not check the actual data structures in the backup.

NOTE **Previous versions and backup verification**

Previous versions of SQL Server also had a *RESTORE VERIFYONLY...* command, which checked the media header and then returned a success or an error. The entire backup set could be invalid, and every other sector on the media could be bad. But as long as the media header was intact, it would return a success. This behavior effectively rendered this command worthless in previous versions because the command didn't actually check anything useful. So, everyone recommended not using this command. However, SQL Server 2005 now performs the necessary checks, so you should execute this command every time you perform a backup.

PRACTICE **Restoring the *AdventureWorks* Database**

Using the backups from Lesson 1, restore the *AdventureWorks* database to the current point in time.

1. If necessary, launch SSMS, connect to your SQL Server instance, and open a new query window.

2. Change the context to the *master* database.

3. Back up the tail of the log by executing the following command:

   ```
   BACKUP LOG AdventureWorks TO DISK = 'C:\TEST\AWTAIL.TRN'
   ```

4. Execute the following *RESTORE* commands to restore the *AdventureWorks* database:

   ```
   RESTORE DATABASE AdventureWorks FROM DISK = 'C:\TEST\AW.BAK' WITH NORECOVERY
   RESTORE DATABASE AdventureWorks FROM DISK = 'C:\TEST\AWDIFF1.BAK' WITH NORECOVERY
   RESTORE LOG AdventureWorks FROM DISK = 'C:\TEST\AW2.TRN' WITH NORECOVERY
   RESTORE LOG AdventureWorks FROM DISK = 'C:\TEST\AWTAIL.TRN' WITH RECOVERY
   ```

5. If you have performed both exercises from Lesson 1, the *AdventureWorks* database should have only a single filegroup, and the *dbo.t1* table should not exist.

6. If you did not perform the filegroup backup from Lesson 1, you need to verify that the *AdventureWorks* database contains all the changes that were made.

Lesson Summary

- SQL Server 2005 provides a flexible and granular way to restore damaged data.
- To recover an entire database, you can perform a full restore along with restoring differential and transaction logs.
- You can use the *STOPAT* option to restore a database to a particular LSN, named transaction, or point in time.
- You can restore individual filegroups, and as long as the primary filegroup is not restored, the rest of the database can remain online and operational.
- You can restore individual pages to fix corruption issues.
- Restore operations can continue past bad sectors within backup media to make a "best effort" to recover as much data as possible.

Lesson Review

The following questions are intended to reinforce key information presented in this lesson. The questions are also available on the companion CD if you prefer to review them in electronic form.

NOTE Answers

Answers to these questions and explanations of why each answer choice is right or wrong are located in the "Answers" section at the end of the book.

---

1. Your database has become damaged. Which of the following can be used to determine which backups can be used to restore the database? (Choose all that apply.)

   A. SQL Server error log

   B. *msdb.dbo.sysbackuphistory* table

   C. *msdb.dbo.backupset* table

   D. Windows Application Event Log

2. The patient claims database at Contoso Limited contains a very sophisticated structure. The database contains six filegroups: PRIMARY, FG1, FG2, FG3, FG4, and FG5. FG4 and FG5 contain the claims table, which is partitioned. Active claims are in FG4, and inactive claims are in FG5. Full database backups are performed once per week on Sunday, with differential backups occurring every 12 hours and transaction log backups running every five minutes. Because of the highly volatile nature of the active claims data, FG4 has a filegroup backup run against it once per day, with filegroup differential backups every hour. Claims are only moved from an active to an inactive state during a maintenance routine that occurs at midnight on Saturday. On Thursday afternoon, a portion of the claims table containing the inactive claims becomes damaged and needs to be restored. Which backups will accomplish this? (Choose all that apply.)

   A. Filegroup backup

   B. Full backup

   C. Transaction log backups

   D. Filegroup differential backup

Lesson 3: Moving a Database

Occasionally, databases need to be moved either within the same server or between servers. SQL Server provides three mechanisms that you can use to move databases. The first method, backup and restore, has already been discussed in the previous two lessons. This lesson will cover the other two methods: using detach/attach and the Copy Database Wizard, which enables you to use detach/attach or SQL Management Objects (SMO).

After this lesson, you will be able to:

■ Choose an appropriate method for moving a database.

Estimated lesson time: 20 minutes

Moving a Database by Using Detach/Attach

You can unmount databases from a SQL Server by detaching them. This process removes the entries in the system tables for this database, causing it to no longer be accessible on the SQL Server instance. Although the database is inaccessible, the files that contain all the objects and data still exist on the operating system in the location in which you created them. After they are detached, you can copy these files to any location on your network because they are no longer being accessed by SQL Server.

To make the database accessible again, you only have to attach it. This process adds an entry in the system tables for the database. And SQL Server then enables access to the database.

NOTE Detach/attach performance

The detach operation requires SQL Server only to close the files and remove an entry in the system tables. And an attach requires SQL Server to simply open the files and make an entry in the system tables. Each operation requires only 1–2 seconds at most to complete.

The following example shows the command required to perform a detach operation:

```
EXEC sp_detach_db 'AdventureWorks', 'true'
```

And the next example shows the command to attach a database:

```
CREATE DATABASE AdventureWorks ON
(FILENAME = 'C:\TEST\AdventureWorks_Data.mdf'),
(FILENAME = 'C:\TEST\AdventureWorks_Log.ldf')
 FOR ATTACH
```

MORE INFO Attach options

For all options that you can use with the detach or attach command, see the SQL Server 2005 Books Online article "CREATE DATABASE (Transact-SQL)."

Using the Copy Database Wizard

IMPORTANT Make sure SQL Server Integration Services is installed

The Copy Database Wizard runs via custom tasks within SQL Server Integration Services (SSIS). To use this wizard, you must have SSIS installed. The proxy account that the package is running under also has to be a member of the *sysadmin* role on both the source and destination instances.

SQL Server's Copy Database Wizard enables you to copy all objects within a database to another instance or to another database within the same instance. This process copies all database objects, users, schemas, and permissions, creating an exact duplicate. You must copy server-level objects such as logins separately.

To access the Copy Database Wizard, right-click a database and select Tasks, Copy Database. When the splash screen appears, click Next. Select the source server from which the database will be copied and click Next. Select the destination server to which the database will be copied and then click Next.

Select either detach/attach or SMO. When you select the detach/attach method, SSIS detaches the database, copies it to the destination, and attaches the database. This process is exactly the same as described previously in this lesson. Selecting SMO leaves the database online and accessible to users while the scripting APIs are used to generate scripts to re-create all objects on the destination as well as move all the data. Copying a database by using SMO is much slower than using either detach/attach or backup/restore.

Click Next to select the databases you want to move or copy. If you specify move, the database is created on the destination and then removed from the source. If you specify copy, the database is created on the destination as well as left on the source. Click Next to display the Configure Destination Database page shown in Figure 11-1.

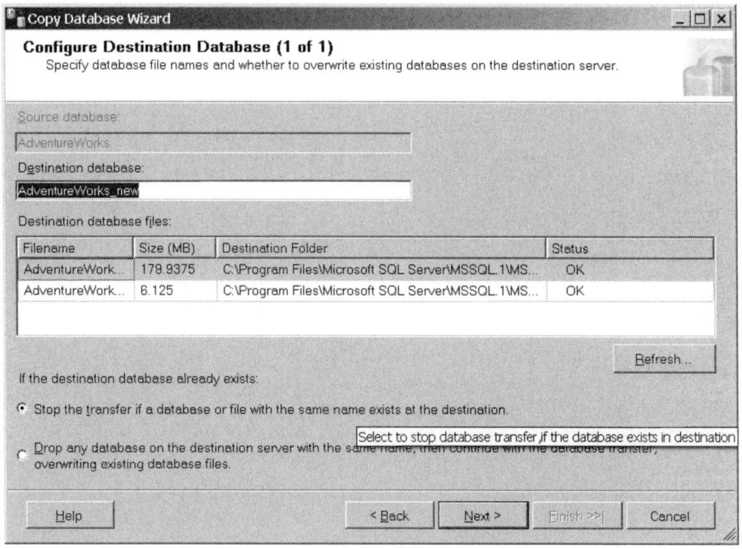

Figure 11-1   Configuring the destination database

You can specify the name of the destination database along with the file locations. If the database already exists on the target, you can specify the copy to either fail or over-write the existing database. Click Next to specify the options for the SSIS package, such as package name and logging options. Clicking Next enables you to specify whether you want the package to execute immediately or at a scheduled time, and specify under which proxy account it should run. Clicking Next enables you to verify the options selected. To complete the wizard, click Finish.

Quick Check

■ What are the three methods to move a database, listed in order of the least amount of time required?

Quick Check Answer

■ The detach/attach method is the fastest possible method because it requires only a modification to a system table, a copy of the files, and then a modification to a system table to bring the database online. Backup/restore is the next-fastest method. It is slower than a detach/attach because the restore operation might have to re-create the files for the database as well as place the pages into the files in order. SMO is the slowest method because it needs to script out all objects, extract all data, re-create all objects, and then load the data.

PRACTICE Using Detach/Attach to Move a Database

In this exercise, you will detach the *AdventureWorks* database, copy it to a new location, and then attach it by using SSMS.

NOTE File names

The actual names of the files in your *AdventureWorks* database might vary. You might also have added filegroups to the database in previous exercises. Therefore, this practice refers to file names in a generic manner. You will need to make appropriate adjustments to match your environment.

---

1. If necessary, launch SSMS and connect to your SQL Server instance.
2. Ensure that no connections have been created to the *AdventureWorks* database.
3. Within Object Explorer, right-click the *AdventureWorks* database and select Tasks, Detach.
4. Click OK.
5. Open Windows Explorer and copy the *AdventureWorks* .mdf, .ndf, and .ldf files to the c:\test directory created earlier.
6. Right-click the Database node in Object Explorer and select Attach.
7. Click Add and select the *AdventureWorks* .mdf file.
8. Click OK.
9. Verify that the *AdventureWorks* database now appears in Object Explorer and that you can access the database and read data from and write data to the database.

Lesson Summary

- Although not a frequent need, you will occasionally have to move databases between instances. SQL Server provides three ways to accomplish this task:
  - □ Using backup/restore
  - □ Using attach/detach
  - □ Using SMO through the Copy Database Wizard
- Using SMO through the Copy Database Wizard will move the database, but any server-level objects such as logins or linked servers that an application needs to work with the database have to be copied separately.

Lesson Review

The following questions are intended to reinforce key information presented in this lesson. The questions are also available on the companion CD if you prefer to review them in electronic form.

NOTE   Answers

Answers to these questions and explanations of why each answer choice is right or wrong are located in the "Answers" section at the end of the book.

---

1. You need to move a large database from Server1 to Server2. During this operation, users still have to be able to execute reports, but they will not be modifying data. Which methods can you use to accomplish this task? (Choose all that apply.)

   A. data pump

   B. detach/attach

   C. backup/restore

   D. SMO

Chapter Review

To further practice and reinforce the skills you learned in this chapter, you can

- Review the chapter summary.
- Review the list of key terms introduced in this chapter.
- Complete the case scenario. This scenario sets up a real-world situation involving the topics of this chapter and asks you to create solutions.
- Complete the suggested practices.
- Take a practice test.

Chapter Summary

- Database backup and restore provides the core capabilities for any disaster recovery planning. Without backups, data cannot be restored if it becomes damaged. Although you might be able to create workarounds by using technologies such as replication, bulk copy program (BCP), or scripting, these processes can be error-prone and can have a high probability of failure.
- Backups provide the following:
  - A way to capture all allocated pages in a database, including all schema, data, and permissions.
  - A way to capture any extents that have changed by using differential backups.
  - A way to capture all incremental transactions with transaction log backups.
  - A way to back up only a portion of a database by using filegroup backups.
- A restore operation can leverage each of these backups in a very flexible manner to restore an entire database, an entire filegroup, a portion of a table, or even a single page.
- SQL Server provides three mechanisms that you can use to move databases: backup and restore, detach/attach, and SMO through the Copy Database Wizard.

Key Terms

Do you know what these key terms mean? You can check your answers by looking up the terms in the glossary at the end of the book.

- active log
- backup device
- backup strategy
- best-effort restore
- corrupt page quarantine
- differential backup
- differential restore
- filegroup backup
- filegroup restore
- full database backup
- full database restore
- log pointer
- media set
- mirrored backup
- partial backup
- partial restore
- point in time recovery
- recovery model
- restore strategy
- tail of the log
- transaction log backup
- transaction log restore

Case Scenario: Designing a Backup Strategy

In the following case scenario, you will apply what you've learned in this chapter. You can find answers to these questions in the "Answers" section at the end of this book.

Contoso Limited, a health care company located in Bothell, WA, has a very volatile database that contains patient claims data. The patient claims data is essential to Contoso's business. Any loss of data would cause severe business damage and, in the worst-case scenario, might cause the company to go out of business. Because of the mission-critical nature of its database, the company has invested in a storage area network (SAN) to ensure that data is always available.

With the rapid growth of its customer base, Contoso's management has finally decided that it needs to hire a DBA to manage its database. Upon joining the company as that DBA, you find out that the data volume is passing the 500-GB mark and rapidly heading toward 1 terabyte. Management has indicated that it needs to ensure that the data is always available; at maximum, the company can have a 30-minute unavailability. That is why the company spent so much money on its SAN.

To your horror, you find out that everything relies on the SAN because management has been convinced by the solution provider who recommended and installed the SAN that the SAN is completely bulletproof and can never fail.

After many discussions, you finally explain to management that guaranteeing zero data loss is a complete impossibility and exists only in the minds of salespeople wanting to sell the company software. Management has agreed that although it would like to avoid all data loss, the company can handle up to five minutes of data loss.

1. What tasks do you immediately need to perform to protect the company's data before something goes wrong?

2. What backups should you implement to ensure that you can recover data?

3. What actions should you take for a longer-term approach to managing the mission-critical data?

Suggested Practices

To help you successfully master the exam objectives presented in this chapter, complete the following practice tasks.

Backing Up a Database

- **Practice 1**   Create and test a backup strategy for your databases that includes full, differential, and transaction log backups.

- **Practice 2**   Create and test a backup strategy for your databases that includes filegroup, differential, and transaction log backups.

- **Practice 3**   Create a database that contains both read-only and read-write filegroups, and back up only the read-write filegroups.

- **Practice 4**   Change the backup strategies created in Practices 1 and 2 to include duplicates of each backup by using the new mirrored backup capability.

Restoring a Database

- **Practice 1**   Test your backups created in "Backing Up a Database" Practice 1 by restoring them.

- **Practice 2**   Test your backups created in "Backing Up a Database" Practice 2 by restoring them.

- **Practice 3**   Test your backups created in "Backing Up a Database" Practice 3 by restoring them.

- **Practice 4**   Test your backups created in "Backing Up a Database" Practice 4 by restoring from a mirror.

- **Practice 5**   Restore a single filegroup (not the primary filegroup) into a database and then observe that any objects in filegroups not being restored can be accessed.

- **Practice 6**   Restore a page into a database to simulate a corrupted page that needs to be restored.

- **Practice 7**   Shut down SQL Server, delete the master.mdf, and then restore the *master* database and verify that all databases are intact and accessible. (You are backing up your *master* database, right?)

- **Practice 8**   Create a Database Snapshot against a database. Make some changes. Restore the database by using the Database Snapshot and verify that your changes no longer exist in the database.

Moving a Database

■ **Practice 1**   Move a database by using the detach/attach method. Determine which other objects also need to be moved to make the database fully accessible to applications.

■ **Practice 2**   Move a database by using the Copy Database Wizard. Select the SMO option and observe the move process. Determine which other objects also need to be moved to make the database fully accessible to applications.

Take a Practice Test

The practice tests on this book's companion CD offer many options. For example, you can test yourself on just the content covered in this chapter, or you can test yourself on all the 70-431 certification exam content. You can set up the test so that it closely simulates the experience of taking a certification exam, or you can set it up in study mode so that you can look at the correct answers and explanations after you answer each question.

MORE INFO   **Practice tests**

For details about all the practice test options available, see the section titled "How to Use the Practice Tests" in this book's Introduction.

Chapter 12
Using Transact-SQL to Manage Databases

Maintaining your databases is often a complex and time-consuming task that involves a multitude of steps you need to perform on a periodic basis. Database administrators (DBAs) often perform their maintenance tasks by using the Maintenance Plan Wizard or the Microsoft SQL Server 2005 main graphical user interface (GUI): SQL Server Management Studio (SSMS). However, this chapter will show you how to accomplish the common maintenance tasks of managing index fragmentation and statistics, shrinking databases, and performing integrity checks by using the power of Transact-SQL.

Exam objectives in this chapter:
- Manage databases by using Transact-SQL.
  - ❑ Manage index fragmentation.
  - ❑ Manage statistics.
  - ❑ Shrink files.
  - ❑ Perform database integrity checks by using DBCC CHECKDB.

Lessons in this chapter:

Before You Begin

To complete the lessons in this chapter, you must have:

- SQL Server 2005 installed.
- A connection to a SQL Server 2005 instance.
- A copy of the *AdventureWorks* sample database.

Real World

Randy Dyess

Having been a DBA for many years in a large variety of environments, I have been responsible for the maintenance of literally thousands of SQL Server databases. The main responsibility of DBAs is keeping their databases up and running in the best possible condition. To achieve this goal, database maintenance is often one of the first tasks new DBAs learn as they begin their career managing SQL Server. The ability to perform database maintenance in a scriptable manner by using Transact-SQL helps newer DBAs transition from managing one database at a time to managing numerous databases at the same time. This multitasking skill is vital to the growth and productivity of DBAs as they efficiently manage applications and serve end users.

Lesson 1: Managing Index Fragmentation

Indexes are an essential component for ensuring optimum query execution. Proper indexing often is the difference between substandard query execution and exceptional query execution. However, unlike other objects created in SQL Server 2005, indexes can lose their effectiveness over time if they are not properly maintained—because of fragmentation of the index pages supporting the indexes. The level of *index fragmentation* and the degree of index maintenance you perform as a DBA often determine which indexes the SQL Server query optimizer uses to execute the query successfully and which indexes the optimizer does not use for any queries. The optimizer could also end up using indexes that have a large degree of fragmentation, which actually hurts a query's performance. This lesson covers the types of index fragmentation your indexes could suffer from, how to identify index fragmentation, and which statements you should issue to correct different types of index fragmentation.

After this lesson, you will be able to:

■ Understand index fragmentation.

■ Identify index fragmentation.

■ Effectively manage index fragmentation levels by using Transact-SQL.

Estimated lesson time: 30 minutes

Understanding Index Fragmentation

Index fragmentation can occur whenever data in a table is modified and this modification affects an index page. Whenever a process performs an INSERT, DELETE, or UPDATE operation against the data in a table, the corresponding clustered and nonclustered indexes for that table are affected as well.

NOTE Index pages and data pages in SQL Server 2005

A SQL Server 2005 index can contain both index pages and data pages. Clustered and nonclustered indexes both contain index pages that hold information about the index key values and information about any pointers to the rest of the data in the table that are needed by the index. However, only clustered indexes contain data pages; the bottom level of a clustered index is actually the table data itself—not index rows containing pointers to the table data, as in nonclustered indexes.

Processes performing DELETE operations often cause space in the underlying index pages to be freed, which can cause an index's pages to contain only a fraction of the index rows they would normally hold if they were full. The condition when pages are not as full as they should be is called *internal fragmentation.*

With internal fragmentation, index pages do not use disk space efficiently, which leads to an increase in the number of pages needed to hold the same number of index rows. This increase in the number of pages causes SQL Server to read a larger number of pages into memory to satisfy a READ operation against an index. *Paging* is the physical act of retrieving the data or index pages from the hard disk subsystem into memory. Because the hard disk subsystem is typically the slowest component on a server, any actions that you can take to reduce the amount of paging improve the overall performance of SQL Server.

INSERT and UPDATE operations can cause SQL Server to create additional index pages if the page in which it needs to place the index row or data row already contains the maximum amount of information a single data or index page can contain.

NOTE   Maximum size of index and data pages

SQL Server 2005 allows a maximum of 8,060 bytes on a single data or index page. The number of data or index rows allowed on a single page is the result of 8,060 divided by the size of the individual data or index row. For example, if you have an index containing 800 bytes of column key values, SQL Server can store only 10 index rows per index page.

When SQL Server needs to place additional rows of data on an index page or data page and that page cannot accommodate the additional row, a *page split* occurs—a new page is added, and SQL Server splits the rows of data or index information on the original page between the original page and the new page. Page splits maintain the logical order of the rows in the index key; SQL Server knows which page the next index key is located on. But page splits do not maintain the physical ordering of the page; the new page usually won't be physically adjacent to the original page on the disk. When pages are not in physical order, there is *external fragmentation.*

External fragmentation is always undesirable in an index, whereas a small amount of internal fragmentation can be desirable in highly transactional databases because it prevents large numbers of page splits. However, large-scale internal and external fragmentations adversely affect the performance of retrieving data.

In the case of internal fragmentation, rows are distributed sparsely across a large number of pages, increasing the number of disk input/output (I/O) operations that SQL Server must perform to read the index pages into memory as well as the number of logical reads it must perform to read multiple index rows from memory.

External fragmentation causes a noncontiguous sequence of index pages on the disk, with new leaf pages far from the original leaf pages and their physical ordering different from their logical ordering. Consequently, when SQL Server performs a range scan on an index that has external fragmentation, it needs to switch between corresponding extents more than what would be ideal. Also, a range scan on an externally fragmented index will not benefit from read-ahead operations performed on the disk. If the pages are arranged contiguously, SQL Server can perform a read-ahead operation to read pages in advance without much head movement.

MORE INFO   Indexes

For information about creating indexes and the types of indexes you can create, see Chapter 4, "Creating Indexes," in this book and the "Indexes" topic in SQL Server 2005 Books Online. SQL Server 2005 Books Online is installed as part of SQL Server 2005. Updates for SQL Server 2005 Books Online are available for download at *www.microsoft.com/technet/prodtechnol/sql/2005/downloads/books.mspx*.

Identifying Index Fragmentation

To help you determine the amount of external and internal fragmentation on indexes that are contained within a database, SQL Server 2005 provides the *sys.dm_db_index_physical_stats* dynamic management function (DMF). By issuing a simple *SELECT* statement against this index DMF, you can check the values contained in the avg_fragmentation_in_percent and avg_page_space_used_in_percent columns, as the following sample query shows, and determine whether your indexes are suffering from fragmentation:

```
--Determine index fragmentation for all tables in the AdventureWorks database
SELECT OBJECT_NAME(dt.object_id), si.name,
dt.avg_fragmentation_in_percent, dt.avg_page_space_used_in_percent
FROM
(SELECT object_id, index_id, avg_fragmentation_in_percent, avg_page_space_used_in_percent
FROM sys.dm_db_index_physical_stats (DB_ID('AdventureWorks'), NULL, NULL, NULL, 'DETAILED')
WHERE index_id <> 0) as dt --does not return information about heaps
INNER JOIN sys.indexes si
ON si.object_id = dt.object_id
AND si.index_id = dt.index_id
```

DBAs should review the value in the avg_fragmentation_in_percent column to determine whether the index contains external fragmentation. External fragmentation is indicated when this value exceeds 10.

DBAs should review the value in the avg_page_space_used_in_percent column to determine whether the index contains internal fragmentation. Internal fragmentation is indicated when this value falls below 75.

NOTE   Test to find the best threshold for your system

These thresholds for determining whether your system is suffering from external or internal fragmentation provide a guideline for determining when you should use either *ALTER INDEX...REORGANIZE* or *ALTER INDEX...REBUILD*. Because the actual thresholds can vary depending on your environment, you should perform tests to determine the best thresholds for your system.

Managing Index Fragmentation

If you determine that your indexes have external or internal fragmentation, you should execute either the *ALTER INDEX...REORGANIZE* or *ALTER INDEX...REBUILD* statements periodically to prevent index fragmentation from affecting query performance.

ALTER INDEX...REORGANIZE

Using *ALTER INDEX...REORGANIZE* reorganizes an index. This statement defragments the leaf level of clustered and nonclustered indexes on tables and views by physically reordering the leaf-level pages to match the logical, left-to-right order of the leaf nodes while compacting the index pages. The level of page compaction is based on the existing fill factor value for the index. You can find the fill factor value in the *sys.indexes* catalog view.

```
USE AdventureWorks;

ALTER INDEX PK_Employee_EmployeeID ON HumanResources.Employee
REORGANIZE;
```

MORE INFO   Fill factor

For information about fill factor, see Chapter 4, "Creating Indexes," in this book and the topic "sys.indexes (Transact-SQL)" in SQL Server 2005 Books Online.

ALTER INDEX...REBUILD

Using the *ALTER INDEX...REBUILD* statement rebuilds an index. This statement removes both external and internal fragmentation by dropping and re-creating the index. This process removes external fragmentation by reordering the index rows in contiguous pages and removes internal fragmentation by compacting the pages based on the specified or existing fill factor setting.

```
USE AdventureWorks;

ALTER INDEX PK_Employee_EmployeeID ON HumanResources.Employee
REBUILD;
```

NOTE   Using the ALL option

By specifying the ALL option on the *ALTER INDEX...REBUILD* statement, you can specify that all indexes on a table be dropped and re-created in a single transaction.

When rebuilding an index, you have the option of performing the *index rebuild* by using the ONLINE option. When this option is ON, the table and associated indexes are available for queries and data modification during the rebuild process.

DBAs can perform concurrent online index operations on the same table only when performing the following index operations:

- Creating multiple nonclustered indexes
- Reorganizing different indexes on the same table
- Reorganizing different indexes while rebuilding nonoverlapping indexes on the same table

Determining Which Statement to Execute

How do you know whether to execute *ALTER INDEX...REORGANIZE* or *ALTER INDEX...REBUILD* against user tables? When your indexes are not heavily fragmented, you can reorganize indexes, which uses few system resources and runs automatically online. For heavily fragmented indexes, you probably need to rebuild the indexes.

To help you determine which statement to use, periodically run a *SELECT* statement against the *sys.dm_db_index_physical_stats* DMF and use the following thresholds as a guideline for your decision:

- Execute *ALTER INDEX...REORGANIZE* to defragment indexes that fall under the following fragmentation thresholds: avg_page_space_used_in_percent < 75 and > 60 or avg_fragmentation_in_percent > 10 and < 15.
- Execute *ALTER INDEX...REBUILD* to defragment indexes that fall under the following fragmentation thresholds: avg_page_space_used_in_percent < 60 or avg_fragmentation_in_percent > 15.

> **Quick Check**
> - What is external fragmentation?
>
> **Quick Check Answer**
> - External fragmentation is the condition in which the physical order of index pages does not match the logical order.

PRACTICE Using ALTER INDEX to Correct Index Fragmentation Levels

DBAs need to learn how to manage index fragmentation levels by using the *ALTER INDEX...REBUILD* and *ALTER INDEX...REORGANIZE* statements. The following two practices take you through the process of correcting index fragmentation levels by using these two statements.

▶ **Practice 1: Use ALTER INDEX...REBUILD to Rebuild an Index**

In this practice, you rebuild an index by using the *ALTER INDEX...REBUILD* statement.

1. Start SSMS.

2. Connect to the instance containing the sample *AdventureWorks* database.

3. In Object Explorer, right-click the *AdventureWorks* database and choose New Query to open the Query Editor pane.

4. In the Query Editor pane, type in the following Transact-SQL statement to view current fragmentation levels, rebuild the indexes on the *HumanResources.Employee* table, and view fragmentation levels after the rebuild:

```
USE AdventureWorks;

--View the current fragmentation levels.
SELECT index_id, avg_fragmentation_in_percent, avg_page_space_used_in_percent
FROM sys.dm_db_index_physical_stats (DB_ID('AdventureWorks'),
 OBJECT_ID('HumanResources.Employee'),NULL, NULL, 'DETAILED')
WHERE index_id <> 0; --does not return information about heaps

--Rebuild all indexes on the table.
--Create the indexes with a fill factor of 90.
--Allow the index operation to take place ONLINE
ALTER INDEX ALL ON HumanResources.Employee
REBUILD WITH (FILLFACTOR = 90, ONLINE = ON);

--View the fragmentation levels after the index rebuilds.
SELECT index_id, avg_fragmentation_in_percent, avg_page_space_used_in_percent
FROM sys.dm_db_index_physical_stats (DB_ID('AdventureWorks'),
 OBJECT_ID('HumanResources.Employee'),NULL, NULL, 'DETAILED')
WHERE index_id <> 0; --does not return information about heaps
```

▶ **Practice 2: Use ALTER INDEX...REORGANIZE to Reorganize an Index**

In this practice, you will reorganize an index by using the *ALTER INDEX...REORGA-NIZE* statement.

1. If necessary, start SSMS and connect to the instance containing the *Adventure-Works* sample database. Open the Query Editor pane.

2. In the Query Editor pane, type in the following Transact-SQL statement to view current fragmentation levels, reorganize the indexes on the *HumanResources.Employee* table, and view the fragmentation levels after the reorganization:

```
USE AdventureWorks;

--View the current fragmentation levels.
SELECT index_id, avg_fragmentation_in_percent, avg_page_space_used_in_percent
FROM sys.dm_db_index_physical_stats (DB_ID('AdventureWorks'),
 OBJECT_ID('HumanResources.Employee'),NULL, NULL, 'DETAILED')
WHERE index_id <> 0; --does not return information about heaps

--Reorganize all indexes on the table.
ALTER INDEX ALL ON HumanResources.Employee
REORGANIZE;

--View the fragmentation levels after the index reorganization.
SELECT index_id, avg_fragmentation_in_percent, avg_page_space_used_in_percent
FROM sys.dm_db_index_physical_stats (DB_ID('AdventureWorks'),
 OBJECT_ID('HumanResources.Employee'),NULL, NULL, 'DETAILED')
WHERE index_id <> 0; --does not return information about heaps
```

Lesson Summary

■ Indexes become fragmented during INSERT, DELETE, and UPDATE operations, and this fragmentation can degrade query performance.

■ Internal index fragmentation occurs when the index pages are not filled to the maximum amount allowed under the current fill factor setting.

■ External index fragmentation occurs when the physical ordering of index pages does not match the logical ordering of the pages.

■ You can check index fragmentation levels by running a *SELECT* statement against the *sys.dm_db_index_physical_stats* dynamic management function.

■ You can correct index fragmentation by executing either the *ALTER INDEX...REORGANIZE* or the *ALTER INDEX...REBUILD* Transact-SQL statement.

Lesson Review

The following questions are intended to reinforce key information presented in this lesson. The questions are also available on the companion CD if you prefer to review them in electronic form.

NOTE Answers

Answers to these questions and explanations of why each answer choice is right or wrong are located in the "Answers" section at the end of the book.

---

1. You are a DBA tasked with maintaining an installation of SQL Server 2005.One of your jobs is to determine the index fragmentation levels for all user tables in your database. Which dynamic management view or function can you use to review index fragmentation levels?

    A. *sys.dm_db_index_operational_stats*

    B. *sys.dm_db_index_usage_stats*

    C. *sys.dm_db_missing_index_details*

    D. *sys.dm_db_index_physical_stats*

2. You are a DBA tasked with maintaining an installation of SQL Server 2005.You need to determine whether your tables contain external fragmentation. Which column would you use to find whether your indexes are externally fragmented?

    A. avg_fragment_size_in_pages

    B. avg_page_space_used_in_percent

    C. avg_fragmentation_in_percent

    D. avg_record_size_in_bytes

3. You are a DBA tasked with maintaining an installation of SQL Server 2005.One of your jobs is to correct the index fragmentation levels for all user tables in your database. During your fragmentation investigation, you determine that an index has external fragmentation levels greater than 30 percent. Which statement would you use to correct this amount of external fragmentation?

    A. *ALTER INDEX...REBUILD*

    B. *ALTER INDEX...REORGANIZE*

    C. *ALTER INDEX...DISABLE*

    D. *ALTER INDEX...SET STATISTICS_NORECOMPUTE = ON*

Lesson 2: Managing Statistics

Another important aspect of achieving top query performance is the statistical information that SQL Server creates about the distribution of values in a column. During its evaluation of a query, the query optimizer uses these statistics to estimate the cost of using an index to satisfy the query. To ensure optimum query performance, you need to understand the importance of *statistics* and decide when to let SQL Server automatically generate and update them, and when to manually generate and update them.

After this lesson, you will be able to:

- Explain the purpose of statistics.
- Manage index and column statistics.

Estimated lesson time: 25 minutes

Understanding Statistics

When SQL Server creates column and index statistics, the database engine sorts the values of the columns on which the statistics are being built and creates a *histogram*. Histograms are based on up to 200 values contained in the column, separated by intervals. The histogram specifies how many rows exactly match each interval value, how many rows fall within an interval, and the density of values contained within an interval. These statistics on column values help the query optimizer determine whether using an index improves query performance.

SQL Server 2005 introduces additional information that is collected by statistics created on *char*, *varchar*, *varchar(max)*, *nchar*, *nvarchar*, *nvarchar(max)*, *text*, and *ntext* columns. This additional information, called a *string summary*, helps the query optimizer estimate the selectivity of query predicates on string patterns, which leads to better estimates of result set sizes when a query uses LIKE conditions.

Automatic Statistics Generation

When a DBA creates an index, the query optimizer stores statistical information about the indexed columns. Additionally, if the AUTO_CREATE_STATISTICS database option is set to ON, the database engine creates statistics on columns that are not contained in indexes but that are used in query predicates.

An additional benefit to having the AUTO_UPDATE_STATISTICS database option set to ON is that the query optimizer also automatically updates statistical information periodically as the data in the tables changes. This statistics update operation is initiated whenever the statistics used in a query execution plan fail a test for current statistics. This test is a random sampling across data pages taken either from the table or the smallest nonclustered index on the columns needed by the statistics. Almost always, statistical information is updated when approximately 20 percent of the data rows have changed; however, the query optimizer ensures that a minimum number of rows are sampled, with tables smaller than 8 MB being fully scanned to gather statistics.

This test is important because when data in a column changes, index and column statistics can become out of date. As a result, the query optimizer might make less-than-optimal decisions about how to process a query, which causes those queries to execute with dramatically substandard performance.

Manual Statistics Generation

You can also manually create statistics. To create statistics on all eligible columns in all user tables in the current database by using just one statement, you can execute the *sp_createstats* system stored procedure. To create statistics on specific table or view columns, you can use the *CREATE STATISTICS* statement. To manually update statistics, you can execute the *UPDATE STATISTICS* statement or execute the *sp_updatestats* system stored procedure. And you can drop statistics by using the *DROP STATISTICS* statement.

A key benefit of creating statistics manually is that you can create statistics that contain densities of values for a combination of columns. By having statistics for a combination of columns, the database engine could make a better estimate for query execution.

Viewing Column Statistics Information

SQL Server 2005 gives DBAs several ways to obtain information about column statistics:

- The *sp_autostats* system stored procedure displays or changes the automatic UPDATE STATISTICS setting for a specific index and statistics or for all indexes and statistics for a specified table or indexed view in the current database.

- The *sys.stats* catalog view displays a row for each statistic of a tabular object of the type U, V, or TF.

- The *sys.stats_columns* catalog view displays a row for each column that is part of *sys.stats* statistics.

- The *STATS_DATE* function returns the date that the statistics for the specified index were last updated.

- The *DBCC SHOW_STATISTICS* statement displays the current distribution statistics for the specified target on the specified table.

Quick Check

- Why are statistics important to query performance?

Quick Check Answer

- During its evaluation of a query, the query optimizer uses the statistical information to estimate the cost of using an index and determine the optimal query plan for a query.

PRACTICE **Manually Creating and Updating Statistics**

The following two practices walk you through the process of manually creating and updating statistics.

▶ **Practice 1: Create Statistics**

In this practice, you create statistics by using the *CREATE STATISTICS* statement.

1. If necessary, start SSMS and connect to the instance containing the *Adventure-Works* sample database. Open the Query Editor pane.

2. In the Query Editor pane, type the following Transact-SQL statement to view which columns in the *HumanResources.Employee* table do not have statistics built on them:

```
USE AdventureWorks;

--Determine which columns do not have statistics on them.
SELECT c.name
FROM  sys.columns c
LEFT OUTER JOIN sys.stats_columns sc
ON sc.[object_id] = c.[object_id]
AND sc.column_id = c.column_id
WHERE c.[object_id] = OBJECT_ID('HumanResources.Employee')
AND sc.column_id IS NULL
ORDER BY c.column_id
```

You might see a result set like the one shown following (actual column names returned will depend upon your database environment):

```
BirthDate
MaritalStatus
Gender
SalariedFlag
VacationHours
SickLeaveHours
CurrentFlag
ModifiedDate
```

3. In the Query Editor pane, type the following Transact-SQL statements to create statistics on the columns in the *HumanResources.Employee* table that do not currently have statistics on them, and then recheck for columns that do not have statistics:

```
--Create statistics for the columns needing statistics.
CREATE STATISTICS st_BirthDate
    ON HumanResources.Employee (BirthDate)
    WITH FULLSCAN;

CREATE STATISTICS st_MaritalStatus
    ON HumanResources.Employee (MaritalStatus)
    WITH FULLSCAN;

CREATE STATISTICS st_Gender
    ON HumanResources.Employee (Gender)
    WITH FULLSCAN;

CREATE STATISTICS st_SalariedFlag
    ON HumanResources.Employee (SalariedFlag)
    WITH FULLSCAN;

CREATE STATISTICS st_VacationHours
    ON HumanResources.Employee (VacationHours)
    WITH FULLSCAN;

CREATE STATISTICS st_SickLeaveHours
    ON HumanResources.Employee (SickLeaveHours)
    WITH FULLSCAN;

CREATE STATISTICS st_CurrentFlag
    ON HumanResources.Employee (CurrentFlag)
    WITH FULLSCAN;
```

```
CREATE STATISTICS st_ModifiedDate
    ON HumanResources.Employee (ModifiedDate)
    WITH FULLSCAN;

--Determine which columns still do not have statistics on them.
SELECT c.name
FROM  sys.columns c
LEFT OUTER JOIN sys.stats_columns sc
ON sc.[object_id] = c.[object_id]
AND sc.column_id = c.column_id
WHERE c.[object_id] = OBJECT_ID('HumanResources.Employee')
AND sc.column_id IS NULL
ORDER BY c.column_id;
```

▶ **Practice 2: Update Statistics**

In this practice, you will manually update statistics by using the *UPDATE STATISTICS* statement.

1. If necessary, start SSMS and connect to the instance containing the *Adventure-Works* sample database. Open the Query Editor pane.

2. In the Query Editor pane, type the following Transact-SQL statements to view when the statistics were last updated, update all statistics on the *HumanResources.Employee* table, and check when the statistics were last updated:

```
USE AdventureWorks;

--View date the statistics were last updated.
SELECT 'Index Name' = i.[name]
, 'Statistics Date' = STATS_DATE(i.[object_id], i.index_id)
FROM sys.objects o
INNER JOIN sys.indexes i
ON o.name = 'Employee'
AND o.[object_id] = i.[object_id];

--Update statistics on all indexes on the table.
UPDATE STATISTICS HumanResources.Employee
WITH FULLSCAN;

--View date the statistics were last updated.
SELECT 'Index Name' = i.[name]
, 'Statistics Date' = STATS_DATE(i.[object_id], i.index_id)
FROM sys.objects o
INNER JOIN sys.indexes i
ON o.name = 'Employee'
AND o.[object_id] = i.[object_id];
```

Lesson Summary

- Statistics on table or view columns play an important role in optimizing query performance; the SQL Server query optimizer uses these statistics to evaluate the cost of using an index to satisfy a query.

- When you create an index, the query optimizer automatically stores statistical information about the indexed columns. You can also set the AUTO_CREATE_STATISTICS database option to ON to have the database engine automatically create statistics on columns that are not contained in indexes but that are used in query predicates and to automatically update statistical information periodically as the data in the tables changes.

- Alternatively, you can manually create and update statistics by using Transact-SQL statements and stored procedures.

Lesson Review

The following questions are intended to reinforce key information presented in this lesson. The questions are also available on the companion CD if you prefer to review them in electronic form.

NOTE   Answers

Answers to these questions and explanations of why each answer choice is right or wrong are located in the "Answers" section at the end of the book.

---

1. Which Transact-SQL function shows the last time statistics were updated for a specified index?

    A. *sys.stats_columns*

    B. *DBCC SHOWCONTIG*

    C. *DBCC SHOW_STATISTICS*

    D. *STATS_DATE*

2. Which Transact-SQL statement allows SQL Server to automatically update statistics?

    A. *sp_autostats*

    B. *sys.stats*

    C. *UPDATE STATISTICS*

    D. *CREATE STATISTICS*

Lesson 3: Shrinking Files

In SQL Server 2005, certain operations such as large delete operations or one-time data loads might leave database files larger than they need to be. SQL Server 2005 enables a DBA to shrink each file within a database to remove unused pages and regain disk space. And although the SQL Server database engine is designed to reuse space effectively, there are times when a database or a database file no longer needs to be as large as it once was. You might then need to shrink the database or file either through a manual process of shrinking all the database files or certain files individually or by setting the database to automatically shrink at specified intervals. In this lesson, you learn how to determine when you should shrink database files and what Transact-SQL statements you can use to shrink databases and database files.

After this lesson, you will be able to:

■ Determine when it is appropriate to shrink database files.

■ Use Transact-SQL statements to shrink databases and database files.

Estimated lesson time: 15 minutes

Shrinking Database Files Automatically

SQL Server 2005 enables you to set a database option that allows the database engine to automatically shrink databases that have free space. When you set the ALTER DATABASE AUTO_SHRINK option to ON, the database engine periodically examines the database's space usage and reduces the size of the database files for that database.

CAUTION   Be careful when allowing AUTO_SHRINK

The AUTO_SHRINK option is set to OFF by default, and you should take care when setting this option to ON. Although the shrink process takes place in the background and does not affect users in the database, the process of shrinking a database can consume system resources, which can degrade the performance of the server. Also, continually shrinking and regrowing a database can lead to fragmentation at the file level, which often cannot be easily addressed in today's 24 x 7 database environments.

Shrinking Database Files Manually

When you need to shrink a database, transaction log, or single database file to recover unused space, it is often a better choice to manually shrink the file rather than to let SQL Server 2005 perform the operation automatically. Manually shrinking the database or database files enables you to choose when the shrink operation takes place, which can dramatically reduce the pressure that the shrink operation can cause on system resources.

BEST PRACTICES   Shrinking databases

As with the automatic shrink setting, the manual shrink process takes place in the background and does not affect users in the database, but the process of shrinking a database can consume system resources and degrade server performance. Also, as with auto shrinks, continually shrinking and regrowing a database can lead to fragmentation at the file level, which can be difficult to fix in busy database environments. DBAs should perform database shrink operations or transaction log shrink operations (covered in a moment) only when they are certain that the unused space being reclaimed will not be needed in the future.

You can manually shrink databases and database files by using the *DBCC SHRINKDATABASE* statement or the *DBCC SHRINKFILE* statement, respectively. Note that when using the *DBCC SHRINKDATABASE* statement, you cannot shrink a database to a size that is smaller than its original size. You also cannot shrink a database file smaller than the used portion of the database. For example, unless you use the *DBCC SHRINKFILE* statement against the individual database files, you cannot shrink a database created with a size of 100 GB to below 100 GB, even if the database contains only 50 MB of data.

MORE INFO   DBCC SHRINKDATABASE and DBCC SHRINKFILE

For full details about executing the *DBCC SHRINKDATABASE* and *DBCC SHRINKFILE* statements, see the SQL Server 2005 Books Online topics "DBCC SHRINKDATABASE (Transact-SQL)" and "DBCC SHRINKFILE (Transact-SQL)," respectively.

Shrinking the Transaction Log

Database transaction logs are created with fixed boundaries in which you can shrink a transaction log file. The size of the virtual log files contained within the transaction log determines the reduction in size that is possible when shrinking the transaction log. This means that you cannot shrink the transaction log to a size less than the virtual log file. Take, for example, a transaction log file that is 10 GB in size and that contains 50 virtual log files, each 200 MB in size. Let's say that shrinking the transaction log would delete unused virtual log files but leave at least two virtual log files intact. In this example, you could shrink the transaction log file only to 400 MB—the size of the two remaining virtual log files. Also note that any virtual log files that are still active and contain uncommitted transactions or unwritten operations will not be part of the shrink process.

Quick Check
- How can you shrink a database without having to shrink each file individually?

Quick Check Answer
- DBAs wanting to shrink an entire database can issue the *DBCC SHRINK-DATABASE* statement against the database.

PRACTICE Shrinking a Database

The following two practices walk you through the processes of setting a database to shrink automatically and manually shrinking a database.

▶ **Practice 1: Set a Database to Shrink Automatically**

In this practice, you will use the *ALTER DATABASE* statement to set a database to shrink automatically.

1. If necessary, start SSMS and connect to the instance containing the *Adventure-Works* sample database. Open the Query Editor pane.

2. In the Query Editor pane, type the following Transact-SQL statements to check the current auto shrink setting for the database, set the database to shrink automatically, and then verify that the auto shrink setting was changed:

```
USE master;

--View the current setting for the database.
SELECT CASE DATABASEPROPERTYEX('AdventureWorks','IsAutoShrink')
   WHEN 0 THEN 'Database is not set to shrink automatically'
   WHEN 1 THEN 'Database is set to shrink automatically'
   ELSE 'Error'
   END;

--Set the database to shrink automatically.
ALTER DATABASE AdventureWorks
SET AUTO_SHRINK ON;

--View the current setting for the database.
SELECT CASE DATABASEPROPERTYEX('AdventureWorks','IsAutoShrink')
   WHEN 0 THEN 'Database is not set to shrink automatically'
   WHEN 1 THEN 'Database is set to shrink automatically'
   ELSE 'Error'
   END;
```

▶ **Practice 2: Manually Shrink a Database**

In this practice, you will use the *DBCC SHRINKDATABASE* statement to manually shrink a database.

1. If necessary, start SSMS and connect to the instance containing the *Adventure-Works* sample database. Open the Query Editor pane.

2. In the Query Editor pane, perform the following operations by typing the Transact-SQL statements that follow the list of operations:

    ❑ View the current size of the database.

    ❑ Create and then drop a table to create unused database space so that you can shrink the database.

    ❑ Check the size of the database.

    ❑ Manually shrink the database.

    ❑ Check the size of the database after shrinking it.

```
USE AdventureWorks;

--View the current size of the database.
SELECT file_id, name, physical_name, size FROM sys.database_files;

--Create a table, fill the table, and then drop to table to create unused database
 space.
CREATE TABLE dropme
(
col1 CHAR(8000)
)

DECLARE @counter INTEGER
SET @counter = 2000

WHILE @counter > 0
BEGIN
    INSERT INTO dropme VALUES (' ')
    SET @counter = @counter - 1
END

--View the current size of the database.
SELECT file_id, name, physical_name, size FROM sys.database_files;

--Drop the table.
DROP TABLE dropme;

--Shrink the AdventureWorks database, leaving no free space.
DBCC SHRINKDATABASE (AdventureWorks, 0);

--View the current size of the database.
SELECT file_id, name, physical_name, size FROM sys.database_files;
```

Lesson Summary

- You can shrink SQL Server 2005 databases to regain disk space.

- DBAs have the option of shrinking the database manually or allowing the database engine to automatically shrink the database.

- You can shrink an entire database by using the *DBCC SHRINKDATABASE* statement or individual database files by using the *DBCC SHRINKFILE* statement.

- As part of your database maintenance, you can also shrink database transaction logs.

Lesson Review

The following questions are intended to reinforce key information presented in this lesson. The questions are also available on the companion CD if you prefer to review them in electronic form.

NOTE Answers

Answers to these questions and explanations of why each answer choice is right or wrong are located in the "Answers" section at the end of the book.

---

1. You are a DBA working at a SQL Server hosting company. You need to ensure that none of your company's client installations wastes disk space. As part of your maintenance tasks, you are charged with periodically shrinking databases. You want to automatically shrink entire databases at a time. How can you achieve this maintenance goal?

   A. Execute the *DBCC SHRINKDATABASE* statement.

   B. Execute the *DBCC SHRINKFILE* statement.

   C. Set each database to shrink automatically by using the *ALTER DATABASE* statement against each database.

   D. You cannot shrink SQL Server 2005 database files automatically.

2. You need to ensure that none of your databases contains unused space because recent database growth is quickly filling up disk space. How can you shrink individual database files during the night when the system is not being used by your end users?

   A. Create a job that will execute the *DBCC SHRINKFILE* statement against the individual files during the night.

   B. Execute the *ALTER DATABASE* statement to allow the database to be shrunk only at night.

   C. Execute the *DBCC SHRINKDATABASE* statement, specifying the time you want the database to be shrunk.

   D. Alter the database to allow the database engine to automatically shrink the database.

Lesson 4: Using DBCC CHECKDB

As part of your regular database maintenance, you need to check your databases for integrity issues. To help you complete this task, SQL Server 2005 provides the *DBCC CHECKDB* database console command. DBAs need to become familiar with this command, its uses, and its output to ensure the stability of their databases. This lesson gives you an overview of *DBCC CHECKDB* and some tips about using it to check the integrity of your database.

After this lesson, you will be able to:

■ Perform database integrity checks by using the *DBCC CHECKDB* command.

Estimated lesson time: 15 minutes

DBCC CHECKDB

The *DBCC CHECKDB* command performs a variety of checks on the database you issue it against to verify the allocation, structural integrity, and logical integrity of all objects in the database. You need to become familiar with the command and the checks that it issues so that you use the appropriate options and so that you don't duplicate the checks it performs during the often-limited maintenance windows found in today's database environment.

The *DBCC CHECKDB* statement performs the following integrity checks:

■ Issues *DBCC CHECKALLOC* on the database

■ Issues *DBCC CHECKTABLE* on every table and view in the database

■ Issues *DBCC CHECKCATALOG* on the database

■ Validates Service Broker data in the database

■ Validates the contents of every indexed view in the database

---

MORE INFO   **DBCC CHECKDB**

To see all the many options available with the *DBCC CHECKDB* command, see the SQL Server 2005 Books Online topic "DBCC CHECKDB (Transact-SQL)."

DBAs should keep in mind the following best practices associated with running *DBCC CHECKDB*:

- Because of the time *DBCC CHECKDB* can take to run against larger databases, you should execute the command with the *PHYSICAL_ONLY* option if you are doing frequent checks on production systems. *PHYSICAL_ONLY* provides a small-overhead check of the physical consistency of the database and can detect torn pages, checksum failures, and common hardware failures that can compromise a user's data.

- To get a full integrity check of your database, periodically execute *DBCC CHECKDB* with no options specified so that you don't limit the check.

- When errors are reported during the execution of *DBCC CHECKDB*, restore the database from a recent database backup chain to resolve the issues. If the database cannot be restored because of its size, a lack of valid database backups, or other issues, consider executing the *DBCC CHECKDB* command by using one of the command's repair options: *REPAIR_ALLOW_DATA_LOSS*, *REPAIR_FAST*, or *REPAIR_REBUILD*. However, using a repair option, which specifies that *DBCC CHECKDB* should repair the found issues, should be a last resort because repair operations do not consider any constraints that might exist on or between tables.

NOTE   **Repair options require single-user mode**

Note that to use one of the three repair options of *DBCC CHECKDB*, the specified database must be in single-user mode.

> ## Quick Check
> - What other *DBCC* statements does the *DBCC CHECKDB* statement execute?
>
> ### Quick Check Answer
> - The *DBCC CHECKDB* statement executes the following DBCC statements: *DBCC CHECKALLOC*, *DBCC CHECKTABLE*, and *DBCC CHECKCATALOG*.

PRACTICE   Executing the DBCC CHECKDB Statement

The following two practices will walk you through the process of executing a *DBCC CHECKDB* statement to ensure database integrity and using that statement to repair any integrity issues found.

▶ **Practice 1: Execute DBCC CHECKDB to Review Integrity Issues**

In this practice, you execute the *DBCC CHECKDB* statement and review the output for database integrity issues.

1. If necessary, start SSMS and connect to the instance containing the Adventure-Works sample database. Open the Query Editor pane.

2. In the Query Editor pane, type the following Transact-SQL statement to execute the *DBCC CHECKDB* statement:

```
USE master;

--Check for database integrity issues.
--Show all error messages.
DBCC CHECKDB ('AdventureWorks') WITH ALL_ERRORMSGS;
```

3. Scroll down the output from the statement to review any error messages.

▶ **Practice 2: Execute DBCC CHECKDB to Review Integrity Issues and Allow for Issue Correction**

In this practice, you execute the *DBCC CHECKDB* statement and allow the statement to correct integrity issues.

1. If necessary, start SSMS and connect to the instance containing the Adventure-Works sample database. Open the Query Editor pane.

2. In the Query Editor pane, type the following Transact-SQL statements to set the database to single-user mode, execute the *DBCC CHECKDB* statement, and allow the statement to attempt to repair any issues found:

```
USE master;

--Check for database integrity issues.
--Allow the statement to attempt to repair issues with possible loss of data.
--Show all error messages.

--Database must be in single-user mode.
ALTER DATABASE AdventureWorks
SET SINGLE_USER;

DBCC CHECKDB ('AdventureWorks', 'REPAIR_ALLOW_DATA_LOSS') WITH ALL_ERRORMSGS;
```

3. Scroll down the output from the statement to review any error messages.

4. In the Query Editor pane, type the following Transact-SQL statement to execute the following statement to set the database back to multiple-user mode:

```
--Remove from single-user mode.
ALTER DATABASE AdventureWorks
SET MULTI_USER;
```

Lesson Summary

- You use the *DBCC CHECKDB* statement to validate database integrity.

- The *DBCC CHECKDB* statement executes *DBCC CHECKALLOC, DBCC CHECK-TABLE,* and *DBCC CHECKCATALOG* statements, making individual execution of these statements unnecessary.

- Although the *DBCC CHECKDB* statement has options to repair issues found during its execution, it is recommended that DBAs attempt to restore the database from valid backup sets before attempting to use *DBCC CHECKDB* to repair integrity issues.

Lesson Review

The following questions are intended to reinforce key information presented in this lesson. The questions are also available on the companion CD if you prefer to review them in electronic form.

NOTE   Answers

Answers to these questions and explanations of why each answer choice is right or wrong are located in the "Answers" section at the end of the book.

---

1. The *DBCC CHECKDB* statement issues which of the following statements?

   A. *DBCC CHECKCATALOG*

   B. *DBCC CHECKIDENT*

   C. *DBCC NEWALLOC*

   D. *DBCC TEXTALLOC*

2. Which *DBCC CHECKDB* option is recommended for frequent checks against large databases?

   A. *NOINDEX*

   B. *REPAIR_FAST*

   C. *PHYSICAL_ONLY*

   D. *NO_INFOMSGS*

Chapter Review

To further practice and reinforce the skills you learned in this chapter, you can

- Review the chapter summary.
- Review the list of key terms introduced in this chapter.
- Complete the case scenarios. These scenarios set up real-world situations involving the topics of this chapter and ask you to create a solution.
- Complete the suggested practices.
- Take a practice test.

Chapter Summary

- To achieve maximum performance for your database queries, you should perform periodic index maintenance to keep index fragmentation in your databases to a minimum level.
- Index and column statistics are key to query performance. Because the query optimizer uses them to determine the execution plan of the query, you need to make sure that statistics are up to date.
- Another important database maintenance task is shrinking databases and database files that contain unneeded and unused space to a smaller size to recapture the unused disk space.
- You need to periodically check the integrity of your databases by using the *DBCC CHECKDB* command and handle errors found during its execution by restoring the database from a valid backup.

Key Terms

Do you know what these key terms mean? You can check your answers by looking up the terms in the glossary at the end of the book.

- external fragmentation
- histogram
- index fragmentation
- index rebuild
- index reorganization
- internal fragmentation
- page split
- statistics
- string summary

Case Scenarios

In the following case scenarios, you apply what you've learned about how to maintain SQL Server 2005 by using Transact SQL. You can find answers to these questions in the "Answers" section at the end of this book.

Case Scenario 1: Defragmenting an Index

You are a DBA for a local book publisher. As part of your job, you must design a method to manage index fragmentation levels. You have decided to create a SQL Server Agent job that checks index fragmentation levels and issues the appropriate *ALTER INDEX* statement to defragment fragmented indexes. To achieve this goal, you need to answer the following questions:

1. What mechanism will your job use to check index fragmentation levels?
2. What threshold will the job use to determine whether the indexes have external fragmentation?
3. What threshold will the job use to determine whether your indexes have internal fragmentation?

Case Scenario 2: Maintaining Database Integrity

You are a DBA for a large phone company. You need to design a database integrity check job in SQL Server Agent. During a planning meeting, your manager asks you the following questions about your integrity job:

1. In large databases, what options will you use with the *DBCC CHECKDB* statement to minimize any performance impact of running the statement?

2. What other options will you use when you run the *DBCC CHECKDB* statement against all databases?

3. How can you make sure that if the integrity-check job finds an issue, you can correct the problem and ensure the database's integrity?

Suggested Practices

To help you successfully master the exam objectives presented in this chapter, complete the following practice tasks.

Managing Index Fragmentation

For this task, you should complete both practices to gain experience in correcting index-fragmentation levels.

- **Practice 1**   Practice executing *ALTER INDEX...REBUILD* to understand how you can issue this statement against indexes needing to be defragmented. Make sure that you understand when to use the statement and how it performs when running as an ONLINE operation.

- **Practice 2**   Practice executing *ALTER INDEX...REORGANIZE* to understand how you can issue this statement against indexes needing to be defragmented. Make sure that you understand the limitations of this statement and how it might not be suited for every table in the database.

Managing Statistics

For this task, complete both practices to gain experience managing statistics on columns in SQL Server 2005 databases.

- **Practice 1**   Review and understand the importance of column statistics by dropping column statistics on tables in a test database and then comparing query execution times before and after the statistics are dropped.

- **Practice 2**   Understand the importance of up-to-date statistics by turning off the capability to automatically update statistics. Then perform a large number of inserts in a table, execute a query, update the statistics, and reexecute the same query. Compare query execution times when the statistics are out of date to when the statistics are up to date.

Shrinking Files

For this task, complete all three practices to gain experience in deciding when to shrink files and the appropriate statement to issue to shrink the files.

- **Practice 1**   Perform a database shrink operation by using the *DBCC SHRINKDATABASE* statement and then watch system resource utilization.

- **Practice 2**   Perform a database shrink operation by using the *DBCC SHRINKFILE* statement and then watch system resource utilization.

- **Practice 3**   Set a database to automatically shrink, and use SQL Server Profiler to watch how many times the shrink operation takes place.

Using DBCC CHECKDB to Perform Database Integrity Checks

For this task, complete both practices to gain experience in deciding when and how to issue a *DBCC CHECKDB* statement and how to read the output.

- **Practice 1**   Perform a *DBCC CHECKDB* statement against all databases, and watch system resource utilization.

- **Practice 2**   Perform a *DBCC CHECKDB* statement with a repair option against a test database to become familiar with setting the database to single-user mode and back to multiple-user mode.

Take a Practice Test

The practice tests on this book's companion CD offer many options. For example, you can test yourself on just the content covered in this chapter, or you can test yourself on all the 70-431 certification exam content. You can set up the test so that it closely simulates the experience of taking a certification exam, or you can set it up in study mode so that you can look at the correct answers and explanations after you answer each question.

MORE INFO   Practice tests

For details about all the practice test options available, see the section titled "How to Use the Practice Tests" in this book's Introduction.

Chapter 13

Working with *HTTP* Endpoints

In today's distributed and often global IT environments, service-oriented applications are in demand. The architecture that supports service-oriented applications relies on *Web services* that can receive requests and send responses in a platform-independent format called *SOAP*. SOAP uses XML as an encoding scheme for request and response parameters and uses HTTP as a transport mechanism.

Within its new endpoints technology for governing connections to Microsoft SQL Server, SQL Server 2005 provides *HTTP endpoints* that enable developers to expose the stored procedures and functions within a database as methods that can be called from any application using the SOAP protocol. This chapter covers the important security considerations for implementing *HTTP* endpoints and then shows you how to create and secure these endpoints so that Web services can securely make direct calls to your database.

Exam objectives in this chapter:
- Implement an *HTTP* endpoint.
  - ❏ Create an *HTTP* endpoint.
  - ❏ Secure an *HTTP* endpoint.

Lessons in this chapter:

Before You Begin

To complete the lessons in this chapter, you must have

- SQL Server 2005 installed.
- A copy of the *AdventureWorks* sample database installed in the instance.

Real World

Michael Hotek

In SQL Server 2000, you could expose stored procedures directly to a Web service. Although this new functionality provided an important capability to applications, the configuration was messy, and you had very little ability to fine-tune security permissions. However, SQL Server 2005 provides an open and straightforward method for exposing stored procedures and functions to Web services by using its new endpoint technology. *HTTP* endpoints in SQL Server 2005 provide a variety of options for securing endpoints while allowing broader access to your database. As more and more organizations require Web services to access data, you can turn to *HTTP* endpoints as a secure mechanism for meeting this business need.

Lesson 1: Understanding *HTTP* Endpoint Security

To communicate with SQL Server, an application must connect to a port number on which that SQL Server is configured to listen. Previous SQL Server versions have left this connection point unsecured as well as unrestricted. However, SQL Server 2005 has redefined its entire connection infrastructure to strengthen communication security. This lesson provides an overview of the flexible and very granular security features that you can take advantage of for an *HTTP* endpoint.

> **After this lesson, you will be able to:**
> - Explain the seven layers of *HTTP* endpoint security.
> - Secure an *HTTP* endpoint.
>
> **Estimated lesson time: 20 minutes**

Seven Layers of *HTTP* Endpoint Security

All connectivity to SQL Server or a feature within SQL Server is accomplished by using endpoints. Lesson 2 walks through the details of creating an *HTTP* endpoint, but you first need to understand the security features that SQL Server 2005 provides for *HTTP* endpoints. You can configure seven layers of security for an *HTTP* endpoint:

- Endpoint type
- Endpoint payload
- Endpoint state
- Authentication method
- Encryption
- Login type
- Endpoint permissions

Let's look at each of these layers in turn.

Endpoint type

The endpoint type defines which types of traffic the endpoint allows. Endpoints can be of two different types:

- **TCP**   Responds only to TCP requests
- **HTTP**   Responds to either HTTP or HTTPS requests

Endpoint payload

The payload setting describes the particular subset of traffic that the endpoint allows. Accepted endpoint payloads are *TSQL*, *SOAP*, *SERVICE_BROKER*, and *DATABASE_MIRRORING*. An *HTTP* endpoint allows only one type of payload: *SOAP*. The options within the *SOAP* payload setting are key to creating a secure *HTTP* endpoint; Lesson 2 covers these important options.

MORE INFO Endpoint payloads

For information about the *TSQL* payload, see Chapter 5, "Working with Transact-SQL." For information about the *SERVICE_BROKER* payload, see Chapter 20, "Working with Service Broker." And for information about the *DATABASE_MIRRORING* payload, see Chapter 17, "Implementing Database Mirroring."

Endpoint state

The possible states for an endpoint are *STARTED*, *STOPPED*, and *DISABLED*. For an endpoint to respond to requests, the state must be set to *STARTED*. An endpoint with a state of *STOPPED* returns an error in response to any connection attempt, whereas an endpoint with a state of *DISABLED* does not respond to any request. To comply with the SQL Server 2005 "off by default" approach to security, the default state is *STOPPED*.

Authentication method

You can use either Windows authentication or certificates as the authentication method for the endpoint connection. You set Windows-based authentication by specifying the *NTLM*, *KERBEROS*, or *NEGOTIATE* option. The *NEGOTIATE* option causes instances to dynamically select the authentication method. For certificate-based authentication, you can use a certificate from a trusted authority or generate your own Windows certificate.

BEST PRACTICES Authentication

When all instances reside within a single domain or across trusted domains, you should use Windows authentication. When instances span nontrusted domains, you should use certificate-based authentication.

Encryption

Endpoints also provide encryption options. The *PORTS* clause enables you to specify whether communication is in clear text or whether Secure Sockets Layer (SSL) is enabled. When you specify the *CLEAR* option, the endpoint sends and receives HTTP traffic. When you specify the *SSL* option, the communication must be accomplished via HTTPS.

Login type

Within the *SOAP* payload, the *LOGIN_TYPE* parameter controls which type of accounts are used to connect to the endpoint. Setting this option to *WINDOWS* allows authentication by using Windows accounts. Setting this option to *MIXED* allows connections to be made using either Windows credentials or a SQL Server login.

Endpoint permissions

Even if you set all of the previous options to the least-restrictive security permissions, all traffic to the endpoint is still restricted. To allow a login to connect to an endpoint, you must grant it *CONNECT* permission on the endpoint.

Quick Check

- You have created an *HTTP* endpoint and specified all security options that are available. You have verified that your application meets all the security permissions, is granted access to the database, and is making the appropriate calls to the *HTTP* endpoint. However, you continue to get access errors. What is the problem?

Quick Check Answer

- Although you have created the endpoint and verified that all options are enabled and compatible for your application, you have an additional step to perform. You must grant *CONNECT* permission to the login that you are using to connect to the endpoint.

Lesson Summary

- *HTTP* endpoints enable you to specify very granular settings across the following seven layers of security.
    - The endpoint type of *HTTP* accepts only HTTP and HTTPS traffic.

❑ The payload must be specified as *SOAP* so that the endpoint accepts only SOAP requests.

❑ The endpoint must be in a state of *STARTED* to respond to requests and return results.

❑ To restrict the types of clients that can send requests, you can specify the enforcement of a specific authentication method such as *NTLM* or *KERBEROS*.

❑ Setting the *PORTS* clause to SSL encrypts all communications and causes traffic to require HTTPS.

❑ The type of login can be limited to *WINDOWS* to restrict access to clients that have been authenticated by Windows.

❑ Finally, the login you are using to connect to the endpoint must be granted the *CONNECT* permission.

Lesson Review

The following questions are intended to reinforce key information presented in this lesson. The questions are also available on the companion CD if you prefer to review them in electronic form.

NOTE Answers

Answers to these questions and explanations of why each answer choice is right or wrong are located in the "Answers" section at the end of the book.

---

1. *HTTP* endpoints are restricted to which of the following elements? (Choose all that apply.)

  A. *SOAP* payload

  B. HTTP or HTTPS traffic

  C. *TSQL* payload

  D. Windows authentication

2. You are working in a very secure environment and must enable *HTTP* endpoints to meet new application needs. You must ensure that only members authenticated to your domain can send requests to the endpoint and that even if someone were to hack into your network, data being sent to clients cannot be read. Which options would you need to enable to meet these requirements? (Choose all that apply.)

    A. *LOGIN_TYPE = MIXED*

    B. *LOGIN_TYPE = WINDOWS*

    C. *PORTS(CLEAR)*

    D. *PORTS(SSL)*

Lesson 2: Creating a Secure *HTTP* Endpoint

You create *HTTP* endpoints to expose stored procedures and functions to SOAP requests from Web services. You can use Transact-SQL statements or SQL Server Management Objects (SMOs) to create and manage *HTTP* endpoints; in this lesson, we will cover the Transact-SQL commands you can use. We will also focus on the *SOAP* payload option, which defines all the actions that are exposed to the Web service and all the formatting options available for the returned results.

After this lesson, you will be able to:
■ Create a secure *HTTP* endpoint.
Estimated lesson time: 20 minutes

Creating an *HTTP* Endpoint

You use the Transact-SQL *CREATE ENDPOINT* statement to create an endpoint, including an *HTTP* endpoint. The statement has two general sections. The first section enables you to specify the transport protocol as either TCP or HTTP; you specify HTTP to create an *HTTP* endpoint. You also set a listening port number and the authentication method for the endpoint as well as other HTTP protocol configuration settings for the endpoint.

In the second section of the *CREATE ENDPOINT* statement, you define the payload that the endpoint supports. As noted in Lesson 1, an *HTTP* endpoint supports only the *SOAP* payload.

The following example shows the general syntax for the *CREATE ENDPOINT* statement:

```
CREATE ENDPOINT endPointName [ AUTHORIZATION login ]
STATE = { STARTED | STOPPED | DISABLED }
AS { HTTP | TCP } (
   <protocol_specific_arguments>
      )
FOR { SOAP | TSQL | SERVICE_BROKER | DATABASE_MIRRORING } (
   <language_specific_arguments>
      )
```

MORE INFO **Protocol-specific arguments**

For information about all the options available for configuring the protocol-specific arguments for an *HTTP* endpoint, see the SQL Server 2005 Books Online article "CREATE ENDPOINT (Transact-SQL)." SQL Server 2005 Books Online is installed as part of SQL Server 2005. Updates for SQL Server 2005 Books Online are available for download at *www.microsoft.com/technet/prodtechnol/sql/2005/downloads/books.mspx*.

Perhaps the most important settings for creating a secure *HTTP* endpoint are in the *language_specific_arguments* section of the *SOAP* payload. We cover the key options for this configuration section later in this lesson.

You use the *ALTER ENDPOINT* statement to add a new method to an existing endpoint, modify or drop a method from the endpoint, or change the properties of an endpoint. And you use the *DROP ENDPOINT* statement to drop an existing endpoint.

Specifying Web Methods

To make an *HTTP* endpoint meaningful, the *SOAP* payload must specify at least one Web method. Web methods simply expose stored procedures and functions as public methods that a Web service can call. In the *WEBMETHOD* portion of the *SOAP* payload's language-specific arguments, you map specific stored procedures and functions you want to expose in the endpoint as Web methods.

The general format of the *WEBMETHOD* portion of the *SOAP* payload is as follows:

```
[ { WEBMETHOD [ 'namespace' .] 'method_alias'
   (   NAME = 'database.owner.name'
     [ , SCHEMA = { NONE | STANDARD | DEFAULT } ]
     [ , FORMAT = { ALL_RESULTS | ROWSETS_ONLY | NONE} ]
   )
```

The *namespace* and *method_alias* that you specify define the name of the Web method that is exposed on the *HTTP* endpoint. The name must be unique for the entire SQL Server instance.

You use the *NAME* clause to specify the fully qualified name of the stored procedure or function that you are mapping to the Web method.

BEST PRACTICES   Object security

The name of the method that is exposed on the endpoint, *method_alias*, should not be the same as the actual stored procedure or function name. Using a different name prevents a hacker from interrogating an *HTTP* endpoint for exposed methods and then using them to attempt to gain direct access to the underlying stored procedures or functions.

The *SCHEMA* option defines whether an inline XML Schema Definition (XSD) will be returned for a *WEBMETHOD* in the SOAP response. The *FORMAT* option controls how results are sent back in the SOAP request. You can choose to send just the result set generated or to also include the row count, along with warning and error messages.

Specifying WSDL Support, Schemas, and Namespaces

Each *HTTP* endpoint includes a clause in the *SOAP* payload to specify *Web Services Description Language (WSDL)* support. When you specify *NONE*, the endpoint does not provide any WSDL support. If you specify *DEFAULT*, a default WSDL is returned for the endpoint.

MORE INFO WSDL

A discussion of WSDL is beyond the scope of this chapter. For information about WSDL and WSDL support, see the SQL Server 2005 Books Online article "Default WSDL."

As part of the *SOAP* payload configuration, you can define a *SCHEMA* for the *HTTP* endpoint. An *HTTP* endpoint has a default *SCHEMA* option that can be overridden by a particular *WEBMETHOD*, if chosen. If you specify *NONE* for the *SCHEMA* option, an inline XSD is not returned in the SOAP request. If you specify *STANDARD*, an inline XSD is returned along with the result set.

NOTE Loading result sets

If you want to load a result set from the SOAP request into a *DataSet* object, an XSD is required.

In addition, the *SOAP* payload area enables you to specify an explicit namespace for an *HTTP* endpoint. The default namespace is the namespace for each *WEBMETHOD*. This option can be overridden within the *WEBMETHOD* definition. If you leave this option at the *DEFAULT* value, which is typical, or don't specify anything for it, the namespace is assumed to be *http://tempuri.org*.

Additional *SOAP* Payload Parameters

You can specify several other parameters for the *SOAP* payload to control various behaviors for the endpoint. Besides the options covered earlier, you can set the following options for the *SOAP* payload:

```
[   BATCHES = { ENABLED | DISABLED } ]
[ , SESSIONS = { ENABLED | DISABLED } ]
[ , SESSION_TIMEOUT = timeoutInterval | NEVER ]
[ , DATABASE = { 'database_name' | DEFAULT }
[ , CHARACTER_SET = { SQL | XML }]
[ , HEADER_LIMIT = int ]
```

The *BATCHES* option controls whether a connection can issue ad hoc SQL queries against the endpoint. When you enable this parameter, a connection to the database can issue any ad hoc SQL query. The commands that a connection can successfully execute are governed by security permissions within the database.

BEST PRACTICES   Enabling ad hoc SQL

You should always disable the *BATCHES* option. Allowing a connection to execute ad hoc SQL que-ries against the endpoint provides an open invitation to hackers to go after your database. For everything that is exposed in an *HTTP* endpoint, you should use the *WEBMETHOD* clause to define a specific set of procedures or functions allowed.

By enabling SESSIONS support, multiple SOAP request/response pairs are treated as a single SOAP session. This allows an application to make multiple calls to the end-point during a single SOAP session.

When you specify a value for the *DATABASE* parameter, the connection to the *HTTP* endpoint changes context to the database that you specified; otherwise, the default database defined for the login is used.

MORE INFO   *SOAP* payload parameters

For a discussion of all possible *SOAP* payload options for an endpoint, see the SQL Server 2005 Books Online article "CREATE ENDPOINT (Transact-SQL)."

Quick Check

1. Which parameter should you specify for the *SOAP* payload to make the endpoint meaningful?

2. Which parameter should never be enabled due to security concerns?

Quick Check Answers

1. The *WEBMETHOD* parameter specifies the procedure or function that is exposed by the endpoint. Each *HTTP* endpoint should always use this parameter to restrict the possible commands that can be executed against it.

2. The *BATCHES* parameter allows a connection to execute ad hoc SQL que-ries against the endpoint; you should disable this parameter to limit the potential exposure to your database from Web service calls.

PRACTICE **Creating an Endpoint**

In this exercise, you will create an *HTTP* endpoint that requires integrated security as well as SSL. The endpoint will expose the stored procedure *uspGetBillOfMaterials* from the *AdventureWorks* database as a Web method.

1. Launch SQL Server Management Studio (SSMS), connect to your instance, and open a new query window.

2. Type the following command to create the endpoint, specifying the endpoint as type *HTTP*, as using integrated authentication, and as using a *PORTS* setting of *SSL*. The statement also specifies the payload as *SOAP* and uses the *WEB-METHOD* parameter to expose the *uspGetBillOfMaterials* stored procedure as a Web method:

```
CREATE ENDPOINT sql_endpoint
STATE = STARTED
AS HTTP(
   PATH = '/sql',
   AUTHENTICATION = (INTEGRATED ),
   PORTS = ( SSL ),
   SITE = 'SERVER'
   )
FOR SOAP (
   WEBMETHOD 'BillofMaterials'
          (name='AdventureWorks.dbo.uspGetBillOfMaterials'),
   WSDL = DEFAULT,
   SCHEMA = STANDARD,
   DATABASE = 'AdventureWorks',
   NAMESPACE = 'http://tempUri.org/'
   );
GO
```

CAUTION   Error creating *HTTP* endpoint

Depending on the specific operating system and the applications that are installed on your machine, you might receive an error message when executing this command. To resolve this issue, see the MSDN article "Guidelines and Limitations in Native XML Web Services" at *http://msdn2.microsoft.com/en-us/library/ms189092.aspx*.

Lesson Summary

- You define *HTTP* endpoints in two sections of the Transact-SQL *CREATE END-POINT* command: one that defines the endpoint as *HTTP* and another that defines the payload as *SOAP*.

- The *SOAP* payload defines the operations allowed for the endpoint as well as how result sets are formatted for the SOAP response.

- The most important parameter within the *SOAP* payload is the *WEBMETHOD* option, which specifies the stored procedure or function that is exposed by the endpoint.

Lesson Review

The following questions are intended to reinforce key information presented in this lesson. The questions are also available on the companion CD if you prefer to review them in electronic form.

NOTE Answers

Answers to these questions and explanations of why each answer choice is right or wrong are located in the "Answers" section at the end of this book.

---

1. Which of the following commands enable a Web service to call the *uspGetBillOf-Materials* stored procedure in the *AdventureWorks* database and ensure that all data remains encrypted? The result set will be loaded into a *DataSet* object.

   A.
   ```
   CREATE ENDPOINT sql_endpoint
   STATE = STARTED
   AS HTTP(
      PATH = '/sql',
      AUTHENTICATION = (INTEGRATED ),
      PORTS = ( CLEAR ),
      SITE = 'SERVER'
      )
   FOR SOAP (
      WEBMETHOD 'BillofMaterials'
              (name='AdventureWorks.dbo.uspGetBillOfMaterials'),
      WSDL = DEFAULT,
      SCHEMA = STANDARD,
      DATABASE = 'AdventureWorks',
      NAMESPACE = 'http://tempUri.org/'
      );
   ```

   B.
   ```
   CREATE ENDPOINT sql_endpoint
   STATE = STARTED
   AS HTTP(
      PATH = '/sql',
      AUTHENTICATION = (INTEGRATED ),
   ```

```
        PORTS = ( SSL ),
        SITE = 'SERVER'
        )
   FOR SOAP (
      WEBMETHOD 'BillofMaterials'
                (name='AdventureWorks.dbo.uspGetBillOfMaterials',
                 SCHEMA = STANDARD),
      WSDL = DEFAULT,
      SCHEMA = STANDARD,
      DATABASE = 'AdventureWorks',
      NAMESPACE = 'http://tempUri.org/'
      );
```

C.

```
CREATE ENDPOINT sql_endpoint
STATE = STARTED
AS HTTP(
   PATH = '/sql',
   AUTHENTICATION = (INTEGRATED ),
   PORTS = ( SSL ),
   SITE = 'SERVER'
   )
FOR SOAP (
   WEBMETHOD 'BillofMaterials'
             (name='AdventureWorks.dbo.uspGetBillOfMaterials'),
   WSDL = DEFAULT,
   SCHEMA = STANDARD,
   DATABASE = 'AdventureWorks',
   NAMESPACE = 'http://tempUri.org/'
   );
```

D.

```
CREATE ENDPOINT sql_endpoint
STATE = DISABLED
AS HTTP(
   PATH = '/sql',
   AUTHENTICATION = (INTEGRATED ),
   PORTS = ( SSL ),
   SITE = 'SERVER'
   )
FOR SOAP (
   WEBMETHOD 'BillofMaterials'
             (name='AdventureWorks.dbo.uspGetBillOfMaterials'),
   WSDL = DEFAULT,
   SCHEMA = STANDARD,
   DATABASE = 'AdventureWorks',
   NAMESPACE = 'http://tempUri.org/'
   );
```

Chapter Review

To further practice and reinforce the skills you learned in this chapter, you can

- Review the chapter summary.
- Review the list of key terms introduced in this chapter.
- Complete the case scenario. This scenario sets up a real-world situation involving the topics of this chapter and asks you to create solutions.
- Complete the suggested practices.
- Take a practice test.

Chapter Summary

- Service-oriented applications are the new "old" architecture currently in vogue. This architecture relies on the creation of Web services that can receive requests and send responses in a platform-independent format called SOAP.
- *HTTP* endpoints enable developers to expose the stored procedures and functions within a SQL Server 2005 database as methods that can be called from any application using the SOAP protocol.

Key Terms

Do you know what these key terms mean? You can check your answers by looking up the terms in the glossary at the end of the book.

- *HTTP* endpoint
- SOAP
- Web service
- Web Services Description Language (WSDL)

Case Scenario: Creating *HTTP* Endpoints

In this case scenario, you will apply what you've learned in this chapter. You can find answers to these questions in the "Answers" section at the end of this book.

Contoso Limited, a health care company located in Bothell, WA, has just contracted with a service provider that will perform research for certain patient claims. The service provider is not allowed access to the Contoso network because of security concerns related to all the company's proprietary and confidential data.

1. How can you create a solution that enables the service provider to access the claims it needs to research as well as to write the results back into the database?

2. How can you ensure that the access meets all company security requirements and that all data is encrypted anywhere on the network?

Suggested Practices

To successfully master the exam objectives presented in this chapter, complete the following practice tasks.

Creating *HTTP* Endpoints

- **Practice 1**   Create an *HTTP* endpoint that exposes each of the stored procedures in the *AdventureWorks* database as Web methods.

- **Practice 2**   Write a Microsoft Visual Studio application that will make calls to the *HTTP* endpoint and display the results of each call in a grid attached to a *DataSet* object.

Take a Practice Test

The practice tests on this book's companion CD offer many options. For example, you can test yourself on just the content covered in this chapter, or you can test yourself on all the 70-431 certification exam content. You can set up the test so that it closely simulates the experience of taking a certification exam, or you can set it up in study mode so that you can look at the correct answers and explanations after you answer each question.

MORE INFO   Practice tests

For details about all the practice test options available, see the "How to Use the Practice Tests" section in this book's Introduction.

Chapter 14

Working with SQL Server Agent Jobs

Microsoft SQL Server features a powerful and flexible job-scheduling engine called SQL Server Agent. This chapter explains how you can use SQL Server Agent to define jobs and schedule them to automatically execute on a scheduled basis. You will see how to create maintenance plans to specify maintenance tasks such as backups to be performed against one or more databases. And this chapter shows you how to define operators to send messages about job success or failure and how to configure alerts, which enable you to monitor the system for specified conditions and execute jobs to proactively address potential issues.

Exam objectives in this chapter:

- Implement and maintain SQL Server Agent jobs.
    - Set a job owner.
    - Create a job schedule.
    - Create job steps.
    - Configure job steps.
    - Disable a job.
    - Create a maintenance job.
    - Set up alerts.
    - Configure operators.
    - Modify a job.
    - Delete a job.
    - Manage a job.
- Monitor SQL Server Agent job history.
    - Identify the cause of a failure.
    - Identify outcome details.
    - Find out when a job last ran.

Lessons in this chapter:

Before You Begin

To complete the lessons in this chapter, you must have

- SQL Server 2005 installed.

- A connection to a SQL Server 2005 instance in SQL Server Management Studio (SSMS).

- The *AdventureWorks* database installed.

- SQL Server Integration Services (SSIS) installed.

Real World

Michael Hotek

As a database administrator (DBA), I need to perform many tasks on a recurring basis. The most common task is performing backups of my databases. All backups need to be done on a scheduled basis, such as running a transaction log backup every five minutes. Fortunately, SQL Server ships with a scheduling engine called SQL Server Agent.

To meet my requirements of executing backups on a regularly scheduled basis, I create jobs that are then executed on the schedules that I define by using SQL Server Agent. Without having a scheduling engine in the database system, I would have to purchase third-party software to accomplish such management tasks.

Executing backups on a scheduled basis is just one way to use SQL Server Agent to improve your productivity as a DBA and to ensure that important management tasks are performed when needed. Anything that you need to execute on a scheduled basis can take advantage of the services that this component offers.

Lesson 1: Creating a SQL Server Agent Job

SQL Server Agent is the scheduling engine within SQL Server. One of the primary purposes of this engine is to execute defined *jobs* at specified intervals. You can define SQL Server Agent jobs to execute a variety of important tasks such as database backups, reindexing, and integrity checks. In this lesson, you will learn how to create a job in SQL Server Agent and how to configure the job options that are available.

> **After this lesson, you will be able to:**
> - Create a job.
> - Set a job owner.
> - Create job steps.
> - Create job schedules.
>
> **Estimated lesson time: 20 minutes**

How to Create a SQL Server Agent Job

A job in SQL Server Agent consists of *job steps*, an owner to provide the security context for the job, and one or more schedules for executing the job.

The high-level steps for creating a new job are as follows:

1. Create a new job and give it a name, a database context, and an owner.
2. Add one or more job steps to the job.
3. Optionally specify a schedule on which to execute the job.

To create a new job, you need to expand the SQL Server Agent node within the Object Explorer in SSMS, as shown in Figure 14-1.

Right-click the Jobs node and choose New Job. The New Job window opens. In this window, you can define several general properties for each job, including name, job category, and description. A job name can be up to 64 characters long. Be sure to use a descriptive job name that clearly identifies the basic purpose of the job.

You can use the job category to group jobs together based on the types of actions they perform. For example, you should specify Database Maintenance as the category for any jobs that execute maintenance tasks. You can use any of the built-in job categories that ship with SQL Server or you can create your own categories.

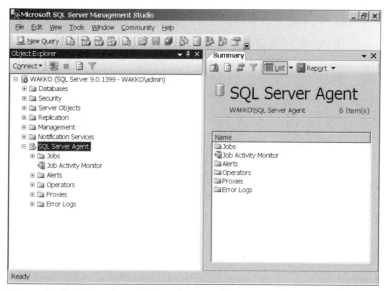

Figure 14-1   Managing all jobs, alerts, and operators from within the SQL Server Agent node

A description text box enables you to enter additional details about a job. If specific business rules govern a job or the way it is constructed, you should specify them in the job description to facilitate future job-maintenance actions. You see the New Job window completed in Figure 14-2.

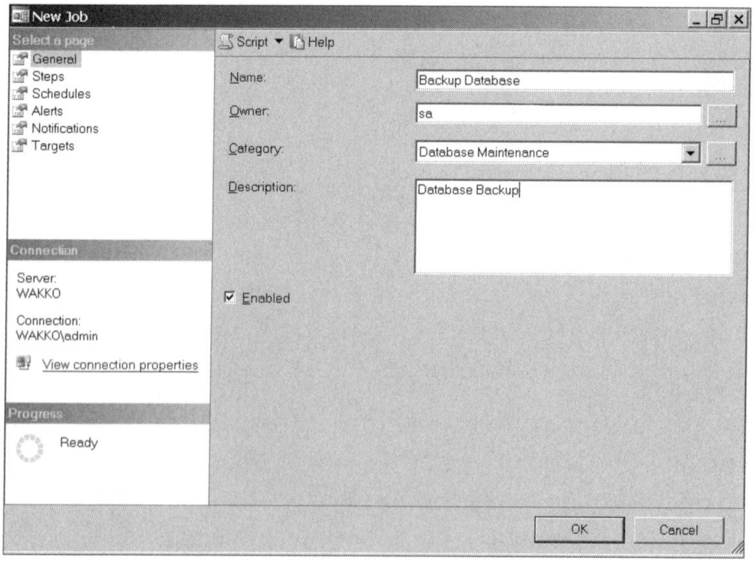

Figure 14-2   Defining a new job from the New Job window

How to Specify a Job Owner

On the New Job General page, you also specify the job owner, which defines the user or group who manages the job. Only the job owner or a member of the *sysadmin* role is allowed to modify a job. If the owner of the job is not a member of the *sysadmin* role, you need to ensure that the job owner has access to any proxy accounts necessary to execute a step within the job.

You use *SQL Server Agent proxy* accounts to control fine-grained permissions to SQL Server Agent. These proxy accounts control access to certain external subsystems within SQL Server such as replication, SSIS, SQL Server Analysis Services, CmdExec, and ActiveX. When a job step requires the use of one of these subsystems, the job owner is validated for access to the proxy. Once validated, SQL Server Agent impersonates the proxy account to allow execution of the job step.

MORE INFO   Proxy accounts

For more information about proxy accounts, see the SQL Server 2005 Books Online article "How to: Configure a User to Create and Manage SQL Server Agent Jobs." SQL Server 2005 Books Online is installed as part of SQL Server 2005. Updates for SQL Server 2005 Books Online are available for download at *www.microsoft.com/technet/prodtechnol/sql/2005/downloads/books.mspx*.

For job steps that execute Transact-SQL statements, the security context for the job step is derived from the job owner.

The SQL Server Agent proxies used, along with the job owner, prevent a user from gaining elevated permissions within SQL Server by using SQL Server Agent.

Quick Check
- Under what security context does a job step run?

Quick Check Answer
- A job step is executed using the security credentials of the job owner. For job steps that access external resources such as the file system, SSIS, and replication, a proxy account is used.

How to Create Job Steps

The core of a job is one or more *job steps*, which define the actual action(s) to be performed within the jobs.

The high-level steps for defining a job step are the following:

1. Create a new job step, specifying a name and type.
2. Define the command you want to execute.
3. Define logging and notification actions.

To define a job step, select the Steps page within the New Job window, as shown in Figure 14-3.

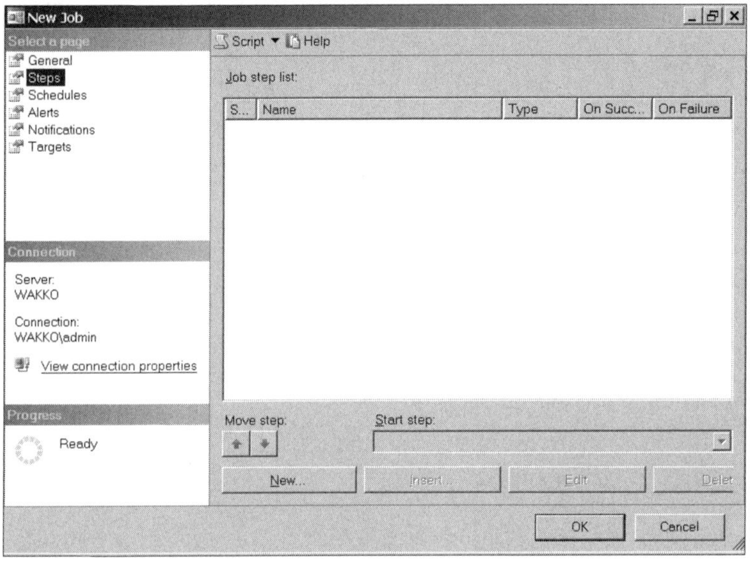

Figure 14-3   Defining a new job step

After clicking New, you can define the job step's properties, as the example shows in Figure 14-4.

For each job step, you need to define a name, which can be up to 64 characters. You also need to define a job step as a specific type.

The most common type of job step is Transact-SQL. With this type of job step, you define the database context in which to run the Transact-SQL batch that you specify. You can define a simple batch of Transact-SQL statements to execute as the job step, but more often you specify a call to a stored procedure. Other types of job steps correspond to SSIS, Analysis Services, replication, and ActiveX calls.

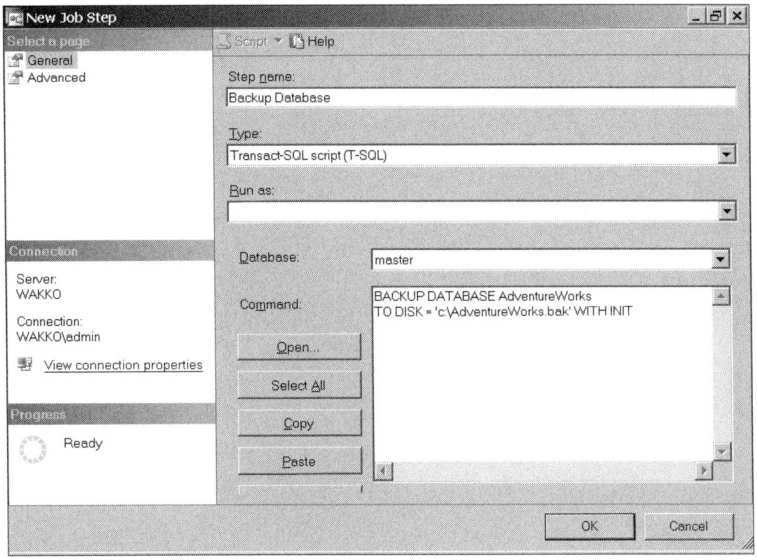

Figure 14-4   Defining job step properties

Depending on the type of job step you select, you have various configuration options available. You access the job step options by selecting the Advanced page in the New Job Step window, as Figure 14-5 shows.

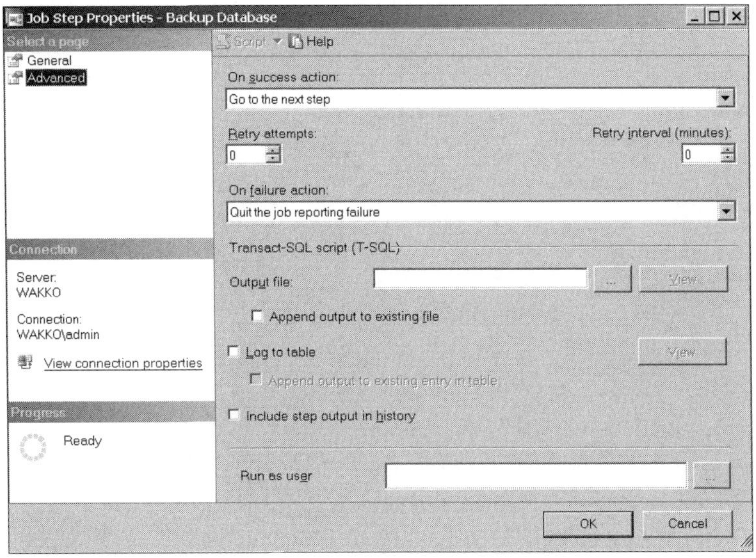

Figure 14-5   Specifying success, failure, and output file options

You can specify actions to take when the step completes successfully, such as Go To The Next Step, and actions to take when the step fails, such as Quit The Job, Reporting Failure. You can define how many times and at what interval to retry the job step. You can also specify logging options, such as writing to an output file.

IMPORTANT   Logging options

DBAs rarely specify logging options for job steps. However, without logging, it is much more difficult to troubleshoot why a job step may be failing. You should always output to a file at a minimum. You can then scan the output file for error messages.

How to Create Job Schedules

After you create job steps for your SQL Server Agent job, you can attach one or more schedules to the job. Without a schedule, a job can be executed only on demand from another process.

To create a new *job schedule*, select the Schedules page in the New Job window and then click New, as shown in Figure 14-6.

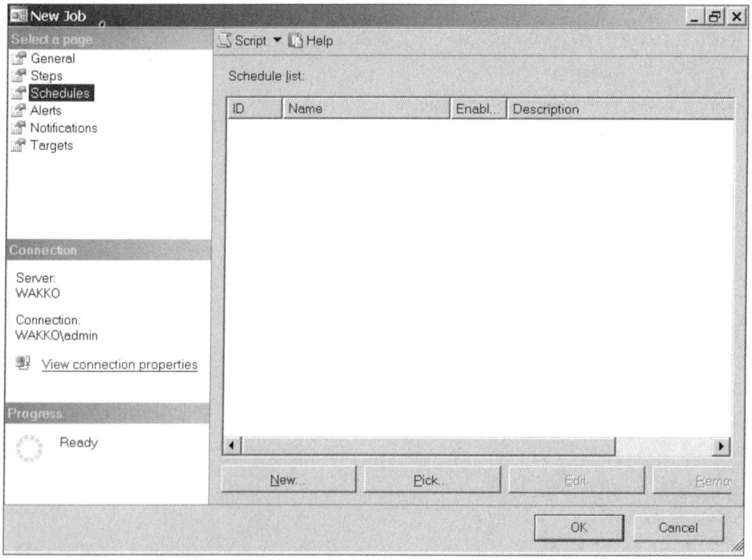

Figure 14-6   Creating a job schedule

On the resulting New Job Schedule dialog box, shown in Figure 14-7, you specify the schedule name, type, frequency, and duration. You can define job schedules to run on a periodic basis—such as daily, weekly, or monthly—with a variety of options available depending on the base interval you choose. The most common job schedule frequency is to run the job daily, and within each day, every *n* hours or *n* minutes.

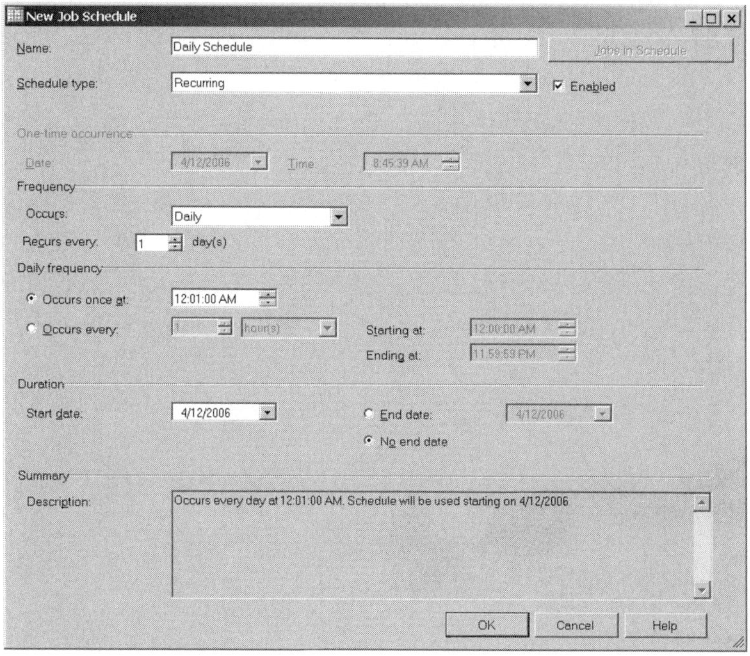

Figure 14-7   Specifying scheduling options

Instead of specifying a time interval for executing the job, you can use the Schedule Type drop-down list to schedule the job to execute based on CPU idle conditions, to execute when SQL Server Agent starts, or to execute only once. In addition, you can specify start and end dates for each schedule, allowing a particular job schedule to remain in effect only within that period.

NOTE   **Job schedule differences in SQL Server 2005**

In SQL Server 2000, job schedules are specific to a given job. In SQL Server 2005, however, job schedules are treated as separate entities. You can create a job schedule once and then use the same schedule for multiple jobs.

Lesson Summary

- SQL Server Agent is a basic scheduling engine included with SQL Server 2005 that enables you to define jobs and the schedules on which to automatically execute them.

- A job in SQL Server Agent consists of job steps: an owner to provide the security context for the job and one or more schedules for executing the job.

- To create a job step, you specify a name and type for the step, define the command to be executed in the step, define notification actions to occur on job step success or failure, and specify logging.

- You can define one or more job schedules to attach to a job, specifying the recurring interval for executing the job.

Lesson Review

The following questions are intended to reinforce key information presented in this lesson. The questions are also available on the companion CD if you prefer to review them in electronic form.

NOTE   Answers

Answers to these questions and explanations of why each answer choice is right or wrong are located in the "Answers" section at the end of the book.

---

1. What is the role of a job owner? (Choose all that apply.)
   - **A.** Categorize a job.
   - **B.** Provide the security context for a job step.
   - **C.** Execute the job.
   - **D.** Control access to the job.

2. Which of the following are valid scheduling options? (Choose all that apply.)
   - **A.** Once per day
   - **B.** When CPU utilization exceeds 80 percent
   - **C.** When SQL Server Agent starts
   - **D.** Every five seconds

PRACTICE Create a SQL Server Agent Job

In this exercise, you will practice creating a SQL Server Agent job to back up the *AdventureWorks* database on a daily basis at 23:00.

NOTE   Naming conventions

The exercises in this chapter do not explicitly specify the names to give entities. Each DBA has specific naming conventions, so all names should follow your standard naming conventions.

---

1. Open SSMS and connect to your SQL Server.

2. Expand the SQL Server Agent node.

3. Right-click Jobs and choose New Job.

4. Give the job a name and set a job owner with the authority to back up the *AdventureWorks* database.

5. Change the category to Database Maintenance.

6. Enter a description for the job.

7. Select the Steps page and click New to begin defining the backup job step.

8. Give the job step a name and specify Transact-SQL as the type.

9. Verify that the *master* database is selected in the Database drop-down list.

NOTE Database context

For exercises involving a database backup, this book specifies the *master* database as the database context because it will always exist on your SQL Server instance. However, there are no particular requirements to set a backup job to a specific database context.

---

10. Type the following command for the job step to run:

```
BACKUP DATABASE AdventureWorks to DISK = '<dirpath>\AdventureWorks.bak'
```

NOTE Backup file placement

Replace *<dirpath>* with the directory in which you want to place the backup file, for example: *m:\ program files\microsoft sql server\mssql.1\mssql\backup\adventureworks\fullbackup\20060201\ adventureworks.bak.*

---

11. Click OK to create the job step.

12. Select the Schedules page and click New to define a new schedule to attach to the job.

13. Give the schedule a name.

14. Specify the following settings:

    ❑ Schedule Type: Recurring

    ❑ Occurs: Daily

    ❑ Recurs Every: One day

    ❑ Occurs Once At: 23:00, or 11:00 PM

15. Click OK to create the new job schedule.

16. Click OK to close the New Job window and create your new backup job.

Lesson 2: Creating a Maintenance Plan

Maintenance plans in SQL Server 2005 have undergone a dramatic rearchitecture. All maintenance plans are now implemented as monolithic SSIS packages, and each package can have only one schedule attached to it. Thus, if you have multiple schedules that you want to attach to a maintenance plan, you will need to create one plan per schedule, which means that you will define many more plans than you had to in SQL Server 2000. Still, if you do not want to write code to perform your maintenance operations, a maintenance plan is a good starting point.

Within a maintenance plan, you can specify tasks for full, differential, and transaction log backups as well as tasks for integrity checks and reindexing operations.

MORE INFO   Database backups

For more information about database backups, see Chapter 11, "Backing Up, Restoring, and Moving a Database." And for more information about integrity checks and reindexing, see Chapter 12, "Using Transact-SQL to Manage Databases."

> **After this lesson, you will be able to:**
>
> ■ Create a maintenance plan.
>
> **Estimated lesson time: 20 minutes**

How to Create a Maintenance Plan

The most straightforward way to create a maintenance plan is to use the SQL Server Maintenance Plan Wizard. The high-level steps that you take to define a maintenance plan within the wizard are the following:

1. Specify the target server.
2. Specify maintenance tasks to perform.
3. Define task properties.
4. Specify SSIS flow control.
5. Create a schedule.
6. Define logging options.

To access the Maintenance Plan Wizard, open the Management node in SSMS, right-click Maintenance Plans, and choose Maintenance Plan Wizard, as shown in Figure 14-8.

Figure 14-8   Launching the Maintenance Plan Wizard

After launching the Maintenance Plan Wizard for the first time, disable the introductory splash screen so that you go directly into the wizard. By clicking Next, you will access the target server definition screen (see Figure 14-9). On this screen, you give your maintenance plan a name and description, select the server on which you want to run the maintenance tasks, and specify how you want to authenticate to that server.

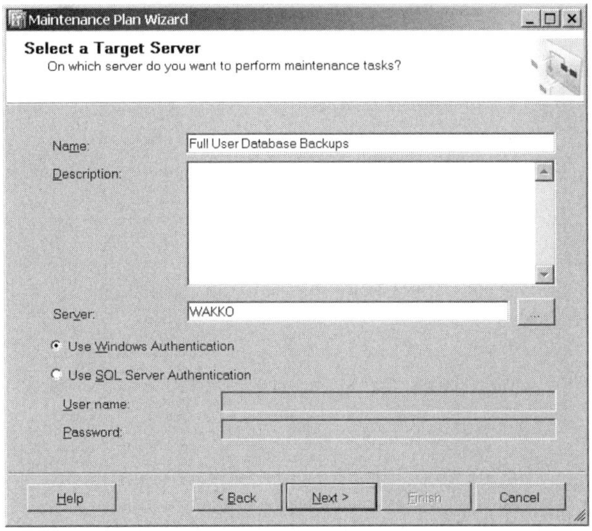

Figure 14-9   Specifying target server and connection parameters

Click Next to display the Select Maintenance Tasks page, which enables you to select the check boxes for one or more maintenance tasks to perform, as shown in Figure 14-10. Table 14-1 lists the available maintenance tasks and their purposes.

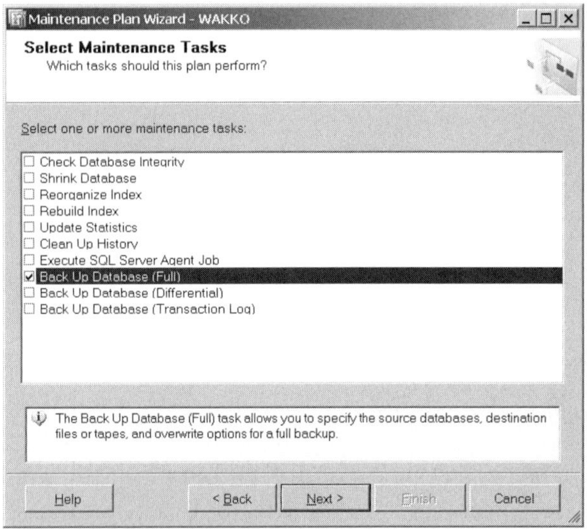

Figure 14-10 Specifying job tasks

Table 14-1 Maintenance Tasks

Task	Purpose
Pointer	Changes the cursor to a point on the design surface
Backup Database Task	Performs a full, differential, or transaction log backup
Check Database Integrity Task	Checks database integrity
Execute SQL Server Agent Job Task	Executes a SQL Server Agent job
Execute T-SQL Statement Task	Executes the specified Transact-SQL statement
History Cleanup Task	Cleans up the job history
Maintenance Cleanup Task	Cleans up backups and reports

Table 14-1   Maintenance Tasks

Task	Purpose
Notify Operator Task	Sends a notification to an operator
Rebuild Index Task	Rebuilds one or more indexes
Reorganize Index Task	Reorganizes one or more indexes
Shrink Database Task	Shrinks a database
Update Statistics Task	Updates the statistics on one or more tables and indexes

NOTE   Each backup plan has only one task

The most common tasks to perform in a maintenance plan are backups. You will never execute full, differential, and transaction log backups on the same schedule. Unfortunately, because you can specify only one schedule for the entire maintenance plan, each backup maintenance plan that you create will have only one task defined within it.

Click Next to display the Select Maintenance Task Order page. Because a maintenance plan can contain multiple tasks, you can specify the execution order for these tasks, as shown in Figure 14-11.

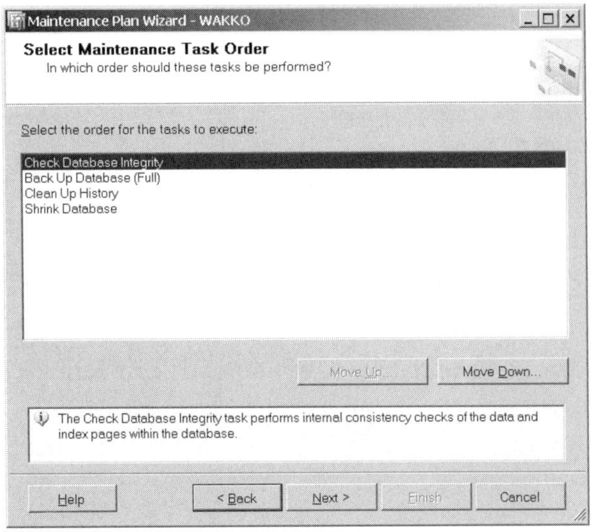

Figure 14-11   Specifying task order

NOTE Can't execute multiple tasks on same schedule

Remember that when creating a maintenance plan, you are in essence creating an SSIS package, so you are defining the flow control definition within the SSIS package. However, you will not be executing multiple maintenance tasks on the same schedule, so this step in the wizard is superfluous.

Depending on the maintenance task you select, the options that you can specify at this point in the wizard vary. If you select a maintenance plan for a database backup, you'll see the option to select the databases to apply the task to, as shown in Figure 14-12.

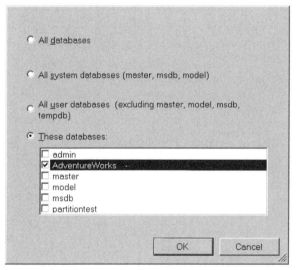

Figure 14-12 Specifying databases to back up

After you select the check box for the databases you want to back up, click OK. You can then specify the folder in which you want to store the backups, along with whether you want to verify the backup integrity, as Figure 14-13 shows. Click Next.

When you have specified all the appropriate task options, you can define a schedule, as shown in Figure 14-14. To access scheduling options, click Change.

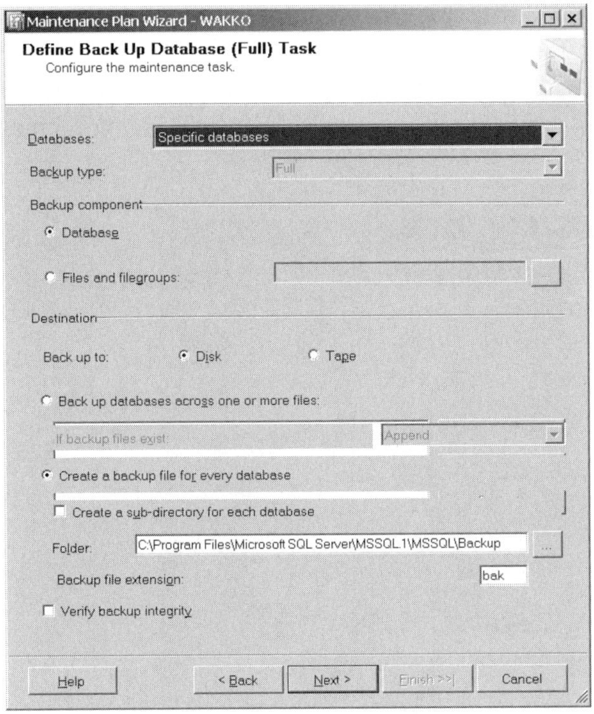

Figure 14-13 Specifying backup options

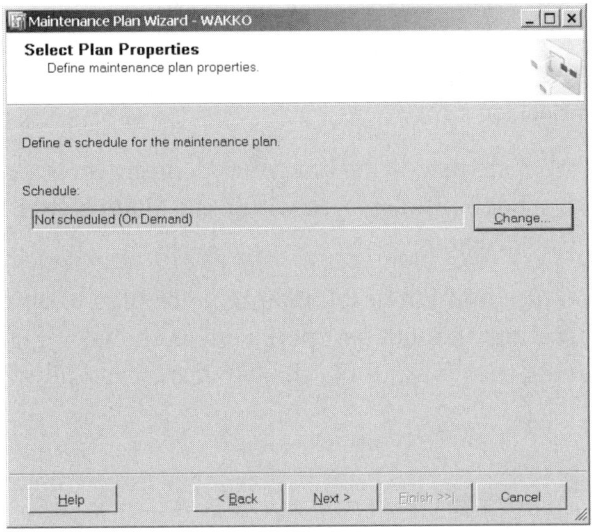

Figure 14-14 Defining one schedule for the entire maintenance plan

The scheduling options available are the same as when you are scheduling a SQL Server Agent job (see Figure 14-15). The difference is that for a regular SQL Server Agent job, you can define multiple schedules for a regular job and reuse previously created job schedules, but you can define only one schedule for a maintenance plan.

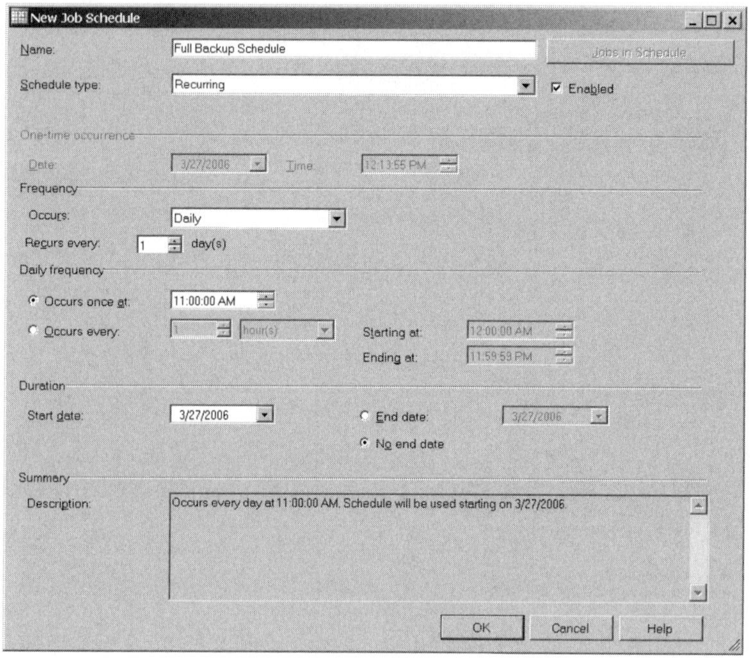

Figure 14-15   Specifying scheduling options

Click OK to close the New Job Schedule dialog box. After defining the schedule, you see a summary of the scheduling options displayed within the Maintenance Plan Wizard, as Figure 14-16 shows. Click Next.

For reporting purposes, you can configure each maintenance plan to write an output file or to e-mail the report about the actions it performs, as shown in Figure 14-17. You will usually specify writing to an output file that you can scan for errors. Click Next.

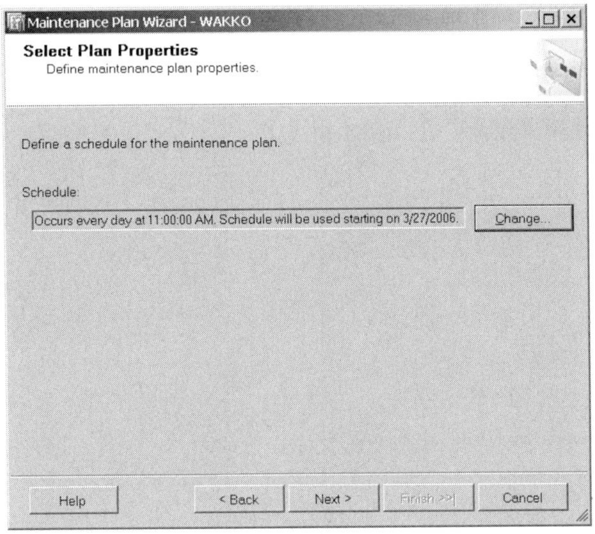

Figure 14-16   Single schedule definition for the maintenance plan

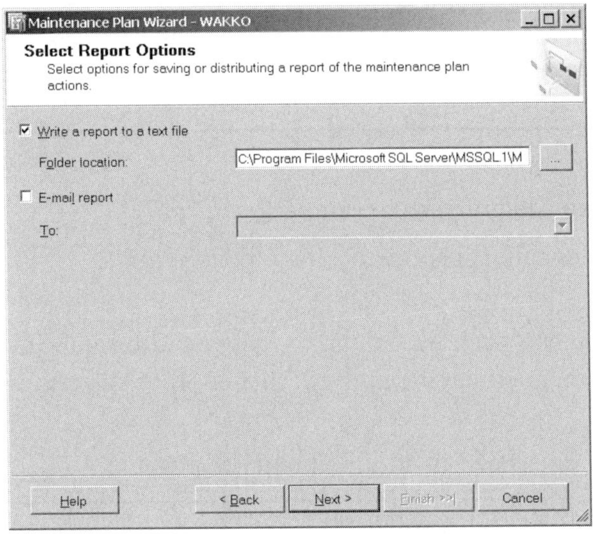

Figure 14-17   Specifying reporting options

At this point, you have completed the creation of a maintenance plan, and the wizard asks you to verify your choices, as Figure 14-18 shows. When you click Finish, the wizard performs the following steps:

1. Generates an SSIS package.

2. Stores that SSIS package within the *msdb* database.

3. Creates a job in SQL Server Agent to execute the maintenance plan.

4. Creates entries in the *sys.dbmaintplan** tables within the *msdb* database.

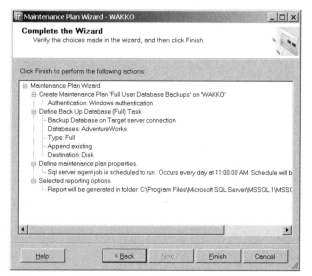

Figure 14-18   Finishing maintenance plan creation

Quick Check

1. What operations can a maintenance plan perform?

2. How many schedules can you apply to a maintenance plan?

Quick Check Answers

1. A maintenance plan can back up databases, delete old backup files from the operating system, maintain indexes, execute another job, and shrink a database.

2. You can apply only one schedule to a maintenance plan.

PRACTICE Create a Maintenance Job

In this exercise, you will practice the creation of a maintenance plan to back up the *AdventureWorks* database. Instead of using the Maintenance Plan Wizard to create the maintenance plan, you will define it from a generic maintenance plan.

1. In SSMS, right-click the Maintenance Plans node in Object Explorer and choose New Maintenance Plan.

2. Specify a name for the maintenance plan and click OK.

3. Click the browser button (...) to the right of the Schedule text box.

4. Configure the maintenance plan to run once per day at 23:00, or 11:00 PM. When you're done, click OK to close the Job Schedule Properties dialog box.

5. Click Connections to open the Manage Connections dialog box. Click Add and specify the server connection options. Click OK to save your changes and then click OK again to close the Manage Connections dialog box.

6. Click Logging and configure the logging options you want to use for this plan.

7. In the Maintenance Plan Tasks toolbox, drag and drop the Back Up Database Task onto the surface of the maintenance plan.

8. Double-click the Back Up Database Task and specify the *AdventureWorks* database to perform a full backup. Click OK to close the Back Up Database Task dialog box.

9. Drag and drop a Maintenance Cleanup Task onto the surface of the maintenance plan.

10. Select the Back Up Database Task.

11. Drag the green arrow from the Back Up Database Task to the Maintenance Cleanup Task, which creates a dependency between the two tasks so that the backup task runs first and the cleanup task runs second.

12. Double-click the Maintenance Cleanup Task and specify saving the backups for one day. When you're done, click OK to close the Maintenance Cleanup Task dialog box.

13. Click Save on the toolbar to save your maintenance plan.

Lesson Summary

- A maintenance plan enables you to graphically configure SQL Server to perform one or more predefined maintenance tasks on a scheduled basis against one or more databases.

- The most common type of maintenance plan that you will create is to back up a database on a regular basis.

- Each maintenance plan is a monolithic SSIS package that can have only one schedule defined for it.

Lesson Review

The following questions are intended to reinforce key information presented in this lesson. The questions are also available on the companion CD if you prefer to review them in electronic form.

NOTE   Answers

Answers to these questions and explanations of why each answer choice is right or wrong are located in the "Answers" section at the end of the book.

---

1. What types of tasks can you define with the Maintenance Plan Wizard? (Choose all that apply.)

    A.   Database creation

    B.   Database backup

    C.   Index rebuilding

    D.   SSIS package execution

Lesson 3: Configuring Operators

The SQL Server Agent subsystem enables you to define *operators* to receive notifications about jobs. You can use this mechanism to enable SQL Server Agent to send a notice when a job has failed, for example, alerting DBAs so that they can quickly evaluate and repair problems.

After this lesson, you will be able to:

■ Configure operators.

Estimated lesson time: 10 minutes

How to Configure an Operator

You configure an operator by naming it and specifying various notification methods for the operator and other parameters, such as an e-mail address to send the notification to. To begin the configuration, in SSMS, right-click the Operators node below SQL Server Agent, and choose New Operator to define properties for an operator, as Figure 14-19 shows.

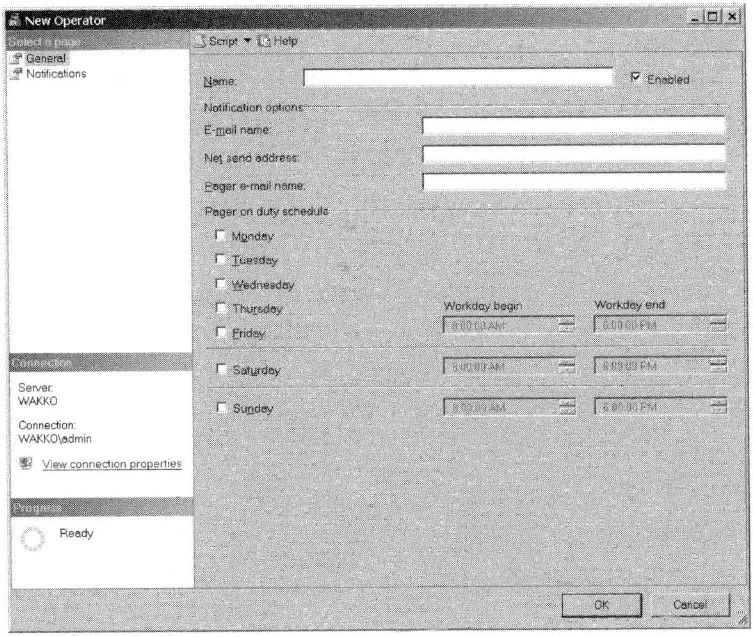

Figure 14-19   Defining operator parameters

Each operator needs a name. You then specify which notification methods—e-mail, net send, and pager—are valid for that operator.

NOTE Enable the Messenger Service

In order to use a net send, the Messenger Service must be enabled.

You specify addresses or numbers for each valid notification method. In addition, you can configure an operator to receive notifications only during specific on-duty hours.

NOTE Specifying a work week

Unfortunately, the graphical user interface (GUI) assumes that the work week is Monday through Friday for everyone in the world.

Selecting the Notifications page displays all jobs and alerts for which a particular operator is configured to receive notifications. Click OK to create the operator.

Quick Check

■ Which notification methods are valid for an operator?

Quick Check Answer

■ You can notify an operator using net send, e-mail, or text messaging.

Managing and Troubleshooting Jobs

You can manage SQL Server Agent jobs within SSMS. To access the list of jobs that are configured on an instance, expand the SQL Server Agent node within SSMS, right-click the Job Activity Monitor item, and choose View Job Activity. The Job Activity Monitor displays a list of the jobs for the instance, along with the date and time the job was last run and the next date and time the job will run.

The Job Activity Monitor also displays whether the job is enabled and whether the last run was successful. You can enable, disable, start, and stop a job by right-clicking it within the job activity grid. The shortcut menu also enables you to access the detailed history for a particular job, including any error messages that might have occurred during job execution.

PRACTICE **Configuring Operators**

In this practice, you will configure an operator to receive e-mail notifications.

1. Expand the SQL Server Agent node.

2. Right-click Operators and choose New Operator.

3. Specify a name for the operator.

4. Specify an e-mail address for the operator.

5. Click OK.

NOTE Sending e-mail

To send e-mail to this operator, you must enable and configure Database Mail. Because text messaging also relies on the mail subsystem, it also requires you to configure Database Mail. For information about configuring Database Mail, see Lesson 2, "Configuring Database Mail," in Chapter 2, "Configuring SQL Server 2005."

Lesson Summary

■ SQL Server Agent enables you to define operators to receive notifications from jobs via e-mail, net send, or pager.

■ Operators provide a convenient way to refer to one or more messaging addresses by a single name.

■ To send e-mail or text messages, you need to have SQL Server Database Mail configured and enabled.

Lesson Review

The following questions are intended to reinforce key information presented in this lesson. The questions are also available on the companion CD if you prefer to review them in electronic form.

NOTE Answers

Answers to these questions and explanations of why each answer choice is right or wrong are located in the "Answers" section at the end of the book.

---

1. Which notification methods are available for an operator? (Choose all that apply.)

   A. cell phone

   B. pager

   C. e-mail

   D. instant messaging

Lesson 4: Configuring Alerts

The *alert* subsystem within SQL Server Agent enables you to notify administrators when specific conditions within an environment are met. SQL Server Agent polls the system on a periodic basis to check for any alert conditions.

> **After this lesson, you will be able to:**
> - Configure alerts.
>
> **Estimated lesson time: 10 minutes**

How to Configure Alerts

The high-level steps for configuring alerts are the following:

1. Create a new alert.

2. Select a type of alert.

3. Configure conditions to monitor.

4. Define an action to be taken when a condition is met.

5. Define additional messaging options.

You find SQL Server alerts in a node under SQL Server Agent. To configure a new alert, right-click the Alerts node and choose New Alert. All alerts should have a name associated with them that describes the purpose of the alert. You also define an alert as based on one of three types of events: performance condition, SQL Server event, or Windows Management Instrumentation (WMI) event.

You base a performance-condition alert on a performance counter. You can specify only one performance counter for an alert, so if you need something more sophisticated that uses multiple counters, you cannot use a SQL Server alert. The example that Figure 14-20 shows specifies an alert condition when the percentage of the transaction log space used in the *AdventureWorks* database exceeds 80 percent.

You base a SQL Server event alert on either an error code or a severity level, as shown in Figure 14-21. You can further refine the particular alert by restricting it to errors that contain a specific string within the error text.

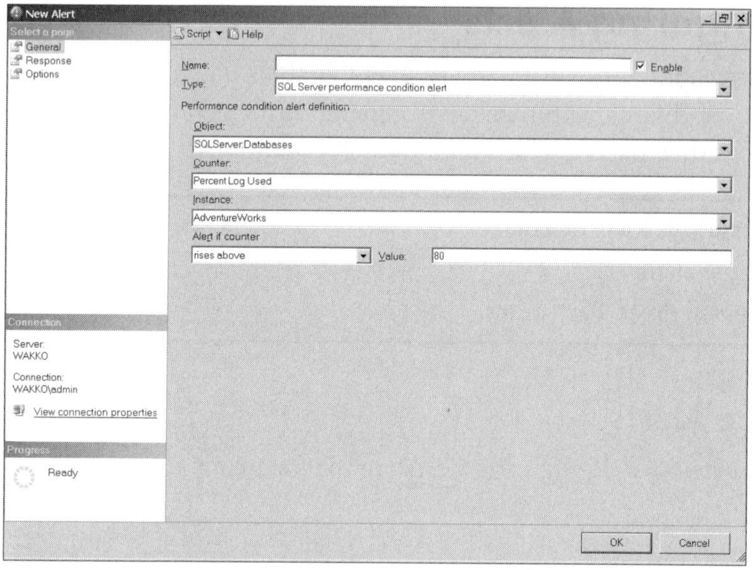

Figure 14-20   Specifying alert parameters for a SQL Server performance condition

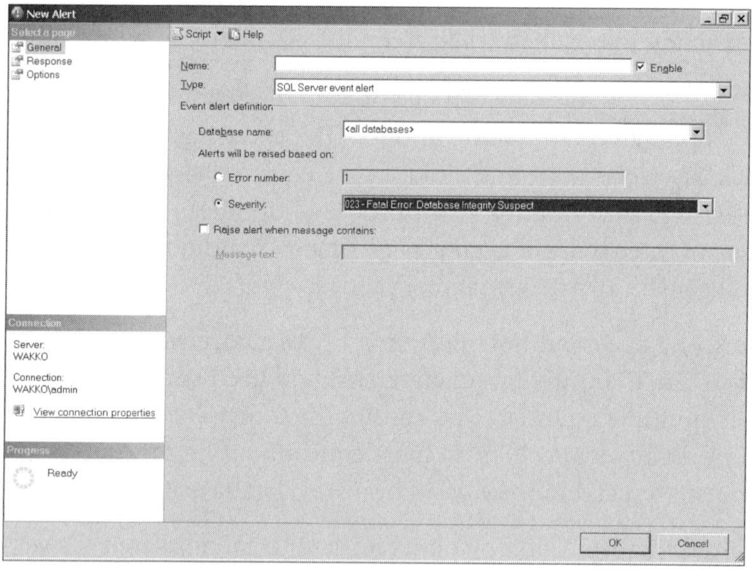

Figure 14-21   Specifying alert parameters for a SQL Server event

Figure 14-22 shows the final type of alert you can create: a WMI event. For this type of alert, you specify a predefined notification query for SQL Server Agent to use or enter your own custom notification query.

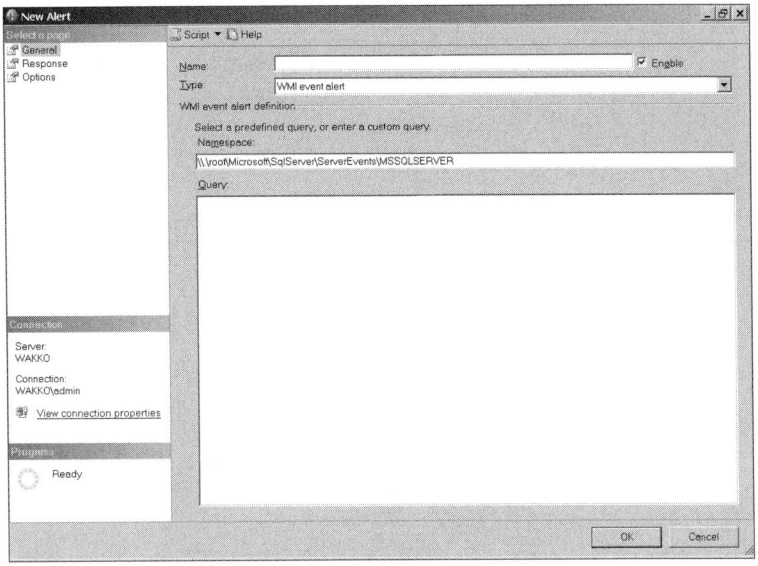

Figure 14-22   Specifying alert parameters for a WMI event

When SQL Server detects that a condition specified by the alert is met, it raises the alert and executes a response based on the response configuration you define. The response to an alert can be as simple as notifying an operator by e-mail, pager, or the net send command. In some scenarios, you can configure SQL Server to respond by executing a job that contains a set of steps designed to address the particular alert event.

If the response to an alert is to notify an operator, you can specify additional options for the notification, as Figure 14-23 shows.

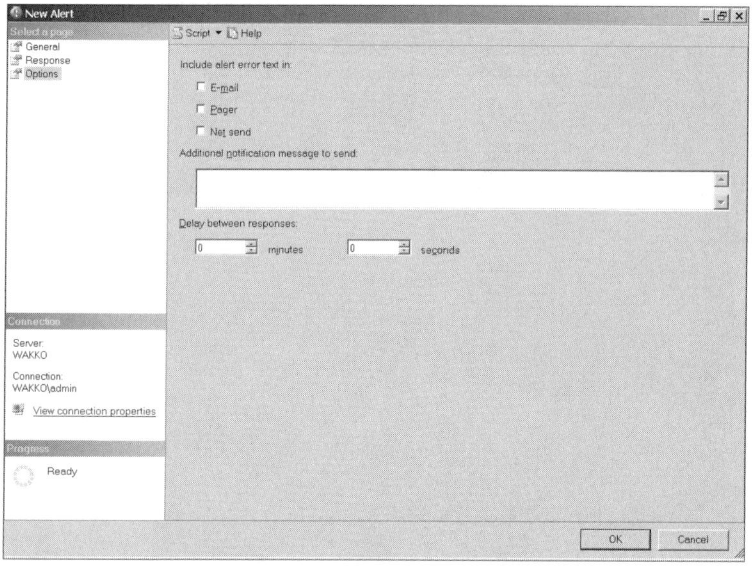

Figure 14-23   Specifying alert options

Quick Check

■ What types of alerts can you define?

Quick Check Answer

■ You can define alerts for a single SQL Server performance counter, SQL Server error code, error severity level, or WMI event.

PRACTICE **Configure Alerts**

In this exercise, you will practice the creation of an alert to notify an operator when the *AdventureWorks* database has a fatal integrity error.

1.   Open the SQL Server Agent node in SSMS.

2.   Right-click Alerts and choose New Alert.

3.   Enter a name for the alert.

4.   In the Type drop-down list, verify that a SQL Server Event Alert is selected.

5.   From the Database Name drop-down list, select the *AdventureWorks* database.

6.   From the Severity drop-down list, select 023–Fatal Error: Database Integrity Suspect.

7. Select the Response page.

8. Select the Notify Operators check box.

9. In the Operator List, select an operator to notify by selecting the operator's E-Mail, Pager, or Net Send check boxes.

10. Select the Options page.

11. Select the E-Mail check box to configure the alert to include the error information in the e-mail it sends to operators.

12. Click OK to save the alert.

Lesson Summary

- Alerts provide a basic monitoring capability within SQL Server.

- You can monitor SQL Server for alert conditions related to performance counters, error codes, error severity levels, or WMI events.

- When an alert is triggered, you can send a notification or configure the alert to execute a SQL Server Agent job that will resolve the situation.

Lesson Review

The following questions are intended to reinforce key information presented in this lesson. The questions are also available on the companion CD if you prefer to review them in electronic form.

NOTE Answers

Answers to these questions and explanations of why each answer choice is right or wrong are located in the "Answers" section at the end of the book.

---

1. What types of alerts can you define? (Choose all that apply.)

   A. Performance conditions for CPU utilization

   B. Performance conditions for SQL Server

   C. Security permissions being changed for a login

   D. Errors generated by an application

Chapter Review

To further practice and reinforce the skills you learned in this chapter, you can

- Review the chapter summary.
- Review the list of key terms introduced in this chapter.
- Complete the case scenario. This scenario sets up a real-world situation involving the topics of this chapter and asks you to create solutions.
- Complete the suggested practices.
- Take a practice test.

Chapter Summary

- SQL Server Agent provides a powerful and flexible scheduling engine within SQL Server.
- By using the capabilities exposed in SQL Server Agent, you can configure operations to automatically execute on a scheduled basis without requiring user intervention.
- You can use the Database Maintenance Plan Wizard to define maintenance tasks, such as database backups or reindexing tasks, to perform against one or more databases.
- You can configure operators to receive notifications such as job failure via e-mail, net send, or pager.
- By combining alerts with the job subsystem, you can use SQL Server Agent to monitor the system for conditions that you specify and then to execute jobs to proactively address potential issues.

Key Terms

Do you know what these key terms mean? You can check your answers by looking up the terms in the glossary at the end of the book.

- alert
- job
- job schedule
- job step

- maintenance job
- maintenance plan
- operator
- SQL Server Agent proxy

Case Scenario: Scheduling Administrative Actions

In the following case scenario, you will apply what you've learned in this chapter. You can find answers to these questions in the "Answers" section at the end of this book.

Contoso Limited, a health care company located in Bothell, WA, has a volatile database containing patient claims data. Contoso is under strict regulation and is required to protect all customer data within a database.

Government regulations allow for minimal data loss in the event of a natural disaster. In the case of Contoso, minimal data loss is defined as no more than 10 minutes of data loss.

In addition, Contoso needs to ensure that performance within its patient claims database is optimal.

Each evening, Contoso receives data feeds from several external vendors that process payments to patients. Frequently, data in the feeds needs to be edited and reimported based on validation scripts that reconcile the data within the patient claims database with the data feeds submitted by the external vendors. While the import processes execute, no other transactions are issued against the patient claims database. The current process creates a full backup of the patient claims database at 23:00 before the import routines are executed.

Contoso also executes a full database backup at 06:00. The exact time that this backup executes is not important as long as it executes before business operations begin for the day.

At 04:00 each day, the system administrators at Contoso shut down the SQL Servers to perform routine maintenance such as applying service packs and hotfixes to the operating system and other software on the server.

Contoso wants to improve its backup strategy to ensure that government regulations are met, as well as requiring a maximum of eight restore operations to recover a database.

1. How does Contoso guarantee that a full backup is created before the patient claims import routines are executed?

2. How do the Contoso DBAs guarantee that a full backup is performed before business operations start in the morning?

3. What backup strategy should be implemented to ensure that a database can be recovered with a maximum of eight restore operations?

Suggested Practices

To help you successfully master the exam objectives presented in this chapter, complete the following tasks.

Create a SQL Server Agent job

For this task, practice creating the following jobs:

■ **Practice 1**   Create a job to perform a differential backup of the *AdventureWorks* database twice per day—at 23:00 and 16:00.

■ **Practice 2**   Create a job to perform a transaction log backup of the *Adventure-Works* database every 10 minutes.

Create a Maintenance Plan

For this task, practice creating the following maintenance plans:

■ **Practice 1**   Using the Maintenance Plan Wizard, create a maintenance plan to perform a differential backup of the *AdventureWorks* database twice per day—at 11:00 and 16:00.

■ **Practice 2**   Using the Maintenance Plan Wizard, create a maintenance plan to perform a transaction log backup of the *AdventureWorks* database every 10 minutes.

Create an Alert

For this task, practice creating the following alert:

■ **Practice 1**   Create an alert to notify an operator when there is a table-integrity error.

Take a Practice Test

The practice tests on this book's companion CD offer many options. For example, you can test yourself on just the content covered in this chapter, or you can test yourself on all the 70-431 certification exam content. You can set up the test so that it closely simulates the experience of taking a certification exam, or you can set it up in study mode so that you can look at the correct answers and explanations after you answer each question.

MORE INFO Practice tests

For details about all the practice test options available, see the "How to Use the Practice Tests" section in this book's Introduction.

Chapter 15

Monitoring and Troubleshooting SQL Server Performance

Monitoring and troubleshooting Microsoft SQL Server is a broad topic that spans a variety of tools and processes. All database administrators (DBAs) eventually face performance issues or errors they have to resolve. In addition, effective monitoring can help DBAs proactively address many issues before they affect applications, users, or customers. This chapter covers the various tools that you can use to monitor the health of your databases, including SQL Server Profiler, Windows System Monitor, the Database Engine Tuning Advisor (DTA), and SQL Server 2005 Dynamic Management Views (DMVs) and Dynamic Management Functions (DMFs). You will also explore the processes for correlating various pieces of data from these tools together to proactively manage databases. A key element in troubleshooting performance problems is understanding SQL Server locking and blocking mechanisms and how to resolve deadlocks, which this chapter also covers. And you will see how to connect to SQL Server via the new dedicated administrator connection (DAC), which guarantees that you will never be locked out of a SQL Server that you need to troubleshoot.

MORE INFO **SQL Server performance monitoring and troubleshooting**

Many books have been devoted to the topic of SQL Server performance monitoring and troubleshooting. This chapter gives you an overview of essential tools and processes and gets you started with the basic and most tried-and-true techniques for finding and resolving performance problems. For complete information about each topic in this chapter, see SQL Server 2005 Books Online. SQL Server 2005 Books Online is installed as part of SQL Server 2005. Updates for SQL Server 2005 Books Online are available for download at *www.microsoft.com/technet/prodtechnol/sql/2005/downloads/books.mspx*.

MORE INFO **Top performance Web sites**

You can also obtain a wealth of performance information from the following valuable Web resources:

- Microsoft SQL Server Customer Advisory Team blog at *http://blogs.msdn.com/sqlcat/*
- Gert Draper's SQLDEV.Net Web site at *www.sqldev.net*, which contains useful utilities and background information

Both these Web sites should be in your Favorites list.

Exam objectives in this chapter:

- Gather performance and optimization data by using the SQL Server Profiler.
    - ❏ Start a new trace.
    - ❏ Save the trace logs.
    - ❏ Configure SQL Server Profiler trace properties.
    - ❏ Configure a System Monitor counter log.
    - ❏ Correlate a SQL Server Profiler trace with System Monitor log data.
- Gather performance and optimization data by using the Database Engine Tuning Advisor.
    - ❏ Build a workload file by using SQL Server Profiler.
    - ❏ Tune a workload file by using the Database Engine Tuning Advisor.
    - ❏ Save recommended indexes.
- Monitor and resolve blocks and deadlocks.
    - ❏ Identify the cause of a block by using the sys.dm_exec_requests system view.
    - ❏ Terminate an errant process.
    - ❏ Configure SQL Server Profiler trace properties.
    - ❏ Identify transaction blocks.
- Diagnose and resolve database server errors.
    - ❏ Connect to a nonresponsive server by using the dedicated administrator connection (DAC).
    - ❏ Review SQL Server startup logs.
    - ❏ Review error messages in event logs.
- Gather performance and optimization data by using DMVs.

Lessons in this chapter:

Before You Begin

To complete the lessons in this chapter, you must have

- SQL Server 2005 installed.
- A copy of the *AdventureWorks* sample database installed in the instance.

Real World

Michael Hotek

The phone rang at 12:30, just as I was heading out for a lunch meeting with a customer. We were going to discuss a possible week-long project to analyze the customer's application for performance issues. It was the customer on the other end of the line.

His ordering system couldn't accept orders. The servers were running, and SQL Server was online. Queries were coming in, but they were taking so long to execute that applications were timing out or customers were going elsewhere. So, 30 minutes later, I was in the company's office instead of at lunch.

While I was driving to the office, I asked the DBAs to launch a SQL Server Profiler trace to begin gathering data. After I reached the office, we saved the current trace data and began the analysis process. We immediately found two stored procedures that were creating most of the issues—but not all of them.

We also found that someone in the marketing department had connected Microsoft Office Access to the company's production database and was running several queries. Unfortunately, the marketing staffer had neglected to join tables together and was executing cross joins instead. Of course, no one in the company would admit to running any queries against production data. After removing the marketing department user's access, customers could suddenly complete orders, but performance was still an issue.

Based on our Profiler traces, we tuned the two procedures that were degrading performance the most. Although these quick fixes didn't solve all of the company's performance issues, which we resolved over the next three weeks, they did patch the performance problems enough that customers could complete orders on the company's Web site instead of taking their business to the competitors.

Lesson 1: Working with SQL Server Profiler

SQL Server Profiler is a powerful but rarely used tool for analyzing database performance issues. By using Profiler to capture traces of database activity, you can analyze query patterns to detect performance problems even before applications are affected. This lesson describes Profiler's role and how to use it to configure *traces* that capture the information you need to resolve performance issues. You will see how to save a trace in a format that enables you to perform advanced analysis and how various trace options affect the data that Profiler gathers. Note that Profiler captures only SQL Server events, not operating system or networking conditions that might be affecting database performance.

After this lesson, you will be able to:

- Define a trace.
- Start, pause, and stop a trace.
- Save a trace log.
- Gather showplan data.
- Create a replay trace.

Estimated lesson time: 45 minutes

Defining a Trace

Inside the database engine, SQL Server provides an event subsystem called *SQL Trace* that is based on an external application programming interface (API). This external API enables you to call SQL Trace by using a variety of parameters that define events and columns of data to capture. The SQL Trace subsystem also enables you to specify optional filters on the data being captured so that you can focus your analysis.

Although you can write the call to SQL Trace by using Transact-SQL code or *SQL Server Management Object (SMO)*, the most common way to work with the SQL Trace API is through the SQL Server Profiler graphical user interface (GUI). Let's look at how to define a trace within Profiler.

You launch SQL Server Profiler from the SQL Server 2005 Performance Tools menu. After it opens, choose File, New Trace. A connection dialog box appears. Connect to the SQL Server instance in which the sample *AdventureWorks* database is installed. You then see the Trace Definition dialog box shown in Figure 15-1.

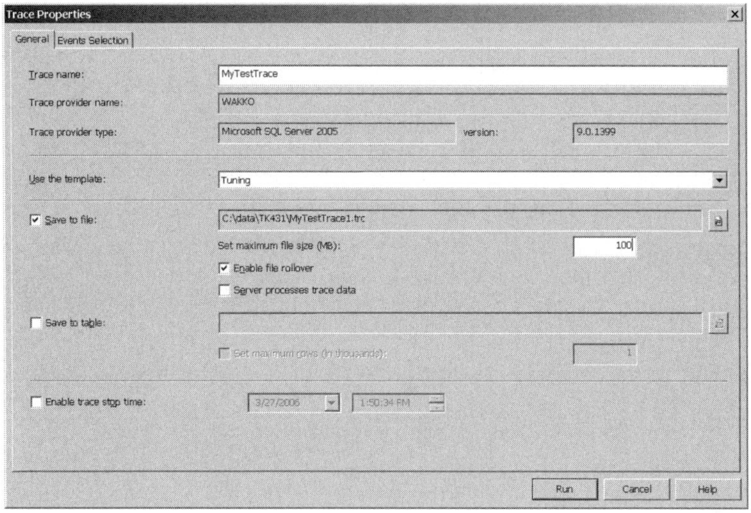

Figure 15-1   Defining the basic attributes for a trace

Each trace that you define must first have a name associated with it. Use a descriptive name that enables you to identify the trace.

Profiler ships with several trace templates designed for common monitoring operations. You can start with a blank template and define all your own options, start from a predefined trace template and then customize the options, or use a predefined trace template without modification. Profiler also enables you to define your own template, save it, and then reuse it.

BEST PRACTICES   Start with a predefined template

Although you can start from scratch and define your own blank template, it is much easier to start with a predefined template. The two most common templates for Profiler traces are Tuning and TSQL_Replay.

You can have the trace data displayed only on the screen within Profiler, saved to a file (SQL Server saves the data in binary format), or saved to a table. If you choose to save to a file or a table, Profiler also displays the data, so traces are rarely displayed only on the screen.

When you specify a file to save the trace data to, you can specify three optional parameters. Setting a maximum size for the trace file enables you to generate trace files that are of a manageable size. The maximum file size setting is always used in conjunction with enabling file rollover. With file rollover enabled, Profiler automatically closes out one file when the maximum size is reached and begins filling a new file. The naming convention for a series of trace files is *<filename>_nx*.trc, where *nx* is a number that starts at 1 and increments infinitely. You can also specify whether Profiler will process the trace or whether the server will process the trace.

BEST PRACTICES   Saving trace data to a file

When I specify a maximum file size, I usually use 500-MB files. This size file is small enough for me to quickly and easily copy or import. And it also captures a large enough amount of data per file so that the number of rollover files is minimal, even when I run traces for an extended period of time on very busy systems.

I never use the option for the server to process the trace. Running a trace against a live SQL Server imposes a performance load due to the active monitoring that is occurring. When the server processes the trace, no events are dropped—even if it means sacrificing server performance to capture all events. Whereas if Profiler is processing the trace, it will skip events if the server gets too busy. I've never seen skipping events to pose an issue because I am not looking for a single event but for a pattern of events over time.

You also have the option to save the trace data directly to a table in SQL Server. When you specify this option, Profiler prompts you to connect to a SQL Server and then specify a table name to store the trace data in.

CAUTION   Avoid saving trace data to a table

It is strongly recommended that you do not choose the option to save trace data to a table. SQL Trace can generate hundreds of thousands of rows of trace data per minute on busy servers. Saving this data directly to a table as it is processed incurs a severe performance penalty. When loading the data into a table, the transaction load can easily be enough to completely saturate the processing on a SQL Server. As you will see in a moment, there are other less-invasive ways to load trace data into a table.

You can enable a trace stop time, which specifies when the trace should be automatically stopped and closed. But you can configure this option only when you are programmatically creating and executing traces.

MORE INFO   Programmatic trace generation

Programmatic generation of traces is beyond the scope of this book, but you can find a wealth of information about this topic by using your favorite search engine.

After you specify how you want to see the trace data, you can click the Events Selection tab, which displays a screen similar to the one shown in Figure 15-2.

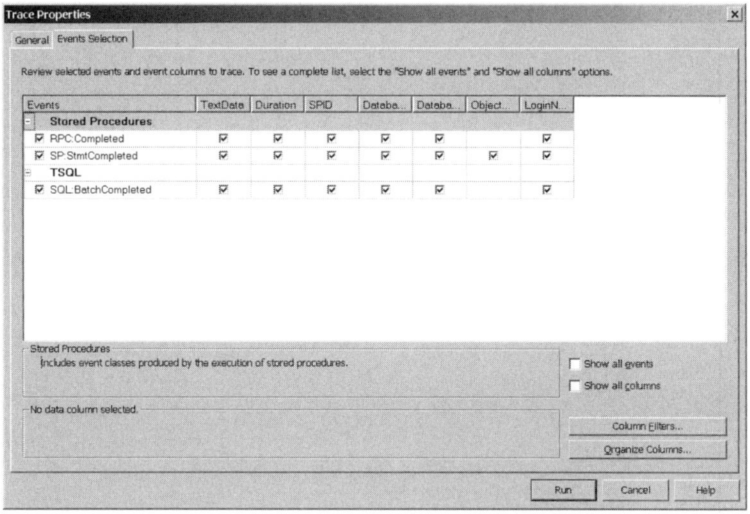

Figure 15-2   Specifying trace events and data columns

Selecting the *trace events* and data columns to capture is the most important step in defining a trace. Omissions at this stage require you to redefine a trace, while gathering too many events can cause you to be completely overwhelmed with data.

CAUTION   Avoid too much data

You never want to set up a trace that gathers all events and all data columns. Such a trace generates so much data that it becomes useless. It can also bring a SQL Server to a halt. Instead, you should start with broad categories related to what you want to investigate and then narrow down your criteria so that you are targeting at a fairly granular level.

Selecting the trace template called Tuning (refer to Figure 15-1) causes a default selection of events and data columns, as Figure 15-2 shows. You can then add other events and select additional data columns. To access all the events that you can define, you can select the Show All Events check box. To display all the columns that you can capture, you can select the Show All Columns check box.

NOTE   *SP: StmtCompleted* and *SP: StmtStarting* events

You should specify the *SP: StmtCompleted* or *SP: StmtStarting* event only after you have narrowed the focus of your trace. These events capture every statement executed within a stored procedure. On high-volume systems, capturing every statement can quickly generate extremely large trace logs.

Note that the trace defined in this lesson does not include any additional events, but it does contain several more columns of data beyond what the default Tuning template specifies. I have added the columns for CPU, Reads, Writes, and RequestID; you will see why later in this chapter.

After you select the events and data columns you want to capture, you can apply filters to your trace to limit the scope of the data that is returned. You specify filters in the same way that you enter criteria for a *LIKE* clause in Transact-SQL. To set filters for a trace, click Column Filters to display the Edit Filter dialog box that is shown in Figure 15-3.

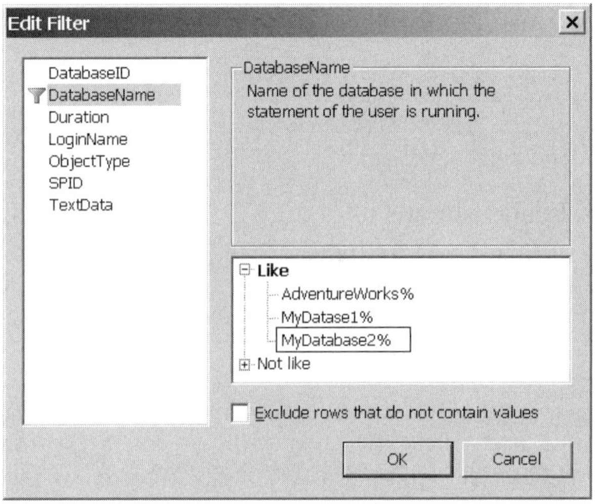

Figure 15-3 Specifying trace filter criteria

BEST PRACTICES Filters

By default, the default Profiler trace templates do not specify any filters. However, it is recommended that you specify filters to target data for your application. Using filters can eliminate all the background processes that issue queries to the system databases. Filters also enable you to isolate your monitoring to a particular database or database-related activity for a single application.

By clicking Organize Columns, you can specify the display order for data within the grid in Profiler. This does not change the internal storage order for the trace data. Figure 15-4 shows the Organize Columns dialog box.

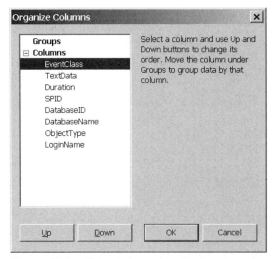

Figure 15-4   Change the order of columns as they are displayed in Profiler.

MORE INFO   **Events and Data Columns**

For a complete list of events and data columns available for capture, see the SQL Server 2005 Books Online articles "SQL Server Event Class Reference" and "Describing Events by Using Data Columns."

At this point, the trace is fully defined. All you need to do is start the trace and begin gathering data. Click Run to launch the trace. Figures 15-5 and 15-6 show a running trace.

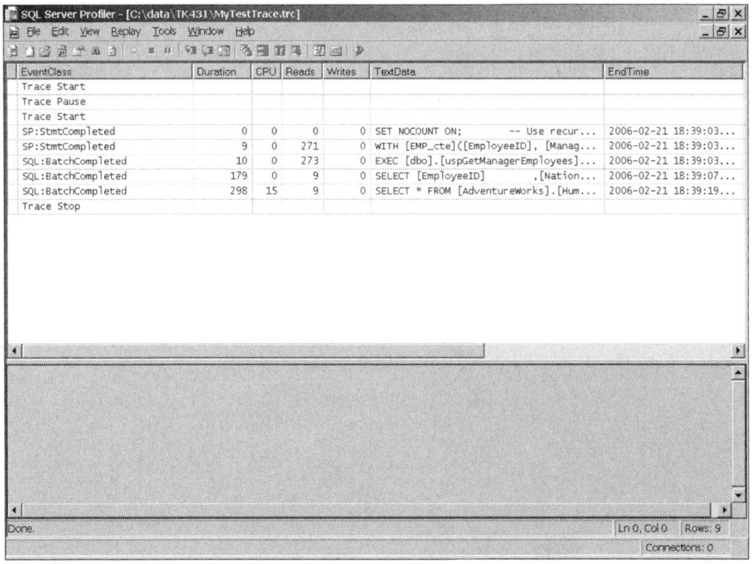

Figure 15-5   Running a trace against an active database

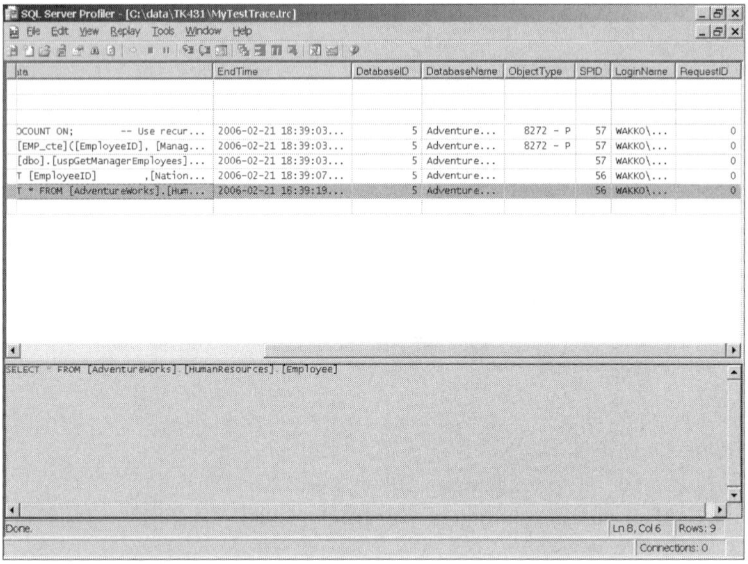

Figure 15-6   Continuation of a tuning trace against AdventureWorks

Starting, Pausing, and Stopping a Trace

After a trace is running, you can control it from within Profiler. In the middle of the toolbar are buttons to start, pause, and stop a trace.

When you click Pause, the data gathering is suspended at the server level. Any events that occur while the trace is paused are not captured. Pausing a trace can be useful when you are looking at a trace in Profiler while data is being captured. Because of the speed at which Profiler logs the data into the grid, it becomes very difficult to look at individual pieces of data. So, you can pause the data capture so that you can investigate trace results for a particular query. Periodically pausing and then restarting a trace is common in the initial stages of investigation, letting DBAs or developers sample query activity to get an idea of where issues might be occurring. You can then redefine the trace with more targeted events and filters.

Stopping a trace closes the trace session. Although you can then restart the trace, the data capture is reset, and all previous data is discarded. Thus, you should stop a trace only when you are finished capturing all of the data you need.

> **Quick Check**
>
> - What capabilities does SQL Server Profiler provide DBAs and developers?
>
> **Quick Check Answer**
>
> - SQL Server Profiler provides a GUI interface to the SQL Trace API. SQL Trace lets DBAs and developers gather data on a variety of events as they occur within the server. They can then use the data gathered for these events to analyze performance or stability issues as well as to track down the causes of errors.

Saving a Trace Log

Capturing trace data has little value unless you can save it and use it as an input for further analysis. There are a variety of ways to save a trace definition or the data it generates.

Saving a Trace Definition

Most environments have traces running either continuously or on predefined intervals. The process of setting up, launching, and closing these traces is automated by using SQL Server Agent jobs. However, writing a trace is not a trivial process. So, you can take a shortcut and let Profiler do all the work for you. After you create a new trace inside Profiler that contains the events, data columns, and filters that you want, click Run and then immediately stop the trace. Under the File menu, go to the option Export, Script Trace Definition. You can use this option to generate a Transact-SQL batch to create a trace for either SQL Server 2005 or SQL Server 2000. You then use this batch as the basis for a stored procedure that SQL Server Agent calls to manage the trace.

Saving Trace Data

This lesson has already covered two methods for saving trace data: save to file and save to table. If during the trace definition you specified to save to a file or table, the trace data is already saved for you. However, you can explicitly write the contents of the grid inside Profiler to either a file or table by accessing the File, Save As, Trace File or File, Save As, Trace Table options. You can also save the trace data in an XML format that can then be parsed by another program.

BEST PRACTICES Saving to a table

The Profiler option to save trace data as a table has an interesting limitation that makes it impractical for production use. Profiler prompts you to create a new table; it does not let you save trace data into an existing table.

So, let's say you have created a trace for your server and specified file rollover. Your trace has been running for awhile and has generated 15 files. All 15 of these files are a single, contiguous trace. To save the trace data to a table, you would first have to open each file and save each to a separate table. After you save each file as a separate table, you would have to manually combine all 15 tables into a single table for analysis.

However, you can eliminate this process with a single line of code. *fn_trace_gettable* is a built-in function that returns the contents of a trace file in a tabular format. There is even an option to iteratively walk down all of the rollover files. Therefore, by creating a statement that performs a *SELECT * INTO <table> FROM fn_trace_gettable ('<filename>')* operation, you can have all 15 trace files loaded into a single table. Later in this chapter, we will see where this function becomes extremely important.

Pulling Out All Transact-SQL Captured by the Trace

Besides saving trace to a file or table, a third way of saving the captured trace data is to pull out all the Transact-SQL captured by the trace. This option is useful if you want to take particular statements and execute them against a test machine to perform further analysis. By selecting File, Export, Extract SQL Server Events, Extract Transact-SQL events, a file is generated that contains all the SQL captured during the trace. You can then load this file into a query window to use as a SQL source.

NOTE Inside SQL Server Management Studio (SSMS)

Most IT professionals using SQL Server perform all their tasks by using SQL Server Management Studio (SSMS). But have you ever wondered what statements SSMS actually executes when you click button X? Have you ever encountered an SSMS feature that did almost what you wanted but didn't quite meet your needs?

Because SQL Trace is an API interface that enables you to capture nearly any event that occurs inside the server, you can use SQL Server's own SQL Trace facility to tell you things about SQL Server. All you need to do is create a Profiler trace with a filter for SSMS. Then, when you execute an action inside SSMS, Profiler displays the Transact-SQL statements that were issued to perform that action. You can also use Profiler to trace what Analysis Services is doing, letting you extract MDX and DMX queries.

Gathering Showplan Data

One of the most critical factors for any analysis process is to have complete information that you can then compare to results on a test machine. For example, SQL Server can generate dramatically different query plans based on the volume of data in a table, skew of the data, statistics that have been automatically generated, index variations, or even which parameters were called for a stored procedure or function. It is common to find a problem query in production and then not be able to reproduce the problem in a test environment. One of the main causes of not being able to reproduce the problem on a test system is having a different query plan generated on the test system.

However, you can gather query plan information, called showplans, in a trace. A *showplan* provides a record of the query that was executed along with the plan that was generated for that execution. By capturing the showplan, you can compare the plans generated for multiple permutations of the same query to determine whether the plan changes over time. You can also use this information to analyze where the performance issues are occurring within the query.

To include showplan information in a trace, you would look under the Performance event class, which provides a variety of options. Figure 15-7 shows the Showplan All and Showplan XML events selected for the trace.

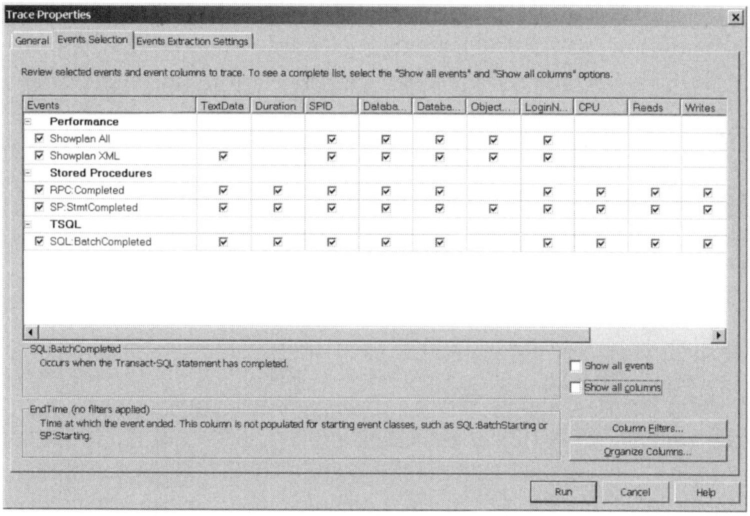

Figure 15-7   Specifying showplan events in a Profiler trace

The Showplan All event provides a text-based query plan in the output. The Showplan XML event, new in SQL Server 2005, provides an extremely powerful and very rich capture of performance data.

When you specify Showplan XML, an additional tab, called Events Extraction Settings, appears. This tab, shown in Figure 15-8, enables you to define special handling for the XML showplan.

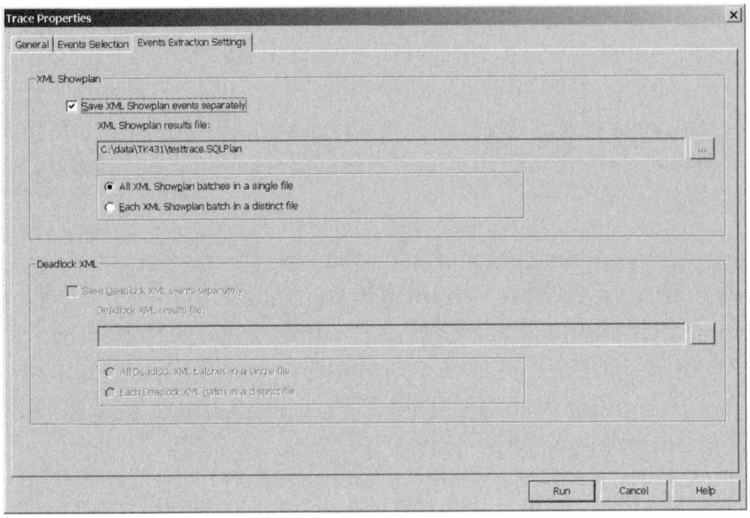

Figure 15-8 Configuring XML extraction handling

You generally leave the output of the Showplan XML event as just another data column in a trace instead of extracting it to a separate file. However, you can directly load Showplan XML data into SSMS and display it as a fully interactive diagram for analysis. This capability is especially useful when getting remote help in tuning a query.

Figure 15-9 shows a trace output with the Showplan XML event displayed.

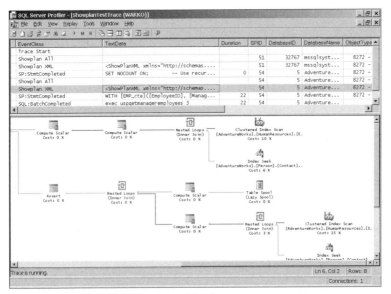

Figure 15-9 Capturing Showplan XML in a trace

Creating a Replay Trace

SQL Server provides a special type of trace called a *replay trace*, which enables you to capture a workload that you can then replay on a test system.

CAUTION **Synching the replay trace with a database backup**

Note that you must synchronize a backup of the database with the replay trace. This action is required because the replay reexecutes the same statements during the replay, and unless the database starts in the correct state, the replay creates many errors.

Profiler contains a multithreaded subsystem to handle the replay of a trace. And there are specific requirements that need to be met for the replay to succeed. You must use SQL Server authentication only and capture specific events as defined in the Replay template. The replay cannot handle Windows authentication because it does not have the ability to impersonate a Windows user.

When Profiler replays a trace, it spawns multiple execution threads that use the same security context as the original execution. Threads are also synchronized to provide a realistic duplication of the workload. The start time, end time, and system process ID (SPID) columns enable Profiler to re-create the exact interleaving of queries that occurred on the original system.

Figures 15-10 and 15-11 show the output for a replay trace.

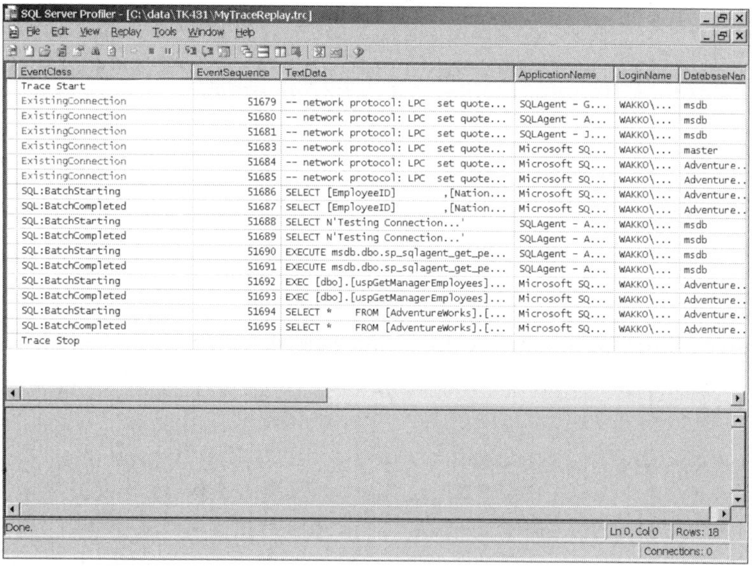

Figure 15-10 Capturing a replay trace

ne	ServerName	BinaryData	SPID	StartTime	EndTime	IsSystem	NTDomainNa...	NTUserNa...	Error
				2006-02-21 18:51:16...					
	WAKKO	0x20000...	51	2006-02-19 04:48:44...			WAKKO	admin	
	WAKKO	0x20000...	52	2006-02-19 04:49:15...			WAKKO	admin	
	WAKKO	0x20000...	53	2006-02-19 04:50:00...			WAKKO	admin	
	WAKKO	0x20000...	55	2006-02-21 18:36:18...			WAKKO	admin	
	WAKKO	0x60080...	56	2006-02-21 18:38:22...			WAKKO	admin	
	WAKKO	0x60080...	57	2006-02-21 18:37:24...			WAKKO	admin	
	WAKKO		56	2006-02-21 18:51:24...			WAKKO	admin	
	WAKKO		56	2006-02-21 18:51:24...	2006-02-21 18:51:24...		WAKKO	admin	0 ...
	WAKKO		52	2006-02-21 18:51:24...			WAKKO	admin	
	WAKKO		52	2006-02-21 18:51:24...	2006-02-21 18:51:24...		WAKKO	admin	0 ...
	WAKKO		52	2006-02-21 18:51:24...			WAKKO	admin	
	WAKKO		52	2006-02-21 18:51:24...	2006-02-21 18:51:24...		WAKKO	admin	0 ...
	WAKKO		57	2006-02-21 18:51:26...			WAKKO	admin	
	WAKKO		57	2006-02-21 18:51:26...	2006-02-21 18:51:26...		WAKKO	admin	0 ...
	WAKKO		56	2006-02-21 18:51:34...			WAKKO	admin	
	WAKKO		56	2006-02-21 18:51:34...	2006-02-21 18:51:34...		WAKKO	admin	0 ...
				2006-02-21 18:51:40...					

Figure 15-11 Continuation of a replay trace

You can replay traces by using the exact timing of the original or execute them without any delays. When you replay a trace by using the exact timing, if SQL Server did not receive any queries for a 15-minute time interval, the replay pauses for 15 minutes before executing the next statement in the trace. Executing without any delays removes this wait period.

A valuable use for this replay capability is to capture realistic workloads against your production environment and then run the workloads against test and quality assurance (QA) environments to enable a level of regression testing for any changes you introduce.

Real World

Michael Hotek

You may have heard about Microsoft's SQL Server Replay Lab. This lab participates in the regression testing of service packs and new versions as well as in various other testing processes. Hundreds of customers have provided database backups along with replay traces for Microsoft to use in the lab. Microsoft constantly replays these traces against new versions and service packs. The results of each run are compared to a baseline run to detect any anomalies. This process enables the SQL Server Development Team to test new code against real-world

---

workloads before releasing the code. The goal of this program is for Microsoft to ensure that it delivers code as bug-free as possible while also maintaining or improving performance with each new code iteration.

PRACTICE Configuring a Baseline Trace

In this practice, you will configure a baseline trace that you can use as the initial investigative trace for performance issues in the *AdventureWorks* database. This type of trace is generally the first step in the data-gathering process, letting you determine which additional filtering or events you need to add to focus on particular performance issues.

1. Launch SQL Server Profiler.

2. From the File menu, choose New Trace.

3. Connect to your SQL Server instance.

4. On the General tab, specify the following options:

   A. Name of the trace

   B. Blank template

   C. Save to file and use the default file name

   D. Maximum file size of 50 MB

   E. Enable file rollover

5. On the Events tab, select the check boxes for the following events:

   A. *SQL:BatchCompleted*

   B. *RPC:Completed*

   C. *Showplan XML*

6. Specify the following additional data columns:

   A. CPU

   B. Reads

   C. Writes

   D. Start Time

   E. End Time

7. Run the trace.

8. Using SSMS, execute several queries against the *AdventureWorks* database and observe what is captured in Profiler.

9. In SQL Server Profiler, stop the trace. Close Profiler.

Lesson Summary

- SQL Server Profiler provides a graphical interface to the SQL Trace API that enables you to capture data for events within SQL Server. You can then analyze the trace data to determine causes of performance degradation, blocking, deadlocking, or other error events.

- The first step in using Profiler to capture data is to define a trace by selecting the events and data columns to capture, choosing any filters you want to enable, and deciding whether you want to save the trace data to a file or table or just display it in Profiler.

- You can start, pause, and stop Profiler traces via buttons on the Profiler toolbar.

- To gather even more complete information about queries that SQL Server is running, you can specify in Profiler that the trace gather showplan information about the query execution plans SQL Server is using.

- You can also create a replay trace to generate a workload that you can replay on a test system.

Lesson Review

The following questions are intended to reinforce key information presented in this lesson. The questions are also available on the companion CD if you prefer to review them in electronic form.

NOTE Answers

Answers to these questions and explanations of why each answer choice is right or wrong are located in the "Answers" section at the end of the book.

---

1. Which types of events can you trace by using SQL Server Profiler? (Choose all that apply.)

   A. CPU utilization

   B. Statements executed within stored procedures

   C. Network input/output (I/O)

   D. Stored procedure recompiles

2. To which formats can you save a trace? (Choose all that apply.)

    A. Binary file

    B. Text file

    C. SQL Server table

    D. Comma-delimited file

3. Which of the following are valid configuration options? (Choose all that apply.)

    A. Trace category

    B. Enable file rollover

    C. Restriction on resources used

    D. Event filters

Lesson 2: Working with System Monitor

System Monitor is the second tool that you can use to gather monitoring data about conditions that might affect database performance. Included with Windows, System Monitor captures counters across a variety of system metrics as well as for any application that you define a set of custom counters for. This lesson explains how to create a System Monitor counter log that you can use to correlate Profiler data with system metrics that Profiler cannot capture. By correlating this data, you can gain a more complete picture of your system's health than either Profiler or System Monitor can provide on its own.

Exam Tip   Although System Monitor is the formal name for this tool, virtually everyone in the industry calls it Performance Monitor, or *PerfMon* for short, because it is used to capture performance counters and you launch it from the Administrative Tools section called Performance. Just remember that on the exam, this tool is always referred to by its formal name of System Monitor. But out in the field, most people call it PerfMon.

> **After this lesson, you will be able to:**
> - Configure a System Monitor counter log.
>
> **Estimated lesson time: 20 minutes**

> ### Real World
>
> *Michael Hotek*
>
> When performance decreases, the database is always the first to receive blame. Thus, the DBA receives the first calls from irate users. One of the first things I do when investigating a performance issue is connect to the SQL Server and look at the results of the *sp_who2* system stored procedure. This stored procedure gives me a basic idea of whether I have a bunch of queries blocking each other and bringing the system to a halt.
>
> At one customer site, I went through this process and didn't see any real issues. The customer had a large number of connections, but requests were being processed very quickly. So, the next step was to open Profiler and run a basic trace to get an idea of the activity on the system and how long most queries were taking.

The Profiler trace also didn't show anything out of the ordinary. Queries were coming through at a very rapid pace, and the average duration of any query was 40 milliseconds. However, the application was still having problems, with extremely slow performance to customers. Many DBAs would become stuck at this point because by all indications, SQL Server was running just fine and was just processing a lot of requests.

However, the DBAs and I opened System Monitor and added the % Processor Time, cache hit ratio, output queue length, page life expectancy, batches/sec, and recompilations/sec counters. What we found was very interesting. The processor was churning at nearly 100 percent, the cache hit ratio was very low, output queue length was above 15, page life expectancy was very low and dropping, batches/sec was at about 1200, and recompiles/sec had skyrocketed to almost 1000.

It turns out that someone had been running baseline performance tests on about 50 stored procedures and decided that it would be a good idea as part of the process to add the *WITH RECOMPILE* clause to the procedure. The procedures then got loaded into the production environment. When database activity increased dramatically in the middle of the day, everything came to a grinding halt. Every procedure being executed was constantly recompiled, which added to the total execution time. And because of this longer execution time, more queries were concurrently executing, so there were more execution plans being generated in the query cache. This, in turn, caused a huge increase in the size of the query cache. Because the query cache and data cache share memory space, the large query cache size was causing data to be ejected from the data cache to allocate more room to the query cache. This forced pages to be read from disk and back into the data cache more frequently, causing the page life expectancy to drop. Everything was hitting a saturation point, so requests were starting to queue up in the IP stack at the server as well.

We immediately started pulling the stored procedures that Profiler was telling us were being executed. We then quickly edited them to remove the *RECOMPILE* clause. Immediately, the processor utilization dropped, the recompiles dropped to almost 0, the page life expectancy quickly started increasing, and the output queue dropped to 0. We also saw that the average duration for queries in Profiler was now about 10 milliseconds.

> Profiler could tell us what was executing on the server, but it couldn't pinpoint the problem. System Monitor could quantify statistics, but it couldn't tell us what was being executed. By using both tools together, we quickly identified a major performance issue and were able to get the system running efficiently again.

Creating a Counter Log

Most administrators open System Monitor, add counters, and start their analyses. There is only one problem: All data is captured in live mode, and there is no option to log it to a file for later analysis. You should always capture System Monitor counters in a log if you plan on doing any analysis of the data or correlating with other tools. Let's look at how to create a System Monitor counter log.

To capture a counter log, you need to launch System Monitor and select Counter Logs below the Performance Logs and Alerts node, as shown in Figure 15-12.

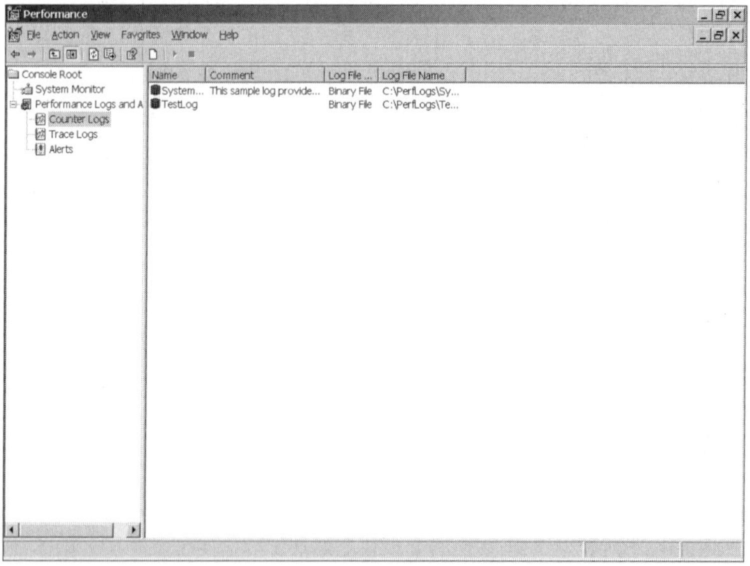

Figure 15-12   Capturing a Performance Counter log

By right-clicking Counter Logs, choosing New Log Settings, and entering a name for the counter log, you start the definition of a counter log, as Figure 15-13 shows.

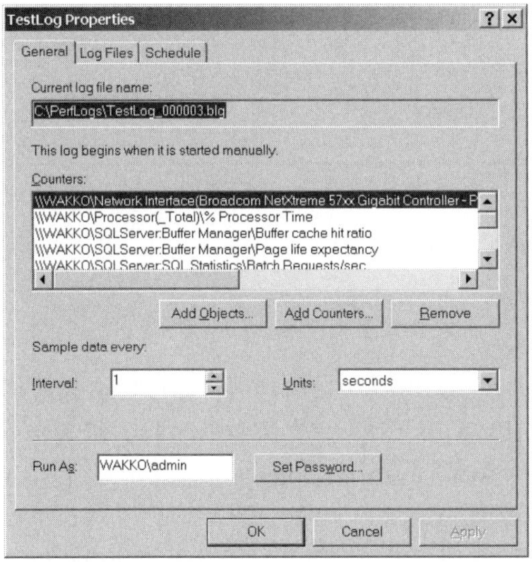

Figure 15-13   Define counters and objects to capture.

There are two buttons in the middle of the screen for defining the counters that you want System Monitor to capture. Clicking Add Objects enables you to gather all counters associated with a particular object; Add Counters enables you to specify individual counters. The sample interval determines how frequently Windows Server 2003 gathers and logs the objects and counters. The Run As field is set to *<Default>*. You should always change it to an explicit Windows user account; otherwise, a counter log normally fails to start.

BEST PRACTICES   Is gathering more counters more expensive?

Many administrators have the misconception that it is more expensive to gather 10 counters than it is to gather 5 counters. Although there is a bit more effort involved in setting up more counters, the resources used to gather counters are almost undetectable. So unless you know the precise counters you need to analyze a problem, you are always better off by clicking Add Objects to gather all counters for a given object.

After specifying the counters for which you want to gather information, you can then specify the format for the log file name as well as optional scheduling parameters. Clicking OK saves your counter log in System Monitor.

If you have specified a schedule for the counter log, Windows Scheduler automatically launches it for you. Otherwise, you need to right-click the counter log and choose Start. System Monitor will then begin to capture counters into a log file in the

C:\PerfLogs directory. You can then open this log file in System Monitor for further analysis, which Lesson 5, "Correlating Performance and Monitoring Data," covers as it explains how to leverage performance counters.

Quick Check

1. How do you launch System Monitor?
2. For what purpose do you use System Monitor?

Quick Check Answers

1. You launch System Monitor from the Start menu by selecting Performance within the Administrative Tools menu on any machine running Windows.
2. You use System Monitor to gather numeric data related to various system and application metrics. System Monitor cannot tell you what is executing, but it can quantify an activity for a given system or application component.

PRACTICE   Configuring a System Monitor Counter Log

In this practice, you will configure a System Monitor counter log, which you will use in Lesson 5 to practice how to correlate data between Profiler and System Monitor.

1. Launch System Monitor by choosing Start, Administrative Tools, Performance.
2. Expand the Performance Logs And Alerts node.
3. Right-click Counter Logs and choose New Log Settings.
4. Specify a name for your log file settings and click OK.
5. Click Add Counters and add the following counters:

    A. Network Interface\Output Queue Length
    B. Processor\% Processor Time
    C. SQL Server:Buffer Manager\Buffer Cache Hit Ratio
    D. SQL Server:Buffer Manager\Page Life Expectancy
    E. SQL Server:SQL Statistics\Batch Requests/Sec
    F. SQL Server:SQL Statistics\SQL Compilations/Sec
    G. SQL Server:SQL Statistics\SQL Re-compilations/Sec

6. Set the interval to one second.

7. Specify a user to run the counter log and enter the user's password.

8. Leave the Log Files and Schedules tabs at their defaults.

9. Click OK. By default, System Monitor stores log files in the folder C:\PerfLogs. If this folder does not yet exist, you are prompted to create it. Click Yes.

10. Right-click your new counter log and choose Start.

Lesson Summary

- System Monitor provides a key tool for gathering statistical data related to hardware and software metrics, which Profiler does not capture.

- You should always capture System Monitor counters in a log if you plan to do any analysis of the data or correlating with other tools.

- To define the counters that System Monitor captures in the counter log, you can use Add Objects to gather all counters associated with a particular object or Add Counters to specify individual counters.

Lesson Review

The following questions are intended to reinforce key information presented in this lesson. The questions are also available on the companion CD if you prefer to review them in electronic form.

NOTE Answers

Answers to these questions and explanations of why each answer choice is right or wrong are located in the "Answers" section at the end of the book.

---

1. A System Monitor counter log can gather which types of information? (Choose all that apply.)

    A. The applications currently running in Windows

    B. Numerical data related to hardware performance

    C. Queries being executed against SQL Server

    D. The number of orders being placed per second

Lesson 3: Using the Database Engine Tuning Advisor

The *Database Engine Tuning Advisor (DTA)* is the greatly enhanced replacement to the Index Tuning Wizard tool that shipped with previous versions of SQL Server. DTA plays an important role in an overall performance solution, letting you leverage the query optimizer to receive recommendations on indexes, indexed views, or partitions that could improve performance.

Hackers have developed sophisticated algorithms for breaking into secure systems, but the most time-honored approach and the one that has a 100 percent success rate is the brute force attack. DTA applies the same concept, taking a *workload file* as an input and then exhaustively testing each query against all possible permutations of indexes, indexed views, and partitions to come up with the best possible solution. This lesson will explain all of the options available in DTA and how to integrate this powerful tool into your performance-tuning work.

After this lesson, you will be able to:

- Build a workload file.
- Configure DTA to analyze a workload.
- Save recommendations from DTA.

Estimated lesson time: 45 minutes

IMPORTANT   If DTA fails to start

There have been many reports of DTA failing to start and displaying a C++ compile error. This is a known issue related to incompatible registry settings that older applications might have added. If you cannot get DTA to start, see the Microsoft article "Bug Details: Database Engine Tuning Advisor" (at *http://lab.msdn.microsoft.com/productfeedback/ViewFeedback.aspx?FeedbackID=631e881c-4b0f-4c5c-b919-283a71cea5fe*) for information about how to fix the problem.

Real World

Michael Hotek

I have been doing performance-tuning work in SQL Server for well over a decade. What I have heard for too long from too many people is that performance tuning is an art form. That could not be further from the truth. Composing the next number one hit, painting a masterpiece, or building an original piece of furniture is an art. Performance tuning is nothing more than the application of knowledge based on a set of rules to produce a result.

Although processor utilization, amount of memory available, and disk I/O can affect database query performance, SQL Server's query optimizer plays a critical role in the performance of any query. SQL Server is a piece of software that is written based on rules. The optimizer applies a defined, but not documented, set of rules to determine how to gather the data that a query requests. We can only deduce these basic rules by understanding how data is organized in SQL Server as well as inspecting showplans to see the query paths that various queries have taken. From these pieces of information, we can start to apply the rules of performance tuning.

At many organizations, gathering and analyzing data to determine where the performance issues are is the first hurdle. The second hurdle is in understanding what to do about the issues to improve performance. Although many performance issues require changes to the code that is executing, many more can be solved simply by adding indexes, dropping indexes, or changing indexes, which is where DTA plays an important role in any environment. It enables you to get at core issues related to indexing without having to spend large amounts of time on analysis.

One of the first things I do at a customer site when dealing with performance issues is to start Profiler and begin capturing queries. I can then take that Profiler trace and feed it directly into DTA. Using the trace I give it, DTA simply takes each query and applies the rules of the optimizer in a nearly exhaustive manner. It uses the query costing values to determine whether a particular query could benefit from having indexes or indexed views created for it or whether partitioning the table would improve performance.

The index recommendations let me zero in on particular areas as well as particular queries that I need to look at. In many cases, running DTA regularly and using its recommendations can help avoid or mitigate performance issues. Although running DTA doesn't eliminate the need for further analysis, as I will describe in subsequent lessons in this chapter, it can at least keep your phone from ringing off the hook with users upset at the responsiveness of a system and let you spend more time doing even deeper analysis to accomplish even better performance.

Building a Workload File

DTA requires you to provide it with a workload that it can analyze. You can provide the workload in a variety of formats, including a trace file, a trace table, or a Transact-SQL script.

The most common workload used within DTA is a trace file. You can generate this trace by using SQL Server Profiler, which ships with a template designed to capture the data DTA needs to perform its analysis. To generate the trace file, launch Profiler, select the Tuning trace template, and save the results to a file. Alternatively, you can load the trace into a table that DTA uses to perform its analysis.

NOTE **Using a Transact-SQL script as a workload file**

A Transact-SQL script makes for an interesting workload file, which simply contains a batch of SQL that you want to analyze. Although there isn't anything earth-shattering about creating a file that contains a batch of SQL, this option takes on a new meaning when you integrate it with your development processes. For example, you can highlight a query in a batch of SQL in the query window within SSMS, right-click the query, and select Send To Database Engine Tuning Advisor. This action launches DTA against the SQL batch you highlighted, letting you perform targeted analysis while you are developing queries.

Configuring DTA to Analyze a Workload

Analyzing a workload in DTA consists of three basic steps:

1. Launch DTA and connect to your server.

2. Select a workfile to analyze.

3. Specify tuning options.

Let's walk through each of these steps. First, launch DTA so that you can configure a new analysis session, as shown in Figure 15-14.

Each session you create will be saved, so you can go back and review previous analysis sessions and view the recommendations that DTA generated. To easily identify sessions, make sure to give each one a descriptive name. You need to specify the workload source along with the database for the workload analysis. You also have to specify the databases and tables that you want to tune within the workload. DTA uses the database you specify for the workload analysis as the basis for making tuning decisions. And by specifying the databases and tables for tuning, you let DTA ignore some of the events in the workload file.

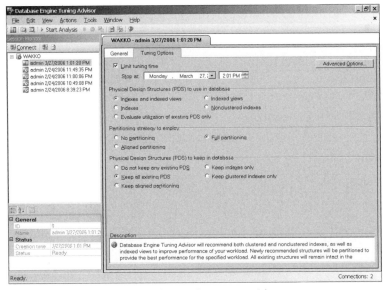

Figure 15-14 Configuring an analysis session

After you specify the general options for the tuning session, click the Tuning Options
tab (see Figure 15-15).

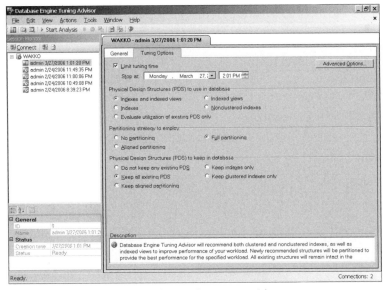

Figure 15-15 Specifying tuning options to consider

One of the most important options to set when configuring a tuning session that involves workloads from production systems is to limit the tuning time. Otherwise, DTA could run for several days before completing.

DTA performs its analysis by loading the specified workload and starting the first command to tune. DTA then interrogates the query optimizer with various options and compares the query cost that the optimizer returns. DTA repeats this interrogation process until it cannot find any options that produce a query plan of a lower cost. DTA then logs any recommendations for that query—such as creating an index, an indexed view, or partitioning the table—and moves on to the next statement to repeat the process.

CAUTION   DTA's performance impact

DTA actively sends requests to the query optimizer, which then returns a query cost. The query cost is based on the live distribution statistics for data within the database being tuned. Therefore, DTA generally uses your production database when it is in an analysis session. Thus, you must be very careful when executing a DTA analysis because the load it puts on the database can affect performance. If possible, restore a backup of your production database on another server and use it for the DTA analysis session.

In general, you will specify that DTA look for both indexes and indexed views to create for better performance. However, you can restrict the structures that DTA will consider.

DTA also analyzes whether partitioning a table might improve query performance. When you are configuring partitioning options in DTA, keep in mind that if you are using the *SWITCH* command with partitioning, you will want to restrict DTA's analysis to aligned partitions only.

MORE INFO   Partitioning

For information about partitioning, see Chapter 6, "Creating Partitions."

The final tuning options you can specify for DTA concern whether to keep physical design structures (PDSs). If you specify the option to keep them all, DTA recommends only creation of indexes, indexed views, or partitioning. If you specify any of the other options, DTA also includes recommendations regarding dropping structures if that could improve performance.

With the Advanced Options page, shown in Figure 15-16, you can specify whether you want to have online or offline recommendations.

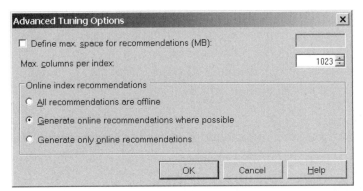

Figure 15-16   Specifying advanced tuning options

NOTE   Restrictions on online operations

Online operations are restricted by the edition of SQL Server 2005 that you are running. See SQL Server 2005 Books Online for more information about the specific capabilities of your edition.

After you configure your DTA tuning session, you can start an analysis by clicking Start Analysis, which displays extended information on the session, as Figure 15-17 shows.

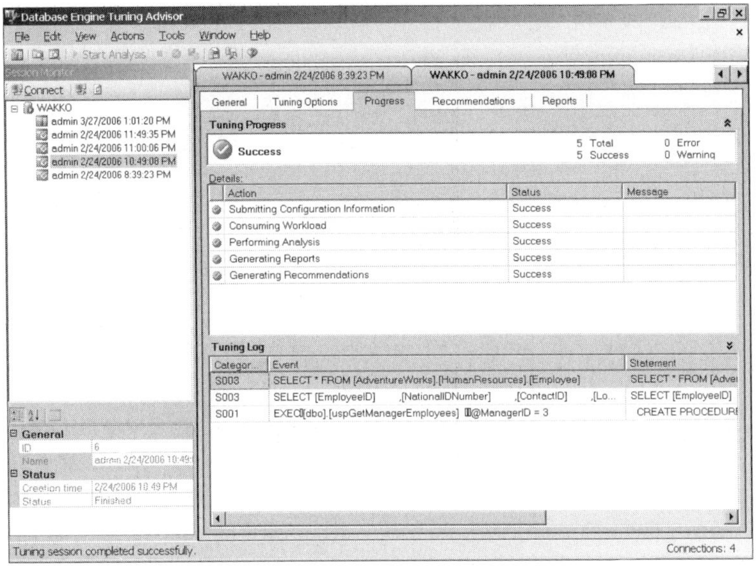

Figure 15-17   Viewing the analysis progress

DTA displays the progress of each action in the middle of the screen; you will notice that the majority of the time is spent on the Performing Analysis action. As DTA completes its analysis of each statement, it displays the statement in the bottom pane. When DTA encounters a statement that it has already analyzed, it increments the Frequency counter for that statement and continues to the next statement in the workload.

To view DTA's performance recommendations, select the Recommendations tab (see Figure 15-18).

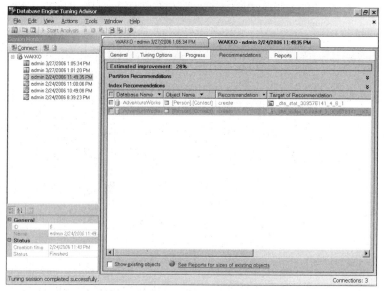

Figure 15-18   Viewing performance recommendations

DTA displays all recommendations, and you can sort and filter them by using the column headers on the grid.

Scrolling to the right displays the definition of each recommendation as a hyperlink (see Figure 15-19). Clicking a hyperlink launches a pop-up window that contains the complete Transact-SQL statement required to implement the recommendation.

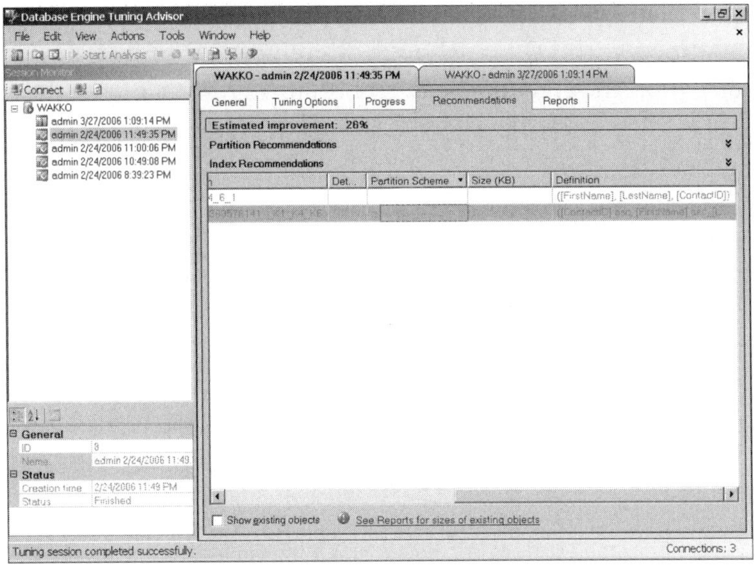

Figure 15-19   Viewing performance recommendations continued

Each analysis session produces several reports that you can view by selecting the Reports tab shown in Figure 15-20.

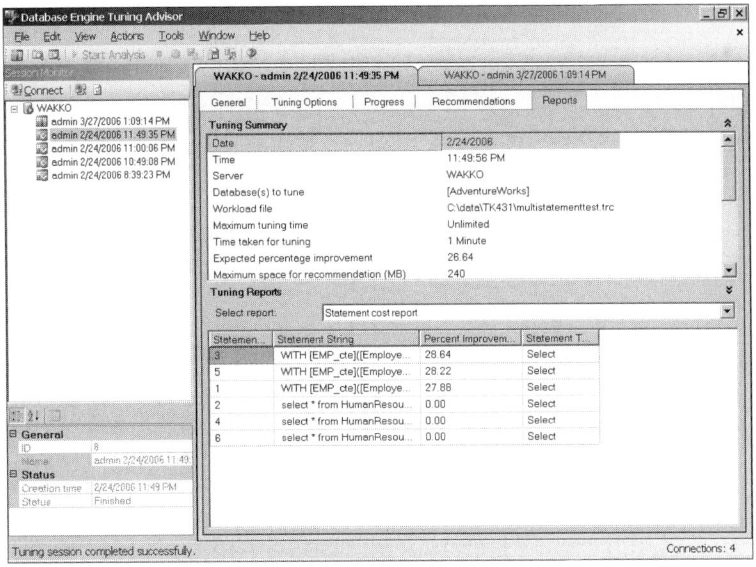

Figure 15-20   Viewing analysis reports

Selecting a report changes the data in the bottom pane. The only reports that you can view are shipped with DTA. Although there isn't an option to add custom reports, you can export the contents of any report to an XML file from the right-click menu.

BEST PRACTICES   Leveraging trace tables

With DTA, using a trace table can actually provide a more powerful, integrated, and automated analysis capability than using a trace file. You can set up a job that periodically launches a SQL Trace to capture a trace and save it to a file. You can then create a second job that explicitly stops the trace after a given interval. After the trace is stopped, you can move the trace file to a central location and use *fn_trace_gettable()* to load the trace into a table. By creating one table per SQL Server instance within a database, you can create a central repository for all traces in your environment. You can then configure DTA to use your trace table as a workload source for analysis. Set up DTA to analyze the workload and quit after approximately an hour.

Of course, incremental traces will get loaded into the table. And based on the portion of the table that DTA has analyzed, you can create a process that executes after an incremental trace is loaded and removes any rows from the trace table corresponding to queries already analyzed, allowing each subsequent run of a DTA analysis to work on queries that have not already been covered. Eventually, after many incremental analysis runs, you will achieve full analysis of the entire workload.

Remember that when you configure an analysis run, each session is saved and preserves DTA's recommendations and reports. You can then clone the session and use the clone to initiate a subsequent analysis run. This capability enables you to quickly and easily use the settings from a previous run against your trace table to execute another analysis run.

Saving Recommendations from DTA

After a DTA analysis session is complete, you can save DTA's recommendations from the Actions menu. When you save recommendations, DTA creates a script file that contains the Transact-SQL code required to implement all the recommendations.

Instead of saving recommendations to a file, you can apply them directly to a database either immediately or by creating a job in SQL Server Agent to apply them. However, applying changes directly to a database through DTA is not recommended because this action does not integrate with your source code control system and does not maintain your source tree. You also generally have multiple copies of the same database in development, testing, and production to which you should apply the changes.

> **Quick Check**
> - How can you use DTA as a primary tool for performance tuning?
>
> **Quick Check Answer**
> - Using a workload file generated by SQL Trace, DTA can analyze each statement run against a database to determine whether performance can be improved by adding indexes, indexed views, partitioning tables, or even possibly dropping indexes, indexed views, and partitions.

PRACTICE Analyzing a Workload in DTA

In this practice, you will create a workload file and then use that workload file as a source for DTA to analyze for performance improvements.

1. Open SSMS and connect to your SQL Server instance.

2. Open a new query window and change the context to the *AdventureWorks* database.

3. Open SQL Server Profiler (choose Tools, SQL Server Profiler), connect to your SQL Server instance, and create a new trace.

4. Specify the trace template called Tuning and set Profiler to save the trace to a file.

5. Start the trace.

6. Switch back to your query window and execute several queries against the *AdventureWorks* database.

7. Stop the trace and close SQL Server Profiler.

8. Close SSMS without saving your queries.

9. Start DTA and connect to your SQL Server instance.

10. If not already created, create a new session.

11. Specify a name for the session.

12. Select the workload file that you just created in SQL Server Profiler.

13. Select the *AdventureWorks* database for workload analysis.

14. Select the check box next to the *AdventureWorks* database and leave the default for all of the tables.

15. On the Tuning Options tab, leave all default options.

16. Start the analysis. (Click Start Analysis on the toolbar.)

17. After the analysis is complete, review DTA's output for recommendations and look at each report DTA generated for the workload.

Lesson Summary

- DTA takes a workload file as input and then exhaustively tests each query in the workload file against all possible permutations of indexes, indexed views, and partitions to come up with the best possible performance recommendations.

- The most common workload used within DTA is a trace file. You can generate the trace file by using SQL Server Profiler's Tuning template, which is designed to capture the data DTA needs to perform its analysis.

- Analyzing a workload in DTA consists of three basic steps: launching DTA, selecting a workfile to analyze, and specifying tuning options.

- When you save DTA's recommendations from the Actions menu, DTA will create a script file that contains the Transact-SQL code required to implement all its recommendations.

Lesson Review

The following questions are intended to reinforce key information presented in this lesson. The questions are also available on the companion CD if you prefer to review them in electronic form.

NOTE Answers

Answers to these questions and explanations of why each answer choice is right or wrong are located in the "Answers" section at the end of the book.

---

1. Which types of workloads can DTA use? (Choose all that apply.)

   A. Profiler deadlock trace

   B. SQL script

   C. Table containing trace data

   D. Counter log

2. Which of the following are valid configuration options for tuning a workload? (Choose all that apply.)

    A. Create views

    B. Drop indexes

    C. Online indexes only

    D. Nonclustered indexes

Lesson 4: Using Dynamic Management Views and Functions

Dynamic management views (DMVs) and *Dynamic management functions (DMFs)* fill an instrumentation gap by providing capabilities that DBAs have long needed to effectively manage SQL Server databases. By leveraging the detailed and extremely granular information that DMVs and DMFs provide, administrators can rapidly diagnose problems and get systems back online. They can also use these new tools proactively to spot patterns and take corrective action before outages occur. Although a full discussion of using DMVs and DMFs is far beyond the scope of this lesson, it will cover the basics of SQL Server 2005's new instrumentation infrastructure and how to begin using these facilities as core data providers within any monitoring process.

After this lesson, you will be able to:

- Understand the categories of DMVs and DMFs.
- Identify key performance and monitoring DMVs and DMFs.

Estimated lesson time: 60 minutes

Real World

Michael Hotek

When SQL Server 2000 was released, the marketing hype was that the database system provided all the functionality of a true enterprise-class database platform. I've always disagreed with that assessment. Although SQL Server 2000 was a very good product that provided a lot of valuable functionality, it fell short of what I consider "enterprise class."

An enterprise-class database platform isn't simply capable of storing a large amount of data. It also needs to have very robust and easy-to-access instrumentation that exposes enough detail to let DBAs quickly diagnose problems and keep the environment working at optimum levels.

SQL Server 2000 essentially provided a black box for DBAs to use. You could solve most performance problems by using SQL Trace to extract data from the black box and then aggregate it to find the queries that were affecting performance. However, this process consumed a large amount of time. In addition, there were entire classes of problems that were extremely difficult to find and solve, as anyone having to use *sp_lock* would know.

During the Consumer Technology Preview (CTP) cycle for SQL Server 2005, I was working with an independent software vendor (ISV) that was benchmarking its application on SQL Server 2005. This was a new version of the application, containing new functionality that hadn't been through rigorous performance testing yet. The purpose of the first phase of the benchmark was to determine whether SQL Server 2005 performance characteristics were going to be good enough to let the ISV aggressively push forward with its plans or if it was going to need to wait for awhile until SQL Server performance caught up with its needs.

We launched the first few tests and received mixed results. The performance was within the ISV's broad target, but it should have been much better. During the third run, we started looking at SQL Server 2005's missing index DMVs and found two indexes that should have been created but were somehow missed. Leveraging SQL Server's new online index creation capability, we added these indexes during the load test to test whether this process would cause the application to crash. The indexes were created without impact, and the application's performance immediately improved.

This entire process took about two minutes from start to finish. In SQL Server 2000 and earlier versions, we would have had to start a SQL Server Profiler trace, captured a significant portion of the queries issued against the test, analyzed the trace output, found the queries we needed to look at, and then evaluated the code to determine what improvements we needed to make. With prior versions, we might have been lucky to complete this process in half a day. After analyzing lots of query plans, we also would have found only one of the indexes that we created. If we had been analyzing a production system, the DMVs and DMFs in SQL Server 2005 would have saved us at least four hours of analysis time that we could have then devoted to other critical DBA tasks such as sleeping.

Key Performance and Monitoring DMVs and DMFs

DMVs and DMFs are divided into dozens of categories that encompass various features, subsystems, and statistical categories. Categorization of the views and functions is achieved by using a standardized naming convention in which the first part of the name, or prefix, indicates the category for a DMV or DMF. Table 15-1 lists the prefixes for each category and the general purpose of the DMVs or DMFs in each category.

Table 15-1   DMV and DMF Prefixes

Prefix	General purpose
*dm_db_* *	Provides general database statistics such as space and index utilization.
*dm_exec_* *	Provides query statistics.
*dm_io_* *	Provides I/O statistics.
*dm_os_* *	Provides hardware-level information.

Database Statistics

You can use one DMV and two DMFs to gather basic index usage information within a database.

The *sys.dm_db_index_usage_stats* DMV contains core statistics about each index within a database. Use this view when you need to find the number of seeks, scans, lookups, or updates that have occurred with an index.

BEST PRACTICES   Using *sys.dm_db_index_usage_stats*

The *sys.dm_db_index_usage_stats* DMV is a good place to start to find any indexes that the query optimizer is not using. If the system has been running for awhile, and an index does not have any seeks, scans, or lookups registered for it, it is a strong possibility that the index is not being used to satisfy any queries. Or an index might show activity but is no longer being used. You can determine the last time an index was used by examining the *last_user_seek, last_user_scan* and *last_user_lookup* columns.

Of much more interest on a day-to-day basis, however, are the *sys.dm_db_index_operational_stats* and *sys.dm_db_index_physical_stats* DMFs.

The *index_operational_stats* function takes four parameters: *database_id*, *object_id*, *index_id*, and *partition_id*. This function displays all the current I/O statistics related to locking, latching, and access. You use this function to find out how heavily a particular index is being used in terms of modifications as well as scans or lookups. You would also reference the output of this function when you are concerned about locking or latching contention in the database.

The *index_physical_stats* function takes five parameters: *database_id*, *object_id*, *index_id*, *partition_id*, and *mode*. This function returns row size and fragmentation information. In previous versions of SQL Server, *DBCC SHOWCONTIG* was used to return this type of data.

The final set of views and functions essentially provide a real-time index analysis. The views beginning with *sys.dm_db_missing_index_** track indexes that could be created against your database. When queries are executed that cause the table to be scanned, and SQL Server determines that it could have taken advantage of an index to satisfy the query, it logs entries in *sys.dm_db_missing_index_details*, *sys.dm_db_missing_index_group_stats*, and *sys.dm_db_missing_index_groups*. The group stats view contains counters for the number of times a particular index could be used as well as the seeks, scans, and some basic costing values. The index details view contains information about the table that should have an index created on it as well as the column for that index. The index groups view provides an aggregation functionality.

By combining these three views together, you can proactively analyze new indexes while a system is operating without requiring workload traces to be generated for analysis in DTA. Although these views are not a replacement for DTA, which also considers indexed views and partitions and provides a more exhaustive analysis of indexes, they can be a very effective initial level of analysis.

BEST PRACTICES   **Calculating the value of proposed indexes**

The most difficult decision to make is which of the indexes proposed by the *sys.dm_db_missing_index** views can provide the most benefit. Applying some basic calculations, you can derive a numerical comparison based on *SELECT* activity only for each of the proposed indexes. The following example shows the code you can use to apply the calculations:

```
SELECT *
FROM
(SELECT user_seeks * avg_total_user_cost * (avg_user_impact * 0.01) AS index_advantage,
 migs.* FROM sys.dm_db_missing_index_group_stats migs) AS migs_adv
   INNER JOIN sys.dm_db_missing_index_groups AS mig ON migs_adv.group_handle =
   mig.index_group_handle
   INNER JOIN sys.dm_db_missing_index_details AS mid ON mig.index_handle = mid.index_handle
ORDER BY migs_adv.index_advantage
```

On operational systems, values above 5,000 indicate indexes that should be evaluated for creation. When the value passes 10,000, you generally have an index that can provide a significant performance improvement for read operations.

This algorithm accounts only for read activity, so you will always want to consider the impact of maintenance operations as well.

Query Statistics

The query statistics DMVs and DMFs encompass the entire group of functionality related to executing a query in SQL Server. This functionality is broken into two distinct groups: connections to the instance and queries executing inside the engine.

Connection information is contained in two DMVs: *sys.dm_exec_requests* and *sys.dm_exec_sessions*. Each connection to a SQL Server instance is assigned a *system process ID (SPID)*, with information about each session available in *sys.dm_exec_sessions*.

You can retrieve session information regarding the user or application creating the connection, login time, connection method, and a variety of information concerning the high-level statistics for the state of the connection.

BEST PRACTICES *sys.dm_exec_sessions*

In previous versions of SQL Server, you would retrieve the information that *sys.dm_exec_sessions* provides by executing the *sp_who* or *sp_who2* system stored procedures, or by retrieving rows from the *sysprocesses* table. However, *sys.dm_exec_sessions* contains significantly more information than previous versions of SQL Server logged.

Each session in SQL Server will normally be executing a single request. However, it is possible for a single SPID to spawn multiple requests. You can retrieve statistics about each executing request from *sys.dm_exec_requests*. The requests DMV forms the basis for resolving many performance issues.

The information contained within this view can be separated into four categories: query settings, query execution, transactions, and resource allocation. Query settings encompass the options that can be applied to each request executed, such as quoted identifiers, American National Standards Institute (ANSI) nulls, arithabort, transaction isolation level, and so on. Query execution encompasses items such as the memory handle to the SQL statement, the memory handle to the query plan, CPU time, reads, writes, the ID of the scheduler, the SPID blocking the request if applicable, and so on. Transactions encompass such items as the transaction ID, the number of open transactions, the number of result sets, the deadlock priority, and related statistics. Resource allocation encompasses the wait type and wait time.

IMPORTANT The DBA's friend: *sys.dm_exec_requests* DMV

Because the *sys.dm_exec_requests* view is used to determine many different operation states, it will become an extremely familiar tool for any DBA managing a SQL Server server.

Detailed query statistics are contained within the *sys.dm_exec_query_stats* and *sys.dm_exec_cached_plans* DMVs. Query stats provides detailed statistics related to the performance of a query as well as the amount of resources the query consumed. Using this DMV, you can determine the number of reads (logical and physical), writes (logical and physical), CPU, and elapsed time for a query. The DMV tracks these statistics based on the SQL handle and also contains the plan handle.

MORE INFO   Query plans, execution plans, and the query optimizer

Every SQL statement that is executed must be compiled. After it is compiled, it is stored in the query cache and identified by a memory pointer called a handle. The SQL Server query optimizer then must determine a query plan for the statement. After the query plan is determined, it is also stored in the query cache and identified by a memory pointer. The compiled plan then generates an execution plan for the query to use. When the query executes, the *sys.dm_exec_query_stats* DMV tracks the SQL handle with the associated plan handle for that execution, as well as all the statistical information for that query. The details of query plans, execution plans, and the query optimizer are beyond the scope of this book, but you can find comprehensive coverage of these topics in the book *Inside SQL Server 2005: The Storage Engine*, by Kalen Delaney (Microsoft Press, 2007).

You use the *sys.dm_exec_cached_plans* DMV, which is similar to *syscacheobjects* in previous SQL Server versions, to retrieve information about query plans. SQL Server query plans can be of two basic types: compiled and execution. A compile plan is generated for each unique SQL statement that has been executed. Parameters and literals are substituted with generic placeholders so that execution of a stored procedure with varying values for parameters, for example, is still treated as the same SQL statement and does not cause the optimizer to create additional plans. Compiled plans are reentrant, meaning that they can be reused.

An execution plan, on the other hand, is created for each concurrent execution of a particular statement. Thus, if 15 connections were executing the same stored procedure concurrently, regardless of whether the parameters were the same, there would be one compiled plan and 15 execution plans in the query cache.

Although the SQL handle and the plan handle are meaningful to the SQL Server engine, they are meaningless to a person. So SQL Server provides two functions to translate the information. The *sys.dm_exec_sql_text* DMF takes a single parameter of the SQL handle and returns in text format the query that was executed. The *sys.dm_exec_query_plans* DMF takes a single parameter of the plan handle and returns an XML showplan.

BEST PRACTICES   **An easier way to translate handle information**

Although it might be interesting to find handles in the query stats or cached plan DMVs and then input them into the DMFs to translate everything into human-readable format, there is an easier way to achieve this translation. The *CROSS APPLY* operator invokes a table-valued function for each row within a table. Thus, you can use the following queries to apply this translation for given rows in the query stats or cached plans DMVs:

```
SELECT * FROM sys.dm_exec_query_stats CROSS APPLY sys.dm_exec_query_plan(plan_handle)
SELECT * FROM sys.dm_exec_query_stats CROSS APPLY sys.dm_exec_sql_text(sql_handle)
SELECT * FROM sys.dm_exec_cached_plans CROSS APPLY sys.dm_exec_query_plan(plan_handle)
```

Because an operational system can easily have thousands of rows in *sys.dm_exec_query_stats* or *sys.dm_exec_cached_plans*, you shouldn't execute the previous queries without providing a *WHERE* clause to restrict the scope.

I/O Statistics

The DMVs and DMFs that deal with I/O track the physical I/O to the data files and the log files for each database.

A key DMF in this category is *sys.dm_io_virtual_file_stats*, which takes two parameters: *database ID* and *file ID* (both of which can be null). This DMF is comparable to the *fn_virtual_filestats()* function in SQL Server 2000, but it contains more granular information to enable you to make better decisions. The virtual file stats DMF breaks down the physical I/O written to each file within a database into reads, writes, bytes read, and bytes written. It also tracks I/O stalls, broken down by reads and writes. The I/O statistics are cumulative from the time the SQL Server instance was started. This DMF helps you evaluate whether you have an I/O imbalance between files for your database. And this information, in turn, enables you to determine whether tables or indexes should be moved to provide better throughput from physical reads or writes.

Another useful DMF in the I/O statistics category is *sys.dm_io_pending_io_requests*, which contains a row for each request that is waiting for an I/O operation to complete. On a very active system, you always find requests that are pending. However, if you find a particular request that has to wait a significant amount of time or you have very large numbers of requests that are pending all the time, you might have a disk I/O bottleneck.

Hardware Statistics

The final category of DMVs covered in this lesson deals with the operating system interface between SQL Server and Windows as well as the physical hardware interaction.

Although you can use System Monitor to gather a variety of counters, the logs gathered are not formatted to allow you to easily extract and correlate the data with a variety of other sources. To get a result set that you can more easily manipulate, you can use the *sys.dm_os_performance_counters* DMV. This view provides all the counters that a SQL Server instance exposes in an easily manipulated result set.

NOTE Accessing hardware counters

Keep in mind that the performance counters DMV provides only SQL Server counters and does not allow access to any hardware counters. To access hardware counters, you have to make Windows Management Instrumentation (WMI) calls to pull the data into a result set that you can then manipulate.

Another key DMV for hardware statistics is *sys.dm_os_wait_stats*, which provides the same data that you could gather by using *DBCC SQLPERF(WAITSTATS)* in SQL Server 2000. This DMV plays an important role in any performance analysis by aggregating the amount of time processes had to wait for various resources to be allocated.

MORE INFO Wait types

SQL Server 2000 had 77 *wait types*. SQL Server 2005 exposes 194 wait types. Although a complete discussion of each wait type is beyond the scope of this book, for details about wait types see Gert Drapers' SQLDEV.Net Web site at *www.sqldev.net/misc/sp_waitstats.htm*.

> **Quick Check**
> - What function do DMVs and DMFs play in a monitoring and analysis system?
>
> **Quick Check Answer**
> - DMVs and DMFs provide a rich granular instrumentation platform for SQL Server 2005, providing the core resources for gathering virtually any type of data for an instance or a database.

Lesson Summary

- Prior versions of SQL Server implemented a basic "black box" approach to the database engine, which made it difficult to manage and monitor. SQL Server 2005 opens up the black box by providing a large set of detailed interfaces that expose virtually every operational statistic within the database engine.

- SQL Server's DMVs and DMFs are broken into four general categories, providing information about database statistics, query statistics, I/O statistics, and hardware statistics.

Lesson Review

The following questions are intended to reinforce key information presented in this lesson. The questions are also available on the companion CD if you prefer to review them in electronic form.

NOTE   Answers

Answers to these questions and explanations of why each answer choice is right or wrong are located in the "Answers" section at the end of the book.

---

1. You notice that performance of certain high-volume queries has suddenly degraded, and you suspect that you have contention issues within your databases. Which DMV or DMF do you use to determine whether you have a contention issue and which users are being affected?

   A. *sys.dm_os_performance_counters*

   B. *sys.dm_os_wait_stats*

   C. *sys.dm_db_index_physical_stats*

   D. *sys.dm_exec_requests*

Lesson 5: Correlating Performance and Monitoring Data

SQL Server Profiler, System Monitor, DTA, DMVs, and DMFs each capture a piece of monitoring data. Although you can use each individually to solve problems, their true value comes when you use all these tools in a cohesive manner to monitor systems. Because SQL Server does not operate in a vacuum, this integration enables you to evaluate data from all layers: from the disk subsystem, to the operating system, through the memory space, into the query optimizer, through the data structures, and out to the client.

The sections in this lesson provide examples of correlating data from multiple sources to understand a performance issue. These examples are intended to provide a starting point to demonstrate how each of the tools fit together; they do not provide an exhaustive treatment of all the ways you can use the tools together, which would easily fill an entire book. Each of the scenarios in this lesson demonstrates how data from one tool could lead you down the incorrect path, whereas correlating multiple pieces of data enables you to pinpoint the correct bottleneck or issue in the system.

> **After this lesson, you will be able to:**
> - Describe the basic processing architecture for queries.
> - Correlate System Monitor data with a SQL Server Profiler trace.
> - Correlate DMVs/DMFs with SQL Server Profiler traces.
> - Correlate DMVs/DMFs with System Monitor data.
> - Correlate several DMVs/DMFs to evaluate performance.
> - Combine data from SQL Server Profiler, System Monitor, DMVs, and DMFs into a consolidated performance view.
>
> **Estimated lesson time: 30 minutes**

Basic Query Processing Architecture

SQL Server uses a *cooperative multiprocessing model* instead of a symmetric multiprocessing model. The main difference between these two processing models is the way processor scheduling is handled. In a cooperative model, only a single thread is executing at one time on a processor, and the thread cedes control of the processor when it does not have work to perform. In this way, it allows multiple threads to cooperate with each other to maximize the amount of actual work being performed.

Controlling this cooperative behavior is the job of the *User Mode Scheduler (UMS)*. When SQL Server starts, it creates one UMS for each logical or physical processor that it is allowed to use on the system. Instead of handing off threads to the operating system to schedule on a processor, SQL Server performs its own scheduling via the UMS.

As connections are made to SQL Server, the corresponding SPID is allocated to a UMS. This allocation process uses a basic balancing algorithm that seeks to spread the processing as evenly among the UMSs as possible. Although requests by a particular connection will generally execute on the same UMS, it is possible for a particular request to be handled by any UMS that is available.

Each UMS uses three queues to process queries: runnable, running, and waiting. When a query is executed, it is assigned a thread and placed into the runnable queue. Threads are taken off this queue on a first in, first out (FIFO) basis. The thread is placed into the running queue and scheduled on the processor. At the instance the thread needs to wait for a resource such as I/O, network, or memory to be allocated, it is swapped off the processor and moved to the waiting queue.

The thread lives on the waiting queue for as long as is necessary to wait for the resource to be allocated to the thread. During this time, SQL Server tracks the amount of time the thread is waiting, as indicated by the wait time, as well as the resource that it is waiting on, as indicated by the wait type.

After the resource is freed up, the thread is swapped off the waiting queue and placed at the bottom of the runnable queue, where it must wait behind all other processes to reach the top of the runnable queue. The amount of time a process spends in the runnable queue before being swapped onto the processor is called the signal wait.

What does all of this information about processor scheduling internals have to do with monitoring or performance? When a query executes, it requires a variety of resources. The query has to be compiled, which requires memory and processor resources. The compiled plan has to be generated and stored in the query cache, which requires memory and processor. The executable plan then has to be swapped onto a processor to execute the query, which requires processor, memory, and potentially disk access. As the query reads and writes data, locks must be established, requiring yet more memory, processor, and possibly disk I/O. Finally, the results of the query have to be packaged and sent back to the client, which requires memory, processor, and network I/O.

All this processing means that memory has to be allocated at least five times. If there is memory pressure on the system, the thread has to wait for memory to be allocated each time it is required, resulting in five trips to the waiting queue along with five trips up the runnable queue. The same goes for processor, disk I/O, memory, locks, and so on. Each of these resource allocations adds time to the overall duration of a query. Thus, identifying anything causing a bottleneck increases overall performance. Writing queries so that they access the minimum amount of data and use the minimum amount of resources also means better performance.

Minimizing all these factors requires correlating many pieces of data together into a single cohesive picture of the processing state within a SQL Server instance.

Correlating System Monitor Data with SQL Server Profiler Traces

The most common use of Profiler is to gather traces related to long-running queries. Although Profiler enables you to capture long-running queries, it does not provide the context to explain why queries might be running long.

Consider that you have configured Profiler to capture queries that are taking longer than three seconds to execute. After capturing several dozen queries that meet the criteria, each one is executed against a test system that mimics production in both hardware and database size. Each of the queries completes in 30 milliseconds or less. Why would these queries take longer than three seconds to complete in production?

To find the answer, you can take advantage of a new capability in SQL Server 2005 to provide context to a trace being captured in Profiler by correlating the trace to a System Monitor counter log. The Profiler trace must include the Start Time as one of the data columns to allow events to be correlated.

After a trace has been stopped and is no longer capturing events, you can correlate it to a counter log by using the File, Import Performance Data menu. After selecting the counter log and the counters to correlate, you see a consolidated screen like the one shown in Figure 15-21.

Using the context provided by the counter logs, you can evaluate further information with respect to the previous trace for long-running queries. You might determine, for example, that every time a query takes more than three seconds to execute, the processor utilization is at 100 percent. So instead of trying to tune the queries, you would investigate the cause of high CPU utilization to improve query performance.

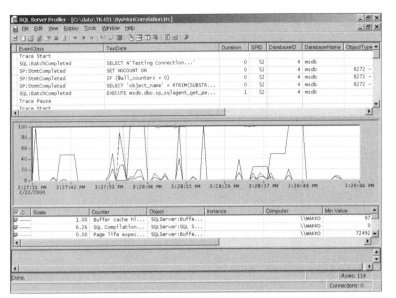

Figure 15-21   Correlating a System Monitor counter log with a Profiler trace

Correlating DMVs/DMFs with SQL Server Profiler Traces

Continuing with the earlier trace for queries executing longer than three seconds, you determine that each query has a less-than-optimal query plan. Instead of using indexes, each of the queries is performing a table scan. However, all the appropriate indexes have been created—the query optimizer is simply not using them.

CAUTION   Don't try to outguess the optimizer

In this case, some developers and DBAs would begin trying to rewrite the queries or, even worse, adding query hints to force the query optimizer to use the indexes. Keep in mind, however, that the optimizer is an extremely intelligent piece of software that is constantly sampling data distributions and making adjustments so that it can process queries with the fewest resources possible. It is extraordinarily rare that anyone is going to outguess the optimizer and force it down a more optimal path than the one it has chosen.

By combining the data from the *sys.dm_db_index_physical_stats* DMV, you might find that the optimizer is not selecting the indexes that are expected because they have become heavily fragmented. Simply rebuilding the indexes to eliminate the fragmentation would cause the optimizer to begin selecting the expected indexes, immediately improving query performance without anyone ever having to change the code or the database structure.

Correlating DMVs/DMFs with System Monitor Data

Via System Monitor, you have noticed that certain CPUs are running at 100 percent utilization, whereas others are sitting nearly idle. The busy CPUs suddenly drop to very low utilization while others are nearly idle. At the same time, users start complaining about performance issues on the order entry database, which is used for purely online transaction processing (OLTP) operations.

You launch Profiler, but it does not show any queries that would exhibit the behavior that you are observing through System Monitor.

By using the *sys.dm_os_schedulers* DMV, you could determine that processing is nearly evenly distributed on each UMS and that no single UMS has been overloaded with executing requests to create a bottleneck. However, the *sys.dm_os_wait_stats* DMV shows that there is currently an extremely high wait time value for the *CXPACKET* wait type. This condition corresponds to thread synchronization for parallel queries, which would explain the behavior of the processors along with the query performance degradation.

Where a SQL Trace would not provide any solutions to this type of performance problem, by using the information from the DMVs, you could determine that you need to change the *max degree of parallelism* value to 1, which eliminates the possibility of having parallel query plans generated. As a result of this change, query performance would almost immediately improve in an OLTP environment because more queries could be executed at any given time. You would still need to investigate why parallel query plans were being selected in the first place. But in the meantime, users wouldn't be calling to complain about performance issues.

Correlating Multiple DMVs/DMFs

Consider a situation in which you have severe blocking. You have analyzed all the queries that are constantly blocking each other. Although some blocking is expected to ensure data integrity as inserts, updates, and deletes are performed against the database, the blocking should not be as severe as what you are seeing in production.

By using the *sys.dm_exec_requests* DMV and the *sys.dm_os_waiting_tasks* DMV, you might find that queries exhibiting the severe blocking are also appearing in this combined list far too frequently to be a coincidence. And the wait type of these problem queries is almost always *WRITELOG*.

By moving the transaction log to dedicated drives that can provide better performance, you can reduce the bottleneck to the transaction log. This would cause a significant decline in the severity of the blocking issues, getting you back to a level typical
for any multiuser system.

Quick Check

■ What is required to correlate information between SQL Server Profiler, System Monitor, and DMVs/DMFs?

Quick Check Answer

■ You need to capture the Start Time data column in the SQL Server Profiler
trace definition to correlate information. Profiler can display a System Monitor counter log alongside a trace as long as the trace has captured the Start
Time data column. DMVs and DMFs can be used in conjunction with this
data as well if the information is also stamped by a time.

PRACTICE Creating a Consolidated Performance View

With the capability to correlate data from multiple tools to fix issues in near real-time,
the big question becomes how to create a longer-term solution.

You can use SQL Server Profiler to create a script that will allow a trace to be executed
programmatically through SQL Server Agent. You can have the trace data output to a
file and loaded into a table by using *fn_trace_gettable*. In addition, the DTA has a command-line interface that allows analysis to be performed programmatically. And
counter logs in System Monitor can be run on a scheduled basis by using the Windows scheduler. You can even log data from DMVs and DMFs to tracking tables to
provide point-in-time snapshots of your system.

By now, you will have worked through a variety of exercises and practices in the chapters within this book. Each of those exercises provided a step-by-step procedure to
create a very specific solution. This exercise takes a different approach.

1. Combine all the information and best practices from this lesson into an automated (or at least semiautomated) process to gather and analyze monitoring
data for your SQL Server 2005 databases.

Lesson Summary

- SQL Server uses a cooperative multiprocessing model instead of a symmetric multiprocessing model for processing queries.

- Controlling this cooperative query processing behavior is the job of the UMS.

- By correlating all the information at your disposal from SQL Server Profiler, System Monitor counter logs, and operational statistics in DMVs/DMFs, you can target the root cause of a performance issue.

- To correlate this information, your SQL Server Profiler trace must capture Start Time data.

Lesson Review

The following questions are intended to reinforce key information presented in this lesson. The questions are also available on the companion CD if you prefer to review them in electronic form.

NOTE Answers

Answers to these questions and explanations of why each answer choice is right or wrong are located in the "Answers" section at the end of the book.

---

1. Which data column is required to correlate a System Monitor counter log to a trace in SQL Server Profiler?

    A. Text Data

    B. End Time

    C. SPID

    D. Start Time

Lesson 6: Resolving Blocking and Deadlocking Issues

If all databases were read-only, we wouldn't have to deal with concurrent access issues. However, we also wouldn't have to worry about any data. Any database that allows multiuser access and data modifications must have mechanisms to maintain data consistency. Having locking and blocking is a desired effect. However, having locking or blocking for an extended period of time or having deadlocks is undesirable and must be resolved. This lesson discusses the locking mechanisms that SQL Server uses to manage concurrent access, how to minimize the effect of blocking, and how to avoid deadlocks.

After this lesson, you will be able to:

- Identify causes of a block by using DMVs.
- Terminate processes.
- Configure SQL Server Profiler for deadlock events.
- Log deadlock chains to the SQL Server error log.
- Analyze deadlock chains.
- Understand how isolation levels affect blocking.
- Understand how transactions can cause blocking in multiuser systems.

Estimated lesson time: 45 minutes

Understanding Locking

To manage multiuser access to data while maintaining data consistency, SQL Server uses a locking mechanism for data. This mechanism arbitrates when a process is allowed to modify data as well as ensuring that reads are consistent.

Locks occur at three different levels and can be of three different types. A lock can be applied at a row, page, or table level. SQL Server manages the resources allocated by locks and determines the appropriate level of the lock based on a relatively aggressive escalation mechanism.

NOTE   Do database-level locks exist?

You might find a database-level lock mentioned in some texts about SQL Server. This type of lock does not exist. Some people use this term simply to indicate that SQL Server has acquired a table-level lock on all tables within a database.

The main decision threshold occurs at approximately three percent to five percent. If SQL Server determines that a query requires locks on three percent to five percent of the rows on a given page, it acquires a page-level lock. Similarly, if SQL Server determines that a query requires locks on three percent to five percent of the pages in a given table, it acquires a table-level lock. Because it is not always possible to accurately predict the percentage of rows or pages that require a lock, SQL Server can automatically promote from fine-grained locks to a coarser level of lock. This process is called *lock escalation.*

NOTE **Lock escalation paths**

It is a common misconception that SQL Server escalates locks from a row level to a page level and finally to a table level. However, lock escalation has exactly two paths. SQL Server escalates row-level locks to table-level locks, and it escalates page-level locks to table-level locks.

In addition to the *locking levels*, SQL Server has three types of locks: shared, exclusive, and update.

A shared lock, as its name implies, allows shared access to the data. An unlimited number of connections are allowed to read the data. However, any piece of data that has a shared lock on it cannot be modified until all shared locks are released.

An exclusive lock, as its name implies, allows only a single connection to access the locked data. SQL Server uses this type of lock during data modification to ensure that other users cannot view the data until it has been committed to the database.

An update lock is a special case. This lock begins as a shared lock while SQL Server locates the rows it must modify within the table. After SQL Server locates the rows, it promotes the lock to an exclusive lock just before it performs the actual modification of the data. This lock promotion during an update is the most common cause of deadlock issues, which we will cover in a moment.

Understanding Isolation Levels

SQL Server 2005 specifies five different *isolation levels* that affect the way transactions are handled and the duration of locks. Table 15-2 describes each of these isolation levels.

Table 15-2   SQL Server 2005 Isolation Levels

Isolation level	Description
READ UNCOMMITTED	This isolation level lets other connections read data that has not yet been committed.
READ COMMITTED	This isolation level prevents other connections from reading data that is being modified until the transaction has been committed.
REPEATABLE READ	Connection 1 is not allowed to read data that has been modified but not yet committed by Connection 2. Additionally, no other connection is allowed to modify any data that has been read by Connection 1 until the transaction completes. This causes shared locks to be placed on all data that is read, and the locks are held until the transaction completes.
READ SERIALIZABLE	This isolation level places all of the restrictions as *REPEATABLE READ* and prevents new rows from being inserted within the keyset range that is locked by a transaction.
SNAPSHOT	Commonly known as "readers do not block writers and writers do not block readers," this isolation level uses row versioning and ensures that a read operation will return the image of the data as it existed prior to the start of a modification.

Understanding Blocking

Because read operations place shared locks on rows, pages, or tables, and update operations need to place exclusive locks on rows, pages, or tables, conflicts can occur between locks—an exclusive lock cannot be acquired against a resource that has a shared lock. This condition is called *blocking* and is a normal operation in multiuser environments to ensure integrity of data and of query results.

Any blocking occurring within an environment should be of a very short duration. Having processes blocked for an extended period of time—generally defined as longer than one second—creates contention, lowers concurrency, and is generally manifested as performance problems within an application.

To determine whether processes are being blocked and to identify the process that is creating the blocking, you would use the *sys.dm_exec_requests* DMV. If a value greater than 0 exists in the *blocking_process_id* column, the process is being blocked by the SPID logged in this column.

You need to carefully monitor blocking issues because they are not actually error conditions. SQL Server is processing requests exactly as intended. However, a blocked process cannot complete until the process that is blocking it has finished and released all the competing locks.

Terminating Processes

In severe cases of blocking, you might need to forcibly terminate a process to allow other processes to complete. Termination should always be a last resort, but it is the only way to allow other processes to complete when they are being blocked by another process.

The command to terminate a process is *KILL spid*, where *spid* is the session ID assigned to the blocking process. This command can be executed only by a member of the *sysadmin* fixed server role. When executed, this command immediately terminates a process. Any open transactions are rolled back, and an error is returned to the application.

Understanding Deadlocking

When a process is blocked, SQL Server still maintains a clear process execution order. After a process that is creating a block has released any competing locks, the blocked process will continue executing. However, it is possible to have a combination of blocks that can never be resolved. This situation is called a *deadlock*.

A deadlock always requires at least two processes, and each of those processes must be making a modification to data. If Process 1 were to acquire an exclusive lock on a row while Process 2 acquired an exclusive lock on a different row, you don't have a problem. However, if Process 1 then attempted to acquire a shared lock on the row that is exclusively locked by Process 2, and Process 2 at the same time attempts to acquire a shared lock on the row that is exclusively locked by Process 1, an impossible scenario is created. Neither process can ever complete because each process relies on the other process completing first. Figure 15-22 illustrates this scenario.

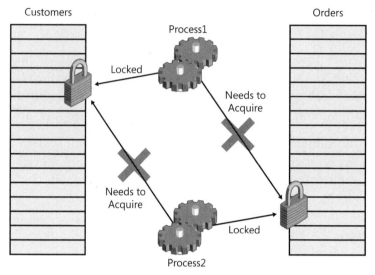

Figure 15-22 Creating a deadlock

Because neither process has the capability to complete a transaction, the locks would be held forever unless there were a way to detect and resolve the deadlock. SQL Server can detect a deadlock and, in response, it applies an algorithm (*deadlock detection*) that selects one of the processes as a *deadlock victim*. SQL Server terminates the victim process, rolls back any open transactions, releases the locks, and returns error 1205 to the application.

The exact error message returned is the following:

```
Msg 1205, Level 13, State 51, Line 1
Transaction (Process ID 55) was deadlocked on lock resources with another process and has
been chosen as the deadlock victim. Rerun the transaction.
```

BEST PRACTICES Detecting a 1205 error

Deadlocks are a timing issue. Essentially, two processes happened to be executing at the wrong moment in time. The data access layer in an application should be coded to detect a 1205 error being returned. When the application detects this error, it should immediately reissue the transaction instead of displaying an error message to a user.

For DBAs and developers, this error message doesn't provide very much information about the cause of the problem. To prevent future deadlocks from occurring, you need to investigate.

Fortunately, SQL Server Profiler provides detailed information about deadlocks via a *deadlock trace*. You create a deadlock trace by selecting the *Locks\Deadlock Graph* event. When a deadlock occurs, this trace produces an output similar to that shown in Figure 15-23.

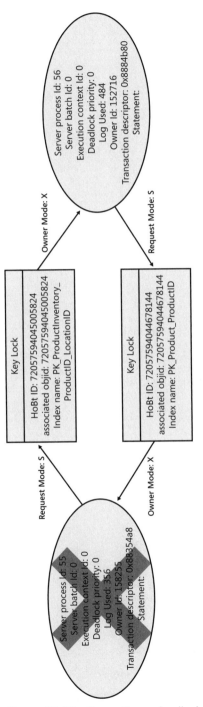

Figure 15-23   Generating a deadlock graph

The deadlock graph is an XML document that you can analyze separately from the graphical display in Profiler. The XML document generated for the deadlock graph shown in Figure 15-23 is as follows:

```
<deadlock-list>
 <deadlock victim="process6b9798">
  <process-list>
   <process id="process6b8f28" taskpriority="0" logused="484"
    waitresource="KEY: 5:72057594044678144 (010086470766)"
    waittime="5859" ownerId="152716"
    transactionname="user_transaction"
    lasttranstarted="2006-03-01T21:52:40.877" XDES="0x8884b80"
    lockMode="S" schedulerid="1" kpid="4384" status="suspended"
    spid="56" sbid="0" ecid="0" priority="0" transcount="2"
    lastbatchstarted="2006-03-01T22:12:39.517"
    lastbatchcompleted="2006-03-01T22:12:35.893"
    clientapp="Microsoft SQL Server Management Studio - Query"
    hostname="WAKKO" hostpid="5988" loginname="WAKKO\admin"
    isolationlevel="read committed (2)" xactid="152716" currentdb="5"
    lockTimeout="4294967295" clientoption1="671090784"
    clientoption2="390200">
    <executionStack>
     <frame procname="adhoc" line="1" stmtstart="24"
      sqlhandle="0x0200000065b7c70eb116ee82532161c54e5244ca43966c00">
SELECT [Name],[ReorderPoint],[StandardCost] FROM [Production].[Product]
WHERE [ProductID]=@1
     </frame>
     <frame procname="adhoc" line="1"
      sqlhandle="0x020000000747301e16f4ac6a5a7d86dd22031822e3d9c3c4">
select Name, ReorderPoint, StandardCost
from Production.Product
where ProductID = 1
     </frame>
    </executionStack>
    <inputbuf>
select Name, ReorderPoint, StandardCost
from Production.Product
where ProductID = 1
    </inputbuf>
   </process>
   <process id="process6b9798" taskpriority="0" logused="356"
    waitresource="KEY: 5:72057594045005824 (0200b8bc7a9c)"
    waittime="1984" ownerId="156255"
    transactionname="user_transaction"
    lasttranstarted="2006-03-01T22:12:29.860" XDES="0x88854a8"
    lockMode="S" schedulerid="1" kpid="6028" status="suspended"
    spid="55" sbid="0" ecid="0" priority="0" transcount="1"
    lastbatchstarted="2006-03-01T22:12:43.393"
    lastbatchcompleted="2006-03-01T22:12:29.860"
    clientapp="Microsoft SQL Server Management Studio - Query"
    hostname="WAKKO" hostpid="5988" loginname="WAKKO\admin"
    isolationlevel="read committed (2)" xactid="156255" currentdb="5"
    lockTimeout="4294967295" clientoption1="671090784"
    clientoption2="390200">
    <executionStack>
```

```
    <frame procname="adhoc" line="1" stmtstart="46"
      sqlhandle="0x02000000c8759f1723746364b90be104dca93fd9cd660dab">
SELECT [ProductID],[LocationID],[Shelf],[Bin],[Quantity]
FROM [Production].[ProductInventory]
WHERE [ProductID]=@1
AND [LocationID]=@2
    </frame>
    <frame procname="adhoc" line="1"
      sqlhandle="0x0200000015377209c7e128bc4aef074f8d4396274ea023a0">
select ProductID, LocationID, Shelf, Bin, Quantity
from Production.ProductInventory
where ProductID = 1
and LocationID = 1
    </frame>
    </executionStack>
    <inputbuf>
select ProductID, LocationID, Shelf, Bin, Quantity
from Production.ProductInventory
where ProductID = 1
and LocationID = 1
    </inputbuf>
    </process>
   </process-list>
   <resource-list>
    <keylock hobtid="72057594044678144" dbid="5"
     objectname="AdventureWorks.Production.Product"
     indexname="PK_Product_ProductID" id="lock3b36500" mode="X"
     associatedObjectId="72057594044678144">
     <owner-list>
      <owner id="process6b9798" mode="X"/>
     </owner-list>
     <waiter-list>
      <waiter id="process6b8f28" mode="S" requestType="wait"/>
     </waiter-list>
    </keylock>
    <keylock hobtid="72057594045005824" dbid="5"
     objectname="AdventureWorks.Production.ProductInventory"
     indexname="PK_ProductInventory_ProductID_LocationID"
     id="lock3b36bc0" mode="X"
     associatedObjectId="72057594045005824">
     <owner-list>
      <owner id="process6b8f28" mode="X"/>
     </owner-list>
     <waiter-list>
      <waiter id="process6b9798" mode="S" requestType="wait"/>
     </waiter-list>
    </keylock>
   </resource-list>
  </deadlock>
</deadlock-list>
```

SQL Server Profiler has three events related to deadlocks. The *Locks\Lock:Deadlock Chain* and *Locks\Lock:Deadlock* events contain little information that is useful for resolving the cause of a deadlock. You should only ever need to use the *Locks\Deadlock Graph* event, which provides all the information required to resolve the cause of a deadlock.

MORE INFO   Deadlocks

For more information about deadlocks, see the SQL Server 2005 Books Online topic "Deadlocking."

> **Quick Check**
> - How is a deadlock created?
>
> **Quick Check Answer**
> - A deadlock is created by two processes acquiring exclusive locks and then requesting a shared lock on the resource that is exclusively locked by the other process. This process produces a blocking situation that cannot resolve itself, so SQL Server will detect the deadlock and select one of the processes as the deadlock victim.

PRACTICE Investigating a Deadlock

In this practice, you will configure SQL Server Profiler to capture the *Locks\Deadlock Graph* event and then produce a deadlock to observe the results.

1. Launch SQL Server Profiler. Create a new trace and connect to your SQL Server instance.

2. Select the blank template.

3. On the Events Selection tab, select the *Locks\Deadlock Graph* event.

4. Click Run to start tracing.

5. Launch SSMS and connect to your SQL Server.

6. Open two query windows and change the database context for both to the *AdventureWorks* database.

7. In query window 1, execute the following query:

```
BEGIN TRANSACTION
UPDATE Production.Product
SET ReorderPoint = 1000
WHERE ProductID = 1
```

8. In query window 2, execute the following query:

```
BEGIN TRANSACTION
UPDATE Production.ProductInventory
SET Quantity = 400
WHERE ProductID = 1
AND LocationID = 1

SELECT Name, ReorderPoint, StandardCost
FROM Production.Product
WHERE ProductID = 1
```

9. Switch to window 1 and execute the following query, making sure that you do NOT issue a *commit transaction* statement:

```
SELECT ProductID, LocationID, Shelf, Bin, Quantity
FROM Production.ProductInventory
WHERE ProductID = 1
AND LocationID = 1
```

10. Switch to Profiler and review the deadlock graph that is generated.

Lesson Summary

- Any system that enables multiple users to change data at the same time must implement a set of rules to ensure data consistency. SQL Server implements these rules by using shared and exclusive locks on rows, pages, and tables.

- When a piece of data is exclusively locked, no other process is allowed to read or modify that data, which inevitably causes blocking to occur as a normal state of operations.

- When blocks are retained for a significant amount of time, end users will begin to complain of slow performance. So it is critical to monitor the *sys.dm_exec_requests* DMV to detect any processes producing excessive blocking. In extreme cases, you might have to terminate the process that is producing the excessive blocking.

- In addition to blocking, design flaws in applications can produce deadlocks. SQL Server will detect a deadlock and automatically select one process to terminate. Capturing a *Locks\Deadlock Graph* event in Profiler and using the information captured to make changes to the application is critical to ensure that your databases continue to operate without errors.

Lesson Review

The following questions are intended to reinforce key information presented in this lesson. The questions are also available on the companion CD if you prefer to review them in electronic form.

NOTE   Answers

Answers to these questions and explanations of why each answer choice is right or wrong are located in the "Answers" section at the end of the book.

---

1. Which of the following are valid locks? (Choose all that apply.)

    A. Shared column lock

    B. Exclusive column lock

    C. Shared table lock

    D. Exclusive row lock

Lesson 7: Resolving Database Errors

There are literally hundreds of errors that can occur within SQL Server, not including errors created in application code. The tools and methods covered in the previous six lessons of this chapter give you the ability to diagnose and fix any error that can occur on your database system. However, to diagnose an issue, you must first be able to connect to the SQL Server. In many cases, the SQL Server can be so busy processing requests that it can no longer allocate memory or processor resources to even allow an administrator to connect.

This situation caused many issues in previous versions of SQL Server. Administrators would become locked out of their own servers and could not investigate or determine the cause of an issue, much less fix the problem. SQL Server 2005 solves this problem by introducing a feature called the *dedicated administrator connection (DAC)*. This lesson explains how to use the DAC and notes that you also need to monitor SQL Server error logs and Windows Application event logs for critical error messages.

> **After this lesson, you will be able to:**
> - Connect to an instance using the DAC.
>
> **Estimated lesson time: 10 minutes**

Using the DAC

The DAC is implemented as a specific TCP endpoint in a SQL Server instance that is always attached to a dedicated UMS. The naming of this feature has already caused a significant amount of unfortunate confusion. The DAC is not intended for use as the connection for all administrative operations. The DAC was created to provide a connection that could always be used by a member of the *sysadmin* role to access a SQL Server instance, thereby guaranteeing that an administrator could not be locked out of SQL Server due to resource allocation issues.

Although it is always running on a dedicated UMS, the DAC has limited resources allocated to it, so the operations that can be performed via the DAC are also limited. Any operation that would spawn multiple threads, such as a backup or restore, are not allowed within the DAC. Only a single connection at a time is allowed. If the connection is already being used, any subsequent connections are refused. Additionally, you create a connection to the DAC in only two ways:

- Via SQLCMD
- Through the Query window in SSMS

The DAC does not allow connections from SQL Server Profiler, the DTA, Object Explorer in SSMS, third-party applications, or any other application.

BEST PRACTICES   DAC: A Last Resort

The DAC is intended as a last-resort connection method. If you can create a connection to SQL Server through normal means, you should use that mechanism, which allows access to anything with the capability to issue queries against SQL Server. Only when connection by any other method is unsuccessful should you use the DAC. You should also use it only for simple operations such as querying DMVs/DMFs and terminating processes.

To connect to the DAC, specify *ADMIN:* and the name of your instance—for example, *ADMIN:MyMachine\Instance1.*

SQL Server and Windows Error Logs

To resolve database errors, you should also review the SQL Server error logs and the Windows Application Event Log for errors. Although a variety of informational messages is logged to each of these locations, any error with a severity level of 16 or higher automatically gets logged to the SQL Server error log and the Windows Application Event Log. Errors with a severity of 16 or higher are critical errors that you need to investigate immediately.

Although you can scan each of these logs manually, it is much more common to point an enterprise monitoring product such as Microsoft Operations Manager at these logs and then have the monitoring tool page an operator when it encounters errors.

PRACTICE Connecting to the DAC

In this practice, you will create a connection to the DAC and determine whether any processes are being blocked.

IMPORTANT   It would be nice to produce a nonresponsive server to demonstrate the ability to always be able to connect to the DAC, but we will skip that step to avoid undue complexity.

---

1. Launch SSMS.
2. Click Database Engine Query.
3. In the Connect To Server dialog box, insert *ADMIN:* before the instance name.

4. After the query window is open, execute the following query to determine whether there are any blocked processes:

```
SELECT session_id, sql_handle, plan_handle FROM sys.dm_exec_requests WHERE
  blocking_session_id > 0
```

Lesson Summary

- When a SQL Server instance is having performance issues but is so busy that an administrator cannot connect to even attempt to fix the issue, the DAC provides a last resort connection method for use by members of the *sysadmin* role. It is always available and cannot be locked out.

- To resolve database errors, you should also review the SQL Server error logs and the Windows Application Event Log, especially for critical errors with a severity level of 16 or higher.

Lesson Review

The following questions are intended to reinforce key information presented in this lesson. The questions are also available on the companion CD if you prefer to review them in electronic form.

NOTE Answers

Answers to these questions and explanations of why each answer choice is right or wrong are located in the "Answers" section at the end of the book.

---

1. Which of the following are valid connection options for the DAC?

    A. *dta* command-line utility

    B. *osql* command-line utility

    C. Object Browser connection

    D. SQLCMD

Chapter Review

To further practice and reinforce the skills you learned in this chapter, you can

- Review the chapter summary.
- Review the list of key terms introduced in this chapter.
- Complete the case scenario. This scenario sets up a real-world situation involving the topics of this chapter and asks you to create a solution.
- Complete the suggested practices.
- Take a practice test.

Chapter Summary

- SQL Server 2005 provides a variety of tools that you can use for both monitoring and troubleshooting.
- SQL Server Profiler provides an interface to SQL Trace, which exposes hundreds of events that occur within the database engine, such as any currently executing queries and their execution statistics.
- A trace that is generated in Profiler can be used as a workload for analysis by the DTA, which exhaustively applies the rules of the query optimizer to determine whether performance can be improved through indexing, indexed views, or partitioning.
- The Windows System Monitor can be used to capture performance counters that can then be correlated to a SQL Trace within Profiler to provide an environment context to the events that were captured.
- The most significant step forward within SQL Server 2005 can be found within DMVs and DMFs, which provide a means of gathering and comparing extremely granular data via a simple *SELECT* statement. This set of instrumentation provides a greater level of detail into the inner operational state of a SQL Server instance than was ever available before.
- By using each of these tools, along with an understanding of the locking mechanisms that govern all data access within SQL Server, you can quickly diagnose problems and maximize availability of data to your users. These tools can also be combined into an automated system that can identify activity patterns and proactively make adjustments to avoid availability issues.

■ To enhance SQL Server's error-resolution capabilities, Microsoft introduced DAC to provide a connection that could always be used by a member of the *sysadmin* role to access a SQL Server instance, thereby guaranteeing that an administrator could not be locked out of SQL Server because of resource allocation issues.

■ In addition to using SQL Server Profiler/SQL Trace, System Monitor, and DMVs and DMFs, you should also monitor SQL Server error logs and the Windows Application Event Log for error messages.

Key Terms

Do you know what these key terms mean? You can check your answers by looking up the terms in the glossary at the end of the book.

■ blocking

■ cooperative multiprocessing

■ Database Engine Tuning Advisor (DTA)

■ deadlock

■ deadlock detection

■ deadlock trace

■ deadlock victim

■ Dedicated administrator connection (DAC)

■ Dynamic Management Functions (DMFs)

■ Dynamic Management Views (DMVs)

■ isolation levels

■ lock escalation

■ locking level

■ locking promotion

■ PerfMon

■ replay trace

■ showplan

■ SQL Server Management Object (SMO)

■ SQL Server Profiler

- SQL Trace
- System Monitor
- system process ID (SPID)
- trace
- trace events
- User Mode Scheduler (UMS)
- wait type
- workload file

Case Scenario: Diagnosing Performance Problems

In the following case scenario, you will apply what you've learned in this chapter. You can find answers to these questions in the "Answers" section at the end of this book.

Contoso Limited, a health care company located in Bothell, WA, has a volatile database containing patient claims data. The company has recently undertaken a massive development process to rewrite the entire patient claims database, currently running on Microsoft Access, in a Microsoft .NET language with the data being stored in SQL Server 2005.

The company's developers could port the Access database and rewrite the patient claims application's entire functionality. However, they did not have any DBAs on the staff to help with any database issues. The developers also have little knowledge about SQL Server. In development and testing, the new application performed much better than the previous application, so testing was cut short, and the application was deployed into production.

At the same time as the new application was put into production, sales signed four major new customers, which increased application activity almost 30 times more than before. By the time the support staff was partially done setting up the first customer, the customer started complaining about some performance issues. And performance declined rapidly as more data was added. Management concluded that it would be impossible to get all four of the new customers running on the new application when it couldn't even handle the load it already had. In addition, the IT staff was facing unexplained deadlock errors.

You have been hired by Contoso Limited to fix the performance issues along with all of the unexplained "deadlock victim" errors. How do you go about fixing this environment?

Suggested Practices

To help you successfully master the exam objectives presented in this chapter, complete the following practice tasks.

Working with SQL Server Profiler

- **Practice 1** Create a trace to capture all the queries being executed against a particular database. Include the reads, writes, duration, and CPU of each query.

- **Practice 2** Create a replay trace and set up a test environment against which you can replay it.

- **Practice 3** Create a trace to capture all the queries being executed against a particular database along with all of the statistics and query plans necessary to analyze performance issues. Save the trace in a table and then find the top 10 queries by frequency, duration, and impact.

- **Practice 4** Create an automated routine executed from SQL Server Agent that will start traces every 15 minutes, run them for 10 minutes, and then load the results into a centralized table.

Working with System Monitor

- **Practice 1** Create a System Monitor counter log to capture the processor, memory utilization (system and within SQL Server), and SQL Server caching counters. Run this counter log while you are executing the traces in the other practices.

Using the Database Engine Tuning Advisor

- **Practice 1** Using the trace generated in "Working with SQL Server Profiler" Practice 3, use DTA to analyze the workload for performance improvements.

- **Practice 2** Build the semiautomated performance analysis system outlined in the best practices within the DTA lesson.

Using Dynamic Management Views and Functions

- **Practice 1** Find the indexes in your databases that are not being used.

- **Practice 2** Starting with the DMV that will show you waiting tasks, return the query that is executing on a process that is tying up a resource, and causing other processes to have to wait for it to be released.

- **Practice 3** Identify indexes that might be good candidates for creation in your database to improve performance.

- **Practice 4** Identify the top two resources that processes have to wait to be allocated. Clear the statistics and gather this data again. Then, using the individual processes already created in this practice, build an automated routine to gather the wait types, wait times, and signal wait times on a 15-minute interval and log the results to a table for further analysis.

Correlating Performance Data

- **Practice 1** Correlate the trace from "Working with SQL Server Profiler" Practice 1 with the counter log from "Working with System Monitor" Practice 1.

- **Practice 2** Correlate the trace from "Working with SQL Server Profiler" Practice 2 with the counter log from "Working with System Monitor" Practice 1. After generating a counter log during the trace replay on the test system, correlate the trace results from the replay with the counter log. Compare the results from the two systems.

Resolving Blocking and Deadlocking Issues

- **Practice 1** Create a deadlock trace.

Using DAC

- **Practice 1** Create several blocked processes. Connect to the DAC by using SQL-CMD and return the SPID that is causing the blocking issue.

Take a Practice Test

The practice tests on this book's companion CD offer many options. For example, you can test yourself on just the content covered in this chapter, or you can test yourself on all the 70-431 certification exam content. You can set up the test so that it closely simulates the experience of taking a certification exam, or you can set it up in study mode so that you can look at the correct answers and explanations after you answer each question.

MORE INFO   Practice tests

For details about all the practice test options available, see the "How to Use the Practice Tests" section in this book's Introduction.

Chapter 16
Managing Database Snapshots

A *Database Snapshot* is a new technology in Microsoft SQL Server 2005 that provides very specific functionality for creating read-only copies of your databases. This chapter explains how to create Database Snapshots, restrictions on their use, and how to integrate Database Snapshots into a recovery strategy.

Exam objectives in this chapter:
- Manage database snapshots
    - ❑ Create a snapshot
    - ❑ Revert a database from a snapshot

Lessons in this chapter:

Before You Begin

To complete the lessons in this chapter, you must have

- SQL Server 2005 installed.
- A connection to a SQL Server 2005 instance.
- A copy of the *AdventureWorks* sample database.

Real World

Michael Hotek

Database administrators (DBAs) are frequently called upon to manipulate data within operational systems. When an organization needs to bulk load data or make mass changes, DBAs are called upon to directly modify data because it is the most efficient way. Before making any change of this nature to a system, I always create a backup so that the state of the database can be reverted in the event of an error during the data change operation.

Creating a backup can account for a significant portion of the maintenance time required to make the changes. With the new Database Snapshot technology, I can quickly save the state of the database before making changes. By eliminating the need to make a full backup, I now have a lot more time to sleep while other DBAs spend endless nights waiting for a backup to complete.

Lesson 1: Creating a Database Snapshot

A Database Snapshot encompasses a set of new technologies in SQL Server 2005 that allow a DBA to quickly create a data snapshot. This lesson will introduce the key concepts of Database Snapshots along with how to create and use them.

After this lesson, you will be able to:

■ Explain the structure of a Database Snapshot.

■ Explain how copy-on-write works.

■ Create a Database Snapshot.

■ Query a Database Snapshot.

Estimated lesson time: 10 minutes

Database Snapshot Structure

You build a Database Snapshot against a *source database*. Because a Database Snapshot is a point-in-time, read-only copy, it does not contain a transaction log and cannot be written to.

At the time of creation, the files underneath a Database Snapshot do not contain any data and consume very little space on disk. This is accomplished by defining the files as *sparse files* within the file system. By leveraging sparse file technology, you can create Database Snapshots nearly instantaneously, even for multiterabyte databases.

All database objects, along with users and permissions, are the same between the source database and the Database Snapshot. Because a Database Snapshot is read-only, you cannot change permissions, add users, or modify any objects or data.

Copy-On-Write Technology

To maintain the Database Snapshot as a point-in-time, read-only copy of a database, as well as satisfy the condition that a Database Snapshot be very fast to create, a mechanism had to be created to maintain the data state.

At initial creation, a Database Snapshot does not contain any pages of data nor does it contain any information from the source database. The file structure is created as a sparse file and the Database Snapshot links back to the source database.

When a data page changes in the source database, SQL Server writes the original image of the page into the Database Snapshot, which preserves the state of the data page at the instant in time that the Database Snapshot was created. Any subsequent changes to the data page in the source database are ignored by the Database Snapshot. This write of the original image of the data page from the source database is called *copy-on-write*.

Quick Check

- What is a Database Snapshot and what information does it contain?

Quick Check Answer

- A Database Snapshot provides a point-in-time, read-only copy of the source database. The only information contained within a Database Snapshot are the pages that changed in the source database since the Database Snapshot was created.

A Database Snapshot contains a unique structure called a *catalog of changed pages*, which is a bitmap that contains a list of the pages within the source database that have changed since the point in time of the creation of the Database Snapshot. When SQL Server writes the original image of a data page to the Database Snapshot, it changes the bit corresponding to that page from 0 to 1 within the catalog of changed pages.

By writing the original image of a data page to the Database Snapshot, it allows the Database Snapshot to maintain the state of the data at the point in time of the Database Snapshot creation. Because a Database Snapshot contains only the original image of pages that were changed since creation, very little overhead is incurred on the system.

Quick Check

- A Database Snapshot is required to maintain the state of the data at a single point in time. How is this requirement satisfied?

Quick Check Answer

- A catalog of changed pages tracks those pages that have been changed since the Database Snapshot was created. This catalog is used during query execution to determine whether data should be retrieved from data pages written to the Database Snapshot or from the source database.

Creating a Database Snapshot

You create a Database Snapshot like any other database within SQL Server, but you must use a special clause in the *CREATE DATABASE* command.

The *CREATE DATABASE* statement for a Database Snapshot must meet some specific requirements:

- You must include an entry for each filegroup in the source database.
- You must define the logical name of each filegroup the same as in the source database.
- You must specify the *AS SNAPSHOT OF* clause with the *CREATE DATABASE* command.

The general syntax for creating a Database Snapshot is as follows:

```
CREATE DATABASE database_snapshot_name
    ON
        (
        NAME = logical_file_name,
        FILENAME = 'os_file_name'
        ) [ ,...n ]
    AS SNAPSHOT OF source_database_name
```

A Database Snapshot has some important restrictions:

- You cannot back up, restore, or detach the Database Snapshot.
- It must exist on the same SQL Server instance as the source database.

NOTE **Database mirroring with Database Snapshots**

A Database Snapshot must exist on the same SQL Server instance as the source database. The mirror database in a Database Mirroring session is not accessible for any operations. However, it is possible to create a Database Snapshot against a mirror database.

This capability can be used to offload reporting activity to the server containing the mirror.

- Full-text indexes are not supported.
- You cannot drop, detach, or restore the source database when a Database Snapshot is present.
- You cannot create Database Snapshots against system databases.
- Structural changes are not allowed, such as adding or removing filegroups.

Retrieving Data from a Database Snapshot

Writing a *SELECT* statement against a Database Snapshot is not any different from writing a *SELECT* statement against any other database.

The result set of a query against a Database Snapshot is obtained from two locations, with the data then combined into a single result set.

- Data that has not changed since the Database Snapshot was created is obtained from the source database.

- Data that has changed since the Database Snapshot was created is obtained from the data pages written to the Database Snapshot.

PRACTICE Creating a Database Snapshot

In this exercise, you will practice the creation of a Database Snapshot against the *AdventureWorks* database.

1. Open SQL Server Management Studio (SSMS).

2. Connect to the SQL Server instance containing the *AdventureWorks* sample database.

3. Click New Query in the toolbar.

4. Type the following code:

```
CREATE DATABASE snapshottest
on
    (
    NAME='AdventureWorks_Data',
    FILENAME='C:\Program Files\Microsoft SQL
     Server\MSSQL.1\MSSQL\Data\snapshottest.ds')
AS SNAPSHOT OF AdventureWorks
```

NOTE No spaces in path

Be sure not to enter any spaces in the paths contained within the single quotes in the previous code.

---

5. Insert data into the *AdventureWorks* database.

6. Observe that this data does not exist when querying the Database Snapshot.

Lesson Summary

- A Database Snapshot is a point-in-time, read-only copy of a source database that exists on the same SQL Server instance as the source database. As pages are changed in the source database, the original image of the data page is written into the sparse files of the Database Snapshot to preserve the state of the data at creation time.

- Although a Database Snapshot can be queried like any other database, you are not allowed to modify data or structural elements. A Database Snapshot also cannot be used for backup/restore operations. Even though it is required to exist on the same SQL Server instance as the source database, a Database Snapshot can be created against a mirror database within a Database Mirroring session.

Lesson Review

The following questions are intended to reinforce key information presented in this lesson. The questions are also available on the companion CD if you prefer to review them in electronic form.

NOTE Answers

Answers to these questions and explanations of why each answer choice is right or wrong are located in the "Answers" section at the end of the book.

---

1. Which operations can be performed against a Database Snapshot?
   A. *BACKUP DATABASE*
   B. *ALTER DATABASE*
   C. *SELECT COLUMN1, COLUMN2 FROM TABLE*
   D. *UPDATE TABLE1 SET COLUMN1 = 4*

2. You can create a Database Snapshot against which types of databases? (Choose all that apply.)
   A. User database
   B. Master database
   C. Another Database Snapshot
   D. Mirror database

3. What data is contained within a Database Snapshot? (Choose all that apply.)

    A. All original pages of the source database

    B. Only the original image of pages changed since the Database Snapshot was created

    C. A catalog of changed pages

    D. Metadata about the database objects

Lesson 2: Reverting a Database from a Database Snapshot

A Database Snapshot provides a point-in-time copy of a source database. Because it provides a copy of the data in the database, you can use it to recover in a variety of situations. In the event of data being accidentally damaged or if an administrative process makes changes that are unwanted, you can extract the original version of the data from the Database Snapshot and move it back into the source database using either an *INSERT* or *UPDATE* statement.

In an extreme case, a DBA might want to restore the state of a database back to a previous point in time. This lesson will explain how to revert a source database to a previous point in time by using a Database Snapshot.

After this lesson, you will be able to:

■ Revert a database from a Database Snapshot.

Estimated lesson time: 10 minutes

Reverting a Database

Reverting a database is a special subclass of restore operation that you can perform against a database. During a restore of a database, you can leave the database in a recovering state to apply subsequent transaction logs to roll a database forward to a specific point in time. Reverting a database will take a database back to a point in time; however, you cannot restore subsequent backups after reverting the database to that point in time.

Using a Database Snapshot to revert a database has some restrictions:

■ Only a single Database Snapshot can exist against a source database.

■ Any full-text catalogs on the source database are dropped and must be re-created.

■ The transaction log is rebuilt, which breaks the log chain.

■ The source database and Database Snapshot are offline during the revert.

The syntax to revert a database from a Database Snapshot is as follows:

```
RESTORE DATABASE <database_name> FROM DATABASE_SNAPSHOT = <database_snapshot_name>
```

> **Quick Check**
> - How many Database Snapshots can exist against a source database when you are restoring?
>
> **Quick Check Answer**
> - Reverting a database using a Database Snapshot causes all the changed pages within a Database Snapshot to overwrite the corresponding pages in the source database. Because this process changes the state of the database, it would immediately invalidate all Database Snapshots except the one used to revert from. Therefore, SQL Server enforces the restriction that only a single Database Snapshot can exist against a source database when you use the Database Snapshot to revert. In this way, it prevents the possibility of having invalid Database Snapshots.

PRACTICE Reverting a Database from a Database Snapshot

In this practice, you will revert the *AdventureWorks* database to a previous version using the Database Snapshot you created in the previous lesson in this chapter.

1. If necessary, open SSMS and connect to the SQL Server instance containing the Database Snapshot you created in the previous lesson in this chapter.
2. Click New Query.
3. Type the following code:

    ```
    RESTORE DATABASE AdventureWorks FROM DATABASE_SNAPSHOT = 'snapshottest'
    ```

4. Verify that the data added to the table in the *AdventureWorks* database during the previous exercise no longer exists.

Lesson Summary

- The *RESTORE DATABASE* command contains a special clause that enables a DBA to revert a database from a Database Snapshot. This operation would invalidate any other Database Snapshots created against the source database, so you must drop all other Database Snapshots before you can perform a revert. Additionally, any operation that relies on a contiguous transaction log chain will be interrupted because the restore process will rebuild the transaction log.

Lesson Review

The following question is intended to reinforce key information presented in this lesson. The question is also available on the companion CD if you prefer to review it in electronic form.

NOTE Answers

Answers to this question and explanations of why each answer choice is right or wrong are located in the "Answers" section at the end of the book.

---

1. Which of the following are required before a database can be reverted from a Database Snapshot? (Choose all that apply.)

    A. Full text catalogs on the source database must be dropped.

    B. Users cannot be accessing the source database or the Database Snapshot.

    C. Log shipping must be stopped.

    D. All Database Snapshots except the Database Snapshot used for the revert must be dropped.

Chapter Review

To further practice and reinforce the skills you learned in this chapter, you can

- Review the chapter summary.
- Review the list of key terms introduced in this chapter.
- Complete the case scenario. This scenario sets up a real-world situation involving the topics of this chapter and asks you to create solutions.
- Complete the suggested practices.
- Take a practice test.

Chapter Summary

- A Database Snapshot is a point-in-time, read-only copy of a source database that can be used for read activities.
- In addition to read activities, you can use a Database Snapshot to revert a database to a previous point in time defined by the instant in time at which you created the Database Snapshot.
- Because Database Snapshots can be used for read operations as well as recovering to a previous point in time, they are ideal for use in situations in which DBAs would normally create an interim backup to eliminate a significant amount of time spent during maintenance operations.

Key Terms

Do you know what these key terms mean? You can check your answers by looking up the terms in the glossary at the end of the book.

- catalog of changed pages
- copy-on-write
- Database Snapshot
- reverting a database
- source database
- sparse file

Case Scenario: Implementing Database Snapshots for Administrative Actions

In the following case scenario, you will apply what you've learned in this chapter. You can find answers to these questions in the "Answers" section at the end of this book.

Contoso Limited, a health care organization located in Bothell, WA, has a very volatile database that contains patient claims data. The patient data is protected by privacy laws, and all access to this data is required to be audited. Audit data is written into a set of audit tables by the stored procedures that control all data access within the patient claims database.

Auditors within the organization, along with external auditors, require access to audit data in the patient claims database at specific points in time.

Each evening, Contoso receives data feeds from several external vendors who process payments to patients. Data in the feeds frequently needs to be edited and reimported based on validation scripts that reconcile the data within the patient claims database with the data feeds submitted by the external vendors. During the time when the import processes execute, no other transactions are issued against the patient claims database. The current process creates a full backup of the patient claims database before the import routines are executed.

1. How can Contoso DBAs reduce the amount of time it takes to import data feeds?

2. What mechanism can Contoso use to provide mutiple point-in-time copies of the data for auditors to query while minimizing the amount of time spent on administering this solution?

Suggested Practices

Database Snapshots are a very specific feature within SQL Server 2005. A Database Snapshot has exactly one way to create it, and there is exactly one way to revert a database using a Database Snapshot. Therefore, no additional practices exist for Database Snapshots beyond those already specified within this chapter.

Take a Practice Test

The practice tests on this book's companion CD offer many options. For example, you can test yourself on just the content covered in this chapter, or you can test yourself on all the 70-431 certification exam content. You can set up the test so that it closely simulates the experience of taking a certification exam, or you can set it up in study mode so that you can look at the correct answers and explanations after you answer each question.

MORE INFO   **Practice tests**

For details about all the practice test options available, see the section titled "How to Use the Practice Tests" in this book's Introduction.

Chapter 17

Implementing Database Mirroring

Database mirroring is a new Microsoft SQL Server 2005 availability technology that lets you maintain a hot or warm standby server with automatic failover and no data latency. Database mirroring, available currently as an evaluation feature that you enable by using a trace flag, operates at the database level to provide a duplicate copy of data on a mirror database and server. This chapter introduces you to database mirroring, which will be included as a supported feature of SQL Server 2005 in a future service pack, and it explains each *operating mode* that you can configure for this long-awaited feature.

MORE INFO   Database mirroring

This chapter covers the basic data mirroring information you need for the 70-431 exam. For full details about database mirroring, see the white paper "Database Mirroring in SQL Server 2005" by Ron Talmage at *www.microsoft.com/technet/prodtechnol/sql/2005/dbmirror.mspx*.

Exam objectives in this chapter:

- Implement database mirroring.
    - ❑ Prepare databases for database mirroring.
    - ❑ Create endpoints.
    - ❑ Specify database partners.
    - ❑ Specify a witness server.
    - ❑ Configure an operating mode.

Lessons in this chapter:

Before You Begin

To complete the lessons in this chapter, you must have

- Three instances of SQL Server 2005 installed.

- Either Standard or Enterprise Edition for all instances.

- A copy of the *AdventureWorks* sample database on one of the instances.

- Trace flag 1400 enabled on all three instances.

NOTE Enabling database mirroring with trace flag 1400

In the release-to-manufacturing (RTM) version of SQL Server 2005, database mirroring is not a supported feature and can be enabled only by using trace flag 1400. In a future SQL Server 2005 service pack, database mirroring will be enabled and fully supported within the product. To set a trace flag, refer to the SQL Server 2005 Books Online article "DBCC TRACEON (Transact-SQL)." SQL Server 2005 Books Online is installed as part of SQL Server 2005. Updates for SQL Server 2005 Books Online are available for download at *www.microsoft.com/technet/prodtechnol/sql/2005/downloads/books.mspx*.

Real World

Michael Hotek

Since I formally entered the database industry more than a decade ago, my primary focus has been on building systems to predictably achieve high levels of availability. In the 1980s and 1990s, this was a rather difficult task. It usually involved complex architectures, complicated components, and a large dose of custom coding. The tools and technologies were immature at best and nonexistent at worst.

You could divide the availability systems that we designed back then into two basic categories. Client-oriented systems would receive a transaction and then write it to multiple destinations. And we generally built server-oriented systems around code to transfer backups between one or more systems.

As technology matured, we gained additional tools that allowed basic data duplication across multiple environments in a timely manner. However, this advancement also introduced latency between the primary and secondary databases, which could lead to data loss. We learned to deal with the potential problem because we simply could not eliminate it.

What we needed was an integrated database technology, transparent to applications, that would maintain a duplicate copy of the data without incurring latency. If the technology could also provide mechanisms to automatically fail over to the secondary database upon failure of the primary database, it would be a significant evolutionary advancement in availability technologies.

With the addition of database mirroring in SQL Server 2005, we finally have a technology that fills a significant gap in availability solutions and does not require custom coding. I can now make a single database within an instance highly available, with automatic failover, no latency between the primary and secondary databases, and transparency to the application. It isn't a perfect solution yet, but database mirroring is well on the way to fulfilling an availability requirement that I've had for well over ten years.

Lesson 1: Understanding Database Mirroring Roles

All new technologies add new terminology to our vocabulary, and database mirroring is no different. In this lesson, you learn many of the key terms for database mirroring, including principal database, mirror database, and witness server. And you see how these different *database mirroring roles* interact with each other in a database mirroring session.

> **After this lesson, you will be able to:**
> - Define what the principal database does.
> - Define what the mirror database does.
> - Define what the witness server does.
> - Understand how the database mirroring roles work together.
>
> **Estimated lesson time: 10 minutes**

Database Mirroring Roles

Database mirroring comprises two mandatory roles and a third optional role. You must define a database in a principal role and another database in a mirror role. You can also optionally define a SQL Server instance in the role of witness server to govern automatic failover from the primary to the mirror database. Figure 17-1 shows a reference diagram for a database mirroring configuration.

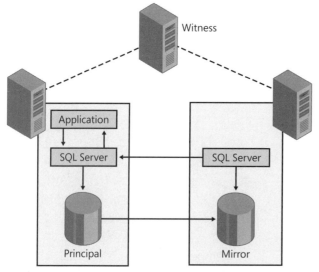

Figure 17-1   Database mirroring components

Principal Role

The database you configure in the *principal* role becomes the source of all transactions in a data mirroring session. The primary database is recovered, it allows connections, and applications can read data to and write data from it. Note that you must specify the Full recovery model for the database to participate in a *database mirroring session*, a requirement that Lesson 2 covers in more detail.

NOTE   Serving the database

When an instance has a database that allows transactions to be processed against it, it is said to be "serving the database."

Mirror Role

The database you define in the *mirror* role is the partner of the primary database and continuously receives transactions from the principal database. The database mirroring process is constantly replaying transactions from the primary database into the transaction log and flushing the transaction log to the data files on the mirror database so that the mirror database includes the same data as the primary database. The mirror database is in a recovering state, so it does not allow connections of any kind, and transactions cannot be written directly to it. However, you can perform a database snapshot against a mirror database to give users read-only access to the database's data at a specific point in time. (See Chapter 16, "Managing Database Snapshots," for information about database snapshots.)

NOTE   Transient operating states

The principal and mirror roles are transient operating states within a database mirroring session. Because the databases are exact equivalents and are maintained in synchronization with each other, either database can take on the role of principal or mirror at any time.

Witness Server

The *witness server* is the third and optional role you can configure within a database mirroring session. You use this server to implement automatic failure detection and failover. You configure the witness server by using the *High Availability operating mode*, which Lesson 4 discusses. Although database mirroring allows a principal and mirror to occur only in pairs (for example, a principal cannot have more than one mirror, and vice versa), a witness server can service multiple database mirroring pairs. Each database mirroring pair that a witness server services has a single row of information in the *sys.database_mirroring_witnesses* catalog view. The sole purpose of the witness is to serve as an arbiter within the High Availability operating mode to ensure that the database can be served on only one SQL Server instance at a time. If a primary database fails, and the witness confirms the failure, the mirror database can take the primary role and make its data available to users.

IMPORTANT   Database-level vs. server-level roles

Database mirroring's principal and mirror roles occur at a database level and must be defined within SQL Server 2005 instances that are either Standard or Enterprise Edition. However, you define the witness role at an instance level. The instance of SQL Server 2005 that you use for the witness server can be any edition, including SQL Server Express Edition, which is why we refer to a principal or mirror *database* but a witness *server*.

> ## Quick Check
> - What are the three database mirroring roles and what functions do they serve?
>
> ## Quick Check Answer
> - The principal database is currently serving the database to applications.
> - The mirror database is in a recovering state and does not allow connections.
> - The optional witness server is an instance of SQL Server that is used for automatic failure detection and failover from a primary to a mirror database.

Lesson Summary

- A database participating in a database mirroring session can be in one of two roles: principal or mirror.
- The principal database is the database that allows connections and transactions to be processed.
- The mirror database is inaccessible to applications and receives transactions sent from the principal database.

- The witness is a SQL Server instance that functions as an arbiter within a database mirroring session. This is an optional component that you use when you want to implement automatic failure detection and failover.

Lesson Review

The following questions are intended to reinforce key information presented in this lesson. The questions are also available on the companion CD if you prefer to review them in electronic form.

NOTE   Answers

Answers to these questions and explanations of why each answer choice is right or wrong are located in the "Answers" section at the end of the book.

---

1. Which role is valid for database mirroring?

    A. Publisher

    B. Principal

    C. Primary

    D. Monitor

2. Which of the following are valid actions for a witness? (Choose all that apply.)

    A. Arbitrates a failover for the High Protection operating mode

    B. Arbitrates a failover for the High Availability operating mode

    C. Serves the database when the principal and mirror are offline

    D. Services multiple database mirroring sessions

Lesson 2: Preparing Databases for Database Mirroring

You configure database mirroring on a database-by-database basis. Each database you define must use the Full recovery model to participate in a database mirroring session. And you must initialize each mirror database to ensure that it is synchronized with the principal before you start the mirroring session. This lesson walks through the four general steps you need to take to prepare for database mirroring:

1. Ensure that databases are set to use the Full recovery model.
2. Back up the primary database.
3. Restore the database to the instance hosting the mirror database by using *NORE-COVERY*.
4. Copy all necessary system objects to the instance hosting the mirror database.

After this lesson, you will be able to:
- Perform the prerequisite steps for enabling database mirroring.

Estimated lesson time: 10 minutes

Recovery Model

SQL Server offers three recovery models for databases: Simple, Bulk-Logged, and Full. The Simple recovery model minimally logs transactions, removing the inactive portion of the transaction log at each checkpoint. The Bulk-Logged recovery model does not fully log certain operations such as *BULK INSERT*, *BCP*, or *CREATE INDEX* operations. Because database mirroring maintains both the primary and mirror databases as exact duplicates, including synchronizing all internal structures such as Log Sequence Numbers (LSNs), the Simple and Bulk-Logged recovery models are incompatible with database mirroring. Therefore, the only recovery model that a database can use to participate in database mirroring is the Full recovery model.

NOTE   Full recovery model required

You cannot configure database mirroring if the participating databases are not using the Full recovery model. In addition, you cannot change the recovery model of a database that is participating in database mirroring.

Backup and Restore

Because the principal and mirror databases are duplicates of each other, a mechanism is needed to ensure that both databases are initialized to the same state. The process of initialization for database mirroring involves performing a backup of the principal database and restoring it to the mirror.

When restoring the database to the mirror, it is essential that you specify the *NORE-COVERY* option for the *RESTORE* command, which guarantees that the starting state of the mirror reflects the state of the principal database, including the LSNs.

You will find that the backup and restore process consumes the most amount of time during database mirroring configuration. However, you probably will not be able to take the primary database offline to initialize database mirroring. Instead, because the database on the mirror is in an unrecovered state, you can apply a chain of transaction logs to bring the mirror up-to-date.

BEST PRACTICES   Initializing the mirror

Instead of performing a backup to initialize the mirror, I always use the last full backup of the primary database and then apply all subsequent transaction logs. After all log backups are taken, I execute a final transaction log backup to capture all remaining transactions and then initiate database mirroring. An alternative method uses log shipping to maintain the two databases in synchronization and as the initialization mechanism for database mirroring. In this case, you might still have to apply at least one transaction log backup before you can initiate the database mirroring session.

BEST PRACTICES   Backup/restore and log shipping

For more information about backup/restore and log shipping, please refer to Chapter 11, "Backing Up, Restoring, and Moving a Database," and Chapter 18, "Implementing Log Shipping."

Copy System Objects

Database mirroring operates at a database level, so it is not responsible for any other objects on the server. So although you can configure database mirroring to automatically fail over to the mirror database, to allow applications to function after a failover, you must ensure that all other objects are transferred to the instance hosting the mirror database.

The most common objects that require transfer are the logins that allow applications to authenticate for database access. You can also have linked servers, SQL Server

Integration Services (SSIS) packages, SQL Server Agent jobs, custom error messages, or other objects configured on the server. Copying all of these objects to the instance hosting the mirror database is the final step in the initialization process.

NOTE   Using SSIS tasks to transfer objects

To transfer objects to the instance hosting the mirror database, you can use SSIS, which includes the Transfer Logins task for transferring logins from one instance of SQL Server to another while keeping any passwords encrypted. SSIS also provides tasks for transferring SQL Server Agent jobs, error messages, and other types of objects.

> ## Quick Check
> - What is the process for preparing a database to participate in a database mirroring session?
>
> ### Quick Check Answer
> - Change the recovery model to Full, back up the primary database, restore to the instance hosting the mirror database with the *NORECOVERY* option, and then copy all system objects such as logins and linked servers.

PRACTICE Preparing Databases for Database Mirroring

In this exercise, you will practice preparing databases for database mirroring using the *AdventureWorks* database.

1. Connect to the instance hosting the *AdventureWorks* database that you want to use as the principal database.

2. Right-click the *AdventureWorks* database and choose Properties. Select the Options page.

3. From the Recovery Model drop-down list, select Full. Click OK.

4. Back up the *AdventureWorks* database.

5. Copy the backup to the machine running the instance on which you want to host the mirror database.

6. Restore the *AdventureWorks* database, ensuring that you specify not to recover the database.

7. Back up the transaction log on the *AdventureWorks* database, copy the backup to the machine running the instance in which the mirror database is being hosted, and restore the transaction log.

8. Transfer to the instance hosting the mirror all logins, jobs, linked servers, and other objects external to the database that are needed for the application to work.

Lesson Summary

- Database mirroring maintains synchronization between the two databases in the mirroring session.

- All databases that participate in database mirroring must be set to the Full recovery model to ensure that all transactions are applied to the mirror.

- You then must initialize the mirror by restoring a backup, ensuring that the *NORECOVERY* option is specified.

- Because database mirroring is responsible only for copying the contents of a database to the server hosting the mirror database, you must separately copy over all other server objects, such as logins, linked servers, and jobs.

Lesson Review

The following questions are intended to reinforce key information presented in this lesson. The questions are also available on the companion CD if you prefer to review them in electronic form.

NOTE   Answers

Answers to these questions and explanations of why each answer choice is right or wrong are located in the "Answers" section at the end of the book.

1. Which of the following is a valid step for preparing a database to participate in a database mirroring session? (Choose all that apply.)

   A. Configure distribution.

   B. Back up the database.

   C. Restore the database with *RECOVERY*.

   D. Restore the database with *NORECOVERY*.

2. Which database setting is valid for database mirroring?

    A. Full recovery model

    B. 80 compatibility level

    C. Read only

    D. Bulk-Logged recovery model

Lesson 3: Establishing Endpoints

SQL Server 2005 introduces a stronger, revamped, multilayer security model. The first layer of security occurs at the connection point to an instance. And *endpoints* control the capability to connect to an instance. Because database mirroring relies on connectivity among up to three instances of SQL Server 2005, you must establish endpoints to enable communications among these instances. In this lesson, you review the concept of endpoints, walk through endpoint options, and see how to configure endpoints specifically for database mirroring.

After this lesson, you will be able to:

- Explain endpoint configuration options and best practices.
- Create endpoints for database mirroring.

Estimated lesson time: 10 minutes

Endpoint Types

In SQL Server 2005, you can create two types of endpoints: *TCP* or *HTTP*. Database mirroring uses *TCP* endpoints for communications. *HTTP* endpoints, on the other hand, service *SOAP* requests.

MORE INFO   HTTP endpoints

For information about *HTTP* endpoints, see Chapter 13, "Working with HTTP Endpoints."

Along with a type definition for an endpoint, you specify a *payload*. *TCP* endpoints can have a payload of *TSQL*, *SERVICE_BROKER*, or *DATABASE_MIRRORING*. For a database mirroring session, you create *TCP* endpoints with a payload of *DATABASE_MIRRORING*. You create an endpoint at the SQL Server instance level instead of at the database level. So for each SQL Server instance, you can create only one endpoint, which has a payload of *DATABASE_MIRRORING*.

MORE INFO   Endpoints

For more information about endpoints, see the SQL Server 2005 Books Online article "CREATE ENDPOINT (Transact-SQL)." SQL Server 2005 Books Online is installed as part of SQL Server 2005. Updates for SQL Server 2005 Books Online are available for download at *www.microsoft.com/ technet/prodtechnol/sql/2005/downloads/books.mspx*.

Endpoint Security

Endpoints provide multiple layers of security that you can configure for your needs. The first level of security is in the type and payload definition, as you just saw. When you create an endpoint for a database mirroring session, the endpoint will not respond to any requests other than for database mirroring. The endpoint will refuse any HTTP, Transact-SQL, or Service Broker requests.

The second layer of security is the TCP configuration of the endpoint. Each *TCP* endpoint requires that you specify a port number. The default port number for a *TCP* endpoint is 5022. You then configure the Listener IP for the *TCP* endpoint. By default, the endpoint accepts connections on any valid IP address (the *ALL* option). But to further restrict the requests to which this endpoint responds, you can specify a particular IP address for it to listen to for requests.

BEST PRACTICES   Port numbers

Because port 5022 is the default port number for a *TCP* endpoint, you should specify a different port number. Not using the default port number helps foil potential hackers—or at least makes their job more difficult—by requiring them to use a port scanner instead of just blindly connecting to port 5022 for a denial of service attack (DoS) or other hacking attack. However, the general recommendation is to leave the Listener IP set to the default of *ALL* because a given instance could have multiple database mirroring sessions running.

The third and fourth layers of security for an endpoint are the authentication method and the encryption setting. You can use either Microsoft Windows–based authentication or certificates. You specify Windows-based authentication by selecting the *NTLM*, *KERBEROS*, or *NEGOTIATE* option. The *NEGOTIATE* option causes the instances to dynamically select the authentication method. You can set up certificate-based authentication by using a certificate from a trusted authority or by generating your own Windows certificate.

BEST PRACTICES   Authentication

When all database mirroring instances reside within a single domain or across trusted domains, you should use Windows-based authentication. When instances span nontrusted domains, you should use certificate-based authentication.

All communications between endpoints can be encrypted, and you can specify which encryption algorithm to use for the communications. The default algorithm is RC4, but you can specify the much stronger Advanced Encryption Standard (AES) algorithm.

BEST PRACTICES Encryption

Use RC4 for minimal encryption strength and best performance. Use AES if you require strong encryption, but note that this algorithm requires more calculation overhead and will affect performance.

The fifth and sixth layers of security regard state options for an endpoint. You have to grant *CONNECT* authority to an endpoint for a connection to be established. Additionally, you must set the state of the endpoint to *STARTED*. An endpoint with a state of *STOPPED* returns an error for any connection attempt, whereas an endpoint with a state of *DISABLED* does not respond to any request. The default option is *STOPPED*.

Database Mirroring Endpoints

Endpoints that support database mirroring are a special implementation of a *TCP* endpoint and have the following characteristics:

- Endpoint type of *TCP*
- Payload of *DATABASE_MIRRORING*
- Only one endpoint supporting database mirroring allowed per SQL Server instance

Database mirroring endpoints establish a seventh layer of security through the use of the *ROLE* option. You can specify that an endpoint be a *PARTNER*, *WITNESS*, or *ALL*. An endpoint specified as *PARTNER* can participate only as the principal or the mirror. An endpoint specified as *WITNESS* can participate only as a witness. An endpoint specified as *ALL* can function in any role.

NOTE Endpoints on Express Edition

If you are creating a database mirroring endpoint on SQL Server 2005 Express Edition, it will support only a role of *WITNESS*.

The following Transact-SQL example shows how to create a database mirroring endpoint:

```
CREATE ENDPOINT [Mirroring]
AS TCP (LISTENER_PORT = 5022)
FOR DATA_MIRRORING (ROLE = PARTNER, ENCRYPTION = REQUIRED);
ALTER ENDPOINT [Mirroring] STATE = STARTED;
```

This code creates an endpoint to service database mirroring sessions on port 5022, responding to requests from all valid IP addresses. The *ROLE = PARTNER* option specifies that the endpoint allows only databases hosted on this SQL Server instance to participate as a principal or mirror using the RC4 encryption algorithm.

NOTE Configuring database mirroring

You typically configure database mirroring within SQL Server Management Studio (SSMS) from the Database Properties, Mirroring page. On this page, you click Configure Security, which launches the Configure Database Mirroring Security Wizard that lets you specify several options. For example, you can use this wizard to specify whether you plan to use a witness server instance in your mirroring configuration. When you're finished with your selections, the wizard executes the two commands shown in the preceding example—*CREATE ENDPOINT* and *ALTER ENDPOINT*—against each instance hosting a database that participates in a database mirroring session.

> ## Quick Check
> - What are the seven levels of security provided by TCP endpoints servicing database mirroring sessions?
>
> ## Quick Check Answer
> - The first layer is the type and payload definition.
> - Layer two defines the TCP options of the port number and Listener IP.
> - Layer three is the authentication method required for the endpoint.
> - Layer four adds encryption options for all communications between partners.
> - Layer five requires that the account authenticating the connection have *CONNECT* permissions.
> - Layer six specifies *STATE* options that determine whether the endpoint will allow or respond to connection requests.
> - Layer seven in the endpoint security model restricts the database mirroring roles that an endpoint supports.

PRACTICE Establishing Endpoints for Database Mirroring

In this practice, you establish the endpoints required for a database mirroring session. You configure endpoints for a principal, a witness, and a mirror to allow the creation of a database mirroring session using any operating mode.

1. Connect to the instance hosting the *AdventureWorks* database that you plan to use as the principal database.

2. Right-click the *AdventureWorks* database and choose Properties.

3. Select the Mirroring page.

4. Click Configure Security to launch the Configure Database Mirroring Security Wizard.

5. On the first screen, the splash screen, select the Do Not Show This Starting Page Again check box. Click Next. You will now define endpoints for all three database mirroring roles: principal, mirror, and witness.

6. On the Include Witness Server page, verify that Yes is selected. This option enables you to configure an endpoint's security for the witness server instance. Click Next.

7. On the Choose Servers To Configure page, you see that the Principal Server check box is selected and unavailable because it is assumed that you are running the wizard from that instance. Verify that the Mirror Server Instance and Witness Server Instance check boxes are also selected. Click Next.

8. On the Principal Server Instance page, by default, the Principal Server instance is already selected. In the Listener Port text box, specify a port number. In the Endpoint Name text box, type a name for the endpoint. Also verify that the Encrypt Data Sent Through This Endpoint check box is selected to ensure secured communications. Click Next.

NOTE   Retrieving endpoint information

If an endpoint for database mirroring has already been created for the instance, SQL Server will retrieve this information and display it in this screen; you cannot edit this information.

---

9. On the Mirror Server Instance page, click Connect, specify the instance name and login credentials for the instance on which you want to host the mirror database, and then click Connect. This creates a connection to the instance hosting the mirror. Specify the port number and a name for the endpoint, and select the Encrypt Data Sent Through This Endpoint check box to ensure secure communications. Click Next.

BEST PRACTICES   Specifying an endpoint name

I always specify Mirroring as the endpoint name, which standardizes the naming convention for these types of endpoints so that I can easily distinguish them from other types of endpoints.

---

10. On the Witness Server Instance page, connect to the witness server instance the same way you connected to the mirror instance in step 9. Specify the port number and endpoint name, and then select the Encrypt Data Sent Through This Endpoint check box to ensure secure communications. Click Next.

CAUTION   Configuring endpoints on different instances

For database mirroring, you must configure the principal, mirror, and witness endpoints on different SQL Server instances.

---

11. On the Service Accounts page, you specify service accounts. This step is optional. If all the instances that you are configuring endpoints for have the SQL Server service running under the same service account, you do not have to specify anything here. Otherwise, specify the service account for the SQL Server service on all three instances. Click Next.

12. On the Complete The Wizard page, review the configuration settings that the wizard will implement. If you have any changes to make, click Back until you reach the appropriate page and then make the necessary changes. If the configuration is correct, click Finish.

13. When the wizard completes, click Close. Click OK to close the Database Properties message box. This message box serves to remind you that mirroring does not begin until you click Start Mirroring on the Mirroring page of the Database Properties dialog box for the primary database. Click OK to close the Database Properties – Adventure Works dialog box.

NOTE   Transact-SQL alternative

All the steps you perform within the Configure Database Mirroring Security Wizard are equivalent to connecting to each SQL Server instance and issuing a *CREATE ENDPOINT* command along with an *ALTER ENDPOINT* command to change the state to *STARTED*.

Lesson Summary

■ Endpoints provide a rich, flexible, and multilayered approach to securing communications.

■ By setting a variety of options for authentication, port number, and encryption, you can create a secure configuration for database mirroring.

■ You can use Transact-SQL to configure endpoints, but the typical approach is to use the Database Properties, Mirroring page of SSMS.

Lesson Review

The following questions are intended to reinforce key information presented in this lesson. The questions are also available on the companion CD if you prefer to review them in electronic form.

NOTE Answers

Answers to these questions and explanations of why each answer choice is right or wrong are located in the "Answers" section at the end of the book.

---

1. Which types of endpoints and payloads can you create? (Choose all that apply.)

    A. *TCP* endpoint with a *TSQL* payload

    B. *HTTP* endpoint with a *DATABASE_MIRRORING* payload

    C. *TCP* endpoint with a *DATABASE_MIRRORING* payload

    D. *HTTP* endpoint with a *TSQL* payload

2. Which of the following are endpoint options that are required for transactions to be exchanged between principal and mirror databases? (Choose all that apply; each answer represents a portion of a solution.)

    A. *STATE* configured with the default option

    B. Port 6083 specified for communications

    C. *COMPRESSSION* set to *ENABLED*

    D. *ROLE* set to *PARTNER*

Lesson 4: Understanding Operating Modes

You can configure database mirroring for three different operating modes: High Availability, High Performance, and High Protection. The operating mode governs the way transactions are transferred between the principal and the mirror databases as well as the failover processes that are available in the database mirroring session. In this lesson, you learn about each operating mode, the benefits of each, and how database mirroring's caching and transparent client redirect capabilities give it advantages over other availability technologies.

After this lesson, you will be able to:

- Explain the differences between each operating mode.
- Choose the appropriate operating mode for your situation.
- Explain how database mirroring's caching and transparent client redirect work.

Estimated lesson time: 10 minutes

Real World

Michael Hotek

One of my customers in the financial services industry had some strict data availability requirements for its application. The company required the database to be available more than 99.995 percent of the time as well as a guarantee of zero data loss—except in the event of a catastrophic failure such as the loss of all or part of a data center due to an environmental disaster. The organization further required that the solution automatically detect any failure of the primary database as well as automatically fail over to a secondary server. The customer also wanted all of this to happen without the application's awareness and without requiring any application code changes.

Replication and log shipping obviously would not work for this set of requirements. Although we could get replication to meet the 0.005 percent downtime requirement, we could not guarantee this level nor could we guarantee zero data loss. Log shipping could approach but likely not meet the 0.005 percent downtime requirement and could not automatically detect failure and provide automatic failover to the secondary server unless we wrote custom code on the back end. In addition, we could not guarantee zero data loss in a log-shipping implementation.

Clustering definitely could not meet the downtime requirements, although it could meet nearly all of the other requirements if we made a couple of simple changes to the data access object to add reconnect logic.

To meet this organization's availability requirements before the introduction of SQL Server 2005, we would have had to write a lot of custom code and make significant changes to the application tier, which the company didn't want. But the new database mirroring functionality operating in High Availability operating mode met all these requirements.

In implementing the data mirroring solution for this customer, we had some initial issues with application performance until we got the networking layer tuned properly. We also had to make a small modification to the data access object in the application to enable the application to detect a disconnect and then automatically reconnect. After we implemented these changes, we had an operating availability solution that met all the customer's availability requirements.

High Availability Operating Mode

Database mirroring's High Availability operating mode provides durable, synchronous transfer between the principal and mirror databases in addition to automatic failure detection and failover.

SQL Server first writes all transactions into memory buffers within the SQL Server memory space. The system writes out these memory buffers to the transaction log and then flushes the log to the data files. When SQL Server writes the transaction to the transaction log, the system triggers database mirroring to begin transferring the transaction log rows to the mirror. The transaction rows continue to flow to the mirror. When the application issues a commit for the transaction, the transaction is first committed on the mirror database. An acknowledgement of the commit is sent back to the principal, which then allows the commit to be issued. After the commit is issued on the principal, the acknowledgment is sent back to the application, allowing it to continue processing. This process guarantees that all transactions are committed and hardened to the transaction log on both the principal and mirror databases before the commit is returned to the application.

NOTE Classic availability method

The High Availability operating mode uses an availability methodology that has been in practice for several decades. The application writes directly to at least two servers and does not process the next request until the transaction has committed to all servers. Database mirroring takes this approach one step further by extending it into the database, thereby making it transparent to applications.

The synchronous transfer of data poses a planning issue for applications. Because a transaction is not considered committed until SQL Server has successfully committed it to the transaction log on both the principal and the mirror database, High Availability operating mode incurs performance overhead. And as the distance between the principal and the mirror instances increases, the performance impact also increases.

High Availability operating mode requires a witness server along with the principal and mirror databases for database mirroring to automatically detect a failure at the principal and fail over to the mirror. To detect failure, High Availability operating mode uses a simple ping between each instance that participates in the database mirroring session.

CAUTION   Ping test limitation

A database can become inaccessible due to a runaway transaction or other operations. However, database mirroring does not detect these as failures; only a failure of the ping test is considered a failure.

When the database mirroring session fails over, SQL Server reverses the roles of the principal and mirror. SQL Server promotes the mirror database to the principal and begins serving the database, and it then demotes the principal database to the mirror. SQL Server also automatically reverses the transaction flow. This process is a significant improvement over other availability methods such as replication or log shipping, which require manual intervention or even reconfiguration to reverse the transaction flow.

In this automatic failover process, the mirror essentially promotes itself to principal and begins serving the database. But first, the witness server must arbitrate the failover and role reversal by requiring two of the three database mirroring roles—or a quorum—to agree on the promotion. A quorum is necessary to prevent the database from being served on more than one instance within the database mirroring session. If the principal were to fail, and the mirror could not connect to the witness, it would be impossible to reach a quorum, and SQL Server would then not promote the mirror to the principal.

NOTE   Split-brain problem

If the mirror were allowed to determine that it should serve the database by itself, it could introduce a situation whereby the database would be accessible to transactions on more than one server. This is referred to as a "split-brain" problem.

High Availability operating mode's automatic failure detection and failover follow these general steps:

1. The principal and mirror continuously ping each other.
2. The witness periodically pings both principal and mirror.
3. The principal fails.
4. The mirror detects the failure and makes a request to the witness to promote itself to the principal database.
5. The witness cannot ping the principal but can ping the mirror, so the witness agrees with the role reversal, and SQL Server promotes the mirror to the principal.
6. The principal server comes back online from the failure and detects that the mirror has been promoted to principal.
7. SQL Server demotes the original principal to a mirror, and transactions begin flowing to this database to resynchronize it with the new principal.

IMPORTANT **Hot standby: witness must be online**

If the witness server is offline, there is no automatic failover. This means that you can use High Availability operating mode to provide a hot standby server only when the witness server is online. Otherwise, you have a warm standby configuration.

High Performance Operating Mode

Database mirroring's *High Performance operating mode* uses a principal and a mirror database but does not need a witness server. This operating mode provides a warm standby configuration that does not support automatic failure detection or failover.

High Performance operating mode does not automatically fail over because the application's transactions are sent to the mirror asynchronously. Transactions are committed to the principal database and acknowledged to the application. A separate process constantly sends those transactions to the mirror, which introduces latency into the process. This latency prevents a database mirroring session from automatically failing over because the process cannot guarantee that SQL Server has received all transactions at the mirror when a failure occurs.

Because the transfer is asynchronous, High Performance operating mode does not affect application performance, and you can have greater geographic separation between the principal and mirror. However, this mode increases latency and can lead to greater data loss in the event of a primary database failure.

High Protection Operating Mode

Database mirroring's *High Protection operating mode* is the same as High Availability operating mode, except that you do not configure a witness server. SQL Server transfers transactions synchronously between principal and mirror, but because a two-out-of-three quorum cannot be achieved without a witness, failover is manual. If the principal fails in High Protection operating mode, you must manually promote the mirror to serve the database.

BEST PRACTICES **High Protection operating mode**

Because High Protection operating mode's synchronous transfer can affect application performance while not offering the benefit of automatic failover, this operating mode is not recommended for normal operations. You should configure a database mirroring session in High Protection operating mode only when you need to replace the existing witness server. After you have replaced or recovered the witness, you should change the operating mode back to High Availability operating mode.

Caching

Each high availability technology available in SQL Server 2005 has performance and possibly application implications during a failover. Clustering avoids the application issues because it uses only one instance; however, the instance must restart on another node, thereby causing the data and query caches to be repopulated. Log shipping requires changes to the application to reconnect to the secondary server as well as requiring the data cache and procedure cache to be repopulated. Replication requires application changes to reconnect to a subscriber and has some performance impact because the query cache and part of the data cache would need to be repopulated.

Database mirroring, however, does not have caching issues. In addition to sending transactions to the mirror, database mirroring also performs periodic metadata transfers. The purpose of these metadata transfers is to cause the mirror to read pages into data cache. This process maintains the cache on the mirror in a "semi-hot" state. The cache on the mirror does not reflect the exact contents of the cache on the principal, but it does contain most of the pages. Thus, when the database mirroring session fails over, SQL Server does not have to completely rebuild the cache, and applications do not experience as large a performance impact as they would if you had used the other availability technologies.

Transparent Client Redirection

One of the most difficult processes of failing over when using either log shipping or replication involves application connections. Applications must be redirected to the secondary server to continue processing. Database mirroring can avoid this necessity under a very particular configuration.

The new version of MDAC that ships with Microsoft Visual Studio 2005 contains a database mirroring–related feature within the connection object called *Transparent Client Redirect*. When a connection is made to a principal, the connection object caches the principal as well as the mirror. This caching is transparent to the application, and developers do not need to implement any code to implement this functionality.

If a database mirroring session were to fail over while an application were connected, the connection would be broken, and the connection object would send an error back to the client. The client would then just need to reconnect, and the connection cache within MDAC would automatically redirect the connection to the mirror server. The application would think it was connecting to the same server to which it was originally connected, when in fact it is connected to a different server.

Quick Check

1. What are the three operating modes for database mirroring?
2. Which mode is not recommended for normal operations?

Quick Check Answers

1. The three operating modes are High Availability operating mode, High Performance operating mode, and High Protection operating mode.
2. High Protection operating mode is not recommended for normal operations because its synchronous transfers have high performance impact without the benefit of automatic failover.

PRACTICE Configuring the Operating Mode

In this exercise, you will practice configuring the *AdventureWorks* database for High Availability operating mode.

1. Right-click the *AdventureWorks* database on the instance that will host the principal database, choose Properties, and select the Mirroring page.

2. Specify the endpoints for principal, mirror, and witness that you configured in the previous establishing endpoints practice.

NOTE   Retrieving an endpoint address

If you do not remember the endpoint addresses, you can retrieve them using one of two mechanisms:

❑ You can query *sys.database_mirroring_endpoints* on each instance to get the endpoint address for each instance.

❑ You can launch the Configure Database Mirroring Security Wizard by clicking Configure Security and walking through each step. Because you have already created the endpoints, the wizard automatically retrieves information about them. When the wizard finalizes, it automatically enters the endpoint addresses into the appropriate fields for configuring database mirroring.

---

3. Verify that the Synchronous With Automatic Failover (High Availability) operating mode is selected.

4. Click Start Mirroring. When mirroring completes, click OK to close the Database Properties – AdventureWorks dialog box.

NOTE   Transact-SQL alternatives for configuring operating mode

This process within SSMS is equivalent to connecting to the mirror database and issuing an *ALTER DATABASE SET PARTNER* Transact-SQL statement and then connecting to the principal database and issuing the statement *ALTER DATABASE SET PARTNER* along with *ALTER DATABASE SET WITNESS*.

Lesson Summary

■ Operating modes govern the way SQL Server transfers transactions between the principal and the mirror databases as well as the failover processes that are available in the database mirroring session.

■ High Availability operating mode synchronously transfers data between principal and mirror, requires a witness, and automatically fails over only when the witness is present.

■ High Performance operating mode asynchronously transfers data between principal and mirror, does not use a witness, and requires a manual failover.

■ High Protection operating mode synchronously transfers data between principal and mirror, does not use a mirror, and requires manual failover.

- Metadata transactions are periodically sent to the mirror to maintain the cache on the mirror in a semi-hot state.

- Transparent Client Redirection allows connections to be transparently redirected to the mirror upon a failover.

Lesson Review

The following questions are intended to reinforce key information presented in this lesson. The questions are also available on the companion CD if you prefer to review them in electronic form.

NOTE Answers

Answers to these questions and explanations of why each answer choice is right or wrong are located in the "Answers" section at the end of the book.

---

1. Which of the following are characteristics of High Availability operating mode? (Choose all that apply.)

   A. Asynchronous data transfer

   B. Synchronous data transfer

   C. Automatic failover

   D. Manual failover

2. Which of the following are characteristics of High Performance operating mode? (Choose all that apply.)

   A. Asynchronous data transfer

   B. Synchronous data transfer

   C. Automatic failover

   D. Manual failover

3. Which of the following are characteristics of High Protection operating mode? (Choose all that apply.)

   A. Asynchronous data transfer

   B. Synchronous data transfer

   C. Automatic failover

   D. Manual failover

Lesson 5: Failing Over a Database Mirror

When you configure a database mirroring session in High Availability operating mode, a failure of the principal triggers an automatic failover to the mirror in all except one scenario: when the witness server is unavailable. You must always perform manual failover for the High Performance and High Protection operating modes. For these reasons, it is important for you to understand how to manually fail over to the mirror to achieve maximum uptime. This lesson explains the failure scenarios requiring a manual failover as well as the commands you use to initiate a failover.

> **After this lesson, you will be able to:**
> - Explain which failure scenarios require manual failover.
> - Fail over a database mirroring session.
>
> **Estimated lesson time: 10 minutes**

Understanding Failure Scenarios

As Lesson 4 explained, a database mirroring session in High Availability operating mode can automatically fail over to the mirror as long as the witness is online and available. Automatic failover requires the presence of the witness to prevent both the principal and the mirror from bringing the database online. However, if the witness is offline and the principal fails, you must manually fail over the database mirroring session at the mirror.

CAUTION   If the witness is not visible from the mirror

If the witness server is not visible from the mirror, you must either reconfigure the operating mode for the database mirroring session or turn off the witness.

Alternatively, you can manually fail over a database mirroring session in High Availability operating mode by issuing the following command at the principal:

```
ALTER DATABASE SET PARTNER FAILOVER
```

BEST PRACTICES   Manual failover

In High Availability operating mode, you would normally issue this statement to manually fail over from the principal to the mirror before taking the principal offline for maintenance.

A failure of the principal in either High Performance or High Protection operating mode leaves the mirror in a restoring state and inaccessible to transactions. When this occurs, you must connect to the mirror and initiate a manual failover from there.

How to Initiate a Failover

The most common scenario for initiating a failover in a production environment is to do so from the mirror. Initiating a failover is a straightforward process. However, you cannot manually initiate a failover at the mirror from the Database Properties page within SSMS because the mirror database is in a recovering state. In this state, the database is inaccessible. Because the only time you can manually initiate a failover from the graphical user interface (GUI) is when the principal is online, which is not the typical situation, you should always use the *ALTER DATABASE* Transact-SQL command to initiate a failover. The complete *ALTER DATABASE* command you issue at the mirror database is as follows:

```
ALTER DATABASE <mirror_database> SET PARTNER FORCE_SERVICE_ALLOW_DATA_LOSS
```

IMPORTANT Data loss possible

Manually forcing the failover can cause data loss. With the original principal unavailable, the partners cannot communicate with each other and therefore cannot synchronize their databases. Until the original principal comes back online and can be used as the new mirror, the database mirroring session is suspended.

Quick Check
- What are the requirements to issue the *ALTER DATABASE* statement at the mirror to initiate a failover of the database mirroring session?

Quick Check Answer
- To initiate a failover from the mirror, the witness must be turned off or connected to the mirror, and the principal must be inaccessible.

PRACTICE Failing Over a Database Mirror

In this exercise, you practice the manual failover of the *AdventureWorks* database from the principal to the mirror.

> **NOTE**   **Use High Performance or High Protection operating mode**
>
> In this exercise, to avoid issues with getting a High Availability operating mode in the proper state to accomplish a manual failover at the mirror, first configure a database mirroring session in either High Performance or High Protection operating mode without a witness server.

1. Stop the instance that is hosting the principal database. (Right-click the instance in Object Explorer, choose Stop, and then click Yes to confirm that you want to stop the instance.)

2. Connect to the instance that is hosting the mirror database.

3. Execute the *ALTER DATABASE* command to initiate the failover to the mirror:

   ```
   ALTER DATABASE AdventureWorks SET PARTNER FORCE_SERVICE_ALLOW_DATA_LOSS
   ```

Lesson Summary

- You can initiate a manual failover at the mirror only when the principal is inaccessible and the witness is either off or connected to the mirror.

- To accomplish the failover of a database mirroring session, you need to issue an *ALTER DATABASE* command at the mirror database using the option of *FORCE_SERVICE_ALLOW_DATA_LOSS*.

- You can force a failover from the principal if you need to perform maintenance on the principal.

Lesson Review

The following questions are intended to reinforce key information presented in this lesson. The questions are also available on the companion CD if you prefer to review them in electronic form.

> **NOTE**   **Answers**
>
> Answers to these questions and explanations of why each answer choice is right or wrong are located in the "Answers" section at the end of the book.

1. Which command, when executed from the mirror, will fail over a database mirroring session?

   A. *ALTER DATABASE SET PARTNER OFF*

   B. *ALTER DATABASE SET WITNESS OFF*

   C. *ALTER DATABASE SET PARTNER FAILOVER*

   D. *ALTER DATABASE SET PARTNER FORCE_SERVICE_ALLOW_DATA_LOSS*

Lesson 6: Removing Database Mirroring

After it is configured, you should remove database mirroring only in extreme cases. By removing database mirroring, you terminate all data transfer between the principal and the mirror databases. In this lesson, you learn when to remove database mirroring and how to perform this task.

After this lesson, you will be able to:
- Remove database mirroring.

Estimated lesson time: 10 minutes

Removing Database Mirroring

You should remove database mirroring only under the following circumstances:

- You no longer want to mirror a database.
- The principal has been damaged to such an extent that it would be easier to reinitialize the entire environment.

You can remove a database mirroring session by clicking Stop Mirroring within the Database Properties, Mirroring page for the principal database. This step immediately terminates the database mirroring session. When you click Stop Mirroring, the GUI issues the following single command to terminate the database mirroring session:

```
ALTER DATABASE <database name> SET PARTNER OFF
```

Instead of using the GUI, you can alternatively issue this command at either the principal or mirror database to remove database mirroring.

Quick Check
- How do you terminate a database mirroring session?

Quick Check Answer
- You can immediately terminate a database mirroring session by clicking Stop Mirroring on the Database Properties, Mirroring page or issuing a single *ALTER DATABASE* command from either the principal or the mirror database.

PRACTICE Removing Database Mirroring

In this exercise, you will practice removing database mirroring.

1. Right-click the *AdventureWorks* database on the principal instance and choose Properties.

2. In the Mirroring page, click Stop Mirroring.

NOTE   Transact-SQL alternative to remove mirroring

Clicking Stop Mirroring in the GUI is equivalent to issuing the *ALTER DATABASE Adventure-Works SET PARTNER OFF* Transact-SQL command from either the principal or the mirror database.

Lesson Summary

- Remove a database mirroring session only in an extreme case, such as when the principal becomes damaged beyond repair, or if you have decided that database mirroring is no longer needed.

- To remove database mirroring, you can click Stop Mirroring on the Mirroring page or issue an *ALTER DATABASE* command from either the principal or the mirror.

Lesson Review

The following questions are intended to reinforce key information presented in this lesson. The questions are also available on the companion CD if you prefer to review them in electronic form.

NOTE   Answers

Answers to these questions and explanations of why each answer choice is right or wrong are located in the "Answers" section at the end of the book.

---

1. To terminate the database mirroring session, you can issue the *ALTER DATABASE* command against which partners? (Choose all that apply.)

   A. Principal

   B. Mirror

   C. Witness

   D. Distributor

Chapter Review

To further practice and reinforce the skills you learned in this chapter, you can

- Review the chapter summary.
- Review the list of key terms introduced in this chapter.
- Complete the case scenario. This scenario sets up a real-world situation involving the topics of this chapter and asks you to create solutions.
- Complete the suggested practices.
- Take a practice test.

Chapter Summary

- Database mirroring provides a major new technology for achieving high availability for your databases. Data is securely synchronized between two databases—a principal database and a mirror database—on separate instances of SQL Server.
- When configured in High Availability operating mode, database mirroring synchronously transfers transactions between the principal and mirror databases. This operating mode requires a witness server, which arbitrates the automatic failover to the mirror when the principal becomes unavailable.
- When configured in High Performance operating mode, database mirroring asynchronously transfers transactions between the principal and mirror databases. Because of the asynchronous transfer, application performance is not affected, but the failover to the mirror requires manual intervention.
- Perform manual failover at the mirror server by issuing a single *ALTER DATABASE* statement with the *FORCE_SERVICE_ALLOW_DATA_LOSS* option.
- Removing database mirroring is an easy step within the GUI or via the Transact-SQL *ALTER DATABASE* statement, but it should be done only in extreme cases or if you do not want to mirror a database any more.

Key Terms

Do you know what these key terms mean? You can check your answers by looking up the terms in the glossary at the end of the book.

- database mirroring
- database mirroring role

- database mirroring session
- database partners
- endpoint
- High Availability operating mode
- High Performance operating mode
- High Protection operating mode
- mirror
- mirror failover
- operating mode
- payload
- principal
- Transparent Client Redirection
- witness (witness server)

Case Scenario: Implementing Database Mirroring

In the following case scenario, you will apply what you've learned in this chapter. You can find answers to these questions in the "Answers section" at the end of this book.

Contoso Limited, a health care company located in Bothell, WA, has a volatile database containing patient claims data. The patient data is protected by privacy laws, and all access to this data is required to be audited. Audit data is written into a set of audit tables by the stored procedures that control all data access within the patient claims database.

Auditors within the company, along with external auditors, require access to audit data in the patient claims database at specific points in time. Contoso has had periods during which patient claims data has been unavailable because of administrative actions on the server or equipment failures. The company needs to implement an availability solution that does not require changes to its existing ASP.NET 2.0 and C# .NET 2.0 applications while also providing automatic failover to a secondary server when the primary goes offline. If Contoso can also use the secondary server to offload the audit reviews, that would be a bonus.

Suggested Practices

To help you successfully master the exam objectives presented in this chapter, complete the following tasks.

Establishing Database Mirroring

To become familiar with database mirroring, practice creating endpoints and configuring database mirroring, including configuration of operating modes. Compare states within the mirroring session as you take various components offline and then practice failing over automatically and manually.

- **Practice 1** Create database mirroring endpoints for a principal, mirror, and witness by using two different methods: the Configure Database Mirroring Security Wizard within the Database Properties, Mirroring page and the *CREATE END-POINT/ALTER ENDPOINT* Transact-SQL commands.

- **Practice 2** Configure database mirroring in High Availability operating mode by using the *AdventureWorks* database.

- **Practice 3** Take the witness offline and observe the state of the mirror database. Then take the mirror offline and observe the effect on the principal database. Bring the mirror and witness back online and observe the various states within the system.

- **Practice 4** Change the operating mode to High Performance and repeat Practice 3.

- **Practice 5** Change the operating mode to High Protection and repeat Practice 3.

- **Practice 6** Perform an automatic failover in High Availability operating mode by shutting down the instance hosting the principal while the mirror and witness are online.

- **Practice 7** Initiate a manual failover in each of the operating modes, using two different methods: SSMS and Transact-SQL.

Creating a Database Snapshot Against a Database Mirror

For this task, practice creating a database snapshot that you can use for reporting purposes.

- **Practice 1** Create a database snapshot against the mirror database. Either drop and re-create the database snapshot or create a series of database snapshots to see how data changes—and how quickly it changes—on the mirror, depending on the operating mode.

Take a Practice Test

The practice tests on this book's companion CD offer many options. For example, you can test yourself on just the content covered in this chapter, or you can test yourself on all the 70-431 certification exam content. You can set up the test so that it closely simulates the experience of taking a certification exam, or you can set it up in study mode so that you can look at the correct answers and explanations after you answer each question.

MORE INFO **Practice tests**

For details about all the practice test options available, see the "How to Use the Practice Tests" section in this book's Introduction.

Chapter 18

Implementing Log Shipping

Log shipping is the automated process of backing up, copying, and restoring the transaction log from one database on a primary server to one or more secondary databases on another server. Using log shipping, you can frequently synchronize the copy of the database with the original, so you can use the copy to distribute query processing for improved performance or as a warm standby database for high availability. This chapter will explain log shipping's components, processes, and requirements. It then will show you how to configure the primary and secondary databases, the various log shipping options, and the optional monitor server for optimal operations.

Exam objectives in this chapter:

- Implement log shipping.

    ❑ Initialize a secondary database.

    ❑ Configure log shipping options.

    ❑ Configure a log shipping mode.

    ❑ Configure monitoring.

Lessons in this chapter:

Before You Begin

To complete the lessons in this chapter, you must have

- A computer that meets the hardware and software requirements for Microsoft SQL Server 2005.

- SQL Server 2005 Developer, Workgroup, Standard, or Enterprise Edition installed.

- SQL Server Agent running and configured with a Microsoft Windows service account.

Real World

Javier Loria

Business users usually like the idea of log shipping because it doesn't require expensive hardware. The first time I explained the benefits of log shipping to one of my customers, she liked the idea so much that she wanted to replace all her clustered servers with a log shipping implementation. I explained that log shipping configurations don't automatically redirect users from one server to another as clustered servers do and that reconfiguring the secondary system as your primary system might take some time. After she reviewed the business objectives of each of her database servers, she chose to use log shipping technology for only three servers that do not run mission-critical applications.

Lesson 1: Preparing to Log Ship

Before you configure log shipping, you need to understand log shipping's architecture and requirements. In this lesson, you'll learn how SQL Server 2005 implements log shipping and its requirements for log shipping.

After this lesson, you will be able to:

- Explain how log shipping works.
- List the server and database requirements for log shipping.

Estimated lesson time: 15 minutes

Understanding Log Shipping

Log shipping synchronizes distributed databases that can reside on different servers or on the same server but within different instances. A log shipping configuration doesn't automatically fail over from the primary server to the secondary server. If you need to switch from the primary database to a secondary database, you bring the secondary database online manually.

SQL Server uses SQL Server Agent jobs to automate log shipping operations. Log shipping defines SQL Server Agent jobs to automate backup, copy, and restore processes at scheduled times. SQL Server then stores information about the history of its execution of jobs in the *msdb* database.

MORE INFO SQL Server Agent

For more information about SQL Server Agent, see Chapter 14, "Working with SQL Server Agent Jobs."

NOTE Log shipping in SQL Server 2005

Unlike in previous versions of SQL Server, log shipping in SQL Server 2005 is not part of the Database Maintenance Plan Wizard.

The recommended log shipping configuration comprises five components: a primary database, a secondary database, a primary server, a secondary server, and a monitor server. Although a separate monitor server is optional, this configuration provides the best setup for effective administration of your log shipping process. Table 18-1 defines each component.

Table 18-1   Log Shipping Terms

Term	Definition
Primary database	The *primary database* is the original database that's distributed to other servers. The primary database receives the updates from the application.
Secondary database	The *secondary database* is the distributed copy of the primary database. The secondary database is frequently synchronized through transaction log restores.
Primary server	The *primary server* is the SQL Server database engine instance that owns the primary database.
Secondary server	The *secondary server* is the SQL Server database engine instance that owns a secondary database. You can configure multiple secondary servers.
Monitor server	The *monitor server* is the SQL Server database engine instance that keeps track of the log shipping process and raises alerts when the process fails.

Figure 18-1 illustrates these components in a typical log shipping configuration.

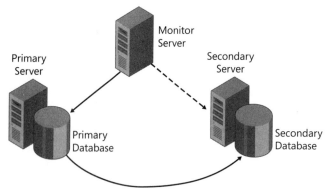

Figure 18-1   Typical log shipping configuration

BEST PRACTICES   Server configuration

The same server can play different roles within the same log shipping configuration or in different log shipping configurations. For example, you could use the same server as both the primary server and the monitor server in the same configuration. However, to create a more fault-tolerant system, you shouldn't use the monitor server as the primary or secondary server in the same configuration.

The log shipping process consists of three main operations:

- Backing up the transaction log of the primary database.
- Copying the transaction log backup to each secondary server.
- Restoring the transaction log backup on the secondary database.

Understanding Log Shipping Requirements

Log shipping requires the following infrastructure:

- You must have at least two SQL Server 2005 database engine servers or two database engine instances in your log shipping implementation. To configure a separate monitor server, you need three servers or three instances. However, for testing and learning purposes, you can configure the same server as the primary, secondary, and monitor server.

- All servers participating in the log shipping process must have SQL Server 2005 Standard, Workgroup, Enterprise, or Developer Edition installed. SQL Server 2005 Express Edition does not support log shipping.

IMPORTANT   SQL Server 2003 log shipping version compatibility

Previous versions of SQL Server cannot participate in a SQL Server 2005 log shipping process.

- SQL Server Agent services should be running and configured with network credentials. You can configure log shipping with SQL Server Agent services stopped, but the process doesn't run automatically.

- The primary database must be configured with the Full or Bulk-Logged recovery model.

- You must have a shared folder to copy the transaction log backups to. The SQL Server Agent service account of the primary server should have read/write access either to the shared folder or to the local NTFS folder. The SQL Server Agent account of the secondary server should have read access to the shared folder.

- The user configuring the log shipping process must have sysadmin access to the participating servers.

> **Quick Check**
>
> - Your manager wants to use SQL Server 2005 Express Edition to monitor the log shipping process. What should you tell him?
>
> **Quick Check Answer**
>
> - Log shipping is not supported in SQL Server 2005 Express Edition.

Lesson Summary

- Log shipping uses SQL Server Agent jobs to automate the process of backing up, copying, and restoring data from a primary database on one server or instance to one or more secondary databases on another server or instance.

- You can use the secondary database either to improve application performance by allowing distributed queries or to improve availability.

- You can also configure a monitor server to record the status and historic information about log shipping jobs.

- Among the prerequisites for log shipping is that the primary database must be in either Full or Bulk-Logged recovery mode.

Lesson Review

The following questions are intended to reinforce key information presented in this lesson. The questions are also available on the companion CD if you prefer to review them in electronic form.

NOTE Answers

Answers to these questions and explanations of why each answer choice is right or wrong are located in the "Answers" section at the end of the book.

---

1. Which SQL Server versions can participate in a SQL Server 2005 log shipping configuration as a monitor server? (Choose all that apply.)

    A. SQL Server 2005 Enterprise Edition

    B. SQL Server 2005 Express Edition

    C. SQL Server 2000 Standard Edition

    D. SQL Server 2005 Workgroup Edition

2. Which of the following database options can be responsible for preventing a log shipping configuration from succeeding?

   A. ANSI NULL Default: True

   B. Compatibility Level: SQL Server 2000 (80)

   C. Quoted Identifiers Enable: False

   D. Recovery Model: Simple

3. Which permissions are required on the backup shared folder to create a log shipping configuration? (Choose all that apply.)

   A. Primary SQL Server Agent service account: full permissions.

   B. Primary SQL Server Agent service account: read/write.

   C. Secondary SQL Server Agent service account: read.

   D. Secondary SQL Server Agent service account: no access.

Lesson 2: Configuring Log Shipping Options

SQL Server 2005 offers three methods for configuring log shipping. The most straightforward method is via SQL Server Management Studio (SSMS), the graphical user interface (GUI) tool that database administrators (DBAs) use to configure, administer, and maintain SQL Server 2005, including log shipping tasks. Alternatively, you can use Transact-SQL statements or SQL Server Management Objects (SMO) to configure log shipping. In this lesson, you will learn how to use SSMS to create a log shipping configuration. The general steps for setting up a log shipping configuration are as follows:

1. Enable the primary database for log shipping.

2. Set log shipping backup options.

3. Enable secondary servers.

4. Set log shipping restore options.

> **After this lesson, you will be able to:**
> - Enable the primary database for log shipping.
> - Set log shipping backup options.
> - Use SSMS to script the log shipping configuration.
> - Enable secondary servers.
> - Set log shipping restore options.
>
> **Estimated lesson time: 40 minutes**

How to Enable the Primary Database

You configure log shipping in SSMS from the Database Properties window. Here's how to enable the primary database for log shipping:

1. To display the Database Properties windows, open SSMS.

2. Connect to the database engine server that hosts the database and navigate to the appropriate database.

3. Select the database you want, right-click the database, and then choose Properties.

4. Below Select A Page, select the Transaction Log Shipping page (see Figure 18-2). Remember that only users with sysadmin access can create log shipping configurations.

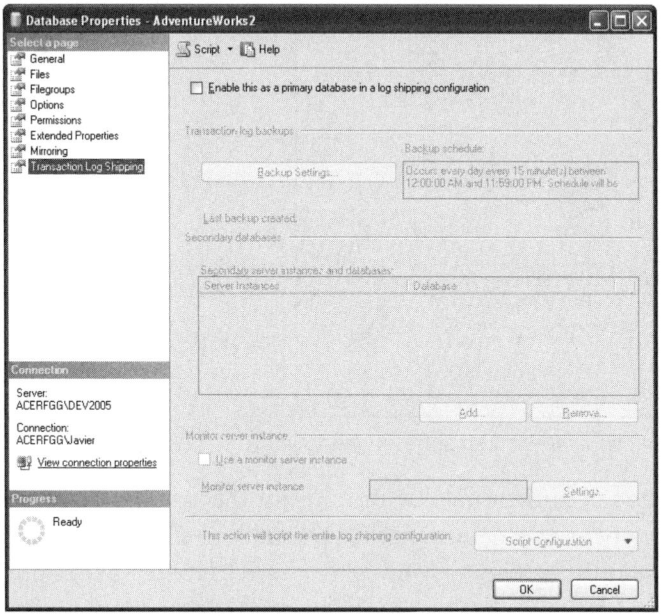

Figure 18-2   SSMS Database Properties window

5. To configure the database as the primary database in your log shipping implementation, select the Enable This As A Primary Database In A Log Shipping Configuration check box.

Defining Log Shipping Backup Options

With the primary database enabled, you can now configure backup settings for the database. When you select the Enable This As A Primary Database In A Log Shipping Configuration check box on the Transaction Log Shipping page of the Database Properties window, the Backup Settings button is enabled. To start your backup definition, click Backup Settings to display the Transaction Log Backup Settings window, shown in Figure 18-3.

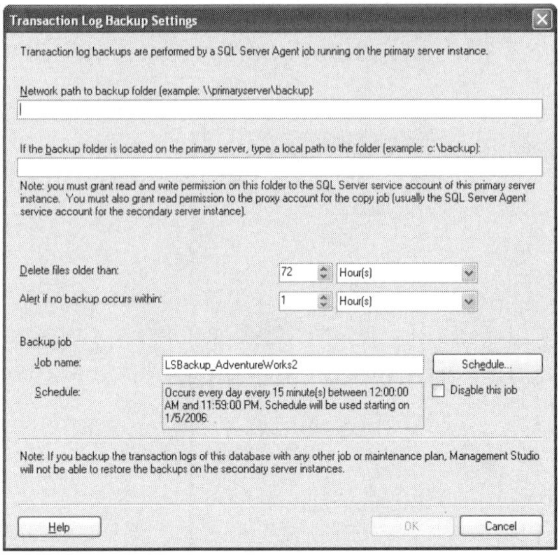

Figure 18-3   Transaction Log Backup Settings window

In this window, you define the backup options for the log shipping process. The available options are network path, local path (optional), retention period, threshold alert, job name, and schedule. The network path is the Universal Naming Convention (UNC) path in which you want to store the backup files for access by secondary servers. The local path is optional, and its default is the network path. To use a local folder to store the backup files, specify it here.

IMPORTANT   Security

When you use a local folder to store backup files, the primary SQL Server Agent must have read/write access to the local folder, and the secondary SQL Server Agents must have read access to the shared folder. When using a remote shared folder, the primary SQL Server Agent must have read/write access to the shared folder, and secondary SQL Server Agents must have read access.

You use the retention period to specify how long the backup files will remain in the shared folder. Log shipping jobs automatically delete the files after the period you specify. You use the threshold alert to specify how long after the last backup an alert will be raised if no other backup occurs. Use the job name to specify the name of the job responsible for the backup task. Click Schedule to display the Job Schedule Properties window, in which you can set the frequency of the task. After configuring the options, click OK.

CAUTION Log backups in a log shipping process

When you're using log shipping, backing up the transaction log independently will disrupt the log shipping process. If you plan to use transaction log backups as part of your recovery plan, use the backup folder as the source of backup files for your recovery plan.

Scripting the Log Shipping Configuration

You can also create a script that enables the primary database and sets the backup options for your log shipping configuration. The advantages of scripting the configuration are that you can use the script to document the configuration and deploy the same configuration for multiple databases, and you can use it as part of the recovery plan.

To use SSMS to generate the script, click Script Configuration at the bottom of the Transaction Log Shipping page in the Database Properties window. Using the options you select in the resulting window, SQL Server generates a script that you can store in a file, display as a query in SSMS, or copy to the Clipboard.

The generated script uses four stored procedures to configure the primary database and the SQL Server Agent backup jobs for log shipping. The core stored procedure, *sp_add_log_shipping_primary_database*, is responsible for most of the configuration except for the schedule definition. The *sp_add_schedule* and *sp_attach_schedule* procedures configure the schedule and attach it to the job. The *sp_update_job* procedure then enables the job for execution. The following code block shows the primary database configuration script:

Primary Database Configuration Script
```
-- Execute the following statements at the primary to configure
-- log shipping for the database [DEMOSRV\DEV2005].[AdventureWorks2],
-- Run the script at the primary in the context of the
-- [msdb] database.
-------------------------------------------------------------------
-- Adding the log shipping configuration
-- ****** Begin: Script to be run at primary: [DEMOSRV\DEV2005] ******
DECLARE @LS_BackupJobId AS uniqueidentifier
DECLARE @LS_PrimaryId AS uniqueidentifier
DECLARE @SP_Add_RetCode As int

EXEC @SP_Add_RetCode = master.dbo.sp_add_log_shipping_primary_database
    @database = N'AdventureWorks2'
    ,@backup_directory = N'C:\LOGSHIP'
    ,@backup_share = N'\\DEMOSRV\LOGSHIP'
    ,@backup_job_name = N'LSBackup'
```

```
        ,@backup_retention_period = 4320
        ,@backup_threshold = 60
        ,@threshold_alert_enabled = 1
        ,@history_retention_period = 5760
        ,@backup_job_id = @LS_BackupJobId OUTPUT
        ,@primary_id = @LS_PrimaryId OUTPUT
        ,@overwrite = 1
IF (@@ERROR = 0 AND @SP_Add_RetCode = 0)
BEGIN
    DECLARE @LS_BackUpScheduleUID As uniqueidentifier
    DECLARE @LS_BackUpScheduleID AS int

    EXEC msdb.dbo.sp_add_schedule
    @schedule_name =N'LSBackupSchedule_DEMOSRV\DEV20051'
    ,@enabled = 1
    ,@freq_type = 4
    ,@freq_interval = 1
    ,@freq_subday_type = 4
    ,@freq_subday_interval = 15
    ,@freq_recurrence_factor = 0
    ,@active_start_date = 20060106
    ,@active_end_date = 99991231
    ,@active_start_time = 0
    ,@active_end_time = 235900
    ,@schedule_uid = @LS_BackUpScheduleUID OUTPUT
    ,@schedule_id = @LS_BackUpScheduleID OUTPUT

    EXEC msdb.dbo.sp_attach_schedule
    @job_id = @LS_BackupJobId
    ,@schedule_id = @LS_BackUpScheduleID

    EXEC msdb.dbo.sp_update_job
    @job_id = @LS_BackupJobId
    ,@enabled = 1
    END
EXEC master.dbo.sp_add_log_shipping_alert_job
```

The *sp_add_log_shipping_primary_database* stored procedure has the same parameters as the SSMS interface to set up the primary database. You can easily change parameters such as *@database*, *@backup_directory*, *@backup_share*, and *@backup_job _name* to create a large number of log shipping configurations. (In fact, if you want to use the previous example script, you should change these parameters to reflect the names of your server, database, backup directory, backup shared folder, and backup job name.) The *@backup_retention_period* sets the number of minutes after which the job will delete backup files—in this script, 4320 minutes or 3 days. The *@backup_threshold* and *@threshold_alert_enabled* specify whether an alert will be raised after a certain period. The *@history_retention_period* sets the time period in minutes after which the job will delete history information from the *msdb* database.

The parameters *@backup_job_id* and *@primary_id* are output parameters needed to configure the schedule.

MORE INFO   **Log shipping system tables**

For complete information about the tables and stored procedures associated with a log shipping configuration, see the "Log Shipping Tables and Stored Procedures" topic in SQL Server 2005 Books Online. SQL Server 2005 Books Online is installed as part of SQL Server 2005. Updates for SQL Server 2005 Books Online are available for download at *www.microsoft.com/technet/prodtechnol/sql/2005/downloads/books.mspx*.

How to Configure Secondary Databases

The log shipping configuration doesn't distribute any data until you configure a secondary server. If you are using log shipping for distributed query processing across multiple servers, you will need to configure multiple secondary databases. Here's how to configure a secondary database in SSMS:

1. Below Secondary Server Instances And Databases in the Database Properties window for the primary database, click Add to open the Secondary Database Settings dialog box, shown in Figure 18-4. This dialog box lets you configure settings in four major categories: connection, initialization, copy files, and restore options.

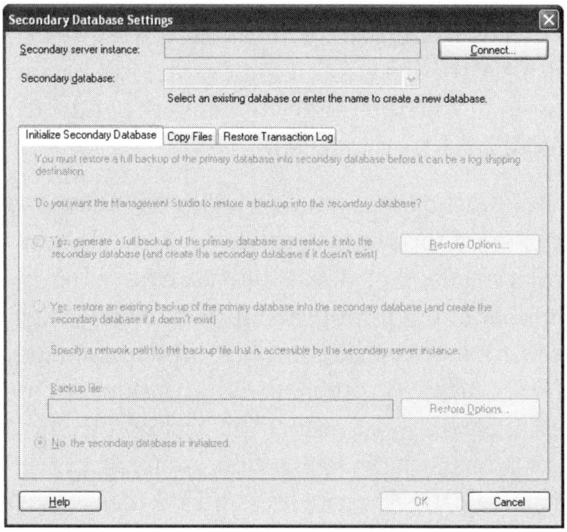

Figure 18-4   Secondary Database Settings dialog box

2. To set up the connection to a secondary database, first select the secondary server that is the owner of the secondary database by clicking Connect to display the Connect To Server dialog box. Provide the required credentials and click Connect. Remember that you need a user with sysadmin access to configure a secondary database.

3. After you specify the secondary server, select the secondary database to use or specify the name of a new database. The default secondary database name is the same as the primary database name.

4. When you specify the connection credentials and database name, SSMS enables the Initialize Secondary Database options. You can select from the following options:

   ❑ Make a full backup of the primary database and restore it in the secondary server.

   ❑ Restore an existing primary database backup in the secondary server.

   ❑ Use an already initialized database.

The Yes, Generate A Full Backup Of The Primary Database option executes a full backup of the primary database. SQL Server stores this full backup in the same folder in which it stores the transaction log backups. After the backup processes, SQL Server uses the file to restore the secondary database to the secondary server. By default, the restore process uses the same path for database files as the primary database. If you want to restore the files to a different path, you can click Restore Options and then specify an alternative path for the data and log files. The full backup option is the default and is appropriate when you have sufficient network bandwidth between servers to copy the full backup file across the network.

You use the Yes, Restore An Existing Backup Of The Primary Database option when you already have a full backup of the primary database, which is often the case when you have multiple secondary servers or when the bandwidth between servers isn't sufficient to copy the file across the network. Some administrators back up the primary database and deliver the backup file to the secondary server using alternate physical media (CD, DVD, or tape). If you choose this option, you must specify the path to the backup file. SQL Server must restore the backup file before the retention period you specified in the primary database configuration expires. With this option, you can also specify alternative paths for data files and log files in the restore process by clicking Restore Options.

You use an already initialized database when the DBA has already created the secondary database and is ready to initiate the log shipping process. This option might be necessary for large databases that might need a customized restore process because they have multiple data files or when creating a new configuration for an already initialized secondary database.

Configuring the Copy Files Task

After initializing the secondary database, your next step is to configure the Copy Files options. The *Copy Files task* is responsible for copying files from the primary server to the secondary server. The task provides three configuration options and a schedule, as Figure 18-5 shows. (You access these options by clicking the Copy Files tab.)

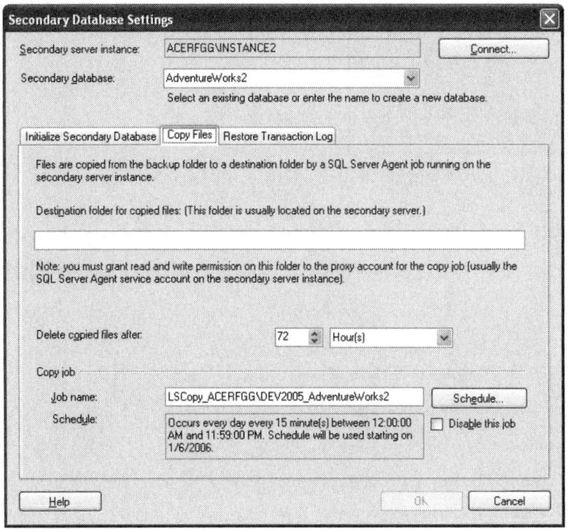

Figure 18-5   Secondary Database Settings—Copy Files tab

The first option you should configure is the destination folder to which the job will copy the transaction log backups. This folder is usually a local directory on the secondary server, but you can also use a shared folder. SQL Server Agent requires read/write access to this folder. Another option you can configure as part of the Copy Files task is the retention period, which is the amount of time that the backup files will remain in this folder. The job responsible for the Copy Files task will delete files older than the time specified in the retention period option. Last, you configure the job name and the schedule for the job responsible for the Copy Files task.

Configuring Log Shipping Restore Options

The last step of configuring the secondary server is specifying the settings for the restore task. You specify these settings on the Restore Transaction Log tab of the Secondary Database Settings dialog box (see Figure 18-6).

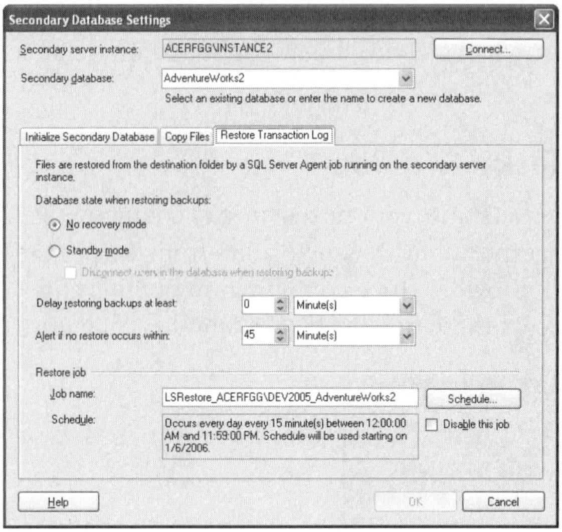

Figure 18-6   Secondary Database Setting—Restore Transaction Log tab

The recovery mode is the most important restore setting, specifying the state of the database after the restoration process. In the next lesson, we will cover the recovery mode in detail.

Other restore settings you can configure are the delay interval, alert threshold, job name, and job schedule. You use the delay interval to set a time gap for executing the restoration process. Use the alert threshold to set how long after the last restore an alert will be raised if no other backup occurs during that interval. You then specify the job name and the schedule of the job responsible for the restoration process.

Quick Check

- You want to implement a log shipping configuration in a wide area network (WAN) environment, and you estimate that the initial full backup/restore process will take several hours. Which option should you choose to initialize the secondary database to speed up the process?

Quick Check Answer

- Create the primary database configuration, back up the database, use physical media (CD, DVD, or tape) to deliver the backup file to the secondary server, and configure the secondary database using the Restore An Existing Primary Database Backup In The Secondary Server option.

> **Real World**
>
> *Javier Loria*
>
> Designing a fault-tolerant environment for the database does not necessarily guarantee that you have a fault-tolerant system. After carefully designing, implementing, and testing a log shipping configuration, I was sure that the main line-of-business application of one of my customers was fault-tolerant. When the primary database server failed, however, we found that the application had the server name hard-coded in it, which prevented failing over to the secondary server we had set up. Fortunately, we managed to rename the server, and the application was online 45 minutes after the crash.

Scripting the Secondary Database Configuration

If you want to create a script to configure the secondary database, click Script Configuration at the bottom of the Database Properties window. Note two important aspects of the generated script:

- The script does not have the required code to initialize the secondary database. The DBA must back up the primary database and use that file to restore the secondary database to the secondary server.

- The script must be divided into two separate files. You must run the first part of the code when you're connected to the secondary server, and you must run the second part of the code while connected to the primary server.

The first part of the script uses the following two main stored procedures to create the log shipping configuration:

- ***sp_add_log_shipping_secondary_primary*** Creates the copy and restore jobs on the secondary server and the primary configuration.

- ***sp_add_log_shipping_secondary_database*** Finishes the configuration process and sets up the secondary database for log shipping.

The following code shows the first part of the secondary database configuration script:

Secondary Database Configuration Script Part 1

```
-- Execute the following statements at the Secondary to configure Log
-- Shipping for the database [DEMOSRV\INSTANCE2].[AdventureWorks2];
-- the script needs to be run at the Secondary in the context of the
-- [msdb] database.
-------------------------------------------------------------------------
```

```
-- Adding the Log Shipping configuration
-- ****** Begin: Script to be run at Secondary: [DEMOSRV\INSTANCE2] ******
DECLARE @LS_Secondary__CopyJobI d AS uniqueidentifier
DECLARE @LS_Secondary__RestoreJobId AS uniqueidentifier
DECLARE @LS_Secondary__SecondaryId AS uniqueidentifier
DECLARE @LS_Add_RetCode As int

EXEC @LS_Add_RetCode = master.dbo.sp_add_log_shipping_secondary_primary
   @primary_server = N'DEMOSRV\DEV2005'
   ,@primary_database = N'AdventureWorks2'
   ,@backup_source_directory = N'\\DEMOSRV\LOGSHIP'
   ,@backup_destination_directory = N'c:\LogShip2'
   ,@copy_job_name = N'LSCopy'
   ,@restore_job_name = N'LSRestore'
   ,@file_retention_period = 4320
   ,@overwrite = 1
   ,@copy_job_id = @LS_Secondary__CopyJobId OUTPUT
   ,@restore_job_id = @LS_Secondary__RestoreJobId OUTPUT
   ,@secondary_id = @LS_Secondary__SecondaryId OUTPUT

IF (@@ERROR = 0 AND @LS_Add_RetCode = 0)
BEGIN
   DECLARE @LS_SecondaryCopyJobScheduleUID As uniqueidentifier
   DECLARE @LS_SecondaryCopyJobScheduleID AS int
   EXEC msdb.dbo.sp_add_schedule
      @schedule_name =N'DefaultCopyJobSchedule'
      ,@enabled = 1
      ,@freq_type = 4
      ,@freq_interval = 1
      ,@freq_subday_type = 4
      ,@freq_subday_interval = 15
      ,@freq_recurrence_factor = 0
      ,@active_start_date = 20060106
      ,@active_end_date = 99991231
      ,@active_start_time = 0
      ,@active_end_time = 235900
      ,@schedule_uid = @LS_SecondaryCopyJobScheduleUID OUTPUT
      ,@schedule_id = @LS_SecondaryCopyJobScheduleID OUTPUT
   EXEC msdb.dbo.sp_attach_schedule
      @job_id = @LS_Secondary__CopyJobId
      ,@schedule_id = @LS_SecondaryCopyJobScheduleID

   DECLARE @LS_SecondaryRestoreJobScheduleUID As uniqueidentifier
   DECLARE @LS_SecondaryRestoreJobScheduleID AS int
   EXEC msdb.dbo.sp_add_schedule
      @schedule_name =N'DefaultRestoreJobSchedule'
      ,@enabled = 1
      ,@freq_type = 4
      ,@freq_interval = 1
      ,@freq_subday_type = 4
      ,@freq_subday_interval = 15
      ,@freq_recurrence_factor = 0
      ,@active_start_date = 20060106
```

```
        ,@active_end_date = 99991231
        ,@active_start_time = 0
        ,@active_end_time = 235900
        ,@schedule_uid = @LS_SecondaryRestoreJobScheduleUID OUTPUT
        ,@schedule_id = @LS_SecondaryRestoreJobScheduleID OUTPUT

    EXEC msdb.dbo.sp_attach_schedule
        @job_id = @LS_Secondary__RestoreJobId
        ,@schedule_id = @LS_SecondaryRestoreJobScheduleID
    END

DECLARE @LS_Add_RetCode2 As int

IF (@@ERROR = 0 AND @LS_Add_RetCode = 0)
BEGIN
EXEC @LS_Add_RetCode2 = master.dbo.sp_add_log_shipping_secondary_database
        @secondary_database = N'AdventureWorks2'
        ,@primary_server = N'DEMOSRV\DEV2005'
        ,@primary_database = N'AdventureWorks2'
        ,@restore_delay = 0
        ,@restore_mode = 0
        ,@disconnect_users= 0
        ,@restore_threshold = 45
        ,@threshold_alert_enabled = 1
        ,@history_retention_period = 5760
        ,@overwrite = 1
END

IF (@@error = 0 AND @LS_Add_RetCode = 0)
    BEGIN
    EXEC msdb.dbo.sp_update_job
        @job_id = @LS_Secondary__CopyJobId
        ,@enabled = 1
    EXEC msdb.dbo.sp_update_job
        @job_id = @LS_Secondary__RestoreJobId
        ,@enabled = 1
    END
```

In this script, *sp_add_log_shipping_secondary_primary* uses the parameters *@primary_server*, *@primary_database*, *@backup_source_directory*, *@backup_destination_directory*, *@copy_job_name*, and *@restore_job_name* in the same manner as SSMS. *@file_retention_period* sets the number of minutes that the job waits before deleting a file.

sp_add_log_shipping_secondary_database finishes the configuration process and configures the secondary database. The first three parameters (*@secondary_database*, *@primary_server*, and *@primary_database*) associate the secondary database with the primary database. *@restore_delay* sets the number of minutes the job will wait before restoring a log backup, and *@restore_threshold* and *@threshold_alert_enabled* specify whether an alert will be raised if after a given time period no restores finish sucess-fully. *@history_retention_period* sets the time period that elapses before the job deletes history information from the *msdb* database. *@restore_mode* and *@disconnect_users* will be explained in the next lesson.

A DBA who needs to configure multiple secondary servers can execute (without any modification) this script on each secondary server and later execute the second part of the script on the primary server multiple times, changing the secondary name to finish the configuration.

As noted earlier, you must run the second part of the script, which is used only to keep a record of secondary databases that have a reference to the primary database, on the primary server. This is important for monitoring purposes. To perform this task, the second part of the script uses the *sp_add_log_shipping_primary_secondary* stored procedure, as the following code shows.

Secondary Database Configuration Script Part 2
```
-- ****** Begin: Script to be run at Primary: [DEMOSRV\DEV2005] ******
EXEC master.dbo.sp_add_log_shipping_primary_secondary
     @primary_database = N'AdventureWorks2'
     ,@secondary_server = N'DEMOSRV\INSTANCE2'
     ,@secondary_database = N'AdventureWorks2'
     ,@overwrite = 1
-- ****** End: Script to be run at Primary: [DEMOSRV\DEV2005]   ******
```

Failing Over to a Secondary Database

If a primary server fails and you need to bring a secondary database online, you must perform the failover manually by following these general steps:

1. Synchronize the primary and secondary databases. You begin by synchro-nizing the secondary database with the primary database, copying any uncopied backup files from the backup share to the copy destination folder of each secondary server. You need to apply any unapplied transaction log backups in sequence to each secondary database; if the primary database is accessible, back up the active transaction log with *NORECOVERY*, and apply the backup to the secondary databases.

2. Recover the secondary database. Recovering puts the secondary database into a consistent state and brings it online.

3. Change the role of the secondary database to primary. After you recover the secondary database, you configure the recovered secondary database to act as a primary database and change the role of the primary database to be the secondary database. Disable the log shipping backup job on the original primary server and the copy and restore jobs on the original secondary server. Configure the secondary database as the primary database by using SSMS.

PRACTICE Creating a Log Shipping Configuration

In these practice exercises, you will create a log shipping configuration that uses a single server for testing purposes.

▶ Practice 1: Prepare the Environment for Log Shipping

In this practice, you will create the file directories and shared folders required for the log shipping configuration. One of the folders will hold the secondary database files, another will store the log shipping backup files, and the last one will hold the secondary copy of the files. You will also create a copy of the *AdventureWorks* database for testing purposes. This database will be in Full recovery mode.

1. Using Windows Explorer, locate the root folder of the C drive and create a folder named **LogShip Practice**. You will use this folder to hold the subfolders for log shipping practices.

2. In the LogShipPractice folder, create three subfolders: **Database**, **LSBackup**, and **Copy**. You will use the Database subfolder to store the secondary server database and log files, the LSBackup folder to store log backups, and the Copy subfolder to store copies of the logs in the secondary server.

3. Right-click the LSBackup subfolder and choose Sharing And Security.

4. Select Share This Folder and click OK. Sharing the folder allows secondary servers to use the UNC path to access the log backups.

IMPORTANT Security

The default right, Everyone read access, is secure enough for testing purposes. In a working environment, you should remove the Everyone group from the shared folder's access control list and add the SQL Service Windows account instead.

---

5. Open SSMS and connect to the default instance of the database engine.

6. Expand the Databases folder.

7. Right-click the *AdventureWorks* database and choose Tasks, Back Up. You are going to back up the *AdventureWorks* database and then use this backup to create a database to use for log shipping.

8. If there are any destination files or backup devices in the destination list box, remove them by selecting each one and then clicking Remove.

9. Click Add to add a destination file. Name the file **AdventureWorks.bak** in the default path and click OK.

10. Click OK to back up the database. Wait for the backup process to complete, and then click OK.

11. Right-click the *AdventureWorks* database and choose Tasks, Restore, Database.

12. In the To Database text box, type **LSTesting** to name the database. You are going to use the *LSTesting* database as the primary database for log shipping.

13. Select From Device, click the browse button (...), and then click Add to select the source file.

14. Select the AdventureWorks.bak file in the default backup path and click OK. Click OK to close the Specify Backup dialog box.

15. Select the AdventureWorks-Full Database Backup check box in the list of backup sets.

16. Select the Options page.

17. In the Restore As column, change the file names of the AdventureWorks_Data and AdventureWorks_Log files to **LSTesting.mdf** and **LSTesting.ldf**, respectively, in the default data directory (C:\Program Files\Microsoft SQL Server\ MSSQL.1\MSSQL\Data). Renaming the files is important to avoid conflicts with the *AdventureWorks* database.

18. Click OK to initiate the restoration process. Then click OK to close the confirmation message displayed when the restore completes.

19. Right-click the *LSTesting* database and choose Properties. (If you do not see the *LSTesting* database displayed in the Databases folder, right-click Databases and choose Refresh.)

20. Select the Options page.

21. Change the Recovery Model to Full. Databases in Simple mode cannot partici-
    pate in log shipping configurations.

22. Click OK to close the Database Properties window.

▶ **Practice 2: Configure the Primary Database**

In this practice, you will configure the *LSTesting* database as the primary database and
create the backup job for the log shipping configuration.

1. In SSMS, select the *LSTesting* database.

2. Right-click the *LSTesting* database and choose Properties.

3. Select the Transaction Log Shipping page.

4. Select the Enable This As A Primary Database In A Log Shipping Configuration
   check box.

5. Click Backup Settings.

6. Specify the UNC path for the backup files in the Network Path To Backup Folder
   text box. For the path, use your computer name and the LSBackup shared
   folder—for example: \\ComputerName\LSBackup.

7. Specify the local directory path for the backup file in the If The Backup Folder Is
   Located On The Primary Server, Type A Local Path To The Folder text box. Use
   the path **C:\LogShipPractice\LSBackup.**

8. Click OK to close the Transaction Log Backup Settings dialog box. By default,
   SQL Server deletes all transaction log backups older than 72 hours, notifies you
   if a backup does not occur within one hour, and backs up the transaction log
   every 15 minutes.

9. Click OK to configure the primary database. Wait for the Save Log Shipping
   Configuration message to appear, and then click Close.

▶ **Practice 3: Configure the Secondary Database**

In this practice, you will configure a secondary database that will be a copy of the
LSTesting database.

1. In SSMS, select the *LSTesting* database.

2. Right-click the *LSTesting* database and choose Properties.

3. Select the Transaction Log Shipping page.

4. Below Secondary Databases, click Add.

5. Click Connect. Use the appropriate credentials to connect to the secondary server. If you are using the same instance as your secondary server, connect to the default server.

6. In the Secondary Database text box, type **LSTesting2** as the database name.

7. Select Yes, Generate A Full Backup Of The Primary Database And Restore It Into The Secondary Database (And Create The Secondary Database If It Doesn't Exist).

8. Click Restore Options and specify a new directory in which you want to restore the database files. Use the **C:\LogShipPractice\Database** path for both the database and log folders. Click OK.

9. Click the Copy Files tab.

10. Type the path **C:\LogShipPractice\Copy** in the Destination Folder For Copied Files text box.

11. Click OK to close the Secondary Database Settings dialog box and confirm your settings.

12. Click OK to close the Database Properties window and implement the new configuration.

13. Wait for the Save Log Shipping Configuration message and finish the configuration process by clicking Close. You should now see the *LSTesting2* database displayed in your Databases folder with a message that states that SQL Server is restoring the database.

Lesson Summary

- SSMS lets DBAs create a log shipping configuration interactively in the Database Properties window.

- You configure the primary database first, setting backup options for the log shipping configuration, and then configure the secondary database and restore options.

- Through SSMS, you can also script your log shipping configuration to document the configuration, deploy the same configuration for multiple databases, and aid in the recovery plan.

- Failing over to the secondary database in case of a primary database failure is a manual process that requires you to synchronize the primary and secondary databases, recover the secondary database, and then configure the secondary database as the primary database.

Lesson Review

The following questions are intended to reinforce key information presented in this lesson. The questions are also available on the companion CD if you prefer to review them in electronic form.

NOTE Answers

Answers to these questions and explanations of why each answer choice is right or wrong are located in the "Answers" section at the end of the book.

---

1. When creating a log shipping configuration, what is the default path of the data files of the secondary database?

   A. C:\Program Files\Microsoft SQL Server\MSSQL.1\MSSQL\Data.

   B. The default path of the secondary database files is the same path as that for the primary database files.

   C. There is no default path; the DBA must specify a file path for each of the data files in the secondary database.

   D. The path of the secondary database is configured at the server level by using the Database Default Location option.

2. Which methods can you use to create a log shipping configuration? (Choose all that apply.)

   A. System stored procedures

   B. Maintenance Plan Wizard

   C. SQL Server Surface Area Configuration tool

   D. SSMS

Lesson 3: Configuring Log Shipping Mode

You can use log shipping to increase either the availability or the scalability of your applications. The log shipping mode you select determines which operational requirement you want to use the technology for. If you choose *No Recovery Mode*, you will use the log shipping configuration for availability reasons only, and the secondary database won't be available for users to query. If you select *Standby Mode*, you allow users read-only access to the secondary database. This configuration increases the scalability of your application by letting you distribute queries across multiple servers and reduces the primary server's workload. In this lesson, you will learn how to configure log shipping's recovery mode.

After this lesson, you will be able to:

- ■ Explain how log shipping's No Recovery mode works.
- ■ Explain how log shipping's Standby mode works.
- ■ Configure the No Recovery and Standby modes.

Estimated lesson time: 30 minutes

How to Configure No Recovery Mode

As you saw in the previous lesson, log shipping uses transaction log backups, copies, and restores to keep the primary and secondary databases synchronized. Seeing how the restoration process handles incomplete transactions will help you understand the purpose of the log shipping mode.

The default behavior of the *RESTORE* command is to read the transaction log backup, apply all the transactions in the log to the database, and roll back all incomplete transactions when the restore finishes reading the log. However, log shipping configurations cannot use this behavior of the *RESTORE* command. If the transactions are rolled back, the database changes will be lost, and at this point, you would not know whether the next transaction log restore would commit or roll back the changes. This *RESTORE* command option is called Recovery Mode, and log shipping doesn't use it.

Instead, log shipping uses the No Recovery Mode of the *RESTORE* command as its default setting. This mode does not roll back incomplete transactions. Incomplete transactions are neither rolled back nor rolled forward; they remain incomplete transactions. One side effect of this option is that the database is not available for user queries.

Here's how to use SSMS to set the No Recovery mode of a log shipping configuration:

1. In SMSS, right-click the primary database and choose Properties. Select the Transaction Log Shipping page.

2. Below Secondary Server Instances And Databases, select the secondary database you want to configure and click the browse button (...). (Or click Add if you want to add a new configuration.)

3. In the Secondary Database Settings dialog box, click the Restore Transaction Log tab. Below Database State When Restoring Backups, select No Recovery Mode, as shown in Figure 18-7.

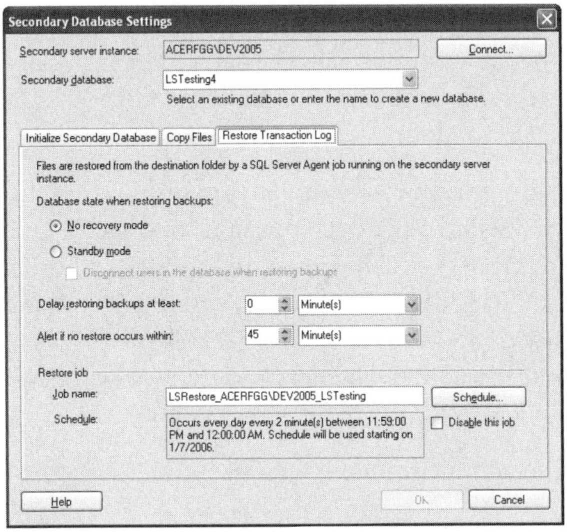

Figure 18-7   Selecting No Recovery Mode

4. Click OK to save your changes and close the Secondary Database Settings dialog box.

5. Click OK to close the Database Properties dialog box for the primary database.

BEST PRACTICES   Availability

When using log shipping for availability reasons only, use No Recovery mode.

> **Quick Check**
>
> 1. What is the default recovery mode setting for log shipping?
>
> 2. When do you use this recovery mode setting?
>
> **Quick Check Answers**
>
> 1. The default setting is No Recovery mode.
>
> 2. You use No Recovery mode when you are using log shipping for availability reasons; this mode doesn't allow user access.

How to Configure Standby Mode

Standby mode is the *RESTORE* command option you use to configure standby servers. In this mode, the secondary database is available for read-only access by users and applications, which enables you to use the secondary database to reduce the workload of the primary database. You cannot use a secondary database in Standby mode to update database information.

A log shipping configuration in Standby mode reads the transaction log backup, applies all transactions in the log to the database, and rolls back all incomplete transactions when the restore process finishes reading the log. The difference between Recovery mode and Standby mode is that Standby mode saves all incomplete transactions in a separate *Transaction Undo File (TUF)*. The restore process uses this file to maintain transactional integrity; when the next restore process occurs, it restores all the committed transactions.

Here's how to use SSMS to configure Standby mode:

1. In the primary database's Properties window, select the Transaction Log Shipping page.

2. Below Secondary Server Instances And Databases, select the secondary database you want to configure and click the browse button (...). (Or click Add if you want to add a new configuration.)

3. In the Secondary Database Settings dialog box, click the Restore Transaction Log tab.

4. Below Database State When Restoring Backups, select Standby Mode, as Figure 18-8 shows.

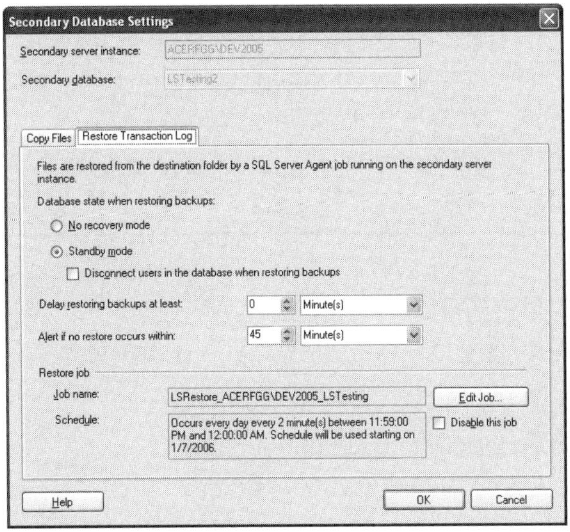

Figure 18-8   Selecting Standby Mode

5. When you select Standby Mode, the Disconnect Users In The Database When Restoring Backup option becomes available. The *RESTORE* command requires exclusive access to the database, so this option is necessary to specify how you want to handle connected users when the restore process begins. The default is to leave users connected to the database, which will cause the restore job to fail. If you select the Disconnect Users In The Database When Restoring Backups check box, the restore will force users off the database after a small delay.

6. Click OK to save your changes and close the Secondary Database Settings dialog box.

7. Click OK to close the Database Properties dialog box for the primary database.

BEST PRACTICES   Scalability

Use Standby mode when you are using log shipping for scalability reasons.

> **Quick Check**
> 1. True or false: Standby mode allows users and applications to access and modify the secondary database.
> 2. True or false: The default setting for Standby mode is to leave users connected to the database when the restore backup operation begins.

> **Quick Check Answers**
> 1. False. Standby mode puts the secondary database in read-only access mode. No database updates are allowed.
> 2. True. This default setting leaves user connected to the database, which will cause the restore job to fail.

PRACTICE Configuring Standby Mode

In these practice exercises, you will review the mode of the previous log shipping configuration and create a new standby configuration.

▶ **Practice 1: Review the Secondary Database Configuration**

In this practice, you will review the log shipping mode of the *LSTesting2* database.

1. In SSMS, select the *LSTesting* database.
2. Right-click the *LSTesting* database and choose Properties.
3. Select the Transaction Log Shipping page.
4. In the Secondary Databases section of the log shipping configuration, click the browse button (...) next to the *LSTesting2* database.
5. Click the Restore Transaction Log tab.
6. Verify that the No Recovery Mode option is selected.
7. Click Cancel to close the Secondary Database Settings dialog box, and then click Cancel to close the Database Properties window.
8. Select the *LSTesting2* database in Object Explorer.
9. Verify that the database *LSTesting2* status is (Restoring ...).
10. Click New Query on the toolbar.
11. In the New Query window, type the following query:

    ```
    SELECT * FROM LSTesting2.HumanResources.Department
    ```

12. Click Execute on the toolbar.
13. Verify that the server returns the following error message:

    ```
    Msg 927, Level 14, State 2, Line 1
    Database 'LSTesting2' cannot be opened. It is in the middle of a restore.
    ```

14. Close the New Query window.
15. Click No to discard the changes in the New Query window.

▶ **Practice 2: Delete the Secondary Database Configuration**

In this practice, you will delete the log shipping configuration of the *LSTesting2* database.

1. In SSMS, select the *LSTesting* database.

2. Right-click the *LSTesting* database and choose Properties.

3. Select the Transaction Log Shipping page.

4. In the Secondary Server Instances And Databases section, select the secondary database and click Remove.

5. In the confirmation message, click Yes to confirm that you want to remove the secondary database.

6. Click OK to close the Database Properties window and save the configuration.

7. In the Save Log Shipping Configuration window, click Close.

8. Select the *LSTesting2* database in Object Explorer.

9. Right-click the *LSTesting2* database and choose Delete.

10. In the Delete Object window, click OK to confirm the deletion.

▶ **Practice 3: Create a Standby Log Shipping Configuration**

In this practice, you will create a new standby log shipping configuration.

1. In SSMS, select the *LSTesting* database.

2. Right-click the *LSTesting* database and choose Properties.

3. Select the Transaction Log Shipping page.

4. Click Add below Secondary Server Instances And Databases.

5. Click Connect; then use the appropriate credentials to connect to the secondary server. If you are using the same instance as the one that contains your primary database, connect to the default server. Click Connect to establish the connection.

6. In the Secondary Database text box, name the database **LSTesting2**.

7. Select Yes, Generate A Full Backup Of The Primary Database And Restore It Into The Secondary Database.

8. Click Restore Options, and type the *C:\LogShipPractice\Database* path for both the database and log folders. Click OK.

9. Click the Copy Files tab.

10. Type the path **C:\LogShipPractice\Copy** in the Destination Folder For Copied Files text box.

11. Click the Restore Transaction Log tab.

12. Select Standby Mode.

13. Click OK to confirm your settings.

14. Click OK in the Database Properties window to implement the new configuration.

15. Wait for the Save Log Shipping Configuration message to appear, and then click Close.

16. Select the *LSTesting2* database in Object Explorer.

17. Verify that the status of the *LSTesting2* database is (Standby/Read Only).

18. Click New Query on the toolbar.

19. In the New Query window, type the following query:

```
SELECT *
FROM LSTesting2.HumanResources.Department
```

20. Click Execute on the toolbar.

21. Verify that the query runs without any error and returns valid data.

22. In the New Query window, replace the previous query with the following command:

```
UPDATE LSTesting2.HumanResources.Department
    SET Name='Testing'
WHERE DepartmentID=1
```

23. Click Execute on the toolbar.

24. Verify that the server returns the following error message:

```
Msg 3906, Level 16, State 1, Line 1
Failed to update database "LSTesting2" because the database is read-only.
```

25. Close the New Query window.

26. Click No to discard the changes in the New Query window.

Lesson Summary

- One of the most important settings in a log shipping configuration is the recovery mode, which you set on the Restore Transaction Log page of the Secondary Database Settings window.

- No Recovery mode doesn't allow users to access the database, so you use it only when you are implementing log shipping for availability reasons.

- Standby mode allows users read-only access to the secondary database. If you are implementing log shipping to improve the scalability and performance of your database, you should select Standby mode.

Lesson Review

The following questions are intended to reinforce key information presented in this lesson. The questions are also available on the companion CD if you prefer to review them in electronic form.

NOTE Answers

Answers to these questions and explanations of why each answer choice is right or wrong are located in the "Answers" section at the end of the book.

---

1. Which of the following statements about log shipping No Recovery mode are correct? (Choose all that apply.)

   A. The secondary database is available for users to query.

   B. The secondary database is not available for users to query.

   C. You can use this mode to increase the scalability/performance of an application.

   D. You can use this mode to increase the availability of an application.

2. Users are complaining about sometimes being disconnected when using the secondary database of a log shipping configuration. How would you explain this behavior?

   A. The secondary server is having performance issues and is losing user connections; you need to increase the secondary server's hardware resources.

   B. This is the default behavior for the No Recovery mode; you need to change the secondary database configuration to Standby mode.

   C. This is optional behavior for the Standby mode. Using SSMS, clear the Disconnect Users In The Database When Restoring Backups check box of the log shipping configuration.

   D. The primary server is having performance issues and is losing user connections; you need to increase the primary server's hardware resources.

Lesson 4: Configuring Monitoring

Log shipping enables you to configure a separate monitor server to capture the history and status of different log shipping operations. The optional monitor server tracks all the log shipping details, including when the transaction log on the primary database was last backed up and when the secondary servers copied and restored the backup files. To make sure that monitoring continues and you have access to this status information if the primary or secondary server is unavailable, you should configure the monitor on a separate server. One monitor server can monitor multiple log shipping configurations. And via SSMS, you can see the current status of any instance involved in the log shipping configuration by accessing the Transaction Log Shipping Status report for that instance.

After this lesson, you will be able to:

- Configure a log shipping monitor server.
- Review log shipping reports.

Estimated lesson time: 20 minutes

Understanding the Role of a Monitor Server

Because the log shipping configuration uses SQL Server Agent jobs to execute backup, copy, and restore tasks, the log shipping jobs always save the status and history of the shipping operations locally. SQL Server Agent stores status and historic information about jobs in the *sysjobactivity* and *sysjobhistory* tables in the *msdb* database. The *sysjobactivity* table records the current activity of SQL Server jobs, and *sysjobhistory* keeps track of the historic execution of jobs. Because backup jobs are executed on the primary server, and copy and restore jobs are executed on the secondary server, the backup history information is stored on the primary server, and copy and restore history information is stored on the secondary server.

MORE INFO   SQL Server agent tables

For more information about job information stored in the *msdb* database, see the SQL Server 2005 Books Online section titled "SQL Server Language Reference-Transact-SQL Reference-System Tables-SQL Server Agent Tables."

Besides these standard SQL Server Agent job records, log shipping records specific log shipping information in the *log_shipping_monitor_error_detail* and *log_shipping_monitor_history_detail* tables. The *log_shipping_monitor_error_detail* table keeps track of error details, and the *log_shipping_monitor_history_detail* table stores information about the history details of log shipping jobs.

One limitation of this job-recording process is that all the monitoring information is stored locally on the same server that executes the job. In case of a server failure, you might lose the database as well as all the recorded information about which jobs executed successfully and which jobs didn't execute—or failed. In such a case, the DBA might not know the status of the secondary database when the primary server fails. Storing historic information about log shipping job execution on a different server helps in the recovery process by providing important status information and helps the DBA to execute the appropriate remaining tasks. This is why log shipping uses a monitor server.

By configuring a monitor server, you force the backup, copy, and restore jobs to write information for the *log_shipping_monitor_error_detail* and *log_shipping_monitor_history_detail* tables on both the local server and the monitor server.

How to Configure a Monitor Server

Here's how to configure a monitor server by using SSMS:

1. In the Database Properties window for the primary database, select Use A Monitor Server Instance and click Settings, which displays the Log Shipping Monitor Settings dialog box.

2. In the Log Shipping Monitor Settings dialog box, click Connect to select the monitor server instance and the authentication credentials you want to use.

> **NOTE** Security
>
> The account connecting to the monitor server must have sysadmin access to the monitor server.

3. Because log shipping jobs (backup, copy, and restore) will store information in the monitor server instance, you must choose how these jobs will authenticate in the monitor server. The default option is to impersonate the proxy account of the job, which means using the SQL Server Agent service account for authentication (see Figure 18-9). You should use this option when both servers are using Windows accounts in the same Active Directory. If you want to provide a SQL Server account, however, select Using The Following SQL Server Login and then specify the login name and password.

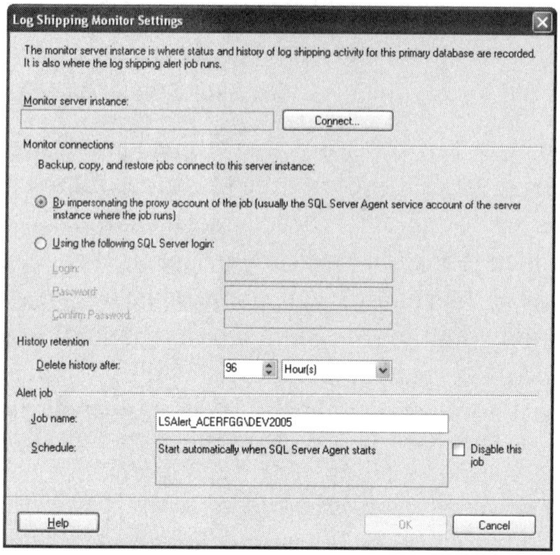

Figure 18-9   Selecting how monitor jobs connect and authenticate

4. Other Log Shipping Monitor Settings options include history retention, which determines how long the log shipping configuration will retain history information about the task, and the name and schedule for the alert job that raises an alert if there are problems in any log shipping jobs. You should use the same schedule as the schedule for the log shipping backup task.

NOTE   Log shipping reports

For the primary, secondary, and monitor servers involved in log shipping, SSMS provides a current log shipping activity report. You can view the Transaction Log Shipping Status report for each server from SSMS. Begin by selecting the server instance you want in Object Explorer. In the Summary (right) pane, from the Report drop-down list, select the Transaction Log Shipping Status report. Viewing the report from the monitor server will give you the most comprehensive information about your log shipping configuration—including the name and status of all primary and secondary servers that are using the monitor server to monitor log shipping operations.

PRACTICE **Creating a Log Shipping Configuration**

In these practice exercises, you will delete the previous log shipping configuration and create a new configuration that uses a monitor server.

▶ **Practice 1: Delete the Log Shipping Configuration**

In this practice, you will delete all the previous log shipping configurations so that you can create a new configuration that includes a monitor server.

1. In SSMS, select the *LSTesting* database.

2. Right-click the *LSTesting* database and choose Properties.

3. Select the Transaction Log Shipping page.

4. Clear the Enable This As A Primary Database In A Log Shipping Configuration check box to disable the configuration and remove all log shipping jobs.

5. Click Yes to confirm that you want to disable the log shipping configuration.

6. Click OK to close the Database Properties window and remove all log shipping configurations. Click Close to close the Save Log Shipping Configuration window.

7. Select the *LSTesting2* database in Object Explorer.

8. Right-click the *LSTesting2* database, choose Delete, and then click OK to delete the database.

9. Using Windows Explorer, navigate to the C:\LogShipPractice\Copy Folder and delete all files.

10. Using Windows Explorer, navigate to the C:\LogShipPractice\LSBackup Folder and delete all files.

▶ **Practice 2: Create a Log Shipping Configuration with a Monitor Server**

In this practice, you will create a new log shipping configuration that uses a monitor server.

1. In SSMS, select the *LSTesting* database.

2. Right-click the *LSTesting* database and choose Properties.

3. Select the Transaction Log Shipping page.

4. Select the Enable This As A Primary Database In A Log Shipping Configuration check box.

5. Click Backup Settings.

6. Specify the UNC path for the backup files in the Network Path To Backup Folder text box. Use your computer name and the LSBackup shared folder—for example, *ComputerName*\LSBackup.

7. Specify the local directory path for the backup file in the If The Backup Folder Is Located On The Primary Server, Type A Path To The Folder text box. Use the path **C:\LogShipPractice\LSBackup**.

8. Click OK to close the Transaction Log Backup Settings dialog box.

9. Below Secondary Databases, click Add.

10. Click Connect. Use the appropriate credentials to connect to the secondary server. If you are using the same instance for the secondary database, connect to the default server.

11. In the Secondary Database text box, name the database *LSTesting2*.

12. Select Yes, Generate A Full Backup Of The Primary Database And Restore It Into The Secondary Database.

13. Click Restore Options so that you can specify the directory in which you want SQL Server to restore the database files. Use the **C:\LogShipPractice\Database** path for both the database and log folders. Click OK.

14. Click the Copy Files tab.

15. Type the path **C:\LogShipPractice\Copy** in the Destination Folder For Copied Files text box.

16. Click OK to confirm your secondary database settings.

17. Select the Use A Monitor Server Instance check box.

18. Click Settings.

19. In the Log Shipping Monitor Server Settings dialog box, click Connect. Use the appropriate credentials to connect to the monitor server. If you are using the same instance as the monitor server, connect to the default server.

20. Click OK to close the Log Shipping Monitor Settings dialog box.

21. Click OK to save the log shipping configuration.

22. SQL Server now backs up the primary database, restores it to the secondary database, and configures monitoring. When this process completes, click Close to close the Save Log Shipping Configuration message box.

▶ **Practice 3: View a Log Shipping Report**

In this practice, you will view the log shipping report included in SSMS.

1. In SSMS, select the database engine instance (server) for which you want to monitor log shipping in Object Explorer.

2. If necessary, select the Summary window or press F7 to display the Summary window in the right pane.

3. On the Summary window toolbar, on the Report drop-down list, select the Transaction Log Shipping Status report.

Lesson Summary

■ You can configure a separate monitor server to capture log shipping information and maintain execution records even when the primary or secondary server fails.

■ In SSMS, you use the Log Shipping Monitor Settings window to configure a monitor server.

■ In SSMS, you can view the Transaction Log Shipping Status report for every server involved in the log shipping configuration.

Lesson Review

The following questions are intended to reinforce key information presented in this lesson. The questions are also available on the companion CD if you prefer to review them in electronic form.

NOTE Answers

Answers to these questions and explanations of why each answer choice is right or wrong are located in the "Answers" section at the end of the book.

---

1. Which of the following is the main reason to configure a separate monitor server in a log shipping configuration?

    A. To provide an automatic failover configuration

    B. To keep track of the results of all tasks in an independent server

    C. To reduce the workload of the primary server

    D. To reduce the workload of the secondary server

2. Which of the following options are available when configuring a monitor server? (Choose all that apply.)

    A. Monitor Database

    B. Operator Name

    C. History Retention

    D. Monitor Instance

Chapter Review

To further practice and reinforce the skills you learned in this chapter, you can

- Review the chapter summary.
- Review the list of key terms introduced in this chapter.
- Complete the case scenarios. These scenarios set up a real-world situation involving the topics of this chapter and ask you to create a solution.
- Complete the suggested practices.
- Take a practice test.

Chapter Summary

- Log shipping uses the SQL Server Agent to automatically synchronize a primary database and one or more secondary databases through a series of jobs that back up the transaction log on the primary database and then copy and restore the log on the secondary databases. However, failing over from the primary database to a secondary database is a manual process.
- In SSMS, you configure the primary database and log shipping backup options. You then configure the secondary databases and log shipping restore options.
- During the configuration process, you select No Recovery mode to create a warm server that doesn't allow user access but instead makes the secondary database part of your availability and disaster recovery implementation.
- You select Standby mode for a secondary database if you want to provide an alternate server for queries and increase the scalability of your solution.
- A resilient log shipping configuration includes a monitor server on a separate system from your primary and secondary servers to monitor and report on the status of the log shipping process.

Key Terms

Do you know what these key terms mean? You can check your answers by looking up the terms in the glossary at the end of the book.

- Copy Files task
- log shipping

- *log_shipping_monitor_error_detail* table
- *log_shipping_monitor_history_detail* table
- monitor server
- No Recovery Mode
- primary database
- primary server
- secondary database
- secondary server
- Standby Mode
- *sysjobactivity*
- *sysjobhistory*
- Transaction Undo File (TUF)

Case Scenarios

In the following case scenarios, you will apply what you've learned about log shipping configuration. You can find answers to these questions in the "Answers" section at the end of this book.

Case Scenario 1: Providing Reporting Scalability

You are working as the DBA of Tailspin Toys, which introduced a line of popular stunt kites three years ago, and business has flourished. To meet customer demand, the company tripled its sales force and customer service staff. Now that the company has grown, the perfomance of the database server has decreased, and some employees frequently complain about how long it takes to perform their daily tasks. A closer look at the system reveals that most of the database server work comes from reporting and Microsoft Office Excel PivotTable queries. To help improve database performance, management has authorized the use of two additional servers with similar hardware configurations as the main database server.

1. How would you configure the new servers to increase the performance of the reporting application and PivotTable queries?
2. Which log shipping mode would you use in this scenario?
3. What database options should you revise before implementing the log shipping process?

Case Scenario 2: Providing Fault Tolerance for Multiple Servers

Fabrikam, Inc., a leading manufacturer of digital cameras, recently acquired a new video products division to expand its product line, increase revenue, and grow overall market share of the company. The new video products division operates in a remote site and should remain as independent as possible. The video products division has four SQL Server 2005 database applications running on four servers. As the DBA of Fabrikam, Inc., you need to increase the availability of these applications under a very tight budget.

1. What technology could you use to increase the availability of the new video products division?

2. Which log shipping recovery mode would you use in this scenario?

3. What database rights must you grant to configure the log shipping process?

Suggested Practices

To help you successfully master the exam objectives presented in this chapter, complete the following tasks.

Create a Log Shipping Configuration

For this task, you should complete at least Practice 1. If you want a more well-rounded understanding of log shipping options and implementation approaches, you should also complete Practices 2 and 3.

- **Practice 1**   Create a log shipping configuration that uses a single database engine instance. Familiarize yourself with the different log shipping options available by using SSMS to create this configuration.

- **Practice 2**   Create a log shipping configuration that uses three separate database engine instances, one for each of the log shipping roles. Notice the SQL Server Agent jobs that are created in each instance to perform the different log shipping tasks.

- **Practice 3**   Create various complex log shipping configurations by using separate database engine instances. Implement log shipping using an already initialized secondary database, using different SQL Agent service accounts, and using stored procedures instead of SSMS.

Take a Practice Test

The practice tests on this book's companion CD offer many options. For example, you can test yourself on just the content covered in this chapter, or you can test yourself on all the 70-431 certification exam content. You can set up the test so that it closely simulates the experience of taking a certification exam, or you can set it up in study mode so that you can look at the correct answers and explanations after you answer each question.

MORE INFO   **Practice tests**

For details about all the practice test options available, see the "How to Use the Practice Tests" section in this book's Introduction.

Chapter 19
Managing Replication

SQL Server database replication is a set of technologies for copying and distributing data and database objects from one database to one or more other databases and keeping the databases synchronized. Using replication technologies, you can increase the availability of your software solutions by geographically distributing your data, making applications more resilient to communication failures. You can also use replication to distribute the data-access workload across multiple servers or to support remote clients.

This chapter gives you a start into replication by exploring the technology's specific terminology and elements as well as which type of replication is appropriate for different business situations. You will learn how to set up a secure replication configuration by using SQL Server Management Studio (SSMS) and how to script the configuration for efficiency and documentation purposes. And you will see how to resolve conflicts that can arise in merge replication setups. Finally, this chapter will give you tips for monitoring and improving the performance of your replication topology.

Exam objectives in this chapter:
- Manage replication
  - ❑ Distinguish between replication types.
  - ❑ Configure a Publisher, a Distributor, and a Subscriber.
  - ❑ Configure replication security.
  - ❑ Configure conflict resolution settings for merge replication.
  - ❑ Monitor replication.
  - ❑ Improve replication performance.
  - ❑ Plan for, stop, and restart recovery procedures.

Lessons in this chapter:

Before You Begin

To complete the lessons in this chapter, you must have:

- A computer that meets the hardware and software requirements for Microsoft SQL Server 2005.
- SQL Server 2005 Developer, Workgroup, Standard, or Enterprise Edition installed.
- SQL Server Agent running and configured with a Microsoft Windows service account.

NOTE Configuring a SQL Server Agent Windows service account

The SQL Server services (SQL Server, SQL Server Agent, Analysis Services, Report Server, and SQL Server Browser), use accounts to authenticate to the local computer and to the network. These accounts are configured when you install SQL Server, but you can use SQL Server Configuration Manager (SSCM) to change the configuration afterwards.

To configure a SQL Server service account using SSCM:

1. Create a Windows user account. Use Local Users And Groups to create the account in the local server's user database, or use Active Directory Users And Computers if the server is a member of an Active Directory domain.

2. Open SSCM. In the console tree, click SQL Server 2005 Services. In the details pane, double-click the service you want to configure.

3. On the Log On tab, select This Account. In the Account Name text box, type the name of the Windows account (or click Browse to browse for and select the user account you just created). Type the user's password in the Password and Confirm Password text boxes. Click OK to save your changes.

4. When prompted, click Yes to restart the service. The service now logs on using the user account and password you specified.

NOTE If you use SSCM to change the SQL Server Agent service account, it is automatically assigned to the SQLServer2005SQLAgentUser$SERVERNAME$INSTANCENAME local group to grant the minimum required rights to operate the service.

Real World

Javier Loria

Distributing data geographically is not an easy task when you don't have the right set of tools. I frequently find customers using complex proprietary solutions to distribute data to multiple sites. Most of these solutions do not provide the manageability that replication does. When that is the case, my message to the customer frequently is "Don't reinvent the wheel!"

SQL Server 2005 provides three replication types and a variety of options within those types so that you can create a customized data-distribution solution for your business needs. SQL Server 2005 also gives you the tools you need to efficiently create, manage, and monitor replication, including SSMS, SQL Server Replication Monitor (SSRM), and Transact-SQL replication stored procedures and Replication Management Objects (RMOs).

And the best part is that this powerful functionality and these management tools come free as integral parts of SQL Server 2005.

Lesson 1: Understanding Replication Types

SQL Server 2005 provides three main types of replication: *snapshot*, *transactional*, and *merge*. These three central types of replication, combined with a variety of options, offer a wide selection of alternatives that you can use to satisfy multiple business needs for distributed computing and high availability. In this lesson, you will learn the key terms and concepts underlying SQL Server 2005 replication and review the three types of replication available.

> **After this lesson, you will be able to:**
> - Understand replication terminology.
> - Explain the three replication types and their advantages and disadvantages.
> - Understand the roles of the different replication agents.
>
> **Estimated lesson time: 20 minutes**

Understanding Replication Terminology

SQL Server replication uses a metaphor from the publishing industry to name components in its architecture. The metaphor of a magazine and its components helps communicate to database architects, administrators, and developers a clear image of the role each component plays in a replication solution.

Publications and Articles

SQL Server replication begins with two elements: an article and a publication. An *article*, the most basic unit of replication, represents the database object that is replicated. SQL Server 2005 replication allows the following articles:

- Tables
- Views
- Filtered tables or views, by column or row
- Indexed views
- Definitions of stored procedures
- Execution of stored procedures

SQL Server groups articles from the same database in a unit called a *publication*. The publication element serves two purposes: It simplifies the configuration and management of the replication process, and it provides a unit to assure the logical relationship and consistency of the data. A publication simplifies management by providing a single point for subscribing to a group of articles, making the replication easier to configure. At the same time, a publication preserves the integrity of the information SQL Server replicates by grouping data that must be kept together. For example, the *Order-Detail* and *OrderHeader* tables are probably better published as a single unit to assure the consistency of the related information.

Server Roles

The publishing metaphor extends to the roles a server can play in the replication topology. You can configure a server as *Publisher*, *Distributor*, and/or *Subscriber*. The relationship between these three servers is shown in Figure 19-1. The Publisher is the original owner of the information that is published. In some scenarios, a Publisher is the only place where data can be modified. However, some replication types allow the propagation of changes from other servers.

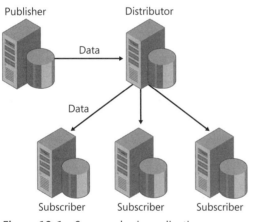

Figure 19-1   Server roles in replication

You also need to configure a server in the role of Distributor. The Distributor is responsible for managing the *distribution* database, which stores replication status data, metadata, and, in some replication scenarios, the actual data that SQL Server replicates. A single database server instance can act as both the Publisher and the Distributor, in which case the Distributor is called a local Distributor. When you configure the Publisher and the Distributor on separate database server instances, the Distributor is called a remote Distributor.

The server that then receives copies of the publication and provides the data to end users and applications is called the Subscriber. In some configurations, Subscribers have a read-only copy of the database; in other configurations, you can update information in the Subscribers and replicate those changes back to the Publisher.

Push and Pull Subscriptions

In replication terminology, you find two types of subscriptions, or ways for Subscribers to get the publication: *push subscriptions* and *pull subscriptions* (shown in Figures 19-2 and 19-3). With a push subscription, the Distributor copies the data to the Subscriber database. With a pull subscription, the Subscriber retrieves the data from the Distributor.

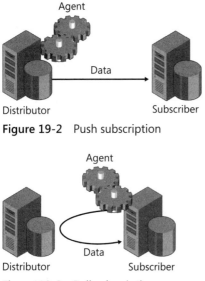

Figure 19-2 Push subscription

Figure 19-3 Pull subscription

When your communication infrastructure has stable and permanent connections among replication servers, a push subscription offers the advantage of providing a central management point to all replication agents that manage the replication process. This results in less administrative overhead and easier troubleshooting procedures.

However, when the replication configuration includes many Subscribers, the distribution process for push subscriptions can tax the hardware resources of a Distributor. Furthermore, servers or clients that connect on demand are better configured as pull subscriptions.

Replication Types

With this terminology foundation laid, let's look at each of the three types of replication that SQL Server 2005 provides. These types are illustrated in Figure 19-4. *Snapshot replication* is the easiest replication type to understand because it is conceptually similar to a full backup and restore. With snapshot replication, the server copies an entire set of data to the Subscribers at scheduled times, rewriting the data at the Subscribers with each copy operation. However, snapshot replication does not operate on the complete database as backup and restore does; snapshot replication copies only the specified articles from the Publisher to the Subscribers. Keep in mind that because snapshot replication copies the entire data set every time it runs, you should use this replication type only when the amount of data is small and rather static.

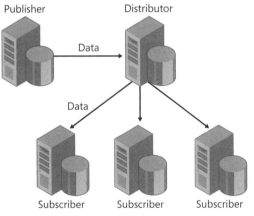

Figure 19-4   Snapshot replication

For more volatile scenarios, *transactional replication* (illustrated in Figure 19-5) provides a better solution because it makes an initial complete copy of the data, and then all subsequent copies transfer modified data only. Transactional replication uses the transaction log to apply to the destination data the same transactions performed on the source data. Because the same modifications are applied at both ends, the information is identical at the Publisher and the Subscriber. This replication type is frequently used for transactional tables, such as an *Order Details* table in a retail database.

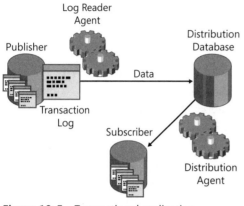

Figure 19-5   Transactional replication

MORE INFO   New in SQL Server 2005: peer-to-peer replication

Peer-to-peer replication is a new kind of transactional replication that lets multiple servers subscribe to the same schema and data, permitting simultaneous changes in multiple servers. For information about peer-to-peer replication, see the SQL Server 2005 Books Online topic "Peer-to-Peer Transactional Replication." SQL Server 2005 Books Online is installed as part of SQL Server 2005. Updates for SQL Server 2005 Books Online are available for download at *www.microsoft.com/technet/ prodtechnol/sql/2005/downloads/books.mspx*.

Transactional replication offers a valuable alternative to snapshot replication when your data is volatile, but it has an important limitation: Transactional replication limits the changes that data can undergo at the destination, and only through a separate communication mechanism can the information updates at the Subscriber database reach the Publisher database.

When your environment requires the ability to support simultaneous data modifications in the Publisher and Subscriber databases, *merge replication* (illustrated in Figure 19-6) offers a solution. With merge replication, the process begins with an initial full copy of the data from the Publisher to the Subscribers. As data changes occur in any server, the replication process takes these changes, resolves any conflicts that might have occurred due to the changes, and applies the changes to all the servers. Unlike transactional replication, merge replication does not rely on the serialization of the database (the transaction log) to synchronize the Publisher and Subscribers. In merge replication, each server modifies the replicated data, and the merge replication process uses a combination of unique identifier columns, triggers, and tables to capture changes in the database. Note that merge replication is the most invasive replication solution because it requires important schema changes in the database.

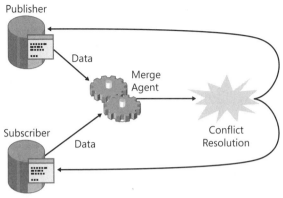

Figure 19-6 Merge replication

Replication Agents

SQL Server uses a group of programs called *replication agents* to execute the replication process. Replication agents, by default, are implemented through SQL Server Agent jobs. SSMS replication wizards automate the creation of these jobs. You can also run replication agents from the command line or from applications that use RMO. You manage replication agents from SSRM (covered in Lesson 5) and SSMS.

SQL Server 2005 replication includes the following key agents:

- **Snapshot Agent (snapshot.exe)** This agent prepares the schemas and the initial copy of the data files. All replication types use the Snapshot Agent as the starting point for the synchronization process. Generally, the Snapshot Agent is run on a regular basis to keep the data files updated. These files are required if the replication synchronization process finds anomalies in the data that cannot be fixed. The Snapshot Agent runs in the Distributor server.

- **Log Reader Agent (logread.exe)** This agent monitors the database's transaction log and copies each transaction that affects the publication to the *distribution* database, in which the transactions are stored until applied to the Subscribers. It is important to note that multiple publications of the same database share the same Log Reader Agent. Log Reader Agents are used only in transactional replication configurations and run in the Publisher server.

- **Distribution Agent (distrib.exe)** This agent performs two tasks: it delivers the initial snapshot to Subscribers and applies transactions stored in the *distribution* database to Subscribers. The Distribution Agent is used in snapshot and transactional replication. The Distribution Agent runs in the Distributor when you configure the publication as a push subscription and in the Subscriber when you configure the publication as a pull subscription.

- **Merge Agent (replmerg.exe)**   This agent delivers the initial snapshot from the Distributor to the Subscribers. It also merges data changes that occur in the Publisher to the Subscribers, and vice versa. When two servers modify the same information at the same time, a conflict occurs; the Merge Agent reconciles the conflict by using a set of rules that you define during replication configuration. The Merge Agent runs in the Distributor when you configure the publication as a push subscription and in the Subscriber when you configure the publication as a pull subscription.

- **Queue Reader Agent (qrdrsvc.exe)**   This agent reads messages stored in queues (SQL Server queues or Microsoft Message Queues) and applies transactions sent to the queue to the Publisher database. The Queue Reader Agent is used only when snapshot or transactional replication is set with the option for queued updating subscriptions.

MORE INFO   Queued updating subscriptions

When you use queued updating subscriptions, SQL Server stores the changes in a queue and then applies the queued transactions asynchronously at the Publisher whenever network connectivity is available. Lesson 2 covers the parameter for setting up updatable subscriptions, but full coverage of queued updating is beyond the scope of this chapter. For complete information, see the "Updatable Subscriptions for Transactional Replication" topic in SQL Server 2005 Books Online.

SQL Server 2005 also includes agents responsible for replication maintenance jobs, including:

- Agent History Clean Up: Distribution
- Distribution Clean Up: Distribution
- Expired Subscription Clean Up
- Reinitialize Subscriptions Having Data Validation Failures
- Replication Agents Checkup
- Replication Monitoring Refresher For Distribution

Quick Check

- Which agent is responsible for delivering the snapshot files to the Subscriber in transactional replication?

Quick Check Answer

- The Distribution Agent (distrib.exe) delivers the snapshot files to Subscribers in a transactional replication architecture.

Lesson Summary

- SQL Server 2005 includes three main replication types: snapshot, transactional, and merge.

- SQL Server uses a magazine publishing metaphor to describe the elements of a replication topology, including articles, publications, Publishers, Distributors, and Subscribers.

- Replication involves one of two types of subscriptions: push subscriptions, which run at the Distributor and send the publication to the Subscribers; and pull subscriptions, which run at the Subscribers and retrieve the publication from the Distributor.

- Replication uses executables called agents to manage the replication process. The main replication agents are the Snapshot Agent, the Log Reader Agent, the Distribution Agent, the Merge Agent, and the Queue Reader Agent.

Lesson Review

The following questions are intended to reinforce key information presented in this lesson. The questions are also available on the companion CD if you prefer to review them in electronic form.

NOTE Answers

Answers to these questions and explanations of why each answer choice is right or wrong are located in the "Answers" section at the end of the book.

---

1. Which replication types rely on the transaction log to monitor changes in the publishing database? (Choose all that apply.)

   A. Snapshot replication

   B. Transactional replication

   C. Merge replication

   D. Peer-to-peer replication

2. Which of the following agents is responsible for monitoring the transaction log in transactional replication?

   A. Snapshot Agent

   B. Distribution Agent

   C. Merge Agent

   D. Log Reader Agent

Lesson 2: Setting Up Replication

The most straightforward method to configure replication is via SSMS. But you can also use Transact-SQL statements or SQL Server RMOs to configure replication. The general steps for configuring replication are as follows:

1. Set up a Distributor for the Publisher to use.

2. Create a publication to replicate that includes the articles you want to copy.

3. Configure the Subscriber and a subscription.

In this lesson, you see how to use SSMS to perform these steps to configure a replication topology. You also see how to generate the equivalent Transact-SQL configuration scripts.

After this lesson, you will be able to:

- Create the *distribution* database.
- Enable a database for replication.
- Create a publication.
- Subscribe to a publication.

Estimated lesson time: 40 minutes

How to Set Up the Distributor

The first step in setting up replication is configuring the Distributor. You can assign each Publisher to only one Distributor instance, but multiple Publishers can share a Distributor. As noted earlier, you can configure the Distributor server to act as the distributor of its own data (local Distributor), which is the default, or as a distributor of data for remote servers (remote Distributor).

BEST PRACTICES   Remote Distributor

You might decide to use a remote Distributor if you want to offload the Distributor processing from the Publisher computer to another computer or if you want to configure a centralized Distributor for multiple Publishers.

Note that the server you choose as the Distributor should have adequate disk space and processor power to support replication and the other activities that need to run on that server.

Here is how to configure the Distributor as a local Distributor:

1. Open SSMS.

2. Connect to the database engine instance you want to configure as Publisher and Distributor.

3. Right-click the Replication folder and choose Configure Distribution.

4. On the Configure Distribution Wizard page, click Next.

5. On the Distributor page, select *server_name* Will Act As Its Own Distributor and click Next.

6. On the Snapshot Folder page, type the path to a local folder or the Universal Naming Convention (UNC) name for a shared folder in which you want to store the files that will hold the publication's schema and data. Click Next.

NOTE   Snapshot folder choices

Consider three important factors as you make your Snapshot folder choice. First, if your subscription topology uses pull subscriptions, use a UNC network path. Second, plan how much space the snapshot files will occupy. And finally, secure the folder and grant permission to only the Snapshot Agent (write) and to the Merge or Distribution Agent (read). Lesson 3 in this chapter provides more details about how to secure replication.

---

7. On the Distribution Database page, type the name of the database and the path of its data and log files, as Figure 19-7 shows. By default, SQL Server names this database *distribution* and places it in the \Program Files\Microsoft SQL Server\ MSSQL.*x*\MSSQL\Data folder, where *x* is the number assigned to the instance on which you are configuring replication. Click Next.

BEST PRACTICES   Configuring the *distribution* database

Transactional replication demands more from the *distribution* database than any other replication type. If you plan to use transactional replication in large and volatile databases, consider placing the log and data files of the *distribution* database in different disk channels, using RAID 1 or RAID 10 for the data files and RAID 1 for the log files.

---

8. On the Publishers page, add other publishers you want to authorize as Publishers to this Distributor, and click Next. By default, SSMS also configures the Distributor as a Publisher.

9. On the Wizard Actions page, you can use the available check boxes to indicate whether you want SSMS to execute the commands now, script them, or both. By default, the Configure Distribution check box is selected. Click Next.

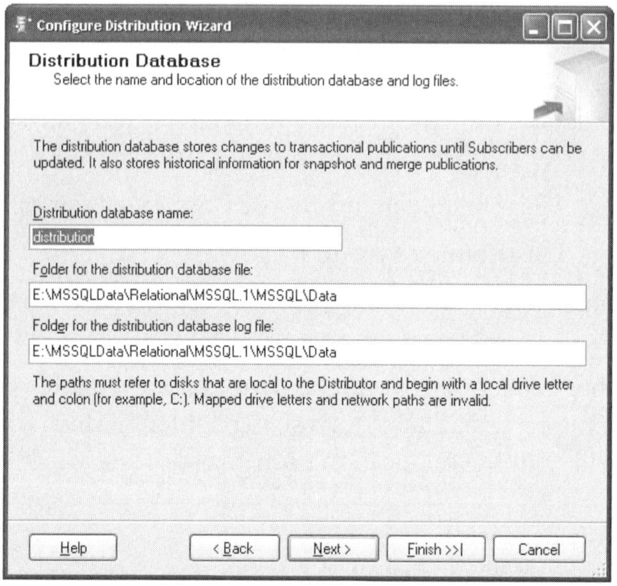

Figure 19-7   Configuring the distribution database

10. If you chose to script the commands, you now see the Script File Properties page. You use this page to configure the name, path, and format of the script. By default, SQL Server creates this script file in your My Documents folder. You can also specify whether you want SQL Server to overwrite an existing script file with the same name or to append this script to it. Click Next.

BEST PRACTICES   Scripting the configuration

Scripting the Distributor configuration is a good idea for documentation purposes; plus, you can use the script in a recovery plan. Additionally, you can use scripts to create more complex database file configurations.

---

11. On the Complete The Wizard page, review the summary of choices you made and then click Finish.

12. Wait for the Configure Distribution Wizard to complete the configuration. After it finishes, click Close.

The following code block shows the Distributor configuration script:

Distributor Configuration Script
```
/*** Scripting replication configuration for server COMPUTERNAME. ***/
/*** Please Note: For security reasons, all password parameters
     were scripted with either NULL or an empty string. ***/
/*** Installing the server COMPUTERNAME as a Distributor.   ***/
```

```
use master
exec sp_adddistributor @distributor = N'COMPUTERNAME', @password = N''
GO
exec sp_adddistributiondb @database = N'distribution'
   , @data_folder = N'C:\MSSQL\Data'
   , @data_file_size = 4
   , @log_folder = N'C:\MSSQL\Data'
   , @log_file_size = 2
   , @min_distretention = 0, @max_distretention = 72
   , @history_retention = 48, @security_mode = 1
GO
use [distribution]
if (not exists (select * from sysobjects
               where name = 'UIProperties' and type = 'U '))
   create table UIProperties(id int)
if (exists (select * from ::fn_listextendedproperty('SnapshotFolder'
        , 'user', 'dbo', 'table', 'UIProperties', null, null)))
   EXEC sp_updateextendedproperty N'SnapshotFolder'
        , N'C:\MSSQL\ReplData', 'user', dbo, 'table'
        , 'UIProperties'
else
   EXEC sp_addextendedproperty N'SnapshotFolder'
        , 'C:\MSSQL\ReplData'
        , 'user', dbo, 'table', 'UIProperties'
GO
exec sp_adddistpublisher @publisher = N'COMPUTERNAME'
        , @distribution_db = N'distribution'
        , @security_mode = 1, @working_directory = N'C:\MSSQL\ReplData'
        , @trusted = N'false', @thirdparty_flag = 0
        , @publisher_type = N'MSSQLSERVER'
GO
```

Be aware that the *@distributor, @data_folder, @log_folder, SnapshotFolder, @working_directory*, and *@publisher* parameters you see in this script are all specific to your environment. The Distributor configuration script that the wizard generates uses three main stored procedures. The first procedure, *sp_adddistributor,* defines the Distributor when the server acts as Publisher. To configure the server as its own Distributor, set the *@distributor* parameter to its own server name; to use a remote server, use the remote server name.

The second stored procedure, *sp_adddistributiondb,* creates the *distribution* database with the specified parameters. If you want to use a *distribution* database with multiple data files or filegroups, first create the database by using a *CREATE DATABASE* statement and set the name in the *@database* parameter. In addition, *sp_adddistributiondb* uses retention parameters to control how many hours SQL Server stores transactions in the database before it erases them (this affects only transactional replication). If the Distribution Agent fails to copy the transactions within the maximum specified period, SQL Server marks the subscription as inactive, and the Snapshot Agent reinitializes the database. Increasing this value increases the space required to hold the transactions, but it can help you avoid making full copies of the publication again, thus losing the advantage of using transactional replication.

The third procedure in the script is *sp_adddistpublisher*. This procedure, executed at the Distributor, configures a Publisher to use the *distribution* database. The script also uses the *sp_addextendedproperty* or the *sp_updateextendedproperty* stored procedure to store the Snapshot folder path as an extended property.

NOTE   Disabling publishing

If you want to disable the publishing on a server, right-click the Replication folder and choose Disable Publishing And Distribution.

> **Quick Check**
> - Which type of replication is more demanding of the *distribution* database?
>
> **Quick Check Answer**
> - Transactional replication is more demanding on the Distributor and the *distribution* database, which stores the data captured from the transaction log for use by transactional replication processes.

How to Create a Publication

After you have configured the Publisher to use a specific Distributor, the next step in setting up replication is to create the publication you want to publish. Here are the steps for creating a publication:

1. Open SSMS.
2. Connect to the database engine instance in which you want to create the publication.
3. Expand the Replication, Local Publications folder.
4. Right-click the Local Publications folder and choose New Publication.
5. On the New Publication Wizard page, click Next.
6. On the Publication Database page, select the database in which you want to create the publication. Click Next.

7. On the Publication Type page, (shown in Figure 19-8), select the type of publication you want to use (Snapshot Publication, Transactional Publication, Transactional Publication With Updatable Subscriptions, or Merge Publication). Click Next.

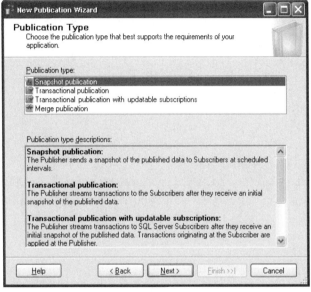

Figure 19-8   Configuring publication type

8. On the Articles page, select the check boxes for the database objects you want to publish. Keep in mind that if you choose objects such as a stored procedure, view, indexed view, or user-defined function (UDF), you must also publish the objects on which those objects depend. For example, if you choose a stored procedure that references two tables, you must include those two tables in the publication. Click Next.

9. On the Filter Table Rows page, you can create a row filter to filter the table you publish. To configure a row filter, click Add. Use the Add Filter dialog box to define the filter, click OK, and click Next.

NOTE   Setting up filters

The Publication Wizard offers two pages that let you set up filters. If you want to filter columns, use the Articles page. If you want to filter by rows, use the Filter Table Rows page.

10. On the Snapshot Agent page, select the Create A Snapshot Immediately And Keep The Snapshot Available To Initialize Subscriptions check box to create a snapshot now. Select the Schedule The Snapshot Agent To Run At The Following Times check box. By default, the New Publication Wizard configures the Snapshot Agent to run on an hourly basis. If you want to change this schedule, click Change to define a new schedule. Click OK to save your new schedule and then click Next to continue.

BEST PRACTICES   Executing the Snapshot Agent

Creating a snapshot can be a demanding process. You should configure the Snapshot Agent to run only at off-peak times.

---

11. On the Agent Security page, click Security Settings to open the Snapshot Agent Security dialog box. Use the options in this dialog box to assign the account by which you want to run the Snapshot Agent process and connect to the Publisher. Click OK to close the Snapshot Agent Security dialog box and then click Next.

MORE INFO   Security

You can configure the Snapshot Agent to run under the SQL Server Agent service account. However, this setup is not recommended because it does not follow the principle of least privilege. For details about how to provide a secure environment for replication, see Lesson 3 of this chapter.

---

12. On the Wizard Actions page, you can use the available check boxes to indicate whether you want SSMS to execute the commands now, script them, or both. By default, the Create The Publication check box is selected. Click Next.

13. If you chose to script the commands, you now see the Script File Properties page. You use this page to configure the name, path, and format of the script. By default, SQL Server creates this script file in your My Documents folder. Click Next.

14. On the Complete The Wizard page, type a name for your publication in the Publication Name text box. Review the summary of your choices, and click Finish to create the publication.

15. Wait for the New Publication Wizard to create the publication. After it completes, click Close.

The following code block shows the publication configuration script that the New Publication Wizard generates:

Publication Configuration Script

```
use [AdventureWorksRepl]
exec sp_replicationdboption @dbname = N'AdventureWorksRepl'
    , @optname = N'publish'
    , @value = N'true'
GO
-- Adding the snapshot publication
use [AdventureWorksRepl]
exec sp_addpublication @publication = N'MSPressRepl'
    , @description = N'Snapshot publication of database ''AdventureWorksRepl'' from Publisher
        ''COMPUTERNAME''.'
    , @sync_method = N'native'
    , @retention = 0
    , @allow_push = N'true'
    , @allow_pull = N'true'
    , @allow_anonymous = N'true'
    , @enabled_for_internet = N'false'
    , @snapshot_in_defaultfolder = N'true'
    , @compress_snapshot = N'false'
    , @ftp_port = 21
    , @allow_subscription_copy = N'false'
    , @add_to_active_directory = N'false'
    , @repl_freq = N'snapshot'
    , @status = N'active'
    , @independent_agent = N'true'
    , @immediate_sync = N'true'
    , @allow_sync_tran = N'false'
    , @allow_queued_tran = N'false'
    , @allow_dts = N'false'
    , @replicate_ddl = 1
    GO
exec sp_addpublication_snapshot @publication = N'MSPressRepl'
    , @frequency_type = 4
    , @frequency_interval = 1
    , @frequency_relative_interval = 1
    , @frequency_recurrence_factor = 0
    , @frequency_subday = 1
    , @frequency_subday_interval = 1
    , @active_start_time_of_day = 0
    , @active_end_time_of_day = 235959
    , @active_start_date = 0
    , @active_end_date = 0
    , @job_login = null
    , @job_password = null
    , @publisher_security_mode = 1

use [AdventureWorksRepl]
exec sp_addarticle @publication = N'MSPressRepl'
    , @article = N'SalesOrderDetail'
    , @source_owner = N'Sales'
```

```
      , @source_object = N'SalesOrderDetail'
      , @type = N'logbased', @description = null
      , @creation_script = null
      , @pre_creation_cmd = N'drop'
      , @schema_option = 0x000000000803509D
      , @identityrangemanagementoption = N'manual'
      , @destination_table = N'SalesOrderDetail'
      , @destination_owner = N'Sales'
      , @vertical_partition = N'false'
GO
use [AdventureWorksRepl]
exec sp_addarticle @publication = N'MSPressRepl'
      , @article = N'SalesOrderHeader'
      , @source_owner = N'Sales'
      , @source_object = N'SalesOrderHeader'
      , @type = N'logbased'
      , @description = null
      , @creation_script = null
      , @pre_creation_cmd = N'drop'
      , @schema_option = 0x000000000803509D
      , @identityrangemanagementoption = N'manual'
      , @destination_table = N'SalesOrderHeader'
      , @destination_owner = N'Sales'
      , @vertical_partition = N'false'
GO
```

As with the previous script for creating the Distributor, this script contains parameters that are specific to your environment. The script that the New Publication Wizard generates uses four stored procedures to create the publication configuration. The first procedure, *sp_replicationdboption*, enables replication in a database. The parameter *@optname* supports the following values: *merge publish* for merge replication, *publish* for snapshot and transactional replication, *subscribe* for subscription, and *sync with backup* for a special type of transactional replication that forces backups of the transaction log before sending transactions to the *distribution* database.

The *sp_addpublication* stored procedure creates the publication when the publication type is snapshot or transactional. The *@sync_method* parameter specifies the format the bulk copy files use. Use native format when the replication includes only SQL Server subscriptions, and use character format when other platforms (such as Microsoft Office Access, Oracle, or IBM DB2) subscribe to the publication.

You use the parameters *@enabled_for_internet*, *@ftp_port*, *@ftp_address*, *@ftp_subdirectory*, *@ftp_login*, and *@ftp_password* when subscribers use the Internet to connect for replicating the database. The *@enabled_for_internet* parameter enables the configuration, and the rest of the parameters set the configuration of the Snapshot folder.

The *sp_addpublication_snapshot* stored procedure configures the job that runs the Snapshot Agent. You configure the job schedule by using the following parameters: *@frequency_type*, *@frequency_interval*, *@frequency_relative_interval*, *@frequency_recurrence_factor*, *@frequency_subday*, *@frequency_subday_interval*, *@active_start_time_of_day*, *@active_end_time_of_day*, *@active_start_date*, and *@active_end_date*. In the sample script, the Snapshot Agent job is set to run once a day every day.

MORE INFO Schedules

If you want a better understanding of the schedule parameters that the Snapshot Agent job uses, review the documentation about *sp_add_schedule* in SQL Server 2005 Books Online. To gain a good understanding of the parameter semantics, you can create a job with multiple schedules and generate a script to review the resulting parameter settings.

The last three parameters of *sp_addpublication_snapshot*—*@job_login*, *@job_password*, and *@publisher_security_mode*—set the security context of the job. You will find more information about replication security in the next lesson.

Finally, the *sp_addarticle* stored procedure is executed multiple times, once per article in the publication, to configure the database objects that will be published. You configure the publication, article name, and object to publish by using the parameters *@publication*, *@article*, *@source_owner*, and *@source_object*. When you want to create a script that configures a large number of articles with the same options, copy and paste this procedure, replacing the parameter values with the appropriate object names.

The *sp_addarticle @type* parameter sets what will be published: the schema, the data, or the execution. For example, to publish table or view data, use the *logbased* value; to copy the schema of a stored procedure or view, use *proc schema only* or *view schema only*, respectively; and to replicate the execution of the stored procedure, use *proc exec*.

NOTE Article types

Some Subscribers support only certain article types. For example, non-SQL Server Subscribers do not support schema-only or stored procedure replication. So take your environment into consideration before specifying article types.

How to Subscribe to the Publication

The final step in the replication configuration process is configuring the Subscriber to receive the publication. To configure a subscription for a Subscriber, follow these steps:

1. Open SSMS.
2. Connect to the Publisher database engine instance.

3. Expand the Replication, Local Publications folder.

4. Right-click the publication to which you want the Subscriber server to subscribe, and select New Subscriptions to start the New Subscription Wizard.

5. On the New Subscription Wizard page, click Next.

6. On the Publication page, you see that the Publisher and publication are automatically selected for you. This occurs because you right-clicked the publication to subscribe to it, so SQL Server knows which publisher and publication to use. Click Next.

NOTE New Subscription Wizard

You can start the New Subscription Wizard at the Subscriber instead of at the Publisher. If you do so, the wizard includes the option to connect to the Publisher server and select the appropriate publication.

---

7. On the Distribution Agent Location page, select the type of subscription you want: push or pull. If you select Run All Agents At The Distributor (Push Subscriptions), the Distribution agent runs on the Distributor; if you select Run Each Agent At Its Subscriber (Pull Subscriptions), the Distribution Agent runs on the Subscriber. Click Next.

8. On the Subscribers page, select the check box for the server or instance you want to subscribe to this publication. From the Subscription Database drop-down list, select the database in which you want to store this publication. (Click New Database if you want to create a new database for the subscription.) By clicking Add Subscriber, you can add SQL Server as well as non-SQL Server (Oracle and IBM DB2) Subscribers. Click Next.

NOTE Non-SQL Server Subscribers

The Subscription Wizard in SSMS provides support only for SQL Server, Oracle, and IBM DB2 Subscriber databases. If you want to use other non-SQL Server Subscribers, use stored procedures to configure the subscription.

---

9. On the Distribution Agent Security page, configure the security context that the agent will use. Click Next.

10. On the Synchronization Schedule page, select the schedule you want the Distribution Agent to use. For snapshot and merge replication, use Run On Demand Only or set a schedule. For transactional replication, use Run Continuously or set a schedule. Click Next.

11. On the Initialize Subscription page, configure the initialization to occur immediately or at first synchronization. Remember that the initial snapshot creates the schema and generates bulk copy files that contain all the publication data and can demand a lot of resources. Click Next.

12. On the Wizard Actions page, you can use the available check boxes to indicate whether you want SSMS to execute the commands now, script them, or both. Make your selection and then click Next.

13. If you chose to script the commands, you now see the Script File Properties page. You can configure the name, path, and format of the script and whether you want SQL Server to overwrite an existing file with the same name or append this script to it. Click Next.

14. On the Complete The Wizard page, review the summary of choices you made and click Finish.

15. Wait for the New Subscription Wizard to create the subscription. After it completes, click Close.

The script that the Subscription Wizard generates uses different stored procedures depending on the publication and subscription type you chose. For a snapshot or transactional publication and a push subscription, the script uses two stored procedures. The *sp_addsubscription* procedure adds the subscription, and the *sp_addpushsubscription_agent* procedure creates a job to run the Distribution Agent, including similar job schedule parameters as *sp_addpublication_snapshot*. The following code example shows a Subscriber configuration script:

Subscriber Configuration Script
```
--- BEGIN: Script to be run at Publisher 'COMPUTERNAME' ---
use [ReplTesting]
exec sp_addsubscription @publication = N'Products'
    , @subscriber = N'COMPUTERNAME'
    , @destination_db = N'SubsTesting'
    , @subscription_type = N'Push'
    , @sync_type = N'automatic'
    , @article = N'all'
    , @update_mode = N'read only'
    , @subscriber_type = 0
exec sp_addpushsubscription_agent @publication = N'Products'
    , @subscriber = N'COMPUTERNAME'
    , @subscriber_db = N'SubsTesting'
    , @job_login = null
    , @job_password = null
    , @subscriber_security_mode = 1
    , @frequency_type = 8
    , @frequency_interval = 1
```

```
      , @frequency_relative_interval = 1
      , @frequency_recurrence_factor = 1
      , @frequency_subday = 1
      , @frequency_subday_interval = 0
      , @active_start_time_of_day = 0
      , @active_end_time_of_day = 235959
      , @active_start_date = 20060226
      , @active_end_date = 99991231
      , @enabled_for_syncmgr = N'False'
      , @dts_package_location = N'Distributor'
GO
---- END: Script to be run at Publisher 'COMPUTERNAME' ---
```

As with the other replication scripts, this script contains parameters that are specific to your environment. The first procedure in the script, *sp_addsubscription*, creates the subscription and should be run at the Publisher using the publishing database. The parameters *@publication*, *@subscriber*, and *@destination_db* define the subscription, given that a server and subscribing database can subscribe to a publication only once. The *@subscription_type* parameter can be either push or pull, depending on where you want the Distribution Agent to run.

The *@sync_type* parameter indicates the initial status of the Subscriber database. The value *automatic* means that the replication process will use the Snapshot Agent to transfer the data and schema to the Subscriber. This value can be used when the connection between servers is good enough to move the snapshot through the network.

The Initialize With Backup option initializes the schema and initial data from a backup of the publication database. The *@backupdevicetype* and *@backupdevicename* parameters set the name or path of the file to restore. These options let administrators back up the publishing database and deliver the backup file to the Subscriber server, using alternative physical media (CD, DVD, or tape).

CAUTION   Initialize With Backup option

The Initialize With Backup option restores in the Subscriber the complete publishing database—not just the articles included in the publication. All information stored in the subscribing database will be lost.

The Replication Support Only option assumes that the Subscriber already has the schema and the initial data. Thus, the replication process will add only objects required to support the replication.

The next section on updatable subscriptions explores the *@sync_type* parameter in greater detail.

NOT FOR REPLICATION Option

Triggers, foreign keys, and the identity property have a special *NOT FOR REPLICATION* option that you can apply to prevent replication in certain situations. The *NOT FOR REPLICATION* option applies only when you are distributing changes by using the replication engine. Three key examples of where you should consider creating objects with the *NOT FOR REPLICATION* option are triggers, foreign key constraints, and columns for which you've enabled the identity property.

Triggers

Triggers fire based on the actions for which they are configured, as Lesson 3 in Chapter 9, "Creating Functions, Stored Procedures, and Triggers," explains. The *NOT FOR REPLICATION* option applies only to *AFTER* triggers created on tables. When user transactions are being issued against a table, the triggers fire as normal. However, when the replication engine is applying a change to a table, the *NOT FOR REPLICATION* option prevents the trigger from firing.

Applying the *NOT FOR REPLICATION* option to triggers is intended to prevent a trigger from firing when the replication engine is processing changes so that the trigger does not end up performing duplicate processing. You should set this option for any triggers that perform operations that will be replicated. However, you should not apply it to triggers that perform operations that will not be replicated or that should be executed regardless of whether a change was made by a user or the replication engine.

Foreign Key Constraints

Any *INSERT*, *UPDATE*, or *DELETE* operations cause SQL Server to check foreign key constraints. *INSERT* and *UPDATE* operations cause SQL Server to check the parent table to ensure that a reference value for the foreign key exists. *DELETE* operations cause SQL Server to check all child tables to make sure that you are not attempting to remove a referenced value from the table. If the replication engine applies the change, it is not necessary to perform these checks because SQL Server would have already validated the foreign key when the user issued the transaction. By adding the *NOT FOR REPLICATION* option to foreign key constraints, you direct SQL Server to bypass the foreign key checks when the replication engine is performing *INSERT*, *UPDATE*, and *DELETE* operations.

You use the *NOT FOR REPLICATION* option for foreign keys to prevent duplicate processing. You should always apply this option for all foreign keys on tables that are participating in replication.

Identity Columns

Columns with an identity property are affected only when an *INSERT* operation occurs. SQL Server uses the *seed* and *increment* values to determine the next number in the sequence to be generated for the new row. You can directly *INSERT* a row into a table and specify a value for the identity column by using the *SET IDENTITY INSERT ON* statement. When you use this statement, SQL Server will *INSERT* the row as long as it does not violate uniqueness. This operation also causes the identity column to be reseeded.

The replication engine must directly insert rows into tables that have identity columns and includes the *SET IDENTITY INSERT ON* clause in any of the replication stored procedures that perform inserts. However, the reseeding of an identity column is problematic for replication configurations that allow inserts to occur at multiple locations. To ensure that these inserts at multiple locations do not violate primary key constraints, each database in which you are inserting rows has its own range of identity values. You can configure these identity values either manually or by using the auto-identity-range management features within replication. If SQL Server permitted the identity column to be reseeded during each explicit *INSERT* operation, errors would cascade throughout the architecture because of duplicate primary keys.

The *NOT FOR REPLICATION* option applied to an identity column prevents this reseeding operation when the replication engine is performing the insertions. You should always use the *NOT FOR REPLICATION* option for identity columns within tables that are participating in replication.

Updatable Subscriptions

The most interesting parameter of the *sp_addsubscription* procedure is *@sync_type*. This parameter configures the updatability of the Subscriber, setting how transactions that occur in the *subscription* database will be propagated to the Publisher. SQL Server uses five different combinations of two communication mechanisms—the two-phase commit and queues—to set how it propagates changes. Using the *@update_mode* parameter, you can set the following options:

Option	Two-Phase Commit	Queued
Read Only	-	-
Sync Tran	First	-

Option	Two-Phase Commit	Queued
Queue Tran	-	First
Failover	First	Second
Queue Failover	Second	First

The Read Only mode does not propagate changes to the Publisher; all changes in the Subscriber are lost the next time the Publisher replicates the information. From the application perspective, consider the data in the Publisher to be read-only.

The Sync Tran option uses a distributed transaction that updates both servers at the same time. If the communication between Publisher and Subscriber fails, the transactions in the Subscriber fail, and the data cannot be read until the communication is reestablished. Only then will updates be allowed. Sync Tran relies on the two-phase commit protocol to update the publisher database.

The Queue Tran option uses queues to store the transactions and asynchronously apply the transactions in the Publisher. Therefore, if the communication between Publisher and Subscriber fails, the transactions in the Subscriber continue to commit properly. And when the Publisher is online again, transactions in the queue will be applied to the published database. However, Queue Tran opens the possibility of updates occurring at both servers simultaneously, and conflicts can occur when applying these changes. Thus, you must configure a conflict-resolution policy when creating the publication.

CAUTION   Schema changes when using the Queue Tran option

When you use Queue Tran mode, the replication process adds a uniqueidentifier column to all tables or underlying tables in the publication. This column is used to control row versions. Some applications might fail because of the additional column.

The Failover option enables the subscription for immediate updating with queued updating as a failover. Data modifications can be made at the Subscriber and propagated to the Publisher immediately. If the Publisher and Subscriber are not connected, you can change the updating mode so that data modifications made at the Subscriber are stored in a queue until the Subscriber and Publisher are reconnected.

The Queue Failover option enables the subscription as a queued updating subscription with the capability to change to immediate updating mode. Data modifications can be made at the Subscriber and stored in a queue until a connection is established between the Subscriber and Publisher.

Replication Backup and Restore

It is important for you to regularly back up your replication databases and test to make sure you can restore those backups. You need to regularly back up the following replication databases: the *publication* database, the *distribution* database, *subscription* databases, and the *msdb* and *master* databases at the Publisher, Distributor, and all Subscribers. If you perform regular log backups, any replication-related changes should be captured in the log backups. If you do not perform log backups, make sure to perform a backup whenever you change a replication-related setting.

You can restore replicated databases to the same server and database on which you created the backup. If you want to restore a backup of a replicated database to another server or database, note that replication settings will not be preserved. In this case, you must re-create all publications and subscriptions after you restore the backups.

MORE INFO Backing up and restoring replicated databases

Replicated databases have special backup and restore considerations depending on the type of replication you are performing. Covering all these considerations and steps is beyond the scope of this chapter, but for detailed information, see the SQL Server 2005 Books Online topic "Backing Up and Restoring Replicated Databases."

PRACTICE Configuring Snapshot Replication

In the following practices, you create a snapshot replication configuration that uses a single server for testing purposes.

▶ **Practice 1: Prepare the Environment for Replication**

In this practice, you create the file directories required to configure snapshot replication. One of the folders will hold the Snapshot folders, and another will hold the scripts. You also create a copy of the *AdventureWorks* database that will be used as a publishing database. Finally, you create an empty database that subscribes to the publication.

1. In the root folder of the C drive, create a folder named **ReplicationPractice**. This folder will hold the subfolders for the replication practices.

2. In the ReplicationPractice folder, create two subfolders: **ReplData** and **Scripts**. The ReplData folder will store the snapshots of publications; the Scripts folder will store replication configuration scripts.

3. Open SSMS and connect to the default instance of the database engine by using your Windows account.

4. Expand the Databases folder.

5. Right-click the *AdventureWorks* database, and select Tasks, Back Up. You will back up the *AdventureWorks* database and use this backup to create a database for testing purposes.

6. If there are any destination files or backup devices in the destination list box, remove them by clicking Remove.

7. Click Add to add a destination file. Name the file **AdventureWorks.bak** in the default backup path, and click OK.

8. Click OK to back up the database. Wait for the backup process to complete, and then click OK.

9. Right-click the *AdventureWorks* database and choose Tasks, Restore, Database. You will use the recently created backup to create a testing database.

10. In the To Database text box, type **ReplTesting** to name the database. You will use the ReplTesting database to create publications.

11. Click OK to initiate the restoration process and then click OK to close the confirmation message displayed when the restore completes.

12. Right-click the Databases folder and choose New Database. You will create an empty database that will subscribe to the publication.

13. In the Database text box, type **SubsTesting** to name the database. Click OK to create the database.

▶ **Practice 2: Configure Publishing and Distribution**

In this practice, you will use the Configure Distribution Wizard to configure your server as a Publisher and Distributor. You will also generate the scripts to document the configuration.

1. If necessary, open SSMS and connect to your server by using Windows authentication.

2. Right-click the Replication folder and choose Configure Distribution. The Configure Distribution Wizard starts.

3. On the Configure Distribution Wizard page, click Next.

4. On the Distributor page, leave the default option (*COMPUTERNAME* Will Act As Its Own Distributor; SQL Server Will Create A Distribution Database And Log)

and then click Next. This option provides steps to create the *distribution* database. If you want to use a remote server, there is no need to create the *distribution* database.

IMPORTANT   Additional steps if SQL Server Agent stops

By default, replication uses SQL Server Agent jobs to execute replication agents. If SQL Server Agent is stopped or configured for manual startup mode, the Configure Distribution Wizard will have to perform additional steps to start SQL Server Agent and to change its configuration to automatic.

---

5. On the Snapshot folder page (see Figure 19-9), set the path to **C:\Replication-Practice\ReplData** and click Next.

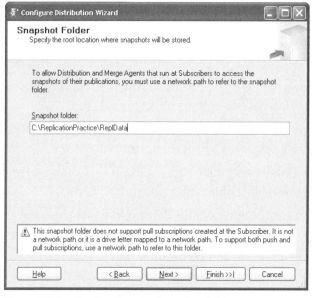

Figure 19-9   Configuring the Snapshot folder

MORE INFO   Snapshot folder path

Specifying a local path for the Snapshot folder limits the replication process to push subscriptions only. In the next lesson, you will use a UNC network path to configure the Snapshot folder, which allows both push and pull subscriptions.

---

6. Review the *distribution* database default settings and click Next. The *distribution* database will store data and log files in the default folder.

7. On the Enable Publishers page, review the authorized publishers. Confirm that the local server is selected and click Next.

8. On the Wizard Actions page, select both check boxes. You will create the *distribution* database, configure the server, and create the script to document the configuration. Click Next.

9. On the Script File Properties page, use the path and file name **C:\Replication-Practice\Scripts\ConfigureDistribution.sql** and select Overwrite The Existing File. (You will use this script in other practices.) Click Next.

10. On the Complete The Wizard page, review the configured options and then click Finish.

11. Wait for the configuration of the Distributor and Publisher to complete and then click Close.

▶ **Practice 3: Configure a Snapshot Publication**

In this practice, you will create a snapshot publication with four articles: three tables and one stored procedure. The tables—*Product*, *BillOfMaterials*, and *UnitMeasure*—will have the schema and data published. You will also publish the schema of the *uspGetBillOfMaterials* stored procedure.

1. If necessary, using SSMS, connect to the server by using Windows authentication.

2. Expand the Replication folder and right-click the Local Publications folder. Choose New Publication. The New Publication Wizard starts.

3. On the New Publication Wizard page, click Next.

4. On the Publication Database page, select the database *ReplTesting* and click Next. This step will configure the publishing database.

5. On the Publication Type page, verify that Snapshot Publication is selected. Click Next.

6. On the Articles page, shown in Figure 19-10, expand Tables and select the BillOfMaterials, Product, and UnitMeasure check boxes. Expand Stored Procedures and select the uspGetBillOfMaterials check box. The publication will copy the schema and data of the tables and the schema of the stored procedure. Click Next.

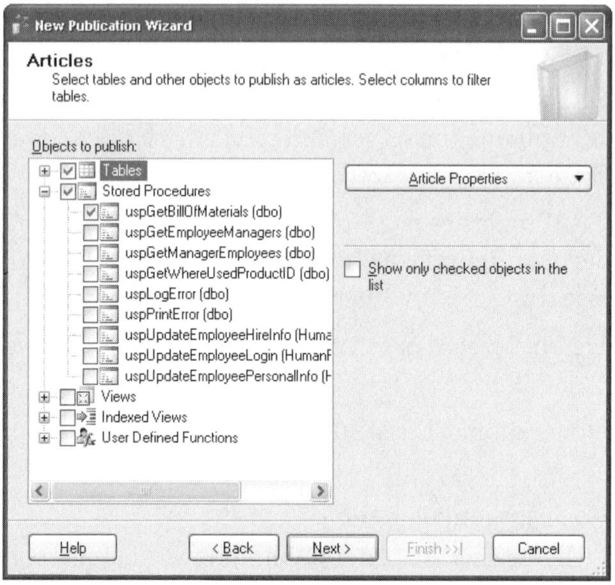

Figure 19-10   Selecting different object types to publish

7. Read the Article Issues warning and then click Next. The warning informs users that the stored procedure depends on other objects that might not be published; it might not behave as expected if objects it depends on do not exist in the Subscriber database. In this case, you are publishing all the required objects.

8. On the Filter Table Rows page, click Next.

9. On the Snapshot Agent page, select both check boxes. You want the Snapshot Agent to run immediately and to create a scheduled job. Click Change to configure the schedule.

10. In the Frequency section of the Job Schedule Properties dialog box, select Weekly from the Occurs drop-down list. Verify that the Sunday check box is selected. In the Daily Frequency section, select Occurs Once At to configure the job to run at midnight. Click OK to confirm the schedule, which schedules the agent to run once a week, every Sunday, at midnight. The Snapshot Agent will generate schema and bulk copy (BCP) files once a week. Click Next to continue.

11. On the Agent Security page, click Security Settings.

12. Select Run Under The SQL Server Agent Service Account and leave the default option, By Impersonating The Process Account, in the Connect To Publisher section. Click OK to confirm the security configuration and click Next to continue.

CAUTION Setting Snapshot Agent security

In this practice, you are configuring the snapshot replication process to run under the SQL Server Agent security context. In a real-world scenario, this is not a recommended practice. The next lesson will discuss security options to configure replication agents.

---

13. On the Wizard Actions page, select both check boxes. You want SSMS to create the publication and a script as a reference to the publication's configuration. Click Next to continue.

14. On the Script File Properties page, set the file name to **C:\ReplicationPractice\ Scripts\CreateProductsPublication.sql**. Select Overwrite The Existing File and click Next.

15. Name the new publication **Products** and review the configuration. Click Finish to create the publication, the job to run the Snapshot Agent, and the script.

16. After the creation of the publication completes, click Close.

▶ **Practice 4: Configure a Subscription**

In this practice, you create a subscription to the Products publication. The subscribing database will receive copies of the three tables, including data and schema, and will receive a copy of the stored procedure code.

1. If necessary, using SSMS, connect to your server by using Windows authentication.

2. Expand the Replication, Local Publications folder.

3. Right-click the Products publication you just created and choose New Subscriptions. The New Subscription Wizard starts. Click Next.

4. On the Publication page, verify that the Products publication is selected. Click Next.

5. On the Distribution Agent Location page, verify that Run All Agents At The Distributor (Push Subscriptions) is selected. Click Next. This process will configure a push agent to distribute the publication.

6. On the Subscribers page, select the check box for your own server. From the Database drop-down list, select the SubsTesting database, which configures *SubsTesting* as the Subscriber database. Click Next.

7. On the Distribution Agent Security page, click the (...) button to configure the agent security context. Use the following options:

   ❑ Select Run Under The SQL Server Agent Service Account.

❑ In the Connect To The Distributor section, verify that By Impersonating The Process Account is selected.

❑ In the Connect To The Subscriber section, verify that By Impersonating The Process Account is selected.

CAUTION Setting Snapshot Agent security

In this practice, you are configuring snapshot configuration to run under the SQL Server Agent security context. In a real-world scenario, this is not a recommended practice. The next lesson discusses security options for configuring replication agents.

---

8. Click OK to configure agent security and then click Next.

9. On the Synchronization Schedule page, from the Agent Schedule drop-down list, select Define Schedule.

10. The New Job Schedule dialog box appears, as shown in Figure 19-11. In the Frequency section, select Weekly from the Occurs drop-down list. Verify that Recurs Every is set to 1 week and select the Sunday check box.

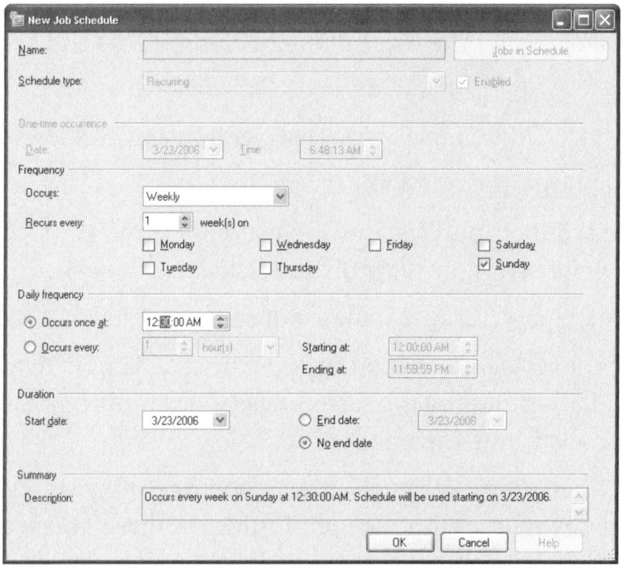

Figure 19-11   Setting the Distribution Agent schedule

11. In the Daily Frequency section, verify that Occurs Once At is selected and set the time to 00:30, or 12:30 AM.

12. Click OK. These settings configure the Distribution Agent to run once a week on Sunday at half past midnight. The Distribution Agent will take the schema and

BCP files created by the Snapshot Agent and bulk copy them into the publishing database. Click Next.

13. On the Initialize Subscriptions page, leave the Initialize Immediately check box selected. Click Next.

14. On the Wizard Actions page, select both check boxes. You want SSMS to create the publication and you also want it to create the script to have as a reference in the documentation. Click Next.

15. On the Script File Properties page, set the file name to **C:\ReplicationPractice\ Scripts\CreateProductsSubscription.sql.** Select Overwrite The Existing File and click Next.

16. Click Finish to create the subscription and the job to run the Distribution Agent.

17. After the creation of the subscription completes, click Close.

▶ **Practice 5: Test the Replication Configuration**

In this practice, you will corroborate that the snapshot publication has been delivered and that the tables and the stored procedure are stored in the *SubsTesting* database.

1. If necessary, using SSMS, connect to the server by using Windows authentication.

2. Expand the Databases, SubsTesting database.

3. Expand the Tables folder and verify that the three tables (*BillOfMaterials*, *Product*, and *UnitMeasure*) exist.

4. Expand the Programmability, Stored Procedures folder.

5. Right-click the *uspGetBillOfMaterials* stored procedure and choose Execute Stored Procedure.

6. In the Value column for *@StartProductID*, type **800**.

7. In the Value column for *@CheckDate*, type **2006-01-01**.

8. Click OK.

9. Check that the procedure runs successfully and returns 88 rows.

Lesson Summary

■ You can use the SSMS Configure Distribution Wizard to configure SQL Server as a replication Publisher and/or Distributor. The wizard also generates scripts for later deployment or documentation purposes.

- Using the SSMS New Publication Wizard or the stored procedure *sp_replicationdboption*, you can enable a database for publication. The New Publication Wizard performs the following tasks:

  - ❏ Creates the publication.
  - ❏ Adds the articles to the publication.
  - ❏ Configures the jobs to run the required replication agents.
  - ❏ Creates the schedules to execute the jobs.
  - ❏ Generates a script with the commands required to create the replication configuration.

- The SSMS New Subscription Wizard simplifies the process of subscribing to the publication, creating the required jobs to execute the subscription agents.

Lesson Review

The following questions are intended to reinforce key information presented in this lesson. The questions are also available on the companion CD if you prefer to review them in electronic form.

NOTE Answers

Answers to these questions and explanations of why each answer choice is right or wrong are located in the "Answers" section at the end of the book.

---

1. You are configuring the Snapshot folder of a Distributor. When is a shared folder compulsory?

   A. When using merge replication

   B. When using transactional replication

   C. When using pull subscriptions

   D. When using push subscriptions

2. Which of the following stored procedures enables databases for publication?

   A. *sp_adddistpublisher*

   B. *sp_adddistributor*

   C. *sp_adddistributiondb*

   D. *sp_replicationdboption*

Lesson 3: Configuring Replication Security

Security is a must-have requirement for all database technologies you implement, including replication. SQL Server 2005 has expanded the roles that can participate in configuring replication and gives you to the tools you need to ensure that no one has more permissions than necessary in the replication environment. In this lesson, you'll learn how to configure replication in a secure environment as well as how to configure replication agents to use the fewest privileges possible.

After this lesson, you will be able to:

- Explain the replication security model.
- Explain replication agents' security requirements.
- Configure replication by using the principle of least privilege.

Estimated lesson time: 20 minutes

Setting Up Replication in a Secure Environment

Creating a secure replication environment begins with the setup process. In previous versions of SQL Server, only sysadmin roles had the rights required to configure replication. With SQL Server 2005, however, roles with lower security levels can configure replication. Expanding the roles that can configure replication is useful for Internet service providers (ISPs), for example, where the database administrator (DBA) can enable replication at the server level, and database owners can create the rest of the configuration. But you need to make sure that you appropriately restrict the permissions of the various roles involved in the replication setup process.

Table 19-1 summarizes the membership levels required to configure replication.

Table 19-1   Member Levels Required to Set Up Replication

		Membership	
Level	Task	Publisher	Subscriber
Server	Configure the Publisher and Distributor	sysadmin	-
Database	Enable publishing	*sysadmin*	-

Table 19-1   Member Levels Required to Set Up Replication

		Membership	
Level	Task	Publisher	Subscriber
Database	Create publications	*db_owner*	-
Database	Subscribe to a publication	*db_owner*	*db_owner*

Using this set of rights, different users can participate in the publishing process as follows:

- A DBA, as part of the sysadmin role, is responsible for configuring the *distribution* database and setting up the Publisher-Distributor configuration at the server level. The DBA is also responsible for enabling the database for publication.

- A Publisher account, at the database owner access level, is responsible for creating the publication.

- Finally, a Subscriber account, with rights to the Publisher and Subscriber, is responsible for subscribing to the publication.

Securing Publications

To secure publications, SQL Server 2005 offers a new mechanism: the publication access list (PAL). The PAL is equivalent to the Windows access control list (ACL). NTFS, printing, and shares all use ACLs to control user access.

The PAL is automatically created with the publication, and you use it to assign a list of logins and groups that have access to the publication. Every time an agent connects to the Publisher or Distributor and requests the publication, the server uses the PAL to verify that the agent account is included in the list.

To access a PAL through SSMS, follow these steps:

1. Open SSMS.
2. Connect to the Publisher database engine instance.
3. Expand the Replication, Local Publications folder.
4. Right-click the Publication and choose Properties.
5. Select the Publication Access List page, as Figure 19-12 shows.

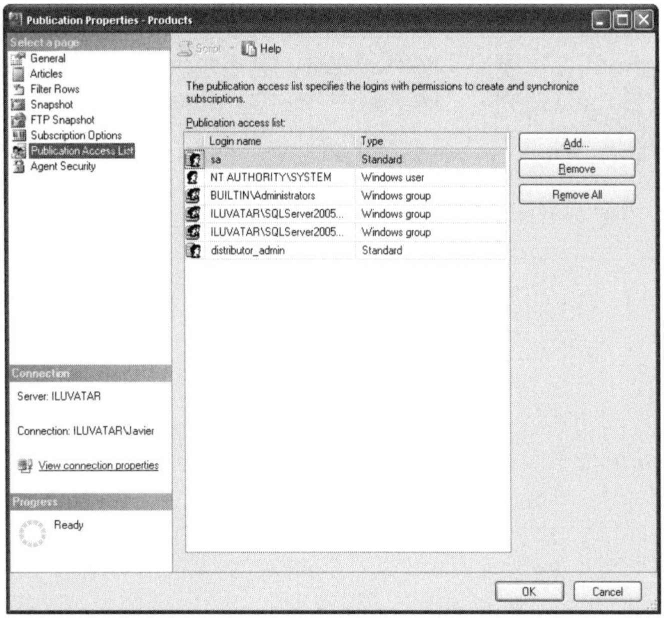

Figure 19-12   Selecting Publication Access List

To access and manage the list by using stored procedures, use the following procedures:

- ***sp_help_publication_access***   Returns the list of logins in the PAL
- ***sp_grant_publication_access***   Adds a login to the PAL
- ***sp_revoke_publication_access***   Removes the login from the PAL

Permissions Required by Agents

The principle of least privilege, or least account, is a key concept in security. The idea is to grant the minimum possible rights or account privileges to permit a legitimate action. This principle gives you greater data and functionality protection from malicious users or hackers. Limiting the level of access that replication agents have is an important task in the process of securing the replication process. Because agents are executables that run under the context of a Windows account, they affect not only the database but also the operating system.

Table 19-2 summarizes the minimum permissions required by each replication agent.

Table 19-2   Replication Agent Permissions

Agent	Publication Database	Distribution Database	Subscription Database	Snapshot Share	PPAL
Snapshot	*dbo_owner*	*dbo_owner*	-	Write	
Log Reader	*dbo_owner*	*dbo_owner*	-		
Distribution (Pull)			*dbo_owner*	Read	Yes
Distribution (Push)		*dbo_owner*	*dbo_owner*	Read	Yes
Merge (Push)	*Public*	*dbo_owner*	*dbo_owner*	Read	Yes
Merge (Pull)	*Public*	*Public*	*dbo_owner*	Read	Yes
Queue Reader	*dbo_owner*	*dbo_owner*	*dbo_owner*		

Quick Check

- You want to secure a transactional pull replication configuration. What rights should you grant the Windows user account that runs the Distribution Agent?

Quick Check Answer

The Windows account should

- Be assigned to the *distribution* database as *dbo_owner*.
- Be assigned to the *subscription* database as *dbo_owner*.
- Have read access to the Snapshot folder.
- Be added to the PAL.

PRACTICE **Creating a Secure Transactional Replication Configuration**

In this practice, you create and configure a new publication, using a secure environment. As a system administrator, you will delete the previous publication, create the accounts and configure the operating system permissions, and finally configure replication at the server level. You will log in as a Publisher user to create the publication and then log in as a Subscriber user to subscribe to the publication.

▶ **Practice 1: Delete the Unsecure Replication**

In this practice, you delete the previously defined replication configuration so that you can create a new configuration that uses security best practices.

1. Open SSMS.

2. Expand the Replication, Local Publications folder.

3. Right-click the Product publication and choose Delete.

4. Click Yes to confirm the removal of the publication and the subscription. SQL Server automatically deletes the snapshot and distribution jobs, along with the publication and subscription information.

5. Navigate to the Databases folder.

6. Right-click the *SubsTesting* database and choose Delete.

7. In the Delete Object dialog box, click OK to confirm the removal of the *SubsTesting* database.

8. Right-click the Databases folder and choose New Database. You will create an empty database that will subscribe to your new secure publication.

9. In the Database text box, type **SubsTesting** to name the database. Click OK to create the database.

10. On the toolbar, click New Query.

11. Type the following command:

```
exec sp_replicationdboption @dbname = N'ReplTesting'
    , @optname = N'publish'
    , @value = N'false'
```

12. This command disables the *ReplTesting* database for publishing. Execute the command and then verify that the server returns the following message:

```
The replication option 'publish' of database 'ReplTesting' has been set to false.
```

13. Right-click the Replication folder and choose Disable Publishing And Distribution. This process deletes the *distribution* database and removes the Publisher configuration.

14. On the Disable Publishing And Distribution Wizard page, click Next.

15. Select Yes, Disable Publishing On This Server.

16. Click Next.

17. On the Wizard Actions page, verify that the default option Disable Publishing And Distribution is selected and click Next.

18. On the Complete The Wizard page, click Finish.

19. After disabling publishing and distribution completes, click Close. SQL Server has now removed the previous configuration.

▶ **Practice 2: Prepare a Secure Environment**

In this practice, you create Windows accounts and define the minimum required rights to configure and run the replication process. These rights include shared folder rights and NTFS rights.

1. Right-click My Computer and select Manage. You will create the Windows local accounts you will assign to user roles and replication agents.

NOTE   **Working in a domain environment**

If you are working in a domain environment, use the Active Directory Users And Computers console to create the Windows accounts.

---

2. Expand System Tools, Local Users And Groups, Users.

3. Right-click Users and choose New User.

4. In the New User dialog box (see Figure 19-13), specify the user name and password and confirm the password. For the user name, type **ReplSnapAgent**, and for password, type **P@ssw0rd**. This account will be used for the Snapshot Agent.

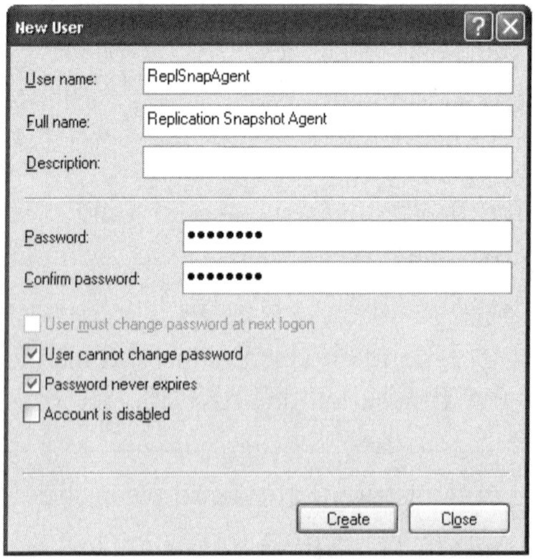

Figure 19-13   Configuring the ReplSnapAgent account

5. Clear the User Must Change Password At Next Logon check box. Select the User Cannot Change Password and Password Never Expires check boxes. These options are frequently used in service accounts. Click Create.

6. Repeat the user-creation process for the following accounts: ReplDistAgent, PublisherUser, and SubscriberUser. ReplDistAgent will be assigned to the distribution agent, and PublisherUser and SubscriberUser represent user accounts that will perform the publishing tasks.

7. Close Computer Management.

8. In the root folder of the C drive, navigate to the ReplicationPractice folder. This folder holds the subfolders for replication practices.

9. Right-click the ReplData folder and select Sharing And Security.

10. Select Share This Folder. Using a shared folder for snapshots enables both push and pull subscriptions.

11. Click Permissions to edit the folder's share permissions.

12. Remove the Everyone group.

13. Click Add.

14. In the Enter The Object Names To Select text box, type **Administrators**; **ReplDistAgent**; **ReplSnapAgent**; **PublisherUser**; **SubscriberUser**.

15. Click Check Names.

16. Verify that all the names are expanded and click OK.

17. Assign the following permissions:

User	Access Level
Administrators	Allow-Full Control
PublisherUser	Allow-Read
SubscriberUser	Allow-Read
ReplSnapAgent	Allow-Change
ReplDistAgent	Allow-Read

Note that you are granting permissions to the user accounts Administrator, PublisherUser, and SubscriberUser only for troubleshooting purposes.

18. Click OK to assign the permissions.

19. Click the Security tab. (The next steps assume that you are working in an NTFS file system partition; if not, skip the following steps.)

BEST PRACTICES   Setting NTFS security

To provide a secure environment for database replication, configure the Snapshot folder on an NTFS partition.

---

20. Click Add to configure NTFS permissions.

21. In the Enter The Object Names To Select text box, type **ReplDistAgent**; **ReplSnapAgent**; **PublisherUser**; **SubscriberUser**.

22. Click Check Names.

23. Verify that all the names are expanded and click OK.

24. Assign the following permissions:

User	Allow
PublisherUser	Read & Execute, List Folder Contents, and Read
SubscriberUser	Read & Execute, List Folder Contents, and Read
ReplSnapAgent	Modify, Read & Execute, List Folder Contents, Read, and Write
ReplDistAgent	Read & Execute, List Folder Contents, and Read

25. Click OK.

▶ **Practice 3: Use Scripts to Configure Publishing and Distribution**

In this practice, you configure your server as a Publisher and Distributor by using the scripts generated in the previous lesson. You will change the scripts to use a shared folder to hold the snapshots. You can alternatively use the Configure Replication Wizard and supply the appropriate parameters.

1. Open SSMS.

2. From the main menu, select File, Open, File.

3. Select the C:\ReplicationPractice\Scripts\ConfigureDistribution.sql file and click Open. This script has the configuration from the previous practice. When prompted, click Connect to connect to your server.

4. Press Ctrl+H to display the Quick Replace dialog box.

5. In the Find What text box, type **C:\ReplicationPractice\ReplData**.

6. In the Replace With text box, type ***COMPUTERNAME**Replication Practice*\\ *ReplData*.** (Replace *COMPUTERNAME* with the name of your server.) You will configure a Network Shared Folder and replace the local path configuration.

7. Click Replace All. Click OK to close the message box that states that three occurrences were replaced.

8. Close the Find And Replace dialog box.

9. Execute the script to configure the server. When the script completes, close it. Do *not* save the script; you will need the original configuration in later practices.

10. Click New Query.

11. Type the following command:

```
exec sp_replicationdboption @dbname = N'ReplTesting'
    , @optname = N'publish'
    , @value = N'true'
```

This command is the only additional step the DBA has to take to configure replication.

12. Execute the command and verify that the server returns the following message:

```
Command(s) completed successfully.
```

13. Close SSMS.

▶ **Practice 4: Finish the Secure Environment**

In this exercise, you will complete the secured configuration of the replication process. These rights include shared folder rights, NTFS rights, and SQL database roles.

1. If necessary, open SSMS and connect to your server by using Windows authentication.

2. In Object Explorer, expand the Security folder. You will grant SQL Server access to the recently created accounts.

3. Right-click the Logins folder and choose New Login.

4. Click Search.

5. In the Enter The Object Names To Select text box, type **ReplDistAgent**.

6. Click Check Names and click OK to select the account.

7. Select the User Mapping page. Create the following user-login mappings and assign the appropriate role membership:

   ReplDistAgent User Mapping

Database	Role
Distribution	*db_owner*
SubsTesting	*db_owner*

   This step creates database user accounts mapped to the login and assigns the account to the database owner role.

8. Click OK to create the login.

9. Repeat the login-creation process for the account ReplSnapAgent:

   ReplSnapAgent User Mapping

Database	Role
Distribution	*db_owner*
ReplTesting	*db_owner*

10. Repeat the login-creation process for the account PublisherUser:

    PublisherUser User Mapping

Database	Role
ReplTesting	*db_owner*

11. Repeat the login-creation process for the account SubscriberUser:

    SubscriberUser User Mapping

Database	Role
SubsTesting	*db_owner*
ReplTesting	*db_owner*

12. Close SSMS.

▶ **Practice 5: Configure a Snapshot Publication**

In this practice, you create a snapshot publication in a secure environment. You use a limited access account with no special rights at the server level and no rights at the *Subscriber* database, and you create a subscription in a database with *db_owner* rights.

You assign a Windows user account to the Snapshot Agent. Finally, you assign the accounts to PAL to allow the Subscriber account to work.

1. Navigate to Start, All Programs, Microsoft SQL Server 2005.

2. Right-click Microsoft SQL Server Management Studio and choose Run As.

3. In the Run As dialog box, select The Following User. In the User Name text box, type **PublisherUser** and type the password **P@ssw0rd**. You will use an account with limited access to configure the publication. Click OK.

4. Connect to the default database engine by using Windows authentication.

5. Expand the Replication folder and right-click the Local Publications folder. Choose New Publication. The New Publication Wizard starts.

6. On the New Publication Wizard page, click Next.

7. On the Publication Database page, verify that the database *ReplTesting* is selected and click Next. You will publish the *ReplTesting* database.

8. On the Publication Type page, verify that Snapshot Publication is selected. Click Next.

9. On the Articles page, expand Tables and select the BillOfMaterials, Product, and UnitMeasure check boxes. Expand the Stored Procedures folder and select the uspGetBillOfMaterials check box. The publication will copy the schema and data of the tables and the schema of the stored procedure. Click Next.

10. Read the Article Issues warning and click Next. The warning informs users that if you publish a stored procedure that depends on other objects, the stored procedure might not work as expected if objects it depends on do not exist in the Subscriber database. In this practice, you are publishing all required objects.

11. On the Filter Table Rows page, click Next.

12. In the Snapshot Agent page, select both check boxes. You want the Snapshot Agent to run immediately and to create a scheduled job. Click Change to configure the schedule.

13. In the Frequency section of the Job Schedule Properties dialog box, select Weekly from the Occurs drop-down list. Verify that the Sunday check box is selected. In the Daily Frequency section, select Occurs Once At to configure the job to run at midnight. Click OK to confirm the schedule, which schedules the agent to run once a week, every Sunday, at midnight. The Snapshot Agent will generate schema and BCP files once per week. Click Next to continue.

14. On the Agent Security page, click Security Settings. You will assign a Windows user account to execute the Snapshot Agent.

15. In the Process Account text box, type *COMPUTERNAME***\ReplSnapAgent**, where *COMPUTERNAME* is your server name.

16. In the Password and Confirm Password text boxes, type **P@ssw0rd**.

17. Below Connect To The Publisher, verify that By Impersonating The Process Account is selected.

18. Click OK and then click Next.

19. On the Wizard Actions page, select both check boxes. You want SSMS to create the publication as well as the script to have as a reference in the documentation. Click Next.

20. On the Script File Properties page, set the file name to **C:\ReplicationPractice\ Scripts\CreateProductsPublicationSecure.sql**. Select Overwrite The Existing File and click Next.

21. Name the publication **Products** and review the configuration. Click Finish to create the publication, the job to run the Snapshot Agent, and the script.

22. Wait until the publication is created and then click Close.

23. Right-click the recently created Products publication and choose Properties.

24. Select the Publication Access List page.

25. Click Add, select the ReplSnapAgent login, and click OK.

26. Click Add again, select the SubscriberUser, and click OK twice.

27. Close SSMS where you are logged on with the PublisherUser account.

▶ **Practice 6: Configure a Subscription**

In this practice, you create a snapshot publication in a secured environment. You use a limited access account with no special rights at the server level and rights at the *Subscriber* database and *subscription* databases. You assign a Windows user account to the distribution agent.

1. Navigate to Start, All Programs, Microsoft SQL Server 2005.

2. Right-click Microsoft SSMS and choose Run As.

3. In the Run As dialog box, select The Following User. In the User Name text box, type **SubscriberUser** and type the password **P@ssw0rd**. You will not use a sysadmin account to create the publication; instead, you will use an account with *dbo_owner* access to the publishing database and no access to the *Subscriber* database. Click OK.

4. Connect to the default database engine by using Windows authentication.

5. Expand the Replication, Local Publications folder.

6. Right-click the recently created Products publication and choose New Subscriptions. The New Subscription Wizard starts. On the New Subscription Wizard page, click Next.

7. On the Select Publication page, verify that the Products publication is selected. Click Next.

8. On the Distribution Agent Location page, verify that Run All Agents At The Distributor (Push Subscriptions) is selected. Click Next. This process configures push agents to distribute the publication.

9. On the Subscribers page, select the check box for your server, and from the Database drop-down list, select the *SubsTesting* database. This process will configure *SubsTesting* as the *Subscriber* database. Click Next.

10. On the Distribution Agent Security page, click the (...) button to configure the agent security context. As Figure 19-14 shows, you will assign a Windows user account to the Distribution Agent. Use the following options:

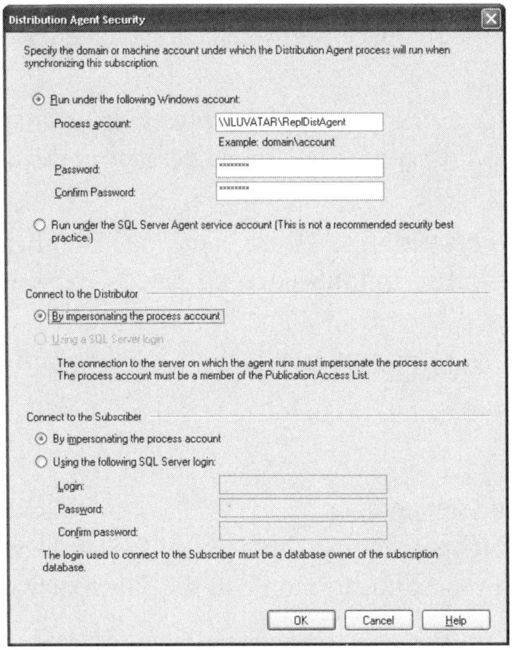

Figure 19-14   Configuring Distribution Agent security settings

❑ Process Account: **COMPUTERNAME\ReplDistAgent** (replace *COMPUTERNAME* with your server name).

❑ Password: **P@ssw0rd**.

❑ Confirm Password: **P@ssw0rd**.

❑ In the Connect To The Distributor section, verify that By Impersonating The Process Account is selected.

❑ In the Connect to the Subscriber section, verify that By Impersonating The Process Account is selected.

11. Click OK to configure the distribution agent's security and then click Next.

12. On the Synchronization Schedule page, from the Agent Schedule drop-down list, select Define Schedule.

13. In the New Job Schedule dialog box, in the Frequency section, verify that Weekly is selected from the Occurs drop-down list. Verify that Recurs Every is set to 1 and then select the Sunday check box.

14. In the Daily Frequency section, verify that Occurs Once At is selected and set the time to 12:30 AM.

15. Click OK. This process will configure the Distribution Agent to run once a week on Sunday at half past midnight. Click Next.

16. On the Initialize Subscriptions page, verify that Immediately is selected. Click Next.

17. On the Wizard Actions page, select both check boxes. You want SSMS to create the publication as well as the script to have as a reference in the documentation. Click Next.

18. On the Script File Properties page, set the file name to **C:\ReplicationPractice\ Scripts\CreateProductsSubscriptionSecure.sql**. Select Overwrite The Existing File and click Next.

19. Click Finish to create the subscription and the job to run the Distribution Agent.

20. Wait for the subscription creation to complete and then click Close.

21. Close SSMS.

▶ **Practice 7: Test the Replication Configuration**

In this practice, you corroborate that the snapshot publication has been delivered and that the tables and the stored procedure are stored in the *SubsTesting* database.

1. Using SSMS, connect to the server by using Windows authentication. (Use your standard Windows account.)

2. Expand the Databases, SubsTesting database.

3. Expand the Tables folder and check that the three tables exist.

4. Expand the Programmability, Stored Procedures folder.

5. Right-click the *uspGetBillOfMaterials* stored procedure and choose Execute Store Procedure.

6. In the @StartProductID Value column, type **800**.

7. In the @CheckDate Value column, type **2006-01-01**.

8. Click OK.

9. Check that the procedure successfully runs and returns 88 rows.

Lesson Summary

■ SQL Server 2005 includes a new security model that allows the configuration of the replication process by using different accounts that might have limited access to SQL Server.

■ Replication agents should be configured with limited access to follow the principle of least privilege. This principle protects data and functionality from malicious users and ill-behaved applications.

■ Using SSMS New Publication and New Subscription wizards, you can assign the Windows user accounts to run the agents, protecting your data and your server.

Lesson Review

The following questions are intended to reinforce key information presented in this lesson. The questions are also available on the companion CD if you prefer to review them in electronic form.

NOTE   Answers

Answers to these questions and explanations of why each answer choice is right or wrong are located in the "Answers" section at the end of the book.

---

1. What is the purpose of the PAL?

    A. Increase publication performance.

    B. Secure the publication.

    C. Provide a fault-tolerance mechanism.

    D. Increase subscription performance.

2. Which role membership level is the minimum necessary to subscribe to a publication? (Choose all that apply.)

    A. *db_datareader* at the *publishing* database

    B. *db_owner* at the *publishing* database

    C. *db_datawriter* at the *Subscriber* database

    D. *db_owner* at the *Subscriber* database

Lesson 4: Configuring Conflict Resolution for Merge Replication

Merge replication enables each server in the replication configuration to modify the data, later sending the changes to the *distribution* database. Therefore, in merge replication, conflicts might occur if two servers update the same data simultaneously. When you configure merge replication, you need to define the rules for how the Merge Agent should resolve any conflicts to maintain data validity and consistency. In this lesson, you will learn how to configure conflict resolution for merge replication and how to use the COM-based resolvers that come with SQL Server 2005 to resolve conflicts.

After this lesson, you will be able to:

- Explain the need for conflict resolution in merge replication.
- Configure conflict resolution for merge replication.
- Use the COM-based resolvers supplied with SQL Server 2005.

Estimated lesson time: 40 minutes

Conflict Resolution Basics

Unlike transactional replication, merge replication does not rely on the transaction log to synchronize the Publisher and Subscribers. In merge replication, each server modifies the replicated data, and the replication process uses uniqueidentifier columns and triggers to capture database activity on each server. When the Merge Agent runs, changes to the data are synchronized between Publisher and Subscribers. If data has also changed in the Publisher or has changed in another Subscriber and is already applied to the Publisher, a conflict occurs.

MORE INFO   **How merge replication works**

If you are interested in understanding the internal workings of merge replication, read the "How Merge Replication Tracks and Enumerates Changes" section in SQL Server 2005 Books Online. Using this information, you can review the triggers code and table schema of merge replication tables and go inside the process.

Conflict Resolution Resolvers

When the Merge Agent is running, and the Publisher and Subscribers are connected, the agent detects any conflict that has occurred since the last synchronization process. If the agent encounters a conflict, it uses a conflict resolver to determine the data that will be propagated to all participants.

A *conflict resolver* is either a Microsoft .NET Framework business component that uses the business logic handler framework included in the namespace *Microsoft.SqlServer.Replication.BusinessLogicSupport* or a COM-based object that implements the *ICustomResolver COM* interface. These components are used to resolve merge replication conflicts. SQL Server 2005 provides 12 COM-based resolvers, which Table 19-3 describes.

Table 19-3   SQL Server 2005 Conflict Resolvers

Name	Description
Additive	Winner determined from the priority value. Specified column set to the sum of the source and the destination column values.
Averaging	Winner is determined from the priority value. Specified column set to the average of the source and the destination column values.
DATETIME (Earlier Wins)	Column with the earlier datetime value determines the winner.
DATETIME (Later Wins)	Column with the later datetime value determines the winner.
Maximum	Column with the larger numeric value determines the winner.
Minimum	Column with the smaller numeric value determines the winner.
Merge Text	Conflict winner is determined from the priority value. The text columns in conflict are set to the merged value, consisting of the common prefix followed by the unique part from the Publisher, then by the delimiter, and finally by the unique part from the Subscriber.
Subscriber Always Wins	Subscriber, regardless of whether it is the source or destination, is the winner.
Priority Column	Column with the larger numeric value determines the conflict winner.

Table 19-3   SQL Server 2005 Conflict Resolvers

Name	Description
Upload Only	Changes uploaded to the Publisher are accepted; changes are not downloaded to the Subscriber.
Download Only	Changes uploaded to the Publisher are rejected; changes are downloaded to the Subscriber.
Stored Procedure	Conflict resolution depends on the logic in the stored procedure you specify.

MORE INFO   Microsoft COM-based resolvers

For more information about Microsoft COM-based resolvers, see the section "Microsoft COM-Based Resolvers" in SQL Server 2005 Books Online. The previous table is a summary of the more detailed one you can find in Books Online.

In some cases, the resolver determines the winner by using a column; in other cases, the winner is determined by the priority, and only the column value will be affected by the resolver.

MORE INFO   Stored procedure conflict resolvers

As an alternative to using a SQL Server 2005 predefined conflict resolver, you can write your own custom conflict resolver as a Transact-SQL stored procedure at each Publisher. During synchronization, this stored procedure is invoked when conflicts are encountered in an article to which the resolver was registered, and information on the conflict row is passed by the Merge Agent to the required parameters of the procedure. Stored procedure resolvers are invoked only to handle row change–based conflicts. They cannot be used to handle other types of conflicts such as insert failures due to *PRIMARY KEY* violations or unique index constraint violations. For information about using a stored procedure conflict resolver, see the SQL Server 2005 Books Online article "How to: Implement a Stored Procedure–Based Custom Conflict Resolver for a Merge Article (Replication Transact-SQL Programming)."

To configure a resolver, use the New Publication Wizard. In the Articles Definition page, select the table for which you want to configure a resolver. From the Articles Properties drop-down list, select Set Properties Of Highlighted Table Article (see Figure 19-15). Note that you can configure the resolver properties for all tables by selecting Set Properties Of All Table Articles instead.

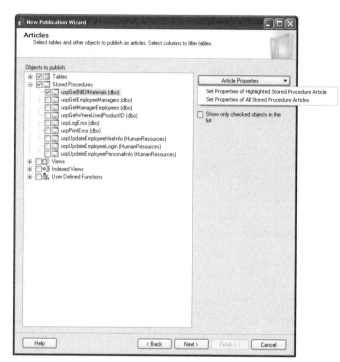

Figure 19-15   New Publication Wizard: Articles page

When you are defining merge replication, the wizard adds a tab to the Article Properties dialog box that you can use to configure the conflict resolver, as shown in Figure 19-16.

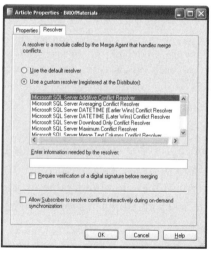

Figure 19-16   Configuring a conflict resolver

You can also use the *@article_resolver* parameter of the *sp_addmergearticle* stored procedure to configure a merge replication resolver by using Transact-SQL code.

Quick Check

- You want to configure a custom resolver. Which options do you have?

Quick Check Answer

- You can use one of the following options:
  - ❏ Create a .NET Framework business component.
  - ❏ Create a COM-based object.
  - ❏ Create a custom Transact-SQL stored procedure to use as a conflict resolver.

PRACTICE Configuring Merge Replication

In this practice, you create and configure a new merge publication. You first delete the previously created secure publication, and then you configure an unsecure merge replication publication with different conflict resolvers. Finally, you test the resolvers and review conflict winners and losers.

▶ **Practice 1: Delete the Previous Replication Setup**

In this practice, you delete the previously defined replication configuration. You won't disable publishing and distribution, but you will grant SQL Server Agent account access to the snapshot shared folder.

1. Open SSMS.

2. Expand the Replication, Local Publications folder.

3. Right-click the Product publication and choose Delete.

4. Click Yes to confirm the removal of the publication and the subscription.

5. Navigate to the Databases folder.

6. Right-click the *SubsTesting* database and select Delete.

7. In the Delete Object dialog box, click OK to confirm the removal of the *SubsTesting* database.

8. Right-click the Databases folder and choose New Database. You will create an empty database that will subscribe to the publication.

9. In the Database text box, type **SubsTesting** as the database name. Click OK to create the database.

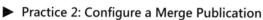 **Practice 2: Configure a Merge Publication**

In this practice, you create a merge publication. As part of the configuration process, you assign two different conflict resolvers.

1. If necessary, using SSMS, connect to the server by using Windows authentication.

2. Expand the Replication folder and right-click the Local Publications folder. Choose New Publication, which starts the New Publication Wizard.

3. On the New Publication Wizard page, click Next.

4. On the Publication Database page, select the *ReplTesting* database and click Next.

5. On the Publication Type page, select Merge Publication. You will create a merge publication to configure conflict resolvers. Click Next.

6. On the Subscriber Types page, verify that the SQL Server 2005 check box is selected and click Next.

7. On the Articles page, expand Tables and select Location, Product, and Product-Inventory. The publication will copy the schema and data of these tables.

8. On the Articles page, select the Show Only Checked Objects In The List check box. This action filters the list and shows only the *Location*, *Product*, and *Product-Inventory* tables. You will configure the *Product* table to use the standard conflict resolver and the *Location* and *ProductInventory* tables to use COM-based resolvers.

9. In the Objects To Publish list, select the *Location* table, and from the Article Properties drop-down list, select Set Properties Of Highlighted Table Article.

10. Click the Resolver tab and select Use A Custom Resolver (Registered At The Distributor).

11. Select the Microsoft SQL Server DATETIME (Later Wins) Conflict Resolver.

12. In the Enter The Information Needed By The Resolver text box, type **Modified-Date**.

13. Click OK. The row modified most recently is set as the conflict winner.

14. Select the *ProductInventory* table, and from the Article Properties drop-down list, select Set Properties Of Highlighted Table Article.

15. Click the Resolver tab and select Use A Custom Resolver (Registered At The Distributor).

16. Select the Microsoft SQL Server Minimum Conflict Resolver.

17. In the Enter The Information Needed By The Resolver text box, type **Quantity**.

18. Click OK. The winning row will always be the Publisher row, but the quantity will always be the minimum of the row.

19. Click Next.

20. Read the Article Issues warning, and click Next. The warning informs users that all merge replication articles must have a uniqueidentifier column, and if they don't have it, the first snapshot adds a column. Some applications might not handle the schema change appropriately and will stop working as expected.

21. On the Filter Table Rows page, click Next.

22. On the Snapshot Agent page, select both check boxes. You want the Snapshot Agent to run immediately and to create a scheduled job. Click Change to configure the schedule. Schedule the Snapshot Agent to run once a week on Sundays at midnight. Click OK to save your changes and then click Next.

23. On the Agent Security page, click Security Settings.

24. Select Run Under The SQL Server Agent Service Account. In the Connect To Publisher section, verify that By Impersonating The Process Account is selected. Click OK and then click Next.

CAUTION   Setting Snapshot Agent security

In this practice, you are configuring the Snapshot Agent to run under the SQL Server Agent security context. In a real-world scenario, this is not a recommended practice; in the previous lesson, you learned how to configure security in a real-world scenario. This practice focuses on merge replication conflict resolvers.

---

25. On the Wizard Actions page, select both check boxes. You want SSMS to create the publication and the script to have as a reference in the documentation. Click Next.

26. On the Script File Properties page, set the file name to **C:\ReplicationPractice\ Scripts\CreateInventoryPublication.sql**. Select Overwrite The Existing File and click Next.

27. Name the publication **Inventory** and review the configuration. Click Finish to create the publication, create the job to run the Snapshot Agent, and create the script.

28. After the publication has been created, click Close.

29. Right-click the Inventory Publication and choose Properties. You will configure the Snapshot folder to the local directory instead of the shared folder because the SQL Server Agent service account does not have access to the shared folder.

30. Select the snapshot page.

31. In the Location Of The Snapshot Files section, clear the Put Files In The Default Folder check box and select the Put Files In The Following Folder check box.

32. Set the folder path to: **C:\ReplicationPractice\ReplData.** Click OK to confirm the new settings.

▶ **Practice 3: Subscribe to the Merge Publication**

In this practice, you create a subscription to the merge publication.

1. If necessary, using SSMS, connect to the server by using Windows authentication.

2. Expand the Replication, Local Publications folder.

3. Right-click the recently created Inventory publication and choose New Subscriptions, which will start the New Subscription Wizard. Click Next.

4. On the Publication page, verify that the Inventory publication is selected. Click Next.

5. On the Distribution Agent Location page, verify that Run All Agents At The Distributor (Push Subscriptions) is selected. Click Next to configure push agents to distribute the publication.

6. On the Subscribers page, select the check box for your own server, and from the Subscription Database drop-down list, select the *SubsTesting* database. This will configure *SubsTesting* as the Subscriber database. Click Next.

7. On the Distribution Agent Security page, click the (...) button to configure the agent security context.

8. Use the following options:

  ❑ Run Under The SQL Server Agent Service Account.

  ❑ In the Connect To The Distributor section, verify that By Impersonating The Process Account is selected.

  ❑ In the Connect to the Subscriber section, verify that By Impersonating The Process Account is selected.

CAUTION **Setting the Snapshot Agent security**

In this practice, you are configuring the Snapshot Agent to run under the SQL Server Agent security context. In a real-world scenario, this is not a recommended practice.

---

9. Click OK to configure the merge agent's security and then click Next.

10. On the Synchronization Schedule page, from the Agent Schedule drop-down list, select Define Schedule. Configure the merge agent to run once a week on Sundays at 00:30, or 12:30 AM.

11. Click OK. This configures the merge agent to run once a week on Sunday at half past midnight. Click Next.

12. On the Initialize Subscriptions page, leave the default option Initialize Immediately. Click Next.

13. Review the default subscription type priority for conflict resolution and click Next. This option sets the subscription priority to 75.00, so changed rows at the subscriber and publisher have the same priority.

14. On the Wizard Actions page, select both check boxes to create the publication and a script to document the configuration. Click Next.

15. On the Script File Properties page, set the file name to **C:\ReplicationPractice\ Scripts\CreateProductsSubscription.sql**. Select the Overwrite The Existing File option and click Next.

16. Click Finish to create the subscription and the job to run the Distribution Agent.

17. Wait for the subscription to be created, and then click Close.

▶ **Practice 4: Verify Merge Conflict Resolution**

In this practice, you verify that the conflict resolution you configured works as expected. (If present, first delete the trigger tuid_ProductAudit from SubsTesting.Production.Product.)

1. Using SSMS, connect to the server by using Windows authentication.

2. Navigate to the Replication, Local Publications, [ReplTesting]: Inventory publication.

3. Right-click the *COMPUTERNAME*.SubsTesting subscription and choose View Synchronization Status.

4. Click Start to initiate the Distribution Agent and synchronize the Publisher and the Subscriber.

5. Wait for the agent to replicate and then click Close.

6. In the toolbar, click New Query.

7. In the Query Editor, type the following update queries:

```
USE ReplTesting
UPDATE Production.Product
    SET Name=Name+'Updated at Publisher'
WHERE ProductID=1

USE SubsTesting
UPDATE Production.Product
    SET Name=Name+'Updated at Subscriber'
WHERE ProductID=1
```

8. Execute the queries and verify that they return the following:

```
(1 row(s) affected)
```

```
(1 row(s) affected)
```

9. Navigate to the Replication, Local Publications, [ReplTesting]: Inventory publication.

10. Right-click the *COMPUTERNAME*.SubsTesting subscription and choose View Synchronization Status.

11. Click Start to initiate the Distribution Agent and synchronize the Publisher and the Subscriber.

12. Wait for the agent to replicate and then click Close.

13. Right-click the [ReplTesting]: Inventory publication and choose View Conflicts.

14. Double-click the *Product(1)* table.

15. In the Microsoft Replication Conflict Viewer dialog box, review the conflict winner and loser.

16. Do *not* submit the winner or loser. Close the Microsoft Replication Conflict Viewer dialog box.

17. Navigate to the Databases, ReplTesting, Tables, Production.Product table.

18. Right-click the table and choose Open Table.

19. Verify that the Name column for the row with a ProductID of 1 is the one updated at the Publisher.

20. Close the Table window.

21. Navigate to the Databases, SubsTesting, Tables, Production.Product table.

22. Right-click the table and choose Open Table.

23. Verify that the Name column for the row with a ProductID of 1 is also the one updated at the Publisher and that both databases have the same value. The merge default conflict resolver chose a winner, and data is consistent in both databases. The conflict winner is always the publisher database.

24. In the toolbar, click New Query.

25. In the Query Editor, type the following queries:

```
USE ReplTesting
UPDATE Production.Location
   SET Name=Name+'Updated at Publisher'
WHERE LocationID=1

WAITFOR DELAY '00:00:15'

USE SubsTesting
UPDATE Production.Location
   SET Name=Name+'Updated at Subscriber'
WHERE LocationID=1

SELECT *
FROM ReplTesting.Production.Location
WHERE LocationID=1
SELECT *
FROM SubsTesting.Production.Location
WHERE LocationID=1
```

26. Execute the queries and verify that the *SELECT* statements return two rows, and that the ModifiedDate column has a 15-second difference.

27. Navigate to the Replication, Local Publications, [ReplTesting]: Inventory publication.

28. Right-click the *COMPUTERNAME*.SubsTesting subscription and choose View Synchronization Status.

29. Click Start to initiate the Distribution Agent and synchronize the Publisher and the Subscriber.

30. Wait for the agent to replicate and then click Close.

31. Right-click the [ReplTesting]: Inventory publication and choose View Conflicts.

32. Double-click the *Location(1)* table.

33. In the Microsoft Replication Conflict Viewer, review the conflict winner and loser. The winner this time is the row updated at the Subscriber because it was the last one you updated.

34. Do *not* submit the winner or loser. Close the Microsoft Replication Conflict Viewer.

35. Navigate to the Databases, ReplTesting, Tables, *Production.Location* table.

36. Right-click the table and choose Open Table.

37. Verify that the Name column for the row with a LocationID of 1 is the one updated at the Subscriber.

38. Close the table window.

39. Navigate to the Databases, SubsTesting, Tables, Production.Location table.

40. Right-click the table and choose Open Table.

41. Verify that the Name column is also the one updated at the Subscriber and that both databases have the same value.

42. In the toolbar, click New Query.

43. In the Query Editor, type the following queries:

```
USE ReplTesting
UPDATE Production.ProductInventory
    SET Quantity=Quantity-20
WHERE ProductID=1 AND LocationID=1

WAITFOR DELAY '00:00:15'

USE SubsTesting
UPDATE Production.ProductInventory
    SET Quantity=Quantity-50
WHERE ProductID=1 AND LocationID=1

SELECT *
FROM ReplTesting.Production.ProductInventory
WHERE ProductID=1 AND LocationID=1
SELECT *
FROM SubsTesting.Production.ProductInventory
WHERE ProductID=1 AND LocationID=1
```

44. Execute the queries and verify that the *SELECT* statements return two rows, that the Quantity column displays different values in each database (the Subscriber is lesser), and that the ModifiedDate column has a 15-second difference.

45. Navigate to the Replication, Local Publications, [ReplTesting]: Inventory publication.

46. Right-click the *COMPUTERNAME*.SubsTesting subscription and choose View Synchronization Status.

47. Click Start to initiate the Distribution Agent and synchronize the Publisher and the Subscriber.

48. Wait for the agent to replicate and then click Close.

49. Right-click the [ReplTesting]: Inventory publication and choose View Conflicts.

50. Double-click the *ProductInventory(1)* table.

51. In the Microsoft Replication Conflict Viewer, review the conflict winner and loser. The winner this time is the row updated at the Publisher, but the Quantity column is the lesser value of both columns and is the value updated at the Subscriber.

52. Do *not* submit the winner or loser. Close the Microsoft Replication Conflict Viewer.

53. Navigate to the Databases, ReplTesting, Tables, *Production.ProductInventory* table.

54. Right-click the table and choose Open Table.

55. Verify that the Quantity column displays the value updated at the Subscriber.

56. Close the table.

57. Navigate to the Databases, SubTesting, Tables, *Production.ProductInventory* table.

58. Right-click the table and choose Open Table.

59. Verify that the Quantity column displays the value updated at the Subscriber and that both databases have the same value.

Lesson Summary

- Merge replication allows simultaneous updates in multiple databases, which might cause data conflicts. To resolve these conflicts, SQL Server lets you create components that define business logic to determine the winning row.

- To configure conflict resolution in merge replication, use the Article Properties page of the New Publishing Wizard in SSMS or the *@article_resolver* parameter of the *sp_addmergearticle* stored procedure.

- SQL Server 2005 provides a set of COM-based conflict resolvers that implement common business rules, but you can also create custom components.

Lesson Review

The following questions are intended to reinforce key information presented in this lesson. The questions are also available on the companion CD if you prefer to review them in electronic form.

NOTE **Answers**

Answers to these questions and explanations of why each answer choice is right or wrong are located in the "Answers" section at the end of the book.

1. What types of conflict resolvers does SQL Server support? (Choose all that apply.)

    A. .NET Framework business object components

    B. COM-based resolvers

    C. UDF-based resolvers

    D. Trigger-based resolvers

2. At what level is conflict resolution configured?

    A. Publisher level

    B. Database level

    C. Subscription level

    D. Article level

Lesson 5: Monitoring Replication

Monitoring is an important part of a DBA's job. And because replication is a distributed activity involving multiple computers, you need to take special care in monitoring replication processes. In SQL Server 2005, the main tool for monitoring replication is the SSRM, although you can also monitor parts of the replication configuration via SSMS. You can also use Transact-SQL and RMO to monitor replication. In addition, you can set up alerts for replication agent events and use System Monitor to monitor replication processes. This lesson focuses on setting up SSRM to monitor replication processes, setting up alerts for replication agent events, and using System Monitor's replication counters and objects.

After this lesson, you will be able to:
- Use SSRM to manage replication.
- Configure replication alerts.
- Use Performance Monitor to monitor replication.

Estimated lesson time: 30 minutes

Using SQL Server Replication Monitor

SSRM is the new graphical tool that SQL Server 2005 provides to help you monitor replication agents and the replication process. Although you can use SSMS to monitor parts of the replication process or use Transact-SQL or RMO, SSRM is the most important tool for monitoring replication, presenting a Publisher-focused view of all replication activity.

You can start SSRM by right-clicking the replication folder in SSMS and choosing Launch Replication Monitor. Figure 19-17 shows the SSRM. Alternatively, you can run SSRM from its default path: C:\Program Files\Microsoft SQL Server\90\Tools\Binn\sqlmonitor.exe.

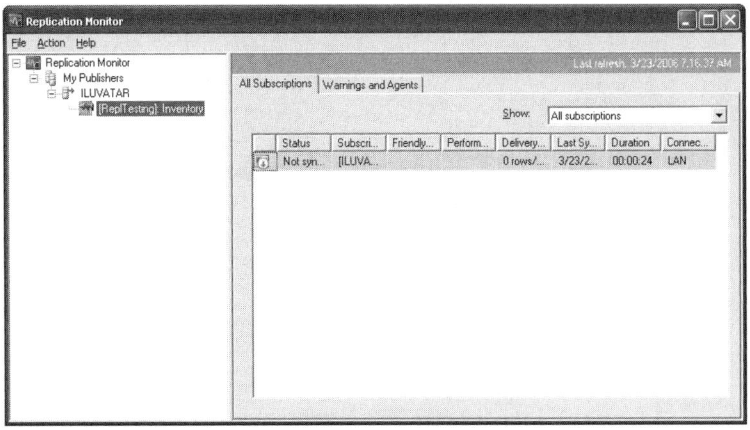

Figure 19-17   SQL Server Replication Monitor

Configuring Non-sysadmin Access to Replication Monitoring

By default, only members of the sysadmin fixed server role can monitor replication, but a system administrator can give non-sysadmin users permission to monitor replication by assigning them to the replmonitor role. The replmonitor role is a fixed database role in the *distribution* database. Here is how to grant users permission to monitor replication processes:

1. Open SSMS and connect to the Distributor server.
2. Navigate to the Security, Logins folder.
3. Right-click the login of the user you want to be able to monitor replication and choose Properties.
4. Select the User Mapping page.
5. Select the *distribution* database in the Users Mapped To This Login Table grid.
6. Select the Map check box for the *distribution* database.
7. In the Database Role Membership For: Distribution section, select the replmonitor check box, as Figure 19-18 shows. Click OK.

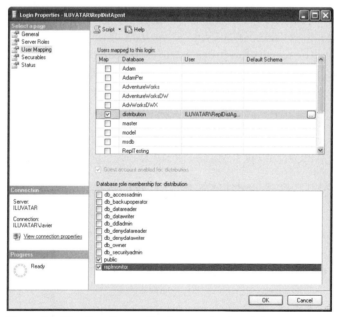

Figure 19-18   Granting replication monitoring rights

NOTE Security

Being a member of the replmonitor database role does not grant the user any other administration rights besides monitoring. Members of this role can monitor replication, but unless additional rights are granted, they cannot change the configuration.

> ### Quick Check
>   - How would you grant a user permission to monitor replication?
>
> **Quick Check Answer**
>   - In the Distributor server, make the user a member of the replmonitor role in the *distribution* database.

Using SSRM to View Replication Status

SSRM lets DBAs monitor replication from a central administration point. Here is how to use SSRM to monitor a Publisher:

1. Open SSRM.
2. In the console tree, select Replication Monitor.
3. Click the Add Publisher hyperlink.
4. In the Add Publisher dialog box, from the Add drop-down list, select Add SQL Server Publisher.
5. Provide the authentication parameters and click Connect.

You can also add all Publishers that use the same Distributor by selecting Specify A Distributor And Add Its Publishers from the Add drop-down list.

After you add the distributor, you can navigate to the server and all its publications. SSRM helps you monitor the replication status and history of replication agents. And if you have the appropriate rights, you can change the configuration of publications and subscriptions. To add new publications or subscriptions, however, use SSMS.

To review the history of the Snapshot Agent, for example, take the following steps:

1. Open SSRM.
2. Expand Replication Monitor, My Publishers, *Publisher Name*.
3. Select the publication you want.

4. In the details pane, click the Warnings And Agents tab.

5. In the Agents And Jobs Related To This Publication grid, double-click the Snapshot Agent.

To review the history of the Distribution or Merge agent, in step 4 click the All Subscriptions tab instead of the Warnings And Agents tab, and then double-click the subscription you want to monitor.

Configuring Alerts with SSRM

SSRM also helps administrators manage replication in a more proactive manner by simplifying the configuration of *replication alerts*. Alerts are automated responses to SQL events—in this case, replication issues. SQL Server Agent monitors the Windows application log for events that have alerts defined for them. If such an event occurs, SQL Server Agent responds by executing a task that you have defined or by sending an e-mail or a pager message to a specified operator. Replication provides a number of predefined alerts for replication agent events, and you can create additional alerts if necessary.

SSRM lets you enable the following alerts:

- Replication: Agent custom shutdown
- Replication: Agent failure
- Replication: Agent retry
- Replication: Agent success
- Replication: Expired subscription dropped
- Replication: Subscriber has failed data validation
- Replication: Subscriber has passed data validation
- Replication: Subscription reinitialized after validation failure

All these alerts are created at the Distributor and disabled by default.

SSRM simplifies the process of enabling the alert and configuring a response. Here is how to use SSRM to configure an alert:

1. Open SSRM.

2. In the console tree, expand Replication Monitor, My Publishers, *Publisher Name*.

3. Select the publication for which you want to configure the alert.

4. Select the Warnings And Agents tab.

5. Click Configure Alerts.

You can also configure alerts by using SSMS and navigating to the SQL Server Agent, Alerts folder.

NOTE   Configure warnings

In addition to creating replication alerts, you can configure a set of warnings to monitor performance and agent status. When you use SSRM to enable a warning, you specify a threshold. When that threshold is met or exceeded, a warning is displayed. You can enable warnings for the following conditions:

- Imminent subscription expiration

- Exceeding the specified latency

- Exceeding the specified synchronization time

- Falling short of processing the specified number of rows in a given amount of time

---

Monitoring Replication with System Monitor

You can use System Monitor's performance objects and counters to set a replication baseline and monitor replication processes. A replication baseline captures a set of measures that you can later compare to measures from the new or modified replication configuration.

SQL Server 2005 adds 5 performance objects and 12 counters to System Monitor, as Table 19-4 shows.

Table 19-4   SQL Server 2005 Performance Objects and Counters

SQL Server: Replication	Counter	Description
Agents	Running	The number of replication agents currently running
Snapshot	Snapshot: Delivered Cmds/sec	The number of commands per second delivered to the Distributor
	Snapshot: Delivered Trans/sec	The number of transactions per second delivered to the Distributor

Table 19-4   SQL Server 2005 Performance Objects and Counters

SQL Server: Replication	Counter	Description
Logreader	Logreader: Delivered Cmds/sec	The number of commands per second delivered to the Distributor
	Logreader: Delivered Trans/sec	The number of transactions per second delivered to the Distributor
	Logreader: Delivery Latency	The current amount of time, in milliseconds, elapsed from when transactions are applied at the Publisher to when they are delivered to the Distributor
Dist.	Dist: Delivered Cmds/sec	The number of commands per second delivered to the Subscriber
	Dist: Delivered Trans/sec	The number of transactions per second delivered to the Subscriber
	Dist: Delivery Latency	The current amount of time, in milliseconds, elapsed from when transactions are delivered to the Distributor to when they are applied at the Subscriber
Merge	Conflicts/sec	The number of conflicts per second occurring during the merge process
	Downloaded Changes/sec	The number of rows per second replicated from the Publisher to the Subscriber
	Uploaded Changes/sec	The number of rows per second replicated from the Subscriber to the Publisher

MORE INFO   **Performance counters and objects**

The previous table is a summary of the one you can find in the "Monitoring Replication with System Monitor" section in SQL Server 2005 Books Online.

DBAs usually add the SQL Server Replication Agents: Running counter to the general performance baseline to gain more information about what is happening in the system. You can also create a specific baseline for each of the agents that runs in the system; this baseline would combine Agent counters with general resource counters to measure processor, memory, network, and input/output (I/O) consumption.

Improving Replication Performance

After you configure replication, take the time to develop a performance baseline so that you can determine how replication behaves with a typical workload in your environment. With such a baseline, you can determine when your environment's performance changes and take appropriate action to maintain an efficient system.

You can use SSRM and System Monitor to determine baseline values for the following key factors in replication performance:

- **Latency** The amount of time it takes for a data change to be propagated between nodes in a replication topology.

- **Throughput** The amount of replication activity (measured in commands delivered over a period of time) a system can sustain over time.

- **Concurrency** The number of replication processes that can operate on a system simultaneously.

- **Duration of synchronization** How long it takes a given synchronization to complete.

- **Resource consumption** Hardware and network resources used in replication processing.

After you have established baseline numbers, set thresholds in SSRM so that you know when these baselines have been exceeded. You can then take appropriate action.

MORE INFO Improving the performance of your replication system

For best practices and tips on how to improve the performance of your replication system, see the SQL Server 2005 Books Online topic "Enhancing Replication Performance."

PRACTICE Using SSRM to Review Agent Status History

In these practices, you configure a non-sysadmin account to access SSRM and then use SSRM to review replication agent status history.

▶ **Practice 1: Grant Monitor Rights**

In this practice, you grant the PublisherUser account rights to monitor the replication process.

1. Open SSMS and authenticate by using your Windows account.
2. Navigate to the Security, Logins folder.
3. Right-click the PublisherUser login and choose Properties.
4. Select the User Mapping page.
5. Select the Map check box for the *distribution* database in the Users Mapped To This Login grid. This creates a new user in the distribution database mapped to the PublisherUser login.
6. Select the replmonitor role check box in the Database Role Membership For Distribution grid, which adds the user to the role and grants the required rights to monitor replication. Click OK.
7. Close SSMS.

▶ **Practice 2: Monitor Replication with SSRM**

In this practice, you, as the PublisherUser, use SSRM to review agent history.

1. Navigate to Start, All Programs, Microsoft SQL Server 2005.
2. Right-click Microsoft SQL Server Management Studio and choose Run As.
3. In the Run As window, select The Following User. In the User Name text box, type **PublisherUser** and in the Password text box type **P@ssw0rd**. You will use an account with limited access to monitor the replication process. Click OK.
4. Connect to the default database engine by using Windows authentication.
5. Right-click the Replication folder and select Launch Replication Monitor.
6. Navigate to the [ReplTesting]: Inventory publication.
7. Right-click the publication and choose Generate Snapshot to try to execute the Snapshot Agent.
8. You should get an error message: EXECUTE Permission Denied On Object 'sp_start_job'. You were granted monitor rights, but you don't have sysadmin rights. Click OK to close the error message box.

9. Double-click the only subscription in the Subscription grid. The Subscription Synchronization History dialog box opens.

10. Review the status and article details of the last synchronizations and then close the dialog box.

11. In SSRM, select the Warnings And Agents tab.

12. Double-click the Snapshot Agent in the Agents And Jobs Related To This Publication grid. The Snapshot Agent Synchronization History dialog box opens.

13. Review the status and article details of the last synchronizations and then close the dialog box.

14. Close SSRM and SSMS.

Lesson Summary

- From SSMS, DBAs and user members of the replmonitor database role can launch SSRM to monitor the replication process.

- You can use SSRM to create replication alerts that automatically respond to replication events.

- Replication adds a set of performance objects and counters to System Monitor that you can use to create a baseline to monitor replication agents.

Lesson Review

The following questions are intended to reinforce key information presented in this lesson. The questions are also available on the companion CD if you prefer to review them in electronic form.

NOTE Answers

Answers to these questions and explanations of why each answer choice is right or wrong are located in the "Answers" section at the end of the book.

1. Which tool is the most appropriate to monitor replication?

   A. SQL Server Management Studio (SSMS)

   B. SQL Server Replication Monitor (SSRM)

   C. SQL Server Configuration Manager (SSCM)

   D. SQL Server Error and Usage Reporting (SSEUR)

2. Which tool should a DBA use to create a baseline to monitor replication?

    A. SQL Server Management Studio (SSMS)

    B. SQL Server Replication Monitor (SSRM)

    C. System Monitor

    D. Event Viewer

Chapter Summary

- Replication is a set of technologies for copying and distributing data and database objects from one database to another and then synchronizing between databases to maintain consistency.

- SQL Server 2005 offers three major replication types: snapshot, transactional, and merge. Snapshot replication copies the whole set of data every time, transactional replication uses the transaction log to replicate changes only, and merge replication uses triggers and additional tables to allow multiple distributed updates of the same data and then uses conflict resolvers to define conflict winners and losers if there are data conflicts.

- SQL Server uses replication agents to implement replication. Replication agents should run with the fewest possible rights and account privileges to follow the important security concept called the principle of least privilege.

- Merge replication requires you to configure conflict resolvers, which are specialized components (.NET or COM) that can implement business logic to resolve data conflicts when replication servers simultaneously modify the same data.

- SSRM is the new monitoring tool that lets administrators supervise corporate-wide replication processes from a single administration point.

Key Terms

Do you know what these key terms mean? You can check your answers by looking up the terms in the glossary at the end of the book.

- conflict resolver
- merge replication
- peer-to-peer replication
- pull subscription
- push subscription
- replication agent
- snapshot replication
- transactional replication

Case Scenarios

In the following case scenarios, you will apply what you've learned about how to configure, secure, and monitor replication in SQL Server 2005. You can find answers to these questions in the "Answers" section at the end of this book.

Case Scenario 1: Providing Local Access to Reports

Fabrikam, Inc., a leading manufacturer of digital cameras, recently acquired a new Video Products division to expand its product line, increase revenue, and grow overall market share of the company. The new Video Products division operates at a remote site and should remain as independent as possible. The marketing department requires weekly reports from the division based on a sales summary view.

1. What type of replication would you use to copy the sales summary data from the Video Products division server to the marketing server?

2. You want to use a pull subscription for the replication configuration. What additional consideration must you take when configuring the replication?

3. You want a member of the Marketing department to be able to monitor the replication processes. How would you grant monitoring access without giving excessive rights to the marketing representative?

Case Scenario 2: Providing Fault Tolerance for Multiple Servers

You are working as the DBA for a large university with seven schools that offer graduate and undergraduate programs. The university's enrollment is growing rapidly, and funds have been approved for seven new servers running SQL Server 2005—one server for each school. The servers will support the enrollment application, developed by in-house developers.

Even when communication within the university network is very good, IT has agreed that each site should remain as independent as possible, and the enrollment application should be available when communication fails. As a rule, students enroll in the school they attend, although sometimes this is not the case.

1. What type of replication would you use to distribute the enrollment database?

2. Before implementing replication, what application considerations do the DBAs need to take into account?

3. In case of a conflict—a very rare case of a student enrolling in two schools at the same time—what alternatives could you give to programmers?

Suggested Practices

To help you successfully master the exam objectives presented in this chapter, complete the following tasks.

Creating Replication Setups

For this task, you should complete at least Practices 1 and 3. If you want a more well-rounded understanding of replication and implementation approaches, you should also complete Practice 2.

- **Practice 1** Create a merge replication configuration that uses a single database engine instance. Become familiar with merge replication options, particularly filtering options at the article and publication levels.

- **Practice 2** Create a merge replication configuration that uses two servers. Configure one as Publisher-Distributor and the other one as Subscriber. Analyze the differences between push and pull subscriptions. Disrupt the process by unplugging the network cable of one of the servers, and then use SSRM to review alerts.

- **Practice 3** Create a transactional replication configuration that uses a single database engine instance. Become familiar with transactional replication options. Configure different objects (tables, views, and stored procedures) and review article options.

Take a Practice Test

The practice tests on this book's companion CD offer many options. For example, you can test yourself on just the content covered in this chapter, or you can test yourself on all the 70-431 certification exam content. You can set up the test so that it closely simulates the experience of taking a certification exam, or you can set it up in study mode so that you can look at the correct answers and explanations after you answer each question.

MORE INFO Practice tests

For details about all the practice test options available, see the "How to Use the Practice Tests" section in this book's Introduction.

Chapter 20

Working with Service Broker

Microsoft SQL Server 2005 introduces Service Broker—a secure, reliable, robust, and highly scalable message-queuing system for distributed applications. By providing the core architectural components for ensuring that messages are received and can be persisted, even through system failure, Service Broker enables the next generation of highly scalable applications.

Developers create most applications by using sequential, synchronous processing. In this model, a transaction is started, data is locked to prevent anyone else from accessing it, the change is made, and the locks are released. This approach works reasonably well for some applications. However, many applications need consistent processing for a business transaction that can span multiple databases, platforms, and even company boundaries. Many more applications simply need to send a request for some processing to be done and do not need an immediate response as long as they can be sure that the request will be processed as soon as possible.

You might think that asynchronous processing would lead to data integrity issues. However, asynchronous processing can actually allow applications to process many more requests than would otherwise be possible because you don't have to expend resources either waiting for a process to complete or periodically checking for status. Obviously, some applications need to ensure that a process completes before continuing, and Service Broker provides a prepackaged capability to manage the entire infrastructure required to create asynchronous distributed systems.

This chapter explains the Service Broker objects—the message types, contracts, queues, and services—that are involved in processing messages. It then looks at the Service Broker mechanisms—conversations, dialogs, and routing—that manage the message traffic and ensure reliability.

MORE INFO Building Service Broker applications

This chapter provides an overview of Service Broker applications. But for a much more detailed discussion of Service Broker and building robust distributed Service Broker applications, we recommend *The Rational Guide to SQL Server 2005 Service Broker Beta Preview* by Roger Wolter (Rational Press, 2005). Although written against the beta version of SQL Server 2005, this book provides a comprehensive review of Service Broker functionality, complete with lots of code samples and practices.

Exam objectives in this chapter:

- Implement Service Broker components.

    - ❑ Create services.

    - ❑ Create queues.

    - ❑ Create contracts.

    - ❑ Create conversations.

    - ❑ Create message types.

    - ❑ Send messages to a service.

    - ❑ Route a message to a service.

    - ❑ Receive messages from a service.

Lessons in this chapter:

Before You Begin

To complete the lessons in this chapter, you must have

- SQL Server 2005 installed.

- A copy of the *AdventureWorks* sample database installed in the instance.

Real World

Michael Hotek

Recently, I worked on one of the most amazing SQL Server systems that I have ever seen. There was nothing really unique about the technical implementation—the table structures, the code within the application, or how transactions were processed. What was unique was the sheer scale of processing that was occurring.

This database application was literally the largest in existence on a SQL Server platform and possibly on any database platform. Some people might want to argue this point. But when you use numbers with 11 zeros to start measuring the

---

database transactions you are processing daily, you might begin to be in the ballpark of this application.

Performance wasn't the problem with this application. The company was expanding its environment into additional markets, with the first market targeting an expected growth of almost double the database application's current load. All users had to have access to all data as well. So the company needed a mechanism to cache data close to the users while also maintaining a centralized database with at least half of the initial writes coming from a few thousand miles away.

The organization could not use distributed data techniques such as log shipping because the databases were never offline, and developers would have to write a significant amount of code to extract just the incremental changes. Although replication can move incremental changes at a rapid enough rate to handle virtually any load, it simply did not have the capacity to move the volume of data necessary.

Because the data would be cached locally, and users would generally find everything they needed in the local cache, it was not critical to have writes committed to the central database in a synchronous manner. So the developers began architecting a reasonably straightforward mechanism to queue changes locally and then send them back to the corporate data center in an asynchronous manner. However, they then realized other issues they had to overcome: issues of durability, backups, synchronization, ensuring that a change is sent only once, and hundreds of other issues that any queue with multiple readers would have.

This scenario was a perfect fit for Service Broker. Although the volume of changes was staggering, the developers could create as many queues and brokers as they needed. Multiple brokers could then read from a single queue, and the volume of changes could be spread across multiple queues. The Service Broker architecture would guarantee that a change was sent once and only once while providing all the other infrastructure elements necessary to manage the changes. SQL Server would provide the means to ensure that the changes were durable and could survive even the complete loss of the queue due to disaster.

With Service Broker providing all the architecture they needed, not only could the developers avoid months of architecting, coding, and testing, but the company could also take advantage of having a robust, distributed, high-performance message queue at no extra cost because it is included with SQL Server 2005. I can't wait to see this Service Broker application go into production processing several billion messages per day.

Lesson 1: Exploring the Service Broker Architecture

Service Broker provides a new architectural service for building asynchronous, highly scalable applications. The first step in building Service Broker applications is to understand how all the components fit together to create a solution. In this lesson, you will explore the components of a Service Broker solution, get an overview of how applications interact with Service Broker, and see how to enable Service Broker's services in SQL Server 2005.

After this lesson, you will be able to:

- Identify the components of a Service Broker solution.
- Understand how Service Broker interacts with an application.
- Enable Service Broker.

Estimated lesson time: 15 minutes

Messaging Overview

Much of the documentation related to Service Broker revolves around messages and how to process them. Unfortunately, most database developers and administrators stop as soon as they see the word *message*. After all, we are talking about database applications, so transactions have to be used to submit, modify, and retrieve data in a reliable manner. Messages belong in an e-mail system, not in a database, right?

This perspective could not be further from the truth. It is simply an unfortunate misunderstanding of what a message really is.

Every computer system ever built deals with messages. It is unavoidable. Data has to be input. Code has to be executed to process the data. And the results have to be returned to something. These are all messages, meaning directives to do something.

In the computing world, this concept can be a bit amorphous. An application sending a message that contains a CustomerID is pretty esoteric. What does it mean? Is the application asking for the name of the customer? Is the application asking for all orders that have been placed by the customer? Is the application asking for the address of the customer? The answer to these questions and many more like them is yes, no, and all of the above. We simply do not know. However, the application sending the message containing the CustomerID doesn't simply broadcast it to the network, it sends the CustomerID to a particular application. And a developer has coded the application that receives the CustomerID to perform a specific action.

So a message without a means to process it is of no value. And an application without any capability to accept input is equally worthless. These two components rely on each other to create value.

What does any of this philosophy of messaging have to do with Service Broker or your business needs? Service Broker provides the mechanisms to process messages, going several steps beyond just accepting any message that someone wants to send and then passing it on to something that processes the data. Service Broker provides the objects and infrastructure to ensure that messages are formatted correctly so that applications can understand them, and it ensures that the only messages that are accepted are those associated with applications that understand how to process the messages.

Service Broker Components

To understand all the pieces required to create a Service Broker application that enables communication to be controlled, reliable, robust, and scalable, let's look at the elements from the outside in.

First, communication must occur between a source and a target. In Service Broker, they are called *endpoints*. The physical implementation of an endpoint is a database. This means that Service Broker *sends* and *receives* data between databases. The endpoint that starts the communication process is known as the *initiator*, and the endpoint that receives the initial request is known as the *target*. Once established, communication can flow in both directions. The initiator and target endpoints can be in the same database, in different databases on the same instance, or in databases on different instances or servers.

The end result of a Service Broker application is to manage *conversations*—exchanges of data—between endpoints. Conversations in Service Broker, just like conversations between people, can be of two different types:

- *monolog*   A conversation that occurs from one endpoint to any number of target endpoints. This conversation type is not currently available in SQL Server 2005.
- *dialog*   A conversation that occurs between exactly two endpoints.

Conversations manage the flow of messages between initiator and target. You would need only this mechanism if resources were always available, always had the capacity to process every message as soon as it arrived, and never failed. But because this is not possible, your applications require a structure to store messages that are submitted so that the applications can continue with other tasks, knowing that the submitted messages will be processed as soon as possible.

This storage mechanism is called a *queue*, which is simply a table. When an application submits a message, it is appended to the bottom of the table. And other applications read messages off the top of the table. After an application retrieves a message, that message is removed from the queue.

You can move queues between databases and between servers because they are, after all, just tables. Larger applications might also need multiple copies of a queue spread across many machines to handle the volume of messages being sent. So Service Broker provides an abstraction layer to isolate applications from the physical storage that contains the messages that need to be processed. This abstraction layer is called a *service*.

Services in a Service Broker application provide a little more than a simple abstraction layer. A service is attached to a single queue to abstract the physical storage. And the service also serves as a constraint on the conversations that are allowed, providing a well-defined interface for applications that describes the processing that the service can perform.

A service constrains the types of conversations that are allowed by specifying the objects, or *contracts*, that can be used. The purpose of a contract is to define the list of messages that can be sent or received.

Service Broker messages are further constrained by a formatting mechanism called a *message type*. The message type ensures that only messages that contain proper formatting are accepted. For example, you can use the message type to ensure that an endpoint that understands only English receives only English messages.

Messaging-Application Interaction

With Service Broker's infrastructure defined, the question of how to use it with your applications still remains. The interface for an application is straightforward.

Instead of inserting a row of data into a table, Service Broker applications push messages onto a queue, and the messages are picked up at a later time and processed. To accomplish this, an application starts a conversation, sends the message to a service, and then closes the conversation. Because the service is linked to a queue, this action places a message onto the queue, and the message can then be processed later without requiring the application to wait for a response.

Figure 20-1 illustrates a basic Service Broker application.

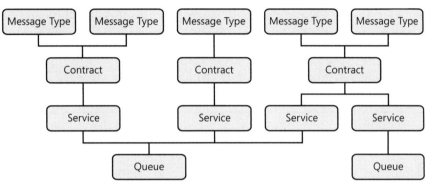

Figure 20-1   Defining the relationship between Service Broker objects

Enabling Service Broker

Like all SQL Server 2005 services that are not required to run the core engine, Service Broker is disabled by default. To use the Service Broker infrastructure, you must enable it. You first need to create a database master key that will be used as the session key for all conversations.

To enable Service Broker, execute the following command:

```
ALTER DATABASE <database_name> SET ENABLE_BROKER
```

CAUTION   Case-sensitive naming conventions

All identifiers in Service Broker use a binary collation and are, therefore, case sensitive, regardless of the collation settings in a particular database or instance.

Quick Check
- What are the components involved in a Service Broker application, and what function does each provide?

Quick Check Answer
- A *message type* provides a name for a message that is allowed to be sent to an endpoint.

- A *contract* provides a list of message types that are allowed to be used.

- A *queue* is the storage structure used to store messages that need to be processed.

- A *service* provides an abstraction layer for an application; it is tied to a queue and restricts the types of messages that are allowed based on contracts it is defined to use.

- A *conversation* is the means by which messages are sent to a queue for processing.

PRACTICE Enable Service Broker

In this practice, you will enable Service Broker and create a database master key to be used as a session key for the Service Broker conversations.

1. Launch SQL Server Management Studio (SSMS), connect to your instance, and open a new query window.

2. Execute the following batch to enable Service Broker and create the master key:

```
ALTER DATABASE AdventureWorks SET ENABLE_BROKER
GO
USE AdventureWorks
GO
CREATE MASTER KEY
ENCRYPTION BY PASSWORD = 'fgU6*%japTwS^3L!#n'
GO
```

NOTE Creating a database master key

If you already created a master key for the *AdventureWorks* database in a previous exercise, you can skip these steps because a database is allowed to have only one master key.

MORE INFO Master keys

For information about creating database master keys, see Chapter 2, "Configuring SQL Server 2005."

Lesson Summary

- Service Broker provides the infrastructure needed to build reliable, secure, and scalable messaging applications.

- Service Broker conversations enable applications to interact with Service Broker services, which are attached to each message queue.

- Services validate messages that are sent to the queue by enforcing contracts and message types.

- After a message has passed this validation, the service places the message on a queue, where it can be processed by a background task.

Lesson Review

The following questions are intended to reinforce key information presented in this lesson. The questions are also available on the companion CD if you prefer to review them in electronic form.

NOTE Answers

Answers to these questions and explanations of why each answer choice is right or wrong are located in the "Answers" section at the end of the book.

---

1. Which of the following are valid Service Broker objects? (Choose all that apply.)

    A. dialog

    B. conversation

    C. queue

    D. message

Lesson 2: Creating Message Types and Contracts

For any communication to succeed, both parties must agree on the acceptable format of the information being exchanged. People accomplish this task without conscious thought. If a question is asked in Spanish, the response that provides the information requested is also in Spanish. If that same question were asked in English, the response would be returned in English. However, if the person asking the question were speaking French and the person being asked understood only German, communication would fail.

In Service Broker, message types ensure reliable communication by enforcing an agreed-upon format for message content that is transmitted between two endpoints. Contracts, in turn, control the message types that are allowed within a conversation, defining both the acceptable input and the acceptable output that will be returned. In this lesson, you will see how to create message types and contracts to define appropriate communication between application components.

After this lesson, you will be able to:

■ Create message types.

■ Create a contract.

Estimated lesson time: 15 minutes

Creating Message Types

A message type is composed of two key components: name and *validation*. The generic form of the command to create a message type is as follows:

```
CREATE MESSAGE TYPE message_type_name
    [ AUTHORIZATION owner_name ]
    [ VALIDATION = {  NONE
                    | EMPTY
                    | WELL_FORMED_XML
                    | VALID_XML WITH SCHEMA COLLECTION
                                            schema_collection_name
                    } ]
```

The *message_type_name* clause can be any name that is valid for an identifier. However, you will want to carefully consider each name that you create. Service Broker applications communicate between two databases that are usually on different instances. You will want to ensure that each message type name is globally unique, so developers usually name them by using a URL.

The *AUTHORIZATION* clause specifies the owner of the message type.

The *VALIDATION* clause specifies whether messages are validated or not when they are submitted. All Service Broker messages have a data type of *VARBINARY(MAX)*. However, messages can be composed of up to 2 gigabytes of data that doesn't have to meet any specific requirements. Table 20-1 describes the validation options that are available for a message type.

Table 20-1   Validation Options for Message Type

Option	Description
EMPTY	Forces the message body to contain no data.
NONE	The message body can contain any data in any format.
WELL_FORMED_XML	The message body is allowed to be only a well-formed XML document.
VALID_XML WITH SCHEMA COLLECTION	The message body must be a well-formed XML document, and the document must conform to one of the schemas in the specified *schema collection*.

When you specify a validation method of either *WELL_FORMED_XML* or *VALID_XML WITH SCHEMA COLLECTION*, the message is loaded into an XML parser and validated when it arrives at either endpoint. This parser validation can add overhead in the processing. If your Service Broker application accepts messages from external sources that you cannot control, you usually specify one of these options. However, if you control all the applications that are creating messages, or your application includes code to handle various messages, you will want to specify *NONE* to eliminate the parser overhead.

Here is an example message type statement specifying a URL name for the message type and the validation option *VALID_XML WITH SCHEMA COLLECTION*:

```
CREATE MESSAGE TYPE [http://broker.SolidQualityLearning.com/test/CheckClasses]
VALIDATION = VALID_XML WITH SCHEMA COLLECTION
[http://broker.SolidQualityLearning.com/test/CourseSchemas]
```

IMPORTANT   Object naming

All names in a Service Broker application are case sensitive. All messages are transmitted with a binary collation to ensure that different collation sequences between endpoints do not cause data loss due to character set compatibility issues.

Quick Check

- What validation options are available for message types?

Quick Check Answers

- *EMPTY* specifies that no data is contained in the message.

- *NONE* specifies that the message can contain any data and is not validated.

- *WELL_FORMED_XML* uses an XML parser to guarantee that a valid XML document is within the message body.

- *VALID_XML WITH SCHEMA COLLECTION* loads an XML parser and validates the message body against the schemas in the specified schema collection.

Creating a Contract

A contract contains a list of message types and the services that are allowed to send them. The generic form of the statement to create a contract is as follows:

```
CREATE CONTRACT contract_name
   [ AUTHORIZATION owner_name ]
      ( {  { message_type_name | [ DEFAULT ] }
          SENT BY { INITIATOR | TARGET | ANY }
       } [ ,...n] )
```

The *contract_name* clause provides a convenient way to refer to a group of message types. The name must conform to the rules for identifiers and, like all other names in Service Broker components, is case sensitive.

The *AUTHORIZATION* clause sets the owner of the contract.

The body of a contract specifies the message types that are allowed as well as which service is allowed to send a given message type. If the *SENT BY* clause specifies *INITI-ATOR*, only the service that started the conversation can use that message type. If the *SENT BY* clause specifies *TARGET*, only the service that is processing messages on the queue can send that message type. If the *SENT BY* clause specifies *ANY*, either service can send a message of that type.

Let's look at an example of defining a contract for several message types.

Let's say you are developing an application that lets a user select a product from a list. The product ID that the user selects will be sent by the application to the database, and the database will return a result set that includes the Bill Of Materials associated with the specified product ID. After the Bill Of Materials is received, additional processing will occur. The sending of the product ID and the returning of the associated Bill Of Materials might take awhile, so you also need to define a mechanism to allow either side to find out the status of their request.

Here is how you can use Service Broker message types and a contract to accomplish this processing. First, you would create a message type of *RequestBillOfMaterials*, which is used to send the product ID to the database; a message type of *ReturnBillOf-Materials*, which is used to return the result set to the application; and a message type of *StatusRequest*. Because all three message types define a logical process, you can combine them into a contract. The process is initiated with a message type of *Request-BillOfMaterials*, so the contract would specify this message type with a *SENT BY INITIATOR* clause because the destination for the message would not have the capability to generate a message that contained the product ID. The database that accepts the product ID input and returns the result set will use the *ReturnBillOfMaterials* message type with a *SENT BY TARGET* clause because the source of the product ID would not have the capability to generate a result set. The *StatusRequest* message type can be used by either one, so you will define it with the *SENT BY ANY* clause because either participant in the conversation can request the status at any time.

Because contracts define the type of messages allowed as well as which side of the conversation can use a particular message type, there is one more requirement for defining a contract. Messages cannot be sent spontaneously. Therefore, every contract must contain at least one message type that can be used by the service that initiates a conversation, meaning that at least one message type must have the *SENT BY* clause specifying either *INITIATOR* or *ANY*.

PRACTICE Creating Message Types and Contracts

In these two practices, you will create the basic message structures required for a Service Broker application.

▶ **Practice 1: Create a Message Type**

In this practice, you create a message type that will be used to request a bill of materials from the *AdventureWorks* database. You also create a message type for the result set that will be returned in response to the request.

NOTE Practice assumptions

All exercises in this chapter assume that the Service Broker application is entirely internal to your environment, which enables us to drop the URL naming convention, leaving you with less typing to do.

---

1. Launch SSMS, connect to SQL Server, and open a new query window.

2. To create the following two message types

   ❑ The requesting message type named *SubmitBOMProduct* with the validation option *WELL_FORMED_XML*

   ❑ The message type to return results, named *ReceiveBillOfMaterials*, which also uses the validation option *WELL_FORMED_XML*

   type the following batch:

```
CREATE MESSAGE TYPE SubmitBOMProduct
VALIDATION = WELL_FORMED_XML
CREATE MESSAGE TYPE ReceiveBillOfMaterials
VALIDATION = WELL_FORMED_XML
```

▶ **Practice 2: Create a Contract**

In this practice, you create a contract for the message types that you defined in Practice 1.

1. If necessary, launch SSMS, connect to SQL Server, and open a new query window.

2. Type the following batch to create the *BillOfMaterialsContract* contract for the message types *SubmitBOMProduct* and *ReceiveBillOfMaterials*:

```
CREATE CONTRACT BillOfMaterialsContract
(SubmitBOMProduct SENT BY INITIATOR,
ReceiveBillOfMaterials SENT BY TARGET)
```

Lesson Summary

■ Message types enforce an agreed-upon format for messages that are transmitted between two endpoints, defining the information that is acceptable in a message body.

■ When creating a message type, you have the option of specifying a value for the *VALIDATION* clause, which specifies whether messages are validated when they are submitted.

■ Contracts restrict the types of messages that can be used in a particular conversation, providing an interface in which the inputs and outputs are completely defined.

■ When you define a contract, you must specify which service is allowed to send a given message type: the initiator, the target, or any.

Lesson Review

The following questions are intended to reinforce key information presented in this lesson. The questions are also available on the companion CD if you prefer to review them in electronic form.

NOTE   **Answers**

Answers to these questions and explanations of why each answer choice is right or wrong are located in the "Answers" section at the end of the book.

---

1. Which of the following are validation options for a message type? (Choose all that apply.)

   A. *NULL*

   B. *ANY*

   C. *WELL_FORMED_XML*

   D. *NONE*

2. What do contracts define?

   A. Valid XML for a message

   B. Where messages are going to be stored

   C. Which messages are valid for a conversation

   D. The services that are valid for a conversation

Lesson 3: Creating Queues and Services

Service Broker queues contain all the information that needs to be processed. Put simply, queues are tables that contain one or more messages. Although you could spend a significant amount of time defining message types and contracts, without queues—and more particularly, something on a queue—a Service Broker application would be worthless. A Service Broker service, in turn, defines a queue for a conversation to use and restricts the types of conversations that are allowed on that queue. This lesson will show you how to define queues and services for your Service Broker infrastructure, highlighting the key options you need to specify.

After this lesson, you will be able to:

- Create queues.
- Create services.

Estimated lesson time: 25 minutes

Creating a Message Queue

Service Broker is designed to facilitate reliable *asynchronous processing*. An application submits a processing request in the form of a message and then continues on with other work. That process accomplishes the asynchronous piece of the processing equation. However, the message has to be stored somewhere so that it is retained for another process to work on. You could store the message by writing the data into a memory structure and then providing a reference to that structure. But any power loss or reboot will cause messages to be lost. Instead, you need a mechanism to safely store the valuable business data that is contained within a message and protect it against failures, including the loss of the server in which the message was originally stored.

A queue is the mechanism that stores all messages within a Service Broker application. SQL Server 2005 implements queues by using a new feature called *hidden tables*. This feature prevents a queue from being directly accessed by an application via *INSERT*, *UPDATE*, *DELETE*, or *SELECT* statements while still allowing the storage engine to treat it as any other table. Because queues are recognized by the storage engine, you can use most of the SQL Server high-availability techniques, including clustering, log shipping, database mirroring, and backup/restore, to ensure that data is not lost from a queue.

The general format of the command to create a queue is as follows:

```
CREATE QUEUE <object>
  [ WITH
    [ STATUS = { ON | OFF } [ , ] ]
    [ RETENTION = { ON | OFF } [ , ] ]
    [ ACTIVATION (
        [ STATUS = { ON | OFF } , ]
          PROCEDURE_NAME = <procedure> ,
          MAX_QUEUE_READERS = max_readers ,
          EXECUTE AS { SELF | 'user_name' | OWNER }
          ) ]
  ]
  [ ON { filegroup | [ DEFAULT ] } ]
```

An example of the simplest form of this command is the following:

```
CREATE QUEUE BOMProductIDQueue
```

Quick Check

- What is the purpose of a queue within a Service Broker application?

Quick Check Answer

- Queues store the messages that need to be processed by a Service Broker application.

The first thing that you should note with this command is the lack of syntax used to define a table. Although a queue is a physical table in the storage engine that consumes disk space, the structure is fixed, and you cannot change it. Because the structure of a queue is fixed, syntax does not need to exist to define the structure.

The *ON* clause of the *CREATE QUEUE* statement functions the same as any other object that stores data. This clause lets you specify the filegroup on which a queue should be created.

BEST PRACTICES   Queue storage

For most Service Broker applications, you should create a dedicated filegroup or set of filegroups for any queues, which facilitates recovery operations and enables you to target backups. Because you can back up and restore filegroups independently, you can maintain availability of data while recovering a queue or recover a queue independently of the remainder of the database. For applications that are processing a high volume of messages, you should isolate the storage to minimize any disk bottlenecks.

MORE INFO   Filegroup backup and restore

For more details about filegroup backup and restore, see Chapter 11, "Backing Up, Restoring, and Moving a Database."

The *STATUS* clause determines whether the queue is enabled. When a queue is set to *STATUS = OFF*, it does not allow any messages to be added to or removed from the queue.

The *RETENTION* clause determines whether messages are automatically removed from the queue after they are processed. When *RETENTION = ON*, all messages in the queue are retained. After the conversation that processed the messages has been explicitly closed, the messages that were processed by the conversation are removed from the queue. So the *RETENTION* value is used to allow a conversation that performs multiple operations to detect errors and perform compensating actions.

The most interesting capability of a queue resides in the *ACTIVATION* clause. Service Broker is used to enable asynchronous applications. And because of the nature of an asynchronous application, an application does not have any direct way to know when new work has arrived and needs to be processed. Without Service Broker's *ACTIVATION* option, you would need to create a process that causes the application to periodically poll for new work. Such a process would result in an enormous amount of wasted time and resources spent just finding out whether work needs to be done.

However, when you define a queue with an *ACTIVATION* clause, a stored procedure is automatically executed when a message is placed on the queue. This functionality eliminates any polling that you would have to create in other message-based applications.

The *STATUS* option for the *ACTIVATION* clause specifies whether a procedure will automatically be executed when a new message arrives. If *STATUS = ON*, the stored procedure specified in the *PROCEDURE_NAME* option automatically launches to begin processing messages. This procedure executes under the security context you specify in the *EXECUTE AS* option.

When a message arrives in the queue, the stored procedure specified in the *ACTIVATION* clause is automatically launched only if there isn't already a stored procedure running to process the messages. This piece of the activation algorithm ensures that resources are not wasted polling for work or launching many copies of a stored procedure. The procedure would then begin processing messages in the queue until the queue is empty; then it would exit.

A second piece of the activation algorithm helps balance the resources available for processing. If a stored procedure is already running to process messages in the queue, the rate at which messages are *dequeued* is compared to the rate at which they are *enqueued*. If Service Broker determines that messages are arriving faster than they can be processed by the existing procedures already running, another copy of the stored procedure is launched, up to the maximum number configured in the *MAX_QUEUE_READERS* option.

Activation is not a requirement for coding Service Broker applications because many methods for processing messages are equally valid. However, queue activation makes it much easier to write automatic processing algorithms.

Real World

Michael Hotek

In mid-2005, I was working with a customer to define the company's adoption path for SQL Server 2005. The firm performed many tuning iterations on its application and was still barely getting by. And the IT staff hoped that SQL Server 2005 would be able to help them increase the capacity of their application because they could switch to a code base written natively in 64-bit code running on new 64-bit dual-core machines.

We started by looking at the types of queries the application was running and the execution statistics for those queries. What we encountered was a relatively interesting distribution of queries in the environment. It turned out that a single stored procedure was responsible for more than 95 percent of the total query volume executed against the core server. This procedure normally ran in a few milliseconds, but the purpose of the procedure was to check for new work to perform. The application managed an automated testing platform. Test administrators would define new tests and then dispatch them. An infrastructure component would then assign the test to a machine, the machine would execute the test, and the results would be returned to the central test dispatcher. We originally thought that tests were pushed out to the target machine, which was an incorrect assumption on our part.

The set of tests to execute were added to a processing queue. Each machine in the architecture would then periodically poll for new work to perform. When tests were found in the queue that had not yet been assigned, the dispatcher would assign the test to a machine so that other machines would not also execute the test. All the metadata related to the test to execute would then be downloaded to the machines. After they received the downloaded metadata, the machines would perform all the tasks necessary to complete the tests and then upload the results back to the dispatcher.

The story doesn't end there, though. Machines could crash, lock up, become unresponsive, and otherwise fail. After all, the company was testing applications to find bugs, and some of those bugs could cause problems on the machines. So after a test was dispatched, another component would periodically poll the machines to ensure that they were still alive and the test was still executing. This polling accounted for another 4 percent of the queries within the architecture.

In summary, a large amount of effort was expended in building a highly scalable and robust system to dispatch tests and receive results. The system had to handle thousands of test machines with hundreds of test administrators, and it would need to be extended into tens of thousands of test machines in the future. The existing system simply could not cope with the volume.

This is where Service Broker—in particular, queue activation—could play an extremely important role. Instead of having to constantly poll for new work, the system could implement queue activation to dispatch work when new messages reach the queue. Because Service Broker ensures that a message is processed only once, the infrastructure was already in place to ensure that two machines wouldn't receive the same test. The semantics available within a Service Broker conversation let a test be aborted when the test machine hasn't responded within a specified period of time while also enabling the infrastructure to send periodic status updates. Because of the transactional nature that you can impose in Service Broker, if a test machine were to crash, the message that initiated the test would be placed back in the queue and could be immediately dispatched to another machine for processing.

This customer's conversion from its previous architecture into a new Service Broker–based architecture is still ongoing. But we will be able to eliminate almost 98 percent of the queries that are currently being executed and replace them with queue activation. The Service Broker infrastructure will also replace all the custom code that needed to be written to manage the custom queue infrastructure. Service Broker will allow the existing platform to scale much further and will provide new features that can drive the testing process even more reliably than before.

Creating a Service

A service defines the endpoint, or queue, that a conversation will use as well as the types of conversations, or contracts, that are allowed on a queue. The general format of the command to create a new service is as follows:

```
CREATE SERVICE service_name
  [ AUTHORIZATION owner_name ]
  ON QUEUE [ schema_name. ]queue_name
  [ ( contract_name | [DEFAULT] [ ,...n ] ) ]
```

As with all Service Broker objects previously discussed, the *AUTHORIZATION* clause defines the owner of the service.

You specify a single queue name in the *ON QUEUE* clause. So for effective communication to occur, you need to create two services: one for the initiator and one for the target. In the body of the *CREATE SERVICE* command, you then specify one or more contracts for the specified queue.

Service Abstraction

You might be wondering why you can't have an application reference a queue directly instead of having to create yet another object that essentially provides a pointer to the queue.

Service Broker applications are designed to be distributed as well as to provide load-balancing capability. A particular service could reference multiple queues on multiple machines to provide scalability and load balancing. It is also possible to back up a queue and move it to another machine in case of a disaster or when you need to increase processing capacity.

If applications directly accessed queues, any infrastructure changes would require you to rewrite the applications. The service provides an interface abstraction for applications. An administrator can then manage the infrastructure as needed to provide the capacity and recoverability required without affecting the application.

A basic example of a statement to create a service is as follows:

```
CREATE SERVICE BOMRequestService
ON QUEUE BOMProductIDQueue
(BillOfMaterialsContract)
```

> **Quick Check**
> - What capability does a service enable for a Service Broker application?
>
> **Quick Check Answer**
> - A service defines the endpoint (queue) that is used for requests and the types of conversations (contracts) that are allowed on the queue, providing an abstraction layer for applications to interact with Service Broker so that changes in infrastructure do not require changes to an application.

PRACTICE Creating Queues and Services

In these practices, you create the message storage system as well as the abstraction interface for a Service Broker application.

▶ **Practice 1: Create a Queue**

In this practice, you create two basic queues to work with the message types and contracts you created in Lesson 2. Because the processing you use these for is manual in nature, you do not need to specify any activation.

1. If necessary, launch SSMS, connect to your SQL Server instance, and open a new query window.

2. Execute the following batch to create two queues named *BOMProductIDQueue* and *BOMResultQueue*:

```
CREATE QUEUE BOMProductIDQueue
CREATE QUEUE BOMResultQueue
```

▶ **Practice 2: Create a Service**

In this practice, you create the two services that will be used in our ongoing example to enable a product ID to be sent to a database and have a Bill of Materials returned.

1. If necessary, launch SSMS, connect to your instance, and open a new query window.

2. Type in and execute the following batch to create two services—*BOMRequestService* and *BOMResponseService*—on the queues you just created and to allow the contract called *BillOfMaterialsContract*.

```
CREATE SERVICE BOMRequestService
ON QUEUE BOMProductIDQueue
(BillOfMaterialsContract)
CREATE SERVICE BOMResponseService
ON QUEUE BOMResultQueue
(BillOfMaterialsContract)
```

Lesson Summary

- Queues store messages until they can be processed.

- Because queues are hidden tables within the storage engine, they can be backed up and even restored to another server in the event of failure, ensuring the reliability of messages that are sent for processing.

- By using the activation capability of queues, you can create automated systems that begin processing messages as soon as they arrive on the queue.

- A Service Broker service defines the main communication path for a conversation, including the endpoint (queue) to use and the types of conversations (contracts) that are allowed on the queue.

Lesson Review

The following questions are intended to reinforce key information presented in this lesson. The questions are also available on the companion CD if you prefer to review them in electronic form.

NOTE Answers

Answers to these questions and explanations of why each answer choice is right or wrong are located in the "Answers" section at the end of the book.

---

1. Which queue feature controls how many applications are available to process messages placed on a queue?

    A. retention

    B. activation

    C. Maximum Number Of Queue Readers

    D. Stored Procedure To Execute

2. Which Service Broker objects are defined by a service? (Choose all that apply.)

    A. message type

    B. dialog

    C. queue

    D. contract

Lesson 4: Creating Conversations

Conversations provide a mechanism for reliable and ordered processing of messages across transactions, server restarts, and even disasters without requiring you to write large volumes of custom code. In this lesson, you will see how to start a conversation for sending messages and then how to define routes for messages that a service sends across a conversation.

After this lesson, you will be able to:

- Create conversations.
- Understand routing of messages on conversations.

Estimated lesson time: 15 minutes

Create a Conversation

One of the more difficult issues to solve with asynchronous applications is ensuring that messages are processed in order. Message order is a bit more flexible than in a strict database transaction. Message ordering ensures that multiple related messages are processed in sequence instead of in random order.

As an example, consider an order entry application. Messages are placed on the queue for each order that is submitted. Individual messages appear for the order header and for each order line item. When the messages are processed by an application, the application must ensure that the order header is processed first, followed by each line item. If a line item were to be processed before the order header, errors would occur. Although the order header and associated line items must be processed in a particular sequence, multiple orders can be processed simultaneously.

To ensure that messages are received and processed in the same order as they are sent, each message has a sequence number. Because this sequence number is persistent, message order is guaranteed, even through a restart of the instance.

Because some messages could be received while communications errors might cause others to not reach the endpoint, Service Broker has a mechanism to retry messages until they are successfully received, guaranteeing that no gaps exist in the message sequence. With other messaging systems, you would have to create your own sequence numbers as well as code the retry logic to ensure that all messages have been received. But again, this capability is built into Service Broker. Applications simply place messages on a queue and take them off a queue for processing. Service

Broker ensures that the messages are delivered to the endpoint and processed in the correct order.

A Service Broker conversation implements this reliable ordered process for delivering messages via services. To start a conversation, you would issue a *BEGIN DIALOG CONVERSATION* command, as the following general syntax shows:

```
BEGIN DIALOG [ CONVERSATION ] @dialog_handle
    FROM SERVICE initiator_service_name
    TO SERVICE 'target_service_name'
        [ , { 'service_broker_guid' | 'CURRENT DATABASE' } ]
    [ ON CONTRACT contract_name ]
    [ WITH
    [ { RELATED_CONVERSATION = related_conversation_handle
      | RELATED_CONVERSATION_GROUP = related_conversation_group_id } ]
    [ [ , ] LIFETIME = dialog_lifetime ]
    [ [ , ] ENCRYPTION = { ON | OFF }  ] ]
```

When a conversation is started, it returns a unique identifier that is used to reference the dialog that has been created. The return value is placed into the *@dialog_handle* variable.

The first two clauses specify the service that is used to initiate the conversation and the service that is the target. After the services are specified, a contract is also required. The *ON CONTRACT* clause specifies which contract defined for the target service will be used for this conversation.

You can also group multiple conversations together to form a logical process. To group conversations, you can use either the *RELATED_CONVERSATION* or *RELATED_CONVERSATION_GROUP* options.

The *LIFETIME* option specifies the maximum number of seconds the conversation is allowed to exist. If the dialog is not explicitly ended at both the initiator and target before this time expires, an error is returned, and any open processing is rolled back. The *ENCRYPTION* option specifies whether messages that are sent and received are to be encrypted.

NOTE Encryption

Messages are encrypted only if they are exchanged between SQL Server instances. If messages are sent and received within the same instance of SQL Server, they are never encrypted.

Quick Check

- What are the elements required to create a conversation?

Quick Check Answer

- A conversation requires you to specify two services and a contract. One service defines the initiator of the dialog; the other service defines the target of the dialog. The specified contract has to be accepted by the target service.

Routing Messages to a Service

When a service sends a message over a conversation, Service Broker uses routes to locate the service to receive the message. When that service responds, Service Broker then uses routes to locate the initiator service.

To determine the route for a conversation, SQL Server matches the service name and the broker instance identifier that you specified in the *BEGIN DIALOG CONVERSATION* statement against the service name and broker instance identifier that are specified in the route. If a route does not provide a service name or broker instance identifier, any service name or broker instance identifier can be a match. For services that do not have a route defined, each database has a default route called *AutoCreatedLocal* that ensures that messages are delivered within the current SQL Server instance.

MORE INFO   Selecting a route

When more than one route matches a conversation, SQL Server uses a complex process to select a route. For information about this process, see the SQL Server 2005 Books Online topic "Service Broker Routing." SQL Server 2005 Books Online is installed as part of SQL Server 2005. Updates for SQL Server 2005 Books Online are available for download at *www.microsoft.com/technet/prodtechnol/sql/2005/downloads/books.mspx*.

When the initiator receives an acknowledgment message from the target, the initiator uses the broker instance identifier in the acknowledgment message to route subsequent messages to the same target.

For each database that contains a service, you can specify a route for the external services that the service communicates with. You use the *CREATE ROUTE* statement to add a new route to the routing table for the current database. You should specify three key components for the *CREATE ROUTE* statement: the name of the service for the route, the broker instance identifier of the database to send the messages to, and the network address of the broker that hosts the service.

For messages on conversations within the local instance, Service Broker determines routing by checking the routing table, *sys.routes*, in the local database. For messages on conversations that originate in another instance, Service Broker checks the routes in *msdb.sys.routes*.

PRACTICE **Create a Conversation**

In this practice, you create a conversation that will use your previously created services and contracts.

1. If necessary, launch SSMS, connect to your instance, and open a new query window.

2. Execute the following batch to begin a conversation between the *BOMRequestService* and the *BOMResponseService*:

```
DECLARE @dialoghandle  uniqueidentifier

BEGIN DIALOG CONVERSATION @dialoghandle
FROM SERVICE BOMRequestService
TO SERVICE 'BOMResponseService'
ON CONTRACT BillOfMaterialsContract

SELECT @dialoghandle
```

NOTE **Using the conversation**

Please leave the query window open for the next exercise, which uses the conversation you just created.

Lesson Summary

- Conversations provide a mechanism for reliable and ordered processing of messages, even across transactions, server restarts, or disasters.

- Conversations define that all messages are exchanged between an initiator service and a target service that is constrained by a particular contract.

Lesson Review

The following questions are intended to reinforce key information presented in this lesson. The questions are also available on the companion CD if you prefer to review them in electronic form.

NOTE Answers

Answers to these questions and explanations of why each answer choice is right or wrong are located in the "Answers" section at the end of the book.

---

1. How does a conversation ensure a message order?

   A. Message ID

   B. Sequence number

   C. Conversation ID

   D. Contract ID

Lesson 5: Sending and Receiving Messages

After building the infrastructure of a Service Broker application, you need a way to place messages onto a queue and take messages off the queue for processing. In this lesson, you will first see how to use the *SEND* command to place messages on a queue for processing. And then you will see how to use the *RECEIVE* command to remove one or more messages from the queue as a result set that is then passed to the calling application for further processing.

After this lesson, you will be able to:

■ Send messages.

■ Receive messages.

Estimated lesson time: 15 minutes

Sending Messages

The message-queuing process begins with a process that places on a queue messages that need to be processed. After the messages are written to the queue, this process is complete and can continue on with other tasks. The syntax for placing messages on a queue, a process called *enqueuing*, is as follows:

```
SEND
    ON CONVERSATION conversation_handle
    [ MESSAGE TYPE message_type_name ]
    [ ( message_body_expression ) ];
```

CAUTION   Command terminator

If the *SEND* command is not the first statement in a batch, the previous statement must be terminated with a semicolon.

The *SEND* command takes the handle of a conversation that was started. You can also specify a *MESSAGE TYPE*, but this is usually left off to push the type checking down to the contract that is in use for the conversation. The main piece of information is the message body.

The *SEND* command places the contents of the message body onto the queue that is active for the conversation. You can then retrieve the contents of a queue by using a *SELECT* statement, as follows:

```
SELECT <column list> FROM <queue name>
```

For example, to retrieve the message body contents from the *BOMResultQueue* queue, you would use the following query:

```
SELECT * FROM BOMResultQueue
```

Receive Messages

After messages have been placed on a queue, they must be processed. The syntax to take messages off the queue, a process called dequeuing, is as follows:

```
RECEIVE [ TOP ( n ) ]
        <column_specifier> [ ,...n ]
        FROM <queue>
        [ INTO table_variable ]
        [ WHERE {  conversation_handle = conversation_handle
                 | conversation_group_id = conversation_group_id } ];
```

CAUTION **Command terminator**

If the *RECEIVE* command is not the first statement in a batch, the previous statement must be terminated with a semicolon.

The *RECEIVE* command returns the requested messages as a result set that is then passed to the calling application for further processing. Although the result set that is returned can be manipulated directly, it is generally written to a table variable and then processed from there.

Because a queue can contain messages from multiple conversations, you can restrict the messages that are retrieved to a particular conversation or *conversation group*. This restriction is useful when a receiving process needs to operate on multiple messages in sequence.

Unless *RETENTION* is specified for a queue, each message that is returned by the *RECEIVE* command is removed from the queue.

MORE INFO **Receive operational details**

For more detailed information on the *RECEIVE* command, see the SQL Server 2005 Books Online topic "RECEIVE (Transact-SQL)."

> **Quick Check**
> - How are messages processed for a Service Broker application?
>
> **Quick Check Answer**
> - The *SEND* command places messages that need to be processed on a queue. The *RECEIVE* command removes one or more messages from the queue as a result set that is then passed to the calling application for further processing.

PRACTICE Send and Receive Messages

In this practice, you will send messages to a queue and receive messages from a queue. This practice performs multiple steps to let you view the contents of the queues at each step. All activity for a conversation is specified by using a conversation handle. This exercise uses a generic placeholder of *<conversation handle>* within the syntax. You must replace this placeholder with the actual conversation handle you are using. (Be sure to enclose the conversation handle in quotes.) If you are not sure what the conversation handle is, you can retrieve it from *sys.conversation_endpoints*.

1. In the Query window within SSMS, view the contents of both queues you created by executing the following batch:

   ```
   SELECT * FROM BOMProductIDQueue
   SELECT * FROM BOMResultQueue;
   ```

2. Observe that both queues are empty.

3. Using the conversation handle generated in the previous exercise, execute the following command to send a message of type *SubmitBOMProduct*:

   ```
   SEND ON CONVERSATION 'conversation handle'
      MESSAGE TYPE SubmitBOMProduct
      (N'<ProductID>6</ProductID>');
   ```

4. Again, view the contents of both queues by executing the following batch:

   ```
   SELECT * FROM BOMProductIDQueue
   SELECT * FROM BOMResultQueue;
   ```

5. Observe that the initiator queue is empty and that the target queue has a row of data. By casting the *message_body* column to an XML data type, you can view the contents in a human-readable format.

6. Using the conversation handle generated in the previous exercise, execute the following command:

```
RECEIVE TOP (1) *
FROM BOMResultQueue
```

7. Observe that you received a result set as output from this command.

8. View the contents of both queues by executing the following batch:

```
SELECT * FROM BOMProductIDQueue
SELECT * FROM BOMResultQueue;
```

9. Observe that both queues are empty again.

Lesson Summary

■ The infrastructure of a Service Broker application would not be useful without a way to place messages on a queue and then pull those messages off the queue for further processing.

■ The *SEND* command places messages on a queue.

■ The *RECEIVE* command pulls off one or more messages for processing.

Lesson Review

The following questions are intended to reinforce key information presented in this lesson. The questions are also available on the companion CD if you prefer to review them in electronic form.

NOTE   Answers

Answers to these questions and explanations of why each answer choice is right or wrong are located in the "Answers" section at the end of the book.

---

1. Which of the following are required for the *SEND* command? (Choose all that apply.)

   A. First statement in batch

   B. Conversation handle

   C. Message type

   D. Queue

2. Which of the following are required for the *RECEIVE* command? (Choose all that apply.)

    A. Contract

    B. Message Type

    C. First statement in batch

    D. Queue

Chapter Review

To further practice and reinforce the skills you learned in this chapter, you can

- Review the chapter summary.
- Review the list of key terms introduced in this chapter.
- Complete the case scenario. This scenario sets up a real-world situation involving the topics of this chapter and asks you to create a solution.
- Complete the suggested practices.
- Take a practice test.

Chapter Summary

- Service Broker provides a robust, scalable, distributed, reliable platform for building asynchronous messaging applications.
- Message types and contracts are used to constrain and validate the formats for messages that applications can deliver.
- A service provides an abstraction layer over a queue that enables you to develop applications without being concerned about the physical implementation.
- Conversations provide a way to place messages on a queue in an ordered and reliable manner.
- The *SEND* and *RECEIVE* commands provide the infrastructure for reliably and predictably sending messages to a service and receiving them from a service, letting developers focus on building the logic of their systems instead.

Key Terms

Do you know what these key terms mean? You can check your answers by looking up the terms in the glossary at the end of the book.

- activation
- asynchronous processing
- contract
- conversation
- conversation group

- dequeue
- dialog
- endpoint
- enqueue
- hidden tables
- message
- message type
- monolog
- queue
- queue reader
- receive
- retention
- schema collection
- send
- service
- transmission queue
- validation

Case Scenario: Building a Service Broker Application

In the following case scenario, you will apply what you've learned in this chapter. You can find answers to these questions in the "Answers" section at the end of this book.

Wide World Importers is an import business that stocks a wide array of products from various countries around the world. The company maintains inventory for more than 80,000 products, which are routinely ordered by wholesale customers through the company's business-to-business Web portal. Customers can directly enter requests in a form or use a Web service to submit their orders via a standard application programming interface (API).

Wide World Importers also enables customers to request several billion additional products from more than 100,000 different suppliers through its brokerage services, which take care of ordering, shipping, customs clearance, and direct delivery to the customer's warehouse. Because of the nature of the business, inventory is never checked before requests are submitted.

After a customer request is submitted, it needs to be validated to determine whether it contains products that are stocked or that need to be brokered. If it contains products that are stocked, further processing is required to determine whether sufficent inventory is available to meet the order and, if so, to allocate the inventory. The allocation process generates an order that contains all the line items that can be immediately processed. This allocation process needs to trigger a restocking notice if inventory levels fall below a predefined threshold.

Orders with available inventory get processed through the normal fulfillment channels that include automatic credit checks, order acceptance notifications, physical pull of inventory, packaging, shipment, delivery, and acceptance by the customer as well as status notifications for the order. Requests for items that are stocked but for which there is insufficient inventory cause a new order to be generated containing the out-of-stock items.

Requests with items that need to be brokered are routed into a separate queue, which requires manual intervention by a user to source the product. After products are sourced with a supplier and a purchase contract is entered, the request is turned into an order tied to the purchase contract and follows a special fulfillment process that tracks the shipment, customs clearance, and delivery to Wide World Importers—and then into the normal fulfillment channel.

Wide World Importers needs to increase efficiency and speed up the release of new services, many of which can't be launched because of lack of resources in the IT department. The IT department employs 35 developers and administrators to monitor and troubleshoot the millions of lines of custom code that were created to manage the business. You are charged with figuring out a way to reduce the number of people working on all this custom code so that they can be allocated to new products that will improve the business. Given the features you have learned about in this chapter, what would you do?

Suggested Practices

To help you successfully master the exam objectives presented in this chapter, complete the following practice tasks.

Configuring a Service Broker Solution

■ **Practice 1** Create an application that lets a user request a particular report to execute. Place the request on a queue and then use the Service Broker infrastructure to process the report in a background task and return the results to the user.

■ **Practice 2** Create a vacation-request application. The application enables employees to request time off. Place each request on a queue for background processing. Design a Service Broker infrastructure that can manage the various processes that need to be performed and that eventually results in an e-mail being sent back to the employee with approval or rejection.

Take a Practice Test

The practice tests on this book's companion CD offer many options. For example, you can test yourself on just the content covered in this chapter, or you can test yourself on all the 70-431 certification exam content. You can set up the test so that it closely simulates the experience of taking a certification exam, or you can set it up in study mode so that you can look at the correct answers and explanations after you answer each question.

MORE INFO **Practice tests**

For details about all the practice test options available, see the "How to Use the Practice Tests" section in this book's Introduction.

Chapter 21
Creating Full-Text Catalogs

SQL Server, like all database platforms, is built to store and retrieve large amounts of data. The system enables efficient data management by imposing a structure on the data it stores in its tables. However, not all data has a well-defined structure, and not all queries conform to basic true/false rules for retrieving data. To manage this type of data and its associated queries, other platforms rely on third-party tools. But SQL Server's Full-Text Search component provides a powerful and flexible feature called full-text indexing to manage queries issued against unstructured data. This chapter provides an overview of full-text search elements and terminology, explains how to create full-text catalogs and indexes, and shows how to populate the indexes and keep them up to date. Then the chapter shows you how to execute full-text queries to search full-text indexed columns for matching words.

Exam objectives in this chapter:
- Implement a full-text search.
    - Create a catalog.
    - Create an index.
    - Specify a full-text population method.

Lessons in this chapter:

Before You Begin

To complete the lessons in this chapter, you must have

- SQL Server 2005 installed.
- Full-text indexing installed.
- A copy of the *AdventureWorks* sample database installed in the instance.

NOTE   Full-text search

SQL Server 2005 provides Full-Text Search as a separately installable component. You can find the option to install full-text functionality under the Database Engine node within the SQL Server 2005 Setup Wizard. If you specify default settings for installing the Database Engine, Full-Text Search is selected and installed. Full-text indexing has its own service, called Microsoft Full-Text Engine for SQL Server (MSFTESQL), for populating and managing full-text catalogs. One instance of full-text indexing is installed for each SQL Server instance, with each instance having its own MSFTESQL service and service account.

MORE INFO   Installing full-text search

For complete information about installing full-text search, see the SQL Server 2005 Books Online article "Installing and Upgrading Full-Text Search." SQL Server 2005 Books Online is installed as part of SQL Server 2005. Updates for SQL Server 2005 Books Online are available for download at *www.microsoft.com/technet/prodtechnol/sql/2005/downloads/books.mspx*.

Real World

Michael Hotek

One of the largest recruiting agencies in the world spent years developing a proprietary application that allowed recruiters to quickly and flexibly search the agency's database for resumes that matched desired criteria. On any given day, agency employees ran thousands of queries against several hundred thousand resumes to fill thousands of openings spanning every industry and job function. To its competitors, this company was the model of success. However, this success came at the cost of hundreds of hard-working research assistants who spent 35–40 hours a week parsing resumes into a massive keyword index because the programming team couldn't keep pace with the industry's rate of change.

Every week, the recruiting agency had to deal with hundreds of new job titles, technology changes, and terminology shifts. The IT team loaded all these changes into the automated parsing routines on which the search system was based. Then the team executed hundreds of tests to ensure accurate results before releasing the new code base. After the new search code was released, the IT team had to reparse the entire database of resumes, compare it with the previous parsing, and then rebuild the keyword index. When the system was originally deployed, this process took two to three days. Two years later, it was taking four to five weeks and growing longer all the time. The company had to find a solution.

I was called in to help, and after spending about three hours gaining an understanding of the company's environment, I asked the IT staff if we could run a simple set of tests on a prototype solution. The staff was hesitant because all previous "tests" they had performed with a variety of vendors required days or weeks of effort and yielded mixed results. But after assuring them that the initial tests should be completed by the end of the day, I was able to proceed.

We installed SQL Server 2000's Full-Text Search component, built a full-text catalog, and added two indexes. The entire process took about an hour on the subset of test data we were using. We then executed hundreds of the IT team's test queries and compared the results with previous results. The results weren't encouraging. Less than 10 percent of the results from the full-text queries matched the results from the proprietary search algorithms. We then looked at the results more closely. It turns out that our full-text queries were picking up thousands of resumes that the proprietary algorithms missed due to misspellings, synonyms, and other factors. The full-text results were also more accurate when dealing with the series of keywords on which recruiters normally searched.

Our simple test turned into a full-blown pilot program. In less than a day, the developers could switch over the application's querying capability to use the full-text index. Three days later, the application was in production with spectacular results. The day the new application went into production, the company shattered all previous records for matching potential candidates to job openings. Over the next two months, the company hit a record for placements, only to break it the following week. The agency no longer needed the position of research assistant, so it moved its research assistants into other roles, with most of them receiving promotions to junior recruiter.

Implementing the full-text feature also let the company eliminate the entire scanning and optical character recognition (OCR) process it previously used. Resumes submitted in plain-text format were loaded into one column. Resumes that were submitted in any other format were converted to Microsoft Word or PDF format and loaded directly into the database. The IT team then used the full-text engine with add-in filters that could break the resumes down into words and index them in native document format without requiring any of the previous time-consuming text conversions.

In one case, one of the agency's sales representatives was visiting a potential new customer, hoping to sign a contract to manage the customer's recruiting efforts. The customer decided to give the agency a test on the spot and handed the representative a profile for a new job title that it was creating based on changes in its industry that had occurred just two weeks earlier. The sales rep did not know the customer was considering four other recruiting agencies. After getting a network connection, the sales rep immediately found 15 potential candidates for the new position. She walked out of the meeting with a contract in hand because none of the competitors could even find a reference to the skill set the customer was asking for.

Over the next two years, this company expanded operations to span the globe, recording a corresponding 50× increase in number of placements. All this success came with very little investment in IT because full-text indexing could adapt itself to any language needed. As we write this book, the recruiting agency is finishing its pilot program for upgrading to SQL Server 2005 and is expecting to reap significant performance improvements.

NOTE   Chapter conventions

As with many technologies within SQL Server 2005, you can use SQL Server Management Studio (SSMS) to administer full-text indexing by pointing and clicking your way through administration screens. And you might choose to use SSMS to manage full-text functionality in your organization. However, walking through the screens in the SSMS graphical user interface (GUI) doesn't explain very much about the functionality you can leverage. Because the SSMS screens and wizards submit Transact-SQL commands to SQL Server to perform the specified tasks, this chapter uses this code to explain what you can do to take advantage of full-text indexing in a variety of situations.

Lesson 1: Creating a Full-Text Catalog

Full-Text Search is based on the technology of full-text indexes. Although you create full-text indexes on columns within tables in SQL Server databases, the full-text indexes are maintained in a structure outside of SQL Server called a *full-text catalog*. A full-text catalog stores one or more full-text indexes. In this lesson, you will see how to use the Transact-SQL *CREATE FULLTEXT CATALOG* command to create a full-text catalog.

> **After this lesson, you will be able to:**
> - Create a full-text catalog.
>
> **Estimated lesson time: 20 minutes**

How to Create a Full-Text Catalog

The first step in creating full-text indexing is to create a full-text catalog to hold the indexes. You create a catalog by using the *CREATE FULLTEXT CATALOG* Transact-SQL command, as the following general syntax shows:

```
CREATE FULLTEXT CATALOG catalog_name
    [ON FILEGROUP filegroup ]
    [IN PATH 'rootpath']
    [WITH <catalog_option>]
    [AS DEFAULT]
    [AUTHORIZATION owner_name ]
<catalog_option>::=
    ACCENT_SENSITIVITY = {ON|OFF}
```

After giving the catalog a name, you specify a filegroup for the catalog, which needs to be part of the database for which the catalog will contain indexes. Although you can put the catalog on the default filegroup, it is a good practice to put a catalog on a secondary filegroup and to use this filegroup only for full-text catalogs. This configuration lets you use filegroup backup and restore to back up and restore a full-text catalog independently of the rest of the database.

You use the command's *IN PATH* clause to specify the root directory in which the full-text catalog will be stored. For full-text catalogs, the filegroup specification simply associates a full-text catalog to a filegroup for use with backup and restore operations. However, the actual catalog is stored within a physical directory structure outside a database. When you create a catalog, a directory with the same name as your catalog is created in this root directory. If a directory that uses the same name as your catalog already exists, a suffix is appended to the name to create a unique directory structure.

Within this directory structure, as indexes are added to the catalog, subdirectories are created to contain them.

You use the command's *WITH* clause to specify accent sensitivity. If you don't specify an option for this clause, the full-text catalog uses the setting from the database's collation. Otherwise, you can explicitly specify whether the catalog should be sensitive to accents. If you change this option later, you must rebuild all full-text indexes within the catalog.

The next clause, *AS DEFAULT*, serves a similar purpose as setting a default filegroup. When you create full-text indexes without explicitly specifying a catalog, SQL Server creates the indexes within the default catalog.

The command's *AUTHORIZATION* clause simply specifies the user or role that owns the catalog.

Quick Check

1. What is the purpose of a full-text catalog?
2. Where is a full-text catalog stored?

Quick Check Answers

1. A full-text catalog provides the basic storage container for one or more full-text indexes.
2. Full-text catalogs, along with their associated indexes, are stored in a directory structure that is external to SQL Server.

PRACTICE   Create a Full-Text Catalog

In this practice, you create a full-text catalog to use with the *AdventureWorks* database.

1. Create a directory on the operating system named C:\test.
2. Launch SSMS, connect to your instance, and open a new query window.
3. Add a new filegroup to the *AdventureWorks* database that you will use for the full-text catalog by executing the following batch:

```
USE master
GO
ALTER DATABASE AdventureWorks ADD FILEGROUP FTFG1
GO
ALTER DATABASE AdventureWorks ADD FILE ( NAME = N'AdventureWorksFT_data',
```

```
FILENAME = N'C:\TEST\AdventureWorksFT_data.ndf' , SIZE = 2048KB , FILEGROWTH =
 1024KB ) TO FILEGROUP [FTFG1]
GO
```

NOTE **Filegroup must have primary file**

Although full-text catalogs and indexes are stored in a directory structure external to SQL Server, the filegroup on which a full-text catalog is placed must have at least one active file. This file cannot be marked *READ ONLY* or taken *OFFLINE*.

---

4. Create a full-text catalog on the FTFG1 filegroup by executing the following command:

```
USE AdventureWorks;
GO
CREATE FULLTEXT CATALOG AWCatalog ON FILEGROUP FTFG1 IN PATH 'C:\TEST' AS DEFAULT;
GO
```

Lesson Summary

- The first step in setting up full-text indexing is to define a catalog to store one or more full-text indexes that are used to process queries.

- You use the *CREATE FULLTEXT CATALOG* Transact-SQL command to create a full-text catalog.

- Although you must associate a full-text catalog with a filegroup for backup and restore purposes, full-text catalogs are stored in a directory structure external to the database.

Lesson Review

The following questions are intended to reinforce key information presented in this lesson. The questions are also available on the companion CD if you prefer to review them in electronic form.

NOTE **Answers**

Answers to these questions and explanations of why each answer choice is right or wrong are located in the "Answers" section at the end of the book.

---

1. Where does the full-text catalog physically exist?

    A. Within the database in which it is associated

    B. In the *msdb* database

    C. In an external directory structure

    D. In a filegroup for the database

Lesson 2: Creating a Full-Text Index

After you have created a full-text catalog, you need to create one or more *full-text indexes* before you can execute full-text queries. In this lesson, you will review the powerful architecture of full-text indexing and then see how to create an index by using the *CREATE FULLTEXT INDEX* Transact-SQL command.

After this lesson, you will be able to:

■ Explain the terminology associated with full-text indexing.

■ Create a full-text index.

Estimated lesson time: 20 minutes

Full-Text Index Architecture

You can build full-text indexes on textual data stored in char, nchar, varchar, nvarchar, varchar(max), text, ntext, image, varbinary, varbinary(max), and xml columns. However, the image, varbinary, and varbinary(max) columns require special handling if you want to use them for full-text processing.

You use multiple *helper services* to build a compact and efficient full-text index. These services include word breakers and stemmers, language files, noise word files, filters, and protocol handlers.

Word breakers are routines that find the breaks between words and generate a basic word list for each row within the column or columns that you are indexing. Stemmers conjugate verbs. Word breakers and stemmers work with *language files* to understand the words that are in the input stream. Language files, in conjunction with word breakers and stemmers, allow full-text indexing to handle multiple languages without requiring translation routines or specialized processing.

Commonly used words in a language are referred to as *noise words*. Noise words are contained in language-specific noise files, which contain basic structural elements that are not useful for search routines. Examples of noise words for the English language are "the," "a," and "an." When the word-breaker routine encounters a noise word for the particular language being processed, it ignores the word. Thus, a full-text index does not include all possible words in a column, but only those that are interesting for queries.

NOTE Configuring noise words

SQL Server ships with a default set of noise word files for each language. These files are stored in $SQL_Server_Install_Path\Microsoft SQL Server\MSSQL.1\MSSQL\FTDATA\. The files are simple text files that you can edit to include noise words specific to your application that you want to exclude. If a word exists in this file, it is not indexed and is excluded from any full-text queries.

At this point, you might be thinking that you can create full-text indexes only on text-based columns. This is not true. You use *protocol handlers* and *filters* when you want to create a full-text index on a varbinary, varbinary(max), or image column. These services let you extract text from Word, Excel, and PowerPoint files as well as PDF and other files that are stored in a native format inside SQL Server. For the filters to work, you need to add a column to the table to contain a value that indicates the type of document stored in the column. The filter then loads up the binary stream stored in the column, strips all the formatting information, and returns the text within the document to the word-breaker routine.

BEST PRACTICES Filters

By taking advantage of filters, you no longer have to convert files to a text-based format before being able to use full-text indexing on them. You can store files in their native format inside SQL Server while still allowing full-search capability.

After the word-breaker routine has a list of valid words for a row within a column, the full-text engine calculates *tokens* to represent the words. A token is simply a compressed form of the original word that saves space and ensures that full-text indexes can be created in as compact a form as possible.

The full-text functionality then builds all the tokens in a column into an inverted, stacked, compressed structure within a file that is used for search operations. This unique structure allows ranking and scoring algorithms to efficiently satisfy possible queries.

How to Create a Full-Text Index

To create a full-text index, you use the *CREATE FULLTEXT INDEX* Transact-SQL command, as the following generic syntax shows:

```
CREATE FULLTEXT INDEX ON table_name
    [(column_name [TYPE COLUMN type_column_name]
        [LANGUAGE language_term] [,...n])]
```

```
KEY INDEX index_name
    [ON fulltext_catalog_name]
[WITH
    {CHANGE_TRACKING {MANUAL | AUTO | OFF [, NO POPULATION]}}
]
```

The first part of this command specifies the table on which you want to create the full-text index. Although you can index multiple columns in a table, only one full-text index per table is allowed.

You then specify the column or columns you want to index. If you specify a column of type varbinary, varbinary(max), or image for indexing, you must also specify the *TYPE COLUMN* clause. This clause refers to the column discussed earlier that you need to add to the table to designate the format of the column's data.

NOTE Type columns

A type column is a character column that contains an abbreviation that corresponds to the contents of a column being indexed. For example, a value of .doc indicates a Word document. This value is entered on a row-by-row basis, so multiple different document types can be stored in a single column. This column is used to load the correct filter for the word-breaker routine when the index is built on a varbinary, varbinary(max), or image column.

As you are specifying the column and column type for the index, you can also specify an explicit language for the column. You might need to specify this clause when you are indexing a table that contains multiple columns in which each column contains different languages, such as a column that is translated into multiple languages.

The command's *KEY INDEX* clause specifies the table's unique column. This column uniquely identifies each row in the table so that the full-text index can be correlated to rows in the table. The key must be a single column in the table; compound keys are not allowed.

The next clause, *ON*, enables you to specify the full-text catalog on which the index is created.

And the final clause specifies whether changes to the indexed data are tracked. With regular indexes, SQL Server always maintains the index in sync with the underlying data by causing changes in the index at the same time as changes to the referenced data are made. Full-text indexes, however, are separated from normal database transaction processes so that changes to data in columns that are full-text indexed are propagated into the index via a background process that does not immediately reflect the data changes.

When the change-tracking value is set to *MANUAL*, changes to the data in the columns need to be propagated into the index either manually or by scheduling a job in

SQL Server Agent to propagate the changes. The default value of *AUTO* causes a change to be propagated into the index by using a background process that occurs outside of the transaction making the change. And when this value is set to *OFF*, SQL Server does not track any changes, which causes the index to become further and further out of date until it is rebuilt either manually or via a SQL Server Agent job. The *OFF* option also includes a *NO POPULATION* clause that you can specify to cause a full-text index to be created without populating the index.

BEST PRACTICES   Initial *catalog population*

Populating a full-text index is a very resource- and input/output (I/O)-intensive operation. The initial creation of a full-text index should usually be performed when activity in the database is very low, so most database administrators (DBAs) create full-text indexes by using the *OFF* and *NO POPULATION* clauses, and then they create a job to populate all full-text indexes when minimal database activity is occurring. After the index is populated, if the column on which the index is created does not change frequently, you can then normally set change tracking to *AUTO* to keep the index up to date.

> ## Quick Check
> - What are the requirements for creating a full-text index?
>
> ### Quick Check Answer
> - Only one full-text index can be created on a table. The columns in a full-text index can be character (all types), varbinary, and image data types. A single-column unique key must exist on the table.

PRACTICE   Create a Full-Text Index

In this practice, you create two full-text indexes. The first index is on a character-based column. The second index takes advantage of the filters that ship with SQL Server to index a column containing Word documents stored in a varbinary(max) column.

1. If necessary, launch SSMS, connect to your instance, and open a new query window.

2. Create a full-text index on the ProductionDescription column in the *Production.ProductDescription* table in the *AdventureWorks* database by executing the following command:

```
CREATE FULLTEXT INDEX ON Production.ProductDescription (Description) KEY INDEX
  PK_ProductDescription_ProductDescriptionID ON AWCatalog WITH CHANGE_TRACKING AUTO;
```

3. Create a full-text index on the Document column of the *Production.Document* table by executing the following command:

```
CREATE FULLTEXT INDEX ON Production.Document (Document TYPE COLUMN FileExtension) KEY
    INDEX PK_Document_DocumentID ON AWCatalog WITH CHANGE_TRACKING AUTO;
```

4. Observe the changes on the file system after the indexes are created.

5. View the full-text catalog and associated indexes inside SSMS.

Lesson Summary

- To create a full-text index, you use the *CREATE FULLTEXT INDEX* Transact-SQL command.

- You can create full-text indexes on a variety of columns, including text-based, binary, and image columns.

- Varbinary and image columns let you store files in their native format within SQL Server while still making these files available for full-text indexing and searching.

- To build a compact and efficient full-text index, you use multiple helper services, including word-breaker routines, language files, noise word files, filters, and protocol handlers.

Lesson Review

The following questions are intended to reinforce key information presented in this lesson. The questions are also available on the companion CD if you prefer to review them in electronic form.

NOTE   Answers

Answers to these questions and explanations of why each answer choice is right or wrong are located in the "Answers" section at the end of the book.

---

1. Which of the following are requirements for creating a full-text index? (Choose all that apply.)

    A. Primary key

    B. Single-column unique index

    C. Image column

    D. Text-based column

Lesson 3: Populating a Full-Text Index

As Lesson 2 noted, because of the external structure for storing full-text indexes, changes to underlying data columns are not immediately reflected in the full-text index. Instead, a background process enlists the word breakers, filters, and noise word files to build the tokens for each column, which are then merged back into the main index either automatically or manually. This update process is called population or a *crawl*. To keep your full-text indexes up to date, you must periodically populate them. This lesson shows you how to perform a full or partial population of a full-text index.

After this lesson, you will be able to:

■ Specify an index-population method.

Estimated lesson time: 20 minutes

Specifying an Index-Population Method

You can choose from three modes for full-text *index population*:

■ Full

■ Incremental

■ Update

A full population causes the full-text engine to read and process all rows from the table for the indexed columns. Because full population is very resource-intensive, you typically use full population for the initial population of the full-text index and then use either an incremental or update population to keep the index up to date.

Incremental population automatically populates the index for rows that were modified since the last population. Incremental population requires a timestamp column on the table, which the full-text engine uses to determine which rows have changed. If any metadata for the index has changed since the last population, the incremental population is performed as a full population.

Update population uses the changes that SQL Server tracks to process any inserts, updates, and deletes since the last time a change-tracked index was populated. With this population mode, you can specify how you want to propagate the changes to the index. Specifying *AUTO* for change tracking enables automatic processing; with *MANUAL* you can implement a manual method for processing changes.

You use the *ALTER FULLTEXT INDEX* Transact-SQL command to populate a full-text index, as the following general syntax shows:

```
ALTER FULLTEXT INDEX ON table_name
    { SET CHANGE_TRACKING { MANUAL | AUTO | OFF }
    | START { FULL | INCREMENTAL | UPDATE } POPULATION
    | STOP POPULATION
    }
```

Populating a Full-Text Catalog

In addition to periodically populating your full-text indexes, you might also need to rebuild or reorganize a full-text catalog to update all the indexes in the catalog. The following syntax shows the *ALTER FULLTEXT CATALOG* Transact-SQL command that enables you to operate on all indexes in a full-text catalog at the same time:

```
ALTER FULLTEXT CATALOG catalog_name
{ REBUILD [ WITH ACCENT_SENSITIVITY = { ON | OFF } ]
| REORGANIZE
| AS DEFAULT
}
```

When you use the *REBUILD* option for this command, the full-text catalog is deleted from the file system and rebuilt. You generally use this option only when you need to change the *ACCENT_SENSITIVITY* setting for the catalog.

Specifying the *REORGANIZE* option causes all indexes in the catalog to have all changes merged. This operation frees up disk and memory resources, and you should run the *ALTER FULLTEXT CATALOG* command with this option periodically to achieve maximum full-text performance.

Quick Check
- Why do you need to periodically perform index populations?

Quick Check Answer
- Full-text indexes are an external structure, so they are not updated at the same time as changes are made to the underlying data columns. A background process enlists the word breakers, filters, and noise word files to build the tokens for each column, which are then merged back into the main index either automatically or manually.

PRACTICE **Populate a Full-Text Index**

In this practice, you perform a full repopulation of the two indexes you created earlier.

1. If necessary, launch SSMS, connect to your instance, and open a new query window.

2. Execute a full population of the full-text indexes on the ProductDescription and Document columns by executing the following batch:

```
ALTER FULLTEXT INDEX ON Production.ProductDescription START FULL POPULATION;
ALTER FULLTEXT INDEX ON Production.Document START FULL POPULATION;
```

3. Explain why the output of these commands was a warning that the commands will be ignored.

Lesson Summary

■ To keep full-text indexes in sync with the columns they are built on and to perform maintenance on the indexes, you must periodically populate the indexes.

■ You can completely rebuild or incrementally populate an individual index by using the *ALTER FULLTEXT INDEX* Transact-SQL command.

■ On a periodic basis, you can also reorganize a full-text catalog to free up disk and memory for all full-text indexes in the catalog by using the *ALTER FULLTEXT CATALOG* command.

Lesson Review

The following questions are intended to reinforce key information presented in this lesson. The questions are also available on the companion CD if you prefer to review them in electronic form.

NOTE Answers

Answers to these questions and explanations of why each answer choice is right or wrong are located in the "Answers" section at the end of the book.

1. Which of the following is a valid population option for a full-text index?

   A. *REORGANIZE*

   B. *INCREMENTAL*

   C. *REBUILD*

   D. *COMPLETE*

Lesson 4: Querying Data by Using a Full-Text Index

Full-text indexes are useful only if they are used to satisfy requests. However, regular Transact-SQL statements will not cause the query optimizer to automatically select a full-text index. You gain full-text query capability by using the *CONTAINS*, *CONTAIN-STABLE*, *FREETEXT*, and *FREETEXTTABLE* full-text query keywords. Full-text query keywords are available in two types: predicate functions and rowset functions. The *CONTAINS* and *FREETEXT* functions are query predicates that return a simple True or False result to limit the result set. The *CONTAINSTABLE* and *FREETEXTTABLE* functions return a rowset that must be joined to another table based on a key value; you can use these functions to extend the capabilities of your queries. This lesson looks at each of these full-text keywords and describes which are appropriate for different needs, showing you the query syntax you need to use as well as query examples to help you understand the different results you can achieve.

> **After this lesson, you will be able to:**
> ■ Explain the differences between the full-text query keywords.
> ■ Submit full-text queries.
> **Estimated lesson time: 20 minutes**

Query Execution

When you execute queries that use full-text functions, SQL Server first parses and compiles them and then hands them to the query optimizer. The optimizer recognizes the full-text functions and routes them to the full-text search engine. The full-text search engine takes the search terms passed and routes them through the dedicated query processor for full-text queries. Before the query processor can search for the keywords in the index, the keywords must be transformed into matching tokens. For this transformation, the full-text query processor launches the word breakers, stemmers, and noise word files discussed previously in this chapter. It also interrogates a thesaurus, which returns a list of synonyms that are also searched.

It is this extended capability for matching on derivatives as well as synonyms that makes full-text searches so powerful and flexible—capable of even handling common word misspellings. Let's look at each of the full-text query keywords in turn.

FREETEXT

The *FREETEXT* function accepts one or more columns to search and a search argument. This function performs a fuzzy search in that it automatically searches for inflectional forms (stemming) as well as related words that the thesaurus identifies. The general syntax of the *FREETEXT* function is as follows:

```
FREETEXT ( { column_name | (column_list) | * }
        , 'freetext_string' [ , LANGUAGE language_term ] )
```

This function does not provide the customization or precision that you typically want in production applications. For example, searching for the keyword "*bike*" by using the *FREETEXT* function would return "*bike*", "*biker*", "*bike riding*", "*bike-riding*", and various synonyms as well as any word that contains the word "*bike*".

Let's say you execute the following query against the *Production.ProductDescription* table using first the *FREETEXT* function and then the *CONTAINS* function:

```
SELECT ProductDescriptionID, Description FROM Production.ProductDescription
WHERE FREETEXT(Description, N'bike');

SELECT ProductDescriptionID, Description FROM Production.ProductDescription
WHERE CONTAINS(Description, N'bike');
```

The *FREETEXT* query returns 16 rows of data as opposed to the 14 rows that the *CONTAINS* query returns.

Search Argument Data Types for Full-Text Functions

When the SQL Server query optimizer decides how to efficiently satisfy a query, it uses an inspection algorithm that looks at value-distribution statistics to determine whether an index should be used for the query. The full-text engine also maintains a set of distribution statistics.

The optimization process includes an algorithm generically referred to as "parameter sniffing," which can handle explicit values as well as values contained within variables. The algorithm gives each potential path a basic score that indicates how selective a given path is for a query. These numbers are then used to determine whether an index seek, index scan, nested loop, or other method is used to satisfy a segment of a query.

What does parameter sniffing have to do with full-text queries? When the full-text optimizer cannot use parameter sniffing for one reason or another, it essentially makes a guess. This educated guess assigns a value based on the number of rows in the table up to a maximum value. In SQL Server 2000, the maximum value for a full-text function was 1,000. In SQL Server 2005, this value has been increased to 10,000. Obviously, guessing in the context of such a large maximum value has a significant potential to generate an inefficient query plan.

You can inspect these estimated values by looking in the TotalSubtreeCost column after using the *SET STATISTICS PROFILE ON* command.

Many people unknowingly prevent the optimizer from using parameter sniffing by the search arguments they use with the full-text functions. The full-text functions expect a Unicode data type for the search argument. Failure to pass in a Unicode argument prevents the optimizer from using parameter sniffing to evaluate distribution statistics. On large tables, this problem is magnified, forcing the optimizer to make an educated guess that can result in a suboptimal query plan.

FREETEXTTABLE

The *FREETEXTTABLE* function works exactly like the *FREETEXT* function except that it returns a rowset that contains a rank column. The RANK column provides a numeric value between 1 and 1,000 that is a relative number indicating how well the row matches the search criteria. The KEY column returns the unique key that is used to identify the row. The general syntax of this function is as follows:

```
FREETEXTTABLE (table , { column_name | (column_list) | * }

     , 'freetext_string'

   [ ,LANGUAGE language_term ]

   [ ,top_n_by_rank ] )
```

The *FREETEXTTABLE* version of the previous *FREETEXT* query would look like this:

```
SELECT PD.ProductDescriptionID, PD.Description, KEYTBL.[KEY], KEYTBL.RANK
from Production.ProductDescription AS PD

INNER JOIN FREETEXTTABLE(Production.ProductDescription,Description,N'bike')
AS KEYTBL ON PD.ProductDescriptionID = KEYTBL.[KEY];
```

Note that the column named KEY in the result set must be enclosed in brackets because it is a Transact-SQL keyword. A higher value for RANK indicates a less-precise match to the search terms. The results of this sample query provide additional insight into why the *FREETEXT* and *CONTAINS* queries return different results. Keys 1187 and 1188 provide close but not exact matches by returning rows that have words with a substring of the search term.

CONTAINS

The *CONTAINS* function lets you use precise as well as fuzzy matching algorithms to satisfy full-text queries. As you can see from the following general syntax for the function, it accepts a variety of parameters to let you specify exact behaviors:

```
CONTAINS
      ( { column_name | (column_list) | * }
          , '< contains_search_condition >'
   [ , LANGUAGE language_term ]
      )
< contains_search_condition > ::=
   { < simple_term >
   | < prefix_term >
   | < generation_term >
   | < proximity_term >
   | < weighted_term >
   }
   | { ( < contains_search_condition > )
   [ { < AND > | < AND NOT > | < OR > } ]
   < contains_search_condition > [ ...n ]
   }
< simple_term > ::=
          word | " phrase "
< prefix term > ::=
   { "word * " | "phrase *" }
< generation_term > ::=
      FORMSOF ( { INFLECTIONAL | THESAURUS } , < simple_term > [ ,...n ] )
< proximity_term > ::=
   { < simple_term > | < prefix_term > }
   { { NEAR | ~ }
   { < simple_term > | < prefix_term > }
   } [ ...n ]
< weighted_term > ::=
   ISABOUT
       ( { {
 < simple_term >
 | < prefix_term >
 | < generation_term >
 | < proximity_term >
 }
  [ WEIGHT ( weight_value ) ]
  } [ ,...n ]
      )
```

```
< AND > ::=
    { AND | & }
< AND NOT > ::=
    { AND NOT | & !}
< OR > ::=
    { OR | | }
```

You can specify search arguments as exact matches or as prefixes. The following query, for example, finds all rows that have an exact match for the word "bike":

```
SELECT ProductDescriptionID, Description FROM Production.ProductDescription
WHERE CONTAINS(Description, N'bike');
```

The next query returns rows that have an exact match for the word "bike" and rows that contain any words that start with "bike". You specify "bike" as a prefix by using an asterisk (*) after the term and enclosing the search term in double quotation marks:

```
SELECT ProductDescriptionID, Description FROM Production.ProductDescription
WHERE CONTAINS(Description, N'"bike*"');
```

The keywords *FORMSOF*, *INFLECTIONAL*, and *THESAURUS* allow matches on variants of a search term. *INFLECTIONAL* causes the search to consider word stems in a search. For example, searching for the word "drive" will also produce matches on "drove", "driven", "driving", and so on. By specifying the use of a *THESAURUS*, the query processor also returns synonyms as matches for the search term. For example, "metal" also returns results for "gold", "aluminum", "steel", and so on.

Examples of each of these queries are as follows:

```
SELECT ProductDescriptionID, Description FROM Production.ProductDescription
WHERE CONTAINS(Description, N' FORMSOF (INFLECTIONAL, drive) ');
```

```
SELECT ProductDescriptionID, Description FROM Production.ProductDescription
WHERE CONTAINS(Description, N' FORMSOF (THESAURUS, metal) ');
```

NOTE Thesaurus files

All thesaurus files are shipped empty. For thesaurus matches to work, these files must be populated. All thesaurus files are XML documents; you can find them in the $SQL_Server_Install_Path\ Microsoft SQL Server\MSSQL.1\MSSQL\FTDATA\ directory. For information about populating thesaurus files, see the SQL Server 2005 Books Online article "Configuring Thesaurus Files."

Word proximity is a common way of searching documents for multiple keywords or phrases. This type of query uses the *NEAR* (~) keyword. The closer words are to each other, the better the match for these types of queries. The proximity is used as part of the RANK calculation for rows matching the search criteria. This keyword is rarely used with the *CONTAINS* predicate because the rank of matched results cannot be evaluated directly. The following two queries are equivalent to each other:

```
SELECT ProductDescriptionID, Description FROM Production.ProductDescription
WHERE CONTAINS(Description, N'mountain NEAR bike');

SELECT ProductDescriptionID, Description FROM Production.ProductDescription
WHERE CONTAINS(Description, N'mountain ~ bike');
```

As if all these options were not enough, you can also assign relative weights to particular search terms. This weighting affects the ranking score that the full-text optimizer returns by causing a particular term to be considered more or less significant. The *WEIGHT* clause, a value between 0.0 and 1.0, has no effect on queries that use *CONTAINS*, but it does affect the RANK value returned with *CONTAINSTABLE*. Because the *AdventureWorks* sample database deals with bikes, the following query uses weighting to place more emphasis on the word "*mountain*" than the word "*bike*":

```
SELECT Description FROM Production.ProductDescription
WHERE CONTAINS(Description,'ISABOUT (mountain weight (.8), bike weight (.2) )' );
```

Also note that you can use multiple keywords in a search. To specify multiple keywords, you separate the terms by the keywords *AND*, *AND NOT*, or *OR* to include or exclude rows.

CONTAINSTABLE

The *CONTAINSTABLE* function has the same capabilities as the *CONTAINS* function. However, like the *FREETEXTTABLE* function, it returns a rowset that contains a RANK and a KEY column that can be used to return the best matches to a search. The general syntax for this function is the following:

```
CONTAINSTABLE ( table , { column_name | (column_list ) | * } , '
< contains_search_condition > '
    [ , LANGUAGE language_term]
  [ ,top_n_by_rank ]
        )
```

> **Quick Check**
> - What is the difference between the *CONTAINS* and *FREETEXT* functions?
>
> **Quick Check Answer**
> - *FREETEXT* is a less-precise way of querying full-text data because it auto-matically searches for all forms and synonyms of a word or words. *CON-TAINS* allows a precise specification for a query, including the capability to search by word proximity, weighting, and complex pattern matching.

PRACTICE Query a Full-Text Index

In this practice, you execute a query by using the full-text indexes that you previously created.

1. If necessary, launch SSMS, connect to your instance, and open a new query window.

2. Execute the following batch:

```
SELECT ProductDescriptionID, Description FROM Production.ProductDescription
WHERE CONTAINS(Description, 'alloy');

SELECT ProductDescriptionID, Description FROM Production.ProductDescription
WHERE CONTAINS(Description, 'same');
```

3. Why does the first query return results, whereas the second query does not?

Lesson Summary

- SQL Server passes full-text queries to the full-text search engine, which routes search terms through the dedicated query processor for full-text queries.

- The full-text query processor provides extended capability for matching on derivatives as well as synonyms, making full-text searches powerful, flexible, and even capable of handling common word misspellings.

- You can use the *FREETEXT* and *FREETEXTTABLE* full-text functions to provide a general sampling of rows that might match the search argument.

- You use the *CONTAINS* and *CONTAINSTABLE* functions in production applications to allow for very precise criteria to target search results.

Lesson Review

The following questions are intended to reinforce key information presented in this lesson. The questions are also available on the companion CD if you prefer to review them in electronic form.

NOTE Answers

Answers to these questions and explanations of why each answer choice is right or wrong are located in the "Answers" section at the end of the book.

---

1. Which of the following is a valid option for a *FREETEXT* or *FREETEXTTABLE* query?

   A. *THESAURUS*

   B. *NEAR*

   C. *WEIGHT*

   D. *LANGUAGE*

Chapter Review

To further practice and reinforce the skills you learned in this chapter, you can

- Review the chapter summary.
- Review the list of key terms introduced in this chapter.
- Complete the case scenario. This scenario sets up a real-world situation involving the topics of this chapter and asks you to create a solution.
- Complete the suggested practices.
- Take a practice test.

Chapter Summary

- SQL Server's Full-Text Search component, based on full-text indexes, lets you efficiently query unstructured data stored within SQL Server.
- To implement full-text indexing, you need to take the following steps:
  - ❑ Create a full-text catalog to contain the full-text indexes.
  - ❑ Create one or more full-text indexes within a full-text catalog.
  - ❑ Specify a method to populate the full-text indexes to keep them up to date with underlying data.
- After you create the full-text indexes, you can execute full-text queries by using the *CONTAINS*, *CONTAINSTABLE*, *FREETEXT*, and *FREETEXTTABLE* functions.

Key Terms

Do you know what these key terms mean? You can check your answers by looking up the terms in the glossary at the end of the book.

- catalog population
- crawl
- filter
- full-text catalog
- full-text index
- helper service
- index population

- language file
- noise words
- protocol handler
- token
- word breaker

Case Scenario: Building Full-Text Indexes

In the following case scenario, you apply what you've learned in this chapter. You can find answers to these questions in the "Answers" section at the end of this book.

Contoso Limited, a health care company located in Bothell, WA, maintains a large database of patient claims records. Each patient claim contains documents for the initial claim, documentation to justify the claim, and supporting documents such as doctor evaluations and records, as well as documents that describe treatments. Contoso has captured and stored all this data within a SQL Server 2005 database. Data exists in the database in a variety of formats: as discrete data in varchar columns, as Word documents, as PDFs, and as scanned images (OCR to text) in image columns.

Now Contoso wants to add several new features within the existing application to enhance the company's analysis capabilities. The company needs to implement a fraud-detection system to find out whether particular doctors are involved in numerous claims, far beyond normal. After doctors in this group are identified, an analyst needs to be able to cross-reference diagnoses and claims by using flexible criteria.

Contoso also needs to be able to check a claim against prior records for the same patient to determine whether this is a recurring injury and whether previous claims were accepted or rejected. The company also wants to analyze claim volumes by company as well as break down the claim amounts by specific type of injury.

How would you implement these features into the application by using the least amount of time and effort?

Suggested Practices

To help you successfully master the exam objectives presented in this chapter, complete the following practice tasks.

Creating Full-Text Indexes

■ **Practice 1**   Build a full-text index on the resumes submitted by job candidates within the *AdventureWorks* database.

Querying Full-Text Indexes

■ **Practice 1**   Query the resumes within the *AdventureWorks* database for a variety of keywords. Perform each keyword search using the *CONTAINS, CONTAINSTABLE, FREETEXT,* and *FREETEXTTABLE* keywords; then compare the results.

■ **Practice 2**   Expand the list of words searched on by the queries in the Lesson 4, "Query Data by Using a Full-Text Index," practice. Perform each keyword search using the *CONTAINS, CONTAINSTABLE, FREETEXT,* and *FREETEXTTABLE* keywords; then compare the results.

■ **Practice 3**   Using the queries from Practice 2, expand or contract the scope of the search by using inflections of words or synonyms.

Take a Practice Test

The practice tests on this book's companion CD offer many options. For example, you can test yourself on just the content covered in this chapter, or you can test yourself on all the 70-431 certification exam content. You can set up the test so that it closely simulates the experience of taking a certification exam, or you can set it up in study mode so that you can look at the correct answers and explanations after you answer each question.

MORE INFO   **Practice tests**

For details about all the practice test options available, see the "How to Use the Practice Tests" section in this book's Introduction.

Answers

Chapter 1: Lesson Review Answers

Lesson 1

1. **Correct Answer: D**

   A. **Incorrect:** Express Edition can use only one CPU.

   B. **Incorrect:** Workgroup Edition can use only two CPUs.

   C. **Incorrect:** Although Developer Edition can use more than four CPUs, it is not licensed for production use.

   D. **Correct:** Standard Edition of SQL Server 2005 can use up to four CPUs.

2. **Correct Answer: C**

   A. **Incorrect:** Express Edition does not allow data partitioning.

   B. **Incorrect:** Workgroup Edition does not allow data partitioning.

   C. **Correct:** Enterprise Edition supports data partitioning.

   D. **Incorrect:** Standard Edition does not allow data partitioning.

3. **Correct Answer: A**

   A. **Correct:** Express Edition is free to distribute and does not require users to purchase a SQL Server license.

   B. **Incorrect:** Workgroup Edition requires users to purchase a SQL Server license.

   C. **Incorrect:** Developer Edition is not licensed for production use.

   D. **Incorrect:** Standard Edition requires users to purchase a SQL Server license.

Lesson 2

1. Correct Answer: D

    A. **Incorrect:** If you're using Windows 2000 Server, your SQL Server 2005 installation requires Windows 2000 Server SP4.

    B. **Incorrect:** If you're using Windows 2000 Server, your SQL Server 2005 installation requires Windows 2000 Server SP4.

    C. **Incorrect:** If you're using Windows 2000 Server, your SQL Server 2005 installation requires Windows 2000 Server SP4.

    D. **Correct:** If you're using Windows 2000 Server, your SQL Server 2005 installation requires Windows 2000 Server SP4.

2. Correct Answer: A

    A. **Correct:** The minimum service pack level required by SQL Server 2005 for Windows Server 2003 is SP1.

    B. **Incorrect:** The minimum service pack level required by SQL Server 2005 for Windows Server 2003 is SP1.

    C. **Incorrect:** The minimum service pack level required by SQL Server 2005 for Windows Server 2003 is SP1.

    D. **Incorrect:** The minimum service pack level required by SQL Server 2005 for Windows Server 2003 is SP1.

3. Correct Answer: A

    A. **Correct:** Express Edition requires only 192 MB of memory.

    B. **Incorrect:** Workgroup Edition requires a minimum of 512 MB of memory.

    C. **Incorrect:** Developer Edition requires a minimum of 512 MB of memory.

    D. **Incorrect:** Standard Edition requires a minimum of 512 MB of memory.

Lesson 3

1. Correct Answer: C

    A. **Incorrect:** You install service packs at an instance level, and this solution does not let each client operate with a different service pack.

    B. **Incorrect:** You can support multiple instances on a single server, with each instance using a different service pack.

C. **Correct:** This solution represents the best solution because each client has its own instance, which lets each of them operate with different service packs. Multiple instances can be placed on one or more servers.

D. **Incorrect:** Although this solution meets the first goal of permitting clients to use SQL Server with different service packs, it requires you to install separate SQL Server servers for each client. In addition, this solution requires you to move a client to a different server if he requires a change in service pack.

2. **Correct Answer: A**

A. **Correct:** There can be only one default instance on a single server.

B. **Incorrect:** There can be only one default instance on a single server.

C. **Incorrect:** There can be only one default instance on a single server.

D. **Incorrect:** There can be only one default instance on a single server.

Lesson 4

1. **Correct Answers: A and C**

A. **Correct:** You need to install the SQL Server Agent service to use an account.

B. **Incorrect:** This agent for transactional replication operates under the security account of the SQL Server Agent.

C. **Correct:** You need to install the SQL Server service to use an account.

D. **Incorrect:** Although there are replication agents, these agents operate under the security account of the SQL Server Agent.

2. **Correct Answer: C**

A. **Incorrect:** This type of authentication does not allow the use of only SQL Server logins.

B. **Incorrect:** This type of authentication allows the use of only Windows logins.

C. **Correct:** This type of authentication allows the use of both Windows logins and SQL Server logins.

D. **Incorrect:** This is a type of account, not an authentication mode.

Lesson 5

1. **Correct Answer: A**

    A. **Correct:** An in-place upgrade is installing SQL Server 2005 on top of the current installation.

    B. **Incorrect:** SQL Server does not allow the sharing of databases between an older version and a newer version of SQL Server.

    C. **Incorrect:** This is a side-by-side installation.

    D. **Incorrect:** This is a side-by-side installation.

2. **Correct Answer: B**

    A. **Incorrect:** This type of data movement does not require the source database to be clear of users.

    B. **Correct:** This type of data movement requires the source database to be clear of users.

    C. **Incorrect:** This type of data movement does not require the source database to be clear of users.

    D. **Incorrect:** This type of data movement does not require the source database to be clear of users.

3. **Correct Answer: D**

    A. **Incorrect:** Successful upgrades often depend heavily on checklists that remind you of all the tasks that must be performed before, during, and after the upgrade.

    B. **Incorrect:** You need to plan for the additional disk space required for copies of your database files, the files you will upgrade, and the final files needed by the upgraded databases. This often means that you need two to four times the amount of disk space during the upgrade as you will need after the upgrade is finished.

    C. **Incorrect:** The upgrade process will stop and start the SQL Server service several times during the upgrade process, and you do not want the startup stored procedures firing multiple times during the upgrade.

    D. **Correct:** You should allow the system databases to autogrow during the upgrade process and make sure they have enough space for this growth.

Chapter 1: Case Scenario Answers

Case Scenario 1: Installing SQL Server 2005

1. You should use Mixed Mode authentication because the current application requires SQL Server logins.

2. Because each store's databases must be separate from the others, you should create multiple named instances of SQL Server. By using all named instances, you have standardized the installation process.

3. For this particular installation, you must use Enterprise Edition because it is the only production-licensed edition that supports eight CPUs.

Case Scenario 2: Upgrading an Instance of SQL Server

1. There are several methods to use when moving databases from one server to another during a side-by-side upgrade. Given that we cannot stop the current installations to detach the databases and move them, we can use the backup/restore, Copy Database Wizard, or manual scripting methods to move the databases to their new locations.

2. As part of the upgrade plan, I have created a rollback process that will let me stop the upgrade at any point during the process and bring the old databases and installations back online until we can solve any problem encountered during the upgrade.

3. Another part of the upgrade plan is an exhaustive testing plan that lets us test all parts of our applications against the new database installation before we make the final switch. Testing will be done not only by the database team but will also include the quality assurance (QA) team, the application-development team, and the business units using the database in the testing scenarios. All teams must approve the validity of the new installation before we turn off the old instance and make the switch.

Chapter 2: Lesson Review Answers

Lesson 1

1. **Correct Answer: C**

   A. **Incorrect:** The *ADD FILE* clause allows you to create a database file.

   B. **Incorrect:** The *MODIFY FILEGROUP* clause allows you modify properties for an existing filegroup.

   C. **Correct:** You can add a filegroup by executing the *ALTER DATABASE* statement with the *ADD FILEGROUP* modifier. Also, you can create a filegroup directly from the *CREATE DATABASE* statement.

   D. **Incorrect:** The *REMOVE FILEGROUP* clause allows you remove a filegroup from a database.

2. **Correct Answer: C**

   A. **Incorrect:** You can gain better performance by separating data files from log files rather than separating the operating system from SQL Server executable files.

   B. **Incorrect:** Storing SQL Server executable files and the transaction log in the same disk does not avoid disk contention.

   C. **Correct:** You have log files in a RAID 5 system and data files in another RAID 5 system. This configuration generally gives you good performance by enabling the database engine to access transaction log and data files simultaneously.

   D. **Incorrect:** RAID 1 provides good read performance, but the transaction log is a write-consuming file.

3. **Correct Answers: A, C, and D**

   A. **Correct:** You can mark a filegroup as read-only so that you cannot modify any database object inside the filegroup.

   B. **Incorrect:** Write-only is not a valid filegroup type.

   C. **Correct:** Each database has a default filegroup that stores database objects that you do not explicitly assign to other filegroups.

   D. **Correct:** The primary filegroup is the filegroup that stores the primary database file.

Lesson 2

1. **Correct Answer: A**

    A. **Correct:** Database Mail uses Service Broker activation to start the external mail program when there are e-mail messages waiting to be processed.

    B. **Incorrect:** Database mirroring is a high-availability technology that Database Mail does not need.

    C. **Incorrect:** Database Mail does not need any Extended MAPI profile on the server. It uses the standard SMTP protocol.

    D. **Incorrect:** Database Mail can use mail accounts from any SMTP mail server.

2. **Correct Answer: A**

    A. **Correct:** Database Mail accesses the SMTP server by using the database engine service account credentials by default.

    B. **Incorrect:** The credentials used to access the SMTP server when Windows authentication is configured are the database engine service credentials.

    C. **Incorrect:** Database Mail does not use SQL Server Browser to perform its actions.

    D. **Incorrect:** Active Directory Helper service does not access the SMTP server for Database Mail.

3. **Correct Answer: D**

    A. **Incorrect:** A Database Mail profile is a collection of accounts.

    B. **Incorrect:** You can create public or private profiles and control which users can access each profile, but there is no mapping between database users and profiles.

    C. **Incorrect:** A profile is a collection of Database Mail accounts, not user accounts.

    D. **Correct:** Each Database Mail profile can use several Database Mail accounts.

Lesson 3

1. **Correct Answer: A**

    A. **Correct:** When a database is in the Simple recovery model, the database engine minimally logs most operations.

    B. **Incorrect:** In a Full recovery model, all transactions are logged.

    C. **Incorrect:** In a Bulk-Logged recovery model, only bulk operations are minimally logged.

    D. **Incorrect:** The Simple recovery model logs transactions only minimally.

2. **Correct Answers: B and C**

    A. **Incorrect:** The recovery model is a database-level configuration, so you cannot change the recovery model by using *sp_configure*.

    B. **Correct:** You can change the database recovery model graphically in SSMS.

    C. **Correct:** *ALTER DATABASE* is the Transact-SQL statement that lets you change the recovery model.

    D. **Incorrect:** You cannot specify the recovery model in the *CREATE DATA-BASE* statement. When you create a database with the *CREATE DATABASE* statement, SQL Server creates it with the recovery model from the model database.

3. **Correct Answers: A and D**

    A. **Correct:** Because the transaction log is truncated in the Simple recovery model, you cannot restore the database to a given point in time.

    B. **Incorrect:** You can restore differential backups because they are database backups and you do not need transaction log information.

    C. **Incorrect:** You can restore full backups because you do not need transaction log information to perform that action.

    D. **Correct:** You cannot restore a data page in the Simple recovery model. A page restore requires an unbroken chain of log backups up to the current log file.

Lesson 4

1. **Correct Answers: B, C, and D**

    A. **Incorrect:** Database users are database-level objects, not server-level principals.

    B. **Correct:** Fixed server roles are server principals that let you assign administrative rights to logins.

    C. **Correct:** Windows logins are server principals that let you give access to Windows users and groups.

    D. **Correct:** SQL Server logins are server principals created, stored, and managed in SQL Server.

2. **Correct Answers: A and C**

    A. **Correct:** By using Windows authentication, SQL Server relies on operating system authentication. You can gain access to all the operating system security features and can implement enterprise-wide policies.

    B. **Incorrect:** SQL Server 2005 lets you apply the local Windows Password Policy to SQL Server logins.

    C. **Correct:** Windows authentication is the default authentication mode.

    D. **Incorrect:** The default authentication mode is Windows authentication.

3. **Correct Answers: B and C**

    A. **Incorrect:** The *FROM* clause is for Windows logins only.

    B. **Correct:** *CREATE LOGIN* is the recommended syntax for creating SQL Server logins in SQL Server 2005.

    C. **Correct:** Although you can create SQL Server logins by using the *sp_addlogin* stored procedure, this procedure is only for backward compatibility. You should use the *CREATE LOGIN* syntax.

    D. **Incorrect:** The *sp_grantlogin* stored procedure grants access to an operating system user.

Lesson 5

1. **Correct Answer: B**

    A. **Incorrect:** The database catalog is defined in the database system tables.

    B. **Correct:** Schemas group database objects and let you perform some administrative tasks, such as grant permissions, together.

    C. **Incorrect:** Schemas do not group databases.

    D. **Incorrect:** Schemas do not define the table catalog.

2. **Correct Answers: B and D**

   A. **Incorrect:** Although you can use the *FROM* clause to create database user Peter mapped to login Peter, you must specify the *LOGIN* clause as well.

   B. **Correct:** You can use *FOR LOGIN* or *FROM* to specify the mapped login.

   C. **Incorrect:** This capability does not exist in the *SQL_LOGIN* clause.

   D. **Correct:** You can create the database user without specifying the login name; the database engine will look for a login with the same name as the database user.

3. **Correct Answers: A and C**

   A. **Correct.** You can nest database roles inside other database roles.

   B. **Incorrect:** You can add user-defined database roles and grant permissions to them.

   C. **Correct:** All SQL Server databases have predefined database roles, but you can add new database roles to group users and grant permissions.

   D. **Incorrect:** The map between logins and users is a one-to-one relationship. You cannot map fixed server roles to database roles.

Lesson 6

1. **Correct Answer: C**

   A. **Incorrect:** The database engine automatically creates the service master key.

   B. **Incorrect:** The service master key can be opened by the service user account.

   C. **Correct:** The service master key is generated automatically for each installation and can be opened only by the SQL Server service account.

   D. **Incorrect:** The service master key is generated automatically.

2. **Correct Answer: A**

   A. **Correct:** This is the correct syntax to create a certificate secured with the database master key.

   B. **Incorrect:** Although the statement is the correct one, the syntax is not valid.

   C. **Incorrect:** The correct statement to use is *CREATE CERTIFICATE*, not *CREATE CERT*.

   D. **Incorrect:** The correct statement to use is *CREATE CERTIFICATE*, not *CREATE CERT*.

3. **Correct Answers: A and D**

   A. **Correct:** The database master key is optional. You can create it if you want to use it to protect certificates and keys.

   B. **Incorrect:** The database master key is not mandatory.

   C. **Incorrect:** The database master key is created manually.

   D. **Correct:** You should create the database master key manually by using the *CREATE MASTER KEY* statement.

Lesson 7

1. **Correct Answer: B**

   A. **Incorrect:** You can access objects of other databases in the same instance without creating an external data source.

   B. **Correct:** You need to create an external data source when you need to access a different instance.

   C. **Incorrect:** You can access objects of different schemas without creating an external data source.

   D. **Incorrect:** You can access objects of other owners without creating an external data source.

2. **Correct Answers: A and D**

   A. **Correct:** You need to define the OLE DB data source to connect to.

   B. **Incorrect:** You need an OLE DB data source so that you can configure a linked server to an external data source.

   C. **Incorrect:** You need an OLE DB Provider to configure a linked server to an external data source.

   D. **Correct:** You need an OLE DB provider that lets you connect to the external data source.

3. **Correct Answers: B and D**

   A. **Incorrect:** You can define the security mode for each linked server.

   B. **Correct:** The database engine creates a self-mapping security context when you create a linked server. You can change this behavior by configuring a security mapping.

   C. **Incorrect:** The default configuration is self-mapping.

   D. **Correct:** You can choose a different security mode for each linked server.

Chapter 2: Case Scenario Answers

Case Scenario 1: Configuring Security

1. Because you need to provide access to Macintosh clients, you need to configure Mixed Mode authentication. You can use Windows logins for the Windows XP users.

2. You should create two database roles: one for Sales users and another one for Marketing users. With this configuration, you need to manage permissions for only these two roles.

3. To configure the encryption architecture, you need to do the following:

   A. Create a database master key for the CRM database.

   B. Create a certificate in the CRM database and protect the certificate with the database master key.

   C. Create a symmetric key that is protected with the certificate, and use the key to encrypt the data.

Case Scenario 2: Configuring a Heterogeneous Environment

1. You need to create a linked server to provide access from the SQL Server database to the Oracle server. You can then execute distributed queries on the Oracle server and return results to SQL Server data consumers.

2. Because the external data source is a non-SQL Server and does not support Windows authentication, the most secure solution for your connection is to map SQL Server logins to remote Oracle users.

3. To send e-mail to branch offices from your SQL Server application, you need to configure SQL Server Database Mail. Because Database Mail is a standard SMTP client, you do not need to change your infrastructure. You need only a valid SMTP account on the UNIX mail server to create a profile in Database Mail that lets you send e-mail using that SMTP account.

Chapter 3: Lesson Review Answers

Lesson 1

1. **Correct Answer: C**

    A. **Incorrect:** A *text* data type can store up to 2 GB of data but does not allow direct comparison of columns.

    B. **Incorrect:** A *varbinary* data type stores binary data.

    C. **Correct:** A *varchar*(max) column can store up to 2 GB of data while still enabling you to use all functions and comparison operators.

    D. **Incorrect:** A regular *varchar* column cannot store 2 GB of data.

Lesson 2

1. **Correct Answers: A and C**

    A. **Correct:** You can use system functions that return a scalar value in a check constraint.

    B. **Incorrect:** Stored procedures cannot be called within a check constraint.

    C. **Correct:** UDFs that return a scalar value can be referenced in a check constraint.

    D. **Incorrect:** Views cannot be referenced in check constraints.

Lesson 3

1. **Correct Answers: B and D**

    A. **Incorrect:** You cannot enable the CLR on a database-by-database basis.

    B. **Correct:** You must enable the CLR by using the Surface Area Configuration utility.

    C. **Incorrect:** You must compile and load into SQL Server a class that conforms to the UDT specification. However, class creation is not limited exclusively to .NET languages.

    D. **Correct:** You can use any CLR-compatible language, including C#, Visual Basic, and Cobol.NET to create a class for a CLR user-defined type.

Chapter 3: Case Scenario Answers

Case Scenario: Designing a Database

1. There are some core tables that are necessary for this database: Customer, CustomerAddress, CustomerContact, Patient, PatientAddress, Doctor, DoctorAddress, and Claims.

2. You need to create each of these core tables with primary keys to ensure that each row can be uniquely identified.

3. You need to link each table together by using appropriate foreign key constraints to enforce rules such as the following: a claim cannot be entered that is not associated with a company, and a patient's address cannot be created without having the patient in the database first.

4. You should implement additional supporting tables to enforce such things as valid lists of states.

5. You need to define check constraints to enforce specific formatting for data such as Social Security numbers, phone numbers, and e-mail addresses.

6. You need to carefully analyze the claims table to determine whether to store documents in native format such as Word or PDF, or to transform them into a standard exchange format and store them in a schema-enforced XML column.

7. All these choices require you to spend time defining all pieces of data that need to be stored and any business rules that need to be enforced.

Chapter 4: Lesson Review Answers

Lesson 1

1. Correct Answers: B and C

   A. **Incorrect:** An index has a single page at the root level that is called the root page.

   B. **Correct:** An intermediate level can contain zero or more pages, and an index can have multiple intermediate levels.

   C. **Correct:** The leaf level can contain one or more pages; there is only a single leaf level, which is at the bottom of the index.

   D. **Incorrect:** B-tree is the name for the structure of the index, not a level in the structure.

Lesson 2

1. **Correct Answer: B**

   A. **Incorrect:** A unique index requires that the data value in each row for the index is not duplicated, but it does not affect the physical ordering of the table.

   B. **Correct:** A clustered index causes the rows in the table to be physically ordered based on the index definition.

   C. **Incorrect:** A nonclustered index does not enforce a physical structure.

   D. **Incorrect:** A foreign key enforces referential integrity between two tables.

2. **Correct Answer: B**

   A. **Incorrect:** *PAD_INDEX* leaves empty space on intermediate-level pages in the index.

   B. **Correct:** *FILLFACTOR* leaves empty space on the leaf level of an index.

   C. **Incorrect:** *MAXDOP* specifies the maximum degree of parallelism used during index creation.

   D. **Incorrect:** *IGNORE_DUP_KEY* causes duplicates to be ignored for unique indexes.

Lesson 3

1. **Correct Answer: A**

   A. **Correct:** *PAD_INDEX* leaves empty space on intermediate-level pages in the index.

   B. **Incorrect:** *FILLFACTOR* leaves empty space on the leaf level of an index.

   C. **Incorrect:** *MAXDOP* specifies the maximum degree of parallelism used during index creation.

   D. **Incorrect:** *IGNORE_DUP_KEY* causes duplicates to be ignored for unique indexes.

Chapter 4: Case Scenario Answers

Case Scenario: Indexing a Database

1. The first step is to verify that each table in the database has a primary key to ensure that rows can be uniquely identified. You implement the primary keys as indexes, and they should be sufficient to satisfy the requirements of data entry.

2. After verifying that primary keys exist on all the tables, you ensure that each table has a clustered index. To simplify things at this point, until you have much more knowledge about the data-access patterns and the volume and pattern of changes, you decide to alter all the primary keys so that they are clustered indexes as well.

3. You then create additional nonclustered indexes that SQL Server can use to quickly satisfy the search criteria that employees are using to locate claims data. The initial stage of this process is to simply get nonclustered indexes in place for use with the most common queries.

4. In a secondary indexing round, you will take a closer look at the nonclustered indexes to determine whether columns can be included to make the indexes covering indexes for the most common queries.

Chapter 5: Lesson Review Answers

Lesson 1

1. **Correct Answers: A, C, and D**

   A. **Correct:** A full outer join returns nonmatching data from both the left and right tables.

   B. **Incorrect:** An inner join returns only matching data.

   C. **Correct:** A right outer join returns nonmatching data from the right table.

   D. **Correct:** A left outer join returns nonmatching data from the left table.

2. **Correct Answer: D**

   A. **Incorrect:** *AVG* returns the average value of the rows.

   B. **Incorrect:** *COUNT_BIG* returns the count of rows as a big integer.

   C. **Incorrect:** *STDEV* returns the standard deviation of the rows.

   D. **Correct:** *COUNT* returns the count of rows as an integer.

3. **Correct Answer: D**

    A. **Incorrect:** This syntax would return only matches for *"Book"*.

    B. **Incorrect:** This syntax would return matches for *"Book*"* (exact string).

    C. **Incorrect:** This syntax would return only matches for *"Book"*.

    D. **Correct:** This syntax would return all words starting with *"Book"*.

Lesson 2

1. **Correct Answers: A, C, and D**

    A. **Correct:** *STR* converts numbers into strings.

    B. **Incorrect:** *STUFF* inserts strings inside other strings.

    C. **Correct:** *CAST* converts between data types.

    D. **Correct:** *CONVERT* converts between data types.

2. **Correct Answer: C**

    A. **Incorrect:** This method does not exist by default.

    B. **Incorrect:** This method does not exist by default.

    C. **Correct:** *ToString* returns the string representation of the UDT.

    D. **Incorrect:** This method does not exist by default.

3. **Correct Answer: B**

    A. **Incorrect:** *STR* is a system function.

    B. **Correct:** The *AS* keyword is used to create a column alias.

    C. **Incorrect:** The *FROM* keyword is used to query a table.

    D. **Incorrect:** The *COLUMN* keyword is used when defining a table.

Lesson 3

1. **Correct Answers: A, C, and D**

    A. **Correct:** Static cursors do not detect any changes to underlying data.

    B. **Incorrect:** A so-called firehose cursor is a name for a type of forward-only cursor supported by some clients; it is not a SQL Server feature.

    C. **Correct:** Dynamic cursors detect all changes to the underlying data.

    D. **Correct:** Keyset cursors detect some changes to the underlying data.

2. **Correct Answer: B**

   A. **Incorrect:** Prefixing the table name with # creates a local temporary table.

   B. **Correct:** Prefixing the table name with ## creates a global temporary table.

   C. **Incorrect:** Declaring a table using *DECLARE* and prefixing with @ creates a local table variable.

   D. **Incorrect:** Using *SELECT INTO* and specifying a table name prefixed with # creates a local temporary table.

3. **Correct Answers: A, B, and D**

   A. **Correct:** *SELECT INTO* can be used to create local temporary tables.

   B. **Correct:** *SELECT INTO* can be used to create permanent tables.

   C. **Incorrect:** *SELECT INTO* cannot be used to insert data into an existing table.

   D. **Correct:** *SELECT INTO* can be used to create global temporary tables.

Lesson 4

1. **Correct Answer: B**

   A. **Incorrect:** *DELETE FROM TRANSACTION* deletes all rows from a table called *TRANSACTION*.

   B. **Correct:** *COMMIT TRANSACTION* is used to save the data from a transaction.

   C. **Incorrect:** *UPDATE TRANSACTION* returns an error because it is updating no columns in a table called *TRANSACTION*.

   D. **Incorrect:** *SELECT TRANSACTION* returns a single row with an unnamed column with the value "TRANSACTION".

2. **Correct Answer: D**

   A. **Incorrect:** The *ERROR_STATE* function returns the state of the error.

   B. **Incorrect:** The *ERROR_MESSAGE* function returns the message associated with the error.

   C. **Incorrect:** The *ERROR_SEVERITY* function returns the severity of the error.

   D. **Correct:** The *ERROR_NUMBER* function returns the number for the error that occurred.

Chapter 5: Case Scenario Answers

Case Scenario 1: Database-Backed Authoring Application

1. Because the data-validation stored procedures throw exceptions if there are errors in the data, this is a natural case for the *TRY/CATCH* error handling syntax. Proseware developers should start a transaction, perform all data modifications in a *TRY* block, and then execute the data-validation procedures. If there are any errors, they will be caught in the *CATCH* block, and the data modification can be rolled back.

2. Proseware developers can use the *COUNT* aggregate function to determine how many submissions each author had. The query can select from the *Submission* table, using the author ID column as the nonaggregated grouping column.

3. The report should use the *PIVOT* operator to generate a weekly summary. First, developers need to create a derived table that includes the author ID and the week of submission date. They can then pivot this derived table, using the *COUNT* aggregate function, for each week of submission that exists in the quarter.

Case Scenario 2: Banking Corporation

1. Northwind Partners should make sure that all funds-transfer logic participates in transactions. Starting a transaction will ensure that if an error occurs after money is withdrawn from one account, but before it is deposited into another account, the withdrawal can be rolled back, thereby restoring the data to its original state.

2. All data-modification code should be put in *TRY* blocks. Logging code can be placed into the associated *CATCH* blocks.

3. The search should use the *FREETEXT* predicate, which will match a search term even if it's not typed exactly as it appears in the data.

Chapter 6: Lesson Review Answers

Lesson 1

1. **Correct Answer: A**

    A. **Correct:** A partition function defines the boundary points used to partition a table, index, or indexed view.

    B. **Incorrect:** A partition scheme defines the physical storage that partitions will be stored on.

    C. **Incorrect:** There isn't a function that returns the values in a partition. To return values in a partition, you would use a *SELECT* statement in combination with the *$PARTITION* function.

    D. **Incorrect:** The function that returns the number of the partition containing a specified value is *$PARTITION*.

Lesson 2

1. **Correct Answer: B**

    A. **Incorrect:** A partition function defines the boundary points used to partition a table, index, or indexed view.

    B. **Correct:** A partition scheme defines the physical storage on which the partitions are stored.

    C. **Incorrect:** There isn't a function that returns the values in a partition. To return the values in a partition, you would use a *SELECT* statement in combination with the *$PARTITION* function.

    D. **Incorrect:** The function that returns the number of the partition containing a specified value is *$PARTITION*.

Lesson 3

1. **Correct Answers: A and B**

    A. **Correct:** You can partition tables, indexes, and indexed views.

    B. **Correct:** You can partition tables, indexes, and indexed views.

    C. **Incorrect:** Regular views do not contain any data, so they cannot be partitioned.

    D. **Incorrect:** Partitioning is internal to a database, so you cannot partition an entire database.

Lesson 4

1. **Correct Answer: D**

   A. **Incorrect:** A partition function defines the boundary points used to partition a table, index, or indexed view.

   B. **Incorrect:** A partition scheme defines the physical storage that partitions will be stored on.

   C. **Incorrect:** There isn't a function that returns the values in a partition. To retrieve the values in a partition, you use a *SELECT* statement in combination with the *$PARTITION* function.

   D. **Correct:** The function that returns the number of the partition containing a specified value is *$PARTITION*.

Lesson 5

1. **Correct Answer: A**

   A. **Correct:** *SWITCH* exchanges a full partition and an empty partition between tables.

   B. **Incorrect:** *MERGE* removes a boundary point in a partition function.

   C. **Incorrect:** *SPLIT* introduces a new boundary point into a partition function.

   D. **Incorrect:** *INTERSECT* is a new Transact-SQL operator that is not used to manage partitions.

Chapter 6: Case Scenario Answers

Case Scenario: Archiving Data

1. You first partition the *Claims* table by using a datetime column that divides the data based on month.

2. At the beginning of each month, you create a new table that exactly matches the structure of the *Claims* table. Create the new table by using the same partition function and partition scheme as the *Claims* table.

3. Use the *SWITCH* operator to move the oldest partition from the *Claims* table to the newly created, empty table.

4. Execute a *MERGE* operation to remove the boundary point for the month that was just removed.

5. Alter the partition scheme to set the *NEXT USED* filegroup to the one that held the data just removed from the table.

6. Execute a *SPLIT* operation to introduce a new boundary point for the new month.

7. Use SQL Server Integration Services (SSIS) to load the data into a staging table in the *Research* database. The staging table has the same structure as the *Claims* table within this database and uses the same partition function and partition scheme, but the staging table does not have any additional indexes created yet.

8. After you load the data into the staging table, you create the rest of the indexes so that the staging table matches the structure of the *Claims* table. You then truncate the table in the claims database.

9. Execute a *SPLIT* operation against the *Claims* table to create a new empty partition that corresponds to the data in the staging table.

10. Execute a *SWITCH* operation to add the data from the staging table into the *Claims* table.

11. Finally, truncate the staging table.

Chapter 7: Lesson Review Answers

Lesson 1

1. **Correct Answer: B**

   A. **Incorrect:** The *CHECK OPTION* parameter forces queries that modify data using the view to conform to any filter criteria specified in the view definition.

   B. **Correct:** *SCHEMABINDING* prevents a table from being dropped without first dropping views that depend on the table.

   C. **Incorrect:** *UNION* is an operator that can be used in a query.

   D. **Incorrect:** *QUOTED_IDENTIFIER* is a setting that must be set to *ON* to create an indexed view.

Lesson 2

1. **Correct Answer: B**

    A. **Incorrect:** *SCHEMABINDING* prevents a base table from being dropped if a view is created over it.

    B. **Correct:** *CHECK OPTION* ensures that changes made through the view conform to the selection criteria of the view.

    C. **Incorrect:** The *ANSI_NULLS* setting does not limit the modifications that can be performed through a view.

    D. **Incorrect:** The *QUOTED_IDENTIFIER* setting does not limit the modifications that can be performed through a view.

Lesson 3

1. **Correct Answers: A and C**

    A. **Correct:** *QUOTED_IDENTIFIER* has to be set to *ON* when the view and any base tables referenced in the view are created.

    B. **Incorrect:** Two-part names are required for all tables referenced in the view.

    C. **Correct:** The view must have been created with *SCHEMABINDING*.

    D. **Incorrect:** *ANSI_NULLS* has to be turned *ON* when the view and base tables referenced in the view are created.

Chapter 7: Case Scenario Answers

Case Scenario: Creating Views

1. The development group should implement views that return data based on various functions that the applications require. The developers can then replace the application code that currently executes the queries with the new views, ensuring that all applications are using the same query.

2. As long as all the requirements are met, the developers could turn the poorly performing queries into views and then add a clustered index to each view to make it an indexed view. Using indexed views would incur a slight overhead when data is written but could improve performance on read operations.

Chapter 8: Lesson Review Answers

Lesson 1

1. **Correct Answers: A and C**

    A. **Correct:** Document order and structure are preserved because the XML data is stored as text. SQL Server does not modify its contents.

    B. **Incorrect:** When storing XML data in a text column, SQL Server does not allow mixing the XML data with relational data as a result of a query. The only way to do this is to extract the XML data from the text column and assign it to a variable of type *XML*.

    C. **Correct:** This is the most efficient scenario. In cases in which the XML data will not be filtered or modified at the node level, storing it as a text column allows for fast retrieval of the complete XML document.

    D. **Incorrect:** SQL Server 2005 does not offer any indexing for text columns.

2. **Correct Answers: B and C**

    A. **Incorrect:** You can create indexes on XML data type columns, but this is not a function of an XML schema.

    B. **Correct:** An XML schema validates an XML instance whenever a typed XML instance is assigned to or modified.

    C. **Correct:** An XML schema provides information about the types of attributes and elements in the XML data type instance. For example, decimal arithmetic operations can be performed on a decimal value but not on a string value.

    D. **Incorrect:** The XML data type includes methods for manipulating XML data and structure; this is not a function of an XML schema.

Lesson 2

1. **Correct Answer: C**

   A. **Incorrect:** The requested XML structure is made of two levels, so a nested query is required. The formatting indications to create elements and attributes do not match the requested structure.

   B. **Incorrect:** Even though a nested query is used, the inner FOR XML query does not use the TYPE instruction to indicate that the result of the inner query should be of the XML data type, so it will be interpreted as text. The formatting indications to create elements and attributes do not match the requested structure.

   C. **Correct:** A nested query is used to generate a two-level XML structure. The outer query uses an aggregate function to calculate the total number of contacts stored for each company. The inner query retrieves each of the contacts for that company. The inner query composes the columns into attribute-centric XML nested under a *<Contacts>* element. The outer query composes the columns into element-centric XML nested under a *<ContactList>* element.

   D. **Incorrect:** The inner query composes the columns into element-centric XML nested under a *<Contacts>* element. The outer query composes the columns into attribute-centric XML nested under a *<ContactList>* element. The formatting indications to create elements and attributes do not match the requested structure.

2. **Correct Answers: A and D**

   A. **Correct:** The *exist()* method can execute the XQUERY expression. It will return 1 if there are any nodes returned from the expression or 0 if there is nothing returned from the expression.

   B. **Incorrect:** The *modify()* method accepts a different type of expression that includes specific commands for XML data manipulation.

   C. **Incorrect:** The *value()* method accepts XQUERY expressions, but it must validate that the expression returns a single scalar value. This is not the case in this example, so the expression would generate a compilation error.

   D. **Correct:** The *query()* method would execute the XQUERY expression and return an XML fragment as output.

Lesson 3

1. **Correct Answer: C**

    A. **Incorrect:** The *exist()* method of the XML data type provides the ability to execute an XPATH or XQUERY expression to check for the existence of nodes.

    B. **Incorrect:** An XML schema collection is used to type the parameters, variables, and columns of the XML data type.

    C. **Correct:** An annotated XML schema uses special annotation keywords to map an XML schema to a relational schema.

    D. **Incorrect:** A relational schema is the term for data in a relational-tabular format; this schema does not map an XML schema to the database schema.

2. **Correct Answers: B and C**

    A. **Incorrect:** An XML schema validates your XML document: if an XML document conforms to what is declared inside an XML schema, the XML document is said to be valid. An invalid XML document does not conform to what is declared inside an XML schema.

    B. **Correct:** XML views and annotation XML schemas are easy to maintain because they are stored as files on the file system; any changes you make to them do not require recompiling the application.

    C. **Correct:** You can offload the XML rendering from your database system by deploying the XML views and annotated XML schemas on a different machine than the database server.

    D. **Incorrect:** An updategram is the mechanism that compares the original and current views of the XML data to create the Transact-SQL commands that synchronize the changes from the XML data into relational data.

Lesson 4

1. **Correct Answer: C**

    A. **Incorrect:** SQLXML-annotated XSD schemas just declare a mapping between an XML schema and a relational schemSQLXML-annotated XSD schemas by themselves do not support updating the XML data; they must be used in conjunction with SQLXML updategrams.

    B. **Incorrect:** SQLXML updategrams allow modification of XML values but do not support modifying the XML structure. SQLXML updategrams take the XML structure as declared on an annotated XSD schema.

    C. **Correct:** XML DML enables you to modify XML values as well as the XML structure. By using XQUERY constructor functions such as *attribute* and *element*, XML DML supports adding a new dynamic structure to the XML document.

    D. **Incorrect:** You use OPENXML to transform an XML instance into a tabular format. It does not support modifying XML data.

2. **Correct Answer: B**

    A. **Incorrect:** The result of executing the XQUERY expression is a collection of nodes. XQUERY is supported by the *insert* XML DML keyword.

    B. **Correct:** The *insert* instruction is composed of two expressions and one operator. The first expression, the XQUERY expression, extracts all the Employee nodes in this location: */Departments/Department[@id=1]/Employees/Employee*. The second expression indicates that the extracted nodes should be copied into the same location (*/Departments/Department[@id=1]/Employees/Employee*), therefore duplicating the nodes.

    C. **Incorrect:** The *[1]* axis applies to the entire path because it is scoped with the parenthesis. The contents of */Departments/Department[@id=1]/Employees/Employee* will be copied into exactly the same location.

    D. **Incorrect:** XML DML is an extension to the XQUERY language, so it supports the FLWOR expression.

Lesson 5

1. **Correct Answers: A, B, and C**

    A. **Correct:** By processing all documents at once, just a single DOM structure is created in memory.

    B. **Correct:** This is the most important performance practice when using OPENXML. The *sp_xml_removedocument* stored procedure will unload the XML structure and free memory resources.

    C. **Correct:** Using smaller XML tag names could provide a slight improvement in performance, especially if the XML tag names used are very large.

    D. **Incorrect:** Splitting the XML data into multiple files is usually not a good idea because you will need to process each of them independently. This process translates into loading multiple DOM structures in memory instead of just one.

2. **Correct Answers: A, B, and C**

    A. **Correct:** When calling the *sp_xml_preparedocument* stored procedure to use OPENXML, the procedure accepts the following data types: *char, nchar, varchar, nvarchar, text, ntext,* or *xml*. But if the data is stored already as XML, using the *nodes()* method would be easier and provide better performance.

    B. **Correct:** OPENXML enables you to extract XML data out of a single source—a single XML document loaded into memory. By using the *nodes()* method, you can merge multiple XML documents coming from different sources into a single result set.

    C. **Correct:** The XPATH implementation in OPENXML and in the XML data type differs slightly, and it is possible that an XPATH function that works in OPENXML won't work in the XML data type—or the other way around.

    D. **Incorrect:** The syntax for writing OPENXML has not changed from previous versions of SQL Server. Therefore, you don't need to migrate code involving XML manipulation via OPENXML unless any of the previously explained reasons apply.

Lesson 6

1. **Correct Answer: C**

    A. **Incorrect:** A PATH secondary index will not help much in this type of query because the expression is not searching for a specific path, and the path is not even fully specified.

B. **Incorrect:** A PROPERTY secondary index will not help much in this type of query because the expression is not filtering on the table's primary key and extracting values by using the *value()* method.

C. **Correct:** A VALUE secondary index will improve the query performance because the query engine will execute a lookup on the secondary index and serve the query without having to access the XML BLOB.

D. **Incorrect:** SQL Server 2005 does not support creating a clustered index on an XML-typed column.

2. **Correct Answer: D**

A. **Incorrect**: Creating new indexes will not help because the application is inserting more information than it is reading.

B. **Incorrect:** Dropping the secondary indexes would bring a slight improvement in performance, but it is not the best answer.

C. **Incorrect:** Creating new indexes would not help because the application is inserting more information than it is reading.

D. **Correct:** Dropping all the indexes on the XML columns would improve performance because SQL Server would not have to maintain them. You could re-create them later, after the heavy insert activity is finished.

Chapter 8: Case Scenario Answers

Case Scenario 1: Troubleshooting XML Performance by Choosing the Correct Indexing Strategy

1. You should use an XML VALUE index if your queries are value-based, meaning that you will filter by the contents of the nodes first and maybe not by the structure of the XML data. Also, you should use an XML VALUE index when the path is not fully specified or if it includes a wildcard. When such conditions exist, an XML VALUE index is optimal because the key columns of the VALUE index are the node value and path of the primary XML index. In our case scenario, even though we are interested in searching on the values (we must search for feeds that contain specific keywords) and not in the structure, the XQUERY written in the *fn_FindKeyword* function filters first by the node structure and then by the values. Therefore, the VALUE index doesn't provide the best performance.

2. The *for $item in /rss/channel/item, $title in $item/title, $desc in $item/desc* decla-ration in the FLWOR expression will filter first by path to find those nodes that must be processed. In this case, an XML PATH index would be much more valu-able because the key columns are the path and then the node value.

3. Another possible alternative in this specific scenario is to use the SQL Server 2005 Full Text Search service to query the text provided inside the XML feeds.

Case Scenario 2: Handling Data as XML or as Relational Representation

Among the many reasons you could give your manager for your recommended solu-tion, here are some important benefits your company could gain from using XML Web services for this application:

■ The type of information you must store requires order preservation. The order in which questions are formulated depends on previous answers. Preserving order is an XML strength.

■ The different schemes for answer types would be hard to represent in a relational structure. XML easily handles semistructured data, in which some structure in the data is constant, and others might be optional or dependent on other parts of the structure.

■ Because this questionnaire must be given in more than 150 countries, it likely will be easier and more scalable and maintainable to distribute the questions as XML Web services. And if the data will be consumed in XML format, why spend the time and effort to transform it into a different format just for storage?

■ Management will want to run different types of reports against this data (for example, which employees are performing above expectations, which are having morale problems, and so on). And you can use XQUERY to create complex que-ries that span different answer choices and answer formats.

Chapter 9: Lesson Review Answers

Lesson 1

1. **Correct Answers: B and D**

   A. **Incorrect:** Modifying data is not allowed within a function.

   B. **Correct:** A function can return the result of a *SELECT* statement.

   C. **Incorrect:** Stored procedures cannot be executed within a function.

   D. **Correct:** Inserts, updates, and deletes are allowed with local table variables.

Lesson 2

1. **Correct Answer: B**

   A. **Incorrect:** The *ENCRYPTION* option causes SQL Server to encrypt the contents of the stored procedure before storing it.

   B. **Correct:** The *RECOMPILE* option causes SQL Server to compile the stored procedure each time it is executed, generating a new query plan for each execution.

   C. **Incorrect:** *VARYING* is a keyword related to the output parameter of the procedure.

   D. **Incorrect:** The *EXECUTE AS* clause specifies the security context for the stored procedure.

Lesson 3

1. **Correct Answer: C**

   A. **Incorrect:** Indexes cannot be created within a trigger when it is used against the table or view that is the target of the triggering action.

   B. **Incorrect:** Backup and restore operations are not allowed within a trigger.

   C. **Correct:** Triggers can be used to insert data into tables.

   D. **Incorrect:** The structure of a database cannot be changed in a trigger.

Chapter 9: Case Scenario Answers

Case Scenario: Creating Triggers, Functions, and Stored Procedures

1. Because all changes need to be audited, Contoso should implement DML triggers behind each table that log all changes in a set of audit tables. The company should also implement DDL triggers that prevent any changes to objects (*CREATE/ALTER/DROP*) within the database so that structural changes can be controlled and audited.

2. Because the patient risk score is a common calculation that should not be left up to each developer to implement, this calculation should be encapsulated in a function.

3. The company should implement stored procedures that *SELECT, INSERT, UPDATE,* and *DELETE* data so that users do not need permissions directly to the base tables within the database.

Chapter 10: Lesson Review Answers

Lesson 1

1. **Correct Answers: A and C**

    A. **Correct:** When the database recovery model is changed from Full to Bulk-Logged, point-in-time recovery capability is lost and is not reestablished until the recovery model is set back to Full and a log backup is performed.

    B. **Incorrect:** Minimal logging does NOT require that a table have a clustered index. In fact, if a table has a clustered index and the table is not empty, minimal logging cannot occur. Also, the database does not have to be in single-user mode for clustered indexes to be created.

    C. **Correct:** A table lock can prevent users from accessing the data in the table during the bulk load.

    D. **Incorrect:** *bcp* can be run at any time.

Lesson 2

1. **Correct Answers: B and D**

    A. **Incorrect:** The *-T* argument specifies that the connection to SQL Server is a trusted connection. Although you need to establish a connection with the SQL Server, it does not necessarily have to be a trusted connection.

    B. **Correct:** The *-t* argument specifies the field terminator or delimiter, and because the default is a tab, not a comma, you must specify this argument.

    C. **Incorrect:** The *-r* argument specifies the row delimiter, which defaults to newline if not specified. Therefore, you do not need to specify this argument.

    D. **Correct:** The *-F* argument specifies which row is the first row *bcp* should read for import; it defaults to the first row. The data file contains a header row as its first row, so *bcp* must start the import at the second row.

Lesson 3

1. **Correct Answer: B**

   A. **Incorrect:** The SQL Server service user account cannot be used to verify permissions because the SQL Server 2005 instance is not running in Mixed Mode.

   B. **Correct:** File access is verified by using the account of the user who executed the *BULK INSERT* command.

   C. **Incorrect:** The only time permissions would be verified by using the SQL Server Agent service account is if the command is executed by SQL Server Agent as part of a job that did not override the credentials.

   D. **Incorrect:** File permissions are always checked because all processes run within a security context.

Lesson 4

1. **Correct Answers: A and D**

   A. **Correct:** You can use the *OPENROWSET* function in place of a table in the *FROM* clause of a query.

   B. **Incorrect:** You cannot use the *OPENROWSET* function as a direct source for import using *bcp*.

   C. **Incorrect:** You cannot use the *OPENROWSET* function as a direct source for import using *BULK INSERT*.

   D. **Correct:** If the data provider supports it, you can use the *OPENROWSET* function as a target of an *INSERT*, *UPDATE*, or *DELETE* query.

Lesson 5

1. **Correct Answer: D**

   A. **Incorrect:** The wizard has the same GUI no matter where you start it from.

   B. **Incorrect:** There are no additional options added to the wizard by starting it from within BIDS; in fact, the Run Immediately option is removed.

   C. **Incorrect:** You can start the wizard from the command prompt by executing DTSWizard.exe from the proper folder.

   D. **Correct:** When you start the wizard from within BIDS, the package created by the wizard is saved as part of the currently open SSIS project, and no Run Immediately option is available from within the wizard.

Chapter 10: Case Scenario Answers

Case Scenario: Fixing a Bloated Transaction Log

1. First, you verify that the *Logging* table is not involved in replication.

2. Because the beginning and ending identity value for each week's load is stored in another table, you modify the delete script to use the identity in its *WHERE* clause by performing a lookup from the other table.

3. You verify that the user that the script executes as has adequate permissions to change the recovery model and drop and re-create the indexes.

4. You modify the scripts so that just before the delete query is run, you remove all the nonclustered indexes from the table, perform the delete query, and then remove the clustered index from the table.

5. You modify the *BULK INSERT* statements so that they are using the TABLOCK hint.

6. You modify the scripts so that they re-create all the indexes, starting with the clustered index, after all the loads are done.

7. After you complete the previous items, the log no longer bloats during the bulk loads, so you modify the backup strategy so that a log backup is done after the loads are done and the database is put back into the Full recovery model.

Chapter 11: Lesson Review Answers

Lesson 1

1. **Correct Answer: C**

    A. **Incorrect:** Adding the user to the *db_accessadmin* role enables the user to alter user permissions or schemas but does not enable backing up the database.

    B. **Incorrect:** A member of the *db_owner* role is granted full authority to perform any operation against a database. Adding the user to this role would grant elevated security permissions.

C. **Correct:** A member of the *db_backupoperator* role is allowed only to back up the database, log, or checkpoint in the database. No other access is allowed.

D. **Incorrect:** A member of the *sysadmin* role can perform any operation on the entire SQL Server instance. Adding the user to this role would grant elevated permissions.

2. **Correct Answer: B**

A. **Incorrect:** The differential change bitmap page(s) contain one bit for each extent that has been changed. The differential backup will contain all pages in an extent that have changed regardless of whether only a single page in that extent has been written to or all pages have been written to.

B. **Correct:** The differential backup will contain all the extents that have had a change. It does not matter if the change was to a single page, multiple pages, or all pages in an extent. The entire extent is still backed up.

C. **Incorrect:** A differential backup contains all changes that have occurred since the last full backup (at midnight), not since the last differential backup.

D. **Incorrect:** A differential backup contains all changes that have occurred since the last full backup (at midnight), not since the last differential backup.

3. **Correct Answer: B**

A. **Incorrect:** A transaction log backup does not capture uncommitted transactions.

B. **Correct:** A transaction log backup captures all committed transaction in the log, starting with the last LSN that was backed up at 09:10 and continuing forward in the log until it reaches the oldest open transaction.

C. **Incorrect:** A transaction log backup does not capture data pages.

D. **Incorrect:** A transaction log backup does not capture extents.

Lesson 2

1. **Correct Answers: A, C, and D**

    A. **Correct:** Each backup places an entry into the SQL Server error log that contains the database name, file name, and first/last LSN for the backup.

    B. **Incorrect:** This is a table in SQL Server 2000 that contains the history of all backups on the instance. This table no longer exists in SQL Server 2005.

    C. **Correct:** The *msdb.dbo.backupset* table is used to track each backup that is generated. It used with the *msdb.dbo.backupfile* table to identify each file that was created during a backup operation.

    D. **Correct:** The same backup information that is written to the SQL Server error log is also written to the Application Event Log.

2. **Correct Answers: B and C**

    A. **Incorrect:** The inactive claims are in FG5, so a filegroup backup of the active claims (FG4) does not do any good.

    B. **Correct:** The last full backup of the database needs to be restored.

    C. **Correct:** After restoring the last full backup, the most recent differential backup should be restored, followed by every subsequent transaction log backup.

    D. **Incorrect:** Because the filegroup differential backup is executed against FG4, it cannot be used to recover FG5.

Lesson 3

1. **Correct Answers: C and D**

    A. **Incorrect:** A data pump task in SSIS only moves data from one location to another. It does not transfer all other objects in a database nor does it transfer users, schemas, or permissions.

    B. **Incorrect:** When a database is detached, it is no longer accessible. Therefore, users would not be able to run reports.

    C. **Correct:** You could use backup and restore to move the database, which would leave the original database on Server1 for reporting while enabling you to create a copy of the database on Server2.

    D. **Correct:** You can use SMO to extract all the elements of the database on Server1 and re-create them on Server2.

Chapter 11: Case Scenario Answers

Case Scenario: Designing a Backup Strategy

1. You need to implement backups of some type immediately, which will mean explaining to management, usually many times, all the ways that a SAN can actually be taken offline or become unavailable. All the rest of the planning and testing can wait for a later time.

2. As an immediate solution, you should implement a strategy of full, differential, and transaction log backups. On a 500-GB+ database, it is unlikely that you will meet the 30-minute downtime threshold, but being able to at least restore the database to either a point in time or up to the point of failure is a major step forward. To meet the five minutes or less of data loss will require transaction log backups. Providing for a margin of error, create transaction log backups that run every two minutes. To minimize the number of transaction log backups that need to be applied, implement differential backups that run every four hours. For now, a full backup every day should be sufficient as long as adequate storage space is available.

3. Thinking longer term, you need to break down the entire database as well as access patterns on the data. Because of the amount of data in the database, restore operations will prove time-consuming, and the situation will only get worse. In many operational systems, data eventually reaches a point at which it is no longer modified. As data continues to age, it is rarely read and then finally reaches a point when it is never again accessed. However, you cannot simply throw it away. You need to determine the aging pattern so that you can implement archival routines that will reduce the volume of data needing to be backed up on a daily basis. You should also change the storage structure within the database through distinct placement of tables on specific filegroups as well as using partitioning. You can switch to filegroup backups that can target a subset of the database and enable your backups to consume less space as well as provide more granular and efficient restores. You need to perform all these tasks within the context of figuring out how to restore all or a portion of the database within business requirements and then designing the backup strategy required to meet those needs.

Chapter 12: Lesson Review Answers

Lesson 1

1. **Correct Answer: D**

    A. **Incorrect:** This view is used to return current low-level I/O, locking, latching, and access method activity for each partition of a table or index in the database.

    B. **Incorrect:** This view is used to return counts of different types of index operations and the time each type of operation was last performed.

    C. **Incorrect:** This view is used to determine information about missing indexes.

    D. **Correct:** This view is used to determine index fragmentation levels.

2. **Correct Answer: C**

    A. **Incorrect:** The avg_fragment_size_in_pages column displays information about the average number of pages in one fragment in the leaf level of an IN_ROW_DATA allocation unit, not external fragmentation levels.

    B. **Incorrect:** The avg_page_space_used_in_percent column displays information about internal fragmentation levels.

    C. **Correct:** The avg_fragmentation_in_percent column displays information about external fragmentation levels.

    D. **Incorrect:** The avg_record_size_in_bytes column displays information about the average record size in bytes, not external fragmentation levels.

3. **Correct Answer: A**

    A. **Correct:** You should use the *ALTER INDEX...REBUILD* statement to correct index external fragmentation levels of greater than 15 percent.

    B. **Incorrect:** You should use the *ALTER INDEX...REORGANIZE* statement only when external fragmentation levels are between 10 percent and 15 percent.

    C. **Incorrect:** You use the *ALTER INDEX...DISABLE* statement to disable indexes, not to correct index fragmentation.

    D. **Incorrect:** You use the *ALTER INDEX SET STATISTICS_NORECOMPUTE = ON* statement to determine whether distribution statistics are automatically recomputed.

Lesson 2

1. **Correct Answer: D**

   A. **Incorrect:** The *sys.stats_columns* catalog view displays a row for each column that is part of *sys.stats* statistics and does not show when the statistics were last updated.

   B. **Incorrect:** *DBCC SHOWCONTIG* displays index fragmentation information.

   C. **Incorrect:** *DBCC SHOW_STATISTICS* shows statistics information, but does not show the date the statistics were last updated.

   D. **Correct:** The *STATS_DATE* function shows the date statistics were last updated.

2. **Correct Answer: A**

   A. **Correct:** The *sp_autostats* system stored procedure displays or changes the automatic *UPDATE STATISTICS* setting for a specific index and statistics or for all indexes and statistics for a specified table or indexed view in the current database.

   B. **Incorrect:** The *sys.stats* catalog view displays a row for each statistic of a tabular object of the type U, V, or TF.

   C. **Incorrect:** The *UPDATE STATISTICS* statement is used to manually update statistics.

   D. **Incorrect:** The *CREATE STATISTICS* statement is used to manually create statistics.

Lesson 3

1. **Correct Answer: C**

   A. **Incorrect:** The *DBCC SHRINKDATABASE* statement will not set a database to shrink automatically; it is a manual shrink statement.

   B. **Incorrect:** The *DBCC SHRINKFILE* statement will not set a database to shrink automatically; it is a manual shrink statement.

   C. **Correct:** Setting each database to shrink automatically by using the *ALTER DATABASE* statement will allow the database engine to periodically shrink the databases.

   D. **Incorrect:** You can use the *ALTER DATABASE* statement to allow the database engine to automatically shrink a database.

2. **Correct Answer: A**

   A. **Correct:** By creating a job and scheduling the job to run at night, you can execute the *DBCC SHRINKFILE* statement against individual database files during the night, when your end users are not using the database.

   B. **Incorrect:** The *ALTER DATABASE* statement, which automatically shrinks a database, cannot be scheduled.

   C. **Incorrect:** The *DBCC SHRINKDATABASE* statement does not let you schedule the operation unless you create a job to execute the statement.

   D. **Incorrect:** The *ALTER DATABASE* statement, which automatically shrinks a database, cannot be scheduled.

Lesson 4

1. **Correct Answer: A**

   A. **Correct:** The *DBCC CHECKDB* statement issues the *DBCC CHECKCATA-LOG* statement during its execution.

   B. **Incorrect:** The *DBCC CHECKDB* statement does not issue the *DBCC CHECKIDENT* statement during its execution.

   C. **Incorrect:** The *DBCC CHECKDB* statement does not issue the *DBCC NEWALLOC* statement during its execution because this statement has been discontinued in SQL Server 2005.

   D. **Incorrect:** The *DBCC CHECKDB* statement does not issue the *DBCC TEXT-ALLOC* statement during its execution; this statement has been discontinued in SQL Server 2005.

2. **Correct Answer: C**

   A. **Incorrect:** Although you can use this option against large databases, the *PHYSICAL_ONLY* option is recommended for frequent integrity checks against large databases because of its small overhead.

   B. **Incorrect:** Although this option can be used against large databases, the *PHYSICAL_ONLY* option is recommended for frequent integrity checks against large databases because of its small overhead.

C. **Correct:** The *PHYSICAL_ONLY* option is recommended for frequent checks against large databases because of its small overhead. This option checks the physical consistency of the database and can detect torn pages, checksum failures, and common hardware failures that can compromise a user's data.

D. **Incorrect:** Although this option can be used against large databases, the *PHYSICAL_ONLY* option is recommended for frequent checks against large databases because of its small overhead.

Chapter 12: Case Scenario Answers

Case Scenario 1: Defragmenting an Index

1. SQL Server 2005 exposes index fragmentation levels through the *sys.dm_db_index_physical_stats* DMF. Your job should call this DMF to check for index fragmentation and determine whether it needs to perform any operations to defragment indexes.

2. Your job should check for external fragmentation by looking for values over 10 percent in the avg_fragmentation_in_percent column returned by the *sys.dm_db_index_physical_stats* DMF.

3. Your job should check for internal fragmentation by looking for values under 75 percent in the avg_page_space_used_in_percent column returned by the *sys.dm_db_index_physical_stats* DMF.

Case Scenario 2: Maintaining Database Integrity

1. When issuing the *DBCC CHECKDB* statement against large databases, your job will use the *PHYSICAL_ONLY* option to lessen the amount of time it takes for the *DBCC CHECKDB* statement to complete.

2. As part of your integrity-check job, you plan to periodically execute the *DBCC CHECKDB* statement with no options to limit the check.

3. Your plan for correcting errors found during the execution of the *DBCC CHECKDB* statement is to first restore the database. If you cannot restore the database for any reason, you plan to execute the *DBCC CHECKDB* statement with one of the repair options to correct the integrity error.

Chapter 13: Lesson Review Answers

Lesson 1

1. **Correct Answers: A and B**

   A. **Correct:** An *HTTP* endpoint allows only one type of payload: *SOAP*.

   B. **Correct:** An *HTTP* endpoint supports either HTTP traffic (specified by the *CLEAR* option) or HTTPS traffic (specified by the *SSL* option).

   C. **Incorrect:** An *HTTP* endpoint allows only the *SOAP* payload. A *TCP* endpoint supports the *TSQL* payload.

   D. **Incorrect:** An *HTTP* endpoint supports Windows authentication or certification-based authentication.

2. **Correct Answers: B and D**

   A. **Incorrect:** Mixed Mode allows both Windows accounts and SQL Server logins to be used. SQL Server logins do not require authentication to the domain.

   B. **Correct:** The Windows login option forces all logins to be Windows logins.

   C. **Incorrect:** This option communicates over HTTP and does not encrypt the data.

   D. **Correct:** This option will create encrypted communications between the client and the endpoint by using HTTPS.

Lesson 2

1. **Correct Answer: C**

   A. **Incorrect:** By specifying *CLEAR* for the *PORTS* parameter, communication occurs on port 80 in an unencrypted format.

   B. **Incorrect:** By specifying a *SCHEMA* option of *STANDARD* in the *WEB-METHOD* clause, an XSD schema is not sent back in the SOAP response because this overrides the *SCHEMA* setting for the endpoint. To load results into a *DataSet* object, an XSD is required.

   C. **Correct:** To ensure encrypted communications, you must specify *SSL* for the *PORTS* parameter. To load the result set into a *DataSet*, an XSD must be returned in the SOAP response.

   D. **Incorrect:** Although this endpoint is created with all of the appropriate options, it is disabled and does not respond to any requests.

Chapter 13: Case Scenario Answers

Case Scenario: Creating *HTTP* Endpoints

1. You need to create two stored procedures in the patient claims database. One stored procedure will retrieve only the subset of data the service provider is allowed to see. The other stored procedure will write into the database any data sent from the service provider.

2. To secure the access, you need to expose these stored procedures as Web methods on an *HTTP* endpoint. The endpoint needs to specify *PORTS(SSL)* to ensure that all traffic is encrypted on the network. The service provider will need to use a *LOGIN_TYPE* of *MIXED* because it is not allowed any direct access to the Contoso network. You will then need to grant this login permission to execute the stored procedures as well as the *CONNECT* permission on the *HTTP* endpoint.

Chapter 14: Lesson Review Answers

Lesson 1

1. **Correct Answers: B and D**
   A. **Incorrect:** A job category is used to categorize a job.
   B. **Correct:** Transact-SQL job steps use the job owner to determine access to database objects. For other types of job steps, the owner is used to determine access authority for proxy accounts that SQL Server Agent impersonates.
   C. **Incorrect:** SQL Server Agent executes jobs.
   D. **Correct:** Only the job owner or a member of the *sysadmin* role can modify or delete a job.

2. **Correct Answers: A and C**
   A. **Correct:** You can specify a job to run on a monthly, weekly, or daily basis.
   B. **Incorrect:** You can create an alert for a performance condition that can execute a job when the condition is met. However, performance conditions are not scheduling options.
   C. **Correct:** Jobs can be specified to execute when SQL Server Agent starts.
   D. **Incorrect:** The smallest scheduling interval that you can specify is once per minute.

Lesson 2

1. **Correct Answers: B and C**

   A. **Incorrect:** A maintenance plan can execute a SQL Server Agent job, and that job can create a database. But database creation is not a task type for a maintenance plan.

   B. **Correct:** You can perform full, differential, or transaction log backups as well as backup history cleanup within a maintenance plan.

   C. **Correct:** You can update statistics, reorganize an index, and rebuild an index.

   D. **Incorrect:** A maintenance plan can execute a SQL Server Agent job, and that job can execute an SSIS package. But package execution is not a task type for a maintenance plan.

Lesson 3

1. **Correct Answers: A, B, and C**

   A. **Correct:** Although a cell phone is not a notification type, it responds to a phone number just like a pager and can receive text messages.

   B. **Correct:** A pager can be specified to receive a text message.

   C. **Correct:** In addition to text message notification, an operator can be configured to receive notifications via e-mail and net send.

   D. **Incorrect:** The notification infrastructure does not currently support instant messaging.

Lesson 4

1. **Correct Answers: B and D**

   A. **Incorrect:** Although you can specify alerts based on performance counters, these counters are limited to SQL Server counters.

   B. **Correct:** SQL Server counters can be used to define a performance condition alert.

   C. **Incorrect:** Changing security permissions cannot be monitored by alerts.

   D. **Correct:** An alert can be created based on an error code, an error severity level, and an error containing a particular string.

Chapter 14: Case Scenario Answers

Case Scenario: Scheduling Administrative Actions

1. The Contoso DBAs should create a job to execute a full database backup every day at 23:00. Alternatively, they could create a maintenance plan to perform a full database backup every day at 23:00.

2. Because Contoso shuts down the servers every day at 04:00, the company cannot count on a job schedule that executes a full backup at a specific time. Instead, the DBAs should add a second job schedule to the full backup job that executes when SQL Server Agent starts. This approach ensures that as soon as SQL Server Agent starts, a full backup is performed.

3. Contoso requirements dictate that the recovery strategy cannot allow more than 10 minutes of data loss. The company also requires a maximum of eight restore operations to recover the database. Contoso already performs full backups at 23:00 and when SQL Server Agent starts. To meet the recovery requirements, the company also needs to configure jobs for differential and transaction log backups. DBAs should create a job to execute a differential backup once an hour and a second job to execute a transaction log backup every 10 minutes. To recover to any point in time, the DBAs need to apply the following backups in this order:

   A. The most recent full backup

   B. The most recent differential backup

   C. Up to six transaction log backups (one of these being a backup of the tail of the log)

Chapter 15: Lesson Review Answers

Lesson 1

1. **Correct Answers: B and D**

   A. **Incorrect:** CPU utilization is a hardware counter that System Monitor can log. Profiler can trace only SQL Server events.

   B. **Correct:** By specifying the *SP: StmtStarting* or *SP: StmtCompleted* event, you can capture any statement executing within a stored procedure.

   C. **Incorrect:** You use System Monitor to capture network I/O statistics, which Profiler cannot capture.

   D. **Correct:** The *SP:Recompile* event logs any recompiles of a stored procedure.

2. **Correct Answers: A and C**

   A. **Correct:** You can save a trace to a file. The format cannot be specified; the content is saved in binary format.

   B. **Incorrect:** A trace is saved in binary format.

   C. **Correct:** You can save a trace into a table.

   D. **Incorrect:** The file format cannot be specified; SQL Server saves a trace in a binary format.

3. **Correct Answers: B and D**

   A. **Incorrect:** You can specify a predefined trace template, which is a collection of events, columns, and filters. But traces do not have categories.

   B. **Correct:** File rollover can be specified when you specify that you want to save the trace to a file. This parameter is used in conjunction with the maximum file size parameter.

   C. **Incorrect:** You cannot limit the resources that a trace uses, such as memory, processor, or network I/O. A trace will consume as many resources as necessary to capture events. However, if the server becomes too busy, some events may be skipped.

   D. **Correct:** You can filter events by defining filter criteria that an event must meet for it to be logged. You use filters to focus a trace on a particular problem.

Lesson 2

1. **Correct Answers: B and D**

   A. **Incorrect:** System Monitor captures only numerical data and cannot be used to capture the applications being launched in Windows.

   B. **Correct:** Windows ships with hundreds of counters related to hardware and Windows performance.

   C. **Incorrect:** You use Profiler to capture the queries being executed in SQL Server.

   D. **Correct:** You can create custom counters for your application that System Monitor can use. If you were to create a counter for the number of orders being placed per second, System Monitor could capture that information.

Lesson 3

1. **Correct Answers: B and C**

   A. **Incorrect:** A deadlock trace does not contain the necessary data for DTA analysis.

   B. **Correct:** You can load a file containing Transact-SQL into DTA as the source for analysis.

   C. **Correct:** By using the Tuning template that ships with SQL Server Profiler, you can generate trace data and save it to a table to be used as a workload source.

   D. **Incorrect:** A counter log is created within System Monitor and cannot be consumed by DTA.

2. **Correct Answers: C and D**

   A. **Incorrect:** DTA can recommend the creation of indexed views, but it will not specify the creation of a regular view.

   B. **Incorrect:** DTA can be used to recommend indexes that can be dropped, but it is not an explicit configuration option.

   C. **Correct:** You can specify online indexes only by using the Advanced Options button.

   D. **Correct:** You can restrict tuning to creation of nonclustered indexes only.

Lesson 4

1. **Correct Answer: D**

   A. **Incorrect:** The *sys.dm_os_performance_counters* DMV returns all the SQL Server performance counters as a result set, but it does not contain any information about blocked processes.

   B. **Incorrect:** Although *sys.dm_os_wait_stats* can indicate whether processes have to wait an excessive amount of time for a resource to be allocated, it does not allow identification of blocking nor can it correlate to specific users.

   C. **Incorrect:** The *sys.dm_db_index_physical_stats* DMV will display detailed statistics for specified indexes within a database, but it does not contain information about blocked processes.

   D. **Correct:** The *sys.dm_exec_requests* DMV contains one row for each executable thread in SQL Server. One of the columns in this view is called *blocking_session_id*. A nonzero value in this column indicates the SPID that is blocking the execution of this request.

Lesson 5

1. **Correct Answer: D**

    A. **Incorrect:** The text data column in Profiler displays the query that was exe-cuted, but cannot be correlated to the statistical information in a System Monitor counter log.

    B. **Incorrect:** Although a System Monitor counter log maintains a time dimen-sion internally, it does not correlate to the End Time column in a trace.

    C. **Incorrect:** The SPID in SQL Server does not have any context outside of SQL Server, so it cannot be understood by a System Monitor counter log.

    D. **Correct:** The Start Time column is used to synchronize events between a System Monitor counter log and a Profiler trace.

Lesson 6

1. **Correct Answers: C and D**

    A. **Incorrect:** SQL Server does not lock individual columns in a table.

    B. **Incorrect:** SQL Server does not lock individual columns in a table.

    C. **Correct:** Shared locks can be acquired at the row, page, and table levels.

    D. **Correct:** Exclusive locks can be acquired at the row, page, and table levels.

Lesson 7

1. **Correct Answer: D**

    A. **Incorrect:** Neither the DTA nor the command-line version, dta.exe, are allowed to connect to the DAC.

    B. **Incorrect:** *osql* was the command-line utility in SQL Server 2000 and can-not connect to the DAC.

    C. **Incorrect:** The object browser in SSMS requires multiple threads, which is not allowed with the DAC.

    D. **Correct:** The DAC can be accessed only from the SQLCMD command-line utility or a query window inside SSMS.

Chapter 15: Case Scenario Answers

Case Scenario: Diagnosing Performance Problems

NOTE **Summary of main activities**

The following answers do not represent a complete solution. They are intended to highlight some of the activities necessary.

---

1. To find the deadlocks, you first need to use SQL Server Profiler to create a dead-lock trace. Use the Tuning template to create the trace and specify that output be sent to a file.

2. After the trace is completed and the trace data is saved to files, load the saved trace files into a table to be used as a workload source for the DTA.

3. Execute a DTA analysis to look for indexes and indexed views that should be created to improve performance.

4. Use the *sys.dm_db_missing_index** views and functions to find indexes that SQL Server has identified as useful for the queries and use this information to determine new indexes to add.

5. Use the *sys.dm_exec** views and functions to identify blocking within the system and quickly target the code that needs to be fixed.

6. Run various queries against the trace files that you loaded into a table to identify the top 15 most expensive queries in descending order, which enables you to target your tuning activity to those queries with the most impact.

7. After you have addressed these immediate performance issues, use SQL Server Agent to create automated solutions to regularly capture traces, load them into tables, and then analyze them to identify queries that the IT staff needs to look at for performance issues.

8. Create automated processes to identify indexes that are not being used so that the IT team can consider dropping them to improve performance of write activity.

Chapter 16: Lesson Review Answers

Lesson 1

1. **Correct Answer: C**

    A. **Incorrect:** You cannot execute a *BACKUP*, *RESTORE*, or *DETACH* operation against a Database Snapshot.

    B. **Incorrect:** Changes are not allowed to any objects or structural elements in a Database Snapshot.

    C. **Correct:** You can execute any type of *SELECT* statement against a Database Snapshot with the exception of full-text queries.

    D. **Incorrect:** A Database Snapshot is read-only and does not allow changes to data.

2. **Correct Answers: A and D**

    A. **Correct:** Any user database can be the source of a Database Snapshot.

    B. **Incorrect:** Database Snapshots are not allowed to be created against system databases.

    C. **Incorrect:** Database Snapshots cannot be created against another Database Snapshot.

    D. **Correct:** A Database Snapshot can be created against the mirror database within a Database Mirroring session.

3. **Correct Answers: B and C**

    A. **Incorrect:** Only pages that have changed since the creation of the Database Snapshot are copied.

    B. **Correct:** The copy-on-write process writes the original image of the data page from the source database when it is first changed following the creation of a Database Snapshot.

    C. **Correct:** The copy-on-write process updates the catalog of changed pages within the Database Snapshot. The catalog of changed pages is used to determine where to obtain data to satisfy a query.

    D. **Incorrect:** A Database Snapshot does not generally contain metadata of its own. Instead, it exposes the metadata from the source database.

Lesson 2

1. **Correct Answers: B and D**

   A. **Incorrect:** You do not need to drop full text catalogs before reverting the database. The full text catalogs are automatically dropped during the revert operation and must be rebuilt.

   B. **Correct:** The revert of the database places both the source database and Database Snapshot into a restoring mode, so no users are allowed to be connected to the database when the restore operation is initiated.

   C. **Incorrect:** Log shipping does not need to be stopped, but because the revert process will rebuild the transaction log and break the log backup chain, log shipping will need to be reinitialized.

   D. **Correct:** Only one Database Snapshot can exist against a source database when a database is reverted from a Database Snapshot.

Chapter 16: Case Scenario Answers

Case Scenario: Implementing Database Snapshots for Administrative Actions

1. The job that creates the full backup prior to the import routines can be replaced with the creation of a Database Snapshot. This eliminates the time required to back up the database while still giving DBAs the option to return the database to the state it was in before the import routines were executed.

2. A job can be created in SQL Server Agent that creates Database Snapshots against the patient claims database at auditor-specified intervals, such as once per hour. Auditors can then choose the version of the data they want to view. Database Snapshots require much less administrative time and effort than any implementation of any other process such as backup/restore, log shipping, or replication while also minimizing the amount of disk space that is potentially used.

Chapter 17: Lesson Review Answers

Lesson 1

1. **Correct Answer: B**

    A. **Incorrect:** A publisher is a role for a database participating in replication.

    B. **Correct:** The principal is one of the roles for database mirroring and specifies the database that is accepting connections and processing transactions.

    C. **Incorrect:** A primary server is a generic role in a High Availability architecture.

    D. **Incorrect:** The monitor server participates in log shipping.

2. **Correct Answers: B and D**

    A. **Incorrect:** The High Protection operating mode does not use a witness.

    B. **Correct:** The High Availability operating mode has a witness that is used to arbitrate automatic failover.

    C. **Incorrect:** The witness cannot serve the database.

    D. **Correct:** A single witness server can service multiple database mirroring sessions.

Lesson 2

1. **Correct Answers: B and D**

    A. **Incorrect:** Distribution is configured when you are implementing replication.

    B. **Correct:** A backup of the primary database is restored to the mirror.

    C. **Incorrect:** If the database is recovered, it cannot participate in the database mirroring session.

    D. **Correct:** The database must be unrecovered to participate in database mirroring.

2. **Correct Answer: A**

    A. **Correct:** The database must be in Full recovery model.

    B. **Incorrect:** Database mirroring requires that you configure the database with the default SQL Server 2005 (90) compatibility level because the database mirroring feature does not exist in previous versions of SQL Server.

C. **Incorrect:** If the primary database is in a read-only state, transactions cannot be issued against it, so it is incompatible with database mirroring.

D. **Incorrect:** The database cannot be placed in Bulk-Logged recovery model while participating in database mirroring.

Lesson 3

1. **Correct Answers: A and C**

    A. **Correct:** You can create a *TCP* endpoint to service *TSQL* requests, which is how the default communications on Port 1433 are implemented in SQL Server 2005.

    B. **Incorrect:** Database mirroring is not supported on the *HTTP* endpoint type.

    C. **Correct:** You must create all endpoints servicing database mirroring with a type of *TCP* and a payload of *DATABASE_MIRRORING*.

    D. **Incorrect:** *HTTP* endpoints service *SOAP* requests, not *TSQL* requests.

2. **Correct Answers: B and D**

    A. **Incorrect:** The default state is *STOPPED*, which does not allow connections to be created.

    B. **Correct:** You must specify a port number for communications.

    C. **Incorrect:** This option is available only for *HTTP* endpoints with a *SOAP* payload.

    D. **Correct:** To exchange transactions between the principal and mirror database, the endpoint created on the instance hosting these databases must be created with a role of either *PARTNER* or *ALL*.

Lesson 4

1. **Correct Answers: B and C**

    A. **Incorrect:** High Performance operating mode has asynchronous data transfer.

    B. **Correct:** High Availability and High Protection operating modes have synchronous transfer.

    C. **Correct:** Automatic failover is available only with High Availability operating mode and only when the witness server is online.

    D. **Incorrect:** High Protection and High Performance operating modes require manual failover.

2. **Correct Answers: A and D**

   A. **Correct:** High Performance operating mode has asynchronous data transfer.

   B. **Incorrect:** High Availability and High Protection operating modes have synchronous transfer.

   C. **Incorrect:** Automatic failover is available only with High Availability operating mode when a witness is present.

   D. **Correct:** High Protection and High Performance operating modes require manual failover.

3. **Correct Answers: B and D**

   A. **Incorrect:** High Performance operating mode has asynchronous data transfer.

   B. **Correct:** High Availability and High Protection operating modes have synchronous transfer.

   C. **Incorrect:** Automatic failover is available only with High Availability operating mode when a witness is present.

   D. **Correct:** High Protection and High Performance operating modes require manual failover.

Lesson 5

1. **Correct Answer: D**

   A. **Incorrect:** Setting *PARTNER OFF* will remove the database mirroring session instead of failing it over.

   B. **Incorrect:** Setting the witness to *OFF* will remove the witness from the database mirroring session but will not cause a failover.

   C. **Incorrect:** The *FAILOVER* option can be executed only from the principal.

   D. **Correct:** The *FORCE_SERVICE_ALLOW_DATA_LOSS* option can be executed from the mirror when the witness is either off or connected to the mirror and the principal is not visible to the mirror.

Lesson 6

1.   **Correct Answers: A and B**

   A.   **Correct:** You can issue this command against either the principal or the mirror.

   B.   **Correct:** You can issue this command against either the principal or the mirror.

   C.   **Incorrect:** The only role of the witness server is to monitor the database mirroring session. You cannot terminate the database mirroring session from the witness.

   D.   **Incorrect:** A distributor is a role in replication and does not participate in database mirroring.

Chapter 17: Case Scenario Answers

Case Scenario: Implementing Database Mirroring

1.   Contoso can configure database mirroring in High Availability operating mode to achieve its availability goals. This mode allows the database to automatically fail over if the principal becomes unavailable. Although this configuration alone does not meet the requirement that the failover be transparent to the application, if a minor change is made to the application's connection logic, Contoso can take advantage of the transparent client redirect capability. To achieve seamless redirection in the event of a failover, Contoso developers would have to trap an error caused by a disconnect and simply reconnect to the server.

2.   Contoso DBAs can offload audit reporting to the mirror by creating a database snapshot of the mirror.

Chapter 18: Lesson Review Answers

Lesson 1

1. **Correct Answers: A and D**

   A. **Correct:** SQL Server 2005 Enterprise Edition supports log shipping.

   B. **Incorrect:** SQL Server 2005 Express Edition does not support SQL Server Agent; therefore, the log shipping process is not supported in this edition.

   C. **Incorrect:** SQL Server 2000 cannot participate in a SQL Server 2005 log shipping configuration because log shipping does not support interversion operations.

   D. **Correct:** SQL Server 2005 Workgroup Edition supports log shipping.

2. **Correct Answer: D**

   A. **Incorrect:** The ANSI NULL Default option does not affect the log shipping configuration.

   B. **Incorrect:** Log shipping can be configured in databases with any compatibility level.

   C. **Incorrect:** The Quoted Identifiers Enable option does not affect the log shipping configuration.

   D. **Correct:** Log shipping requires the primary database to be in either Full or Bulk-Logged recovery model.

3. **Correct Answers: B and C**

   A. **Incorrect:** The primary server's SQL Server Agent service account does not require full access to the shared folder for backups; only read/write access is required.

   B. **Correct:** Log shipping requires the primary server to write the backup files to the backup shared folder.

   C. **Correct:** Log shipping requires the secondary server to read the backup files in the backup shared folder.

   D. **Incorrect:** Log shipping requires the secondary server to access the backup shared folder.

Lesson 2

1. **Correct Answer: B**

   A. **Incorrect:** The restore process, by default, preserves the path of the primary database files.

   B. **Correct:** By default, the restore process maintains the database file paths between the primary and secondary databases.

   C. **Incorrect:** The restore process, by default, preserves the path of the primary database files.

   D. **Incorrect:** The Database Default Location applies only to new databases, not to restored databases.

2. **Correct Answers: A and D**

   A. **Correct:** You can use the *sp_add_log_shipping_secondary_primary* and *sp_add_log_shipping_secondary_database* system stored procedures to create a log shipping configuration.

   B. **Incorrect:** You use the Maintenance Plan Wizard in SQL Server 2000 databases to create log shipping configurations, but not in SQL Server 2005 databases.

   C. **Incorrect:** You don't use the SQL Server Surface Area Configuration tool to configure log shipping.

   D. **Correct:** In SSMS, you use the Database Properties window to configure a log shipping process.

Lesson 3

1. **Correct Answers: B and D**

   A. **Incorrect:** When the secondary database is in No Recovery mode, users cannot query it.

   B. **Correct:** When the log shipping configuration is in No Recovery mode, the secondary database is not available for users to query.

   C. **Incorrect:** Because the secondary database is not available for user queries, you can't use the secondary server to increase the scalability/performance of your application.

   D. **Correct:** Because the secondary database is not available for user queries, you can use it as a standby server to increase the availability of your application.

2. **Correct Answer: C**

   A. **Incorrect:** Disconnecting users from the secondary database is one of the options for Standby mode.

   B. **Incorrect:** When log shipping is in No Recovery mode, users cannot query the secondary database.

   C. **Correct:** The DBA must decide whether users will be disconnected from the secondary database during the restore log task or whether to leave users connected.

   D. **Incorrect:** Disconnecting users from the secondary database is one of the options of Standby mode.

Lesson 4

1. **Correct Answer: B**

   A. **Incorrect:** Log shipping does not provide an automatic failover configuration.

   B. **Correct:** A monitor server provides a central location to store combined detail and historic records of log shipping tasks on the primary and secondary servers.

   C. **Incorrect:** The monitor server does not reduce the workload of the primary server; it only keeps a record of log shipping tasks.

   D. **Incorrect:** The monitor server does not reduce the workload of the secondary server; it only keeps a record of log shipping tasks.

2. **Correct Answers: C and D**

   A. **Incorrect:** The log shipping configuration is always stored in the *msdb* database.

   B. **Incorrect:** The monitor server configuration does not include any operator configuration.

   C. **Correct:** The History Retention option determines how long the results of log shipping tasks will be stored.

   D. **Correct:** The Monitor Instance option sets the name of the database engine instance responsible for tracking the log shipping process.

Chapter 18: Case Scenario Answers

Case Scenario 1: Providing Reporting Scalability

1. Use a log shipping configuration consisting of one primary server and two secondary servers.

2. Use Standby mode and then redirect reports and PivotTable queries to the secondary servers.

3. You need to make sure that the recovery model of the primary database is set to either Full or Bulk-Logged; log shipping is not supported in the Simple recovery model.

Case Scenario 2: Providing Fault Tolerance for Multiple Servers

1. Use four log shipping configurations to copy databases from each of the primary servers onto a single secondary server that you will use as a standby server for high availability. This strategy minimizes cost while still providing Fabrikam, Inc. with increased reliability for its database applications.

2. Use No Recovery mode to increase the availability of the applications.

3. The secondary server must have access to the network backup shared folder of each configuration. Each primary server must have read and write access to its shared folder.

Chapter 19: Lesson Review Answers

Lesson 1

1. **Correct Answers: B and D**

   A. **Incorrect:** Snapshot replication publishes all data every time; it does not require monitoring changes in the publishing database.

   B. **Correct:** Transactional replication uses the Log Reader Agent to monitor the transactional log and capture data changes.

   C. **Incorrect:** Merge replication uses a combination of uniqueidentifier columns, triggers, and tables to capture changes in the database.

   D. **Correct:** Peer-to-peer replication is a special implementation of transactional replication; therefore, it uses the transaction log to monitor changes in the publishing database.

2. **Correct Answer: D**

    A. **Incorrect:** The Snapshot Agent is responsible for creating the snapshot.

    B. **Incorrect:** In transactional replication, the Distribution Agent delivers the snapshot and applies changes to the publishing database.

    C. **Incorrect:** The Merge Agent delivers snapshots only in merge replication.

    D. **Correct:** The Log Reader Agent monitors the transaction log and captures the changes in published articles.

Lesson 2

1. **Correct Answer: C**

    A. **Incorrect:** A shared folder is not required in merge replication.

    B. **Incorrect:** A shared folder is not required in transactional replication.

    C. **Correct:** A pull subscription configures the Merge or Distribution Agent to run at the Subscriber. So you must use a shared folder to access snapshot information.

    D. **Incorrect:** A push subscription configures the Merge or Distribution Agent to run at the Distributor, so you can use a local folder to access snapshot information.

2. **Correct Answer: D**

    A. **Incorrect:** The *sp_adddistpublisher* stored procedure configures a Publisher to use a specified *distribution* database.

    B. **Incorrect:** The *sp_adddistributor* stored procedure registers a remote or local server as the Distributor of this Publisher.

    C. **Incorrect:** The *sp_adddistributiondb* stored procedure creates the *distribution* database by using the parameters you specify.

    D. **Correct:** The *sp_replicationdboption* stored procedure sets replication database options, including enabling publishing.

Lesson 3

1. **Correct Answer: B**

    A. **Incorrect:** PAL provides security to the publication.

    B. **Correct:** PAL is equivalent to the Windows ACL, except that it secures publications.

    C. **Incorrect:** PAL provides security to the publication.

    D. **Incorrect:** PAL provides security to the publication.

2. **Correct Answers: B and D**

    A. **Incorrect:** Subscribing to a publication requires *db_owner* membership at the *publishing* database. The *db_datareader* access level is not enough.

    B. **Correct:** Subscribing to a publication requires *db_owner* membership at the *publishing* database.

    C. **Incorrect:** Subscribing to a publication requires *db_owner* membership at the *Subscriber* database. The *db_datawriter* access level is not enough.

    D. **Correct:** Subscribing to a publication requires *db_owner* membership at the *Subscriber* database.

Lesson 4

1. **Correct Answers: A and B**

    A. **Correct:** NET Framework business object components are written in managed code to resolve replication conflicts.

    B. **Correct:** COM components are written in unmanaged code (for example, C and C++) to resolve replication conflicts.

    C. **Incorrect:** SQL Server does not support conflict resolution through user-defined functions (UDFs).

    D. **Incorrect:** SQL Server does not support trigger-based conflict resolution.

2. **Correct Answer: D**

    A. **Incorrect:** Conflict resolvers are configured at the article level.

    B. **Incorrect:** Conflict resolvers are configured at the article level.

    C. **Incorrect:** Conflict resolvers are configured at the article level.

    D. **Correct:** Conflict resolvers are configured at the article level in each publication.

Lesson 5

1. **Correct Answer: B**

    A. **Incorrect:** SSMS can be used to configure and monitor replication, but SSRM simplifies replication monitoring even further.

    B. **Correct:** SSRM is designed to simplify the DBA's replication monitoring tasks.

    C. **Incorrect:** SSCM is the services configuration tool; it does not help the DBA monitor replication.

    D. **Incorrect:** SSEUR is a tool that lets SQL Server users authorize Microsoft to collect information about features usage and serious errors.

2. **Correct Answer: C**

    A. **Incorrect:** SSMS does not help DBAs create a replication baseline.

    B. **Incorrect:** SSRM does not help DBAs create a replication baseline.

    C. **Correct:** System Monitor lets DBAs capture performance counters to create a replication baseline, which you can later use to compare the performance of the modified replication process against.

    D. **Incorrect:** Event Viewer is an important tool in the monitoring activity, but it does not help DBAs create a replication baseline.

Chapter 19: Case Scenario Answers

Case Scenario 1: Providing Local Access to Reports

1. Because you need to replicate a summary table, which is small in size and contains relatively static information, you can use snapshot replication.

2. If you use pull subscription, the Snapshot folder must be a shared folder. And in this case, you do not need to grant any rights to the *distribution* database.

3. Make the user's login a member of the replmonitor database role in the *distribution* database.

Case Scenario 2: Providing Fault Tolerance for Multiple Servers

1. Merge replication is the best alternative because it offers great site independence and the possibility of changes at every site.

2. Merge replication changes the schema of tables by adding a uniqueidentifier column, if none exists, to all tables or underlying tables. Some applications will not handle the schema change and might fail or behave unexpectedly.

3. Programmers can use Microsoft COM-based conflict revolvers, create a .NET business component, or create a COM-based conflict revolver to resolve data conflicts if the same data is modified at the same time. They can also use the Stored Procedure Microsoft COM-based conflict resolver and create the required logic in Transact-SQL.

Chapter 20: Lesson Review Answers

Lesson 1

1. **Correct Answers: B and C**

   A. **Incorrect:** A dialog is a type of conversation.

   B. **Correct:** A conversation provides the means for placing messages on a queue.

   C. **Correct:** A queue stores messages until they are processed.

   D. **Incorrect:** A message is data that is sent, but it is not a Service Broker object that you can define.

Lesson 2

1. **Correct Answers: C and D**

   A. **Incorrect:** A validation option of *EMPTY* specifies that the message body should be *NULL*. But *NULL* is not a valid option.

   B. **Incorrect:** *ANY* is an option for the *CREATE CONTRACT* statement.

   C. **Correct:** Specifying this validation option causes a parser to be loaded to ensure that a valid XML document is in the message body.

   D. **Correct:** When a value of *NONE* is specified, the message body can contain any data in any format. It is up to the application to understand the format of the message body.

2. **Correct Answer: C**

   A. **Incorrect:** Valid XML for a message is determined by the definition of a message type.

   B. **Incorrect:** Messages are stored on queues, and the *CREATE QUEUE* command defines where they are stored.

   C. **Correct:** A contract specifies a list of allowed message types that will be valid for a conversation that uses the contract.

   D. **Incorrect:** When a conversation is started, it defines specifies the services that it will be using along with the contract the services will be bound by. But a contract defines only which service can use a particular message type, not the actual services involved.

Lesson 3

1. **Correct Answer: B**

   A. **Incorrect:** The *retention* parameter specifies whether to keep messages until the conversation that processed them has been explicitly closed or whether to discard the messages as soon as they are processed.

   B. **Correct:** *Activation* causes a stored procedure to be launched when a new messages arrives on a queue, as long as a stored procedure is not already running. This feature will launch additional procedures up to a configured maximum if the rate of inbound messages exceeds the rate at which they are being processed.

   C. **Incorrect:** The *MAX_QUEUE_READERS* option limits the number of procedures that are activated but does not activate them to process messages.

   D. **Incorrect:** The stored procedure that is specified for activation processes messages on the queue and does not launch new instances of itself.

2. **Correct Answers: C and D**

   A. **Incorrect:** A contract defines the message types that are allowed.

   B. **Incorrect:** A dialog is a type of conversation that specifies the services to use along with the contracts to use that are defined for those services.

   C. **Correct:** A queue is defined for each service, specifying the endpoint for a conversation.

   D. **Correct:** One or more contracts are defined for the service to restrict the types of conversations in which the service can participate.

Lesson 4

1. **Correct Answer: B**

   A. **Incorrect:** The message ID uniquely identifies the message but does not provide an order to messages.

   B. **Correct:** Each message is tagged with a sequence number that is used to ensure that messages are processed in order.

   C. **Incorrect:** A conversation can contain many messages; therefore, the conversation ID cannot provide a way to order messages.

   D. **Incorrect:** The contract ID uniquely identifies the contract being enforced for the conversation but does not have any capability to order messages.

Lesson 5

1. **Correct Answers: A and B**

   A. **Correct:** The *SEND* command must be the first statement in a batch. If it is not the first statement in a batch, the previous command must be explicitly terminated with a semicolon.

   B. **Correct:** To place a message on a queue, the conversation has to be specified in the *SEND* command by using the conversation handle.

   C. **Incorrect:** The message type is an optional parameter. To build implementation-independent applications, the message-type checking should be left up to the contract and message type elements.

   D. **Incorrect:** The queue is not specified for the *SEND* command because the conversation provides the necessary infrastructure to determine the correct queue to use.

2. **Correct Answer: C and D**

   A. **Incorrect:** The *RECEIVE* command does not perform any type checking via the contract because that capability is handled when a message is placed on the queue.

   B. **Incorrect:** The *RECEIVE* command does not perform any type checking via the message type because that capability is handled when a message is placed on the queue.

   C. **Correct:** The *RECEIVE* command must be the first statement in a batch. If it is not the first statement in a batch, the previous command must be explicitly terminated with a semicolon.

   D. **Correct:** The *RECEIVE* command is built to generically process messages on a queue. However, it needs to know which queue to process to retrieve messages.

Chapter 20: Case Scenario Answers

Case Scenario: Building a Service Broker Application

1. Although the business has rather complex processes and routing requirements, from an IT perspective, it is actually quite straightforward. The entire side of the business that deals with customer orders and inventory is simply a very large message queue. You would convert all the custom code into a Service Broker application. Converting all the code, however, shouldn't be a single-step operation. You should accomplish the conversion in stages to minimize the impact on operations.

2. The first piece to convert is customer requests. Instead of the requests being submitted via the existing code, requests should be submitted to a Service Broker queue. Messages in this queue would then be forwarded to the custom code handling the next part of the process.

3. The second piece to be converted is the logic required to process a request. This logic evaluates the request and generates one or more orders, along with possibly forwarding all or part of a request to a user. The advantage in this step is that Service Broker can be used to manage the process that generates the orders processed by the existing code and to drop the restocking notices on a queue for later processing. Within the same conversation, Service Broker can also be used to send messages to Notification Services with order status updates, restock notices, and brokerage requests. This integration produces a more proactive process that alerts applications and people to processing that needs to be done instead of requiring them to poll for new work.

4. You would then continue replacing custom code with Service Broker functionality for each additional business process down the chain. You could also layer in Notification Services to handle all the customer and internal notifications so that all the custom code for this could be eliminated, freeing up developers even more. Service Broker would provide the messaging infrastructure, with SQL Server providing the security and availability aspects of the solution. And eventually, you would eliminate all the custom code with a request being managed from submission to customer delivery using Service Broker. This implementation would free up significant resources to focus on other projects.

Chapter 21: Lesson Review Answers

Lesson 1

1. **Correct Answer: C**

    A. **Incorrect:** A full-text catalog is a storage structure that is external to a database.

    B. **Incorrect:** The *msdb* database does not contain full-text catalogs.

    C. **Correct:** A full-text catalog is an external storage structure that is created in a specified directory on disk.

    D. **Incorrect:** The specification of a filegroup links a full-text catalog to a database, but the catalog is stored in an external directory structure.

Lesson 2

1. **Correct Answers: B and D**

    A. **Incorrect:** You can use a primary key column, but the requirements for a full-text index are much stricter. Not only does the column have to be unique, but the index can contain only a single column.

    B. **Correct:** A single-column, nonnullable, unique index is required for a full-text index.

    C. **Incorrect:** Although you can use an image column, doing so requires you to add to your table a character column to identify the type of file stored in the column.

    D. **Correct:** You can create a full-text index on any column of a text-based data type.

Lesson 3

1. **Correct Answer: B**

   A. **Incorrect:** *REORGANIZE* is an option for a full-text catalog, not an individual full-text index.

   B. **Correct:** Full-text indexes can specify *FULL*, *INCREMENTAL*, or *UPDATE* as the population mode.

   C. **Incorrect:** *REBUILD* is an option for a full-text catalog, not an individual full-text index.

   D. **Incorrect:** A *FULL* population does a complete rebuild, but there is no option setting called *COMPLETE*.

Lesson 4

1. **Correct Answer: D**

   A. **Incorrect:** *THESAURUS* is an option for *CONTAINS* and *CONTAINSTABLE* queries.

   B. **Incorrect:** *NEAR* is an option for *CONTAINS* and *CONTAINSTABLE* queries.

   C. **Incorrect:** *WEIGHT* is an option for *CONTAINS* and *CONTAINSTABLE* queries.

   D. **Correct:** The *LANGUAGE* option specifies which noise word and language files the word breaker should use for the search arguments in the query.

Chapter 21: Case Scenario Answers

Case Scenario: Building Full-Text Indexes

1. Because of Contoso's large volume of text-based data and documents, this scenario is a perfect application for SQL Server 2005 Full-Text Search. The claims database might have discrete columns for items such as doctor name, company name, and injury, but these columns are likely incomplete. This situation isn't due to lack of input on the part of Contoso employees, but instead because multiple doctors or even multiple companies might be involved in a single claim, with that data being contained in the supporting documentation.

2. By building full-text indexes over the various columns that contain textual data and documents, analysts can execute accurate queries that do not depend on a user extracting data from potentially large volumes of data. In addition, the supporting documents can simply be added to the database, and the full-text indexing process will take care of indexing all the data as well as synonyms and derivatives of words.

Glossary

activation   The process by which stored procedures are automatically launched when messages are placed into the queue. This process also controls whether a single stored procedure is launched or multiple procedures are necessary to keep up with the load.

active log   The portion of a transaction log that contains committed transactions that have not yet been backed up. It also contains any open transactions.

aggregate function   A function that operates on sets of rows instead of on individual values.

alert   A system state that triggers a response, such as notifying an operator or executing a job.

alignment   Occurs when all the indexes for a table as well as the table itself are partitioned by using the same partition function.

asymmetric key   Combines a private key and its corresponding public key. An asymmetric key is stronger than a symmetric key, but it is also more resource-intensive. (*See also* certificate; symmetric key.)

asynchronous processing   An operation that is started and left to run while other work is performed. The initiator of the operation does not control the timing or execution of the operation.

authentication   The process of validating that the user attempting to connect to SQL Server is authorized to do so.

backup   A copy of a database, filegroup, file, or transaction log that can be used to restore data, typically after a serious database error or a system failure. Backups can be used alone or as part of a sequence.

backup device   A predefined pointer to a backup location. Instead of dynamically specifying a tape or disk location within the backup command, a backup device assigns a name to the physical location, and this name can then be reused.

backup file   A file that stores a full or partial database, transaction log, or file and filegroup backup.

backup strategy   The combination of backups that are used for a given database to ensure that it can be restored to meet business requirements. (*See also* restore strategy.)

bcp   The bulk copy program command-line utility. An external program that runs outside of the SQL Server process to bulk copy data either into or out of SQL Server.

best-effort restore   The general term for enabling the *CONTINUE_AFTER_ERROR* option of the restore command. This process enables a restore to continue even if errors in the backup media are found.

blocking   A multiuser access control mechanism. SQL Server uses locking mechanisms to control the integrity of data when it can be accessed by multiple users. A block occurs when a process requests data while that data is exclusively locked by another process.

boundary points   The values used to determine where the data in a table or index is divided into partitions.

broken ownership chain   A permission conflict between dependent objects that prevents an object from being used.

B-tree   A balanced tree structure on which indexes are built. Because a B-tree is symmetric, any query requires the same amount of resources to locate a given value.

BULK INSERT   A Transact-SQL command to insert data into a SQL Server table or view.

Bulk-Logged recovery model   A process in which the database engine minimally logs bulk operations such as *SELECT INTO* and *BULK INSERT*. In this recovery model, if a log backup contains any bulk operation, the database can be restored to the end of the log backup, not to a point in time. The Bulk-Logged recovery model is intended to be used temporarily during large bulk operations. (*See also* Full recovery model; Simple recovery model.)

case expression   A Transact-SQL construct that lets developers express complex switch logic anywhere in Transact-SQL in which a valid expression can be used.

catalog of changed pages   A list of the pages that have changed in a source database since a Database Snapshot was created. This catalog is used to determine which page to retrieve data from: the page in the source database or the page in the Database Snapshot.

catalog population   A background process that loads word breakers, noise word files, language files, and (optionally) filters and protocol handlers to parse text and image columns to extract a list of unique words contained in one or more columns, tokenize them, and build them into an index. (*See also* index population.)

certificate   A public key certificate is a digitally signed statement that maps the value of a public key to the identity of the person, device, or service that holds the corresponding private key. A certificate is the strongest encryption mechanism offered by SQL Server. SQL Server 2005 can create self-signed certificates that follow the X.509 standard. (*See also* asymmetric key; symmetric key.)

clustered index   An index that causes the rows on data pages as well as data pages themselves to be sorted according to the clustering key. A table can have only one clustered index.

clustering key   The column(s) used to define a clustered index.

code page   For character and Unicode data, a definition of the bit patterns that represent specific letters, numbers, or symbols (such as 0x20 representing a blank space and 0x74 representing the character "t"). Some data types use 1 byte per character; each byte can have 1 of 256 different bit patterns.

collation   A set of rules that determines how data is compared, ordered, and presented. Character data is sorted using collation information, including locale, sort order, and case sensitivity.

composition   The process of transforming a set of relational tables into XML data.

conflict resolver   A .NET Framework (managed code) or COM (unmanaged code) component that is designed to resolve conflicts that might occur in merge replication.

constraint   A means for enforcing specific business rules, such as boundary points on data values or uniqueness.

contract   A component within a Service Broker application that defines the message types allowed for a conversation as well as the endpoint that is allowed to use a message type.

conversation   A one-way or two-way ordered exchange of messages between endpoints in a Service Broker application.

conversation group   A logical organization of conversations. It can contain a single conversation or multiple conversations that are related to each other based on application logic.

cooperative multiprocessing   The process that SQL Server uses internally to schedule threads for execution on a processor. This process causes a single thread at a time to execute on a processor and manages the flow of threads to ensure that threads waiting on resources to be allocated do not monopolize a processor.

Copy Files task   The option responsible for copying files from a primary server to a secondary server during a log shipping process.

copy-on-write   The technology used to copy the before image of a data page into a Database Snapshot to maintain the point-in-time state of the data.

corrupt page quarantine   The process that marks a page as corrupted, which enables subsequent actions against the table that do not need to interact with the given page to succeed instead of the entire table or database being taken offline.

covering index   An index used to satisfy a query in its entirety.

crawl   The process that performs a full or partial population of a full-text index.

cross-tabulation   A common business report format in which rows are made into columns.

DAC   *See* Dedicated administrator connection.

data definition language (DDL) trigger   Trigger that fires in response to DDL operations such as *CREATE*, *ALTER*, and *DROP*.

data file   A file that contains data and objects such as tables and indexes. (*See also* log file.)

data manipulation language (DML) trigger   Trigger that fires in response to *INSERT*, *UPDATE*, and *DELETE* operations.

Database Engine Tuning Advisor (DTA)   A tuning tool that ships with SQL Server 2005. It takes a SQL Server Profiler trace as an input and analyzes it against a live database to determine whether structural changes such as indexes, statistics, or partitioning can improve query performance.

Database Mail   The new solution for sending messages from the SQL Server 2005 database engine.

Database Mail account   Contains the information that SQL Server uses to send e-mail messages to the Simple Mail Transfer Protocol (SMTP) server, such as the SMTP server name, the authentication type, and the e-mail address.

Database Mail profile   A collection of Database Mail accounts. Database Mail profiles can be private or public. For a private profile, Database Mail maintains a list of users that can use the profile. For a public profile, members of the *msdb* database role *DatabaseMailUserRole* can use the profile.

database master key   An optional symmetric key that you can create at the database level to encrypt certificates and keys in a database.

database mirroring   A SQL Server 2005 high availability technology configured between a principal and mirror database and an optional witness server. It maintains close synchronization of data and the database schema and offers the option of automatic failover.

database mirroring role   Defines the operating state of each participant in a database mirroring session. There are three possible roles: principal, mirror, and witness.

database mirroring session   A principal database, mirror database, and optional witness server configured to exchange data by using one of three operating modes: High Availability, High Performance, or High Protection.

database partners   The term for a pair of principal and mirror databases participating in a database mirroring session.

database restore   A multiphase process that copies all the data and log pages from a specified backup to a specified database (the data-copy phase) and rolls forward all the transactions that are logged in the backup (the redo phase). At this point, by default, a restore rolls back any incomplete transactions (the undo phase), which completes the recovery of the database and makes it available to users.

database role   A set of built-in database roles provided by each user database. You can use it to group database users for improved management. You can also create your own database roles to group database users and assign permissions on a per-group basis.

Database Snapshot   A point-in-time, read-only version of a source database. Data returned from a Database Snapshot is fixed to the instant in time when you created the Database Snapshot.

DDL trigger   *See* data definition language (DDL) trigger.

deadlock   A situation that occurs when two processes acquire competing locks on data in a way that does not allow either process to complete the transaction.

deadlock detection   The algorithm that SQL Server uses to select the deadlock victim to resolve a deadlock.

deadlock trace   A special trace captured via SQL Trace that identifies the processes and transactions that created a deadlock.

deadlock victim   The process that is chosen to be terminated to resolve a deadlock.

Dedicated administrator connection (DAC)   A connection created as a special TCP endpoint that can be accessed via SQLCMD. Using a DAC, a database administrator can always connect to a SQL Server even when the server is too busy to allow other connections.

default filegroup   When you create a database object and do not specify a filegroup, the object will be allocated to the default filegroup.

dequeue   The process of removing messages from a queue.

derived table   A special kind of subquery that can be selected from and joined to like a table.

destination   *See* target or destination.

deterministic function   A function that always returns the same value when called. The SQL Server built-in function *COS*, which returns the trigonometric cosine of a specified angle, is an example of a deterministic function. (*See also* nondeterministic function.)

dialog   A conversation that occurs between two endpoints.

differential backup   A process that backs up all data pages that have changed since the last full backup.

differential restore   A restore operation that uses a differential backup.

DMFs   *See* Dynamic Management Functions (DMFs).

DML trigger   *See* data manipulation language (DML) trigger.

DMVs   *See* Dynamic Management Views (DMVs).

Document Object Model (DOM)   A World Wide Web Consortium (W3C) specification for the way an application programming interface (API) traverses XML documents.

domain   In Windows Server 2003 security, a collection of computers that are grouped for viewing and administrative purposes and that share a common Active Directory directory services database.

DTA   *See* Database Engine Tuning Advisor.

Dynamic Management Functions (DMFs)   A set of functions that works with the SQL Server instrumentation to display additional data such as query plans.

Dynamic Management Views (DMVs)   A set of views that is dynamically populated with a variety of SQL Server instrumentation. These views provide a granular view across many internal operations.

Edge Table   A construct that represents the structure for an XML tree in tabular format. Each row identifies the properties for each of the nodes that form the XML structure.

endpoint A connection mechanism that is used by any process that needs to access the SQL Server engine to process transactions. A conversation endpoint defines the two database instances participating in a conversation. A Service Broker endpoint is a payload type for a more general SQL Server endpoint that allows Service Broker applications to send and receive messages across SQL Server instances. For database mirroring, you create *TCP* endpoints on every instance involved in the database mirroring session.

enqueue The process of placing messages on a queue.

external fragmentation The degree to which index pages are out of order physically.

extraction, transformation, and loading (ETL) A general term for tools that are used to perform extraction, transformation, and loading functions and more. Examples of ETL tools include SQL Server 2000 Data Transformation Services (DTS) and SQL Server 2005 Integration Services (SSIS).

filegroup A logical structure that lets database administrators group data files and manage them as a logical unit.

filegroup backup A process that backs up the individual filegroups within a database.

filegroup restore A process that restores one or more filegroups to a database.

filter A service that loads during a full-text index population operation that needs to parse varbinary and/or image columns. Filters are available for specific file types such as Word, PowerPoint, and Excel.

fixed server role A role such as sysadmin or securityadmin that enables you to assign administrative privileges to logins.

flat file A file that is not hierarchical in nature or a file that contains data meant for a single table in a database.

FLWOR expression The most important XQUERY expression, which enables developers to write complex querying logic that iterates through a set of nodes that match a specified filter. For each matching node, different data-manipulation functions, extraction methods, and constructors can be applied.

foreign key The structure used to enforce referential integrity by ensuring that values cannot be entered into a column unless they already exist in a related table.

full database backup A process that backs up all data pages in a database that have been allocated to store data.

full database restore A process that recovers an entire backup, replacing anything that existed previously.

Full recovery model A recovery model in which all operations are logged in the transaction log and the database engine never truncates the log. You should perform transaction log backups to truncate the transaction log. The Full recovery model lets you restore a database to the point of failure (or to an earlier point in time in SQL Server 2005 Enterprise Edition). (*See also* Bulk-Logged recovery model; Simple recovery model.)

full-text catalog An external storage structure that contains one or more full-text indexes.

full-text index An external structure contained within a full-text catalog. A full-text index is an inverted, compressed stack of tokens that represents a set of words found in one or more columns specified for indexing for a table.

function A programmatic object that can return either a table variable or a scalar value but is not allowed to execute any command that changes the state of a database.

helper service   A group of services enlisted for populating full-text indexes and performing full-text queries. These services include word breakers, noise word files, and language files.

hidden tables   Tables that exist within SQL Server and that are fully recognized by the storage engine. You cannot issue *INSERT*, *UPDATE*, *DELETE*, or *SELECT* statements directly against them. They also cannot be indexed, have their structure altered, or have triggers created against them. Hidden tables are exposed by a view.

High Availability operating mode   A database mirroring operating mode that requires a principal, mirror, and witness; synchronously transfers data from the principal to the mirror; and allows automatic failure detection and automatic failover as long as the witness server is accessible when the failure occurs.

High Performance operating mode   A database mirroring operating mode that requires only a principal and mirror, asynchronously transfers data from the principal to the mirror, and allows only a manual failover.

High Protection operating mode   A database mirroring operating mode that requires only a principal and mirror, synchronously transfers data from the principal to the mirror, and allows only a manual failover.

histogram   Specifies how many rows exactly match each interval value, how many rows fall within an interval, and a calculation of the density of values or the incidence of duplicate values within an interval.

HTTP **endpoint**   An endpoint type that enables developers to expose the stored procedures and functions within a SQL Server 2005 database as Web methods that can be called from any application using the SOAP protocol.

index fragmentation   The degree to which index pages are out of order physically or the degree in which index pages are partially filled.

index population   A build process that is performed for a single full-text index. (*See also* catalog population.)

index rebuild   The process of rebuilding an index to remove fragmentation by dropping and re-creating the index.

index reorganization   The process of defragmenting the leaf level of clustered and nonclustered indexes on tables and views. The reorganization physically reorders the leaf-level pages to match the logical, left-to-right order of the leaf nodes while compacting the index pages.

indexed view   A view with a clustered index created on it so that returned data is materialized on disk for faster performance.

inner join   When working with multiple tables in a query, a type of join that returns matching rows from both tables involved. (*See also* outer join.)

input parameter   A variable that is passed to a stored procedure or function.

intermediate level   One or more levels within a B-tree created to ensure that a single page resides at the root of the index.

internal fragmentation   The degree to which index pages are partially filled.

isolation levels   ANSI standard locking behaviors that guarantee data and query integrity.

job   One or more tasks to execute. You can optionally configure a job to execute on a scheduled basis or in response to a user action or condition in the system.

job schedule   Provides the execution parameters required to automatically execute a job based on a date- or time-based trigger.

job step   A block of code to execute. Each job step usually executes a single discrete business operation.

language file   A file used to designate language-specific attributes for a full-text index or full-text query.

leaf level   The bottom level within an index.

linked server   A server that lets you access external data sources—such as a remote SQL Server; another instance in your server; or an Access, Oracle, or other database—from your local Transact-SQL code.

local system account   A Windows OS account that has full administrator rights on the local computer but has no network access rights. This account could be used for development or testing servers that do not need to be integrated with other server applications or interact with any network resources. But because of the privileges granted to this account, it is not recommended that this account be used for the SQL Server service or the SQL Server Agent service.

lock escalation   The process by which SQL Server dynamically switches from a fine-grained lock to a coarser-grained lock, such as changing from a page-level lock to a table-level lock.

locking level   The level of lock that is acquired on a resource, which can be either row, page, or table.

locking promotion   A process that occurs with an update lock. This type of lock starts as a shared lock and then is changed to an exclusive lock just before the data is modified.

log file   A file that contains a transaction log. (*See also* data file.)

log pointer   A reference used by the lazywriter process to keep track of the location in a transaction log where the next write should occur. This is an internal structure that has no visibility and cannot be manipulated.

log shipping   The automated process of backing up, copying, and restoring a transaction log from one database on a primary server to one or more secondary databases on another server.

log_shipping_monitor_error_detail **table**   A log shipping table that keeps track of error details.

log_shipping_monitor_history_detail **table**   A log shipping table that stores historic information about log shipping jobs.

maintenance job   A job created within SQL Server Agent as the output of the Maintenance Plan Wizard.

maintenance plan   An SQL Server Integration Services (SSIS) package consisting of one or more tasks related to maintenance on a database, such as backups or reindexing.

media set   A list of files and/or tapes on which a backup is stored.

MERGE   An operation that removes a boundary point from a partition function.

merge replication   A type of replication that allows multiple servers to modify replicated data and uses uniqueidentifier columns, triggers, and tables to monitor data changes in multiple servers.

message   The fundamental unit of data within a Service Broker application. It contains all the information that needs to be processed.

message type   The name for a particular implementation of a message. It defines the possible formats allowed within a message body.

mirror   The database within a database mirroring session that is in a recovering state, does not allow any connections, and is receiving changes from the principal.

mirror failover   The process whereby a mirror database is promoted to principal and recovered. This process also automatically demotes the principal to become the mirror within the database mirroring session.

mirrored backup   A process that enables SQL Server to back up data once but create multiple copies of a database that occur in a single backup operation.

Mixed Mode authentication One of two mechanisms for validating attempts to connect to instances of SQL Server. Users must specify a SQL Server login ID and password when they connect. The SQL Server instance ensures that the login ID and password combination are valid before allowing the connection to succeed. You can create SQL Server logins that are not mapped to an operating system user. You use Mixed Mode authentication when you need to provide access to non-Windows users. (*See also* Windows authentication.)

monitor server A SQL Server database engine instance that keeps track of a log shipping process and raises alerts when the process fails.

monolog A conversation that occurs between a single endpoint and any number of target endpoints. This conversation type is not currently available in SQL Server 2005.

named instance An installation of SQL Server that has been given a name to differentiate it from other named instances and from the default instance on the same computer. A named instance is identified by the computer name and instance name.

nested trigger A trigger that executes code that causes another trigger to fire.

Network Service account A special built-in system account that is similar to authenticated user accounts. This account has the same level of access to system resources and objects as members of the Users group. Services that run under this account access network resources using the credentials of the computer account. It is not recommended that this account be used for the SQL Server service or SQL Server Agent service account.

No Recovery mode A mode that you use when you are using a log shipping configuration for availability reasons only. No Recovery mode makes the secondary database unavailable for users to query.

noise words Commonly used words in a given language—such as "the," "a," and "an"—that are ignored by index population as well as full-text queries.

nonclustered index A type of index that does not cause data pages within a table to be sorted. You can create up to 249 nonclustered indexes per table.

nondeterministic function Function that can return a different value each time the function is called. The SQL Server built-in function *GETDATE()* , which returns the current system date and time, is an example of a nondeterministic function. (*See also* deterministic function.)

online index creation A process that uses row-versioning technology to enable you to build an index while read and write operations are occurring in the underlying table. This feature is available only in SQL Server 2005 Enterprise Edition.

operating mode A configuration that governs how a database mirroring session synchronizes transactions and which failover options are available. You can choose from three operating modes: High Availability, High Performance, or High Protection.

operator Defines the notification mechanisms and parameters required to send a message to a person or group of people.

outer join When working with multiple tables in a query, a type of join that returns all rows from one or both tables and non-matching rows from the other table. (*See also* inner join.)

output parameter A scalar value that is returned from a stored procedure.

ownership chain A cascading set of permissions that goes from a parent object to one or more dependent objects.

page split   The process that occurs when a page is filled with data and another row needs to be written to that page to maintain the data order. SQL Server then allocates a new page to the index or table and moves half the data on the full page to the new page.

parse   To analyze and traverse an XML structure.

partial backup   The process of backing up only a portion of a database.

partial restore   The process of restoring only a portion of a database.

$PARTITION   A function that returns the partition number of a value for a particular partition function.

partition function   A stand-alone object that defines the boundary points for dividing data into partitions.

partition scheme   Maps a partition function to physical storage.

payload   Restricts the allowed operations for an endpoint, which can have a specified type of either *TCP* or *HTTP*.

peer-to-peer replication   A new kind of transactional replication that allows multiple servers to subscribe to the same schema and data, permitting simultaneous changes in multiple servers.

PerfMon   *See* System Monitor.

point-in-time recovery   The capability of a database using the Full recovery model to use transaction log backups to recover a database to a specific time that does not have to coincide with when the backup was taken. If a full database backup is done at midnight and a log backup is done at 04:00, the database can be recovered to any specific time between midnight and 04:00, such as 03:41 or 02:22.

primary data file   A mandatory data file that contains information for a database catalog and points to the other files. The recommended extension for the primary data file is .mdf. (*See also* secondary data file.)

primary database   The original database that is distributed to other servers with log shipping. The primary database receives the updates from the application. (*See also* secondary database.)

primary filegroup   The filegroup that contains the primary data file. All system tables are allocated to the primary filegroup.

primary key   A type of constraint that uniquely identifies each row in a table, which is important for accurately retrieving and modifying data.

primary server   The SQL Server database engine instance that owns the primary database. (*See also* secondary server.)

principal   The database within a database mirroring session that is recovered and online and that allows transactions to be processed against it.

protocol handler   A process that uses one or more filters to extract text data from varbinary and image columns for a word breaker.

pull subscription   A subscription in which the Distribution Agent or Merge Agent runs at the Subscriber and pulls the subscription from the Distributor to the Subscriber.

push subscription   A subscription in which the Distribution Agent or Merge Agent runs at the Distributor and pushes the subscription from the Distributor to the Subscriber.

queue   A hidden table within SQL Server that contains all the messages being sent or received.

queue reader   An object that receives messages from a queue. This object can be a stored procedure or another application.

RAID 0   Also known as disk striping because it creates a disk file system called a stripe set. RAID 0 improves performance for read and write operations because it spreads these operations across all the disks in the set. RAID 0 does not provide fault tolerance.

RAID 1   Also known as disk mirroring, it provides a redundant copy of the selected disk. RAID 1 improves read performance but can degrade the performance of write operations.

RAID 5   The most popular RAID level, which stripes data across the disks of the RAID set as does RAID 0, but RAID 5 also adds parity information to provide fault tolerance. Parity information is distributed among all the disks. RAID 5 provides better performance than RAID 1. However, when a disk fails, read performance is decreased.

read-only filegroup   A filegroup configured to hold database objects that should not be modified, such as historical tables. All filegroups can be configured as read-only except the primary filegroup.

receive   To dequeue a message.

recovery model   A database option that controls how transactions are logged, whether to back up the transaction log, and what restore options are available. Also, the model under which a database is operating for recovery purposes.

recursive trigger   A trigger that causes itself to be called either directly or indirectly.

replay trace   A special type of trace that is created to replay a workload against a test system.

replication agent   A program that executes the replication process. The most important replication agents are Snapshot, Log Reader, Distribution, Merge, and Queue Reader.

restore strategy   The process that is designed to ensure that a database can be recovered while meeting business requirements for the allowed amount of downtime and maximum data loss. Without a restore strategy, backing up a database has virtually no purpose.

retention   Forces a queue to preserve all messages related to a conversation until the conversation is explicitly closed.

reverting a database   The process of recovering the source database from a Database Snapshot.

root node   The single page that resides at the top of a B-tree.

SAX   *See* Simple API for XML (SAX).

scalar function   A function that returns a single value.

schema   A collection of database objects that form a single namespace. The main benefit of schemas is the separation of schemas and users.

schema collection   One or more XML schemas that are bound together through a name. Used to validate the body of a message in a Service Broker application.

secondary data file   Optional files that contain objects and data. A database can contain a maximum of 32,766 secondary files. The recommended extension for secondary data files is .ndf. (*See also* primary data file.)

secondary database   The distributed copy of a primary database that results from log shipping. SQL Server frequently synchronizes the secondary database through transaction log restores. (*See also* primary database.)

secondary server   The SQL Server database engine instance that owns a secondary database. You can configure multiple secondary servers. (*See also* primary server.)

semistructured data   XML data that can change from instance to instance and that defines optional elements. The schema is heterogeneous and might not be easily represented using a relational structure. (*See also* structured data; unstructured data.)

send   To enqueue a message.

service   The name assigned to one or more tasks used to process Service Broker messages.

service master key   A symmetric key generated automatically when you install a SQL Server 2005 instance. The database engine uses the service master key to encrypt linked server passwords, connection strings, account credentials, and all database master keys.

showplan   A graphical or text-based graph of a query plan generated by the query optimizer.

shredding   The process of transforming XML data into a format suitable for storage in relational tables.

Simple API for XML (SAX)   An application programming interface (API) used to traverse an XML structure. Instead of loading the whole XML structure in memory and re-creating a graph, SAX navigates the tree on a node-by-node basis and raises an event for each parsing event of a navigated node, such as the start of a node or the end of a node.

Simple recovery model   A recovery model in which the database engine minimally logs most operations and truncates the transaction log after each checkpoint. In a Simple recovery model, you cannot back up or restore the transaction log. Furthermore, you cannot restore individual data pages. (*See also* Bulk-Logged recovery model; Full recovery model.)

SMO   *See* SQL Server Management Object (SMO)

snapshot replication   A type of replication that copies all the data every time it runs to synchronize the Subscriber and the Publisher.

SOAP   A platform-independent data-access protocol that uses XML as an encoding scheme for request and response parameters and uses HTTP as a transport mechanism.

source   When loading a database, the place from which the data is coming. For loading a database table from a flat file, the flat file is the source. (*See also* target or destination.)

source database   The database against which a Database Snapshot is created.

sparse file   A file that contains at least one region of unallocated space within its structure. The allocation table lists the file with the size specified at creation, but the size on disk is much lower because of the unallocated regions within the file.

SPID   *See* system process ID (SPID).

SPLIT   An operation that adds a new boundary point to a partition function.

SQL Server Agent proxy   A security structure that you configure to enable a job step to access various subsystems within SQL Server, such as the SQL Server Integration Services (SSIS) execution engine or the replication engine.

SQL Server Management Object (SMO)   A class library designed to be used with development environments such as Microsoft Visual Studio 2005. It provides a programmatic interface to objects within SQL Server.

SQL Server Profiler   A performance monitoring tool that ships with SQL Server and provides a graphical user interface (GUI) for SQL Trace.

SQL Trace   The event application programming interface (API) in SQL Server that enables you to gather data on virtually every processing subsystem within SQL Server.

Standby mode   A mode used to give users read-only access to a secondary database. This configuration increases the scalability of your application by letting you distribute queries across multiple servers, thereby reducing the primary server's workload.

statistics   Statistical information created by SQL Server 2005 regarding the distribution of values in a column.

stored procedure   The name for a batch of Transact-SQL or CLR code that is stored within SQL Server and can be called directly by applications or within other programming constructs.

string summary   Additional information that is collected in statistics created on char, varchar, varchar(max), nchar, nvarchar, nvarchar(max), text, and ntext columns.

structured data   XML data that conforms to a strict. It is easily represented using a relational structure. (*See also* semistructured data; unstructured data.)

subquery   A query that can be used as part of a larger query to return data from another table or source.

SWITCH   An infinitely scalable operation that exchanges two partitions between tables.

symmetric key   A key used to encrypt and decrypt data. It is the fastest encryption mechanism and is suitable for encrypting frequently accessed data. (*See also* asymmetric key; certificate.)

sysjobactivity   A table in the *msdb* database that SQL Server Agent uses to record the current activity of SQL Server jobs.

sysjobhistory   A table in the *msdb* database that SQL Server Agent uses to keep track of the historic execution of jobs.

System Monitor   A Windows-supplied performance-monitoring tool used to capture performance counters for hardware, Windows subsystems, and any other applications that expose statistical counters. System Monitor is commonly known as PerfMon.

system process ID (SPID)   A number that uniquely identifies each connection to a SQL Server server.

table   The basic storage structure within a database that holds all the data stored by applications.

table-valued function   A Function that returns a table variable.

tail of the log   The portion of a transaction log that contains committed transactions that have not yet been backed up.

target or destination   When loading a database, the place to which the data is going. For loading a database table from a flat file, the database table is the target or destination. (*See also* source.)

temporary table   A table that can be defined temporarily, making it easier to build complex queries.

token   A specialized compressed representation of a word within a full-text index.

trace   The events and data columns that are output when a specific SQL Trace is executed.

trace events   Actions that are executed within SQL Server, such as stored procedures executing, database files or logs growing or shrinking, or query plans being generated.

transaction log backup   A backup of the active portion of a transaction log. This backup contains only committed transactions and removes the portion of the log that has been backed up so that the space can be reused.

transaction log restore   A restore operation that uses one or more transaction log backups.

Transaction Undo File (TUF)   The file in which Standby Mode saves all incomplete transactions. The restore process uses this file to maintain transactional integrity. When the next restore process occurs, it restores all the committed transactions.

transactional replication   A type of replication that uses the transaction log to log changes in the published articles and then applies the changes to the Subscribers.

transmission queue   A temporary queue that contains messages that are in the process of being sent. This queue also holds messages for retry in the event of unavailability of an endpoint.

Transparent Client Redirection   Process that describes the functionality built into the new MDAC connection library that ships with Visual Studio 2005 and that allows principal and mirror connections to be cached in the connection object. Failure of the principal uses this code to redirect a client connection to the mirror without developer intervention or custom coding.

trigger   Special case of a stored procedure that does not accept any input parameters. The code is automatically executed in response to the data definition language (DDL) or data manipulation language (DML) operation that is specified.

TUF   *See* Transaction Undo File (TUF).

typed XML data   An XML document or fragment that is structured based on the declarations in an XML schema file.

UMS   *See* User Mode Scheduler (UMS).

unstructured data   XML data that does not conform to any specific structure. Every instance can follow a completely different structure, so it is not easily searchable and it is impossible to represent in a relational structure. (*See also* semistructured data; structured data.)

untyped XML data   An XML document or fragment that does not conform to the declarations in any XML schema file, so its structure cannot be validated.

updateable view   A view that allows data modifications to a single underlying table. You use the *WITH CHECK OPTION* clause on the *CREATE VIEW* command to constrain the changes to only the set of rows that match the view's *WHERE* clause.

updategram   An XML structure used to formulate Transact-SQL operations based on the appearances of XML elements. The operations are defined by comparing an original image of the XML with a current image of the XML. Ddepending on the changes detected, specific operations are executed.

User Mode Scheduler (UMS)   A subsystem internal to SQL Server that manages allocation of processor resources. Instead of delegating the allocation to Windows, SQL Server handles all thread scheduling on processors internally. One UMS is created for each physical or logical processor on a machine.

user-defined filegroup   A type of filegroup is created by the database administrator to group secondary files. A database can contain up to 32,766 user-defined filegroups.

validation   The mechanism that is applied to a message body to ensure that it meets formatting requirements.

view   A named *SELECT* statement stored in SQL Server.

wait type   A symbolic value that indicates the type of resource a process is waiting on to complete execution.

Web service   A piece of code that receives requests and sends responses by using the platform-independent SOAP protocol.

Web Services Description Language (WSDL)   See *www.w3.org/TR/wsdl20/* for the detailed specification.

Windows authentication   The default and recommended authentication mode for SQL Server 2005. Only authenticated Windows users can gain access to the SQL Server instance. You need to add a Windows login for each Windows user or group that needs access to a SQL Server instance. (*See also* Mixed Mode authentication.)

Windows collation   A set of rules that determines how SQL Server sorts character data. It is specified by name in the Windows Control Panel and in SQL Server 2005 during setup.

witness (witness server)   The arbiter within the High Availability operating mode. The purpose of the witness is to guarantee that the database cannot be served on more than one instance at the same time.

word breaker A routine that extracts valid words from within a column that is full-text indexed. This routine is used during index population and full-text querying.

workload file The SQL Server Profiler trace that is used as an input to the Database Engine Tuning Advisor (DTA).

WSDL (Web Services Description Language) See *www.w3.org/TR/wsdl20/* for the detailed specification.

XML validation The process of determining whether an XML instance conforms to the definitions defined by an XML schema file.

XPATH A World Wide Web Consortium (W3C) specification that defines a mechanism for searching for specific nodes within an XML instance, validating both the XML structure and the XML content.

XPATH axes Represent a step in an XPATH expression that defines the set of nodes that the expression should return.

XPATH predicates Represent a conditional filter applied to the collection of nodes defined by the axes in an XPATH expression. Only matching nodes will be returned by the XPATH expression.

XQUERY A World Wide Web Consortium (W3C) specification that defines a declarative programming language used to query XML data.

Index

Symbols

System Requirements

We recommend that you use a computer that is not your primary workstation to do the practice exercises in this book because you will make changes to the operating system and application configuration.

Hardware Requirements

The following hardware is required to complete the practice exercises:

- Personal computer with a 600 MHz Pentium III–compatible or faster processor; 1 GHz or faster processor recommended
- 512 MB of RAM or more; 1 GB or more recommended
- 8 GB of available hard disk space

NOTE   Four volumes necessary for some practice exercises

To complete some of the practice exercises in this book, you will need four volumes on your computer. We recommend that you make the C volume the largest, and then use volume sizes of 650 MB for the D, E, and F volumes.

- DVD-ROM drive
- Super VGA (1,024 x 768) or higher resolution video adapter and monitor
- Keyboard and Microsoft mouse, or compatible pointing device

Software Requirements

The following software is required to complete the practice exercises:

- One of the following operating systems:
    - Microsoft Windows 2000 Server with Service Pack (SP) 4 or later
    - Windows 2000 Professional with SP 4 or later
    - Windows XP with SP 2 or later
    - Windows Server 2003 Standard Edition, Enterprise Edition, or Datacenter Edition with SP 1 or later
    - Microsoft Windows Small Business Server 2003 with SP 1 or later

- ❏ Microsoft Windows Server 2003 Standard x64 Edition, Enterprise x64 Edition, or Datacenter x64 Edition with SP 1 or later

- ❏ Windows XP Professional x64 Edition or later running in Windows on Windows

■ SQL Server 2005 (A 180-day evaluation edition of Microsoft SQL Server 2005 Enterprise Edition is included on DVD with this book)

CAUTION Networked computers

If your computer is part of a larger network, verify with your network administrator that the SQL Server instances installed will not interfere with network operations. All instances configured for exercises within this book should be set to allow local connections only to ensure that they will not interact with other resources on your network.

■ Microsoft Internet Explorer 6.0 SP 1 or later

IMPORTANT Evaluation edition is not the full retail product

The 180-day evaluation edition of Microsoft SQL Server 2005 Enterprise Edition provided with this training kit is not the full retail product and is provided only for the purposes of training and evaluation. Microsoft and Microsoft Technical Support do not support this evaluation edition.

Information about any issues relating to the use of this evaluation edition with this training kit is posted to the Support section of the Microsoft Press Web site (www.microsoft.com/learning/support/books/). For information about ordering the full version of any Microsoft software, please call Microsoft Sales at (800) 426-9400 or visit www.microsoft.com.

What do you think of this book?
We want to hear from you!

Do you have a few minutes to participate in a brief online survey? Microsoft is interested in hearing your feedback about this publication so that we can continually improve our books and learning resources for you.

To participate in our survey, please visit:

www.microsoft.com/learning/booksurvey

And enter this book's ISBN, 0-7356-2271-X. As a thank-you to survey participants in the United States and Canada, each month we'll randomly select five respondents to win one of five $100 gift certificates from a leading online merchant.* At the conclusion of the survey, you can enter the drawing by providing your e-mail address, which will be used for prize notification *only*.

Thanks in advance for your input. Your opinion counts!

Sincerely,

Microsoft Learning

Microsoft | Learning

Learn More. Go Further.

Save 15%
on your Microsoft® Certification exam fee

Present this discount voucher to any of 5,000 testing centers worldwide for 15% off one Microsoft Certification exam fee. Or, use the discount code on the voucher to register online or via phone with the Microsoft Certified Exam Provider of your choice.

Microsoft

Microsoft | Learning

Good for 15% off one exam fee in the Microsoft Certified Professional Program
Offer expires 12/31/2010

Your voucher discount code

Redeemable at Microsoft Certified Exam Providers worldwide.
For locations, visit: www.microsoft.com/mcp/exams

Promotion Terms and Conditions:

- Offer good for 15% off one exam fee in the Microsoft Certified Professional Program.
- Voucher code can be redeemed online or at Microsoft Certified Exam Providers worldwide.
- Exam purchased using this voucher code must be taken on or before December 31, 2010.
- Inform your Microsoft Certified Exam Provider that you want to use the voucher discount code at the time you register for the exam.

Voucher Terms and Conditions

- Expired vouchers will not be replaced.
- Each voucher code may only be used for one exam and must be presented at time of registration.
- This voucher may not be combined with other vouchers or discounts.
- This voucher is nontransferable and is void if altered or revised in any way.
- It may not be sold or redeemed for cash, credit, or refund.

X11-56768